The Making of a Court Society

This is the first full-length study of the Portuguese royal court in the fourteenth and fifteenth centuries. It describes the fundamental importance of the court in defining the social position of kings, and shows how kings and nobles redefined one another, despite many celebrated political rivalries within the broader Iberian context. The book contains a detailed comparative analysis of the way royal courts were organised, and of the status, professional and gender groups inside the Portuguese court. The characteristics of the court society as a whole, however, were rooted mostly in the dynamics of hierarchy and interdependence – in other words, in the specific ways the different parts and the individuals were bonded to each other. These bonds are dis[illegible] [illegible]ht of late medieval concepts and theories. The book als[illegible] [illegible]ment of this complex community in the g[illegible] [illegible] at court was shaped by ceremonial duties [illegible]

First published in 1995 as *A co*[illegible] [illegible]*lia*, the book has been extensively revised [illegible]

RITA COSTA GOMES is Professo[illegible] [illegible]sboa, Portugal.

The Making of a Court Society

Kings and Nobles in Late Medieval Portugal

RITA COSTA GOMES

Translated by
ALISON AIKEN

CAMBRIDGE
UNIVERSITY PRESS

CAMBRIDGE UNIVERSITY PRESS
Cambridge, New York, Melbourne, Madrid, Cape Town, Singapore, São Paulo

Cambridge University Press
The Edinburgh Building, Cambridge CB2 8RU, UK

Published in the United States of America by Cambridge University Press, New York

www.cambridge.org
Information on this title: www.cambridge.org/9780521800112

First published 2003
This digitally printed version 2007

A catalogue record for this publication is available from the British Library

Library of Congress Cataloguing in Publication data

Costa Gomes, Rita.
[A Corte dos reis de Portugal no final da idade média. English]
The making of a court society: kings and nobles in late medieval Portugal / Rita Costa Gomes; translated by Alison Aiken.
p. cm.
Includes bibliographical references and index.
ISBN 0 521 80011 0
1. Portugal – Court and courtiers – History. 2. Nobility – Portugal – History. I. Title.
KKQ250 .G6613 2002
305.5′223′09469 – dc21 2002067727

ISBN 978-0-521-80011-2 hardback
ISBN 978-0-521-03695-5 paperback

To Richard, *sempre fitando o sol*

Contents

Figures

Maps

Abbreviations

ALF	Humberto Baquero Moreno, *A Batalha de Alfarrobeira*, 2 vols., Coimbra: Imprensa da Universidade, 1980
ANTT	Arquivo Nacional da Torre do Tombo
Ash	Ashburnam
BGUC	Biblioteca Geral da Universidade de Coimbra
BL	British Library
BLAU	Biblioteca Medicea-Laurenziana
BNL	Biblioteca Nacional (Lisbon)
BNM	Biblioteca Nacional (Madrid)
BPE	Biblioteca Pública de Évora
BPS	Biblioteca Pública de Santarém
Brasões	Anselmo Braamcamp Freire, *Brasões da Sala de Sintra*, 3 vols., Lisbon: Imprensa Nacional–Casa da Moeda, 1973
CDA	*Chancelarias Portuguesas: D. Afonso IV*, ed. Centro de Estudos Históricos da Universidade Nova de Lisboa, 2 vols., Lisbon: INIC, 1990–92
CDP	*Chancelarias Portuguesas: D. Pedro I*, ed. Centro de Estudos Históricos da Universidade Nova de Lisboa, Lisbon: INIC, 1984
CE	Colecção Especial
Cod	Códice(s)
CPA	*Cortes Portuguesas: Reinado de D. Afonso IV (1325–1357)*, ed. Centro de Estudos Históricos da Universidade Nova de Lisboa, Lisbon: INIC, 1982
CPF	*Cortes Portuguesas: Reinado de D. Fernando (1367–1383)*, ed. Centro de Estudos Históricos da Universidade Nova de Lisboa, Lisbon: INIC, 1990

CPP	*Cortes Portuguesas: Reinado de D. Pedro I (1357–1367)*, ed. Centro de Estudos Históricos da Universidade Nova de Lisboa, Lisbon: INIC, 1986
CR	*Corporações Religiosas*
CR 1344	*Crónica Geral de Espanha de 1344*, ed. Luis Filipe Lindley Cintra, 4 vols., Lisbon: Imprensa Nacional–Casa da Moeda, 1983–90
CR 1419	*Crónica dos Sete Primeiros Reis de Portugal*, ed. Carlos Silva Tarouca, 3 vols., Lisbon: Academia Portuguesa da História, 1952–53
CR Afonso V	Rui de Pina, 'Chronica do Senhor Rey D. Affonso V', in *Crónicas*, ed. Manuel Lopes de Almeida, Oporto: Lello and Irmão, 1977, pp. 577–881
CR Ceuta	Gomes Eanes de Zurara, *Crónica da Tomada de Ceuta*, ed. Francisco Esteves Pereira, Coimbra: Academia das Ciências, 1915
CR Duarte	Rui de Pina, 'Chronica do Senhor Rey D. Duarte', in *Crónicas*, ed. M. Lopes de Almeida, Oporto: Lello and Irmão, 1977, pp. 477–575
CR Fernando	Fernão Lopes, *Crónica de D. Fernando*, ed. Giuliano Macchi, Lisbon: Imprensa Nacional–Casa da Moeda, 1975
CR João I	Fernão Lopes, *Crónica del Rei D. João I*, ed. Anselmo Braamcamp Freire and William Entwistle, 2 vols., Lisbon: Imprensa Nacional–Casa da Moeda, 1977
CR João II	Rui de Pina, 'Chronica d'elRei D. João II', in *Crónicas*, ed. Manuel Lopes de Almeida, Oporto: Lello and Irmão, 1977, pp. 883–1033
CR Nuno	*Estória de Dom Nuno Álvrez Pereira*, ed. Adelino Almeida Calado, Coimbra: Imprensa da Universidade, 1991
CR Pedro	Fernão Lopes, *Crónica de D. Pedro I*, ed. Giuliano Macchi, Rome: Edizioni dell'Ateneo, 1966
CRO (Ayala)	Pero López de Ayala, *Crónicas*, ed. José Luiz Martin, Barcelona: Planeta, 1991
CRO Alfonso XI	*Gran Crónica de Alfonso XI*, ed. Diego Catalán, 2 vols., Madrid: Gredos, 1977
CRO Pedro (Ayala)	Pero López de Ayala, *Corónica del Rey D. Pedro*, ed. C. and H. M. Wilkins, Madison: The Hispanic Seminar of Medieval Studies, 1985

CUP	*Chartularium Universitatis Portugalensis*, ed. Artur Moreira de Sá, 12 vols., Lisbon: Instituto de Alta Cultura/INIC, 1966–85
DCH	*Documentos das Chancelarias reais relativos a Marrocos anteriores a 1531*, ed. Pedro de Azevedo, 2 vols., Lisbon: Academia das Ciências, 1915–34
DEHP	*Dicionário enciclopédico da história de Portugal*, 2 vols. published, Lisbon: Alfa, 1985
Desembargo	Armando Luís de Carvalho Homem, *O Desembargo Régio (1320–1433)*, Lisbon: INIC, 1990
DEV	*Documentos históricos da cidade de Évora*, ed. Gabriel Pereira, 3 vols., Évora, 1885–91
DHDA	Francisco Marques de Sousa Viterbo, *Dicionário histórico e documental dos arquitectos, engenheiros e construtores Portugueses*, 3 vols., Lisbon: Imprensa National–Casa da Moeda, 1988
DHP	*Dicionário de história de Portugal*, ed. Joel Serrão, 4 vols., Lisbon: Iniciativas Editoriais, 1971
DLM	*Dicionário da literatura medieval Galega e Portuguesa*, dir. Giulia Lanciani and Giuseppe Tavani, Lisbon: Caminho, 1993
DMA	*Dictionary of the Middle Ages*, ed. Joseph Strayer, 12 vols., New York: Scribner's, 1984
DP	*Descobrimentos Portugueses: documentos para a sua história*, ed. José Martins da Silva Marques, 5 vols., Lisbon: INIC, 1988
Elucidário	Frei Joaquim Santa Rosa de Viterbo, *Elucidário das palavras, termos e frases que em Portugal antigamente se usaram, e que hoje regularmente se ignorão*, ed. Mário Fiúza, 2 vols., Oporto: Civilização, 1962
f.	folio
Gav	*Gavetas*
GTT	*As Gavetas da Torre do Tombo*, 12 vols., Lisbon: Centro de Estudos Históricos Ultramarinos, 1960–77
HFAC	*História florestal, aquícola e cinegética*, ed. Carlos Manuel Baeta Neves, vols. I–IV, Lisbon: Ministério da Agricultura e Pescas, 1981–83
Leges	*Portugaliae Monumenta Historica a saeculo octavo post Christum usque ad quintum decimum, Leges et Consuetudines*, 2 vols., Lisbon: Academia Real das Ciências, 1856–68

Livro Vermelho	*Livro Vermelho do Senhor Rey D. Afonso V, Collecção de livros ineditos de história Portugueza dos reinados de D. João I, D. Duarte, D. Affonso V e D. João II*, ed. Abade Correia da Serra, Lisbon: Academia Real das Ciências, 1793, vol. III
LL	*Livro de Linhagens do Século XVI*, ed. António Machado de Faria, Lisbon: Academia Portuguesa da História, 1956
LL Conde	*Livro de Linhagens do Conde D. Pedro*, ed. José Mattoso, 2 vols., Lisbon: Academia das Ciências, 1980
LN	*Leitura Nova*
LP	*Livro das Leis e Posturas*, ed. Nuno Espinosa Gomes da Silva and Maria Teresa Campos Rodrigues, Lisbon: Faculdade de Direito, 1971
M	Maço
MH	*Monumenta Henricina*, ed. António Joaquim Dias Dinis, 15 vols., Coimbra: Comissão Executiva das Comemorações do V Centenário da Morte do Infante D. Henrique, 1960–74
MPV	*Monumenta Portugaliae Vaticana*, ed. António Domingues Sousa Costa, 3 vols. published, Braga/Oporto: Edições Franciscanas, 1968–70
NA	*Núcleo Antigo*
OA	*Ordenações Afonsinas*, ed. Mário Júlio de Almeida Costa and Eduardo Borges Nunes, 5 vols., Lisbon: Fundação Calouste Gulbenkian, 1988
OD	*Ordenações de D. Duarte*, ed. Martim de Albuquerque and Eduardo Borges Nunes, Lisbon: Fundação Calouste Gulbenkian, 1988
PA	*Livro das Posturas Antigas*, ed. Maria Teresa Campos Rodrigues, Lisbon: Câmara Municipal, 1974
Provas	*Provas da história genealógica da casa real Portuguesa*, ed. António Caetano de Sousa, 12 vols., Coimbra: Atlântida, 1946–54
Quadro	Visconde de Santarém, Luis Augusto Rebelo da Silva, *Quadro elementar das relações políticas e diplomáticas de Portugal com as diversas potências do mundo*, 18 vols., Lisbon: Academia Real das Ciências, 1842–60
REL	Luis Suárez Fernández, *Relaciones entre Portugal y Castilla en la época del Infante Don Enrique, 1393–1460*, Madrid: Consejo Superior de Investigaciones Científicas, 1960

Res	Reservados
Russell	Peter E. Russell, *The English Intervention in Spain and Portugal in the Time of Edward III and Richard II*, Oxford: Clarendon, 1955
Supl.	Suplemento
v	verso

Genealogical tables

1 The Avelar family and Queen Beatriz

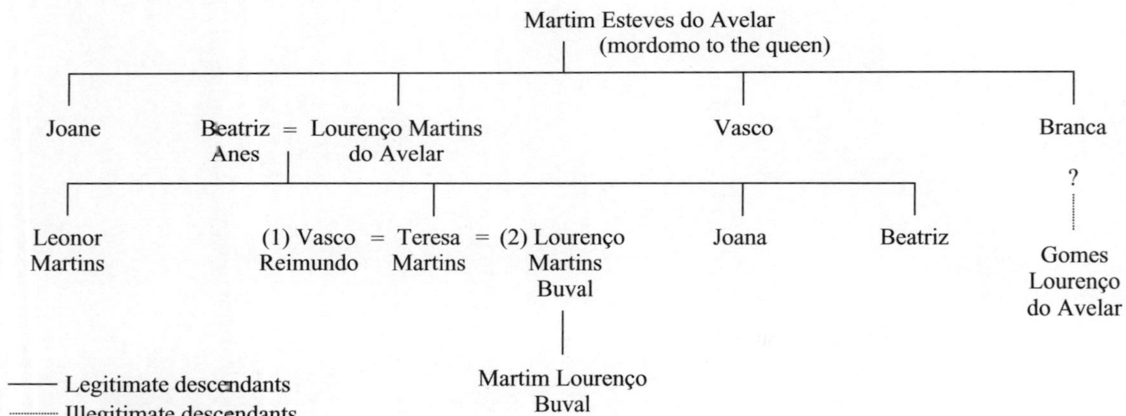

2 The de Meira family and Queen Leonor Teles

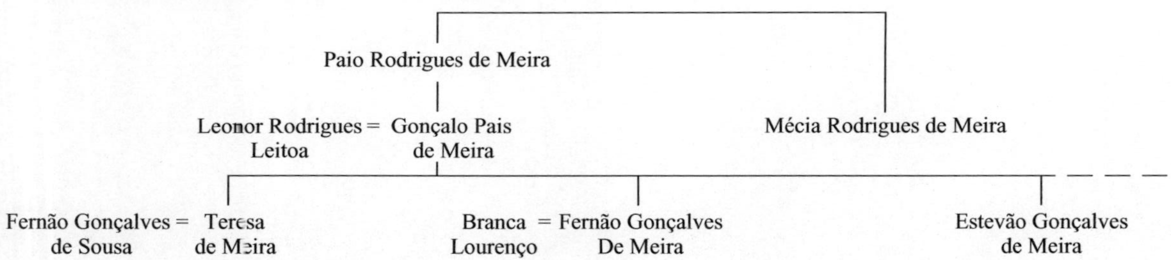

3 The Mirandas and Queen Philippa of Lancaster

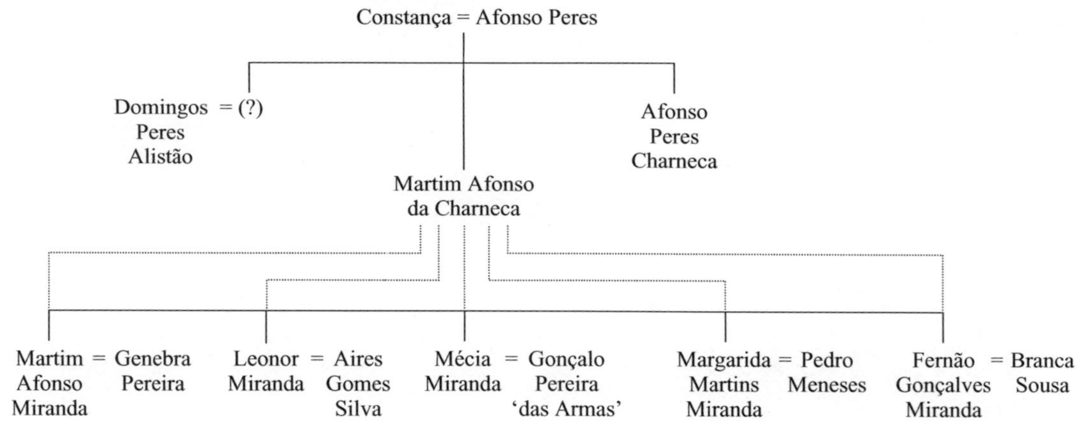

4 The 'da Guerras'

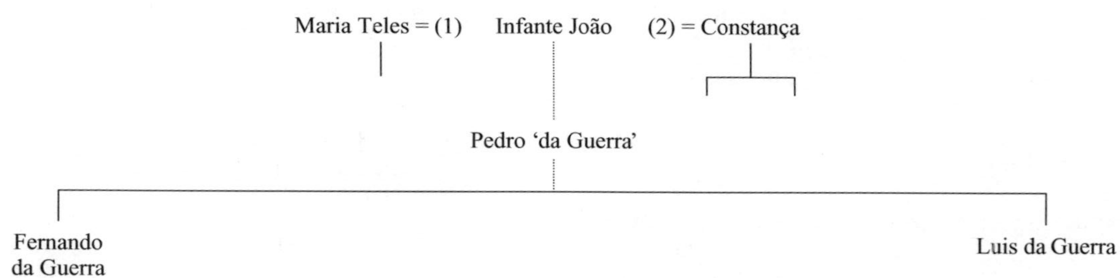

5 The 'de Braganzas'

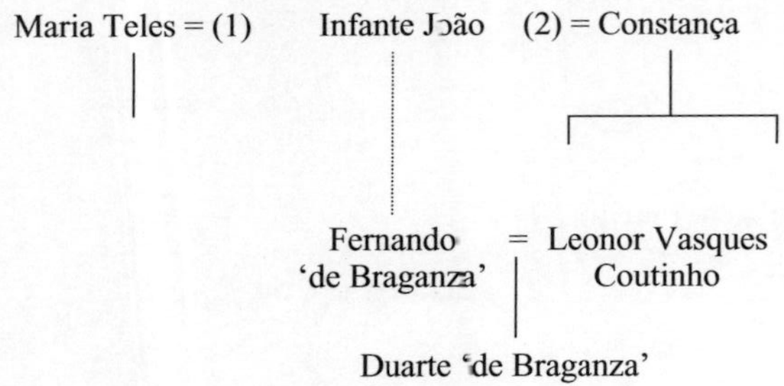

6 The 'de Cascais'

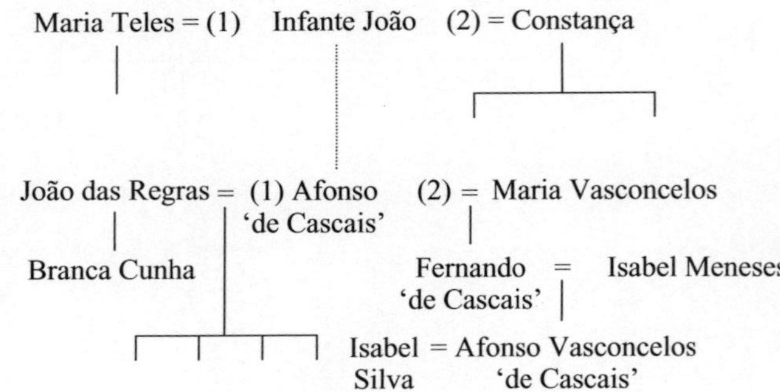

7 The 'de Eças'

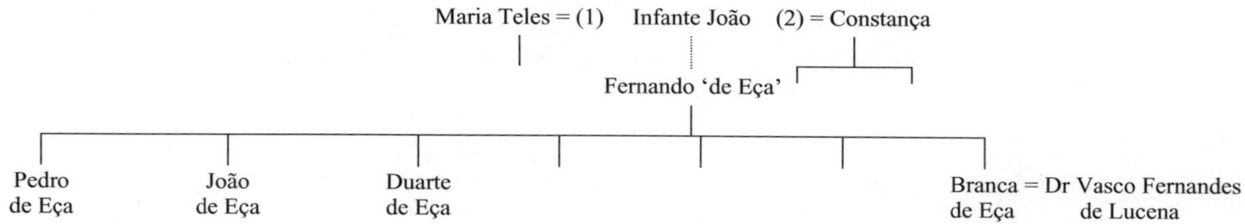

8 The Henriques

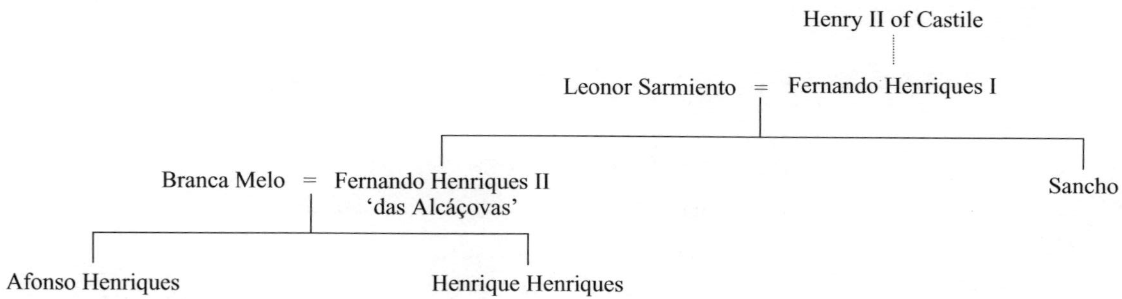

9 The Braganzas

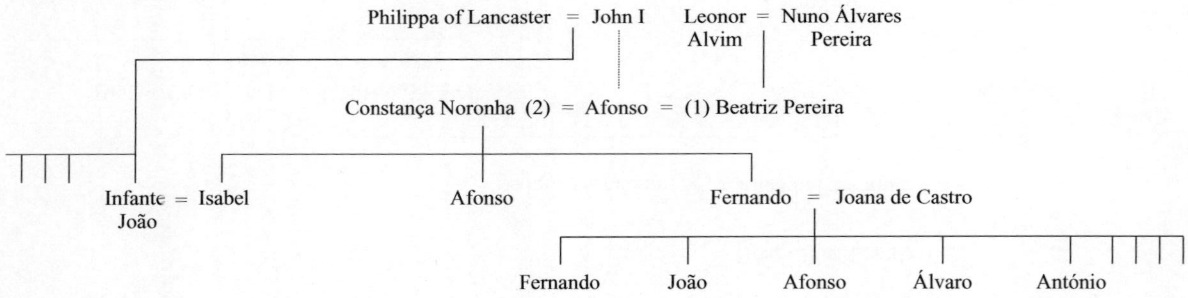

10 The Noronhas

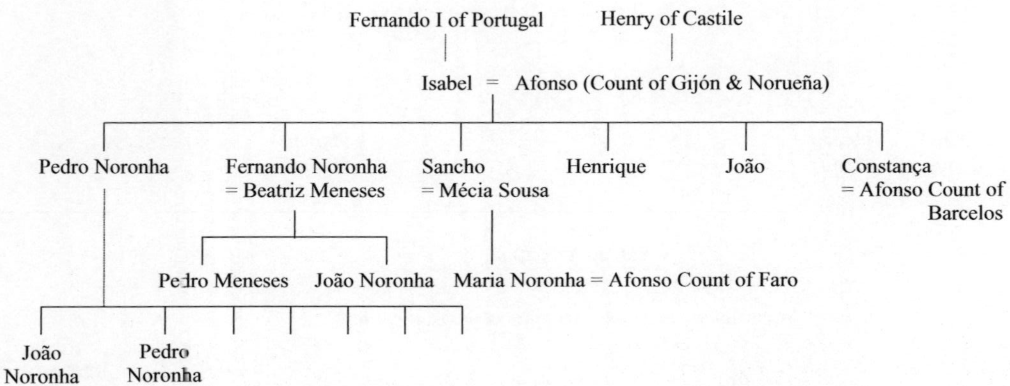

Glossary

Aia	Nurse
Alcaidaria	Governorship of a city
Alcaide	Governor of a city
Alferes	Standard bearer
Almotacé	Inspector of weights and measures
Almoxarife	Collector of the crown taxes
Ama	Nurse/wetnurse
Anadel	Commander
Caça	Hunt
Câmara	Chamber
Camareiro/camareira	Gentleman/gentlewoman of the chamber
Carta	Letter or charter
Casa	House/household
Casamento	(Literally) marriage – the moment at which a couple 'took' their household
Colheita	(Literally) harvest – dues in kind to the monarch
Condestável	Constable
Corregedor	Magistrate
Desembargador	High court judge/senior crown magistrate
Dona	Lady
Donzela	Young (unmarried) lady
Escrivão	Scribe or clerk
Escudeiro	Squire
Esmoleiro	Almoner
Estrebaria	Stable
Falcoeiro	Falconer
Fidalgo	Nobleman
Juiz de fora	District magistrate
Manceba	Young woman/handmaid
Mantimento	Subsistence allowance

Marechal	Marshal
Moço/moça	Boy/girl; groom
Montaria	Big-game hunting
Monteiro	Huntsman
-mor (as a suffix)	head of a department/master
Ordenação	Code of laws
Ouvidor	Crown or circuit judge
Privado/privança	One who had the king's ear/favourite
Procurador	Attorney
Quantia	Feudal rents or income
Quitação	Payment
Real/reis	Low-value unit of money
Regimento	Directive
Rico homem/rica dama	(Literally) rich man/rich woman
Sisa	Excise
Vedor	High officer

Introduction

The aim of this book is an in-depth study, on the scale of a small country, of an historic problem which on many occasions is dealt with in a generic or essentially theoretical manner: the emergence of a specific social form, that is the court in Europe, prior to the nineteenth century. It is an attempt which concentrates systematic research of sources upon a defined period (between 1300 and 1450) while at the same time resorting to the widest possible comparison of the phenomena being studied within the larger sphere of the existence of the medieval courts.

The sociologist Norbert Elias, to whom we are indebted for a fundamental contribution towards the definition and study of the court as a social form of the past, did not consider its existence exclusively in the form of an absolutist court, although he mentions the growing importance which it assumed during the modern period of European history (between the fifteenth and eighteenth centuries). Among the many passages of his writings which he dedicated to the problem, the book concerning the French court of Louis XIV, published for the first time in 1969, stands out, as do the important chapters on the emergence of the noble and royal courts during the medieval period contained within the ambitious construction of his work 'on the process of civilisation', which appeared in a number of versions across several decades (between 1930 and 1970).[1]

The greatest value of the work of Norbert Elias towards the realisation of this study resulted, however, from a number of fundamental contributions of his sociological theory, besides the conclusions resulting from the empirical cases which he mentioned or analysed in greater detail.[2] In spite of the increasingly

[1] Norbert Elias, *The Civilizing Process*, 2 vols. (Oxford: Blackwell, 1978–82); Norbert Elias, *The Court Society* (Oxford: Blackwell, 1983).

[2] Norbert Elias, *What Is Sociology*? (London: Hutchinson, 1978); Norbert Elias, 'Figuration', 'Soziale Prozess', 'Zivilisation', in Bernhard Schäfers (ed.), *Grundbegriffe der Soziologie* (Opladen: Leske und Budrich, 1986), pp. 88–91, 234–41, 382–97; Norbert Elias, *The Society of Individuals* (Oxford: Blackwell, 1991).

critical tone which one detects on the part of some historians regarding these empirical results and even the cultural framework and the presuppositions from which there emerges the thesis on the 'process of civilisation',[3] I believe that the contributions of Norbert Elias are too important to be overlooked. I refer to the concepts of configuration and process on the one hand and, on the other, to his suggestions as to a sociology of royalty.

To consider the medieval court as a social configuration or a 'network of interdependent human beings, with shifting and asymmetrical power balances' implies for the historian the construction of a new subject.[4] Some results considered to have been learnt through social history and through the institutional and political history of Europe must become the object of a critical eye when one studies the interactions between the kings and the nobility and the way in which their mutual dependence became established in the Middle Ages, in particular during the later period. Rather than setting off with an analysis and description merely external to the social groups, for example of the nobility, and accepting, without questioning them historically, the criteria (juridical or otherwise) of classification used by sources available, this is an assessment as to how social relations were formed by which groups, and even individuals. The court is seen as the place and the context from which many of these criteria of classification appeared, as well as the values associated with the nobility. In other words, we find that royalty and the nobility became mutually engendered at the end of the Middle Ages, although the conflict and bitter battles that appear to have placed them one against the other and that occupied the first level of political events in Portugal, as in the majority of European countries, weighed heavily. Far from constituting an immutable entity closed in upon itself, the medieval court affirms itself as a process, or a dynamic sequence of conditions leading to the constitution of a centre from which there emerge determined values and categories that are shared diversely by society both in time and in space.

The proposals of Norbert Elias, which examined a sociology of royalty, in turn challenge the study of the figure of the medieval king solely by his qualities and attributes, as an *a priori* fact of ancient societies or the mysterious emanation of the political doctrines of the past, contrasting it with the notion of a royalty which is 'constructed' through concrete, social mechanisms that can be analysed. To study the court implies detecting what practices and what processes led to the specific position of the kings, or reconstructing among the functions of this

[3] For example, Jeroen Duindam, *Myths of Power: Norbert Elias and the Early Modern European Court* (Amsterdam: Amsterdam University Press [1994]); Daniel Gordon, *Citizens without Sovereignty: Equality and Sociability in French Thought, 1670–1789* (Princeton: Princeton University Press, 1994).

[4] Godfried von Benthem van den Berg, *The Structure of Development: An Invitation to the Sociology of Norbert Elias* (The Hague: Institute of Social Studies, 1971); Artur Bogner, 'The structure of social processes. A commentary on the sociology of Norbert Elias', *Sociology*, 20 (1986), 3, 387–411.

human configuration one which appears to me to be fundamental: the making and maintaining of royalty itself. Such was the medieval concept, as we shall see, which created a necessary link between the court and the king, with one reality being unable to exist without the other.

The interpretation of royalty in this progressive perspective by an analysis of how its position of supremacy grew, separated as it was from society, implies the reconstruction of the functions that the court performed. The main obstacles to this functional study reside in the mixed and enduring character of the organisation of the court. Mixed because the medieval court challenges the categorical distinction, which has as its origin Greco-Latin thought, between the government of the household and the government of the public thing, between *oikos* and *polis*, between *domus* and *res publica*.[5] This presents a formidable obstacle, since these categories still remain subjacent to the historical explanation of European monarchic institutions, as they were also used by medieval thinkers when forging theoretical instruments and the concepts which allowed them to think and to explain power. On the other hand, the formal organisation which presided at the medieval courts, with its internal structure in distinct departments, survived and reproduced itself not only in space but also in time throughout the medieval period and even beyond the fifteenth century, in long lines and internal cores, in spite of the changes which made the court the centre of a larger, more complex web of relations and institutions, giving body to the ever-changing and intermittent reality of the bureaucratic state of the *ancien régime*.

Since it was not an institutional reality in the juridical and formal meaning of the word, as long as the court was a human configuration it remained in an indistinct state between public and private – John of Salisbury suggested that the king himself played a part in the two spheres – and so became hard to individualise. The actual medieval definition therefore served as a starting point: the court was the place of the presence of the king, and the group of individuals who accompanied him (chapter 1). It was a physical, concrete space within which not only the members of the restricted circle of *familiares* of the king and queen moved, but also all those who became the body that mediated between the powers of the monarch and the kingdom, becoming a part of his entourage. It was, therefore, inevitable that other institutions should rise from within this tapestry of diverse functions exercised in the early court, and this led to the formation of bureaucracies and autonomy in various spheres of activity. But besides being a simple sum of all these institutional mechanisms, the court remained an indivisible human configuration in that dual entity which the medieval texts suggest – a space, a group of individuals. How this space became organised in Portugal, who these individuals were and 'in which ways

[5] Aloys Winterling, *Zwischen 'Haus' und 'Staat': Antike Höfe im Vergleich* (Munich: Oldenbourg, 1997), pp. 1–9, 11–25.

they were bonded to each other', these are the questions which this book seeks, above all, to answer.

The perspective of the study of the old courts that Norbert Elias termed 'genetic' thus inspired in me a new examination of the concrete forms of the human organisation which surrounded the medieval kings, termed in a restricted and somewhat pejorative way 'domestic' by the majority of authors. The comparison of these organisational forms allows for the detection of common regularities and principles within the western European profile. This will be not only a description of these but, as suggested by Fredrik Barth, an attempt to explain the similarities, by studying the social processes which cause these regularities of forms that can be observed historically, since they govern and determine the constraints and the incentives beneath which men group and interact within this particular formation.[6] The construction of royalty, with the permanent tension of power relations that constitute court society, seems to be one of these processes. With regard to this problem, it is important to return to the large number of classic studies of Percy Schramm and Ernst Kantorowicz because of the attention which they give to an interpretation of medieval royalty in its link with the complex of ideas, practices and traditions stemming from late antiquity, namely through the Byzantine transmission and synthesis with barbarian royalties, which complex is constantly reinterpreted and 'translated' by fundamental and paradigmatic institutions that were, for the Middle Ages, the papacy and the Empire. The European medieval court is not contained outside this cultural complex of multi-secular density, becoming as it does a group of intercommunicating practices and devices, beyond the actual plan of a country and a period. This perspective allowed me to break from an overspecialised vision of the Portuguese court, which is based upon unproven postulations of isolationism and incipient structure of the monarchic institutions. If we recognise that a royalty exists in Portugal from the middle of the twelfth century, then we must examine the processes which allow for its reproduction and, among these, the emergence of the human configuration which is the court then appears as one of the most important, indeed the essence.

This book does not propose entirely to resolve the general questions which have been advanced. It is important to emphasise, however, that they are subjacent to the strength of understanding of an actual case, that is the Portuguese kingdom at the end of the Middle Ages. This study is limited to dealing as deeply as possible with the problems raised by the use of this chosen perspective. The study today of medieval Portugal, its obstacles and inherent insufficiencies, and also the wealth of an historiographic tradition in constant change, all define the necessary context of this research. Choices as to sources and methods used are, of course, dictated in many cases by this historiographic context. Portuguese

[6] Fredrik Barth, *Models of Social Organisation* (London: Royal Anthropological Institute, 1971).

sources of the medieval period, as is well known, remain largely unpublished. In the particular case of sources produced by royal institutions, the problem is aggravated by a periodic interruption and distortion of the written transmission itself, accompanying as it does the vicissitudes of the memory of royalty, with many of the medieval sources being successively truncated and rewritten, in particular in the fifteenth and sixteenth centuries.

The Iberian context to which I systematically return, which places the kingdom of Portugal in parallel with those of Leon, Castile and Aragon, does not however appear as a mere subtlety or easy solution in the face of the fragmentary and heterogeneous character of Portuguese sources. The texts and customs that originated from the several kingdoms of the Iberian Peninsula formed part of the cultural horizon of the Portuguese of the age, and moulded and played a part in their perception of things. For this reason, many problems need to be interpreted within an Iberian framework where they find their possible significance, and rejection or neglect of this framework is scientifically indefensible. By crossing the perspectives, it seems to me that the court of the Portuguese kings could in turn clarify in several ways the existence of human configurations which are similar in the other territories contained within modern Spain.

In approaching this complex social medium, that is the court of the end of the Middle Ages, I turned to two valuable work tools: genealogy and prosopography. Each complements the other in this attempt to reconstruct court society with an analysis of individual biographies, as well as family recollections and the use of criteria of social classification as defined by the age itself. It is a matter of approaching the status groups, gender groups, professional groups and family groups within the dynamic of their relationships and the framework of a social formation with its own mechanisms of cohesion, its own hierarchies and even, following the hypothesis of Norbert Elias, with its distinctive modes of being and behaving. A detailed reconstruction of this type demanded a prosopographic examination in which the data relative to the identification and chronology of hundreds of individuals, the positions held and functions performed in the royal service were investigated, as also were the terms relative to their status and to the interpersonal relationships of varying types which appeared. For the study of family recollections of the nobility, I was able profitably to put to use the rich Portuguese genealogical literature, particularly the *Livro de Linhagens do Conde D. Pedro* (*c.* 1340, with two later versions, both in the fourteenth century) and the *Livro de Linhagens do século XVI*, and studied and added to the data stemming not only from these, but also from other sources, both factual and narrative, of varying types and origins. From the methodological point of view, recourse to the collation of these various sources was an option that I considered, so abandoning the hypothesis of construction of a prosopographic series based on one sole documentary typology.

The detailed framework described in this book aims to display the principal results reached, outlining Portuguese court society in its development across one and a half centuries. The principal challenge that the description has to confront is the necessary articulation of the several scales of analysis, given that the research had as its departure point an inquiry which was, by its minute nature, destined to reconstruct the dense mosaic of family and individual histories. I therefore sought a thread necessary for the construction of an image of the group of court society (chapter 2). Such an image does not, however, result from the simple juxtaposition of these family or individual histories or from the generalisations that can be drawn from them. This study was intended not to remain constrained by systematic investigation of the trajectories of individuals and groups but rather simultaneously to reflect on that 'network of human interrelations which reproduced itself during successive generations' (Elias), which was the royal court. For this very reason, I analysed the court not simply of one monarch, but of a succession of monarchs, encompassing in the period studied an important dynastic change. The description of the several groups interacting in the Portuguese court of the fourteenth and fifteenth centuries is completed by an analysis and explanation of the interwoven relationships between themselves and the king, resulting in this particular configuration (chapter 3). As will be seen, different ways of existence of the court correspond to the various types of interaction, and these interactions are in turn fundamental to the explanation of the hierarchies, the internal tensions and even certain features of the organisation of the court.

A second part is added to the principal body of the text, in which other important aspects of medieval court society are explored, in particular the forms of life which characterise it. Since this is also a spatial reality, as written of in medieval texts, the royal court must be viewed in its characteristic mobility, with an analysis of the progresses when the monarch symbolically appropriated territory, so manifesting his presence (chapter 4). This space, which can be topographically placed successively on a chronological axis, is a true site of power and reveals in its relations with the physical reality of the country an entire geography of royalty. The medieval monarchs appear thus as true agents of change of the countryside, stamping upon it signs of conquest, possession and realisation of resources. At the end of the Middle Ages Portuguese kings prolonged more and more their stay in certain places, and these progressively became different from the great stopping posts; places began to compete with each other, so generating a hierarchy from which was finally to emerge a capital: Lisbon. The medieval court appears not only as a particular human configuration but also as a spatial-temporal complex which the royal presence reproduced in several ways, for example in relation to the city, through the urban palace, and through the royal entry. Or it might lead to territory that was a privileged dominion of a relationship of royalty with the natural world, carefully delineated through hunting. Or again in the use of the multiplicity of palaces and residences which were spread across the kingdom where the memories of certain monarchs as well as other dynastic or religious memories were incorporated.

Finally, particular attention was given to ritual and ceremonies because of their importance in the regulation of the collective life of the courtier, and I sought to unravel a specific rhythm of the times of court (chapter 5). My perspective is not, however, that of a 'ritualistic' vision, in the sense described by Mary Douglas, of functions performed by this social configuration.[7] The performance of rituals and ceremonies constitutes one of these modes of 'fabrication' of royalty already referred to, but it is not the only one. In this process, which includes multiple factors, ceremonies cannot be seen as the product of an entirely independent and 'self-contained' activity, since it is only one mode of activity among others. The perspective of analysis chosen does not follow the diverse paths of this enormous subject, but rather seeks to reduce it to a precise, problematic axis. The various rites and ceremonies were what ordered time at court, and this generated determined cycles of a framework of fundamental life whose global design we must find once again within a larger framework. I could not, therefore, limit my study to the more spectacular royal ceremonies or those that appear to project more clearly the society of court in relation to that which was exterior to it. Although the knowledge that we possess of them is very unequal, I tried also to identify the more modest ceremonies and rites, unravelling their systematic arrangement based on a typology that distinguishes the temporal modalities that arise. From this perspective, the search for possible meanings becomes related to the whole not simply at the level of isolated ceremonies. The problem of rites gains by being examined in conjunction with the processes of configuration and formal organisation of the organism that surrounded the kings, which can be studied as a true system of social roles where the courtier became the agent of a 'leitourgia' (in its etymological meaning of 'service') of royalty. The ritual function was a duty which, being in many cases central to the establishment of its identity, did not, as we shall see, exhaust all the aspects of its activity.

The text that follows is a revised and enlarged version of the first edition in Portuguese of 1995, with the more significant changes being concentrated in chapters 2 and 5. I should like to express my thanks for all the criticism made during the intervening years that allowed me not only to improve on it in many detailed aspects but also to make more clear and precise the expression of my ideas. In essence, the principal argument of the book remains the same.

The writing of the first version of this book owes much to José Mattoso who followed the project from the beginning, discussing my hypotheses and making important criticisms and suggestions. In so many cases there can be

[7] Mary Douglas, *In the Active Voice* (London: Routledge and Kegan Paul, 1982), pp. 34–8.

seen the mark of his insight, his empathy and his knowledge. The seminars and work sessions with Vitorino Magalhães Godinho, which I had the privilege of attending during the 1980s, were always a fundamental stimulus for my investigation. To him I owe my introduction to the sociological work of Norbert Elias as well as the example of an unfailing attention to a method of critical and creative thought that ignores disciplinary barriers and the comfort of already formed ideas. For welcoming me to his seminars in Florence and the sessions at the Laboratorio di Storia, I owe to Sergio Bertelli my introduction to a stimulating atmosphere, rich in concrete possibilities for work, as well as countless ideas and leads that resulted from the wealth of his comparative vision of the European courts. Francisco Bethencourt, friend and intellectual companion of many years, as well as my friends and colleagues Diogo Ramada Curto, Vanda Anastácio, Luis Krus, Lurdes Rosa, Paola Ventrone, Joaquim Caetano, Alfred Opitz, Armando Luis de Carvalho Homem and João Gouveia Monteiro contributed with reading and bibliographic leads as well as suggestions for research, well-founded criticism and animated discussions which led to the final version. To Peter Linehan and the Instituto Português do Livro, in the person of its Director Teresa Gil, I owe my thanks for all the support they gave to the initiative of the translation of this book into English. The burden of the task fell on Alison Aiken, always gracious and unflinching in the face of an ever growing original. I should like to express here my recognition of her fine work.

1. *The court: outlining the problem*

THE MEDIEVAL CONCEPT

The Middle Ages used a diverse group of words when speaking of the court of the kings. From the point of view of the history of concepts, it is of interest to distinguish carefully the span of social and political meanings and experiences that can be expressed by these words, paying particular attention to the rise of new meanings in old words or of neologisms. With a valid and historically coherent definition of the subject of this book in mind, these are, in general, valuable indicators of important changes. As Koselleck states, we can interpret human history in a restricted sense through the concepts of the past, even if the words that are related to these concepts are still in use today. This task requires a work of critical distancing which accompanies both the fundamental historicity and the sedimentation, which is evident in the vocabulary of a given society, of successive uses of a constellation of words. For such, the author reminds us, past uses of a concept should in some way be redefined by the historian.[1]

While Latin predominated as the written language in the medieval west, texts resorted to several names for the court – *curia*, *aula*, *palatium*, *schola* – at the same time as the binominal of words was to emerge that was to take precedence over all these: *cors/curtis*.[2] The formation of a synonym between 'curia' and 'court' is a first aspect deserving our attention. In classical Latin, *curia* and *cohors* (from *cors* and *curtis* in medieval Latin) were far from being synonymous. *Cohors* initially meant the empty, restricted space in the interior of a residential complex and, at the end of the classical age, the use of the term extended to military language to mean a certain group of soldiers (six centuries), possibly by association with the space occupied in the camp by each of these units. This use later led to *cohors* becoming the common name given

[1] Reinhart Koselleck, *Le Futur passé: contribution à la sémantique des temps historiques* (Paris: Ecole des Hautes Etudes en Sciences Sociales, 1990), pp. 99–118.

[2] Egbert Türk, *Nugae Curialium: le règne d'Henri II Plantagenêt et l'éthique politique* (Geneva: Droz, 1977), pp. 3–5; Aurelio Roncaglia, 'Le corti medievali. Premessa', in *Letteratura Italiana* (Turin: Einaudi, 1982), vol. I, pp. 33–6.

to groups of armed men such as a praetorian guard (*cohors praetoria*), and was then handed down to the Middle Ages by numerous texts. More important for us, however, is the evolution which led *cohors* to become *cors/curtis*, a word which during the High Middle Ages served to mean the centre of an agrarian complex both in its materiality (still existing today in the Portuguese 'corte', a synonym for a courtyard or stable area), and in evoking the centre of noble power.[3]

As for the word *curia*, its most frequent use in the Latin world was in the institutional and political sphere as a synonym for *senatus*, or the municipal government. From here comes its association, for example, with *decurio*, while the *curialitas* in imperial Roman society was merely an alternative meaning for the order of decuries. In *Lex Visigothorum* or in Isidore of Seville, for example, as also in the Merovingian texts, the use of *curia* and *curialis* prevails when used to refer to municipal institutions. But, as Georges Duby remarks, 'from the eighth century in those texts which we have, *curia* tends to be confused with *curtis*, meaning the fortification from which public power is legitimately driven back, while the scribes and the better-educated inversely used the word *curtis* when speaking of the royal palace: *in curte nostra*, as Charlemagne said in the most important decrees'.[4]

Thus, during the High Middle Ages, two words began to approximate each other and be used to mean respectively: the material centre of the household (or, by extension, a domestic group) and an organism comprising men who acted 'collectively' and were invested in some form with public authority. The two versions that today clearly are opposites of the public and the private therefore appear to become associated in this binominal of words. We can also conclude by analysis that other names were given to the court of the kings, for example *palatium* and *aula*. In turn, these refer to the materiality of the house, of the royal residence. The word *palatium* meant, in particular in the Low Empire, the magnificent imperial residence built on the Palatine, which was evoked in their common name by all the royal or princely residences of the medieval west.[5]

[3] There are several examples in J. F. Niermeyer, *Mediae Latinitatis Lexicon Minus* (Leiden: Brill, 1977) s.v. 'curtis'; J. Corominas and J. A. Pascual, *Diccionario crítico etimológico Castellano e Hispánico* (Madrid: Gredos, 1980) s.v. 'corte'; Ramón Lorenzo, *Sobre cronologia do vocabulário Galego-Português* (Vigo: Galáxia, 1968). On the name given to the housing of animals: Alberto Sampaio, *Estudos económicos* (Lisbon: Vega, 1979), vol. I, p. 78.

[4] Georges Duby (ed.), *Histoire de la vie privée* (Paris: Seuil, 1985), vol. II, p. 30. Later, 'technical' Latin of the universities returned to the original name of 'curia', which is found in the texts of Justinian Law. However, the word appears not to have been much used outside the juridical sphere: Pierre Michaud Quentin, *Universitas: expressions du mouvement communautaire dans le moyen âge latin* (Paris: Vrin, 1970), pp. 141–2.

[5] C. D. Du Cange, *Glossarium Mediae et Infimae Latinitatis*, ed. L. Fabre (Paris: Librairie des Sciences et des Arts, 1938), vol. VI, pp. 98–107. On this subject, the essay by Alain Labbé, *L'Architecture des palais et des jardins dans les Chansons de Geste: essai sur le thème du roi en majesté* (Paris: Champion-Slatkine, 1987).

Its use is very common in the semantic field of judicial activities, uniting, as does the binominal *curtis/curia*, the royal residence intended for the exercise of public power. *Palatium*, like the Castilian *palacio* which derives from it, and the Portuguese *palácio* and *paço* were words which were frequently used during the entire medieval period to mean the court, and in the same way the adjective 'palatine' replaced 'cortês' in many texts.[6] As for *aula*, which is a common name given to a vast space or room where a collection or group of individuals would meet (and let us not forget that the term could also mean the entire space of the church), its use was metonymic, for it was used for the totality of the court, while it also served to designate merely one of its parts. However, it meant an essential part, for the word evoked the space put aside for the meeting of the king with his men.[7] The word 'sala', of German origin, had a similar connotation.[8] As Alain Labbé stated, in the texts of medieval epic tradition there is clearly to be seen the reductive identification of the palace as the *aula* or *sala*, that is precisely the place where the image of sovereign majesty related to a fundamental archetype of royalty took root. Finally, in the word *schola*, which is by far the least used and the one whose meaning is the most restricted, we find again the idea of the armed entourage that appeared in *cohors*, with two words that medieval texts also placed closely in meaning.[9]

What does the history of this group of words tell us? The court of the kings of the Middle Ages was, above all, the household of the monarchs, a magnificent residence or palace where they lived with the domestic community, their *familia*.[10] There is also present in these words the idea of the meeting of several men for process of judgment or, simply, exercising together a power

[6] For the semantics of 'palacio' and 'corte' in medieval Castilian: Bernardo Blanco González, *Del cortesano al discreto* (Madrid: Gredos, 1962), vol. I, pp. 161–6. For the Portuguese '*paço*': Joseph M. Piel, *'Paço' e 'milhafre': história de duas palavras e de alguns termos congéneres*, offprint of *Revista da Faculdade de Letras de Lisboa* (Lisbon, 1971), and the general observations of Henrique de Gama Barros, *História da administração pública em Portugal nos séculos XII a XV* (Lisbon: Sá da Costa, 1945–54), vol. III, p. 200.

[7] Du Cange, *Glossarium*, vol. I, p. 481. Before the thirteenth century, the meeting of the king with his dependants and vassals was often also called *consilium* in the kingdoms of the Western Peninsula, a word Sánchez-Albornoz considered a synonym of *curia*: Claudio Sánchez-Albornoz, *La Curia Regia Portuguesa: siglos XII y XIII* (Madrid: Centro de Estudios Históricos, 1920), pp. 17–18; Claudio Sánchez-Albornoz, 'El *Palatium Regis* Asturleonés', *Cuadernos de Historia de España*, 59–60 (1976), in particular 8–9.

[8] Joseph M. Piel, 'Considerações sobre o hispano-godo **Sala*, Gal.-Port. *Sáa*, *Sá*, etc', in *Estudos de linguística histórica Galego-Portuguesa* (Lisbon: Imprensa Nacional–Casa da Moeda, 1989), pp. 123–7.

[9] Du Cange, *Glossarium*, vol. VI, pp. 349–50. This word is used to mean the court of Leon in the eleventh century: Evelyn S. Procter, *Curia and Cortes in León and Castile, 1072–1295* (Cambridge: Cambridge University Press, 1980), pp. 8–9. In the Charter of Coimbra of 1111, *schola* meant the entourage of the Count of Portucale, D. Henrique. The word also appears in vernacular in *El Cid* ('Oidme escuelas e toda la mi cort!').

[10] Karl Bosl, 'La "familia" come struttura fondamentale della società medievale', in *Modelli di società medievale* (Bologna: Il Mulino, 1981), pp. 131–61.

that is, in origin, public. Some evoke the presence of armed men. It should be emphasised, however, that these words almost always required a denominative (*palatium regis*, *aula regis*, *schola regis*), for they were not used exclusively for the court of the kings, but could also suggest other organisms, such as the house or entourage of a bishop or nobleman.

In texts which come from the medieval Iberian Peninsula, as in the rest of Europe, all these Latin terms are found, with their derivatives, to mean the royal court and its members (*familiares*, *curiales*, *aulici*, *palatini*).[11] With the rise of the vulgar vernacular, as in other Romance languages, 'corte' became, without doubt, the most used word. The important family of medieval terms related to the word – in particular *courtois*/courtier, *courtoisie*/courtesy – also meant within the Iberian context a form of life and a particular literary model.[12] The flowering of Peninsular literature from the twelfth century gives ample testimony to the acceptance and power of this model, principally in the Portuguese case.[13] It should be noted that the men and women who lived at court were not yet, in the Middle Ages, called 'courtiers', a word whose first occurrences with this semantic value, for example in the Latin vocabulary (*curtisanus*), appear to date only from the fourteenth century. The creation of this new word reveals the difficulty in including a far larger group of meanings and experiences within the system of words existing until then. Whether this word had been introduced in the Iberian languages through Occitan or through Italian from the fifteenth century, its generalised use became indivisible from the diffusion of a sixteenth-century ideal of court life, and had already replaced the by-then vulgarised and overrestricted word 'cortês'.[14] In the sixteenth century only this new word appeared to be capable of conveying the entire diversity of aspects of court life in a necessarily polysemic concept, and it bore associations with distinctive behavioural models which were consciously innovative, and which led to the flowering of a true written tradition about the figure of the 'courtier'.

[11] See, for example, the semantic study of 'curialis' by José Antonio Maravall, 'Los "hombres de saber" o letrados y la formación de su conciencia estamental', in *Estudios de historia del pensamiento Español: edad media* (Madrid: Cultura Hispánica, 1983), pp. 359–61.

[12] For an introduction to this problem see Reto Bezzola, *Les Origines et la formation de la littérature courtoise en occident, 500–1200* (Paris: Honoré Champion, 1958–63), or, more recently, C. Stephen Jaeger, *The Origins of Courtliness: Civilizing Trends and the Formation of Courtly Ideals, 939–1210* (Philadelphia: University of Pennsylvania Press, 1985). For the Iberian Peninsula, see Jole Scudieri Ruggieri, *Cavalleria e cortesia nella vita e nella cultura di Spagna* (Modena: Mucchi, 1980).

[13] See António Resende de Oliveira's essay, *Depois de Espectáculo Trovadoresco: a estrutura dos cancioneiros peninsulares e as recolhas dos séculos XIII e XIV* (Lisbon: Colibri, 1994).

[14] Besides statements by Corominas and Pascual in their *Diccionario crítico etimológico*, s.v. 'cortesano' and António de Morais Silva, *Grande dicionário da lingua Portuguesa* (Lisbon: Confluência, 1949–59), s.v. 'cortesão'; see also Margherita Morreale, *Castiglione y Boscán: el ideal cortesano en el Renacimiento Español* (Madrid: Real Academia Española, 1959), vol. I, p. 114; and Peter Burke, *The Fortunes of the Courtier: The European Reception of Castiglione's Cortegiano* (Cambridge: Polity Press, 1995), pp. 67–8.

This brief analysis of the multiplicity of names given to the court is therefore justified by a quest for the medieval concept that cannot be achieved without reference to texts. Because of its importance I selected a work that aims precisely to clarify the norm, to synthesise traditions – including those of the classical world – and to be the receptacle of doctrine: the *Siete Partidas* of Alfonso X of Castile.[15] In the form of an encyclopaedic synthesis, so popular during the thirteenth century, this text includes several passages in which there is a definition of the court. The influence of this work in Portugal is well known, mainly as a source of fifteenth-century Portuguese legislative texts; this is particularly the case in the Second Book, from which I have extracted texts for analysis.[16]

The *Partidas* distinguish the 'Court' (object of Law XXVII, Title IX of the Second Part) from the 'Palace' (Law XXIX). In the first place, the text presents some considerations of an etymological nature: thus, 'corte' was to derive from 'cohors', meaning 'ayuntamiento de compañas', and from 'curia', or 'logar do es la cura de todos los fechos de la tierra'. But also, 'according to the language of Spain', 'corte' is used, 'porque alli es la espada de justicia con que se han de cortar todos los males'.[17] The text defines the court as 'logar do es el rey, et sus vassallos et sus oficiales con él, que le han cotidianamente de consejar e de servir, et los otros del regno que se llegan hi ó por honra del, ó por alcanzar derecho, ó por fazer recabdar las otras cosas que han de ver con el'. As for the palace, it is 'aquel logar do el rey se ayunta paladinamente para fablar con los homes; et esto es en tres maneras, ó para librar los pleytos, ó para comer, ó para fablar en gasajado'. In both definitions we understand the importance of the spatial element for the concept of court and palace: both are 'places', which seems obvious in the latter case, but which gives rise to some interesting problems in the former. The presence of the king defines the 'court': it is an actual space, but it is also a group of individuals who accompany the monarch, an organism whose configurations are fluid, and which includes all those who are within this space, even if temporarily. Meanwhile, the 'palace', with its evocation of specific times and activities, appears as a way of life particular to the court, evoked around three aspects which are associated with the royal presence: the exercise of justice; the distribution of food; the use of the word.[18]

[15] *Las Siete Partidas del Rey Alfonso el Sabio, cotejadas con varios Códices antiguos* (Madrid: Real Academia de la Historia, 1807), vol. I, pp. 56–8.

[16] For this influence see, for all, Nuno Espinosa Gomes da Silva, *História do direito Português* (Lisbon: Fundação Calouste Gulbenkian, 1985), vol. I, pp. 161–2, and the bibliography listed.

[17] *Las Siete Partidas*, vol. I, pp. 82–3. For the encyclopaedic meaning of etymologies in the Alfonsine text, see Hans J. Niederehe, *Alfonso el Sabio y la linguística de su tiempo* (Madrid: Sociedad General Española, 1987), pp. 214–16.

[18] On the use of the word at court, the theorisation of the *Partidas* (in particular Law XXX of Title IX) develops the statements of the Speculum: 'quien quissiere rretraer antel rey deue dezir palabras buenas e apuestas de las que ssolíen dezir ante los rreys por que los omnes sson llamados corteses, e palaçianos eran preçiados e onrrados'. G. Martínez Díez (ed.), *Leyes de Afonso X*, vol. I (Ávila: Fundación Claudio Sánchez-Albornoz, 1985), p. 124. For an in-depth analysis of

In fact, we see several models, several traditions which the theorisation of the *Partidas* regarding the court sought to harmonise, all being superimposed in these texts. Besides the courtly theme, in this definition of the palace we can detect the archetype of a court marked by the *familiaritas*, a term in which is captured, as was the case in the Carolingian court, 'the dual connotation of companionship and patrimonial authority over the household (*familia*), which increase in size during annual assemblies and which include the totality of the political kingdom'.[19] As Janet Nelson states, these assemblies in the Carolingian world were an occasion for principal rites of eating together, hunting, the exchange of gifts, a reaffirmation of ideas of political consensus, and of peace and solidarity among magnates. The physical proximity of the king and the sharing of some moments of his life thus became characteristics of a way of life called, in the texts of Alfonso, 'palaciano' and 'cortês'.

On the other hand, in the *Partidas* we also have an original theorisation that seeks to capture the essence of the subject to be defined – the court – emphasising its connection with space. We are, in this case, faced with a construction which seems to arise from the world of jurists, parallel to that which Frederick II Hohenstaufen suggested in his formula 'ibi sit Alemanie curia, ubi persona nostra et principes Imperii nostri consistunt'.[20] This definition of the court as 'the place where the king is' is perhaps connected to one of the first formulations of a central idea of medieval juridic thought: the idea that the *corpus mysticum* of the Church (or of the kingdom) is where its head is. Thus Gaines Post states, 'any city in which a king had his *sedes* became the capital, because of the *regis potentia* or the powers of the king as the head of the realm'.[21]

In fact, many functions that today we would call 'capital' were concentrated in this itinerant organism that was the royal court. The theorisation of the medieval jurists sought to reflect on this relationship between imperial (or royal) power and space, having recourse to a defining element: the physical presence of the monarch. That this mode of thought produced some problems of interpretation and could lead to doubts is what is concluded from the glossary of one of the versions of the text of the *Partidas* which I have studied; 'otrosi es corte la su chancelleria, aunque el no va hi'. Could the presence of the monarch be

these texts, see Francisco López Estrada, 'Corte y literatura en las *Siete Partidas*', in *Littérature et institutions dans le moyen âge espagnol*, ed. Monique de Lope (Montpellier: Université Paul Valéry, 1991), pp. 9–46.

[19] Janet L. Nelson, 'The Lord's anointed and the people's choice: Carolingian royal ritual', in David Cannadine and S. Price (eds.), *Rituals of Royalty: Power and Ceremony in Traditional Societies* (Cambridge: Cambridge University Press, 1987), p. 165.

[20] On the use of this text (dated 1226) in medieval juridical thought, and the parallelism with the later formula of Baldo, 'ubi est fiscus, ibi est imperium', see Ernst Kantorowicz, *The King's Two Bodies: A Study in Political Medieval Theology* (Princeton: Princeton University Press, 1957), p. 204 and note 34.

[21] Gaines Post, *Studies in Medieval Legal Thought: Public Law and the State, 1100–1322* (Princeton: Princeton University Press, 1964), p. 389.

manifest in any way, other than physical? This idea was not entirely absent in the juridic theory after the thirteenth century. It was also stated that: 'where the emperor is, there is Rome' (Baldo). And as Ernst Kantorowicz and Gaines Post have observed, 'to be sure, this means in one sense that the king is the realm wherever he may go. But there is also, perhaps, the meaning that the king's government and the king are present everywhere in the realm, even though the king remains in the *regia civitas* and in his palace.'[22]

To summarise, when seeking to define the court in its relationship with the king and with the space of the kingdom I detect in this major work on the medieval Hispanic tradition a strong influence of the categories of contemporary juridic thought. One could say that, when speaking of the 'palace', the *Partidas* are referring in particular to the type of relationship which is established with the king at the interior of the court, taking the endogenous point of view, while the book defines that same 'court' in its relationship with other realities which were external to it, making use of innovative juridic concepts which become entwined with a more traditional vision of royalty. In their extraordinary wealth these texts, which are so profoundly influential in the political and juridic culture of the late Middle Ages, present us with several facets of a medieval notion of court which is compatible with the new conceptual synthesis that results from its combining with Roman Law, while simultaneously developing some aspects which have already been evoked by this approximation to the history of the words which expressed it.

First must be emphasised the impossibility of separating clearly, in the medieval definition of the royal court, the public from the private. The court is structured around the person of the king and the king is, even according to the categories of political and juridic thought after the twelfth century, *gemina persona*, that is simultaneously a public and a private person.[23] To this dual nature there corresponded in an analogous form the 'mixed' nature of the court, which was simultaneously *curia* and *curtis*. The second aspect to be emphasised is the absence of precise frontiers: the Middle Ages conceived the court more as a centre of attraction in permanent motion, a grouping of varying composition which accompanied the monarch, than as a stable, delineated entity. Two distinctions can perhaps be established at its core, according to the *Partidas*. One of these would be between those who 'continuously served' the king, a small nucleus of companions whose presence was constant, and those who 'approached' the monarch but who did not remain beside him. In Peninsular Latin documentation, for example, *familiares*, *aulici* and *palatini* could belong to one or the other

[22] Post, *Studies in Medieval Legal Thought*, pp. 387–8 and note 51. See also Rita Costa Gomes, 'Invocar o rei na idade média: breve nota de antropologia jurídica', *Revista Portuguesa de História*, 31 (1996), 195–207.

[23] Kantorowicz, *The King's Two Bodies*, pp. 96 and 172; Ernst Kantorowicz, 'Kingship under the impact of scientific jurisprudence', in *Selected Studies* (New York: Augustin, 1965), pp. 151–66.

group. The other possible distinction would be between 'vassals' and 'officers', which should lead one to reflect upon the variety of relationships that connected the king with his companions and servants within the court. Finally we should emphasise the fact that the medieval concept of the court was based upon a principal element: the physical presence of the monarch, which determined the existence of a space and of a group of men around him. It is worth once again remembering on this point the observations of Gaines Post:

> there was, to be sure, much that was private in the royal household. But at the same time, just as in his office the king was a *persona publica*, just as he enjoyed a public as well as a private *status*, so the royal *domus*, *hostel*, household shared in the public aspects of kingship. Perhaps, indeed, the very joining of status to *hostel*, *l'estat del hotel*, resulted from the concept of *palatium* in the Roman and Canon Law and in the legists and canonists. The imperial palace was 'sacred' and like all *sacra* was a subject of public law.[24]

While, on the one hand, the medieval king seemed to 'segregate' or to cause, simply through his presence, this space or place as Le Goff[25] has more recently stated, on the other hand royalty maintained itself by means of this human network that sustained it and powerfully contributed, in a constant and daily form, towards its reproduction.

STRUCTURES AND INSTITUTIONS

The complexity of the medieval concept of court, the actual plurality of its names, but more than ever the fact that we are able to detect in it categories which contradict central distinctions of the constitutional theory based on the Aristotelian tradition, that is the distinction between the domestic government and the dominion of the 'politic', all led historians towards a separation of this important structure of society of the age into diverse objects to be dealt with separately. For this reason we have available some important elements for the definition and study of the court, but these result from distinct fields of research. These results must be the intent of a type of reconstruction that forms them into a new object, without which the relevance of their contribution might be lost.

The most significant force for the study and investigation of the court of the kings in the Middle Ages owes itself to a large degree to institutional history. However, following the global interpretative synthesis of nineteenth-century historians, the court has been viewed, almost exclusively, as a matrix of administrative and bureaucratic structures of an early stage of the monarchy that, little by little, was becoming free of that matrix.[26] Starting off from abstract and

24 Post, *Studies in Medieval Legal Thought*, p. 387.

25 Jacques Le Goff, 'Le roi dans l'occident médiéval: caractères originaux', in Anne J. Duggan (ed.), *Kings and Kingship in Medieval Europe* (London: King's College, 1993), p. 9.

26 See the influential works of Paul Viollet, *Histoire des institutions politiques et administratives de la France* (Paris, 1890–1903); Achille Luchaire, *Manuel des institutions françaises: période*

timeless notions of state functions, history of institutions thus began 'emptying' the medieval royal court, and through the resistance of the object – for the more that was removed from it, the more there 'remained' something – it considered as merely residual aspects all that which was not indispensable to those functions. These 'remainders' were, for example, an obscure (and certainly necessary) domesticity, and a political dimension which was becoming more visible during the final period of the Middle Ages.

In this approach, which must be recognised and understood to be limited for my purposes, the court is seen merely as a *curia*, an embryo of a future reality – the total emancipation of the exercise of public power. It could be thought that, in a large part, the 'invisibility' of the medieval court in European historiography until the 1980s owes itself to this explanation, the fruit of a 'survival of developmental typologies of the nineteenth century'.[27] It is important to emphasise the singularity of the court of the kings when addressing historiography of the medieval state rather than to compare it with other contemporary organisms, such as the households of important nobles, the monastic family or the ecclesiastical dignitaries and the papal curia. Being attentive to the regime of court duties during the several periods, institutional history presupposes, however, an evolution which would have come about through progressive specialisation and through a rational division of functions, such as the administration of justice or the collection of taxes, in an attempt to attribute to these positions a certain solidity and coherence within a division into periods which leans towards an explanation of the exclusive exercise of functions whose nature is that of a 'state'.

For my part, I shall make my point of departure the structure of the Carolingian court, and shall leave aside all the polemics that surround the origin of court duties and their concrete characteristics, its continuity with or rupture from late imperial institutions or the Germanic *comitatus*.[28] The organisation of the court of Charlemagne, as described to us in the treatise *De Ordine Palatii*, attributed to Hincmar of Rheims, appears as an original synthesis and at the same time as a harmonious vision which is full of political intent, of an organism which includes several of its own elements of 'barbarian' royalties of

des Capétiens directs (Paris: Hachette, 1892). Also on English historians for the derivative of the 'royal household', T. F. Tout, *Chapters in the Administrative History of Mediaeval England* (Manchester: Manchester University Press, 1967), in particular vol. I, pp. 18–31. For the Iberian Peninsula, Luis García de Valdeavellano, *Curso de historia de las instituciones Españolas: de los orígenes al final de la edad media* (Madrid: Revista de Occidente, 1977), p. 202; or A. L. Carvalho Homem, *Conselho real ou conselheiros do rei? A propósito dos 'privados' de D. João I*, offprint of *Revista da Faculdade de Letras* (Oporto, 1987), pp. 19–20.

27 Susan Reynolds, *Kingdoms and Communities in Western Europe, 900–1300* (Oxford: Clarendon Press, 1997), e.g. pp. 335–7; Susan Reynolds, 'The historiography of the medieval state', in Michael Bentley (ed.), *Companion to Historiography* (London: Routledge, 1997) pp. 117–38.

28 See for example Eugen Ewig, 'La monocratie dans l'Europe occidentale (Ve–Xe siècles)', in *La Monocratie*, Recueils de la Société Jean Bodin 21 (Brussels: Université Libre, 1969), vol. II, pp. 57–105; also Herwig Wolfram, 'The shaping of the early medieval kingdom', *Viator*, 1 (1970), 1–20.

western Europe, and others which arose in a probable dialogue with the conservationary and complex characteristics of Byzantine usage.[29] Two aspects of the ordinance of the court that are referred to in this source are particularly relevant: its hierarchic sense and the functional separation into three distinct nuclei of servants – hall, chamber and chapel. The service of the hall is supervised by the trilogy of *senescalcus*, *buticularius* and *comes stabuli*, while the chamber is under the supervision of the *camerarius*, and the chapel that of the *apocrisiarius* or *archicapellanus*, to whom the *cancellarius* was subordinate.[30]

Without doubt, the organisation of this court seems simple when compared with the Byzantine court, in which there are known to have been dozens of subservient duties in several hierarchies (some of which were simply honorary), evoking certain aspects of oriental courts in its elaborate ceremonies and the use of eunuchs.[31] The historians of the Byzantine Empire have emphasised 'the power of cultural continuity' embodied in such a court as being 'in many ways a living archaism'.[32] Byzantium certainly served as a repository of objects, memories and practices which, however, lent themselves merely to a fragmentary reception not lacking in ambiguities, for while it was a human configuration giving body and sense to these elements, the court in its internal complexity remained in a large part inimitable in its own grandeur and liturgical context.[33] The extraordinary prestige of Carolingian royalty formed a closer and, in its relative modesty, more accessible model of the structure described by Hincmar. In the history of the medieval western courts after the eleventh

[29] Thomas Gross and Rudolf Schieffer (eds.), *Hincmarus De Ordine Palatii (editio altera)*, Monumenta Germaniae Historia. Fontes Iuris Germanici Antiqui in usum scholarum separatim editi (Hanover: Hahnsche, 1980), pp. 56–82; Louis Halphen, 'Le *De Ordine Palatii* d'Hincmar', *Revue Historique*, 183 (1938), 1–9; Janet L. Nelson, 'Kingship and empire in the Carolingian world', in Rosamond McKitterick (ed.), *Carolingian Culture: Innovation and Emulation* (Cambridge: Cambridge University Press, 1994), pp. 52–87.

[30] On the use of seals in relation to royalty, Brigitte Bedos-Rezak, 'Ritual in the Royal Chancery: text, image, and the presentation of kingship in medieval French diplomas (700–1200)', in Heinz Duchhard *et al.* (eds.), *European Monarchy: Its Evolution and Practice from Roman Antiquity to Modern Times* (Stuttgart: Steiner, 1992), pp. 27–40.

[31] Byzantine uses are described in the 'Book of Ceremonies' of Constantine Porphyrogenite, a compilation dating from the tenth century; Albert Vogt (ed.), *Le Livre des Cérémonies de Constantin VII Porphyrogénète* (Paris: Les Belles Lettres, 1967). On this text, Averil Cameron, 'The construction of court ritual: the Byzantine Book of Ceremonies', in David Cannadine and Simon Price (eds.), *Rituals of Royalty: Power and Ceremony in Traditional Societies* (Cambridge: Cambridge University Press, 1987), pp. 106–36, and the comparison with Fatimid Egypt in M. Canard, 'Le cérémoniale fatimide et le cérémonial byzantin: essai de comparaison', *Byzantion*, 21 (1953), 355–420. It should be emphasised that Du Cange does not appear to have consulted this source for his well-known *Glossarium* (printed in 1658 and revised in 1733–36).

[32] Alexander P. Kazhdan and Michael McCormick, 'The social world of the Byzantine court', in Henry Maguire (ed.), *Byzantine Court Culture from 829 to 1204* (Washington, DC: Dumbarton Oaks, 1997), pp. 195–6.

[33] Janet Nelson deals with the limits of this cultural transmission by means of an actual ritual: 'Symbols in context: ruler's inauguration rituals in Byzantium and the West in the early Middle Ages', in *Politics and Ritual in Early Medieval Europe* (London: Hambledon, 1986), esp. p. 266.

century, the vulgarisation of this model performs a fundamental function, as stated by Georges Duby.[34] It is therefore not surprising that one of its main aspects, the distinction between the hall and the chamber, is also found in the noble and ecclesiastical *familiae*. How should this coincidence of forms which has been noted by the historians of the Middle Ages for so long be interpreted?

Some important suggestions stem from the anthropology of royalty, particularly following suggestions of Frazer and Hocart.[35] The organisation of court duties must be related to the ritual which certainly surrounded the Carolingian sovereigns, and also to the 'proxemic' rules which regulated a gradual access to the person of the king,[36] to the materialisation of a distancing necessary for the establishment of the actual power of the monarch. The king, as a being who had to be kept 'outside the group', was permanently guarded by a nucleus of servants who comprised the core of the court: the chamber, an organism similar to the Byzantine 'Kubukleion'. But the Carolingian monarch was also the dispenser of food and drink, which is reflected in the functions of organisation and performance of rituals of eating together, by the dual *senescalcus/buticularius*. Besides this, the king supplied his retinue with or maintained horses needed for his itinerance and for war, and this lay within the dominion of the *comes stabuli*. His relationship with the religious sphere, the place where his peculiar nature of *rex-sacerdos* was affirmed, was in turn placed under the authority of the *apocrisiarius*, a high ecclesiastical dignitary.[37] The similarities between the formal organisation of the several medieval courts therefore have roots in the actual ritual processes which led to royalty in the High Middle Ages and which contributed towards its retention, in a manner which is enduring and imbued with tradition. This aspect will be taken up at greater length in the final chapter of this book.

[34] Georges Duby, 'La vulgarisation des modèles culturels dans la société féodale', in *Niveaux de culture et groupes sociaux. Actes du Colloque* (Paris: Mouton, 1967), pp. 33–41. See also the important general observations on the empire by Karl Ferdinand Weber, 'L'historien et la notion d'état', in *Eheit der Geschichte: Studien zur Historiographie* (Sigmaringen: Thorbecke, 1999).

[35] James G. Frazer, *The Golden Bough: A Study in Magic and Religion* (abridged edition) (London: Macmillan, 1922); Arthur Hocart, *Kings and Councillors: An Essay in the Comparative Anatomy of Human Society* (Chicago: University of Chicago Press, 1969); Arthur Hocart, *Kingship* (London: Oxford University Press, 1970). See also Claude Tardits, 'L'invitation au comparatisme. Marc Bloch et les anthropologues', in Hartmut Atsma and André Burguière (eds.), *Marc Bloch aujourd'hui: histoire comparée et sciences sociales* (Paris: Ecole des Hautes Etudes en Sciences Sociales, 1990), pp. 135–6; Rita Costa Gomes, 'A reflexão antropológica na história da realeza medieval', *Etnográfica*, 2 (1998), 133–40.

[36] I am using here the concept of 'proxemics' suggested by Edward T. Hall, *The Hidden Dimension* (New York: Doubleday, 1966). I must thank Sergio Bertelli for having brought to my attention the use of this conceptualisation.

[37] This name, of Greek origin (corresponding to the Latin *responsalis*), alludes to one of his early functions, that is communication between the emperor and the pope, and also to the duty of mediation at the palace between the sovereign and the other bishops. In the Carolingian era, however, the names *archicapellanus* or *summus capellanus* were already used: Louis Thomassin, *Ancienne et Nouvelle Discipline de l'église* (Bar-le-Duc: Guérin, 1864–66), vol. II, pp. 386–99.

Some of these duties fell in earlier times to men from more humble backgrounds, but the importance associated with the services or the *ministeria* of the Carolingian court made them desirable and coveted, and simultaneously promoted those who performed them. Therefore the new tie of vassalage replaced the old dependency of the familiar who was charged with a particular group of duties. From a sociological point of view, this transformation meant an appropriation of this system that caused the monarch to be surrounded by the aristocracy, and the injection of new values into the actual concept of court 'service'. We can relate this transformation on the other hand to the creation of a system of payment to court servants which resulted from the amalgamation of two methods of payment: the *praebenda* (food, 'sustenance' and clothing, which were periodically distributed) and the *beneficium* (land concession).[38]

The very general picture sketched above forms an indispensable basis for the appreciation of the variety presented by the royal courts of the medieval west in their organisation after the eleventh century. From early on, we witness the phenomena of hereditary transmission and the sharing or duplication of duties as their appropriation by magnates and nobles intensified. A comparative history of institutions, which still sorely needs to be carried out, would perhaps show the distinction between two structural groups of courts, as suggested by Petit-Dutaillis or Bryce Lyon: one which was characterised by the relative independence of the various services (with the king able to be the direct head of each one), of which there is a good example in the Anglo-Saxon court; the other being the group of 'continental' courts, or of the Iberian courts, in which one person only (the *maiordomus*) supervised all the servants or, at least, several different sectors.[39]

By taking the evolutionary point of view of institutional history, to which I initially referred, we should see emerging: from the chamber (an organism which permanently accompanies the monarch), the keeping of the treasury and, later, the germ of financial institutions; from the chapel (a clerical organism *par excellence*), the offices of the written word and the chancery; from the hall (which, as has been said, evokes the periodic meeting of the king with his servants and vassals), the duties related to the exercise of justice, military organisation and even, perhaps (as suggested by Sánchez-Albornoz), the germ of

[38] Heinrich Mitteis, *The State in the Middle Ages: A Comparative Constitutional History of Feudal Europe* (Oxford: North Holland, 1975), pp. 164–5; Benjamin Arnold, 'Instruments of power: the profile and profession of the *ministeriales* within German aristocratic society, 1050–1225', in Thomas N. Bisson (ed.), *Cultures of Power: Lordship, Status and Process in Twelfth-Century Europe* (Philadelphia: University of Pennsylvania Press, 1995), pp. 36–55.

[39] Charles Petit-Dutaillis and Georges Lefebvre, *Studies and Notes Supplementary to Stubb's Constitutional History* (Manchester, Manchester University Press, 1930), pp. 348–54; Bryce Dale Lyon and Mary Lyon, *The Wardrobe Book of William Norwell, 1338–1340* (Brussels: Académie Royale de Belgique, 1983), pp. i–xlvii. See also Mitteis, *The State in the Middle Ages*, pp. 154–5 and 194.

representative assemblies. Without wishing radically to challenge this evolutionary framework which, within its general lines, is accepted by the majority of authors, I propose to introduce to it the attention due to the 'domesticity' of the kings, attempting a global vision of the organisation of the courts which does not consider this aspect as a mere archaic residue of lesser importance, clearly separated from the remaining spheres of activity which develop in the royal retinue. In my opinion the selection of concrete characteristics that fell to the diverse duties of the medieval courts should not be considered in too restrictive a way. As we shall see, the 'service' of the king took many forms. Many offices had a variety of spheres, both administrative and fiscal but, at the same time, 'domestic' and even ritual. It is in the unity of all of them that the prestige attributed to royal service by men of the period can be understood. My research sought therefore to question once again the terminology of the sources, seeking not only to understand the regime of court positions, the way in which they were transmitted and the norms which governed them, but also to put in perspective their effective function through a study of those who held the posts and the concrete activities which they performed.

Sources that allow a global picture necessary for a first approach to the organisation of the courts, although relative to the later medieval period, seem to be small in number. Therefore recourse to normative texts as well as other types of sources, such as those of a proto-financial character (for instance lists of payments to members of court), was inevitable for an attempt to fill in the lacunae and to ascertain the problems of interpretation that arose. I constructed four graphic diagrams, starting with known texts, which would allow for the evaluation, beyond the general framework already shown, of the variety of forms of concrete organisation of the royal European courts between the twelfth and fifteenth centuries.[40] It is only by concentrating on the global context that we shall be able correctly to interpret the data available on the Portuguese court.

The construction of these diagrams suggests the clarification of two points for the reader. The first is in respect of the use, without translation, of the vocabulary found in the sources. In fact, I would suggest that translations of the terminology are risky, since at times information is lost in an attempt at clarity. Simple translation can in this case lead to loss, since there is recourse to

[40] For an elaboration of Fig. 1: Richard Fitz Nagel, 'Constitutio Domus Regis', in Charles Johnson *et al.* (eds.), *Dialogus de Scaccario: Constitutio Domus Regis* (Oxford: Clarendon Press, 1983), pp. 129–35. For Fig. 2: *Las Siete Partidas*, vol. I, pp. 56–87. For Fig. 3: Próspero de Bofarull y Mascaró (ed.), 'Ordenacions fetes per lo molt Alt Senyor en Pere Terç, Rey Darago, sobra lo Regiment de tots los officials de la sua cort', *Colección de Documentos Inéditos del Archivo General de la Corona de Aragón*, vol. V (Barcelona, 1850). For Fig. 4: the text of Olivier de la Marche, 'L'Estat de la Maison du Duc Charles de Bourgoigne, dit le Hardy', in Henri Beaune and J. D'Arbaumount (eds.), *Mémoires d'Olivier de la Marche* (Paris: Renouard, 1888), and the Ordinations of 1419/21, 1426/27, 1431–32/33 and 1437, edited by Werner Paravicini, 'Die Hofordnungen Herzog Philipps des Guten von Burgund. Edition', *Francia*, 11 (1983), 257–301; 15 (1987), 183–231; 18 (1991), 111–23.

an identification and correspondence between diverse duties and posts that are not always diachronically acceptable. This is a common result when translating from medieval Latin, as has on occasion been found when analysing the way in which, in the Portuguese case, the names of some earlier posts were translated into the vulgar language in the texts of the fourteenth and fifteenth centuries, without taking note of changes which occurred in the profile and characteristics of the old offices. More problematic still is the translation, for example, into the English language of names of posts that existed in other institutional systems, where the characteristics and regime of services performed diverge substantially at times. All translation in this case presupposes a parallelism in the organisational forms which, on the contrary, could eventually result from an actual historic interpretation, never postulating it at the outset. It is also important to draw attention to the fact that the sources, which were selected because of their heterogeneous nature, do not allow for a direct comparison of the resulting graphics for the deduction of a linear evolution of organisational forms of the medieval court. On the contrary, what is dealt with here is images which demand a synchronic vision, although they are presented in chronological succession, identifying forms whose coexistence is able to reveal different historicities and durations, and which include recent duties and other, older ones, the survival of some and the introduction of others at the organisational level of the respective courts.

A schematic vision of the organisation of the English court based on the *Constitutio Domus Regis*, a document that can be dated 1135–36, allows one to detect its principal orders and groupings (Fig. 1). In it we find a list of the various duties with their respective wages, information that is of an unparalleled hierarchical value. Two phenomena found in this source are brought to our attention: the relative independence of the chancery in relation to the chapel, and the separation between the services of the hall and the chamber.[41] The complexity that this source reveals in these two areas, traditionally associated with the 'domesticity' of the kings, is notable. What must be emphasised is the separation with respect to the hall between the services of food and those of drink, which are placed under the control of the dual *dapifer/pincerna*. The distinction between the various duties was based upon two essential vectors: for whom the food was intended, and with what type of food it was concerned. Therefore, the food intended for the king was kept apart in its preparation from the food for the court – and we then have a *cocus privatorum regis*, independent of the *magna coquina*. The administration of bread and wine acquired an enormous importance, and justified the presence of a *dispensator panis* and of a *dispensator*

[41] On these posts, see Chris Given-Wilson, *The Royal Household and the King's Affinity: Service, Politics and Finance in England, 1360–1413* (New Haven: Yale University Press, 1986); James Willard and William A. Morris (eds.), *The English Government at Work, 1327–1336* (Cambridge, MA: Medieval Academy of America, 1940), vol. I, pp. 206–49.

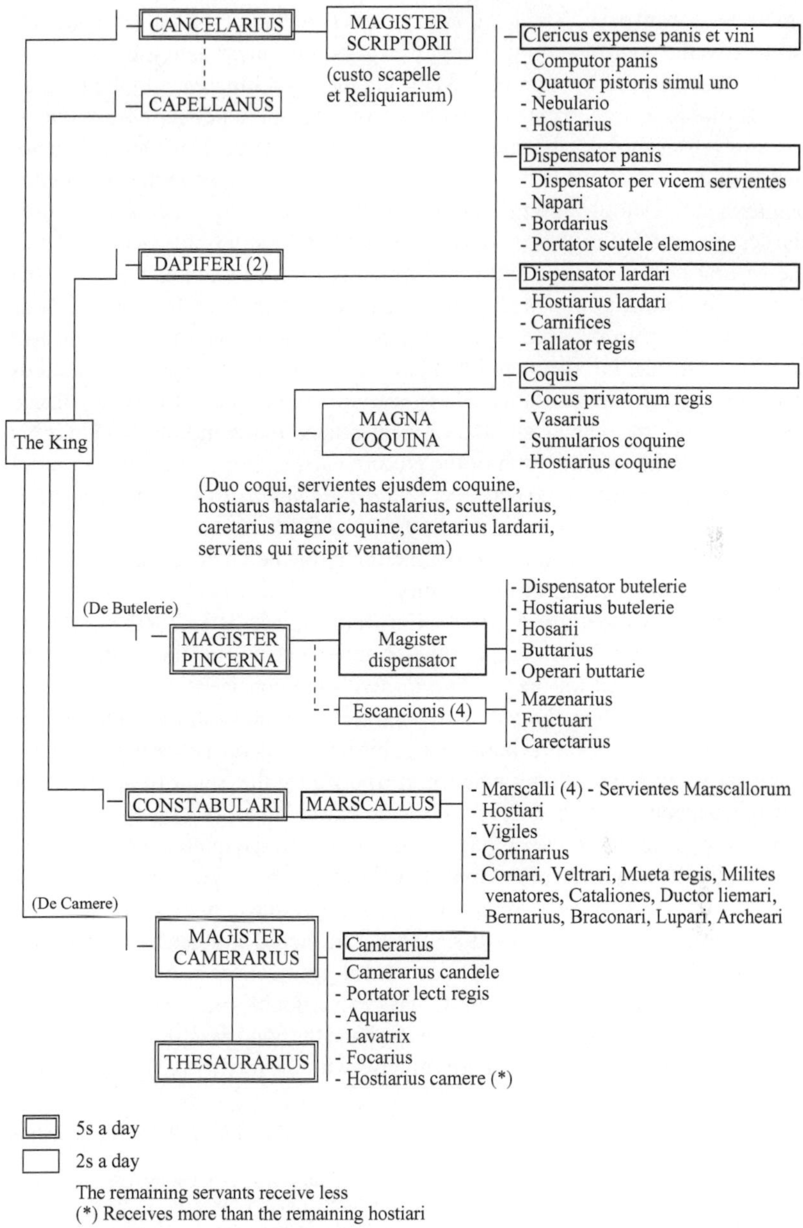

Fig. 1 The English court according to the *Constitutio Domus Regis* (twelfth century)

butelerie, as well as a *clericus expense panis et vini*, all of whom were officials deputed to the control and recording of expenses for these activities.

The abundant distribution of food during the royal itinerance in the English case allows to a large extent an evaluation of the importance of these services. We know, for example, that at the end of the thirteenth century Queen Eleanor distributed the respectable quantity of 9036 individual meals to the poor in one single year, this simply during her travels apart from the king.[42] In all probability, the services related to the royal hall had as a duty not only the distribution of the several rations of food and drink which fell to members of the court, but also the fact of eating together, with which the *portator scutele elemosine* was connected. Certain provisions in particular, such as meat, fruit and salt, had servants connected to them, and this gave rise to a complex system of records and accountancy. The same logic of association between related activities placed the servants of the stables and the services related to the military and hunting retinues under the supervision of the *constabularius*. For its part, the world of the chamber became shared between a *magister camerarius* and a *thesaurarius*, and the presence of servants such as the *portator lecti regis*, or the *aquarius* and *lavatrix*, should be noted in the hierarchy of the chamber, as should the autonomy of the services of the treasury.[43]

With regard to the ordinance of the Castilian court at the end of the thirteenth century, it is possible to compare the relative accuracy of the profile of the English court, based on the *Constitutio*, with the conciseness of a source of doctrinal intent such as the *Partidas*. This text, written from the point of view of the king himself, uses the metaphor of his body to describe the court and distinguishes between the duties which corresponded to the 'sentidos que obran en poridat, asi como imaginando, et pensando et rembrándose'; the duties whose function was similar to the organs 'de dentro del cuerpo quell ayudan a vevir'; and finally those which 'obran mas defuera del cuerpo a guardamiento et amparanza del' or, as stated further on, 'en las cosas que pertenescen à honra, et à guardamiento et à amparanza de su tierra'.[44] It should be noted how this classification, which starts from the philosophical-political *topos* of a comparison between society and the human body, plays with a double meaning of the organic metaphor, considering as it does on the one hand the court as a 'sensorium' of the royal body and, on the other, identifying this with the totality of the kingdom.[45]

42 John Carmi Parsons, *The Court and Household of Eleanor of Castile in 1290* (Toronto: Pontifical Institute of Medieval Studies, 1977), pp. 8–9.

43 The identification of this *thesaurarius* is unanimously suggested as being the later 'keeper of the wardrobe'. On the relationship between the 'wardrobe' and the 'exchequer' (the department which centralised accounts): Lyon and Lyon, *The Wardrobe Book of William Norwell*, pp. xxv–xxvi.

44 *Las Siete Partidas*, vol. I, pp. 57–8.

45 Otto Gierke, *Political Theories of the Middle Ages* (Cambridge: Cambridge University Press, 1987), pp. 22–5. On this idea in John of Salisbury (one of the most common sources): Fumagalli

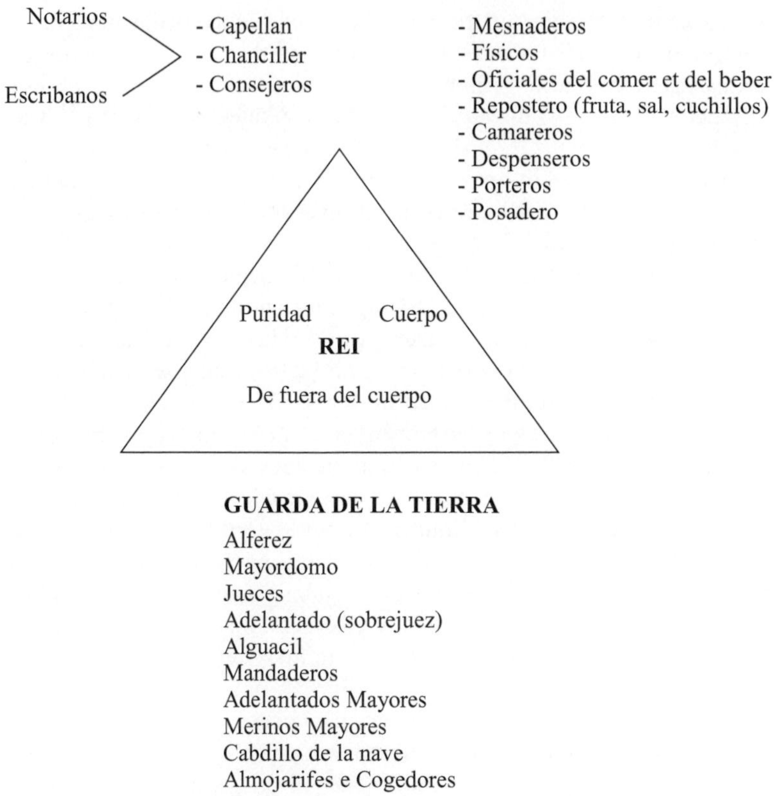

Fig. 2 The Castilian court according to the *Partidas* (thirteenth century)

Reproduced graphically, the ordinance suggested by the *Partidas* clearly reveals an entire schematic (Fig. 2). The text merely mentions the principal duties of the court, and simplifies to the most elementary expression 'domestic' order, not allowing for a clear view of the hierarchy existing among them.

Two aspects must be emphasised, for they evoke the essential originality of the Iberian courts before the fourteenth century: the predominance of the *mordomo* and the independence of the *alferes*. The first aspect, which was detected by Sánchez-Albornoz from the reign of Alfonso III of Asturias (866–910), has been related to influence from beyond the Pyrenees, which was accentuated with the advent of the Navarre dynasty in the westernmost regions of the Peninsula in

Beonio Broccheri, 'Grande e piccole virtù', in *Le Bugie de Isotta: immagini della mente medievale* (Bari: Laterza, 1987), pp. 49–68.

the eleventh century.[46] This 'monocephalic' character of the Peninsular courts remained, even though the French sovereigns had abandoned it. The adoption of the *senescalcus* by the Carolingians has been interpreted as a precaution because of the earlier supremacy of the *maiordomus* in the retinue of the kings.[47] The Anglo-Saxon court, like the English court later on, never had such a hierarchy. Besides, when the name of this position appeared and spread across the Iberian Peninsula, it was already considered an archaism beyond the Pyrenees, as noted by García de Valdeavellano.

While in Capetian France the tendency towards heredity in access to the position of *senescalcus* was stressed, leading to the unfilling of this position at the end of the twelfth century as an attempt to combat the political influence of those who held the post,[48] the supremacy of the Peninsular *mordomo* never apparently posed a threat to the Iberian monarchs. The post held no military prerogatives (as was the case with the French *senescalcus*), nor during the earlier periods was it hereditary. Probably it was in the coexistence of the *mordomo* and the *alferes* that there lay one of the reasons for this apparent equilibrium. Therefore, while we speak of the influence from beyond the Pyrenees in the adoption of the *maiordomus* by the Christian kings of the Iberian Peninsula, we may also allow for the analogy with the Muslim institutions of Al-Andalus, where we find the retention of this duality of offices, that is a distinction and a complementarity between leadership of the military retinue and that of the household of the monarchs.[49]

It is not known whether the replacement that occurred in documents from Leon in the twelfth century of the Latin names *signifer* and *armiger* by the Arab *alferez*, the name given to the leader of the king's gentlemen, indicates a significant change in the functions of this post. The new name seems to relate it not solely and exclusively to the carrying of the insignia and royal standard, but

[46] Sánchez-Albornoz, 'El *Palatium Regis* Asturleonés', pp. 11–16 and 26; Luis García de Valdeavellano, *Historia de España: de los orígenes a la baja edad media* (Madrid: Alianza, 1980), vol. II, pp. 92–5. For a later period see Nilda Guglielmi, 'La curia regia en León y Castilla', *Cuadernos de Historia de España*, 33–4 (1955), 116–267; 38 (1958), 43–131.

[47] J. M. Wallace-Hadrill, *The Long Haired Kings* (Toronto: University of Toronto Press, 1982), pp. 231–48.

[48] Ferdinand Lot and Robert Fawtier, *Histoire des institutions françaises au moyen âge*, vol. II, *Institutions royales* (Paris: PUF, 1958), pp. 52–3. For the Capetians, Eric Bournazel, *Le Gouvernement capétien au XXIIe siècle, 1108–1180* (Paris: PUF, 1975), pp. 111–19; John W. Baldwin, *The Government of Philip Augustus: Foundations of French Royal Power in the Middle Ages* (Berkeley: University of California Press, 1986), pp. 104–6.

[49] E. Lévi-Provençal, *Histoire de L'Espagne musulmane* (Paris: Brill, 1950), vol. II, pp. 128–30; Rachel Arié, 'España musulmana (siglosVIII–XV)', in Manuel Tuñón de Lara (ed.), *Historia de España* (Barcelona: Labor, 1984), vol. III, pp. 60–5; Mohamed Meouak, 'Notes historiques sur l'administration centrale, les charges et le recrutement des fonctionnaires dans l'Espagne musulmane (2e/VIIIe–4e/Xe siècles)', *Hesperis-Tamuda*, 30 (1992), 9–20. On the distinction between the 'offices of the sword' and the 'offices of the pen' see Ibn Khaldun, *The Muqaddimah*, ed. Franz Rosenthal (Princeton: Princeton University Press, 1967), pp. 213–14.

also to skill in mounted combat. In fact, the Arab word meant the 'champion' who launched the challenge against the enemy army, and this identity was carefully preserved for posterity by historians when relating episodes of war.[50] The Christian kings of the Peninsula used the Arab name for this post in the same way as they appear to have adopted the combat techniques of the Muslim armies.

In spite of their relative brevity, the *Partidas* allow us to confirm the importance of the trilogy *mordomo/alferes/chanceler* in positions which were hierarchically superior in the Castilian court during the thirteenth century. The structure of the hall and the chamber under the supervision of the *mordomo* is briefly referred to in the text. To the first of these there belonged the 'oficiales del comer et del beber', the 'despenseros', who controlled the expenses, and the 'porteros' whose judicial duties are emphasised in the text. To the second were connected the 'físicos', the 'camareros', the 'repostero' who was to protect items from 'poridat', the 'posadero' who organised the itinerance of the court and, most probably, the small armed retinue which permanently guarded the body of the king – the 'mesnaderos'. The text also does not fail to mention the 'capellan'. These posts, however, played a reduced part in the chapters of the *Partidas*, which concentrate on the offices 'de fuera del cuerpo', that is in the relations which the court maintained with the kingdom and, consequently, in its judicial, military or fiscal activities. A comparison of this sketch in the *Partidas* of the 'domestic' functions with the greater complexity demonstrated in another almost contemporaneous source such as the accounts of Sancho IV is illuminating. In this latter text, which is very different in nature, it is possible to find, for example, that in Castile there existed a separation between the 'cocina del cuerpo del rey' and the 'cocina' of the court (much the same as the English court), as well as the characteristics of the various officials 'do comer e beber'. This financial documentation shows that there existed an internal hierarchy in the chapel and we can also gather a few indications as to the service of the stables and hunting.[51]

The organisation of the court of Aragon in the middle of the fourteenth century is one of those of which we know most for the medieval period, thanks largely to the 'Ordenacions' of Pedro the Ceremonious (Fig. 3).

[50] On the *armiger* of Leon, see Sánchez-Albornoz, 'El *Palatium Regis*', pp. 21 and 24; Josefina Mateu Ibars, 'La *confirmatio* del *signifer*, *armiger* y *alferez* según documentación Asturleonesa y Castellana', *En la España Medieval*, 1 (1980), 263–316. On the Arab term and the use of combat evoked, *Encyclopédie de L'Islam* (Leiden: Maisonneuve et Larose, 1954–98), vol. II, pp. 800–1. See also António Dias Farinha, 'Contribuição para o estudo das palavras portuguesas derivadas do árabe hispânico', *Portugaliae Historica*, 1 (1983), 253–4; Inés Carrasco, *Los cargos de la Hueste Real en tiempos de Alfonso X: estudio onomasiológico* (Granada: Universidad de Granada, 1922).

[51] 'Libro de diferentes cuentas de Don Sancho IV (1293–1294)', in Mercedes Gaibros de Ballesteros (ed.), *Historia del reinado de Sancho IV de Castilla* (Madrid: Tip. Archivos Bibliotecas y Museos, 1922), vol. I, pp. i–cxlvii. See also Asunción López Dapena, *Cuentas y gastos (1292–1294) del Rey D. Sancho IV el Bravo* (Cordoba: Caja de Ahorros, 1984).

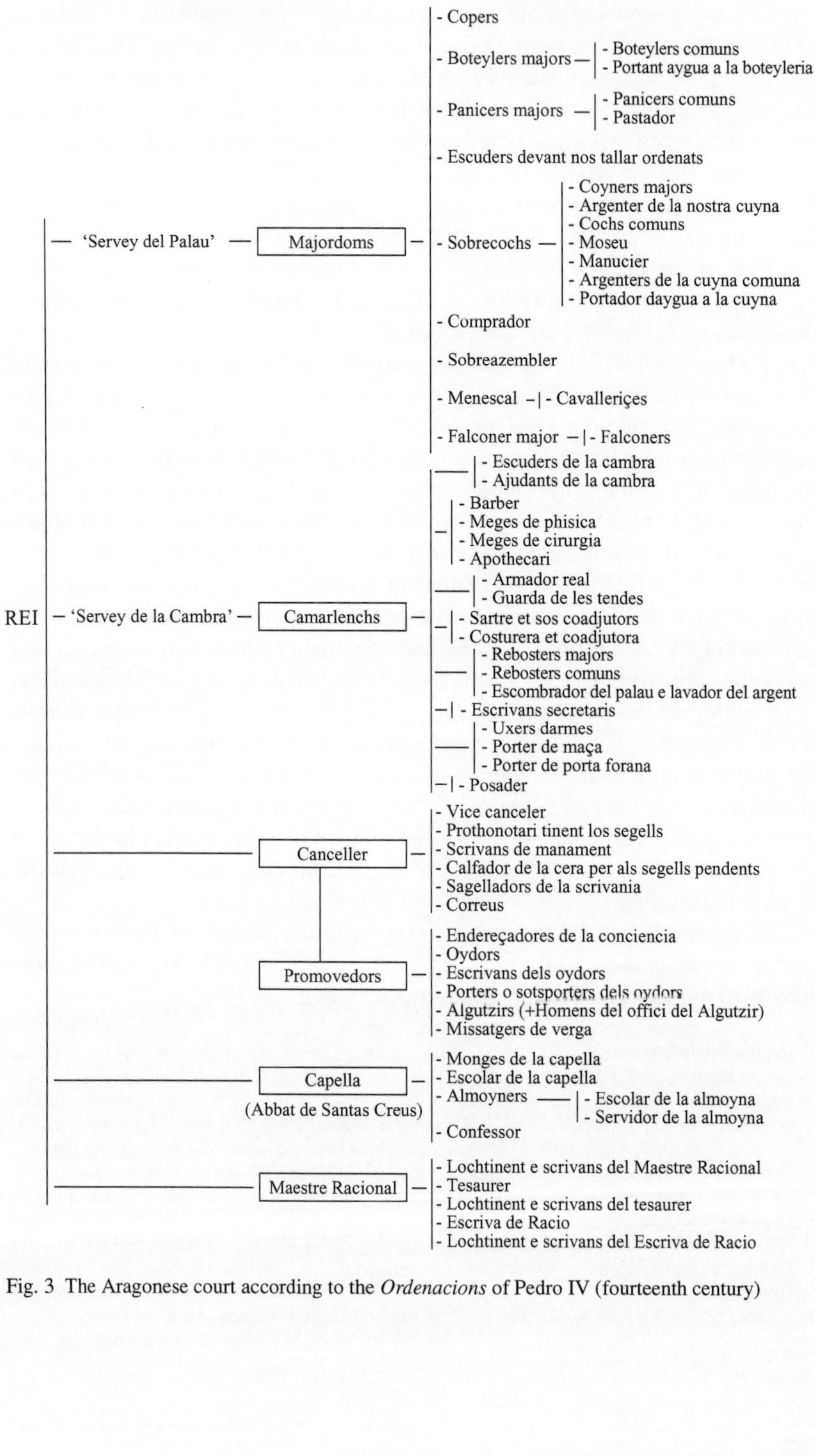

Fig. 3 The Aragonese court according to the *Ordenacions* of Pedro IV (fourteenth century)

The circulation of this text is seen as being exceptional among the few court rulings which we have to hand: the Latin version was known in the middle of the fourteenth century at the French court, while the Catalan version circulated in the Castilian court during the 1380s.[52] The mention 'Liuro dos offiçios da casa d'algũ rey' which is made in the list of books in the library of the Portuguese king, Duarte, must refer also to this text.[53] In fact it was a translation, made in 1344 at the initiative and under the probable organisation of Pedro IV, of the *Leges Palatinae* proposed by James III of Majorca (1324–49).[54] In this text, the court ordination is laid out by the monarch himself, with each duty being the subject of a detailed description of its attributes and hierarchical position. However, there is no passage relating to the post of the *alferes* included in the 'Ordenacions' of 1344, though we know of its existence from other, contemporary directives.

In my diagram we see, once again, the growing independence of the chancery and the emergence of a financial post in Aragon which, from the end of the thirteenth century, was placed under the supervision of the 'Maestre Racional'.[55] The supremacy of the *mordomo*, who ruled in the sovereign house of Aragon in much the same way as he did in the Castilian household, was to be replaced in these 'Ordenacions' by a new hierarchy, in which the 'majordoms' headed the services of the hall and the 'camarlenchs' those of the chamber. We find once again the distinction that was made in the first case between the service of the king (or of the 'body') and of the court ('common'), made clear in the separation of the services of drink ('boteylers'), of distribution of food ('panicers'), or of the kitchen ('coyners'). With its growing independence from the authority of the 'majordom', the Aragonese chamber of the fourteenth century appears in turn as a complex organism, which included its own body of scribes, a large number of persons related to the security and health of the monarch, and a group of artisans

[52] Olivetta Schena, *Le Leggi Palatine de Pietro IV di Aragona* (Cagliari: Istituto sui Rapporti Italo-Iberici, 1983), pp. 29–30 and 44–6; Olivetta Schena and Joseph Trenchs, 'Le Leggi Palatine de Giacomo III di Majorca nella corte di Pietro IV di Aragona', *XIII Congrès d'Història de la Corona d'Aragó* (Palma de Mallorca: Institut d'Estudis Baleàrics (1990)), vol. II, pp. 11–19. On the tradition of these rulings in Aragon: J. Jordán de Urríz y Azara, 'Las Ordenaciones de la Corte Aragonesa en los siglos XIII y XIV', *Boletín de la Real Academia de Buenas Letras de Barcelona*, 13 (1913), 220–9, 284–92.

[53] J. J. Alves Dias and A. H. Oliveira Marques (eds.), *Livro dos Conselhos de El-Rei D. Duarte* (Lisbon: Estampa, 1982), p. 207. I shall return to the subject of the diffusion of the 'Ordenacions' in Portugal in the final chapter.

[54] James III, King of Majorca, *Leges Palatinae*, facsimile edition (Bloomington: Indiana University Press, 1994); G. Kerscher, 'Die Strukturierung des mallorquinischen Hofes um 1350 und der Habitus der Hofgesellschaft', in Holger Kruse and Werner Paravicini (eds.), *Höfe und Ordnungen 1200–1600*. 5 Symposium der Residenzen-Kommission der Akademie der Wissenschaften in Göttingen (Sigmaringen: Thorbecke, 1999), pp. 77–89.

[55] On this position, which originates from Sicily: Enrique Cruselles, *El maestre racional: función política y desarollo administrativo del oficio público* (Valencia: Edicions Alfons el Magnànim, 1989), pp. 28–30; Alan Ryder, *The Kingdom of Naples under Alfonso the Magnanimous: The Making of a Modern State* (Oxford: Clarendon Press, 1976), pp. 19–21.

for making his clothes. The services of the 'reboster' and of the 'posader', which were included here, involved duties close to those of the Castilian officials known as 'reposter' and 'posader' as described in the *Partidas*.

Above all, this directive allows us to detect yet another interesting phenomenon as it describes diverse ways in which the same duty was performed. It shows, for example, the existence of four different 'majordoms': three (one for Aragon, another for Valencia and Majorca, and a third for Cataluña) with functions which were, primarily, honorary in the domestic sphere, for they only served in the royal hall on solemn occasions and had a position in the royal council; and the fourth, which accompanied the king on ordinary service. During the later Middle Ages some duties of the higher hierarchy of the court, therefore, witnessed an increase in the number who held such posts and who shared the same functions in time (each one serving for a part of the year) or in space, as was the case of the three 'majordoms' referred to above. Service in rotation is mentioned in several sources after the eleventh century, such as the *Constitutio* (where it appears to a limited extent), and the existence of a correspondence between the diverse territories of the kings and the duties of the court is also found to have been studied in the case of Aragon, where we can detect this correspondence in the last years of the twelfth century.[56]

The court of the Dukes of Burgundy, according to a description of 1474 in the 'Mémoires' of Olivier de la Marche, is a later example (Fig. 4). I chose it, among other reasons, for the diffusion of the text in the Iberian Peninsula, although some manuscripts dating from the modern period allow us to relate this diffusion to a later influence of the customs of the Burgundian court on the Spanish Habsburgs.[57] A systematic study of the origins of the manuscripts of de la Marche to be found in Spain and Portugal would be necessary, since it has been noted that there are several examples in the collections of the National Library of Madrid, of the Archives of the Torre do Tombo and of the Library of the Ajuda Palace in Lisbon.

[56] Ana Isabel Sánchez Casabón, 'Los cargos de mayordomo, senescal y dapifer en el reinado de Alfonso II de Aragón,' in *Aragón en la edad media*, vol. VIII, *Homenage al Profesor Emerito Antonio Ubieto Arteta* (Saragossa: University of Saragossa, 1989), p. 605.

[57] The problematic of the 'Burgundian influences' was fully reviewed by the important criticisms of Werner Paravicini, 'The court of the Dukes of Burgundy. A model for Europe?', in R. G. Asch and A. Bircke (eds.), *Princes, Patronage and Nobility* (London: Oxford University Press, 1991), pp. 69–102. On the adoption of the uses of Burgundy in the court of Carlos V and Philip of Spain, see J. H. Elliot, 'The court of the Spanish Habsbourgs: a peculiar institution?', in P. Mack and M. Jacobs (eds.), *Politics and Culture in Early Modern Europe: Essays in Honour of H. G. Koenigsberger* (Cambridge: Cambridge University Press, 1987), pp. 5–58; also the new information presented by Rafael Domínguez Casas, *Arte y etiqueta de los Reyes Católicos: artistas, residencia, jardines y bosques* (Madrid: Alpuerto, 1993), pp. 557–616. On the limits of the adoption of this point of view of the organisation of the court, the pertinent observations of Mia Rodríguez-Salgado, 'Honour and profit in the court of Philip II of Spain', in Maurice Aymard and Marzio A. Romani (eds.), *La Cour comme institution économique* (Paris: Maison des Sciences de l'Homme, 1998), pp. 68–9.

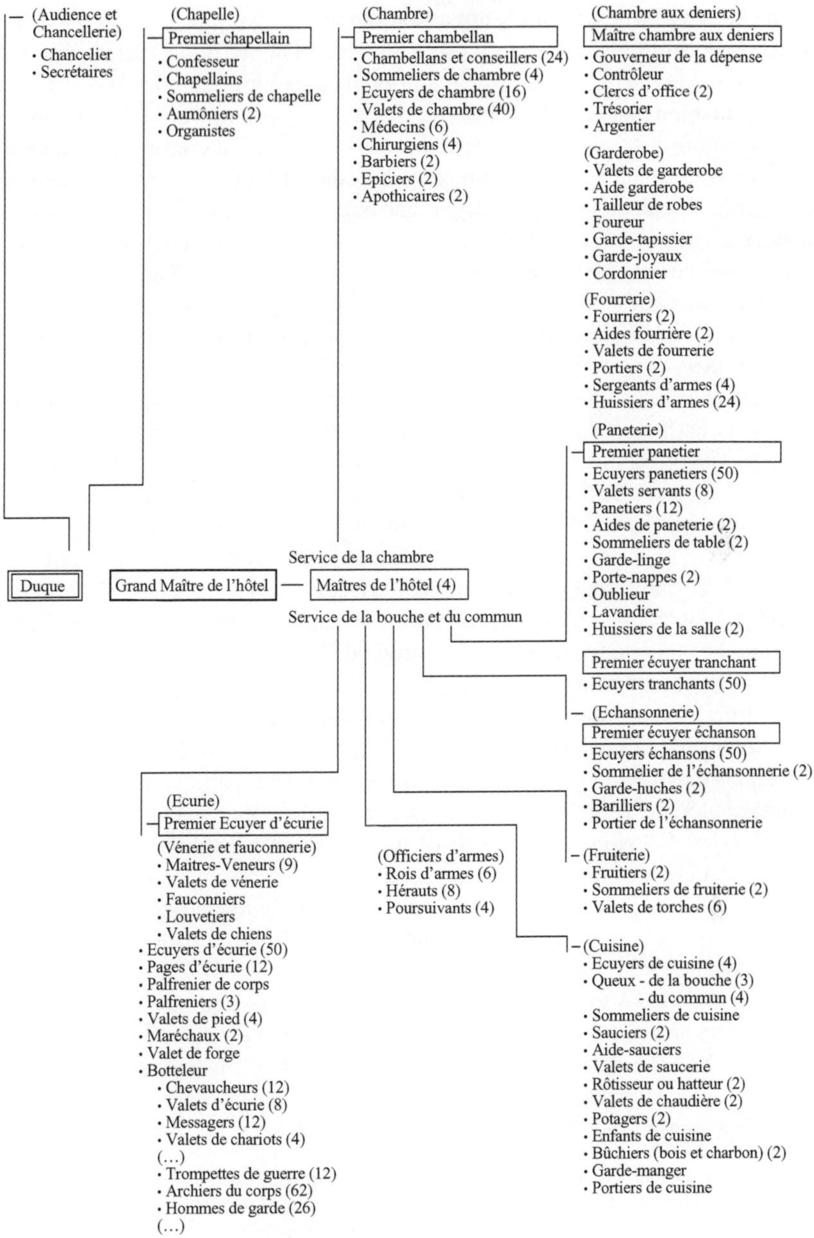

Fig. 4 The Burgundian court according to the *Mémoires* of Olivier de la Marche (fifteenth century)

The sharing of court duties, already referred to regarding Aragon, is very clearly seen in this court: the numbers to which Olivier de la Marche refers shown in the figure represent in the majority of cases a total number of servants. Bearing in mind that service 'par quarts de l'an' or 'par terme' is very common, the true number of those who serve at the same time could therefore be obtained by dividing this total by at least four or by three, according to which case is being dealt with. As can be seen, the Burgundian court developed in an extraordinary manner a custom of sharing of duties, so giving the opportunity to many to 'serve' the duke. This aspect has been stressed by Werner Paravicini, who relates it either to the use that the Burgundian rulers made of this mechanism to recruit nobles from territories which were distinct, from a political and cultural point of view, or to a more precise definition of a 'Burgundian model' for the late-medieval court. The universal presence of this 'model' in fifteenth-century Europe is an historiographic commonplace which needs reconsideration, as does that other commonplace, the diffusion of a 'Spanish model' for the modern period. According to Paravicini, while there are paradigmatic aspects in the organisation of the court of Burgundy, one of these is this conscious use, taken to the limit of material resources available, of the so-called 'service in rotation', and not from the actual organisation of services and departments, which was found to be very close to the contemporary structure of the court of the French kings and cannot be regarded as truly original.[58]

Let us examine the generic configuration of the court of Burgundy following the distinction which de la Marche establishes between 'service de la chambre' and 'service de la bouche et du commun'. This second area (which of course corresponds to the hall) was composed of five separate departments: 'paneterie', 'échansonnerie', 'fruiterie', 'cuisine' and 'écurie', similar to that found in the French court following the reforms of the middle of the thirteenth century.[59] The same norms of association among the several services were practised in Burgundy. Thus, for example, the 'écurie' was strictly related to the service of hunting (also called 'vénerie et fauconnerie'), and in the text of de la Marche it is associated with the 'officiers d'armes', whose role was indispensable in the organisation of tourneys and jousts, and with the central nucleus of the Burgundian army comprising the military entourage of the duke. In its turn, the 'fruiterie' had charge of the provision of fruit and other fresh products, as well as tallow, which formed an important part of the ration paid to the servants of the court. 'Paneterie' and 'échansonnerie' suggest the constant distinction which

[58] Werner Paravicini, 'Expansion et intégration. La noblesse des Pays-Bas à la cour de Philippe le Bon', *Bijdragen en Medelingen betreffende de Geschiedenis der Nederlanden*, 95 (1980), 298–314 and also Paravicini, 'The court of the Dukes of Burgundy', esp. 86–7.

[59] Otto Cartellieri, *The Court of Burgundy: Studies in the History of Civilization* (New York: Haskell, 1970), pp. 52–74; Werner Paravicini, 'Structure et fonctionnement de la cour bourguignonne au XVe siècle', in J. M. Cauchies (ed.), *Le Duc, son entourage, son train* (Turnhout: Brepols, 1998), pp. 1–8. On the legislation of the thirteenth century and the origin of the 'métiers' of the house of the kings of France, Lot and Fawtier, *Institutions royales*, pp. 66–70.

existed in the medieval courts between the distribution of bread and that of wine. The structure of the chamber appears in this text to be very close to what is known of the French court of the same period: independence of the accountancy mechanisms in the service of the 'chambre aux deniers', the organisation of the itinerance by the 'fourrerie' (from *fodrum*), and the making and upkeep of the vestuary and jewels by the 'garderobe'.

What can be concluded from these descriptions?

If we return to the 'domestic sphere' and the duties traditionally associated with it by an analysis of these schemes, it becomes clear that the late-medieval court is an extremely complex organism from the point of view of its formal organisation. In spite of the variety which the examples illustrate, it is possible to speak of the diverse functional groups in the royal 'domesticity' by presenting a larger or smaller internal coherence according to each case. Even though, from a descriptive point of view, the tripartite hall/chamber/chapel is not clearly presented in these sources, it still emerges as an organisational principle in all cases analysed, and shows the existence of a regime of 'domestic' duties in the medieval courts. If one supposes that the problems which a criticism of these sources affirms are overcome or resolved, then the study of this regime would perhaps lead to the construction of yet another subject – the 'household' of the king – which thus occupies its place beside the other, better-known examples such as the central administration, the royal finances or (in a logic which is more centred on precise institutional arrangements) the tribunal of the court, or the chancery. The residual, secondary aspect presented by 'domesticity' in the court of the kings would perhaps be overcome and would once more become an important sphere of this organism of the end of the Middle Ages.[60] But, once again, this would mean separating the composite object to which the medieval concept makes reference into artificially formed dominions.

In fact, a difficult definition of the 'king's household' as a subject of study always leads to already known obstacles, particularly when one attempts to explain the presence of institutional mechanisms which operate at its core, being the irreversible face of the question originally postulated. For if 'domestic logic' is detected in the bureaucratic/administrative institutions related to the development of 'state' functions, then the performance of certain 'domestic duties' also suggests increasingly from the twelfth to the fifteenth centuries a group of highly varied characteristics which almost always include the performance of bureaucratic duties and accountancy. To evaluate the complexity of these characteristics, it is sufficient to consider the descriptions that the sources provide, for example, of the duties connected to the position of the 'boteyler major' of Aragon, or those of the 'premier écuyer d'écurie' of the Duke of Burgundy.[61]

[60] There is a good example in Given-Wilson, *The Royal Household*, or more recently C. M. Wolgar, *The Great Household in Late Medieval England* (New Haven: Yale University Press, 1999).

[61] *Ordenacions... Pedro IV*, pp. 20–3; *L'Estat de la maison...*, pp. 58–63.

Are there not, however, important differences between the duties related to the sustenance, itinerance and daily life of the court, and those studied by the history of institutions relating to justice or to the administration of the kingdom? As I have already stated, I do not wish with these observations to minimise the phenomena of specialisation and differentiation which led to the emergence of true institutions at the heart of the medieval courts. The distinct organisation and finality, the permanence in time, the relation to a system of norms, all these elements of the classic definition of the concept of 'institution' can certainly be found in the court tribunals, in the chanceries, in the centralised financial organisms of the end of the Middle Ages and even in some aspects of the 'domestic' organisation of the households of the kings. But this institutional complex is simultaneously a complex of configurations composed of actual individuals, with the participation of many of them in the social world of the court being an important aspect of its history, which has not yet been sufficiently taken into account.

The court, in turn, is not simply the place that results from the sum of all these institutional mechanisms, as has been made clear from the examples analysed. On the other hand, it is also not merely the 'monarch's household', however complex and tending towards independence the formal definition of the 'domestic' duties might appear to us.[62] Organised around the physical presence of the king, the medieval court can be seen as a human configuration that is the central site of a larger structure, connecting the monarch to the kingdom through a group of complex relations, and by this implying a system of institutions which materialise the necessary mediation of his power. But since the power of the king is introduced and constructed in many ways, it is connected, in no less decisive a manner than it is to the institutional system, to the maintenance of this permanent human nucleus which constitutes a heterogeneous mechanism which is variable in time and space and which allows for the existence of royalty.

THE PORTUGUESE COURT

The claiming of royal dignity by the first monarch of Portugal in the twelfth century was naturally accompanied by the structure of the court following uses common to the westernmost areas of the Peninsula. Therefore we find at the court of the Counts of Portucale as later at the court of the first king, Afonso Henriques, the distinction already spoken of between the *maiordomus* and *armiger* (also known as *alferes* in documents relating to the latter) which characterises the Iberian courts.

The organisation of the hall during the first reigns has left little documentary evidence, although this has served to challenge the interpretative art of

[62] Sergio Bertelli, 'Il concetto di corte', in J. C. Margolin *et al.* (eds.), *Ragione e civilitas: figure del vivere associato nella cultura del 500 Europeo* (Milan: Angeli, 1986).

historians.[63] Most noteworthy are the theories of Claudio Sánchez-Albornoz, who in his first lines defines an evolution which should lead us from the meeting of the primitive Portuguese *curia*, expressly called by the monarch and to which all his vassals who were connected by feudal duty of *consilium et auxilium* would come, to the later development of two types of meeting ('ordinary' and 'extraordinary') in which the Spanish historian saw the origins of the royal council and of the Cortes (Parliaments) respectively. This doctrine underlines the judicial functions of the Portuguese royal hall of the twelfth and thirteenth centuries, but what interested him most of all was the dynamic and the 'modernity' of the corporate and representational principle, of which the Cortes/Parliaments were to be the expression and whose genesis eventually constituted the true object of investigation of the author. The theories of Sánchez-Albornoz refer to the origin of the Cortes, more than to the organisation or the nature of the primitive Portuguese curia.[64]

The publication of the documents of the first Portuguese kings led, on the other hand, to another set of problems because of the mention which appears in them of the diverse duties of the primitive court. In his essay based upon the oldest royal documentation known, Rui de Azevedo identified up to the end of the twelfth century several offices within the ambit of the hall – a *dapifer*, a *pincerna* and a *dispensator*, who were in all probability under the supervision of the *maiordomus*. He also suggested the presence of the *alferes*.[65] Likewise, Avelino de Jesus da Costa emphasised the connection of the chapel to the chancery of the first kings of Portugal, which were both successively under the supervision of the clergy of Braga, the Cathedral of Coimbra and the community of the Observant Canons of Santa Cruz, also in Coimbra.[66]

Little more can be added as to the organisation of the Portuguese court in the period prior to the thirteenth century. The supremacy of three posts (*mordomo*,

[63] See the essay by Barros, *História da administração pública em Portugal*, vol. III, pp. 199–286. Also José Mattoso, *Identificação de um país* (Lisbon: Estampa, 1985), vol. II, pp. 99–119.

[64] Claudio Sánchez-Albornoz, *La curia regia Portuguesa . . . siglos XII y XIII* (Madrid: Centro de Estudios Históricos, 1920); Claudio Sánchez-Albornoz, *Investigaciones y documentos sobre las instituciones Hispanas* (Santiago: Edición Jurídica de Chile, 1970), pp. 456–69. On the reception of his theories in Portugal, see Torquato de Sousa Soares, 'Cúria Régia', *DHP*, vol. I, pp. 774–5.

[65] Rui de Azevedo, 'Funcionários da corte nos documentos régios', in *Documentos medievais Portugueses: documentos régios* (Lisbon: Academia Portuguesa da História, 1958), vol. I, pp. cxv–cxxvii. The identification suggested between the functions of the *maiordomus* and the *dapifer* in the court of the first Portuguese king is, however, an unproven hypothesis. The proximity of the *dapifer* to the *senescalcus*, in the French case, and the identification between this and the *maiordomus* suggested by Du Cange appear to have been the origin of Azevedo's hypothesis. For a criticism of Du Cange on this point, see Ludovico Antonio Muratori, *Dissertazioni sopra le antichità Italiane* (Monaco: Agostino Olzati, 1765), vol. I, pp. 20–8. In the context of Portuguese historiography, the solution proposed by Rui de Azevedo picks up that already proposed a century earlier by José Castello Branco, *O mordomo do rei* (Lisbon: Academia Real das Ciências, 1851). See also on the subject the notes of Alfredo Pimenta, *Idade media: problemas e soluções* (Lisbon: Edições Ultramar, 1946), pp. 81–128.

[66] Avelino Jesus da Costa, 'La chancellerie royale portugaise jusqu'au milieu du XIIIe siècle', *Revista Portuguesa de História*, 15 (1975), 143–69.

alferes and *chanceler*) mentioned in the *Partidas* is confirmed in a famous law of Afonso II (1222) where it was established that, in the absence of any one of them (in the service of the king, in their own service, or through illness) those who held the posts were to find a replacement or to be replaced by the monarch.[67] The general picture of the supremacy of these three court duties was the subject of a careful reconstruction in the study by Leontina Ventura of the court of Afonso III, but it goes back to the first century of the Portuguese kingdom. This author established definitively the fact that the principal magnates of Portugal occupied the posts of *mordomo* and *alferes* of the kings.[68]

Legislative production and the greater quantity of royal documents during the thirteenth century allow for the first time a greater 'visibility' of the structure of the diverse duties of the Portuguese court. In the court of Afonso III and Dinis, for example, we are able to distinguish various services within the ambit of the hall: *cozinha*, *copa* and *escançaria*, *ucharia*, *estrebaria*, *caça* and *montaria*. Besides these there also appear the services of the chamber, and those of the *repostaria* and the chapel.

From legislation of 1258 we clearly find in the kitchen the separation known in other courts between the 'cozinha del-rei de seu corpo' and the 'cozinha do paço', a separation which perhaps already existed in the simultaneous mention of a *dapifer curie* and a *dapifer dominis regis* in the twelfth century, as noted by Rui de Azevedo.[69] Several references to cooks and to the clerk of the kitchen point to a relative independence of this department in Portugal and to the existence of directives relating to its function.[70] The *copa* and *escançaria*, which were under the supervision of a *copeiro-mor* and an *escanção-mor*, were charged with the service of wine for the court and the king as well, of course, as the guarding of the associated tableware.[71] The service placed under the supervision of the *uchão* seems to be one of the more complex, as it is connected to the court supplies of cereals and various provisions. According to José Pedro

67 *Leges*, vol. I, p. 179.

68 Leontina Ventura, 'A nobreza de corte de Afonso III' (Doctoral thesis, University of Coimbra, 1992), vol. I, pp. 43–53.

69 *Leges*, vol. I, pp. 198–200, or the version of *OD*, p. 56. On the twelfth century, Azevedo, 'Funcionários da corte', p. cxvi *et passim*. The contemporary courts of Castile and France also had this separation between the two kitchens: 'Libro de diferentes cuentas de Sancho IV', p. cv; Lot and Fawtier, *Institutions royales*, p. 68.

70 See for example the document of 1279 published by João Pedro Ribeiro, *Dissertações cronológicas e criticas sobre a historia e jurisprudencia eclesiástica e civil de Portugal* (Lisbon: Academia Real das Ciências, 1810–36), vol. III, pp. 83–4.

71 The *copa* is referred to several times in the legislation of Afonso III, particularly in the laws of 1258. On his expenses and the safekeeping of the tableware, see 'Inventários e contas da casa de D. Dinis (1278–1282)', ed. Anselmo Braamcamp Freire, *Arquivo histórico Português* 10 (1916), 41–59, in particular pp. 51–4 on the separation which existed between the *copa* and the *escançaria*. Afonso II had made a gift to his *escanção-mor*: Maria Teresa Nobre Veloso, 'D. Afonso II: relações de Portugal com a Santa Sé durante o seu reinado' (doctoral thesis, University of Coimbra, 1988), vol. I, p. 91.

Machado, the word 'uchão' is derived from the medieval French 'huche', a generic term given to the wooden chests that were a form of storage in general use.[72] This post is mentioned in the documentation of Afonso II. The accounts of the *ucharia* between 1257 and 1270 show supplies of an appreciable quantity of meat and fish (arising from 'colheitas' owed to the king) in the court *ucharia*, and also document a certain complexity in the book-keeping of this service, in which expenses incurred by the *comprador* led to records which would be checked with the accounts of the clerk of the kitchen presented to the *mordomo* and the *chanceler*.[73] The *saquiteiro*[74] and the *mantieiro*[75] were connected in turn with bread and its distribution, while bread-making for the royal table was the duty of the *regueifeira*.[76] We can see in the *ucharia* a service which corresponded in the main to the contemporary French 'paneterie' or the English 'pantry', and like them we must also relate it to the rituals of eating and distribution of cereal rations and other food for members of the court. This group of duties associated with the kitchen, the *copa*, the *escançaria* and the *ucharia*, corresponded to the generic term used by the *Partidas* of 'oficiales del comer et del beber'. In the *estrebaria* there was the *estrabeiro-mor* and the *cevadeiro-mor* with their dependants (grooms and carters) who supplied horses and barley to the court – the latter in all probability also being distributed in rations.[77] To be included in hunting and game hunting are the several *monteiros* and *homens de montaria*, *falcoeiros* and *açoreiros* who are mentioned from time to time in Portuguese royal documents.[78]

The services of the chamber and the *repostaria* are sufficiently recorded in diplomatic sources relating to the thirteenth century to allow for some observations as to their organisation. In the case of the former we should include the *camareiros*, the tailor, the washerwoman, the physician and the barber, who are mentioned in published documentation, as also occurs in the organic of

[72] The etymology of the word also explains its varied spelling, particularly the use of the 'y' in 'ychão' and 'eychão'. On this subject, Victor Gray, *Glossaire archéologique du moyen âge et de la Renaissance* (Paris: Picard, 1928), vol. II, p. 40.

[73] The accounts had been published by João Pedro Ribeiro, *Dissertações cronológicas*, vol. III, pp. 83–4.

[74] The post of *saquiteiro* appears in a law of 1211: *Leges*, vol. I, pp. 175–6 (or *LP*, p. 18; *OD*, p. 51). See also the *Elucidário*, s.v. 'saquiteiro' and 'saquetaria', vol. II, pp. 68 and 548.

[75] On the *mantieiro*, whose function must be related to the food rations distributed at court, see the mention 'de pane de manuterjiis' in the 'Inventários e contas de D. Dinis', p. 59. But also see Carolina Michaëlis de Vasconcelos in her 'Glossário do cancioneiro da Ajuda', s.v. 'manteer', *Cancioneiro da Ajuda* (Lisbon: Imprensa Nacional–Casa da Moeda, 1990), vol. I, p. 52.

[76] On the king's *regueifeira*, see the law of 1258: *OD*, p. 55. And again, the 'Inventários e contas de D. Dinis', p. 57.

[77] In the accounts of Dinis, the *estrabeiro-mor* receives various sums 'pro ad expensam strabarie': 'Inventários e contas de D. Dinis', p. 47. As to the *cevadeiro-mor*, he is mentioned in the law of 1211, with other servants who are rewarded by Afonso II; *Leges*, vol. I, pp. 175–6 and Veloso, 'D. Afonso II', vol. I, p. 91.

[78] The law of 1261 refers to the services of hunting in its relationship with the stable: *Leges*, vol. I, pp. 200–1.

contemporary courts already analysed.[79] There should also be connected to the area of the chamber the service of *pousador* or *aposentador*, who was charged with the itinerance of the king and the court.[80]

More interesting from the comparative point of view, however, is the department of the *repostaria* (or *reposte*), which is mentioned as early as the will of Sancho I regarding the protection of precious objects and the chamber's treasures.[81] In the thirteenth century, reference to the *repostaria* is more frequent than that of the chamber in Portuguese royal documents. We thus have evidence of the activities of the *reposteiro* regarding the handing over of large sums of coinage and other objects in the treasury of Afonso III deposited in the monastery of Santa Cruz in Coimbra.[82] The lists of payments of the court of Dinis, in turn, show the *reposteiro* receiving various sums of money and objects which were delivered by local agents of the royal finances, the 'almoxarifes' of Lisbon, Santarém and Guimarães and Faro, as well as the king's *tesoureiro* ('pro ad expensam de reposte'), all of which movements had to be registered in the 'libro de reposte', which is also mentioned in these documents.[83] All these facts point to the formation of the *repostaria* as a department with important financial duties related to the functioning of the court. It was a department which was closely connected to the king's treasury which, as seen in the case of Afonso III, tended to be sited in a precise location, while the *repostaria* accompanied the monarch on his journeys. In the laws of 1261, among the duties of the *reposteiro* are mentioned the supervision of the granting of 'rations' in the king's house and the levy of fines related to these.[84] I have already stated that in the *Partidas* the 'repostero' had highly varied duties: 'el ha de tener las cosas que el rey manda guardar en poridat: et aun ha de tener otras cosas guardadas que tañen à la guarda del cuerpo del rey, asi como la fruta, et la sal, et los cuchiellos con que

[79] The *camareiro* and the physician of Dinis are referred to in a document of 1321: *HFAC*, vol. I, p. 65. The tailor is mentioned in the law of 1211 (*Leges*, vol. I, pp. 175–6) and again with the king's *lavadeira* in the law of 1258 (*OD*, p. 55). Afonso II also gave a reward to one of his barbers: Veloso, 'D. Afonso II', vol. I, p. 91.

[80] It is possible that the mention of the 'estalageiro' in the law of 1211 refers to this position. The adoption of the names 'pousadeiro' and 'pousador' is not strange, because of the influence of the *Partidas*, already referred to: see, for example, the general chapters of the *Cortes* of 1361, *CPP*, p. 68.

[81] José Mattoso, 'Testamentos de D. Sancho I', in Alexandre Herculano (ed.), *História de Portugal desde o começo da monarquia até o fim do reinado de D. Afonso III* (Final note III) (Lisbon: Bertrand, 1980), vol. III, pp. 570–4.

[82] Pedro de Azevedo, 'O Tesouro de D. Afonso III no Mosteiro de Santa Cruz de Coimbra', *Boletim da Segunda Classe da Academia das Ciências de Lisbon*, 7 (1912–13), 230–63. The documents transcribed dating from the period 1270–75 give ample information on this function of the *reposteiro*, who is assisted by the *copeiro* and the *porteiro*.

[83] 'Inventários e contas de D. Dinis', p. 46. Alexandre Herculano used a meaning which is close to my interpretation when he distinguished the books 'do Recabedo Regni' from those books 'do Reposito' among the records of the monarchs of the thirteenth century on which he had information: Alexandre Herculano, *Opúsculos* (Lisbon: Tavares Cardoso, 1987), vol. VI, p. 289.

[84] *Leges*, vol. I, pp. 202–10 and *OD*, pp. 60–71, in particular pp. 63–4.

tallan ante él, et algunas cosas otras que son del comer quell traen en presente que el han de guardar'.[85] According to this description from the *Partidas*, we should also place the Portuguese *fruteiro* in the *repostaria*, for we find from the accounts of Dinis that the *reposteiro* received cinnamon, several types of sugar 'e outras specias', as well as fruit.[86]

The characteristics of this service are therefore much like those of the French 'chambre' or the papal *camera*, but it is closest of all to the English 'wardrobe' of the thirteenth century. The importance of the wardrobe in the financial organisation of the English court has been the subject of several studies, notably the global interpretation of T. F. Tout who, for the first time, described in detail the relation between this organism, which controlled a large part of the court expenditure, the treasury of the monarchs which was situated in Winchester and the department for the general control of accounts, the exchequer, which was also located in one place.[87] Unfortunately we have no financial documentation for the Portuguese court allowing for such a detailed and complete view of the duties of the *repostaria*. I believe, however, that the relationship which this shows with the king's treasury, as well as its later development in the fourteenth and fifteenth centuries, allows for an approximation which leads to a comparison of its function with that of the English 'wardrobe'. The importance of the *reposte* in the thirteenth century appears clearly from an analysis of the legislation of Afonso III: besides the *alferes*, the *chanceler* and the *mordomo*, only the *reposteiro-mor* could call an opponent to be judged at court.[88] The slight attention which Portuguese historiography has paid to this organism is doubtless due to the fact that it is only referred to in passing in legislative documents of the fifteenth century, which have almost exclusively served as a basis for the study of the organisation of the court in Portugal, without comparing the normative sources with other documentation of administrative and financial practice of the age. In turn, the Manueline directive of 1506 for the *reposteiro-mor*, of which manuscripts have survived, documents a later moment of evolution of the duties of the *repostaria*, in which the financial functions of this service became very restricted owing to the development of bureaucratic organisms connected to public finances.[89]

85 *Las Siete Partidas*, vol. I, p. 68.

86 It is possible to confirm that there was a *fruteiro* in the court of Dinis, for example in the document referred to above of 1321: *HFAC*, vol. I, p. 65.

87 Tout, *Chapters in the Administrative History*, vol. I, pp. 12 and 68, on the chamber/wardrobe relationship in the thirteenth century, and pp. 229–32 for a comparison with the French 'garderobe' and the 'vestiarium' of the papal court. A description of the wardrobe as a financial department at the turn of the fourteenth century can be found in Lyon and Lyon, *The Wardrobe Book of William Norwell*, pp. xxvii–xxviii and lvii.

88 *OD*, p. 118. As will be seen later, this prerogative of the important offices was to be restricted under later legislation.

89 Note in particular the absence of a title for the duty of *reposteiro* in the *Ordenações Afonsinas*, although it is frequently referred to in documentation of the fourteenth and fifteenth centuries. The Manueline directive is known to us in manuscript form dated 1613: ANTT, Laws M.2, no. 19.

In contrast, the frequent occurrence in legislative sources of the word 'ovençal' has led to the construction of an historiographic theory according to which the 'ovençais' played an important role in the Portuguese court in the thirteenth century, and this word served for the duties or functions which were specific to this organisation. If we examine again the legislation attributed to Afonso II, for example: besides the generic references, there are in fact listed among the 'ovençais' officers of the court such as the *porteiro*, the *alfaiate*, the *reposteiro*, the *saquiteiro*, the *cevadeiro*, the *escanção*, the *uchão* and the *estalageiro* (this last being an archaic name for the *estrabeiro* or the *pousador*).[90] But on the other hand, as has already been observed by several historians from Gama Barros onwards, in this same legislation we find that the monasteries and the lay lords also had their 'ovençais'. It is highly probable that during the thirteenth century there occurred a diffusion of practices, of monastic origin, reserving a certain part of income or patrimony for particular costs or expenditure, and that this was the original meaning of the word *obedentiales*. *Obedentia* (Portuguese 'ovença') was the name given to this mechanism of granting funds to the different organisms whose duty was the various aspects of the life of the community.[91] With this interpretation, the 'ovençais' cannot be considered separately from or cumulatively with the other duties to which sources refer during the period as an integral part of the court of the Portuguese kings. It would be more correct to say that certain servants in the thirteenth century were also called 'ovençais', as suggested already by the historians Paulo Merêa and Marcelo Caetano, and that this name was a strong indication that there was recourse to the mechanism of the 'ovença' in the court, in this case the granting of a precise part of the king's income for the costs of the various departments which, one assumes, had direct financing separate from other departments, as was the case in so many medieval courts.

The lack of more precise elements as to the performance of the various duties of court 'que teem algũa ovença', as stated in the laws cited, does not allow us to ascertain how this system was linked with the circulation of money and kind within the court itself, referred to in sources such as the accounts of Dinis. What connection in the thirteenth century did the various quantities of meat and fish resulting from tributes paid in kind (*colheitas*) have with the 'ovença' of the *uchão*, or the sums distributed by the *tesoureiro* to the *reposteiro* and the *estrabeiro* with the existence of the respective 'ovenças'? The question becomes still more complicated if we consider that the mechanism of the 'ovenças'

[90] *Leges*, vol. I, pp. 175–6 and also *OD*, pp. 51, 57 and 142.

[91] Du Cange, *Glossarium*, s.v. 'obedientia'; Joseph M. Piel, *Sobre a origem do antigo Galego-Português 'ovença' e 'ovençal'*, offprint of *Revista Portuguesa de História* (Coimbra, 1978). On the monastic use of 'obedientia', Jacques Hourlier, 'Famiglia', in *Dizionario degli Istituti di Perfezione* (Rome: Edizioni Paoline, 1975), vol. II, pp. 1390–95. On 'obedientia' in the monasteries of the Iberian Peninsula, José Mattoso, *Le Monachisme ibérique et Cluny: les abbayes du diocèse de Porto de l'an mil à 1200* (Louvain: Publications Universitaires, 1968), pp. 259–61.

continued to exist at least until the fifteenth century: in Lisbon, the mention of 'ovençais do rei' is well known in local documentation during the 1300s, but also in 1360 Pedro for example sent a charter 'a uos meus ouençaaes daallem dos montes', referring to the officials of the regions of Trás os Montes.[92] These facts point to the use of the 'ovença' in different regions and in distinct territories of the kingdom. In the *Regimento dos Contos* given to Gonçalo Caldeira in 1434, Duarte ordered: 'per esta guisa farees fazer dous liuros em que sejam postas todas as ouenças do Reino cada hũ almoxarifado sobre ssy'.[93] However, it is necessary to go further and to recognise that there is nothing which allows us to relate the 'ovenças' exclusively to the expenses of the various services of the court. It is clear that this entire subject will only be clarified when a more thorough study is made of the organisation of the medieval royal finances, taking into account these and other processes of the assignment of income from various sources paid throughout the kingdom for uses which had already been determined. In this analysis of the organisation of the court, it did not seem that the name 'ovençais' should be taken into account, since it does not refer to a particular post but means merely a mechanism of finance and perhaps of control of accounts used in various areas and also, perhaps, beyond the court and even the royal administration.

So let us return to the description of the Portuguese court of the thirteenth century, even though this is of necessity concise, owing to the manifest lack of published or listed documentary records. There is scant information as to the royal chapel of Afonso III and Dinis. According to Fleckenstein, in a definition of the medieval imperial or royal 'chapel', we must take note of the three distinct realities which the word encompasses: the group of liturgical objects used in rites; the ecclesiastics connected to the rites; the place or space reserved for this in the interior of the imperial or royal *domus* (which could also be papal or cardinalate).[94] It can be said that the first two aspects are generically better documented in the Portuguese case than is the last, thanks in particular to the mention of liturgical objects in the wills of Portuguese kings and queens, which objects certainly came from their respective chapels. The use of chaplains, apparently in no different a manner than that of other clerics at court, as clerks and even as guards of the royal seal, seems to have occurred in Portugal only during the twelfth century, and this practice was abandoned later when the chancery became organised as an autonomous body.[95]

[92] Marcelo Caetano, *A administração municipal de Lisboa durante a 1a dinastia (1179–1383)* (Lisbon: Academia Portuguesa da História, 1981), pp. 47–9. The charter of Pedro: *CDP*, p. 376.

[93] Virginia Rau, *A Casa dos Contos* (Coimbra: Faculdade de Letras, 1951), pp. 463–9, in particular p. 468.

[94] Josef Fleckenstein, *Die Hofkapelle der Deutschen Könige* (Stuttgart: Hiersemann, 1959); Agostino Paravicini-Bagliani, *La Cour des Papes au XIIIe siècle* (Paris: Hachette, 1995), pp. 142–6.

[95] Costa, 'La chancellerie royale', p. 156.

The precise mention of the *capelão-mor*, the almoner and the king's confessor, as being among those who accompanied the monarch attests, however, to the permanence of specific functions related to the rites among the group of those known as 'clérigos d'el-rei'.[96] The inclusion of the confessor in the royal chapel is somewhat debatable since, as we shall see, his functions were much like those of the chamber, placing him among the closest servants of the king. This unravelling is all the more interesting if, for example, we consider the example of Dinis who, during the final period of his reign, retained the same person as his chaplain and confessor,[97] a practice rarely found with other monarchs. The organic of the chapel of the thirteenth century included, on the other hand, a special post devoted to alms. The connection of the duties of the almoner to the Cistercians of Alcobaça, confirmed at least from the reign of Afonso III,[98] shows, in turn, a preoccupation with the organisation of this important aspect of court life through recourse to the experience of the monks, just as the sovereigns of Aragon did with the Cistercian abbots of Santa Creus and Poblet.[99]

With regard to the relatively complex organisation evoked and perfectly framed within the general panorama of the medieval courts sketched above, it would not be out of place to mention the fluid character and the uncertainty which, in spite of everything, seem to surround the duties of some positions of the Portuguese court at the turn of the fourteenth century. Besides the lacunae and doubts which the interpretation of known sources occasions, it is also probable that it is not possible to attribute to them carefully defined spheres of competence. In many cases there is no express mention of the hierarchic relations which certainly existed between them. On the other hand, the tendency in many medieval organisations towards the multiplicity of terms for the same group of duties is well known, as occurred in Portugal at the time, for example with the services connected to the itinerance of the court. The superimposition, which could be described as stratigraphic, of older offices on the newer ones can also be seen. This is due to a logical respect for tradition, and there will be several examples of this tendency, which hinders a general reconstruction of the structure of the various organisations.

It is known that in the courts of Afonso III and Dinis the performance of various duties was entrusted to the same individuals, either successively or even cumulatively. Some would have had their own dependants who would perform the various duties within their remit, and would be responsible to the

96 Mattoso, *Identificação de um país*, vol. II, pp. 105–6.

97 *HFAC*, vol. I, p. 65 and also ANTT, *LN*, Reis, Book 1, ff. 104–7.

98 Azevedo, 'O Tesouro de D. Afonso III', p. 240. During the Cortes of Leiria of 1254, Afonso III's *mordomo-mor* regularised with the monastery of Alcobaça and the almoner several accounts relating to the previous reigns: Marcelo Caetano, 'O significado das Cortes de Leiria', in *Páginas inoportunas* (Lisbon: Bertrand [1959]), pp. 93–111, in particular p. 105.

99 Quintin Aldea Vaquero (ed.), *Diccionario de historia eclesiástica de España* (Madrid: CSIC, 1972), vol. I, pp. 338–9, s.v. 'capilla real de Aragón'.

king for their performance and receive various rations related to those duties.[100] I shall not spend time now on the consideration of these problems, for to my mind this is only, as has already been stated, a preliminary sketch, in general terms, of the organisation of the court of the Portuguese kings during the period immediately prior to the age to be studied in more detail, that is the fourteenth and fifteenth centuries.

Were one to seek to characterise the evolution of the court from the formal point of view, one could say that during these last two centuries of the Middle Ages it is marked first by a process of *bureaucratisation* and *rationalisation* of functions, in particular in the sphere of judicial, administrative and financial activities which had a place at its core. The process is one that is beginning to be studied in depth thanks to the works of the historian Carvalho Homem. The process is accompanied by a modification of the military role, linked to the existence of fluid boundaries between the royal host and the court. As we shall see, other images of royalty became possible beyond that of the traditional war leader associated with the reconquest. It could be said as we observe a greater 'divisibility' or internal compartmentalisation of the royal court that the external frontiers of this organism become, certainly in my view, more permeable and less precise. In spite of our knowing now much more as to the way in which the court, as a central organism, is related to the periphery of the kingdom, it is more difficult to evaluate the alterations experienced by the configuration of the more restricted nucleus surrounding the monarch.

Some modifications in this central nucleus are found in the sphere of the chamber, which at the end of the medieval period had highly diverse functions and which, together with various institutional systems, constituted the central core of the royal court. In my opinion, these new functions of the complex related to the chamber indicate what Weber was to call a 'persönlisches regime' in the administration of the Portuguese kings which was formed from the middle of the fourteenth century, and beyond doubt flowered with the monarchs of the fifteenth, being particularly important for Duarte. How should we characterise this regime? In the first place, the growing intervention of the chamber in the sphere of production of decrees and royal charters through a post connected to the chamber should be noted: that of the *escrivão da puridade*. The origins of this new structure are related to the use of a seal whose safekeeping remained under the direct control of the monarch, the seal of 'puridad' in Castile and Portugal, also known in the fourteenth century in Portugal as the 'selo de camafeu'.[101]

The origins of the use of this second seal, along with the one in the safe-keeping of the chancellor, were exactly contemporaneous, in Castile, with the reflection based on the actual concept of 'puridad', which was then arising in

[100] These aspects can be deduced from various sections of the Laws of 1258: *Leges*, vol. I, pp. 198–200 or *OD*, pp. 54–8.

[101] *Desembargo*, p. 161. In a law attributed to John I retained in the *Ordenações Afonsinas*, the use of the seal 'de camafeu' is placed on a par with the 'selo das quinas': *OA*, vol. II, p. 220.

the semantic sphere of politics. Found in works intended for the aristocratic public of the thirteenth century, as for example the 'Castigos' attributed to King Sancho, is the entire casuistic complex on the occasions on which a 'privado', or a man 'de merced', might violate the 'secrecy' of his lord: 'Mientra la poridat tovieres guardada en ti, é la non andodieres sembrando en otras partes, serás tu señor de la poridat, é non te verná dapno della; é desque la hobieres descobierta, será la poridat señora de ti, é tu siempre estarás a sospecha que to verná mal della . . . Más vale mentir teniendo poridat, que decir verdat descobriendo la poridat.'[102] At the turn of the fourteenth century, in the face of the collective ideal of the lord among equals, evoked by the royal hall, there appeared a further sphere, that of interpersonal relations, a source of power and a justification for the value of individual interest to be pursued alongside the king. This was the sphere of 'puridade', a word which we also see appear in the *Partidas*, a sphere whose place, through excellence, would at court be the chamber or the council, both organisms of daily contact with and proximity to the king. These texts from the thirteenth century, which were intended for a lay and a court public, sought to express the diverse modalities of action, some being more distant from, others closer to the king, which were open to men who lived at court, and there was a recourse to this concept of 'puridad' or 'secrecy' which became associated with a distinct form of behaviour.[103] It is to my mind significant that there appears a vocabulary associated to the duty whose genesis is of interest to us.

Within this intellectual context in which there was emerging the use of the 'selo da puridade', the power of the written word when used as an instrument of the *regis potestas* was at times seen as somewhat threatening to the monarch himself:

> El poder del rey todo es en tres cosas: lo primero, en la su palabra, lo segundo en la su peñola con que escribe las sus cartas, de lo que él ha de mandar; la tercera, en la su espada con que apremia a los sus enemigos e con que faze justiçia en los suyos, ca la espada taja por premia e por justiçias las cabeças de los que mal facen; *e la peñola, si non escribe como deue, el rey deuele cortar a ella la cabeça.*[104]

In fact, we can see that the safekeeping of the seal, which was the duty of the *chanceler*, was almost always threatened by political agitation. In Portugal, this occurred during the crisis which marked the end of the reign of Sancho II,[105]

[102] Agapito Rey (ed.), *Castigos y documentos para bien vivir ordenados por el Rey don Sancho* (Bloomington: Indiana University Press, 1952), pp. 144–6 (and in general chapter 29 in its entirety, 'que fabla como debe home meter mientes á quien descubre su puridad'). For a general presentation of these texts, Denis Menjot, 'Enseigner la sagesse. Remarques sur la littérature gnomique castillane du moyen âge', in Nilda Guglielmi and Adeline Rucquoi (eds.), *El discurso político en la edad media* (Madrid: CSI/CNRS, 1995), pp. 217–31.

[103] José Bustos Tovar, 'Notas para el léxico de la prosa didáctica del siglo XIII', in *Studia Hispanica in Honorem Rafael Lapesa* (Madrid: Gredos, 1974), vol. II, pp. 149–55.

[104] *Castigos y documentos*, p. 83.

[105] Costa, 'La chancellerie royale', p. 155.

as also later, at the beginning of the reign of Dinis[106] or during the conflicts between his son, the future Afonso IV, and his bastard brother.[107] The use of a 'small seal', an expedient also used by medieval monarchs outside of the Iberian Peninsula, therefore became a common option from the beginning of the fourteenth century for the validation of acts arising in the sphere of 'secrecy' and as an alternative to the power of the chancery.[108] According to Carvalho Homem, in Portugal the origins of this structure may be found during the reign of Dinis, although it is only with Afonso IV that reference to the post is expressly made in royal documentation.

Did the use of the new seal signify an effective downgrading of the importance of the post of *chanceler*, as is traditionally stated? In the particular case of the Portuguese court, the interpretation of the specific position of the medieval scribe of 'secrecy' was, until very recently, overstated because of events that occurred much later. This was due to the force that developed during the seventeenth century for the historical legitimisation of the prerogatives of a post that was 'rediscovered' at the time.[109] In fact, the figure of the seventeenth-century *escrivão da puridade* is closer to that of a 'valido' or minister, who was a typical figure during the *ancien régime*, than that of the earlier post of the same name of the late Middle Ages.[110] Data relative to the fourteenth and fifteenth centuries show the *escrivão da puridade* merely superintending the various *escrivães da câmara*, who were at times also called 'secretários', and who kept the seals which were used there (and from here stems the alternative name, which appears in the documents of the reign of Fernando, of 'chanceler da puridade'), and who were present at the meetings of the royal council.[111] The *chanceler* continued, however, to have more effective duties which were exclusive to him and which, according to the commands of Afonso's Ordinations, implied the

106 José Antunes *et al.*, *Conflitos políticos no Reino de Portugal entre a Reconquista e a Expansão*, offprint of *Revista de História das Ideias* (Coimbra, 1984), pp. 113–14.

107 *Desembargo*, p. 211, note 16.

108 This comparative aspect was suggested by Evelyn S. Procter, 'The use and custody of the secret seal (sello de la puridad) in Castile from 1252 to 1369', *English Historical Review*, 217 (1940), 194–221, in particular 207–8.

109 Francisco Manuel Trigoso Aragão Morato, 'Memória sobre os escrivães da puridade dos reis de Portugal, e do que a este officio pertence', *Memórias da Academia Real das Ciências*, 12 (1837), 91–107; Conde de Tovar, *Estudos históricos* (Lisbon: Academia Portuguesa da História, 1961), vol. III. None of these studies emphasises clearly the difference that the seventeenth-century post, which was included in a system which was far from similar to the medieval in organic and practice, naturally demonstrates in relation to the *escrivão da puridade* of the Middle Ages.

110 I. A. A. Thompson, 'The institutional background of the rise of the minister-favourite', in J. H. Elliot and L. W. Brockliss (eds.), *The World of the Favourite* (New Haven: Yale University Press, 1999), pp. 13–25.

111 These duties are described by the old royal servant Álvaro Gonçalves in 1450, in his report 'do que se praticava' in the time of John I: Tovar, *O escrivão da puridade*, pp. 158–61. Also in the personal notes of Duarte it is stated that there must be present at the meetings of the council 'hũ escriuão da Camara que screua os acordos segundo a cousa for de que se trautar conselho': *Livro dos Conselhos*, p. 14.

exercise of justice regarding members of court, the supervision of the complex structure of the royal chancery and the preservation of writs or the control of the king's notaries all around the country.[112]

Another area in which the chamber of the end of the Middle Ages became increasingly involved was that of the royal finances. Once again, the creation of a structure that was physically independent of the court for the control of accounts, called the 'casa dos contos', whose origin stems from the beginning of the fourteenth century, implied the existence of a direct connection to the monarch, which was naturally through the chamber. Following the verification of accounts by trained personnel, the techniques of which have been explained by Virginia Rau, the final examination of these accounts fell to the monarch, who was assisted by the *vedores da fazenda* and the *contador-mor*, who were in turn aided by the *escrivão da puridade*.[113] This of course did not mean that the fourteenth- and fifteenth-century *repostaria* did not also play an important part in the finances of the king, though it was connected more directly to the functioning of the court itself. This was a department whose accounting tended to remain independent: in a directive dated 1407, John I established that expenses relating to dwellings, to the 'reposte' and to the 'vestires', as well as 'despesas nom certas' of the court *despenseiro*, were to remain solely under the supervision of his *vedor da fazenda*, and that its own register be drawn up 'em hũ livro que andase em as arcas que andam na nossa camara'.[114] In an entry retained in the 'Livro dos Conselhos', Duarte also refers to the complexity in the functioning of the court of the financial activities of the *tesoureiro*, the *despenseiro*, the *reposteiro* and the servants of the *guarda-roupa*, which led to each having its own register, as well as the issue of warrants and their supervision by the *vedores da fazenda*.[115] Unfortunately, nothing remains of these records, although some signs of this court activity, particularly the 'cartas de quitação', can be found in the financial documentation of the Portuguese monarchs of the fifteenth century. It should be emphasised that this involvement of the chamber in financial matters occurred just as much in those areas of 'public finance' as in the more restricted area of the finances of the court itself, in a logical coherence with what has already been seen to have existed in the thirteenth century.[116]

One final aspect that allows us to evaluate the changes in the organisation of the chamber during the final stages of the Middle Ages is related to its military

[112] *OA*, vol. II, pp. 15–23. See the synthesis of the known facts on the position: *Desembargo*, pp. 100–10.

[113] Rau, *A Casa dos Contos*, p. 55. See also the description of Álvaro Gonçalves: Tovar, *O escrivão da puridade*, p. 159.

[114] Royal charter of 1410, recorded in the Books of Accounts, describing measures taken 'ha dous anos vai em tres estando em estremoz', that is before the Cortes of 1408 during which the decision was made to form the Casas dos Infantes: ANTT, *Ch. João I*, 5, f. 72.

[115] *Livro dos Conselhos*, pp. 15–17.

[116] Vitorino Magalhães Godinho, 'Finanças públicas e estrutura do estado', in *Ensaios* (Lisbon: Sá da Costa, 1968), vol. II, pp. 25–63.

duties. The *cavaleiros* who served in the royal 'troop' during the reigns of Afonso III and Dinis for the protection of the person of the monarch were followed in the reign of Afonso IV by the vassals known as 'da guarda', who were soon placed under the supervision of a 'guarda-mor'.[117] To these were added a body of foot and mounted fighting men who were selected for the permanent service of the monarch, and in the fifteenth century a small personal retinue was established, which numbered crossbowmen and 'ginetes' to be added to the bodyguard, as well as the 'guardas da câmara'.[118]

In conclusion, it can be said that the number of principal posts in the chamber of the fourteenth and fifteenth centuries evokes a group of actual departments with a multiplicity of servants who were more or less specialised and who were headed, as shown in Figure 5, by the *camareiro-mor* (with the *guarda-roupa* under him), the *reposteiro-mor*, the *escrivão da puridade*, the *guarda-mor* and the *pousador-mor* (or *aposentador-mor*).[119]

The royal chapel, which in turn was completely independent of the chancery, saw during this period an increase in the number of elements under the supervision of the *capelão-mor* and the *esmoler-mor* and, in particular during the fifteenth century, it acquired a growing ceremonial importance, as will be shown in detail later.

The consideration for the final centuries of the Middle Ages of the existence of a link between the various posts of the old royal hall is, in contrast, a hard challenge. There is a general impression of a pulverisation of the old organic which was, as sources show, due on the one hand to the changes in the way of life of the court itself and, on the other, to the known process of the emergence of institutions developing from the organic. This brought about the development of preferential areas of activity with specialised officials. If we remain attentive to the concepts of the age, we should find once again a group of posts that generally accompany the monarch more assiduously, forming part of the royal court, even though they might equally perform in other institutional structures. We are able to distinguish these posts from those of the chamber since, in general terms, they are related to forms of common service rather than solely to the person of the king, and therefore assume the essential distinction between the hall as an organism resulting from the meeting of the sovereign with his vassals and servants, and the chamber as an organ of separation from and consequently control of access to the presence of the monarch.

117 *CDA*, vol. I, p. 387 (doc. of 1335); *CDP*, p. 6 (doc. of 1357). João Gouveia Monteiro, *A guerra em Portugal nos finais da idade média* (Lisbon: Editorial Notícias, 1998), pp. 14–22.

118 Augusto Cardoso Pinto, *A Guarda del Rei Dom João II: notas e documentos para a história das Guardas Reais Portuguesas* (Lisbon: Centro Tipográfico Colonial, 1930).

119 Sketches of 'Rulings' relating to the *camareiro-mor* and the *aposentador-mor* had been included in the *Ordenações Afonsinas: OA*, vol. I, pp. 337–40 and 348–50. As to the post of the *reposteiro-mor*, a succession of fifteenth-century *cartas de quitação* reveal the complexity of this department: ANTT, *LN*, Extras, ff. 45v to 46, 55v, 10v to 41, 5v to 5 (letters relative to the periods 1451–61 and 1462–73).

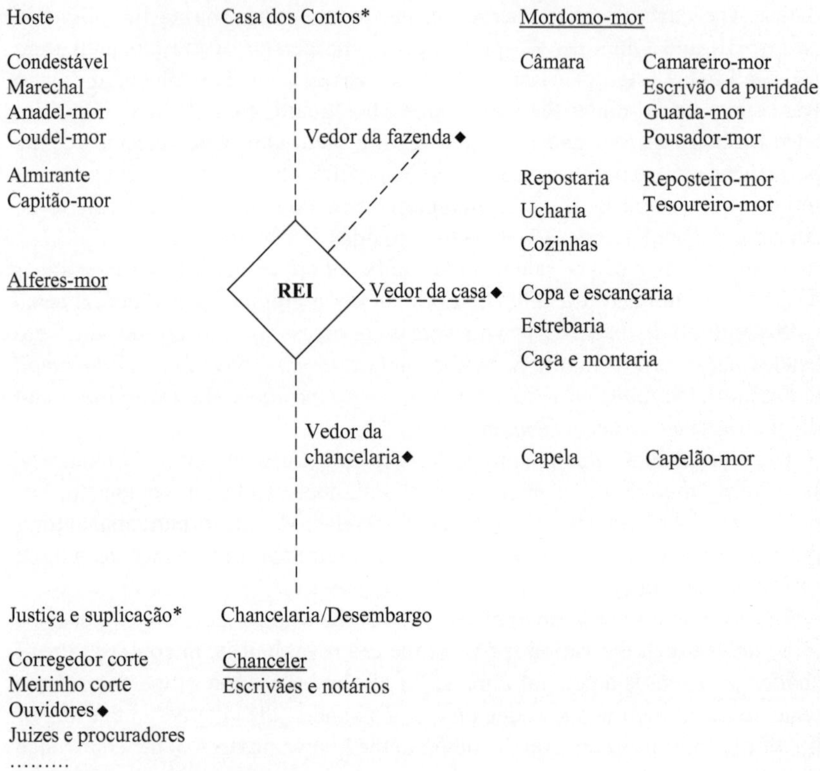

Underlined – charges existing since the thirteenth century
* – institutions developed in the fourteenth and fifteenth centuries
◆ – new royal agents

Fig. 5 The Portuguese court in the fifteenth century (attempted reconstruction)

Thus, the old offices 'do comer e do beber' of the earlier age, to which I have already referred, were succeeded by various departments during the fourteenth and fifteenth centuries. Under the supervision of the *uchão-mor* there existed a multiplicity of servants.[120] Besides those belonging to the *ucharia* itself there were also the services of the *mantearia*, the *saquitaria* and the *requeixaria*. Unfortunately little is known as to the duties of the *requeixaria*, and I therefore adopt the hypothesis of an analogy with the Aragonese 'museria', which was the area in which articles for the royal table were kept separately. Not only does the most probable etymology of this Portuguese word point

[120] See in particular *cartas de quitação* of the *uchão* of Afonso V, Álvaro de Barros, relative to the earlier period to 1462: ANTT, *LN*, Extras, f. 43.

to the notion of 'closed space, recess',[121] but the doubtful information which we have as to the functioning of this area points equally to the control of victuals and, most of all, to their storage or reserves. Similar processes of multiplication of posts arise in the sectors under the control of the *cozinheiro-mor*, the *copeiro-mor* and the *escanção-mor*, to which can also be added the departments of the *estribeiro-mor* and the *cevadeiro-mor*. The characteristics of these organisms were, simultaneously, more complex and more restricted than those of the posts which preceded the thirteenth century, for there became generalised at the interior of the court new forms of remuneration of the servants of the king which were characterised in general by payments in money.

Regarding these changes which, as we shall see, caused the court at the end of the Middle Ages to become a place of intensity of exchange and an economic centre of growing attraction, the new practices of intervention in urban economic life led during the fifteenth century to the creation of a post for the establishment of prices in those places where the court was installed. This was to be the *almotacé-mor*. The directive of this office as written in the Manueline Ordinations resulted, according to Armindo de Sousa, from the palatine elaboration of regulations during the entire fifteenth century, which came about following constant pressure of complaints from the legal representatives of the people.[122] An attempt was made to respond to the chorus of protests of the men 'da governança' of the cities as to the presence of the court and its disruptive effect on local prices and supplies. The idea was to adopt the point of view of the citizens themselves, or to consider the court as a market, therefore placing it under the authority of an *almotacé*. Since the sphere of activity of this official came to supersede in several ways the local *almotacé*, his existence also became highly contested by the same cities, who persistently criticised the royal politics – while the court naturally tended to place the interests of its supplies above all others.

The ceremonial dimension of court life of the fourteenth and fifteenth centuries which will be analysed more thoroughly is, in turn, related for example to the expansion of the body of musicians who accompanied the king, and to new posts which appear within the ambit of the hall. Among these must be emphasised the appearance of heraldic officials and also posts such as that of the *mestre-sala* and the carver. The case of the officials of arms is a direct reflection of the more complex palatine rituals: the emblematic language of arms

[121] Julio Cejador, *Vocabulario medieval Castellano* (Madrid: Visor, 1990), s.v. 'Requejar' and 'Requejo, -xo'. In a published document dated 1286, for example, mention is made of the need to have a market or a slaughter-house in Évora 'mais largos, que os açouguis que hi a son requeixados' (a word which I interpret as a synonym for 'apertados'): *DEV*, vol. I, p. 33. The hypotheses of Viterbo in his *Elucidário*, where he links the *requeixaria* with the word 'queijo', do not appear to have much foundation.

[122] The first rulings relative to this post date from 1417: Armindo de Sousa, *As Cortes medievais Portuguesas (1385–1490)* (Lisbon: INIC, 1990), vol. I, p. 129, note 74.

stemming from fields of battle invaded the social court medium at the end of the Middle Ages, making necessary the presence of the heraldic specialist in the royal hall.[123] The role of these agents of the court in the normalisation and order of this language and in the register of arms was codified by the Portuguese kings, and accompanied restrictive measures as to the use of arms from 1466. But the presence of the officer of arms, the herald, who seems to appear in Portugal in the fourteenth century, was characterised not only by these disciplinary functions and the register of arms that appear relatively late, but most of all for the ceremonial and diplomatic duties that fell to him from early on. The adoption of the hierarchy 'king of arms/herald/pursuivant' during the fifteenth century demonstrates the full participation of the Portuguese court in a larger cultural complex of European courts of the end of the Middle Ages, where these forms of common language, of communication and of distinction were developing.[124]

The services related to hunting demonstrate a curious evolution, and provide a good example of the institution of the court as the centre of a system which tended, through a process of creation of interrelated territorial units, to subordinate the peripheries of the kingdom. Thus the various *monteiros-mores* of the districts who controlled the defined spaces where the king hunted were connected to the *monteiro-mor* who accompanied the court.[125] However he also had control of the *monteiros da câmara*, the *monteiros de cavalo*, the *moços do monte* and other personnel who remained near the monarch and who were permanently ready for the hunt.[126] The *falcoeiro-mor* seems for his part to have headed a similar structure, although its hierarchy is less clear, and from the middle of the fifteenth century he appears to have been under the supervision of the *monteiro*.[127]

123 Michel Pastoureau, *Les Armoiries: typologie des sources du moyen âge occidental*, fasc. 20 (Turnhout: Brepols, 1976), pp. 29–37; Gert Melville, 'Hérauts et héros', in Heinz Duchhard, Richard A. Jackson and David Sturdy (eds.), *European Monarchy: Its Evolution and Practice* (Stuttgart: Steiner, 1992), pp. 17–25.

124 On the officers at arms in the Iberian Peninsula: Martí de Riquer, *Cavalleria fra realtà e letteratura nel Quattrocento* (Bari: Adriatica, 1970), pp. 13–15. Also the highly generic observations of the editor A. Augusto Nascimento, *Livro de Arautos (De Ministerio Armorum)* (Lisbon, 1977), pp. 43–6. Among the numerous visits to the Portuguese court by foreign officials, from the reign of Fernando, are listed those of the herald Arundel and, during the reign of John I, of Bourbon, Aragon (on several missions) and Catalonia, of the King of Arms, Flanders and of several poursuivants, among whom during the reign of Afonso V, was Loland of Denmark. In the list of expenditure of this monarch published by Jorge Faro, there are mentioned missions to Rome and England of his officials at arms, in particular the heralds 'Alcácer', 'Lisbon' and 'Coimbra', and the King of Arms, Portugal.

125 Barros, *História da administração pública*, vol. VI, pp. 49–52 and also the ruling in *OA*, vol. I, pp. 398–405.

126 Direct information on these posts can be found in John I's *Livro de Montaria*, in M. Lopes de Almeida (ed.), *Obras dos Príncipes de Avis* (Oporto: Lello, 1981), pp. 1–132.

127 C. M. Baeta Neves, *Subsídios para a história da falcoaria em Portugal*, offprint of *Boletim da Sociedade de Geografia de Lisboa* (Lisbon, 1984).

A further area in which we are able to observe important changes is that which was organised under the supervision of the *porteiro-mor*. According to the *Partidas*, the 'portero' was responsible for the performance of a group of duties related to his particular position, while his post was connected to communication with the exterior of the palace or court. This post implied the transmission of messages, the publication of royal decrees and participation in the sphere of the execution of justice. This generic profile came to be disseminated among other organisms from the thirteenth century, so that we are able to maintain that, at the end of the Middle Ages, even within the court itself all generally had one or more 'porteiros': the royal chamber, the chancery, the *casa dos contos*, the *casa da justiça* (or the *casa da suplicação*), etc. Were we to analyse the duties of all these 'porteiros' and compare them one with the other as they are described by normative sources, we should see that these functions were very similar, and that they denoted the influence of the same organisational archetype, which was that of the royal palace. As to the old *porteiro do paço*, a post which from the thirteenth century had been related to the collection of royal dues, he appears in the fourteenth and fifteenth centuries as heading a true department, which encompassed specialised agents in the judicial sphere whose functions in the area of the contentious *fazenda* up to the middle of the fourteenth century, for example, have been established today.[128] With the reorganisation of the tribunals of the court in the fifteenth century this role of the *portaria do paço* began to decline in the spheres of justice and the *fazenda*, while it retained those functions related to the communication and execution of the orders of the king, namely the bestowal of castles, the transmission of messages and the calling together of vassals to court for a variety of reasons.[129]

From all the above, it can be deduced that the changes in the organisation of the hall at the end of the Middle Ages implied in general the retention of almost all the posts which were known in the preceding period, whose configuration meanwhile suffered processes of change which were commonplace in medieval organisations: the supremacy of new posts over those which already existed, and the 'internal' transformation which tended towards a greater complexity in the functioning of the various departments. The principal innovation, from an organisational point of view, lay in the appearance of another type of official at the heart of the court: the *vedor*. Along with the *chanceler*, the *vedor da chancelaria* appeared from the second decade of the fourteenth century, and was charged more directly with the functioning of this structure, while the

[128] *Desembargo*, pp. 119–33.

[129] See the law of Afonso IV on the generic validity of the 'portarias': *OD*, p. 381 and *OA*, vol. II, p. 219. The doctrine registered by the Alfonsine texts should also be remembered: 'dezimos ssegunt ffuero antigo dEspana que otro ninguno non puede auer portero para dar o rreçebir castiello ssinon rrey ssolamiente': *Leyes de Alfonso X*, vol. I, pp. 137.

chanceler retained his traditional prerogatives.[130] A parallel relationship was established between the *mordomo-mor* and the *vedor da casa*, whose existence is evident from the reign of Pedro, and whose duties were far more restricted than those of the *mordomo-mor*.[131] From at least 1369, if not before, there appeared *vedores da fazenda*, whose number became fixed at two during the first quarter of the fifteenth century, although this increased in the middle of the century, a fact that Magalhães Godinho associates with the establishment of *sisas*, which were the first general fiscal imposition and applied to all, without distinction.[132]

It could be said that in this way the Portuguese monarchs sought, in various organisms of the court or particularly important sectors, to make use of agents who, while at times there remained an apparent duplication of functions with traditional duties, were characterised precisely for their more direct contact with the king and by an 'interstitial' activity regarding the structure of older functional groups. It cannot easily be accepted, however, that this use of the *vedores* meant that many old posts became merely 'honorary', as some authors rush to suggest. The *vedor* appears as a type of agent who is more specialised, as suggested by Caetano when speaking of the emergence of the distinction between 'ouvidores' and 'veedores' in the fourteenth century, resulting from an embryonic opposition between judicial and administrative duties.[133] In the Portuguese court this distinction had much reason to exist. With the exception of activities relative to *sisas* in the case of the *vedores da fazenda*, this type of agent was in the main to be found distanced from the exercise of justice. In the related areas, this fell to the *chanceler* rather than to the *vedor da chancelaria*; it was the duty of either the *mordomo*, the *ouvidores da portaria* or the *juiz dos feitos d'El-Rei*, but not the *vedor da casa*. On the other hand, from the middle of the fourteenth century it was not uncommon to see the same individual being simultaneously or successively the *vedor da chancelaria* and the *vedor da fazenda*, or the *vedor da casa* and *da fazenda*, a fact which was justified perhaps by a parallel between the duties of this post as well as its extreme specialisation.

Owing to the more specific character of his activities, this type of agent could not carry out the varied group of duties which, according to tradition, fell to the more archaic positions at court, compared with which the *vedores* appear almost always in a hierarchically inferior position. This seems to be the case of the relationship existing between the *chanceler* and the *vedor da chancelaria*, or between the *mordomo* and the *vedor da casa*, in which the first-named had reserved to them those duties which, according to the values of the age, were seen as more prestigious. The appearance of the *vedores* thus signified the introduction of a diverse and transverse logic in the several spheres of activity of the court, and in the performance of the duties whose existence had commenced

130 *Desembargo*, pp. 100–6. 131 *CDP*, p. 472
132 Magalhães Godinho, 'Finanças públicas e estrutura do estado'; *Desembargo*, pp. 129–33.
133 Caetano, *História do Direito Português* (Lisbon: Verbo, 1980), p. 308.

in the previous period. Just as for these it was not possible before to function without the panoply of officials of the written word (who were linked to the existence of the necessary records), and of the judicial or accounting agents, so the king could not, in all probability, control the functioning of the exchequer, the household or the chancery without the respective *vedores*, who logically formed part of the court since they were frequently alongside the monarch and became integrated within the various ambits of the organisation.

Although, as has been said, we are able to consider them as emancipated from the royal hall, several bureaucratic and judicial organisms such as the chancery, the central tribunals and, to a lesser degree, the *casa dos contos* also participated in this human nucleus because of the presence of some part or even the totality of their number. These accompanied the king almost constantly and were therefore known as belonging to the court. I have already spoken of the *chanceler*, whose permanence in the royal entourage was evident, in a general manner, during the fourteenth and through to the middle of the fifteenth centuries, although there was an occasional tendency towards a centralised location of the institution situated under his control (the chancery) whose mobility must have become problematic as the number of servants and records increased.[134] The duties concerning the exercise of justice, with the structuring of a multiplicity of tribunals in the fourteenth century, and later with the creation of the so-called 'casa da justiça da corte' or 'casa da suplicação', constituted another important component of court organisation.[135] The *corregedor da corte*, the *ouvidores*, the judge and *procurador dos feitos d'El-Rei*, and also the *meirinho-mor*, the *meirinho da corte* and even the chief rabbi played a part in different areas in this sphere of activity. These were social positions in the court world, and at times lay at the centre of larger structures that tended to include in their fabric the multiple social and physical spaces of the kingdom. This was the case with the *corregedor* or the rabbi, while at other times the area of their activity was restricted merely to the territorial and human reality of the court.

In the fourteenth and fifteenth centuries the king usually did not in fact exercise justice in person. As the historian Kantorowicz states, on gradually monopolising the administration of justice the legal professionals began to usurp the position of the king himself in his capacity as judge:

> It is true, the king was the fountain of justice; he was supposed to interpret the law in case of obscurity; the courts were still the 'king's court' and the king was still considered the judge ordinary of his realm whereas the judges,

134 *Desembargo*, pp. 156–9; A. L. Carvalho Homem *et al.*, 'Percursos na burocracia régia', in F. Bethencourt and D. Ramada Curto (eds.), *A memória da nação* (Lisbon: Sá da Costa, 1991), pp. 403–23.

135 Caetano, *História do direito Português*, pp. 308–11 and 482–6; Martim de Albuquerque (ed.), *O Regimento quatrocentista da Casa da Suplicação* (Paris: Fondation Calouste Gulbenkian, 1980), and the observations of António Manuel Hespanha, *História das instituições: épocas medieval e moderna* (Coimbra: Almedina, 1982), p. 335 and note 670.

> who derived their power from him, acted only as delegate judges. For all that, the custom arose that the king should not pass judgement himself: *Rex aut Imperator non cognoscunt in causis eorum*, says Andrea de Isernia . . . Indeed, it was common opinion that in cases pertaining to the fisc the prince could be *iudex in causa propria*, and, as Bracton shows, also in cases of high treason.[136]

Thus the judicial duties of the royal hall as described for the first century of the Portuguese kingdom by Sánchez-Albornoz, where the monarchs could participate directly in the exercise of justice, underwent a radical transformation owing to the emergence and the growing independence of the tribunals of the court. To those better-known aspects of the configurations of these judicial positions studied by the history of institutions there must be added, however, the common but little-studied factor which is their participation in the court's social and cultural universe, of which, according to the concept of the age, they formed a part. As the prologue of the Law of 1330 on audiences stressed, the court of the king '*que he com el hũa cousa* . . . he cabeça E cima de todallas justiças do seu Regno . . . he lugar hu todos ham de vjir demandar E pedir direito . . . he fonte de que naçem e hi se emçarram todollos conprimentos de direito E de justiça'.[137] While justice was administered by the delegates of the king, the court was still the natural place for its exercise, and it remained the hierarchical apex of the entire judicial apparatus of the kingdom. In the same way, I have already referred to the presence of the *contador-mor* at court, who was normally accompanied by the *contador da casa* and the *escrivão da fazenda*, who were constantly present in the royal chamber, mainly because of their role in the necessary relationship of the monarch with the independent structure of the *casa dos contos*, which was located in Lisbon.

Finally, there remain to be mentioned in this brief description of the principal posts of the Portuguese court of the fourteenth and fifteenth centuries those related to the exercise of war. I have already stated that these underwent important changes in a role which had previously been performed by the direct entourage of the monarch. In fact the transformations which war saw with the fourteenth century, particularly those related to the long European conflict of the Hundred Years War, made inevitable for the Iberian monarchs the adoption of the customs of countries beyond the Pyrenees in the organisation of their armies.[138]

136 Kantorowizc, 'Kingship under the impact of scientific jurisprudence', pp. 155–6.

137 *OD*, p. 311 (my italics).

138 The adoption of these positions in the Iberian royal armies has been attributed by Portuguese historians to the English influence, in the wake of Gama Barros, and by Spanish historians to the French influence in Castile. It is more correct to see this as a use common both to the English and the French, as recognised by António Caetano do Amaral, *Memória para a história da legislação e costumes de Portugal* (Oporto: Civilização [1945]), pp. 190–1 and as Peter E. Russell suggested when speaking of 'Anglo-French' customs; Russell, pp. 333–4. See the chronology of the appearance of the post in the several Peninsular kingdoms in Juan

The new posts of *condestável* and *marechal* appeared at the end of the fourteenth century in the Portuguese court, although their specific field of activity was the royal host, or a structure of men recruited from among local communities and the nobility (through a system analogous to the English 'retinue' or French 'retenue'), not to be confused with the court 'at arms', although it can encompass it.[139] It was in the latter that the position of *alferes-mor* continued to retain its old supremacy, although within the royal army its military position from then on became insignificant.[140] The army was, in contrast to the court, a temporary organism. Its nominal leadership however, as in the court organism, fell to the monarch. If we examine for example the detailed description of the duties of the Portuguese duality of the *condestável/marechal* in some texts such as the 'Regimento da Guerra' of the fifteenth century, we rapidly come to the conclusion that the *condestável* was a type of *mordomo-mor* of the royal army. His duties included the exercise of justice, the organisation of lodgings and the conscription and control of men of war, all with the assistance of various servants who were headed by the *marechal*. In the court itself, his functions were almost nonexistent outside times of war, as though the post were 'deactivated' when the royal host was dissolved.[141] We can also approximate the duties of *almirante* to this position, in spite of the specificity of its area of activity, and even of its judicial nature, for we see that, much like the role of the *condestável*, a close comparison of those who held the position in the royal court of the fourteenth and fifteenth centuries made him fully part of the royal entourage.[142]

Torres Fontes, 'Los condestables de Castilla en la edad media', *Anuari de Historia del Derecho Español*, 41 (1971), 57–112. On Portugal, the essay by Monteiro, *A guerra em Portugal*, pp. 317–26.

139 Philippe Contamine, *La Guerre au moyen âge* (Paris: PUF, 1980), pp. 275–86.

140 *OA*, vol. I, pp. 333–5. On the *Partidas*, a direct source of the Portuguese Ordinations in this passage, Carrasco, *Los cargos de la Hueste Real*, pp. 59–69.

141 *OA*, vol. I, pp. 285–306 and 'Regimentos' of the Condestável and Marechal, pp. 306–18.

142 Vitorino Nemésio, *Almirantado e portos de Quatrocentos* (Lisbon: Faculdade de Letras, 1961).

2. *Individuals and groups*

We find a highly heterogeneous group of individuals surrounding the king and sharing the diverse modalities of his presence. Based to a large extent on prosopographic data, my research attempts to define this heterogeneity by combining the possible reconstruction of individual and group family lines with a necessary understanding of the configurations of the court as a particular social world. This was a question of isolating and identifying, as far as possible, the numerous individuals surrounding the Portuguese monarch, whose presence was shown through the performance of court duties and by their mention in contemporary lists of names, so making their presence indisputable. Examination of their biographies shows, more than anything, the variety of individuals in their social standing, as well as the specific, variable position that they occupied within the court.

To this general characteristic of the court must also be added another, no less important, which is related to the construction of hierarchies, and is an essential criterion of ordinance in the light of the concepts of the actual age. Viewed globally, the court was a social, hierarchic universe both at its interior and because of the verifiable articulation between its internal divisions and those of society at the end of the Middle Ages. By starting off from a vast group of biographical lines spanning almost two centuries, it was possible to confirm that the careers of the servants of the king played a part in these logics which lie beyond the individual and enclose him within the more or less consistent fabric of a group, characterised by distinct forms of being and behaving and marked by the global design of the actual positions which fell to each one. These logics are not always sufficiently clearly discernible, nor do they appear sufficiently solid for us to consider them as a secure basis for the establishment of a true group within the interior of the medieval court, apart from some more elementary criteria of classification related to the differences of type, status and function. These are the criteria that serve as a basis for my description.

MEN AND WOMEN

One of the main distinctions to be made for a description of the internal diversity of the social medium of the Portuguese court of the thirteenth and fourteenth centuries is that which confronted men and women within this organism. As has been observed by several historians, the medieval royal courts are generally described as organisms predominantly, if not exclusively, made up of men. Indeed, the majority of posts whose description I sought to sketch in the previous chapter were performed by men. This historiographic practice appears not to take seriously the image which medieval literature following the twelfth century suggests, for in this literature the opposition and complementarity between the masculine and the feminine worlds at the heart of the court appear to be an indispensable cog of the actual mechanisms of palace life.

The presence of women was always considered as a distinctive feature of court society at the end of the Middle Ages, and was connected in a precise manner to the queen, who was the central personage of this feminine world, and whose *familia* had an autonomous organisation. The majority of servants of the medieval queens were, certainly, men. But, besides this numerically dominant element of her entourage, it was considered that the queen should be accompanied by a reasonably high number of women of varied standing who were permanently to follow her. Thus we could say that the principal originality of this group within the interior of the court organism resided, in the main, within the uncommon figure of a *familia* whose leadership always fell to a woman, and whose central nucleus (at least from a symbolic point of view) comprised a household of women. Ultimately it lay in its being a relatively unstable group which demonstrated a structural organisational fragility – for, with the death of the queen, the relationship which united the elements of her entourage would be dissolved and reintegrated within the patrimony of the monarchs. This last aspect constituted in all probability the principal element for the explanation of the relatively innocuous character which the much talked of independence of the medieval queens might portray, for it constituted a natural limitation to her capacity for political intervention, which was undeniable and has been underlined by more recent historiography.[1] In this, as in other aspects, we can contrast the situation of the queen with that of the other elements of the royal family, whose more or less substantial patrimonies could, on the contrary, be transmitted to respective descendants, so establishing the basis of a more lasting power.

My intention, however, is not to study the Portuguese 'queen's household' as an institution within itself but rather to understand its participation in the social

[1] Louise Olga Fradenburg (ed.), *Women and Sovereignty* (Edinburgh: Edinburgh University Press, 1992); John Carmi Parsons (ed.), *Medieval Queenship* (New York: St Martin's Press, 1993); Anne J. Duggan (ed.), *Queens and Queenship in Medieval Europe* (Woodbridge: Boydell, 1997).

world of the court of the end of the Middle Ages through the constitution of a female nucleus within it. I shall not, however, spend time on describing the patrimonial and organisational characteristics of this organism, which is largely independent of the court of the monarchs. The Portuguese 'queen's household' was granted its own tradition of organisation and financing at the beginning of the fourteenth century; this arose in the first reigns during which matrimonial alliances of the monarchs were made only rarely beyond the Iberian sphere.[2] During the period which is of interest to us, the households of Queens Beatriz of Castile (1309–59), Leonor Teles (1372–85), Philippa of Lancaster (1387–1415), Leonor of Aragon (1428–45) and Isabel (1447–55) are those which stand out. I shall remain occupied with detailing more thoroughly the female element of the respective entourages in the perspective which is of interest to us.

The first problem to be outlined would of course be that of the co-participation or 'fusion' of this element within the court of the kings or rather that of the actual presence of the Portuguese queens alongside the monarchs of the fourteenth and fifteenth centuries. This is one problem which cannot be resolved either completely or definitively, given the difficulty of establishing itinerances of the queens of the period. While we are able to make use of some elements attesting to this 'fusion' of both entourages at given moments in time, equally we can make use of strong indications of the existence of an itinerance of the queens which is separate from that of the monarchs. A diversity of factors may have influenced the alternance of these two movements, be this in the union with the entourage of the kings or the spatial distancing of the queen in relation to the court: different practices in the management of the patrimony itself, for example; unknown criteria of preference or characteristics of salubriousness in certain regions of the kingdom; or possible reasons of a political nature. On the other hand, we cannot exclude a development of the attitude of the queens regarding this problem during the period studied here: we could contrast the royal nature of Beatriz of Castile who, much like her predecessors of the thirteenth century,[3] was very close to her own land and the monasteries preferred by her, with the 'courtly' royalty of a Leonor Teles, whose intense matrimonial relationship

[2] Francisco Fonseca Benevides, *Rainhas de Portugal* (Lisbon: Tip. Castro e Irmão, 1878–79), vol. I. A *maidordomus reginae* is documented in Leon from the tenth century: Claudio Sánchez-Albornoz, 'El *Palatium Regis*', pp. 16–23. For a comparison with France, Marion Facinger, 'A study of medieval queenship: Capetian France, 987–1237', *Studies in Medieval and Renaissance History*, 5 (1968), 1–47; for England, Hilda Johnstone, 'The Queen's household', in J. F. Willard and W. Morris (eds.), *The English Government at Work, 1327–1336* (Cambridge, MA: The Medieval Academy of America, 1940), vol. I, pp. 250–99; also John Carmi Parsons, *The Court and Household of Eleanor of Castile* (Toronto: Pontifical Institute of Medieval Studies, 1977).

[3] This is found in the petition to be allowed to enter convents of the Clarites and Dominicans with her entourage, *causa devotionis et spiritualis recreationis*, dated 1344, *MPV*, vol. I, p. 27. A description of her stays in S. Clara de Coimbra with the queen mother, D. Isabel, is suggested by the fourteenth-century hagiography: Frei Salvado Martins, *Vida e milagres de D. Isabel*, ed. by J. Joaquim Nunes (Coimbra: Imprensa da Universidade, 1921), p. 59.

so evokes the contemporary situation of Philippa of Hainault at the English court,[4] or the growing political and diplomatic intervention of the queens of the fifteenth century which made it difficult for them to distance themselves from the court, and which is so clear in the case of Philippa of Lancaster or Leonor of Aragon.[5]

Prosopographic research can contribute indirectly to a response to this question through the identification of the largest possible number of servants of these queens. We have seen that, from the earliest example (that of the wife of Afonso IV), some posts in their households were performed by the king's servants, whose presence alongside the monarch is beyond doubt. Beatriz's *chanceler*, for example, was Lopo Fernandes Pacheco, a central personage of the royal court during the first half of the fourteenth century,[6] who was succeeded by the Bishop of Lisbon, Lourenço Martins;[7] her *mordomo* was the master of the military order of Aviz, Martim Esteves do Avelar.[8] More significant still seems to be the fact that a Master Martinho do Rosmaninhal is mentioned as *medico domini regis et suo*,[9] which suggests a close relationship between the *câmara* of the queen and that of the monarch. The same coincidence can be seen, for example, concerning the servants of Leonor Teles: her *ouvidores* Afonso Martins and Gil Anes were, respectively, *vedor da casa* of the king and court *corregedor*.[10] In this case we also find an aggregation of duties related to the function of the royal hall, for the *mantieiro* of Leonor Teles was, simultaneously, Fernando's *cevadeiro-mor*.[11] The examples from the fifteenth century are, naturally, still more numerous. In the household of Philippa we find Lourenço Anes Fogaça, the king's *chanceler*, as her *vedor da fazenda*,[12] while the queen's *reposteiro-mor* was the noble courtier Fernão Lopes de Abreu[13] and João Rodrigues, the king's *saquiteiro*, served as her *uchão*.[14] During the reign of Duarte, a significant point is that the monarch's *aposentador-mor* was the same Rui Mendes de Cerveira who served as *aposentador* to Duarte's wife,

[4] J. W. Sherborne, 'Aspects of the English court culture in the later fourteenth century', in V. J. Scattergood and J. W. Sherborne (eds.), *English Court Culture in the Later Middle Ages* (London: Duckworth, 1983), pp. 1–27.

[5] W. J. Entwistle and P. E. Russell, 'A rainha Dona Felipa e a sua corte', in *Congresso do Mundo Português* (Lisbon: Comissão Executiva dos Centenários, 1940), vol. II, pp. 317–46. The activities of Eleanor of Aragon are well documented in *MH*, particularly vol. III, p. 331 *et passim*.

[6] *Desembargo*, p. 353. [7] *Provas*, vol. I, p. 352.

[8] *Provas*, vol. I, pp. 350, 352. As will be seen, Martim Esteves do Avelar was present at the court of Afonso IV, and moved to Barcelona as ambassador for the marriage of the Infanta D. Leonor and signed the agreement between the king and the Infante Pedro in 1356. The queen mentions that he was her 'criado' and named him in her will, leaving him two silver goblets and two jugs from her treasury.

[9] *MPV*, vol. I, p. 278. [10] *Desembargo*, pp. 271, 306.

[11] ANTT, *Ch. D. Fernando*, 2, f. 44v. [12] *Desembargo*, p. 365.

[13] ANTT, *Ch. D. João I*, 2, f. 4v; *CR João I*, vol. II, p. 210.

[14] ANTT, *Ch. D. João I*, 5, f. 97.

Leonor.[15] Finally, among the servants of the young Queen Isabel we find well-known courtiers of Afonso V, such as Fernando de Meneses, who served as the queen's *mordomo*,[16] or Dr Vasco Fernandes de Lucena, who was her *ouvidor*.[17] All these examples make clear a situation to be found in many contemporary courts: that of the interdependence existing between the queen's household and the court regarding the duties which resulted from a 'fusion' of both entities throughout a large part of their existence. Thus, even while we can admit that the presence of the Portuguese queens at court did not retain a permanent character at the end of the Middle Ages (which could only be concluded through an eventual reconstruction of the respective itinerances), it can be said that the actual function of their households demonstrates a certain proximity to the monarchs.

Just as we see a performance of the duties in the service of the queen by a section of members of the court, either cumulatively or successively with other services for the king, we also see an analogous relationship between the feminine element of her entourage, which is of interest to us now, and the remaining elements of court society. It could be said that it is rare to find among the women who surrounded the Portuguese queens any who did not belong to families whose presence is confirmed at court, and this can in particular be confirmed when dealing with noble families. Thus, there is every indication that the recruitment of the court 'female household' was performed within the same social universe, following criteria of proximity of the respective families to the king.

Let us look, for example, at the formation of the entourage of Beatriz of Castile by examining the legacies made in her will in 1358: of the various women named in the document, we find mention of a relative of hers (her niece, Maria Girona), three women of the de Avelar family (Branca Lourenço do Avelar, Joana Martins do Avelar and Beatriz Martins, her sister), one member of the Velho family (Leonor Gonçalves Velha), and two women related to servants of the king: Constança Nogueira (the daughter of Master João das Regras, the *desembargador* and counsellor of Afonso IV) and Maria Durães, who was certainly related to the *vedor da chancelaria*, João Durães, who was also the king's counsellor.[18] In royal documentation I have found references to more women of this queen's household, such as a *camareira*, Maria Dias, and her *aia*, Maria Rodrigues, whose families cannot be easily identified, although they were very probably wives of noblemen.[19] The complex network of family relationships and court positions can be seen in the best-documented case of

[15] ANTT, *Ch. D. Duarte*, 3, ff. 4 and 5; 1, f. 145.
[16] *MH*, vol. XII, p. 147.
[17] ANTT, *Ch. D. Afonso V*, 5, f. 99.
[18] On Master João das Leis: *Desembargo*, p. 344. The ascendance of Constanza is indicated in the will: *Provas*, vol. I, p. 349. On João Durães: *Desembargo*, p. 334. The presence of this individual in the council of D. Afonso IV was mentioned by Diogo Lopes Pacheco in his testimony of 1385 on the events surrounding the death of Inês de Castro: ANTT, drawer XIII, M 3, no. 8.
[19] ANTT, *Ch. D. João I*, 2, f. 56; *Provas*, vol. I, p. 349.

the Avelar family, shown in Table 1. (The genealogical tables are grouped at the beginning of the book, pp. xv–xx.)

Among the children of Beatriz's *mordomo* I found two well-known members of the queen's household: Branca Lourenço, the queen's *criada*, who is mentioned in her will, and Lourenço Martins, her *copeiro*, named in her will in 1358. He perhaps married twice, and certainly one of his wives, Beatriz Anes,[20] was a relative of the queen, as possibly was Sancha Dias, the heiress of Estevão da Guarda, a well-known courtier of Dinis, and a counsellor of Afonso IV.[21] Among the children of Lourenço Martins were Leonor, Joana and Beatriz, the last two of whom were young women named in the queen's will, as was Teresa Martins, who was married to Vasco Reimondo and then to Lourenço Martins Buval. This second marriage was very probably contracted with the involvement of the queen.[22] An analysis which exists of the supplications made by Beatriz to the pope for the promotion of her servants shows her protection of Martim Lourenço Buval, the son of Teresa Martins, and that of Gomes Martins do Avelar, her *alumnus* (or dependant, who was supported by her), asking for the granting of benefices.[23] As a result, we see in the case of the de Avelar family two successive generations of women associated with the female household of the court between the 1330s and the 1360s, through their presence alongside Beatriz of Castile. But the family was in this environment both because of the masculine component, through the performance of court duties, and in the more restricted sphere of the queen's household.

Identification of those women who gravitated around Leonor Teles is a little more complete, and therefore allows for similar conclusions. We must bear in mind the mention made by Fernão Lopes to the marriages 'arranged' by her: those of Beatriz Nunes de Góis, Mécia Vasques Coutinha, Teresa de Meira, Leonor Gonçalves de Azevedo and Sancha de Andeiro, all of whom were daughters of nobles whose presence at the court of Fernando and, in some cases, that of his predecessor, is well-documented.[24] We are also able to add to this group 'her relative', Inês Dias Botelha; her sisters, Maria Teles and the bastard Joana Teles; the daughter of the archbishop of Braga, Branca Lourenço, and a widow of means, Leonor Rodrigues, who had been married to a Cogominho,

[20] *LL Conde*, 44U, pp. 6–7.

[21] Lourenço Martins do Avelar (or a relative of the same name) claimed the possessions belonging to Estevão da Guarda: *CDP*, p. 426. See also ANTT, *NA*, 314, ff. 111–111v; ANTT, *CR*, S. Vicente de Fora, M 26, no. 2; ANTT, *NA*, 274, ff. 68–9.

[22] *LL Conde*, 44U, pp. 6–7 (which, however, does not mention Joana and Beatriz). Leonor Gonçalves Velha, the *dama* of D. Beatriz mentioned above, was also married to a member of this Buval family: *LL Conde*, 42H, p. 11.

[23] *MPV*, vol. I, pp. 30, 277–8, 481.

[24] Respectively, the daughters of Nuno Martins de Góis (present at the court of D. Pedro and D. Fernando), of Vasco Fernandes Coutinho, of Gonçalo Pais de Meira, of Gonçalo Vasques de Azevedo (a great 'privado' of D. Fernando) and of the controversial Galician, João Fernandes Andeiro. On the marriages: *CR Fernando*, p. 229.

a family whose presence at the Portuguese court is documented from Afonso IV's youth. Isabel and Beatriz, the daughters of the magnate Álvaro Peres de Castro, are also to be found serving Leonor Teles.[25]

What was the fate of this group of women when the widowed queen had to leave the kingdom in 1384? Her *camareiras*, Mor Afonso, Constança Anes and Maria Peres, must have accompanied Leonor Teles into exile,[26] although not all those women who were close to her did so, as we shall have occasion to see. Let us look at Table 2 for the example of the de Meira family in its many connections with the queen.

The presence of Gonçalo Pais de Meira at the courts of Pedro and his successor, King Fernando I, is documented from 1355, and he himself died in 1383. He was married to an illegitimate daughter of the Master of the Order of Christ and, according to Fernão Lopes, his children Teresa de Meira and Fernão Gonçalves had marriages 'arranged' by the queen, Leonor Teles. These were to Fernão Gonçalves de Sousa and to the daughter of the archbishop of Braga respectively. Teresa was mentioned as being in the queen's favour on other occasions having, according to Fernão Lopes, served as *aia* to her only surviving daughter, the Infanta Beatriz, future queen of Castile.[27] Another son of Gonçalo Pais de Meira, Estevão Gonçalves, is listed in several documents as the Master of Santiago during the 1370s.[28] One must also bear in mind the letter of pardon obtained in 1383 by Mécia Rodrigues de Meira, in which Leonor Teles confirms her lifting of 'todo o queixume que della auemos', an enigmatic expression certainly relating to the intense conflict to be found within the court of Fernando and Leonor Teles (a matter which will be dealt with in greater detail later), and which points to a close relationship with the queen.[29] Yet again, the example of the de Meira family proves that the female presence in the entourage of the queens accompanied the presence at court of other members of the same family. Will this phenomenon only be found in the case of female members of the nobility? Examples shown in the household of Beatriz of Castile appear to negate this, but as we depart from the small number of families studied during this period the more uncertain becomes identification of female personages who are of noble birth, giving a highly uncertain character to the prosopographic data, so that a more complete answer must be sought through other sources.

[25] *CR Fernando*, pp. 365 or 559.

[26] ANTT, *Ch. D. Fernando*, 2, f. 80v (Mor Afonso); 3, f. 73v (Constança Anes); *CR João I*, vol. I, p. 139. I do not know whether the 'criada' Senhorinha Fernandes do Amaral also served as *camareira*, which would seem probable bearing in mind the granting of food and clothing made her by D. Leonor: ANTT, *Ch. D. Fernando*, 3, f. 45v.

[27] ANTT, *Ch. D. Fernando*, 3, f. 47v; *CR João I*, vol. I, p. 294.

[28] ANTT, *Ch. D. Fernando*, 4, f. 18v is an example. As will be seen, the swing displayed by the Portuguese king at the time between obedience to Rome or Avignon also influenced the appointment of higher positions in the Military Orders, so that at times different individuals appear as claiming the same position.

[29] ANTT, *Ch. D. Fernando*, 3, f. 87.

Regarding the female entourage of Philippa of Lancaster, through the roll of *moradoras* in her household we find sufficient elements to allow for a final argument in favour of what has been stated up to now. For the first time, we also have available a strong indication as to the numerical relationship between the 'female household' and the masculine element which resided permanently at court – with the small number of between thirty and thirty-eight names of women being listed contrasting with about 390 male individuals believed to be among the king's *moradores*, and a total of merely 180 for the queen's household.[30] This record is fairly analogous to that confirmed by rolls relating to the English court in 1368, with a total of thirty-one women as compared with the 375 names recorded.[31] Among the women named on Philippa's roll are several members of the Moura family (besides Beatriz Gonçalves, her *aia*, we have Leonor Gonçalves de Moura, Isabel Fernandes de Moura and another, whose name was the same as that of the *aia*, Beatriz de Moura), of the Coutinho family (Mécia Vasques Coutinho, Leonor Vasques Coutinho), the Ataíde family (Catarina Vasques de Ataíde, Filipa de Ataíde), the Pereiras (Leonor Pereira, Beringela Pereira), the Melos (Beatriz de Melo), the Cunhas (Maria da Cunha), and the Albuquerques (Joana de Albuquerque). So we find named on this list the most important families of court nobility of the reign of John I. However, we also find members of families who were probably of no importance, but whose proximity to the court dated back several generations, as was the case with the Resendes (Maria Resende), the Teixeiras (Catarina Teixeira), the do Casal family (Inês do Casal) and the Leitão family (Leonor Leitoa). Once again the presence of the bastard children of bishops who were close to the court is found, as was the case of Margarida Martins Miranda, the daughter of Martim Afonso da Charneca, the archbishop of Braga. This list also allows us to confirm, within the female household of the court, the presence of women who were related to the more modest servants of the monarchs, whose noble standing was more recent or even unlikely, such as Catarina Fernandes de Barros, Beatriz Afonso Goriza or the anonymous wife of the king's *mantieiro*, Gonçalo Anes Penteado.[32] With an analysis of Table 3, which relates to the Miranda family, the example chosen to illustrate the complexity of the relations between the women in the entourage of Philippa and the court of John I can be linked to the various cases of the so-called 'new nobility' studied by Braamcamp Freire.

The oldest member of this family to be documented is Afonso Peres (Charneca), an official at the court of Fernando who served as his *escrivão*

[30] *MH*, vol. I, pp. 280–93; vol. IV, pp. 226–34 (on these sources, see note 126, p. 242). Several women of the household of D. Philippa are named by Fernão Lopes: *CR João I*, vol. II, p. 210.

[31] Richard Firth Green, 'The familia regis and the familia cupidini', in Scattergood and Sherborne (eds.), *English Court Culture*, p. 98.

[32] Several *moradores* with the surname Barros or Teixeira appear in the list relating to the court of John I. On the Gorizos: *MH*, vol. III, pp. 76–8; vol. IX, p. 156, note 4, and also ANTT, *LN*, *Estremadura*, 5, f. 102v.

da puridade.[33] He was the father of (at least) two men who were close to John I, as well as a daughter who married Domingos Peres Alistão, Fernando's *almoxarife das ovenças* in Lisbon:[34] these sons are Afonso Peres da Charneca who, according to a report of Fernão Lopes, was made a *cavaleiro* at the battle of Aljubarrota,[35] and Martim Afonso, who was successively bishop of Coimbra (1386–98) and archbishop of Braga (1398–1416).[36] The many children of the latter appear to be well placed in the court environment, both for the duties which they performed and, more importantly, by their marriages. This was the case of Martim Afonso Miranda, who married Genebra Pereira. There were also the daughters of the archbishop: Leonor Miranda, the wife of Aires Gomes da Silva; Mécia Miranda, who married Gonçalo Pereira, nicknamed 'das Armas'; and Margarida Martins Miranda, who is listed among the *moradoras* referred to earlier and who married Pedro de Meneses. In these three cases we find alliances between these women and nobles of higher standing at the court of John I. To these we are able to add another element of this family group, Fernão Gonçalves de Miranda, who was probably the youngest and who, after 1433, married Branca de Sousa at court.[37] The adoption of the family name 'Miranda' must have been through the maternal side, as occurred more frequently during the fifteenth century, particularly in the case of illegitimate children.[38]

I shall not spend any further time on this study, particularly the identification of some family connections on the female side in the households of Leonor of Aragon and Isabel, the wife of Afonso V, in relation to both of whom there are problems of greater interest which are dealt with later. It is sufficient to read the chronicles and other narrative sources which speak of the Portuguese court during the middle of the fifteenth century to see that the infrequent mention of the women who surrounded the queens is made on many occasions in the context of their family ties, be these with the queens or with other members of court society. This small-scale analysis of the family connections of some women who were part of the entourage of the queens and at the Portuguese court confirms the generic description which has been transmitted by literary texts of the period and by some educational and normative sources. Among the latter, produced within the Spanish ambit and circulated in Portugal at the time, I shall emphasise examples regarding the household of the queens in the

[33] *Desembargo*, p. 272. Besides documents named in this: ANTT, *Ch. D. Fernando*, 2, f. 101v.

[34] ANTT, *Ch. D. João I*, 5, f. 36v.

[35] *CR João I*, vol. I, p. 301; vol. II, p. 84. Afonso Peres da Charneca had already died in 1389: ANTT, *Ch. D. João I*, 2, f. 70v.

[36] Having studied in Bologna where he graduated in 1382, Martim Afonso was a member of the *Desembargo* and the council of John I between 1384 and 1414: *Desembargo*, p. 365. See also A. D. Sousa Costa, *Portugueses no Colégio de S. Clemente e Universidade de Bolonha no século XV* (Bologna: Real Colegio de España, 1990), vol. I, pp. 268 and 372.

[37] *LL*, pp. 326, 66–7 and 332; *Brasões*, vol. I, p. 126; vol. II, p. 49.

[38] Marcel Nassiet, 'Parenté et succession dynastiques aux 14e et 15e siècles', *Annales HSS*, 50 (1995), 621–44.

original synthesis, that is the Alfonsine work, in particular the *Espéculo*. As this text states so succinctly, 'la reina es tenuda de criar e casar assí como el rey de criar e de armar'.[39] That is, the presence of the women alongside the queen demonstrates more than anything her protection (and that of the king) of the respective families; marriage appears as the equivalent, within the female sphere, of royal protection which led to the knighthood of a young male court servant. This is a way of perceiving the existence of the court's female household and the relations between the queen and her women, naturally reflected in an internal hierarchy which stratified them, based not only on their family background and their eventual material wealth, but also on their matrimonial status, which was the main difference between 'donas' and 'donzelas'.

Throughout the entire period studied, this distinction of status retained its functionality in sources analysed, placing women in a hierarchy according to the diversity and the autonomy of their spheres of activity. The *donzela*, whose presence at court almost always had as its objective the peculiar type of relationship evoked by the succession of 'criação' and of 'casamento', appeared thus to be more dependent on the queen, and with a sphere of activity which was still more reduced, or generally unimportant. To the *dona*, on the other hand, there were reserved roles of greater autonomy and authority, at times linked to the 'secrecy' (*puridade*) of the queen, in particular those of her *camareira* or *aia*. We know little as to the concrete functions which fell to these women at court, but some rare examples show that they were *donas* and on many occasions widows, as was the case of Philippa of Lancaster's *aia*, Beatriz Gonçalves de Moura,[40] or Leonor of Aragon's *camareira-mor*, the Castilian Constança de Tovar,[41] and the *aia* of the young Queen Isabel, D. Beatriz de Meneses.[42] A greater proximity to and influence upon the queens must have acted as the principal factor of attraction for these positions of the *câmara* which, as was the case in the kings' department of the same name, at times implied the presence and participation of these women in transactions of varying importance relating to the patrimony and incomes of the queens. A good example of this is the acquisition by Beatriz

[39] *Leyes de Alfonso* X, vol. I, *Espéculo*, p. 171 (and all Title XV of vol. II).

[40] Vasco Fernandes Coutinho, the husband of Beatriz, was at the court of D. Pedro and D. Fernando and had already died in 1390: ANTT, *Ch. D. João I*, 2, f. 8. On his position in Philippa's household, see the statements of Fernão Lopes, *CR João I*, vol. II, p. 210; also ANTT, *Ch. D. João I*, 5, f. 66; 3, f. 129v. Following Philippa's death in 1415, Beatriz Gonçalves continued in the service of her daughter, D. Isabel: ANTT, *Ch. D. João I*, 4, f. 96v.

[41] Constança was the widow of the Count of Castile, Rui Lopez d'Avalos, and her presence at the Portuguese court caused some problems and criticism from the king, D. Duarte: *MH*, vol. XV, p. 264.

[42] The wife of Aires Gomes da Silva and an important figure in the household of the Infante Pedro, father of the queen, Beatriz de Meneses was widowed in 1454: *ALF*, vol. II, pp. 1063–71. On her relationship with the queen, ANTT, *Ch. D. Afonso V*, 5, ff. 77, 85v. In her will of 1452, the young queen stated that at her death all the objects of her house be given to her: *Provas*, vol. II, p. 63.

Gonçalves de Moura of an estate in Cantanhede for Queen Philippa in 1392.[43] In the various matrimonial agreements of which there are details for the fifteenth century, the patrimony of the Portuguese queens is almost always known as 'câmara'.[44] Thus, it is not surprising that, when speaking of D. Guiomar de Castro, who was at the time the widow of the Count of Atouguia and the *aia* of the king's sister, D. Leonor, Afonso V said in 1454 that she 'sempre travalhara por sua fazenda [of the Infanta] seer proueuda encaminhada e acreçantada como milhor podia'.[45] The age and the social position of these powerful noblewomen appear very different from those of the *donzelas da rainha*, a name used for the women of varying status, as seen in the examples shown earlier.

According to the *Espéculo*, the name 'ricas-fenbras' or 'ricas-donas' was reserved for the daughters of 'ricos-homens' who already had their own households, even though they were 'donzelas', or for the wives and widows of the 'ricos-homens' of the court. Thus this source refers to yet another hierarchy also spoken of at the Portuguese court which emphasises, within the women's household, the greater freedom and independence in relation to the queen which material wealth, evoked by the existence of a household and patrimony, allowed. This term appears in some Portuguese texts, in particular in the wills of the Portuguese queens, as a valid criterion of distinction. Beatriz of Castile confirmed the fact in 1358 in her list of endowments to the women of her household: the *ricas-donas* (a category which included her relative Maria Girona, who was still single at the time) received 1000 *libras* for their marriage, after whom were the *donas* and the *donzelas* 'assi grandes, como pequenas', who were to receive merely 500 *libras*.[46] While the use of this term *rica-dona* became more rare in the fifteenth century, indications remain as to the difference between the *donas* and the *donzelas* of the court, for example through the difference in the value of dowries 'por casamento' in the households of Philippa of Lancaster, Leonor and Isabel.

There was no lack, either, of religious women in this female world, or those 'de ordem' as they were called at the time. Once again, we are able to give the example of the privileged relations between Beatriz of Castile and some women of the mendicant communities and the Franciscan abbesses who were related to the royal family, such as D. Isabel de Cardona, who was, at the time of the queen's will, the superior of the convent of S. Clara in Coimbra.[47] According to the hagiography of Isabel of Aragon, five Clarites lived with Beatriz, and the

43 ANTT, *Ch. D. João I*, 2, f. 64.

44 See the contract of 1428: *GTT*, vol. VI, pp. 529–43, or 456–69, or *MH*, vol. III, pp. 254–5. On the contract of 1447: *GTT*, vol. VI, pp. 525–8 or *MH*, vol. IX, pp. 243–7.

45 ANTT, *LN*, extras, ff. 65v–66.

46 *Provas*, vol. I, pp. 349–50.

47 *Provas*, vol. I, p. 354. Henrique David, 'A família de Cardona e as relações entre Portugal e Aragão durante o reinado de D. Dinis', in *XIII Congrès d'Història de la Corona d'Aragó* (Palma de Mallorca: Institut d'Estudis Baleàrics, 1989), vol. IV, pp. 273–9.

queen herself frequently visited the convent in Coimbra.[48] Up to the middle of the fourteenth century this community housed a certain number of tombs of the women of the royal family, such as Isabel, the daughter of Afonso IV, who died in infancy; Maria, the daughter of Constança Manuel and Pedro; and also Inês de Castro, until her removal to her marvellous tomb at Alcobaça. As is known, some of these religious communities had very close ties to the court, not only because of the frequent visits to the convents by the queens, but also because of the ties of material protection which the queens gave, as was the case with the Franciscan nuns of Coimbra and Santarém.

The group of convents protected and visited by the Portuguese queens which are of importance to this study also includes communities living under the rule of St Augustine, as at Chelas, or the community of Cistercians such as the Donas de Almoster and Odivelas. However, the preference demonstrated for the mendicant communities is seen as a constant throughout the period studied, a prime example of which is the convents where, under the Treaty of Alcáçovas (1479) it was proposed that they could give lodging to the politically embarrassing figure of the Excellent Lady: besides those communities whose connection to the Portuguese queens dated from the thirteenth century, such as S. Clara in Coimbra or S. Clara in Santarém, there were others to be considered.[49] This was the case with the Dominican nuns of S. Salvador in Lisbon, whose origin at the end of the fourteenth century was connected to members of the court of Fernando, for it was a community which was frequently visited by Queen Leonor of Aragon; or there are the Dominicans of Aveiro, who were also connected to women of the court of Duarte and Afonso V, as well as the royal family itself; or again the monastery of the Conception at Beja, which had recently been founded by the brother of the king, Fernando, and his wife.[50] At a chronological moment which can serve as our point of arrival on this subject, these communities therefore constituted the group of suitable places for the residence of a princess for whom the political vicissitudes of the time, rather than a deliberate choice for a monastic life, imposed a type of semi-enclosure. By including these, we see the areas where it occurred that the members of the women's household of the court lived under the same roof as members of religious societies during this later period.

The permanence of religious women at court can be confirmed above all in the case of the Sisters of St James, in particular the women of the monastery of Santos in Lisbon. A reconstruction of the list of the heads of the religious orders of the fourteenth and fifteenth centuries allows for the confirmation of a true continuity between the entourage of the queens and the environment from which the leaders of this particular community came. Recent studies have

[48] Martins, *Vida e milagres*, p. 60. [49] *CR Afonso V*, p. 870.

[50] BLAU, Ash 1792 (1716), I, fasc. II, nos. 2 and 3. Frei Luís de Sousa, *História de São Domingos*, ed. M. Lopes de Almeida (Oporto: Lello, 1977), vol. I, pp. 739–40 and 1001–15.

demonstrated that the peculiar way of life of these 'sisters' and their exclusive recruitment from among the nobility explain, in part, this homogeneity. Since they were not subject to the vow of celibacy or any form of enclosure, were able to enjoy great independence in the management of their patrimony, and could also keep their daughters with them, the sisters of St James were a fine example of the diversity of the situation of those women who were close to the court.[51] Joana Teles, the illegitimate sister of the queen and the daughter of a member of the Santos community, was the religious leader of that convent from at least the 1370s. According to the chronicler Fernão Lopes, she abandoned the community in order to marry at court, under the protection of Queen Leonor.[52] At the same time, Fernando established a daily 'allowance' for the religious of this convent, which was to be paid by the *almoxarife dos ovençais* of Lisbon.[53] Inês Peres, the mother of the Count of Barcelos and the mistress of John I, was also the religious leader of the Santos convent between 1405 and 1439.[54] While, as we shall see, the presence of nobles connected to the Military Orders at the court of the Portuguese kings was a characteristic of the final period of the Middle Ages, the case of the women of St James can be seen as a corollary, or as a type of 'female counterpart' of this presence.

However, we must recognise the divided character of an image of the feminine world at the court which only takes into account the small nucleus of women of higher social standing in the queen's household, who play a more visible part in the *câmara* of the queens. Some less prestigious roles related to the queen appear to have been reserved for women 'de pequena sorte', or 'mulheres baixas', as sources call them, in particular the 'covilheiras', the 'mancebas' and the 'amas'. In the first of these, we have a curious name through which there was retained a possible archaic distinction between the services of the *cubiculum* and of the *câmara* itself, as occurred for example at the papal court.[55] The *covilheira*

51 Alan Forey, 'Women and the Military Orders in the twelfth and thirteenth centuries', in *Military Orders and Crusades* (London: Variorum, 1994), vol. IV, pp. 63–92. María Echaniz Sanz, *Las mujeres de la Orden Militar de Santiago en la edad media* (Salamanca: Junta de Castilla y León, 1992).

52 ANTT, *CR*, Mosteiro de Santos, M 53, no. 1074; *CR Fernando*, p. 229.

53 ANTT, *CR*, Mosteiro de Santos, M 6, no. 94. This gift was confirmed in 1392 by John I; ANTT, *CR*, Mosteiro de Santos, M 1, no. 17.

54 See among the numerous documents referring to this religious leader: ANTT, *CR*, Mosteiro de Santos, M 49, no. 1019; M 51, no. 1044; M 53, no. 1067; M 50, no. 1030. It is probable that his daughter Beatriz, the future Countess of Arundel, was also connected to this community, and was simultaneously at court. On the part played by Philippa in the negotiations for her marriage, see Entwistle and Russell, 'A rainha Dona Felipa', pp. 345–6.

55 Ludovico Antonio Muratori, *Dissertazioni sulle antichità Italiane* (Monaco: Agostino Olzati, 1765), vol. I, pp. 159–65; Gaetano Moroni, *Dizionario de erudizione storico-eclesiastica* (Venice: Tip. Emiliana, 1840–1979), vol. VII, pp. 20–49 (s.v. 'camerieri (cubicularii)') and pp. 57–85 (s.v. 'camerlengo (camerarius)'); Paravicini-Bagliani, *La Cour des Papes*, pp. 73–6. This distinction was also held in the French court of the eleventh and twelfth centuries: Luchaire, *Manuel des institutions françaises*, pp. 528–9.

(from *cubicularia*) was, therefore, a servant who was closely linked with the physical intimacy of the queen, in the service 'de seu corpo', whose function was different from that of the *camareira* who, as we have seen, might have duties related to the management of the patrimony of the queens, although at times sources oscillate in their use of both these names. This is a distinction that appears to be confirmed by the identification of noble women in general among the *camareiras*. If we refer once again to the general description of the Alfonsine *Espéculo*, among the various *covilheiras* ('covigeras'), the *covilheira* who 'guardasse as arcas e os panos da rainha' deserved special importance, as did the *covilheiras* of the infantes. There should in turn be linked with the presence of these children of the monarchs, as well as the sons and daughters of nobles 'que se crían en casa del rrey', the presence of the *amas*, women who are named quite frequently in the sources of the age because of the successive favours and gifts with which, as adults, the Portuguese monarchs rewarded them for their services.[56] This component of the queen's entourage was invested with greater importance for the survival of the children.

Queen Beatriz of Castile, for example, kept with her between 1313 and 1347 her seven young children, of whom only two daughters (Maria and Leonor) and the heir to the throne (Pedro) lived beyond the first years of life. Also, in all probability, she kept with her the two children of D. Constança Manuel following her death in 1349, which is apparently confirmed by the mention of Maria Durães, a woman of her household, as 'covilheira do infante D. Fernando meu neto'.[57] Leonor Teles, of whose successive pregnancies Fernão Lopes constantly writes, not only kept her own surviving daughter with her, but we also have reference to her keeping children who served as hostages, a practice much in use during the Hundred Years War.[58] Philippa of Lancaster appears to have kept her children with her during their early infancy, although the list of her residences of 1405 shows that the older survivors (Duarte and Pedro), who were at the time about thirteen or fourteen years old, had a group of their own servants of the *câmara*, the *estrebaria* and the *repostaria*, which suggests a certain autonomy of their entourage. The influence of the English queen on the infantes when still children, which is an essential element of the myth of the Golden Age, is an historical problem still to be resolved by use of contemporary sources, as made clear by the anachronisms which continue to be repeated regarding this queen, and which were the subject of Jorge de Sena's harsh criticism in his article on the 'Victorianisation' of the figure of

56 F. M. Sousa Viterbo, *Amas, amos e colaços de pessoas reaes e personagens illustres*, offprint of *Revista de História* (Oporto: 1914).

57 *Provas*, vol. I, p. 342.

58 The son of D. Juan I of Castile was, for example, given to Leonor Teles at the age of two: *CR Fernando*, p. 567. See also the list of hostages in the peace and marriage treaties of D. Beatriz (1383): *GTT*, vol. VII, p. 228.

Philippa.[59] Leonor of Aragon also had nine children during the ten years of her marriage, of whom five survived, and whom she kept with her until her exile in 1440. For the first time, we have information for this queen on her use of a midwife, who is identified among her servants.[60] Finally, the short life of Isabel, who was married to Afonso V as an adolescent, was marked by three difficult pregnancies during her eight years with her husband.[61]

The relationship between the women's house and the young children who were associated with the female world of the court, as well as the proximity of these servants with the world of the body, birth and sex, may contribute to the explanation of the fundamental ambiguity which appears to be associated with the figure of the *covilheira* and the *ama* transmitted to us particularly through court literature of the thirteenth century. In the *cantigas de Santa Maria*, 'covilheira' is frequently synonymous with 'alcoviteira', an intermediary in furtive sexual meetings. With regard to the *ama* in early Portuguese lyrics, particularly in the *cantigas de escárnio*, we see an antithetic counter-image of the 'lady', with the enormously explicit satirical duty regarding her 'easy' life and her improper position in 'courtly' love.[62] These women were an essential component in the female world of the queens' households because of their constant presence and their important functions, all of which can be confirmed through documentary sources. Through their association with an obscure, permissive femininity they appear in literary sources as a curious reverse side of the courtly world associated with the 'ladies' chamber'. As is well known, this world did not grant any value to the reproductive and nutritive function as criteria for the differentiation of the feminine. On the contrary, and as Scaglione reminds us, it actually implied a certain 'androgynisation' of the figure of the lady, who possessed virtues entirely similar to those of the man (*cortezia*, *pretz*, *umildat*, etc.).[63] Texts after the thirteenth century insist, as had already the Afonsine treatises, on the 'cleanliness' and the 'honesty' of the *amas* and 'covilheiras' (or *camareiras*), and so alluded to the ambivalence traditionally associated with these roles, which the chronicler Fernão Lopes used most interestingly in

[59] Jorge de Sena, 'O vitorianismo de D. Filipa de Lancaster', in *Estudos de História e de Cultura* (Lisbon: Revista Ocidente, 1967), pp. 93–100.

[60] D. Leonor left her eldest sons in Portugal and went into exile with only the youngest infanta, D. Joana, who was born in 1439: *MH*, vol. VIII, pp. 266–8, 272–3 and 275–7; vol. IX, pp. 55–6, 79 and 84; vol. XV, pp. 403–4. Her midwife, Catarina Afonso, was a resident in Évora and was still alive in 1446; ANTT, *Ch. D. Afonso V*, 5, f. 67.

[61] João Ramos, 'Genealogia dos reis de Portugal', *Biblos*, 10 (1934), 331–57 and 608–34.

[62] S. Moreta Velayos, 'La sociedade imaginada de las Cantigas', *Studa Historica – Historia Medieval*, 7 (1990), pp. 136–7; Jorge Alves Osório, 'Cantigas de escarnho Galego-Portuguesas: sociologia ou poética?', *Revista da Faculdade de Letras – Línguas e Literaturas*, 3 (1986), 153–99; Yara Frateschi Vieira, 'O escândalo das amas e tecedeiras nos cancioneiros Galego-Portugueses', *Colóquio-letras*, 76 (1983), 18–27.

[63] Aldo Scaglione, *Knights at Court: Courtliness, Chivalry and Courtesy from Ottonian Germany to the Italian Renaissance* (Berkeley: University of California Press, 1991), pp. 106–7.

episodes told in his chronicles as, for example, the celebrated narrative of the loves of the Infante João with Maria Teles.[64]

The *mancebas* of the queens, who were the lowest in the hierarchy of servants in her household, remain in anonymity in almost the entire female world of the courts of the time. Their status differed, as far as can be deduced from some sources, from that of the servants who were not free, who were domestic slaves known as 'servas' and 'mouras' whom the Portuguese queens also used. Beatriz, the wife of Afonso IV, mentioned them in her will, with her 'dwarf', who was possibly also a *serva*. The death of the queen meant release from slavery for these women, as was also the case in the wills of noble women of the thirteenth century.[65] Since, as we know from other sources, the use of slaves in the domestic sphere increased in fifteenth-century Portugal, it is natural that the number of servants of the Portuguese queens who were not free remained relatively high during this final period of the Middle Ages.[66]

Because of its diversity, this group of women who accompanied the queen was a clearly discernible feminine nucleus within the core of the court, and held importance as a centre of attraction and even as a defining element of the court. So much so, that we should ask ourselves whether the court could survive without its women's household, without an attempt, for lack of a queen, to regroup at its centre, based around another woman of royal blood whose standing might approach that of the queen. In this aspect also the situation appears highly diverse according to circumstances.

Throughout the earliest period studied here – the first half of the fourteenth century – one can speak of a true complex which reunited the several nuclei of women at the Portuguese royal court, and which was structured around Beatriz of Castile, for she had been very close to the mother of the king, Isabel, until her death in 1336, as far as we can judge from fifteenth-century chroniclers,[67] and between 1328 and 1340 she kept with her Branca of Castile, who was to become the rejected betrothed of Pedro. Almost certainly, after 1349 she also kept her grandchildren near her.[68] Because of the scarce documentation

[64] *CR Fernando*, p. 356.

[65] Leontina Ventura, 'Testamentária nobiliárquica (séc. XII). Morte e sobrevivência da linhagem', *Revista de História das Ideias*, 19 (1997), 155 and note.

[66] Charles Verlinden, *L'Esclavage dans l'Europe médiévale, I, Péninsule ibérique. France* (Bruges: De Tempel, 1955), pp. 546–632; Jacques Heers, *Escravos e servidão doméstica na idade média* (Lisbon: Dom Quixote, 1983), pp. 99–100 and 132.

[67] According to the *Hagiografia de Dona Isabel de Aragão*, this had also happened to her, Beatriz of Castile: 'a rainha Dona Beatriz a qual trouverom moça pera Portugal e criarom-na elrey D. Dinis e esta rainha Dona Isabel, segundo compria de se fazer em criança de filha de rey', Martins, *Vida e milagres*, ed. Nunes, p. 29.

[68] *CR 1419*, vol. II, p. 165. According to testimonies given in 1385 by Vasco Martins de Sousa and the abbot of S. Julião de Montenegro (who 'vivera com Fernão Gonçalves Cogominho privado do rei D. Afonso'), the marriage to D. Branca would have been consummated by the heir, D. Pedro. Given the particular political circumstances of this enquiry, however, the declarations should be treated with caution: ANTT, drawer XIII, M 3, no. 8, f. 2v.

available regarding D. Constança Manuel, it is not easy to determine whether the household of the wife of the heir to the throne became an independent nucleus during the short nine-year period (1340–49) of her life spent in Portugal.[69] A witness account of Diogo Lopes Pacheco at the Cortes of Coimbra at the end of the century regarding the famous Inês de Castro seems also to allude to a grouping of the several female nuclei surrounding the women of the royal family when it says: 'don Tareyja madre de dom joham Affonso dalboquerque A criara por sa filha E que por sa filha A vijra chamar e Auer depoys *em casa da Raynha dona biatriz e de ElRey dom Affonso*'.[70] This is a situation of relative power for the female court household, which was not repeated, at least with such clarity, following the death of Queen Beatriz in 1359. Between that date and 1372, that is throughout the marriage of Fernando and Leonor Teles, there is a more obscure period in the history of female presence at the Portuguese medieval court.

With the death of Constança Manuel and Inês de Castro, and the absence of Pedro's sisters (Maria who was in Castile and Leonor in Aragon), the court of this monarch seems not to have known an organised women's household.[71] The lack of women at the time in the royal family itself made this understandable, for D. Maria, the daughter of the monarch, had married in 1354 and left Portugal. When alluding to the situation at court on this theme prior to the tempestuous career of Leonor Teles, the chronicler Fernão Lopes refers to the importance which the entourage of D. Beatriz, the daughter of Inês de Castro, would have had: 'tragia . . . gram casa de donas e donzellas, filhas d'algo e de gram linhagem, porque hi nom avia rrainha nem outra iffante por estonce a cuja mercee se ouvessem d'acostar'. The modern historian Dias Arnaut re-evaluated the position of D. Beatriz at her father's court, accepting the view of the chronicler, although he rightly notes that we have no information as to endowments which might have been a patrimonial basis for her household, which is a fact included within the overall context of the scarcity and fragmentation of available sources. If we take the date of 1354 for the birth of this infanta, she would have been only thirteen years old when her father died. In 1373, D. Beatriz was to marry the noble Sancho de Albuquerque in Castile and she, too, left the kingdom.[72]

69 The lands of Viseu, Montemor-o-Novo and Alenquer were given to her as a source of income for her household: *Provas*, vol. I, p. 414; *MPV*, vol. I, p. 133.

70 ANTT, drawer XIII, M 3, no. 8, f. 1 (my italics). The Dona Teresa referred to is Teresa Martins de Melo, wife of the bastard son of D. Dinis, Afonso Sanches, and mother of João Afonso de Albuquerque 'o do Ataúde', who was a central personage at the Castilian court of the same period. On the connections of Albuquerque to the Portuguese court: *CRO Pedro* (Ayala), pp. 30–1 or 50–1.

71 D. Maria returned to the kingdom in 1356 and died in Évora the following year: *CRO Pedro* (Ayala), p. 81. D. Leonor died in Aragon in 1348, a year after her marriage. She maintained contact with her mother during this time, as indicated by the several objects she would have sent to D. Beatriz, referred to in the latter's will: *Provas*, vol. I, pp. 347 and 349.

72 *CR Fernando*, p. 198. Salvador Dias Arnaut, *A crise nacional dos fins do século XIV, I, A sucessão de D. Fernando* (Coimbra: Faculdade de Letras, 1960), 18 and note.

A clearer situation was that which occurred between 1415 and 1428, the period between the death of Philippa of Lancaster and the arrival of Leonor of Aragon in Portugal. Once again, the chronicles of the age emphasise the importance which the future Duchess of Burgundy, the Infanta Isabel, had at the time in the continuity of the women's household at the court of John, where she would have occupied the central position which had previously belonged to her mother.[73] In fact, in the same month in which Philippa died, the monarch made a gift to his daughter of the entire estate of the dead queen, and there is a quantity of documentary evidence as to the management by the princess of this estate.[74] Everything indicates that this was a valuable experience for D. Isabel, who was to become known, when Duchess of Burgundy, for her financial competence and who was included by her husband the duke in several instances of government for the control of accounts and the drawing up of important budgets relating to the Burgundian public finances.[75]

The seven-year period of agitation (1440–47) between the exile of Leonor, the widow of Duarte, and the formation of the household of D. Isabel, the daughter of the regent Pedro, constitutes a further type of problem because of the division which resulted within the women's household at court. One group of women had followed the queen to Castile, while the other had remained in the kingdom. We know from correspondence of the Aragonese monarchs that the attitude of the Portuguese regent was firm regarding the exclusion of one group of the queen's followers. Maria of Aragon wrote in a letter that, following the death of his opponent Leonor, Pedro had sent a list of the names of those persons who would be allowed to return to the kingdom, while the remainder must 'buscar seus partidos' elsewhere. She comments: 'paresce a la dicha senyora huna gran inhumanjdat desterrar e ayrar duenyas e donzellas qui naturalmente no han defension nj puden ir descorriendo por el mundo sin gran notamente e jnfamja de qui assi las fiziesse yr'.[76] The breaking up and disbandment of the female group who accompanied the queen during this period were, therefore, less recognised aspects of the political crises which marked the regency of the Infante Pedro, and it was only following the death of Duarte's widow, when the constitution and patrimonial endowment of the household of the young Isabel became legitimised, that the situation was resolved.[77]

[73] *CR Ceuta*, pp. 132–3.

[74] Manuela Santos Silva, *A região de Óbidos na época medieval – Estudos* (Caldas da Rainha: Património Histórico, 1994), pp. 85–109. See, for example, *MH*, vol. VII, pp. 250–1.

[75] Monique Sommé, *Isabelle de Portugal, Duchesse de Bourgogne: une femme au pouvoir au XVe siècle* (Villeneuve d'Ascq: Presses Universitaires du Septentrion, 1998), pp. 408–19.

[76] *MH*, vol. IX, pp. 79–80, 88 and note. The situation of growing isolation in the exile of D. Leonor, particularly during the final stages of her life referred to by the Portuguese and Castilian chronicles, would seem to indicate that her female entourage must have been reduced in number.

[77] See the gift to the young queen of land belonging to D. Leonor dated in the same year, 1445: *MH*, vol. VIII, pp. 263–4.

Naturally, these periods which are marked by the absence of the central person of the queen were particularly interesting times in the history of the court at the end of the Middle Ages, even though sources of the period refer, as we have seen, to a possible substitution of the queen by other figures, who then acted as an alternative fulcrum within the fabric of relations woven by the circle of women at court. Some of the aspects (referred to at the beginning of this chapter) of the existence of a queen's household, particularly in the patrimonial, organisational and financial spheres, are not detectable, as already seen, for all the infantas. These are factors which are reflected in the importance and varying complexity of the women's household, which represented periods of greater power and attraction, compared with others of relative decline and less importance in court life, as inevitably occurred when there was no queen.

While being the symbolic centre of the female sphere in the entourage of the king, marked by the establishment of a true group of relationships among the individuals who formed the entourage, the entourage of the queen was not, however, the only place at court where women were to be found. Of the various servants who accompanied the monarchs, some, of greater or lesser significance, took with them their wives and other female members of their family, although the identities of these are not to be found. As Green states, women did always form only a small part of the entirety of the identifiable royal entourage – although we know that the majority of the court did not practise celibacy – but this for the simple reason that the mention of these women is rare in available sources. As already seen, some biographical data allow one to link the majority of those women who formed the female household of the Portuguese queens with the permanence at court of the men of the same families. It is impossible to know whether the entourage of the queen, however, included the entirety or even the majority of the women connected with those men who served at court – indeed this seems improbable – nor what were the exact criteria concerning their employment.

If we study the protests repeatedly presented at the Cortes, the number of women led to a great increase in the size of the court.[78] To give an idea of the importance of this world which could be termed 'spectral', we have the list, which Manuel approved at the Cortes of Lisbon in 1498, of all those who were allowed to bring 'mulher e toda sua casa' to court. These were the *mordomo-mor*, the *camareiro-mor*, the *escrivão da puridade*, the *vedores* and *escrivães da fazenda*, the *desembargadores*, the *procuradores*, the *escrivães*, the *meirinhos*, the *físicos* and *cirurgiões*, the *cozinheiro-mor* and the *vedor da casa*. During this later period, the distinction resulted from the express desire to restrict the

[78] See, for example, at the Cortes of 1472–73 the argument by the people against the 'moradores casados' of the court who caused 'sobejidam d apousemtadoria e aa partida bestas de cargua guasto de mantimentos e outros empedimentos': ANTT, Supl. De Cortes, M I, no. 9, f. 65v.

size of the court, without however referring to the traditional prerogatives of some of these posts, in particular through the distinction between the 'cargos maiores' and the others, which had already been mentioned in legislation of the thirteenth century.[79] For the moment, it is worth noting that the royal court was also evidently a possible framework of existence for other women besides those who were specifically related to the queen and her household.

This was also the case for the small number of posts reserved for female duties in the service of the monarchs, encompassed within the two areas of specific activity of the royal *câmara* and the services of the *ucharia* and *mantearia*. Within the first sphere, we find this female participation with the presence of *covilheiras* and *camareiras* of the Portuguese monarchs. A record of a *quitação* dated 1378 made to Guiomar Esteves, who had been a *covilheira* to Fernando certainly since the beginning of that decade, shows that the functions of these servants were close to those already outlined for those in the service of the queens.[80] Their small number (it is rare to find for the same monarch mention of more than two or three servants of this type), and the varying of the name between 'camareiras', 'covilheiras' or 'amas', may serve to indicate that this service represented the continued presence of these women alongside the kings from infancy or adolescence.[81] On the other hand, there also appears the mention of 'criadas' who served in the *câmara*, a fact which takes on particular significance in the case of Pedro I, who refers in his will to two of these women, Beatriz Dias and Inês Afonso, who are well favoured by the king during his lifetime and even during that of his son, Fernando. Fernão Lopes spoke of Beatriz Dias as the 'manceba' of Pedro, which suggests that not always did the female presence within this area of the court comprise only women who were older than the monarch, but that it might also include a young concubine. This would, however, be an exception to the general rule, not only of the 'criadas' of the kings, but also the actual royal concubines.[82] The concubines of the Portuguese kings were traditionally selected from well-known noble families linked to the court, as had already been the case during the thirteenth century.[83]

[79] Visconde de Santarém, *Memórias e alguns documentos para a história e teoria das Cortes Gerais* (Lisbon: Imprensa de Portugal-Brasil, 1924), pp. 261–2.

[80] ANTT, *Ch. D. Fernando*, 4, f. 18: discharge 'de todo Aquello que por nos e por nosso mandado Recebeu e ouue de ueer e procurar des o tempo que conosco fycou ataa o dia da dada desta carta E que outrosy emtregou a Nosa Camara per noso mandado todo Aquello que ajnda sobre sy tynha'.

[81] Maria Peres, a servant of D. Fernando, is in turn called 'sua camareira' in 1380 and 'sua ama' in 1382: ANTT, *Ch. D. Fernando*, 2, ff. 59 and 24v; 3, f. 23v. According to Fernão Lopes, she left the kingdom with Leonor Teles: *CR João I*, vol. I, p. 139. See also the mention of the income of the king which she had before her exile: ANTT, *Ch. D. João I*, 1, f. 71.

[82] *Provas*, vol. I, p. 409. It is possible that one of these women was the mother of a bastard daughter of D. Pedro who, at the date of the king's will, lived in S. Clara de Coimbra: Ramos, *Genealogia dos reis de Portugal*, p. 353. On Beatriz Dias: *CDP*, pp. 583, 220, 365, 486 and 482; ANTT, *Ch. D. Fernando*, 4, f. 2. On Inês Afonso: *CDP*, p. 487; ANTT, *Ch. D. Fernando*, 1, ff. 2 and 35v.

[83] Ventura, 'A nobreza de corte de Afonso III', vol. I, p. 231.

The most typical case I have been able to reconstruct that proves the dominant image of the advanced age of these women is that of the *aia* of Afonso V, Beatriz Anes, the wife of Pero Lourenço de Távora. Her husband had been *reposteiro-mor* of John I until 1421, and died in 1432. Even if one considers the age difference of this couple, which may have been large by present standards, we must remember that the son of Beatriz, Álvaro Peres, was *reposteiro* between 1421 and 1433, that he married in about 1432, and that in 1440 he already had several children from his first marriage who were more or less the same age as Afonso V (and of these, Martim Távora was also the king's *reposteiro*).[84] The figure of this *dona* was, therefore, closer to the maternal archetype, or even a grandmother of the king, than a young woman of his own age. In 1456, when the monarch was only twenty-four years old, Beatriz Anes died. Therefore, whether they were older or younger, these servants who were called *covilheiras*, *aias* and *camareiras*, without forgetting also the more rarely identified king's *lavadeira*, were occupied mostly with his body and his clothes, as were the servants of the queen who held positions of the same name. However, their inclusion in an organism whose hierarchy was exclusively masculine, in what can be seen as being a true *Männerhaus* of the court, as was the king's *câmara*, made them most probably servants in a low, marginalised position, in contrast with those employed in the queen's *câmara*.

As for the services of the *ucharia* and *mantearia*, we find in these evidence of the female presence. For instance, bread-making, which was 'à boca' of the monarch, the queen and their children, was reserved for the *regueifeiras* of the court. I have already mentioned the 'taboo' surrounding the food for the monarch, with the constant strict separation of food for the king and queen from that of the rest of the court community. This aspect makes particularly interesting the preference accorded to female hands for bread-making for the king and the royal family, particularly since the women seem in general to have formed a minority in the services of the kitchen and the *ucharia*, where the other offices for which there is information were all performed by men.[85]

Finally, we must not overlook, at the lowest level of the court based on the perspectives of the time, the presence of the whores or prostitutes in the entourage of the Portuguese kings. We know of some legislative measures which attempted to eliminate or to regulate their presence among the courtiers, particularly in rulings attributed to King Afonso III incorporated in the Afonsine

[84] *CR Pedro*, p. 124. Her name was Beatriz Anes, not Esteves as Braamcamp Freire would wish: *Brasões*, vol. III, pp. 115–16. See also *MH*, vol. X, p. 110 and vol. XII, pp. 316–17. On Martim Távora, ANTT, *Ch. D. João I*, 4, f. 136.

[85] ANTT, *Ch. D. João I*, 1, f. 95, or *MH*, vol. I, p. 288. The monarchs at times called this service 'minha amassaria' and we see only women working in this sphere: ANTT, *Ch. D. Afonso V*, 5, f. 69v.

Ordinations, which established that the whore should be expelled from court 'com pregom na audiencia', and that anyone who brought a whore to court should lose the support of the king.[86] I believe, however, that these restrictive measures were applied merely to the 'supernumeraries' or, as expressly referred to in the law, to those who lived with married men, for just as this occurred in other European courts and in the better-known case of the army of the Portuguese kings, single women 'que fazem por seus corpos' were of a fixed number and their profession was regulated by the authorities. The case of the English court is well known, where this type of prohibition (see an Ordination of 1318) also coexisted with proper regulation of prostitution among young women, whose control was the duty of one of the marshals: as Given-Wilson states, 'something in practice not far removed from an organised brothel seems to have been attached to the royal household'.[87] In France, in the same way, we know of the existence of a fixed group of 'filles de joie suivant la court'.[88] In the Portuguese case, I believe that a royal charter of 1485 is referring to these when it orders the *meirinho* of the court to deal with the lodgings of the 'mancebas solteiras que andam na corte', as was to be done with the 'regatães', and the 'carniçeiros', who were to be housed in specifically reserved areas.[89] In the middle of the fourteenth century the demanding and critical spirit of the bishop of Silves, Álvaro Pais, had risen against this behaviour in the Hispanic courts in a vehement outpouring full of biblical echoes: 'os reis da Espanha em suas casas e séquitos recebem um grande número de meretrizes públicas, e a algumas destas, chamadas estipendiárias, dão dinheiros e pensão em seu palácio, e permitem e consentem que outros seus familiares as recebam, sendo assim a sua corte, em parte, prostíbulo, lupanar e alcouce, como outrora o Templo de Jerusalém'.[90]

Thus we see that the distinctions formed by gender barriers ordered the social world of the court at its several levels of articulation and in its several organisational strata, leading to particular territories for female activity, while there were others where the presence of women was less frequent or simply tolerated, and yet others where they had no place whatsoever. I believe that the character of this environment lies in the particular value of the formation of groups organised around the queen which were exclusively female and whose

[86] *OA*, vol. V, 36. [87] Given-Wilson, *The Royal Household*, p. 60.

[88] R. J. Knecht, 'The Court of Francis I', *European Studies Review*, 8 (1978), 3.

[89] ANTT, *LN*, extras, f. 124. See the ruling of 1421 on the *meirinho de corte*: 'Jtem onde quer que nos formos sseja dada bairro ao meirinho Pera El e pera os seus homeens E Pera os dito Regatãees E Carniçeiros que na corte andarem E ell lhe de as pousadas como vyr que conpre': *OD*, p. 642. This association of prostitutes with the 'impure' professions such as the *carniçeiro* is common.

[90] *Espelho dos Reis* was written between 1341 and 1344 and dedicated to the Castilian king, Alfonso XI: Álvaro Pais, *Espelho dos reis (Speculum Regum)*, ed. Miguel Pinto Meneses (Lisbon: Instituto de Alta Cultura, 1955), p. 270.

function in the social universe of the court was of greater importance. Also of interest is the way in which the association of certain spheres which were seen as being specific to female activity (reproduction, the care of children, the making of food) was articulated in the court, with a clear predominance of men, both in organisation and probably in numbers, and that this presence of women was moulded within the regime of court duties. Men and women were therefore distinguished at the royal court according to a system of classification of sexual division which was articulated with that of medieval society, although it demonstrated some specific aspects which make the environment somewhat unique in the definition of social roles in the configuration of the groups and the life of individuals according to their gender.

THE NOBILITY

How should we reconstruct the extraordinary wealth and diversity of experience of the nobles within the context of the royal court? The aim of my analysis has been, above all, to retain a perspective of social relations and historical process on this problem. My option was that of seeking to study above all the plurality of movements and of social distinctions which formed the nobility of the court as a group rather than a fixed roll of individuals present at court who may have occupied a particular place, that of the nobility, in the socio-juridic stratification of the society of the age. As Oexle reminds us regarding the use of Weber's inspiration in the study of medieval society, 'ce ne sont pas les ordres – la noblesse, les paysans, etc. – qui sont l'objet de recherche, mais les groupes sociaux qui développent une qualité d'ordre (*ständische qualität*)'.[91] The nobility at court was a clear example of what, in Weberian terminology, are known as 'status groups' (*stände*).[92] It is necessary to try to understand what were the processes of construction of this status group, what is not 'exterior' or superimposed on the social condition of the individual (in this case, on a 'noble state' earlier postulated) but which truly constituted it in the web of social relations. This perspective implied the acceptance of a degree of uncertainty in the construction of my data, which was inevitable in view of the multivalence of medieval words used to denote the condition and status of individuals and groups, tending to be replaced by the specificity and by the categorical opposites of contemporary definitions.[93] Some important elements for the critical use of modern classifications arise from the semantic study of social names used

[91] Otto Gerhard Oexle, 'Les groupes sociaux au moyen âge et les débuts de la sociologie contemporaine', *Annales HSS*, 47 (1992), 761.

[92] Max Weber, *Economy and Society* (Berkeley: University of California Press, 1978), vol. II, pp. 932–8.

[93] Howard Kaminski, 'Estate nobility and the exhibition of estate in the later Middle Ages', *Speculum*, 68 (1993), 684–709.

during the period, and also from the reconstruction of the actual mechanisms of characteristics of this status and of these distinctions, as well as how they were processed in precise social contexts.

Before describing the multifaceted panorama of the court nobility, however, and before showing the variety of questions to which this gives rise, it is also necessary to clarify some aspects of the methodology used in this research and of its objectives. Any prosopographic collection on medieval nobility has to begin, most surely, with the reconstruction of genealogies and with the particular method demanded by genealogical science in its classification of family ties. Without wishing to minimise the correctness and importance of the conclusions which this science allows, and which I have had the opportunity to confirm regarding the identification of persons through their family ties, I should like to make clear that my objective does not lie in the identification of family relationships and their classification, which have already been historically proven and are pertinent to the values of the period. The genealogical reconstruction was, for me, merely an instrument of research whose aim was to locate another type of problem. In the 'dark woods' of genealogical literature relative to the late-medieval period, it was necessary to find safe criteria which would allow me to answer the questions, at times minutely, which arose from this type of investigation.

On rereading the ironic writings of Braamcamp Freire on the investigation of the history of the nobility during the medieval and modern periods, written at the beginning of the twentieth century, today's historian can still find a guide in the principal elementary criticisms which surround genealogical research for the 'Brasões da Sala de Sintra': to consider documentary data as important, to refer to recent genealogy as a secondary source and to refrain from deduction regarding undocumented family ties. As will be proved by results shown later, it was not essential to respond to all the questions which the genealogist poses for the detection of the importance of a family, of a lineage or of a link between certain circles of relatives within the context of the court. I attempted to work directly and at first hand on data collected from fourteenth- and fifteenth-century sources, going as far as these permitted in the reconstruction of biographies of the nobles in the royal entourage, but always keeping in mind the principle of simply researching the family relationships with the help of actual problems, and rejecting immediately any temptation for a global reconstruction which within this area could easily become an end in itself. I accepted some of Braamcamp's conclusions and those of other modern genealogists and historians whose list (which was restricted) can be found in the critical apparatus of this text for the cases in which such a reconstruction can be sketched. I decided to reject reconstructions suggested by authors later than the sixteenth century, whose methods and presuppositions demanded a lengthy critical study, and were unsuitable within the ambit of this investigation, but are indispensable to those who wish to make use of the abundant Portuguese and Hispanic genealogical literature with a minimum of scientific rigour. I obtained results which were perhaps flawed from a genealogical point of view, as can be seen by simply thumbing through the simplified genealogical figures in this text, which have been drawn up simply to help the reader. However, I obtained useful material which I saw as heuristically valid for the study of the nobility of the royal court, which was always the main objective of this research.

I shall begin by analysing the presence of the nobility in court society through the reconstruction of family lines throughout the fourteenth and up to the middle of the fifteenth centuries. The history of several families allows us then to progress to a formulation of the problems of interpretation which are more relevant to the study of court nobility. Indeed, by identifying the individuals who accompanied the monarch according to the various families who claimed to belong to his entourage, an initial general view of this presence is made possible before a closer consideration of interactions within this environment and the specific position and type of roles performed by the nobility alongside the king, which are to be the subject of deeper study in the next chapter. I isolated a total of 118 noble families in the Portuguese court at the end of the Middle Ages, covering a large variety of situations from the succession of many individuals through several generations over the entire period of 1300–1450 to the sporadic presence, which is sparsely documented, of one sole person. In this complex and crowded world, I centred on two principal criteria: on the one hand, that of the continuity of their presence at court and, on the other, that of the traditional distinction between families of the highest nobility (who were to become related to the Peninsular royal families) and families of lesser note and more modest standing. These are the criteria that we shall follow in this presentation.

The relatives of the kings

At the time when this analysis begins, that is during the first decades of the fourteenth century, the magnetism of the entourage of the kings had been felt within the Portuguese and the Peninsular context for several generations and, according to José Mattoso, this led to the formation of a court nobility in Portugal from 1250, in which naturally the origins of one part of the families to be studied here were to become immersed. Studied in detail by Leontina Ventura for the reigns of Sancho II and Afonso III (that is between 1223 and 1279), this nobility encompassed a relatively small group of families stratified through their lineage, whose influence was in the majority of cases felt simultaneously in several regions of the country, either through the localisation of patrimonial nuclei or through the retention of tenancies in distinct areas of the kingdom.[94] In general,

[94] Ventura, 'A nobreza de corte de Afonso III'; see also, by the same author, two chapters in a collection on this subject: 'Portugal em definição de fronteiras (1096–1325). Do Condado

because families died out, or less frequently because of exile or departure from court, a large number of these families did not succeed in reproducing their position of proximity to the monarchs beyond the end of the thirteenth century. Others, as will be seen in the case of the Sousas, saw their position at court and even the succession of their lineage strengthened through descendants of royal blood.

The importance of royal blood as a source of supremacy at the heart of the aristocracy is a structural principle of court society. Since the succession to the throne itself was through primogeniture and preferentially through the male line, the remaining sons and daughters of the monarchs (called 'infantes' in Portugal), whether legitimate or not, became hierarchically ordered according to dynastic criteria. This greater or lesser proximity to the throne contributed towards a recognised restlessness in the political activity of these blood relatives of the monarchs, of which a clear example is the activity of the bastard sons of Dinis in the context of the civil war of 1319–24,[95] and the conflict at the court of Fernando in which the children of Pedro I and Inês de Castro played a part during the 1370s,[96] and even the conflicts which accompanied the regency of the Infante Pedro. Because the close relatives of the kings held important estates and eventually dominated territories linked to noble houses, they had a presence at court that was more or less constant and active according to circumstances. Of these it is possible to say that the acceptance of the position of interdependence relative to the monarchs was always ambiguous, mainly because it held an essentially political significance. A complete absence from court circles, meantime, could mean a dangerous lack of importance in position, and a marginalisation unfitting to one's 'status'.

Frequently the descendants of the 'infantes' remained at court and were the origins, through a genealogical *mise-en-scène* in which they became 'founders' of new lineages, of some of the principal families among the high nobility of the end of the Middle Ages. This process can also be seen as a continuation of what is known of the earlier periods, although this is more difficult to perceive owing to the effect of a break between the period of the Aviz dynasty and the period which preceded it. This was deliberately constructed by some sources, in the main by the fifteenth-century chronicler (who was supported by an expurgatory reform of the royal *chancelaria*) and in certain cases by texts from the later phase of genealogical literature. There existed therefore a high nobility which was

Portucalense à crise do século XIV', in Maria Helena Cruz Coelho and Armando Luís de Carvalho Homem (eds.), *Nova história de Portugal* (Lisbon: Presença, 1996), vol. III, pp. 104–44 and 206–24.

95 José Mattoso, 'A guerra civil de 1319–1324', in *Portugal medieval: novas interpretações* (Lisbon: Imprensa Nacional–Casa de Moeda, 1992), pp. 293–308.

96 A fundamental aspect suggested by Arnaut's investigation, *A crise nacional*, and later studied further by Maria José Ferro Tavares, 'A nobreza no reinado de D. Fernando e a sua actuação em 1383–1385', *Revista de História Económica e Social*, 12 (1983), 45–89.

directly related to the royal houses of Portugal and Castile and which performed an essential function at court, particularly in the second half of the fourteenth century, as well as to some new families that appeared in the following century. In general this concerned lineages originating from a bastard line, as was the case with the numerous offspring of the Infante João (the son of Inês de Castro) and also with the Henriques, Braganza and Noronha families.

The Infante João, the son of Pedro and Inês de Castro, became during the 1370s the leader of a strong faction at the court of Fernando, and besides the ambitions which his royal ascendancy accorded him, he assumed the leadership of the influential family of the Castros, to whom I shall refer later. The exile of the infante to Castile after 1380 did not, however, mean the total disappearance of this privileged political position, an echo of which we find to a certain degree in the court presence of his descendants. Thus, alongside John I, there are prominent some sons of his half-brother of the same name, who had held a far more important position at court than the Master of Aviz himself during the last quarter of the fourteenth century. The descendancy of the Infante João helped to prolong this importance in Portugal at the court of the fifteenth century, even through some bastards (for the daughters of his marriage in exile were in Castile). Three of these bastards were the founders of several fifteenth-century court families: Pedro 'da Guerra', who was in Portugal from the end of the 1380s;[97] Fernando, lord of Braganza, who in 1407 married into the Portuguese court;[98] and the youngest, D. Afonso, lord of Cascais, whom the king ordered to marry, within the court, the daughter of his man of letters, João das Regras.[99]

From the first of these, D. Pedro 'da Guerra', descended two of the most important bishops who were close to John's court, where they appear to have been resident at the beginning of the century (Table 4).

These were the brothers, D. Luis da Guerra, the bishop of Guarda, and D. Fernando da Guerra, who was successively bishop of Silves and of Oporto, and archbishop of Braga, and an important figure in Portuguese political society until the reign of Afonso V. D. Luis, who appears to have been the younger, studied in France and Italy until 1429, and participated at several solemn occasions in the life of the court of Duarte and AfonsoV. He died in 1458. As for D. Fernando da Guerra, who was also absent from the kingdom between 1407 and 1414 while studying law in Bologna and Padua, his presence alongside the monarch must have been confined to limited periods, usually annually between 1420 and 1428, and becoming more widely spaced during the reign of Duarte until 1441. However, he remained connected to the court almost constantly from then until 1461, and held the important posts of *chanceler-mor* and *regedor da casa da*

97 *CR João I*, vol. II, p. 269; Arnaut, *A crise nacional*, p. 231.

98 ANTT, *Ch. D. João I*, 3, ff. 92v and 103v.

99 ANTT, *Ch. D. João I*, 3, f. 103v. Branca da Cunha was the daughter of the doctor, but took his mother's name.

suplicação, and confirmed himself as one of the most powerful members of the kingdom.[100]

D. Fernando and his son D. Duarte 'de Bragança' (Table 5) were equally prominent in the reigns of both John and Duarte.[101] As for D. Afonso 'de Cascais' (Table 6), who was close to the heir to the throne Duarte at John's court, he later followed Queen Leonor of Aragon with his son Fernando 'de Cascais' into exile and died in Castile at the beginning of the 1440s.[102] Following this brief eclipse, which coincided with the regency of the Infante Pedro, the family regained its position of importance from 1450, with Afonso Vasconcelos 'de Cascais', the future Count of Penela, and this was one of the most important noble successes of the second half of the fifteenth century. This success has been studied by the historian Costa Lobo and included an involvement in the developing financial activity of exchange during the second half of the fifteenth century.[103] At the court of Afonso V we also find some sons of D. Fernando 'de Eça' (another descendant of the Infante João) who, with the new Vasconcelos family, became the successors of the lords of Cascais, the two lineages which were to survive from those several branches stemming from the son of Inês de Castro in the Portuguese court circle (Table 7).[104]

The relatives of the kings of Castile were also present at the Portuguese court as a result of a movement parallel to that which attracted the Portuguese nobles to the court of the neighbouring kingdom and which was facilitated by the repeated matrimonial alliances between both royal houses. In the final period of the reign of Fernando we see a characteristic example of this mobility with the court career of D. Henrique Manuel, the maternal uncle of the king and also the bastard son of the Castilian infante, D. Juan Manuel. D. Henrique came to Portugal, according to Braamcamp Freire's theory, with his sister, D. Constança Manuel. It was only at the court of Fernando, however, that he became known, and received from the king the title of Conde de Seia. We also know that he was a Castilian agent at the Portuguese court at the beginning of the 1380s.[105]

The Henriques had similar origins, although not in the same line (Table 8). Fernando Henriques, the bastard son of Henry II of Castile, came to Portugal

[100] José Marques, *A propósito dos recomendados de D. Luis da Guerra (1434)*, offprint of *Bracara Augusta* (Braga, 1977), pp. 10–13; José Marques, *A Arquidiocese de Braga no século XV* (Lisbon: Imprensa Nacional–Casa da Moeda, 1988), pp. 68 *et passim*.

[101] ANTT, *Ch. João I*, 3, f. 92v; *Ch. Duarte*, 3, f. 81. *MH*, vol. I, pp. 208 and 314; *CR Duarte*, p. 523; *CR Afonso V*, pp. 630 and 689.

[102] ANTT, *Ch. João I*, 3, f. 103v; *Ch. Duarte*, 1, ff. 32 and 194v. *Provas*, vol. I, pp. 176–8. *MH*, vol. VII, pp. 91–2 and 169–70.

[103] António S. S. Costa Lobo, *História da sociedade em Portugal no século XV* (Lisbon: História Crítica, 1979), pp. 372–4.

[104] *MH*, vol. XII, p. 147. *Provas*, vol. II, pp. 30 and 50. ANTT, *Ch. Afonso V*, 12, f. 14v; 38, f. 78v.

[105] ANTT, *Ch. D. Fernando*, 1, f. 82v; f. 95v; ff. 133 and 124; *CR Fernando*, pp. 228, 271, 340, 407, 542, 556, 602; *CR João I*, vol. I, pp. 216 and 288; vol. II, p. 150. *CRO* (Ayala), p. 701 (Año 1390). See also Arnaut, *A crise nacional*, pp. 356–7.

at the beginning of the fifteenth century, and was granted the most important *moradia* at John's court.[106] His descendants, who were made lords of Alcáçovas, remained alongside the Portuguese monarchs throughout the fifteenth century, and allied themselves through marriage with other members of the nobility at court, occupying a position of great importance there.[107] In both this case and that of the descendants of the Infante João it is highly probable that their presence at the court of John was included in peace treaties negotiated with the neighbouring kingdom of Castile. According to Fernão Lopes, this would also have occurred with the bastard son of João, D. Afonso, who was handed over within the context of agreements made in 1393.[108] The position of these young men was apparently equivocal, for they were linked by blood to the rival party to that of their protector, from whom they were descended, and their delivery as a hostage served on several occasions as a guarantee of political agreements, reflecting simultaneously their important position as relatives of the royal house and the use to which they were put as negotiating pawns in the politics of the age.

The lineage of the Braganzas is well-enough known, and I therefore shall not make a detailed reference to the various members of the family (Table 9). Their position at the Portuguese court during the middle of the fifteenth century can simply be compared with the fame of the great families of the court such as the Castros and the Teles in the previous century.

The Braganzas had many points in common with the examples already shown, particularly because of their origins from a royal bastard and because of the protection afforded them by the successive monarchs of the house of Aviz. However, they were also a special case, first because of their material wealth throughout the century, which was inseparable from Afonso's matrimonial alliance with the heiress of Nuno Álvares Pereira, and also as a result of the strength and astuteness of the political positions of his sons Afonso and Fernando, the Counts of Ourém and Arraiolos, who were well-known courtiers at the time of Duarte and Afonso V. Their participation in the royal council and in the various war and diplomatic initiatives of the monarchs is well documented by contemporary chronicles, for there is important written evidence of the authority of these powerful men in the form of 'epistles' of counsel to the kings.[109] The Braganzas were also prominent because of the spread of their lordly interests throughout the kingdom, which lay well beyond the territorial areas of their counties and which certainly gave them a profile analogous to that of traditional high nobility

[106] *MH*, vol. I, p. 280; vol. IV, p. 232.

[107] ANTT, *Ch. Duarte*, 3, f. 59; *Ch. Afonso V*, 19, p. 94. *MH*, vol. VII, pp. 83–4. *Provas*, vol. II, pp. 49 and 50.

[108] *CR João I*, vol. II, p. 315.

[109] The epistles of both, dated 1432, are quoted as an example: *MH*, vol. IV, pp. 99–108 and 129–33.

at court whose influence on a supra-regional scale stemmed exclusively from their relationship with the king (whether or not accompanied by the holding of posts at court).[110]

Parallel to the Braganzas, we find the origins of the family of the Noronhas in the marriage of Isabel, the bastard daughter of the Portuguese king Fernando, to Afonso 'de Gijón', the bastard son of Henry II of Castile (Table 10).

The descendants of these two, in particular the three brothers Pedro, Fernando and Sancho de Noronha, attended the Portuguese court from the reign of John I. Pedro de Noronha, the archbishop of Lisbon, was well known because of the conflicts which confronted the Portuguese court following the death of Duarte, and he was prominent as an important supporter of Queen Leonor. In fact, the three brothers became associated with Duarte when he was infante. The archbishop had already been involved, with his young brother Sancho, in the negotiations for his marriage and in the arrival of the infanta in Portugal, while Fernando de Noronha was Duarte's *camareiro-mor*, a position he held both before and after his employer's succession to the throne. During the reign of Duarte, the two younger sons played an active part in the royal council.[111] Following the political reversal which the Noronha family suffered during the regency of the Infante Pedro, we find the family once again part of the high nobility at the court of Afonso V, in particular with the presence of Fernando's son, Pedro de Meneses (Conde de Vila Real), and the bastard sons of the archbishop, João and Pedro de Noronha.[112]

Because of their direct relationship with the Portuguese and Castilian royal houses, this relatively restricted group of powerful men represented a factor in the fundamental hierarchy within the court nobility, seeking to become allied in a variety of ways to these families. In analysing the matrimonial practices of the Braganzas, Mafalda Cunha proved endogamy within this group (particularly between the Braganzas and the Noronhas) which, however, relaxed in future generations as they became still less close in their family ties with the monarch. The process of overlap which occurs in the seeking of alliances between these families by the remaining nobles and which can be seen as recurrent in the configuration of the nobility of the medieval court thus resulted in the fifteenth century in the supremacy which continued to be given by the monarchs of the Aviz family to these families who were related to the kings. The prestige associated with royal blood determines the central position of the bastard children and their descendants of the fourteenth century, like that of the great families of the Braganzas or Noronhas during the fifteenth.

110 Mafalda Soares da Cunha, *Linhagem, parentesco e poder: a casa de Bragança (1348–1483)* (Lisbon: Fundação da Casa de Bragança, 1990).

111 ANTT, *Ch. Duarte*, 3, f. 73; *GTT*, vol. VI, 5, pp. 32–533; *MH*, vol. III, p. 223, 263–75; vol. IV, p. 226; *CR Duarte*, p. 572; *CR Afonso V*, pp. 597, 630 and 692.

112 ANTT, *Ch. Afonso V*, 32, f. 152; 5, f. 18v; *MH*, vol. XII, p. 133. *Provas*, vol. II, pp. 30 and 49.

While the tendency towards homogamy within this highly restricted group (which was accompanied by a constant search for royal favour in order to retain 'status') seems to have influenced positively the fortune of the Braganzas and the Noronhas, this could not always be maintained in successive generations. As the royal blood relationship became more distant in time, supremacy tended to wane, and the action of the monarchs was marked by frequent recourse to the favouring of marriages into lower strata. I shall now illustrate a complex line in the case of the de Sousa family, whose biological succession was interrupted but which came to be 'attracted' to the orbit of the royal family through consanguinity with the king which allowed for the survival of their court position. The old de Sousa family was a notable example of the moulding force of court membership within the context of the history of Portuguese nobility. Although their roots go back to the tenth century, it was in the 200 years from the end of the eleventh to the end of the thirteenth century that their continuing involvement with the monarchs reinforced the strength and power of this lineage, and the de Sousas could consider themselves the principal Portuguese court family in this earlier period.[113] Their involvement with the Portuguese kings is demonstrated in the association with military duties linked to the royal army and the leadership of the court organisation, such as the *mordomos* and *alferes*. It was at the end of the thirteenth century that a crisis arose within the family, biological extinction owing to lack of a male line, which very soon caused a reaction from the monarchs. Afonso III had twice married his bastard daughter to two members of the family who could prove to be the potential heirs of the family fortune[114] and in 1287 Dinis started a complicated process of inquiry as to the estates which were included in the extensive patrimony of the de Sousas, his aim being to circumscribe more precisely the configurations of the patrimony and at the same time to reaffirm royal authority as a basis for the future retention of this patrimony.[115] The 'honour' and the antiquity associated with the name of de Sousa, however, had also determined the need for continuity of the family through new lines which had developed through consanguinity with the monarchs.

In fact, the de Sousa family was still present at court at the end of the Middle Ages through two lines which were related to the bastard children of Afonso III – the descendants of Martim Afonso 'Chichorro' and of Afonso Dinis.[116] Their positions were, however, infinitely more modest than those of the antecedents of

[113] José Mattoso, *Ricos-homens, infanções e cavaleiros: a nobreza medieval Portuguesa dos séculos XI e XII* (Lisbon: Guimarães Editores, 1982), pp. 46–50.

[114] Ventura, 'A nobreza de corte', vol. I, pp. 159–61.

[115] Luis Krus, 'O Rei herdeiro dos Condes: D. Dinis e a herança dos Sousas', in *Passado, memória e poder na sociedade medieval portuguesa: estudos* (Redondo: Patrimonia, 1994), pp. 59–99. José Augusto de Sotto Mayor Pizarro, *D. Dinis e a nobreza nos finais do século XIII*, offprint of *Revista da Faculdade de Letras* (Oporto, 1993).

[116] The principal sources used as a basis for the prosopography of noble families are mentioned in many hundreds of notes which accompany the original text of my doctoral thesis. This is held in the main Portuguese public libraries, and I refer the specialist reader to it.

whom they claimed to be the successors. In the first case this presence is shown alongside the future king, Pedro, through Vasco Martins de Sousa 'Chichorro', who had already appeared close to the then infante in 1341, and who was later to be his *chanceler-mor*. The possessions which had been confiscated 'for treason' from Pero Coelho during the reign of that king were returned to him. His participation in the wars of Fernando is mentioned by Fernão Lopes and was, certainly, related to the bestowal of 'quantias' in 1369 and 1375 although this was not sure proof of his presence at the court of Fernando. He had no heirs, and it was through the sons of his brother Martim Afonso de Sousa I that the continuation of the participation of the Sousa/Chichorro family occurred in the fifteenth century, with Gonçalo Anes de Sousa at the court of John I, as well as his sons, who attended Duarte and Afonso V. At the court of John were also the bastard son Martim Afonso de Sousa II and his offspring, Rui de Sousa and Fernão de Sousa.

The other line of the de Sousas, that of the descendants of the bastard infante Afonso Dinis and Maria Pais Ribeira, also seems to have led to certain standing within the social circle of the court. The brothers Rodrigo Afonso de Sousa and Diogo Afonso de Sousa attended the court of Afonso IV, and the first of these extended his presence with Pedro and perhaps even with Fernando. We also find Gonçalo Rodrigues and Fernão Gonçalves de Sousa, descendants of Rodrigo Afonso through a bastard line, at the court of Fernando, but the events of 1383–85 meant the exile of both to Castile. As for Diogo Afonso de Sousa, who died during the reign of Afonso IV, his sons Álvaro Dias de Sousa and Lopo Dias de Sousa I succeeded him at court, although both were exiled in 1365 for reasons which are difficult to clarify. Only Lopo Dias returned, with Fernando, although his position was unimportant.

It was, however, the descendants of Álvaro Dias, through the numerous offspring of his son Lopo Dias de Sousa II, the Master of Christ, who were the side of the family of greatest prominence at the court of the monarchs of Aviz following the relative decline at the end of the fourteenth century. The female line of the Master married into the most favoured court nobility of John: in particular there were Leonor, who married Fernão Martins Coutinho; Violante, who married Rui Vasques Ribeiro; and Isabel, the wife of Diogo Lopes Lobo. But there were also the sons of the master, Rui Dias de Sousa and Diogo Lopes de Sousa, who attended the courts of John and Duarte. It was through the descendants of Diogo Lopes, who was *mordomo-mor* of the latter, that this important post was retained through heredity, and his son Álvaro de Sousa and grandson Diogo Lopes de Sousa II were successively *mordomo-mor* to Afonso V.

The example of the de Sousas during the fourteenth and fifteenth centuries shows us, therefore, the realigning effect which matrimonial alliance with the royal family could have on the establishment of court hierarchies. It was an effect, however, which did not prevent an instability of positions, which could become aggravated as future generations grew further from the ties of consanguinity. It was necessary for the de Sousas to recover during the fifteenth century the prestige associated with the performance of the duty of *mordomo*, and to reaffirm it as the polarising nucleus of a continuity of family tradition, to regain and obtain a renewed supremacy which had in the past been projected through the assumption of a post at court having the same name as the position held by the old de Sousas of the time of the first kings of Portugal.

In conclusion, we can say that the families and descendant lines of relatives of the kings present an example of a varied spread of situations and lines, all of which demonstrate the known general tendency towards 'ennoblement' of this aristocratic group; that is, for this group to assume and adopt forms of family and patrimonial structure characteristic of the nobility. The kings favoured this structure, either by interlinking of families through matrimonial alliances, or by the systematic granting of titles, even though they might be relatively modest (as was the case with several descendant lines of the son of Inês de Castro, or of the king of Castile), or through the granting of titles associated with gifts of territory of the kingdom (in particular the title of Count). Occasionally, these nobles held court posts, always of importance in the hierarchy – *chanceler-mor*, *mordomo*, *alferes*. Royal protection, as clearly shown by the history of the Braganzas and the Noronhas, was the principal factor in the retention of positions of importance.

The important families

Let us now concentrate our attention on the most long-lasting nucleus of the court nobility, consisting of about thirty families who were present almost without interruption at the court of the Portuguese kings from the end of the reign of Dinis to the personal government of Afonso V. This group of nobles who were most frequently at court allows us a good sample of the arguments I should like to formulate. Among these families there existed different important hierarchies, particularly owing to the characteristics of a growing diversity of titles granted by the monarchs. In the nucleus of the important court families I include seven of the best-known of the medieval nobility, although their importance at court naturally varies with time: the Meneses and the Albuquerques (two branches descending from the Teles family), the Pachecos, the Castros, the Pereiras, the Cunhas and the Silvas.

With the Meneses and the Albuquerques, we find the best-known examples of mobility of the families among the high nobility of the period at both the Portuguese and the Castilian courts. This is a movement which I shall have occasion to analyse for other families of more modest standing. The origins of both stem from the Teles family, lords of Albuquerque, whose presence alongside the kings of Portugal had been established during the thirteenth century. The Meneses are characterised by a vigorous ascent in Portugal throughout the fourteenth century, which culminated in the reign of Fernando. João Afonso Telo III, who must have been born in the first decade of the century,[117] formed the basis for his position at the Portuguese court during the 1350s through his links with the young prince Pedro, through his marriage to the daughter of the great lord of Afonso's court, Lopo Fernandes Pacheco, and by the performance of the important duties of *alferes-mor* and *mordomo-mor* at the court of the new king.

For the same period, or a little before, his brother, the first-born Martim Afonso Telo, became prominent at the Castilian court through a career which was in many ways similar, being alongside the Portuguese queen, the mother of Pedro the Cruel. With the tragic death of Martim Afonso in 1356 his descendants, who were nephews of João Afonso Telo III, went to the Portuguese court, where in a manner diametrically opposite to that which occurred with the family in Castile, the influence of the Teles/Meneses did not cease to increase. These descendants of Martim Afonso, together with the young sons of João Afonso Telo III, came to be the most powerful group of nobles at the court of Fernando, being connected by their dual family proximity and by their court *criação*. The county of Barcelos, which the son of Inês de Castro had held since 1356 (with the peace following the conflicts between the opposing factions of the prince, D. Pedro and the old monarch), was granted to João Afonso Telo III in 1357, when the king came to the throne. This would have been the reason for the magnificent celebrations which are described by Fernão Lopes as an example of the magnanimity of Pedro towards the nobles of his 'privança'.[118]

During the reign of Fernando, the influence of João Afonso at court was uniquely prolonged, as was that of another dominant figure in the Portuguese political panorama of the fourteenth century, Álvaro Peres de Castro. Contrary to that which occurred during his father's reign, the central positions of the court of this king seem to have been occupied by persons who were considerably older than the king himself, with the development of an agglomeration of several family clans based upon the leadership of the old power-holders, to whom the later chroniclers, particularly Fernão Lopes, attributed well-defined strategies for the control of the monarch's will.[119] One of the first projects of the (later annulled) matrimonial alliance in 1368 of João Afonso Telo V to Isabel, the bastard daughter of the king, was followed by the king's marriage to Leonor Teles, who was queen from 1372. The following two decades marked the apogee

[117] Fernão Lopes states that in 1370 he 'seria de hidade de saseenta anos': *CR Fernando*, p. 165.

[118] *CR Pedro*, pp. 144–5. Arnaut, *A crise nacional*, pp. 75 and 88 (where he places the feasts mentioned between June and July 1357). It should be noted that in his *Crónica de D. Fernando* Lopes describes other feasts celebrated in 1373 and 1376, but this time in honour of João Afonso Telo V, the son of the count. At these feasts there would have been an 'arruido' caused by the existence of two rival groups among the nobility. The opposition between the feelings of the two courts in the description of the chronicler could not be more alive: that of D. Pedro was festive and cohesive, that of his successor divided and in conflict.

[119] *CR Fernando*, pp. 121 and 158.

of the Teles/Meneses family at the Portuguese court, as is made clear by the various counties granted them by the monarch: the county of Ourém, as well as that of Barcelos, to João Afonso Telo III, which was then passed on to João Afonso Telo IV, his nephew; the county of Neiva to Gonçalo Telo, who was also a brother of the queen; and the county of Viana do Alentejo to João Afonso Telo V.[120]

Clearly, the events of 1383–85 were a shock for this generation of the Meneses, through the deaths of João Afonso Telo IV and João Afonso Telo V, which had been preceded shortly before by the disappearance of the old count, who followed his son Afonso Telo, at the beginning of the decade. There followed the exile of the majority of the remainder of the family.[121] Only Gonçalo Telo attempted, with little success, a compromise with the new powers. His adherence to the cause of the future John I is referred to by Fernão Lopes, and is indirectly confirmed by the series of gifts recorded between August and October 1384 to several *cavaleiros* who were 'vassals' of Gonçalo Teles or members of his household, such as Estevão Lourenço da Grade, Afonso Álvares, Afonso de Castro, Diogo Gonçalves Peixoto, the *vedor* of his household Gil Gonçalves 'Tripeiro', Álvaro Domingues de Oliveira and Afonso Gil Coreixas.[122] This attempt was in part successful for his son Martinho, whose marriage was celebrated at the new court to Teresa Vasques Coutinha, a lady of Philippa's household, and he received from the new monarchy of the dynasty of Aviz a 'quantia' in exchange for military service. But the position of Gonçalo Teles was very fragile, as was that of his son, and in 1384 they were accused of plotting against the new monarchy of Aviz. Following the premature death of Martinho de Meneses, we find his children Fernando de Meneses and Beatriz de Meneses at the court of Duarte and Afonso V. Beatriz was *aia* to the future queen Isabel, holding a position of relative importance, although this was far from the prestige of earlier periods. Their descendants, in particular João de Meneses, who died during his father's lifetime, and Martinho de Meneses II were among the *cavaleiros* at the court of Afonso V during the 1460s, as was the youngest, Pedro de Meneses II.

Prominent among the descendants of João Afonso Telo II was his grandson Pedro de Meneses I, a captain of Ceuta and Duarte's *alferes* whose court career during the 1420s and 1430s owed much to the protection of his king, both when he was infante and following his accession to the throne. This protection is clearly revealed by the ability to hand down titles, benefices and positions under the beneficence of the king to the bastard son of the 'captain', D. Duarte

120 Besides Arnaut, *A crise nacional*, see also Maria José Ferro Tavares, 'A nobreza no reinado de D. Fernando e a sua actuação em 1383–1385', *Revista de História Económica e Social*, 12 (1983), 45–89.

121 From Afonso Telo we learn that he died during the lifetime of the old count, his father, who died in 1381. João Afonso Telo IV died at Aljubarrota and the Count of Viana, João Afonso Telo V, died in 1384: *Brasões*, vol. I, pp. 108–12 and 117–21.

122 *CR João I*, vol. I, p. 212 and ANTT, *Ch. D. João I*, 1, ff. 26, 31, 32v, 33v, 38v, 51v and 64.

Meneses. The descendants of this branch of the Meneses were also present at the court of Afonso V, in particular through Henrique de Meneses. And of course we must note the important descendancy through the female line, who were particularly involved (through the artistic and literary protection of Leonor, the daughter of D. Pedro, captain of Ceuta) in the construction of renewed family 'fame' through the glory of successes in Morocco. As has been noted by António José Saraiva, this process culminated in the writing of the private chronicles of the principal members of the family by the royal chronicler Zurara, as well as the construction of a family pantheon in a church at Santarém, both initiatives in which this lady played a prominent part.[123]

The example of the Albuquerques was, in a certain way, parallel to that of the Meneses because of their dual influence in Portugal and Castile during the fourteenth century, although in this case the importance of the family had always been greater in the neighbouring kingdom than in Portugal. João Afonso de Albuquerque, 'o do Ataúde', was one of the most powerful men of the Peninsula during the first half of the fourteenth century, as is made quite clear by his position of *aio* and *mordomo-mor* of Pedro I of Castile at the beginning of his reign. As the son of Afonso Sanches, the bastard son of the Portuguese king Dinis, he had important connections with the Portuguese court, and this was a political ace throughout his entire troubled career, besides also providing him with a convenient refuge in difficult moments. His wife, Isabel de Molina, and his son Martinho (who died without issue) held property and interests in Portugal, and João Afonso was connected to the Portuguese court circle during the time of Afonso IV and Pedro through the Pachecos and the Castros.

However, it was the bastard descendancy represented at the court of Fernando by Fernando Afonso de Albuquerque and his sisters Beatriz and Maria which was the branch to hold the greatest fortune in Portugal. The sisters were married respectively to João Afonso Telo IV and Gonçalo Telo, and it was at this time that, by living under the protection of their relatives the Meneses, the position of the Albuquerques attained its highest point among their generation at the Portuguese court. According to Fernão Lopes, Fernando Afonso owed his mastership of Santiago to Leonor Teles, and his adherence to the Master of Aviz in 1383 took him to England, where he remained until 1386 as the Master's diplomatic representative, meanwhile contracting numerous debts and becoming involved in commercial activities.[124] He died shortly after returning to Portugal.

[123] On the cultural activities of Leonor: *Brasões*, vol. I, pp. 127–8; Carlos da Silva Tarouca, *A Graça de Santarém. Fundadores e fundações*, offprint of *Brotéria* (Lisbon, 1942).

[124] Russell, pp. 370–2 and 378. Aspects upon which the chronicler Lopes did not fail to comment: 'o Mestre vinha muy garnido de roupas e armas e apostamentos de casa, como aquell que o bem fazer podia segundo o poder que levava de tirar emprestado sobre as mercadorias no regno em quamto tempo la esteuesse': *CR João I*, vol. II, p. 200.

The continuity of this bastard line at the court of the fifteenth century was compromised by Albuquerque's death, for there remained only the female, illegitimate line. However, this was split into a variety of branches, all based on the female line, and continued to flourish within the court. We find that a daughter of Fernando Afonso, Joana de Albuquerque, was among the women who accompanied Philippa of Lancaster. Both branches of descendants of his other, older daughter, Teresa de Albuquerque, also ensured the continuity of the family, who were present at the court of John I, Duarte and Afonso V. This is the case of the Albuquerques descended from Pero Vasques da Cunha, João de Albuquerque I and, most importantly, Pedro de Albuquerque, who was a courtier of Afonso V. Also, though, were Gonçalo and João, sons of Leonor de Albuquerque, the granddaughter of Teresa, who married the *escrivão da puridade*, João Gonçalves de Gomide. Because of the infamy of the name of their ancestor, they were to adopt the maternal surname, claiming also to be descendants of the unfortunate Master of Santiago, who was the 'privado' of Fernando and John I.

An analysis of the line of the Pachecos at the Portuguese court allows us to pinpoint yet another case of fourteenth-century ascendancy which was to be interrupted in the following century, and which progressed far more brilliantly at the court of Castile. The Pachecos of the thirteenth century were already present at the court of the kings of Portugal, but they appear at the time to have been placed at the margin of the powerful family of Riba de Vizela, which was later to die out.[125] Lopo Fernandes Pacheco was among the companions of Afonso IV when infante, and he retained a discreet position during the civil war of 1319–24. During the first half of the century, his presence alongside the king was close, and he occupied the posts of *meirinho-mor*, *mordomo* of the Infante Pedro between 1335 and 1338 and then queen's *chanceler*. He travelled as the monarch's ambassador to the curia of Rome in 1330 (possibly accompanied by his son Diogo) and on several occasions to the court of Alfonso XI of Castile.[126]

With Pedro's accession to the throne, Diogo Lopes was forced into exile, which also meant the confiscation of his goods, allegedly because of his part in the death of Inês de Castro. In the service of Henry of Trastâmara for a decade, Diogo Lopes lived in France and in Aragon in the entourage of his protector, and he made several diplomatic missions: in 1362–63 once again to the Roman curia, and in 1367 to Portugal.[127] Between 1367 and 1372 or 1373 he made his first attempt to return to the Portuguese court, at which he not only was successful, but he also had his property restored and the 'fama'

[125] Ventura, 'A nobreza de corte', vol. I, pp. 460–1.

[126] Mattoso, *Portugal medieval*, pp. 293–308.

[127] The biography of this individual was described in general terms by Maria Yolanda Costa in 'Diogo Lopes Pacheco. Subsídios para o estudo da acção política de um magnate português do século XIV' (unpublished dissertation, University of Coimbra, 1967). On his action as Trastâmara's ambassador: *MPV*, vol. I, pp. 415–16 and 426.

which Fernando granted him as well as the bestowal of lands in 'quantia'. The newly emerging situation following the marriage of the king to Leonor Teles determined, possibly, the second exile of Diogo Lopes with his children, on which there is a substantial amount of information. This exile ended only with his return to Portugal as a member of the Castilian army in 1384. When he was captured at Almada by the Master of Aviz, the old grandee allied himself with the new king, and became part of his council until his death in 1393.

His son João Fernandes Pacheco and the illegitimate Lopo Fernandes Pacheco II served John I during the final decades of the fourteenth century, and distinguished themselves in particular by initiating the alliances which led to the battle of Trancoso and, in the case of João Fernandes, in what was probably a diplomatic mission to the north of Europe as *guarda-mor*, as well as by being a member of the royal council. Following an initial reorganisation of posts after the Cortes of Coimbra and Aljubarrota, there came a new age of emigration among the nobility of the court, which marked the beginning of the reign of John I and which, in 1398, included both descendants of Diogo Lopes. Particularly in the case of João Fernandes Pacheco they experienced a brilliant future with the Castilian king. It is enough to say that among his descendants was Juan Pacheco, the marquis of Villena, one of the most powerful Castilian grandees of the reign of Henry IV of Castile, who was brilliantly portrayed by Fernando de Pulgar in his *Claros Varones de Castilla.*[128] Some Pachecos were certainly at the Portuguese court during the first half of the fifteenth century, but the offices they held were relatively modest – *escrivão da câmara da puridade*, *tesoureiro* – nothing to restore the prestige which had, until then, characterised the family, and it is doubtful whether they were directly related to the branches of the family written of above. Both João Pacheco and Gomes Pacheco, who were mentioned as being among the faithful *cavaleiros* of the 1460s at the court of Afonso V, must, I suppose, have been related to these servants of John I and Duarte.

The continuing presence of the Castros alongside the Portuguese kings during the fourteenth and fifteenth centuries is a final example of an enormous family whose principal sphere of influence lay outside the kingdom. The Castros were an extraordinarily powerful family grouping in Leon and Castile, and were in evidence from the twelfth century in the entourage of the monarchs of the westernmost kingdoms of the Peninsula.[129] The Castros who permeated the Portuguese court were descended from Pero Fernandes de Castro 'da Guerra',[130] a Galician

[128] Fernando de Pulgar, *Claros varones de Castilla*, ed. R. B. Tate (Madrid: Taurus, 1985), pp. 105–9; Juan Torres Fontes, 'La conquista del Marquesado de Villena', *Hispania*, 13 (1953), 37–151; Emilio Mitre Fernández, 'La emigración de nobles Portugueses a Castilla a fines del siglo XIV', *Hispania*, 26 (1966), 513–25.

[129] Simon Barton, *The Aristocracy in Twelfth-Century León and Castile* (Cambridge: Cambridge University Press, 1977), pp. 154–5.

[130] On this member of Castilian court society: José García Oro, *La nobleza Gallega en la baja edad media* (Santiago de Compostela: Bibliófilos Gallegos, 1981), pp. 11–14. On his presence

grandee, both through the offspring of his son Fernando de Castro and through the line of his bastard son Álvaro Peres de Castro.

Fernando de Castro was the most prominent personage in the neighbouring kingdom during the reign of Pedro I of Castile and, after Montiel, he became the principal leader of Pedro's cause. He was only in Portugal between 1369 and 1373, and then fled to England. He died in Gascony in 1377, but his concubine Mília or Mélia Gonçalves and their descendants remained in the Portuguese kingdom, where they had retreated following the peace agreements of 1371 between the Portuguese and the Castilians.[131] Some indications point to an active protection which the Infante João, son of Inês de Castro, lent to these relatives during the 1370s.[132]

The participation of this branch of the family at the court of Fernando, although probable, has left no significant traces, and this relative quiet remained during the reign of John I with regard to Álvaro de Castro II, the son of the legitimist hero.[133] His descendants were prominent during the first decades of the fifteenth century in the court circle, in particular because of this closeness to the infantes of the house of Aviz: Pedro de Castro II and Álvaro de Castro III were connected to the Infante Henry; Fernando de Castro, 'O Cegonho', to the Infante Fernando (he then went into the service of Afonso V); and Fradique de Castro with the Infante Pedro. It is highly probable that it is this Fernando de Castro who was the dedicatee mentioned on the title page of the Portuguese translation of the *Confessio Amantis* by John Gower, recently discovered in the library of the palace in Madrid.[134] The brother of these men, Diogo de Castro, was a *cavaleiro* at the court of Afonso from the period prior to the battle of Alfarrobeira, and he and his son Pedro de Castro III were granted a *moradia* in the 1460s. João de Castro II, who was also a descendant of Pedro de Castro II (the lord of Roriz), is documented among the *cavaleiros* of Afonso V.

in the Minho in 1337 during an incursion in the service of Afonso XI: Luis Krus, *A concepção nobiliárquica do espaço ibérico (1280–1380)* (Lisbon: Fundação Calouste Gulbenkian, 1994), pp. 100–1, notes 172 and 175.

131 On the successive marriages of Fernando de Castro and the political significance attributed to these: García Oro, *La nobleza Gallega*, pp. 15–16. Also Eduardo Guevara y Valdés, 'Los Castro Gallegos del siglo XIV. Apuntes para un análisis de su proyección en la historia política de Castilla', *Hispania*, 45 (1985), 161 and 477–511.

132 As Braamcamp Freire has already stated, and referred to in documentation of 1384: ANTT, *Ch. D. João I*, 1, f. 24v.

133 Although he took part in the conquest of Ceuta with his eldest son, Alvaro de Castro II is not listed among the *moradores* of John I, nor does he perform any duties at the court of this king. Cf. *Brasões*, vol. I, pp. 144–5. He was still alive in 1424: ANTT, *Ch. D. João I*, 4, f. 72.

134 Antonio Cortijo Ocaña, 'La traducción Portuguesa de la Confessio Amantis de John Gower', *Euphrosyne*, 23 (1995), 457–66. Not only is the chronology of this individual, whom we still find at the court of Afonso V in the 1460s, compatible with the dates suggested for the manuscript, but also the connection to England of this branch of the Castros had a family tradition. On the other hand, the well-known governor of the same name at the house of the Infante Henry (who belongs to the other branch of the Castros) died in 1441, and is named by the chroniclers and nobles as 'o velho', as opposed to the name 'o moço' which appears in the title page of the manuscript.

The importance of this family at the Portuguese court of the end of the Middle Ages was demonstrated most clearly through the legitimate line of D. Pedro de Castro, through Álvaro Peres de Castro and Inês de Castro. Both had been in the company of the young Infante Pedro from the 1350s, and their presence in the entourage of Afonso IV and the future king was an important cause of conflict.[135] Many aspects of their activity in Portugal, and most importantly the political significance of the various alliances and positions of Álvaro Peres de Castro both before and after the murder of his sister, still remain little known. On the other hand, his involvement during the 1350s and 1360s with his brother Fernando de Castro, whom I have mentioned above in the political conflicts of the neighbouring kingdom, is indisputable.[136]

The position of greatest relevance of Álvaro Peres at the Portuguese court seems to date from the reign of Fernando, and corresponds on the one hand to his increasing presence in Portugal (which is made all the more obvious by his being granted the county of Arraiolos) and, on the other hand, to the importance of his nephews, the sons of Inês, whose power and influence at the court as brothers of the king appear to have been deliberately obscured by Fernão Lopes.[137] Once again, during the 1370s and 1380s, this grandee was deeply involved in military and political activities, as was his son Pedro de Castro, and both successively took positions which were more distant from those of the Portuguese king and Leonor Teles. This distancing is detectable, above all, from the time of the last war of Fernando's reign of 1381–82, when he acted as supreme commander, and this perhaps revealed the intention of Álvaro Peres to safeguard the interests of his exiled nephew, the Infante João.[138] This attitude would also have dictated the initial adherence of this grandee to the cause of the Master of Aviz in 1383 and 1384 and, driven by probable discontent caused by the growing independence of the Master, would be the reason for the distancing of Pedro de Castro from the revolutionaries in this final year, 1384.

In his *Crónica de D. João I*, Fernão Lopes stresses the participation of some members of the family in the Master's entourage in 1383, when they received a 'mantimento' as members of his household – particularly Afonso and Beatriz de Castro (who were children of Álvaro Peres) and Leonor de Meneses (the

[135] A synthesis on this subject can be found in José Antunes et al., *Conflitos políticos no reino de Portugal entre a Reconquista e a Expansão*, offprint of *Revista de História das Ideias* (Coimbra, 1984), pp. 128–9.

[136] *CRO Pedro*, pp. 45–6 and 152, a version which must be compared with that stated by Fernão Lopes in *CR Pedro*, pp. 260 and 264.

[137] We owe the clarification on this highly important point to the original investigation by Salvador Dias Arnaut, not only for the understanding of the political events of 1383–85 but also for the study of the court of Fernando: Arnaut, *A crise nacional*. See also Marcelo Caetano, *A crise nacional de 1383–85* (Lisbon: Verbo, [1985]), pp. 50–2, note III. It was only with her work in the 1980s that Maria José Ferro Tavares returned to the research of archives on this subject, which during the 1960s and 1970s had been the subject of important interpretative studies, but all based exclusively on Fernão Lopes.

[138] Arnaut, *A crise nacional*, p. 183.

wife of Pedro de Castro).[139] One detects in the work of the chronicler a preoccupation from the beginning with connecting this ambiguous adherence of the Castros to the revolutionary Master with the presence of the descendants of Álvaro Peres and the Infante João at the fifteenth-century court. In fact, Pedro de Castro would have been absent from the kingdom between 1384 and 1388, during a (temporary) eclipse at court marked by the usual confiscation of goods, although his children, particularly João de Castro and Fernando de Castro, were prominent at the outset of the new century among the *moradores* of John I.

The first of these, who married the rich widow of Dr João das Regras, died prematurely in the disaster of Tangier. Fernando de Castro is an interesting example of the career of a fifteenth-century courtier, and was prominent in the service of John I and Duarte in the several areas of political, military and diplomatic activity, while simultaneously cultivating, from 1411 until his disappearance in 1441, a privileged connection with the Infante Henry. His children, Álvaro de Castro IV (Conde de Monsanto) and Garcia de Castro were prominent at the courts of Duarte and Afonso V. This was due in particular to the first of these acting as *camareiro-mor* from the 1440s and by the participation of both men in the king's council following Alfarrobeira. Likewise, Henrique de Castro II became integrated in the court after 1460, having prior to this been connected to the entourage of Henry.

The family of the Pereiras, with the many branches which have to date been identified, constitutes one of the most numerous groups of nobles who were interrelated and who attended the court of the Portuguese kings during the fourteenth and fifteenth centuries. Using as a point of departure the common origin of the descendants of the count Gonçalo Pereira,[140] I shall distinguish the lines stemming from his sons, Vasco Pereira and Gonçalo Pereira, from that of the descendants of his bastard son, Rui Gonçalves Pereira.

In the first case we find Vasco Pereira among the courtiers of Afonso IV at the beginning of the period studied, as well as his son Rui Vasques Pereira, who was present at least from the 1350s. The reign of Pedro was a time of some obscurity in the life of Rui Vasques, whose presence at the Portuguese court cannot be proved. For somewhat hazy reasons, perhaps to do with the exile mentioned above of the Sousa family in about 1365, we find him in the entourage of Pedro I of Castile in 1368 (that is if we are not dealing with an individual of the same name), serving as 'Ballestero Mayor' for the monarch. The beginning of the new reign marked his possible return to the court of Fernando, where he received 'quantias' from the Portuguese king in 1372 and 1373. In 1375 he

[139] *CR João*, vol. I, pp. 89 and 133; vol. II, pp. 270 and 284–7.

[140] On the Pereiras of the thirteenth century: José Mattoso, *Identificação de um país* (Lisbon: Estampa, 1985), vol. I, p. 210 and also *DEHP*, vol. II, pp. 100–1.

once again fell into disgrace, with the confiscation of his goods 'por erros que fez na nossa terra', in the words of the royal decree.

His son, João Rodrigues Pereira, was already at the court of Fernando according to Fernão Lopes, and was among the company of the brother of the queen, Gonçalo Telo (Count of Neiva). He then became an adherent of the new king of Aviz, whom he served until his death in 1398. It is only with Gonçalo Pereira 'das Armas' and Rui Vasques Pereira II that this branch of the family attained positions of importance at court. At least until the regency of the Infante Pedro, Gonçalo and Rui easily maintained their importance in this circle, and were prominent for their service to Duarte and Queen Leonor of Aragon. During the 1450s and 1460s, their descendants João Rodrigues Pereira, the illegitimate sons Vasco Pereira II and Martim Mendes de Berredo and also Rui Vasques Pereira III all held positions of importance in the service of Afonso V.

Let us now look at another group of the Pereiras mentioned above, descending from the bastard Rui Gonçalves Pereira, who was also a contemporary of Afonso IV. At the courts of Pedro and Fernando we find the presence of his sons Álvaro, Gonçalo and Rui Pereira, who witnessed solemn acts and received rents and lands 'em quantia', in particular during the period of the wars in the reign of Fernando. According to the chronicler Lopes, Álvaro and Rui were, during the 1380s, members of a 'company' which was organised by the prior of the Hospital, Pedro Álvares Pereira, for the defence of Lisbon, which seems to indicate a close link between the several branches of the family. Similarly, we find the young Álvaro Pereira II, the nephew of the man of the same name, in 1385 and 1386 as *marechal* of John I, and he took part in the royal council prior to his death in combat. His descendants remained at court during the first decades of the fifteenth century, in particular his daughters Leonor and Beatriz, who were in the entourage of Philippa of Lancaster, and João Álvares Pereira who, with his sons Fernão and Gonçalo Pereira II, was in the company of Duarte. At the court of Afonso V the two successive generations of this lineage were to live together, with the presence of Fernão and his sons Galiote and Rui Pereira II (Gonçalo Pereira II was to die shortly after Alfarrobeira) and that of Vasco Pereira, who was accompanied by his son Gonçalo Pereira III.

It remains to mention the third branch of the Pereiras who were in evidence during this period, whose peculiar characteristics are due to an almost complete lack of legitimate succession, a factor which hinders greatly the identification of individuals. The most important figure of this branch was, without doubt, the prior of the Hospital, the grandee of Portuguese nobility of the fourteenth century Álvaro Gonçalves Pereira, the son of the archbishop of Braga, Gonçalo Pereira. He reappeared at court during the reign of Afonso IV, where he remained until the end of the century. The participation of the prior in the successive wars of the century, particularly in those which took place between 1369 and 1380 (the year of his death), became fundamental because of the military power which his post in the Order of Hospitallers afforded him, and which was increased by a charismatic leadership quality, evidence of which remains in legend.[141]

As has been emphasised by several authors (in particular Díaz Martín on Castile and Mattoso on Portugal), the control of the Military Orders in the Peninsula through the attraction of the Masters to the court and also the influence of their nomination and confirmation by the popes were fundamental strategies for the monarchs of the fourteenth century when confronted by the changes in war methods existing at the time. Since they formed professional bodies of fighting men, the knights of the Orders played an essential part in the royal armies.[142] This had already been demonstrated at the battle of Salado, which is a central element of the legends regarding the prior and the glorification of the Pereira line.[143] The presence of Álvaro Gonçalves Pereira, as that of other Masters at the Portuguese court, would naturally have led to protection by the king of some of his many descendants.

Of those who 'se criaram' with his father the prior, we know that Pedro Álvaro Pereira owed his leading position as head of the Order following 1380 to the intervention of D. Fernando, and he was included by Fernão Lopes among the influential individuals of the entourage of Leonor Teles. Of the descendants of the long relationship of the old prior with Iria Gonçalves do Carvalhal, prominent was Nuno Álvares Pereira, a 'criado' of Fernando, possibly with his youngest brother Rodrigo Álvares Pereira 'Olhinhos'. Nuno Álvares Pereira withdrew from the court following his marriage in the 1370s.[144] The reason for this withdrawal is little explained by the chronicle, and seems to be confirmed by the royal documentation which has survived; it would have coincided with the most important decade of the infante, the son of Inês de Castro, at the court of Fernando. The decisive action of Nuno Álvares during the events of the dynastic crisis is well known.

The presence of Nuno Álvares in John's entourage following 1385 is, however, one of the controversial aspects of his career, in spite of the fact that we know that he held two of the most important posts at court during the reign

141 On the legends on his tomb in Flor da Rosa: Vergílio Correia, *Três túmulos: uma arca tumular do museu de Santarém. Sepultura de Fernão Gomes de Goes em Oliveira do Conde. Moimento do Primeiro Marquês de Valença* (Lisbon: Portugália, [1921]), p. 24 and note.

142 Luis Vicente Díaz Martín, *Los oficiales de Pedro I de Castilla* (Valladolid: University of Valladolid, 1987), p. 169; José Mattoso, *Fragmentos de uma composição medieval* (Lisbon: Estampa, 1987), pp. 287–9.

143 Krus, *A concepção nobiliárquica*, p. 140 and note 299. On the importance of this battle: Bernardo Vasconcelos e Sousa, 'O sangue, a cruz e a coroa: a memória do Salado em Portugal', *Penélope*, 2 (1989), 227–48.

144 The prior had at least half a dozen known children by Iria Gonçalves. It is possible that his connection with the court was strengthened through his mother, whom the fifteenth-century chroniclers include in the entourage of the daughter of Leonor Teles. The theme of the 'criação' of Nuno Álvares at the court of Fernando is a subject upon which the chronicler Lopes insists (*CR Fernando*, pp. 429 and 433), which takes up the *Crónica do Condestabre*, which he used as a source (*CR Nuno*, pp. 3–7).

of this monarch from that date – that of *condestável* and *mordomo-mor* – and he was also a member of his council. However, it is legitimate to doubt his constant presence at the court of John, at least up to the end of the 1390s, when the most intense cycle of war was coming to an end, with the commencement of a serious conflict against the monarch whom he had helped to promote. Between 1400 and 1422–23 his presence at court is at least more probable, according to a reconstruction of his itinerary given by the fifteenth-century chronicle of his deeds.[145] The enormous power of this individual who was central to the events leading to the institution of the new dynasty may have contributed to the retention of a certain capacity to retire from court circles, which was a sign of his independence and demonstrated a type of intermittent relationship with the court similar to that of the powerful masters of the orders of the previous century, such as his father. The same situation of returning to court after 1400 is sketched in the instructions dated 1414 by the king of Aragon to the ambassadors whom he sent to the Portuguese court, which stressed the importance of the presence of Queen Philippa and the count Nuno Álvares at the audience of the king; both were central figures in John's politics during this first decade of the fifteenth century, whose support had always to be achieved.[146]

Although we are not able to relate them precisely to any of the lines of descent so far described, we must include one final group of courtiers of the fifteenth century in the family grouping of the Pereiras. There is Diogo Pereira, a *morador* at the court of John I, and then *vedor* to the Infante João, the *comendador* of Santiago; or Duarte Pereira, who was less known, but who was also a *morador* at the court of this monarch at the beginning of the new century. Henrique Pereira, who was also connected to the Order of Santiago, attended the court of Duarte and Afonso V. Lisuarte and Afonso Pereira were successively *reposteiros-mores* at the court of Afonso from the 1450s until at least 1475, and at the same time were members of the royal council.

With the Cunhas and the Silvas I shall conclude this in-depth circumnavigation of the most notable families who remained assiduously at the Portuguese court throughout the entire period studied. In the first case, we are able to group the diverse individuals in two distinct lines of succession: the descendants of Martim Lourenço da Cunha and those of Vasco Martins da Cunha.

Martim Lourenço da Cunha and his cousin João [Anes] da Cunha are stated to have been at the court of Afonso IV, but we know nothing of them during the reign of Pedro to allow us to place them with certainty among the nobles

[145] Manuel Maria Vermers, 'Nun'Álvares Pereira. A sua cronologia e o seu itinerário', *Lusitania Sacra*, 5 (1960–61), 7–99; J. Cordeiro de Sousa, 'Andanças de Nun'Álvares (1373–1422)', *O Instituto*, 129 (1967), 108–55. The absence of his daughter Beatriz in the list of *moradores* of Philippa of Lancaster should be noted – she would, according to the *Crónica do Condestabre*, have been handed to Iria Gonçalves, her grandmother, following the death of her mother, Leonor de Alvim.

[146] *MH*, vol. II, pp. 107 and 110.

of his entourage. However, the presence of this line at the Portuguese court was certainly apparent during the previous century, and one can say that they owed certain promotion to this court connection.[147] A discrete position in this environment would also be, according to the vision of the court of Fernando which Fernão Lopes has given us, that of João Lourenço da Cunha, the son of Martim, who was the first husband of Leonor Teles and who was forced into exile in the 1370s. Some indications relate him to the Infante João, the brother of the king and the son of Inês de Castro, in whose close circle he seems to have been.[148] João Lourenço, with other members of the court, was accused by Fernando of attempting to poison him 'com peçonha' following the marriage to Leonor Teles, and lost his possessions some years later, but it is impossible to put a precise date on these troubled events which suggest his connection to the royal court.[149] In 1384, João Lourenço da Cunha was, according to Fernão Lopes, in the service of the rebel Master of Aviz at the order of the Infante João, his lord, and was accompanied by his son, Álvaro da Cunha (or Álvaro de Sousa).

Álvaro was to remain in Portugal during the reign of John, when at least his descendant Rodrigo Afonso de Melo or Rui de Melo was a member of the king's *câmara*, and a *morador*. Through the succession of his wife Beatriz Pereira (the heiress of the Pessanha family), he held the hereditary post of *almirante*. It was this same Rui de Melo who had a certain fame during the period following Alfarrobeira, although his presence at the court is poorly documented in the 1450s and 1460s, which is perhaps connected to the fact of his privileged relationship with the Infante Henry, whom he served as *camareiro*. His illegitimate son Álvaro da Cunha II meanwhile was among those listed as *moradores* at the court of Afonso V during the 1470s. The relatively modest positions which, perhaps because of their stormy history, this line of the Cunhas seems to have held at court contrast with the success to be detected among the descendants of Vasco Martins da Cunha.

Martim Vasques da Cunha accompanied the royal entourage during the 1320s, and had married a daughter of the grandee Lopo Fernandes Pacheco, whose importance in the court has already been stated above. It was with this last that Vasco Martins da Cunha I rose, following the death of his father *c.* 1342, and appeared during the reign of Pedro, from whom he received a 'quantia' and the important *alcaidaria* of Lisbon. Of his many children, whose futures were so varied, among the eldest the most notable are Martim Vasques da Cunha II and Vasco Martins da Cunha II and, of the youngest, Gil Vasques da Cunha and Lopo Vasques.

[147] Ventura, 'A nobreza de corte', vol. I, p. 358. [148] Arnaut, *A crise nacional*, p. 179.

[149] There is information on this conflict in a document of the later date of 1379: ANTT, *Ch. D. Fernando*, 2, f. 45v. In this charter, it is mentioned that the king had forgiven an earlier revolt (following his marriage?).

Because of the relatively distant position attributed to him by Fernão Lopes during the events of 1383–85 until the battle of Trancoso, and above all because of his holding of the *alcaidarias* of the Beira Interior during the 1370s and 1380s, Martim Vasques II has been seen as a typical representative of a provincial noble family of Beira, apparently distanced from the royal court.[150] His connection to the king's entourage appears, however, to have been most probable. Besides his involvement in the wars during the reign of Fernando and the receipt of 'quantias', which confirm his inclusion in the royal army, from early on we can detect his proximity to the infant children of Inês de Castro. This connection is demonstrated not only by the position of Martim Vasques II at the Cortes of Coimbra but perhaps far earlier, by the mention of the removal in 1375 of his jurisdiction over his lands. As well as an involvement with the court circles, there is the matrimonial connection of Martim Vasques II with Maria Girona, whom we are able to identify as the niece of Queen Beatriz, and this alliance was certainly contracted at court, and confirmed also by the gift of goods 'em casamento' by the monarch.

The receipt of the *alcaidarias* of Beira completed in some manner the regional settlement of this lineage whose patrimony was situated there also, but cannot in itself be a proof of a withdrawal of Martim and his brothers from the circle of court nobility during the reign of Fernando. The most probable theory remains, in my opinion, that of a retreat of these individuals governed by circumstances during the 1380s related to the marriage of Leonor Teles (who, it must be remembered, had 'repudiated' a Cunha) and/or the later withdrawal from court of the sons of Inês de Castro. However this might be, the entirely different course of the descendants of Vasco Martins da Cunha I, following the death of Fernando, determined the continuity of the presence of this family at the Portuguese court in the following century.

Martim Vasques II, the first-born, following lukewarm obedience to Beatriz in 1383, joined the Master's rebels and received from the new king an impressive quantity of land and rents during the 1380s and 1390s, as well as participating in his council. Martim Vasques, who was the main defender during the Cortes of Coimbra of the pretensions of the Infante João, and who was then imprisoned in Castile, seems following this date to have acceded to the definitive autonomy of the Master of Aviz and his ascent to the throne. However, we find him selling and exchanging a large part of his possessions received between 1394 and 1396, the date of his final exile to the Castilian court, where he took the helm of a 'Portuguese party' opposed to John I. His brothers Gil and Lopo also belonged to this party.[151] Among the descendants of Martim Vasques, only his daughter

[150] Arnaut, *A crise nacional*, esp., pp. 76 and 136.

[151] On his position as leader of the party of exiles in Castile, which was strengthened by the marriage to the daughter of the dead Infante D. João: Arnaut, *A crise nacional*, pp. 209–10.

Leonor da Cunha was definitely at the court of John at the beginning of the following century.

Gil Vasques was the only member of this family who returned to John I after 1402, and he remained in Portugal until his death in 1418.[152] We also find the presence of his children at court, in particular João Pereira 'Agostim', who from the 1420s followed the Infante Henry. Lopo Vasques was, however, the origin of the important line of the Acuña family in Castile, and his descendants were among the best-known examples (as were the Pacheco and the Pimentel families) of successful integration of exiled Portuguese into the Castilian court of the fifteenth century.[153]

The route taken by Vasco Martins da Cunha II and his youngest brother, Pedro Vasques da Cunha, was in total contrast to that chosen by the group of Cunhas who elected for exile. Vasco Martins and his sons Luis and Martim Vasques da Cunha III were at the court of John I during the first two decades of the fifteenth century. Pedro Vasques, who 'se criara' with the Master, received a part of the patrimony of his father, brothers and nephews who were in exile in Castile. As already noted, his descendants remained at the court but abandoned their surname, adopting instead the more prestigious Albuquerque. Martim Vasques da Cunha III died early, before the end of John's reign, and it was his brother Luis Vasques who was at the court of Duarte; a further Cunha had the same name (Martim Vasques da Cunha IV, who was perhaps illegitimate). Fernão Vasques da Cunha, the son of Gil Vasques, who died during the expedition to Tangier, also took part at the Portuguese court.

With the reign of Afonso V, perhaps owing to the progressive depletion of the male line, we see the ascent at court of a branch of the family descending from Vasco Martins da Cunha through his son Estevão Soares, which had until then been the most obscure. Both he and his descendant Vasco da Cunha had contracted marriages outside the nobility, although they were not vastly distant from the servants of the court, for the wife of Vasco was the daughter of Dr Rui Fernandes, the *chanceler* during the final years of John's reign. During the 1460s we find his descendant Aires da Cunha as a *cavaleiro* at the court of Afonso and he too married a daughter of a Lisbon burgher, Afonso Lopes Bulhão. As to the line of Vasco Martins da Cunha II, 'o Moço', the companion of the Master of Aviz, this was represented by his grandson of the same name, Vasco Martins da Cunha III, whose presence alongside Afonso V is shown following the regency, as is his participation in the council of Afonso during the 1470s.

At the end of the Middle Ages, the da Silva family retained a presence at court which dated back to the twelfth and thirteenth centuries, when they were already

152 His marriage must date from the period following the 'return', with the *morador* of D. Philippa's household, Leonor Gonçalves de Moura.

153 Mitre Fernandes, 'La emigración de nobles Portugueses'.

playing a major part in the entourage of the monarchs. Two contemporary individuals, who had married two sisters who were in fact members of their own family, form the starting point of the distinct branches of this family, prominent between 1300 and 1450. Aires Gomes da Silva I, named in the *Crónicas* and the *Livros de Linhagens* as 'o Velho' or 'o Grande', was an important courtier who accompanied Afonso IV. Through information available relating to the end of the century we learn that his involvement in the conflicts with the young Infante Pedro must have been the cause of the destruction of some of his possessions 'que el rei depois pagou'. The ascent to the throne of the rebel infante must have brought some problems for this grandee, of whom we know only that he controlled the important *alcaidaria* of Santarém at the beginning of the reign, but of whose continuing attendance at court there is no proof.

His sons Fernão and Afonso later appear, during the reign of Fernando, as receiving 'quantias' and other benefits. Afonso Gomes was in particular involved in the court circle close to the monarch, who spoke of him 'da nossa criação', and was also one of the most important vassals known of the Infante João, brother of the king. According to his own testimony, however, a protracted argument opposed the da Silvas and the Teles family during the reign of Fernando, and the former received no justice, owing to the 'gram poderio' of the lineage to which the queen belonged. This suggests an animosity and tension between this branch of the da Silva family and that which formed the more powerful noble line at the court in the second half of the fourteenth century, a fact which, combined with the connection to the son of Inês de Castro, contributed to a number of possible reasons for the exile of Afonso and Fernão following the events of 1383–85. Among these reasons was the fact that these da Silvas remained attached to the 'Portuguese party' at the Castilian court which advocated the accession to the throne of Portugal of the Infante João.[154]

We do not find any sign of this branch of the family at the fifteenth-century court, but we do find the descendants of João Gomes da Silva. Aires Gomes da Silva II (or 'o Moço') seems to have begun his stay at court as *aio* of Fernando when he was still infante. As such, we find him referred to in documentation of Pedro from the beginning of his reign. He was an important figure at the court of Fernando, being *alferes-mor* of the monarch and, according to Fernão Lopes, one of the principal members of his council. His brother Gonçalo Gomes, who was also among those who received 'quantias' from the king during the period of the wars of 1369–71 and 1372–73, is also placed among the entourage of Fernando by the chronicler.

[154] On his opposition to the Master of Aviz: *CR João I*, vol. I, pp. 201 and 303. Successive gifts and confiscation of possessions between 1384 and 1386 suggest a radical change of positions: ANTT, *Ch. D. João I*, 1, f. 167v. (confiscation from Afonso); f. 156v (a later gift); f. 157 (restitution of all his possessions); f. 170 (final confiscation of all his possessions; 2, f. 26v (confiscation of the possessions of Fernão, referring to the 'pardon' previously granted).

Unlike Aires Gomes, Gonçalo remained with the cause of the Master of Aviz, and left the court on a diplomatic mission following the Cortes of Coimbra on a journey similar to that of his contemporary, Fernando Afonso de Albuquerque. From the early years of the fifteenth century, the descendants of Gonçalo Gomes became prominent at the court of John, just like members of the hypothetical descendants of Aires Gomes, among them his son Rui Gomes da Silva.[155] Therefore, João Gomes da Silva was *alferes-mor* to John I and a member of his council, living until the end of the reign of Duarte, during which time he appears close to the Infante Pedro, as was his son Aires Gomes da Silva III. Fernão da Silva, his brother, was *estrabeiro-mor* to Duarte, and Rui Gomes da Silva, who by this time was among the *moradores* of John I, also continued at the court of his successor. He died following Alfarrobeira.

In the entourage of Afonso V we find two successive generations of this branch of the da Silvas, represented by Pedro Gomes da Silva and Afonso Teles de Meneses, the sons of Rui Gomes da Silva and, from the other side, both João da Silva and Fernão Teles de Meneses through the descendants of Aires Gomes da Silva III. Also connected to the court of Afonso are the bastards Pedro da Silva, a doctor of law and a distinguished member of the royal *desembargo*, and Diogo da Silva, who was the king's *tesoureiro* in the middle of the 1450s. In turn Rui Gomes da Silva II only became one of the nobility at court following the death of the Infante Henry, to whose household he had belonged before 1460.

A lengthy analysis of this group of more important families (who were also the better known) who accompanied the Portuguese kings constantly leads to some observations as to the overall characteristics of the nobility at court during the fourteenth and fifteenth centuries. First, we find that the period of their presence, which is confirmed by the succession of generations of the same family in the royal service, was accompanied by a process of broadening and diversification in the sphere of activity and actual functions performed by the nobility. For the earlier period, we find a preference for some palace posts and positions of prestige, particularly those of *mordomo* and *aio*, but we also find them as *meirinho* or *alferes* and, in a general manner, holding posts in the royal army, which were to be shared by the family group described whose roots had already settled at court in the thirteenth century (see the Silva and the Teles families). However, the fifteenth century witnessed an extraordinary expansion of the areas of noble participation in all spheres of the court organisation, and it must be emphasised that many of the old families of the court nobility did not shy away from the new roles related to the development of the royal finances and the *desembargo*, as testified by the Castros, the Cunhas and the Silvas.

155 I believe the ascendance of Rui Gomes is only hypothetical, since although the *Nobiliários* tends to identify him as a son of the same name of Aires Gomes da Silva I, there are some serious chronological problems, since Rui Gomes was still alive in 1452: *LL*, p. 118. I would accept the second hypothesis of a descent from Aires Gomes da Silva II, suggested by Braamcamp Freire, since I feel this to be probable: *Brasões*, vol. II, p. 17.

A permanent sign of their being attracted to the court lies in the importance of the military function of the nobles, which was related to the frequency and the scale of wars in which the royal army was involved from the middle of the fourteenth and throughout the entire fifteenth century. This constant fact of war in the life of the court nobles, which is so characteristic of the European situation at the end of the Middle Ages, is, in the Portuguese case, connected to a real process of the Military Orders becoming a part of court life. This is easily detectable in the growing number of those connected to the orders who formed part of the entourage of the monarchs at the end of the Middle Ages, as can be ascertained by recourse to the Pereira family, who were a fine example of this. There are several facets to be distinguished during this integration into court life of the knights of the orders. The presence of the masters at court, for example, is indivisible from the influence of the monarchs in their appointment, to which I have already referred, and which appears in Portugal in the middle of the fourteenth century. Most characteristic of the situation during the fourteenth century appears to be the preferential recruitment of *cavaleiros* from among the middle and lower nobility and those less favoured by family succession, which meant that their more modest situation freed them for a permanent position alongside the monarch and for service in the royal army. On the other hand, the growing control of governing of the Military Orders by the king and the royal family was to have as a consequence during the fifteenth century the granting of titles and positions in these institutions in repayment for services given by the courtiers. In the first case, it was in their position as *cavaleiros* that the more modest nobles were attracted to the court; in the second it would be the courtiers who became knights of the orders who therefore received other revenue and social distinctions. This movement corresponded to a growing attention by the monarchs and the masters of the fifteenth century to the 'reform' of the orders by making them flexible instruments of redistribution of status and of income. In both cases, it is in the process of their being integrated into the court, which grew during the troubled time of the fourteenth-century wars, that a factor can be found in the important explanation of the transformation which the Military Orders as well as court society itself underwent during the later medieval period. The historian Luis Adão Fonseca, postulating a community of interests among all the members of these military orders, suggested that the modern sociological concept of a 'pressure group' should be applied to the Military Orders of the fifteenth century, since these were merely an 'institutional framework' of groups of this type. However, alongside the community of interests a close interaction is another characteristic which is indispensable to pressure groups, and is an inverse factor of their continuation. That is, the members of pressure groups tend to become intensely interrelated for short periods, around specific objectives, or else they easily become disbanded. The reforms of the orders at the end of the Middle Ages appear simply to tend, according to more recent studies, to organise them in local commanderies, a fact which makes this intensity of interaction far less probable and the dispersion of the knights more common than ever before.[156]

However, a connection to war activity under the king's orders is not only confirmed in the case of the members of the Military Orders. The same connection with war is characteristic of the career of the Cunhas or the Pachecos, whose position at court at the turn of the fifteenth century, while they were military leaders, appears to be closely related to their importance in the king's army. It is also made clear in the many 'quantias' received by the members of these families, expressed by the high number of 'lances' with which they served. The same process is also seen in the case of the court supremacy of the descendants of the Teles family in the fifteenth century, which is connected to their military action in Morocco. However, these families were not regularly associated with the orders, unlike the Pereiras.

Finally, we find a structural tendency of society at the court in Portugal in the circulation of the nobles among the various courts of the Peninsula, which can already be observed in the thirteenth century.[157] This was a movement that to a slight extent during the final period of the Middle Ages connected the entourage of the Portuguese kings in particular to that of the Castilians. This circulation, which is clear in the line of the Meneses and the Albuquerques, as well as the Castros and even the Pachecos at the Portuguese court of the fourteenth century, precedes a parallel movement of involvement of Portuguese lineages in the Castilian court in the fifteenth century. It is a strong argument in favour of the existence of a true Peninsular, noble, court *koiné*, not merely based, as suggested by genealogists, upon the spatial contiguity of the two kingdoms or on the existence of family relationships established through marriage alliances. It seems to me to be based also on the dispersal of patrimonies and revenue which court life favoured, so acting as a powerful factor of displacement of lineages and a growing mobility among the nobility. In my opinion, the interest demonstrated by the monarchs of the fifteenth century, whether in Portugal or in Castile, by the promotion of strategies of setting roots of lineages through practical facts of succession such as the *morgadios/mayorazgos*, actually counteracts this tendency and acts as a 'taking root' of the nobility at court, which appears equally beneficial to the political interests of the kings.[158]

The analysis used to approach the vicissitudes of these families for a longer period, covering one and a half centuries, also allows for a better detection

[156] Luis Adão da Fonseca, 'Algumas considerações a propósito da documentação existente em Barcelona respeitante à Ordem de Avis: sua contribuição para um melhor conhecimento dos grupos de pressão em Portugal em meados do século XV', *Revista da Faculdade de Letras* (Oporto), 1 (1984), 19–56.

[157] Henrique David and José Augusto Sotto Mayor, 'Nobres Portugueses em Leão e Castela (século XIII)', *Revista de História* (Oporto), 7 (1987), 135–50.

[158] Rita Costa Gomes, 'A curialização da nobreza', in Diogo Ramada Curto (ed.), *O tempo de Vasco da Gama* (Lisbon: CNCDP–Expo 98, 1998), pp. 245–64 and 387–8.

of circumstances that were marked by a great instability of positions for the nobility of the court. This instability nurtures this type of pendular movement between Portugal and Castile and is made clear in the description of the lines of this small group of relationships prominent at the Portuguese court. Events such as the dynastic mutation and rebellions of 1383–85 in Portugal are more visible times of change, but are only seen as 'strong times' within a greater period, whose beginning can be dated from the 1350s, and this involved these nobles in successive waves of rupture in their careers, emigration and reintegration at court, all of which culminated in the troubled final period of Fernando's reign.

Between 1373 and 1375, and again in 1381–82, two available sets of information relative to exile, imprisonment and confiscation of goods of courtiers express this conflict more clearly. Thus we have in 1373 the exile of Gomes Lourenço de Avelar, the *guarda-mor* of the king[159] and, around 1375, there are several confiscations of possessions concerning Vasco Martins de Sousa, Lopo Dias de Sousa I, Martim Vasques da Cunha II, Lançarote Pessanha, João Lourenço da Cunha and Diogo Lopes Pacheco (the last two of whom were affected perhaps in 1372 or 1373) and also Rui Vasques Pereira.[160] Between that year and 1380 we know, too, of the withdrawal of two more modest individuals, Domingos Anes 'Arrepiado' and the *vedor da fazenda*, Pero Afonso Mealha.[161] I have already referred to conflicts occurring throughout the same period in the household of Leonor Teles, which placed her in opposition to other noblewomen of her entourage.[162] Between 1381 and 1382 Gonçalo Vasques de Azevedo and the bastard brother of the king, the Master of Aviz, also fell into disgrace, and were followed by other nobles connected to the Infante João, the son of Inês de Castro, such as Diogo Gonçalves Barreto, Rodrigo Afonso Lobo, or the Galician, Garcia Afonso de Sobrado.[163]

However, downstream of the crisis the agitation within this circle is also evoked by the events of 1397–98, which led to the exile of the Cunha, the

159 ANTT, *Ch. D. Fernando*, 1, f. 124.

160 See, respectively, ANTT, *Ch. D. Fernando*, 1, f. 176v; ANTT, *Ch. D. João I*, 1, f. 59v; ANTT, *Ch. D. Fernando*, 1, ff. 169v, f. 171; 2, f. 45v; ANTT, *Ch. D. João I*, 1, f. 62v; ANTT, *Ch. D. Fernando*, 1, f. 165v. In the work of Maria José Ferro quoted, the majority of these documents had already been used, but the connections to court are not systematically identified.

161 It was stated of Domingos Anes, the *amo* of the Master of Christ Nuno Freire de Andrade, that 'andava trautando casamento' between the Infante D. João and D. Maria Teles: ANTT, *Ch. D. Fernando*, 4, f. 28v. Fernão Lopes, on the other hand, named a member of the Pereira family as being involved in these treaties: *CR Fernando*, p. 356. On the *vedor* Pero Afonso Mealha: ANTT, *Ch. D. João I*, 1, f. 114v and also *Desembargo*, p. 371.

162 Besides the example referred to above of Mécia Rodrigues de Meira, the conflict with her sister Maria Teles can be quoted, which led to the sale of the possessions of the latter 'por justiças': Arnaut, *A crise nacional*, p. 132 (where the author suggests that there were financial debts).

163 The facts relating to the Master of Aviz are much referred to by Fernão Lopes: *CR Fernando*, pp. 487–500. On the remainder: ANTT, *Ch. D. Fernando*, 2, ff. 89 and 90; *CR Fernando*, pp. 369 and 380. See also Maria José Ferro Tavares, 'A revolta dos mesteirais de 1383', in *Actas das III Jornadas Arqueológicas* (Lisbon: Associação dos Arqueólogos Portugueses, 1978), pp. 359–83.

Pimentel and the Pacheco families and some others and, in a more diverse way, this agitation is also evoked by the reorganisation of the actual entourage of the Portuguese king, which continued until 1408.[164] This second phase of instability was no less important, in the context of the court, than that which had occurred during the reign of Fernando or that of the mutations that occurred owing to the interregnum. According to Peter Russell, the crisis of 1397–98 must have been enormous, and indeed led to a request for help by the new king to his relative, Richard II of England. In June or July of 1398 Richard authorised the purchase of a variety of military equipment destined for Portugal as well as the departure from Dartmouth of an English captain with 150 men at arms and archers to assist John.[165] In the social universe of the court, the chronology of the successive moments of conflict and change thus allows us to place the better-known instability which accompanied the dynastic crisis in a circumstantial tendency which is not limited to the short period of 1383–85. On the other hand, from the point of view of this group of families, in spite of the effervescence of political behaviour of some nobles and the general climate of social revolt, the interregnum of 1383–85 did not necessarily mean a decline in positions occupied at court. As we have seen, a reasonable number of elements of various noble families survived this particularly troubled time or even the entire period and both maintained and even reinforced their positions.

Studied more closely, the linear structure of these families is seen as one of the factors of highly effective adaptability, although in a way it is obscured by the genealogical narrative in its systematic reinterpretation of this structure, according to criteria of hierarchy of the various lines of descent. Through a characteristic reasoning of retro-projection, these texts suggest a static interpretation of the hierarchic position of the family, which genealogical narrative may wish to see immobilised and 'crystallised' in the mythical time of its origins, suggesting a series of tales connected to legendary or historical occurrences, or to particularly charismatic common antecedents. The reality of the family lines in the social context of the age reveals, however, a picture of greater dynamism and plasticity. The decline of a line of succession was frequently accompanied by a simultaneous ascent of other descendant lines of the family, as in the particular example of the Cunhas. In other cases, the succession through the female line or even the pure and simple reclaiming of the succession by collateral lines reinforces a characteristic process of social promotion of the time: the seeking by nobles of any form of ancestry which might place them close to the prestigious horizon of the older families of the kingdom. Although they owed much of their position both to military and to court functions of the more recent family

164 Mitre Fernández, *La emigracón de nobles Portugueses*. His theme is taken up again by Humberto Baquero Moreno, 'La lutte de la noblesse portugaise contre la royauté à la fin du moyen âge', *Arquivos do Centro Cultural Português*, 26 (1989), 49–65.

165 Russell, pp. 547–8.

members, court families claimed a supremacy based on blood and ascendancy. To this inextricable complex of social and textual logic we owe the fascinating palimpsest of late-medieval genealogical literature with the systematic retelling of preserved family memories operating on successive reconstructions.[166]

The serving nobility

I have placed the remaining group of noble families as being in a hierarchically inferior position. They are characterised by their continued presence at court through various political vicissitudes as well as natural, involuntary extinction or emigration which occurred throughout these troubled years. Among these are the Vasconcelos, the Avelar, Azevedo, Meira, Moura, Abreu, Pessanha, Ataíde, Azambuja, Resende, Coutinho, Góis, Pimentel, Camelo, Coelho, Andrade, Brito, Barreto, Cerveira, Fonseca, Melo, Távora and Teixeira families. As we shall see, all these have in common a systematic association with various posts and organisations within the Portuguese court, that is the effective service of the monarchs which was in general the structural core of their presence at court.

Similar to the lines described for the Cunhas or the Silvas in the diversity of posts which they held and in the multiple lines of descent which developed in parallel within the court, we find some Portuguese families who progressed in the royal service such as the Azevedos, the Ataídes, the Coutinhos, the Fonsecas, the Melos or the Vasconcelos. Frequently interrelated, through their proximity to the monarchs these nobles acquired an increasing position and importance at the end of the Middle Ages.

This was the case with the Azevedos, who were with Afonso IV and Pedro and who lived through the difficult situation of the final decades of the fourteenth century, strengthening their presence in the court of the monarchs of the house of Aviz. During the fourteenth century those who are prominent are Gomes Pais de Azevedo and his sons Gonçalo (the *alferes* at the battle of Salado) and Rui, as well as Diogo Gonçalves de Azevedo, who was in the entourages of Afonso IV and Pedro. The same line continued at the court of Fernando, with Álvaro Gonçalves Azevedo and the bastard son of a nun in the family, Gonçalo Vasques de Azevedo, who was *marechal*. With John I we find Martim Gonçalves de Azevedo, the son of Fernando's *privado*, and Pero Lopes de Azevedo. Luis de Azevedo served Duarte and Afonso V (this also during his regency) as the *vedor da fazenda*, while in the 1460s his descendants prospered at the court of Afonso. These were the bastard João Rodrigues de Azevedo, Rui Gomes de

[166] Gabrielle Spiegel, 'History, historicism and the social logic of the text', in *The Past as Text: The Theory and Practice of Medieval Historiography* (Baltimore: Johns Hopkins University Press, 1997), pp. 3–28. See on this problem the important contribution of Luis Krus, *A concepção nobiliárquica do espaço Ibérico (1280–1380)* (Lisbon: Fundação Calouste Gulbenkian, 1994).

Azevedo and Gonçalo Gomes, as well as Rui Dias de Azevedo, who were all related to each other.

In the case of the Ataídes, we see their influence growing in the shadow of the Teles family during the reign of Fernando, such that they became integrated in the group of the 'Great' in the list of *moradores* at the court of John and, by occupying a multiplicity of posts with the Aviz infantes, they became confirmed in hierarchical positions of importance in the heart of the court nobility of the fifteenth century. So it was that the brothers Nuno and Martim Gonçalves de Ataíde I accompanied Afonso IV, while Gil Martins de Ataíde was a member of the entourage of his son, the Infante Pedro. At the court of Fernando, Martim Gonçalves de Ataíde II and Gonçalves Viegas de Ataíde were protected by Leonor Teles. The descendants of both these accompanied John I and his sons. These were Álvaro Gonçalves de Ataíde with his brother Vasco Fernandes, Pero Nunes and Nuno Gonçalves de Ataíde. In the entourages of Duarte and Afonso V were descendants of Nuno Gonçalves de Ataíde, such as Pero de Ataíde II. Also present, however, was the line of Álvaro Gonçalves: Martinho de Ataíde and the priors of the Hospital, João and Vasco de Ataíde, and Álvaro de Ataíde II. Among the younger generations of this family, around the middle of the fifteenth century, were Filipe de Ataíde and Pedro de Ataíde III.

In the mid-fourteenth century the Coutinhos began an upward trajectory, and were also prominent in the royal army, where in the following century one of the branches held the important post of *marechal*. Vasco Fernandes Coutinho accompanied Pedro and perhaps Fernando, with whom his son Gonçalo Vasques was also to be prominent. He was *marechal* to John I, as were his descendants Vasco Fernandes Coutinho I and Fernando Vasques Coutinho, and all were members of the royal council during the fifteenth century. We also find at the court of John their relatives, Luis Gonçalves and Álvaro Gonçalves Coutinho as well as João Rodrigues Coutinho, who died in Tangier. Fernão Coutinho and Diogo Soares Coutinho are suggested as having served Duarte. Finally, Gonçalo Vasques Coutinho and his son of the same name served at the court of Afonso V, as did the youngest sons, Álvaro Coutinho II and João Coutinho.[167]

Although it is less clear, the fortune of the Fonsecas seems also to have been with the royal army in the various branches of this family at court from the fourteenth century. Fernão Martins da Fonseca and his brother Gonçalo Martins were with Afonso IV, as were Lourenço Vasques and his son Vasco Lourenço da Fonseca. At the court of Pedro and Fernando, Rui Peres da Fonseca of the Order of Santiago and his son Pero Rodrigues da Fonseca were prominent. Several Fonsecas also served the monarchs of the house of Aviz.

In the case of the large Melo family we find several lines claiming the succession of the posts of *guarda-mor* and *copeiro-mor* from the reign of Duarte, and

[167] On the Coutinhos, see Luis Filipe Oliveira, *A Casa dos Coutinhos: linhagem, espaço e poder (1360–1452)* (Cascais: Patrimonia, 1999).

this is perhaps the moment of their greatest importance. As with the Cunhas, this family saw one of its branches decline with the dynastic change. The earlier origins of the Melo family seem to lie in the prestigious twelfth-century family of Riba de Vizela. Their connection with the court of the kings of Portugal is found in the middle of that century, with one of the antecedents of the Melos named as 'privado' of Afonso III.[168] Still in the fourteenth century we find, with Pedro and Fernando, Martim Afonso de Melo I with his sons Vasco Martins de Melo I and Martim Afonso de Melo II and his successors, Pedro and Fernando. With the monarchs of Aviz it was the descendants of Vasco Martim I who became prominent at court, while the remaining members of the family chose to go into exile. This branch of the Melos seems to have improved its position substantially following the crisis of 1397–98, in particular Martim Afonso de Melo III (who had earlier been connected with Nuno Álvares Pereira), who was the *guarda-mor* of John I. He was the father of Duarte's *guarda-mor* and also of João de Melo, who became *copeiro-mor* following Alfarrobeira.

The sole exception in this general panorama of promotion is the line of the Vasconcelos, whose presence at the court dates back to the reign of Dinis.[169] The curious relationship of the brothers Mem Rodrigues de Vasconcelos, the *meirinho-mor* to Dinis, with Nuno Rodrigues (*mordomo* of the bastard Afonso Sanches) and João Rodrigues (*mordomo* to the Infante Afonso) seems to have controlled important positions in the court circle from the beginning of the fourteenth century. At the court of Afonso IV we once again find Mem Rodrigues de Vasconcelos, with his son Gonçalo Mendes I, as well as João Rodrigues de Vasconcelos II and João Mendes de Vasconcelos, who continued in the entourage of Fernando as did the son of João Mendes, Mem Rodrigues II. The family seems, however, not to have remained so constantly at court in the fifteenth century. Mem Rodrigues de Vasconcelos II, the Master of Santiago at the court of John I, was perhaps the most notable member of the line at the time of the new dynasty. However, at the court of John we find only his bastard nephew Rui Vasques Vasconcelos (or Ribeiro) residing at court. His descendants were then to accompany Duarte and Afonso V, and were to take this other surname, which came through the female line.

Constantly and more than occasionally connected to the Military Orders, as was the case of the families referred to above, we find in the service of the king at court the Pimentel, the Andrade, the Góis, the Camelo and the Avelar families, who are all perfect examples of the process of 'courtisation of warriors', in this case of the knights of the Orders. In the first of these, the

[168] Isabel Castro Pina, 'Linhagem e património: o senhorio de Melo na idade média', *Penélope*, 12 (1993), 9–26.

[169] On the Vasconcelos of the thirteenth century, see Ventura, 'A nobreza de corte', vol. I, pp. 368–70.

Pimentel family, their presence alongside the monarchs was to date from the fourteenth century, and to strengthen in the reign of Fernando, with distinct adherence to the cause of the opponents of Trastâmara, who took refuge at the Portuguese court.[170] The exile of João Afonso Pimentel, the principal member of this family at the court at the end of the fourteenth century, determined their decline in Portugal and their consequent ascent at the court of Castile in a trajectory analogous to that of the Pachecos.

As for the Andrade family, who originated from Galicia, their connection to the Portuguese kings was due in great part to the court career of the Master of Christ, Nuno Rodrigues 'Freire', who was with Pedro and Fernando, and this determined the participation of his direct descendants in the royal entourage up to the reign of Afonso V. Nuno Freire was in fact one of the principal individuals at the fourteenth-century court, and among his descendants are Rui Freire, Gomes Freire and João Freire, who attended the court of John I. João Freire de Andrade II, the *aposentador-mor*, and Gomes Freire II and his son Luis Freire are the best-known courtiers of this family during the reigns of Duarte and Afonso V.

The de Góis family, a bastard branch of the Farinhas, was connected to the Order of Hospitallers from the first decades of the fourteenth century and became prominent in the *câmara* during the reign of Pedro, in particular Pedro Vasques de Góis, the *escrivão da puridade*. Both Álvaro Vasques de Góis II and the son of the clerk Pero Vasques da Pedra Alçada (or Góis), who were vassals of the Teles family at the end of the century, moved to the service of the monarchs of the house of Aviz and retained their connection with the Order, as also occurred in the case of the prior of the Hospital, Nuno Gonçalves de Góis, a faithful follower of Leonor of Aragon.

Finally, the Camelos, whom we find in the entourage of Afonso IV, appear connected to the Pereiras and also the Hospitallers during the second half of the fourteenth century. Álvaro Gonçalves Camelo I, who disputed the priorship of Crato with Pedro Álvares Pereira during the reign of Fernando, became prominent during the period 1383–85 through his assistance to the Master of Aviz. He took part in the council of the new king and was his *marechal* and *meirinho-mor* until the political crisis of 1397–98. He was temporarily in exile in Castile but returned to the service of John I at his court where there was also his son of the same name, Álvaro Gonçalves Camelo II, whose descendants attended court during the reigns of Duarte and Afonso V, and in the meantime abandoned their family name.

The Avelar family demonstrates a similar trajectory following their relative good fortune with Beatriz of Castile in the middle of the fourteenth century to

170 The progress of the Pimentel family and their connection to the Military Orders are perfectly explained by Bernardo Vasconcelos e Sousa, *Os Pimentéis: percursos de uma linhagem medieval Portuguesa (séculos XIII–XIV)* (Lisbon: Imprensa Nacional–Casa da Moeda, 2000).

which I have already referred, and through their connection with the Order of Aviz they were yet another example of the attraction to court of the knights of the Orders. As well as the group of relatives who have already been studied regarding the entourage of the queens, who remained with the Master of Aviz Martim Esteves de Avelar, there is the career of Gomes Lourenço de Avelar at the court of Fernando between 1367 and 1373; the uppermost point of his trajectory was the post of *guarda-mor*. During the fifteenth century his descendants, Sancho Gomes de Avelar and João Gomes de Avelar, were at the court of John I and Duarte.

Here must be emphasised the retention during the entire period studied of a certain series of posts among this group of families connected to the Military Orders, demonstrated in their scant access to the more important posts at court, which contrasts with the exceptional progress shown above of one of the branches of the Pereiras. The continuity found, through this study, of a multiplicity of biographies both at court and in the royal armies is a fundamental problem since these relationships are frequently characterised by a presence in both sectors. The royal army, being a human configuration that had no permanent character similar to that of the court was, however, an important field of action for those who joined it, for it could influence decisively their position at court. Participation in the army meant improvement in social standing, as we shall see. This participation may have played a no less important part as a means to nobility, as was the case in other medieval kingdoms such as England.[171] The theory of a general economic crisis affecting the entire nobility at the end of the Middle Ages based on the fall in income from land has been the subject of a balanced reappraisal, in particular in the wake of the works of, among others, Vale and Génicot.[172] McFarlane remarks, with regard to the English case, that neither the monarchs nor the nobility needed to 'live on their own' exclusively, for they had an increasing range of resources, many of which did not depend on income from land.[173] In this context, war played an extremely important part after 1350, owing to the tendency towards the generalisation of turning to stipendiary pay, and this was the case in Portugal. Added to this was the real possibility of access to other gains through sacking and pillaging and the general practice of ransom and imprisonment, particularly when war was

[171] João Gouveia Monteiro, *A guerra em Portugal nos finais da idade média* (Lisbon: Editorial Notícias, 1998), pp. 22–52.

[172] Malcolm Vale, *War and Chivalry: Warfare and Aristocratic Culture in England, France and Burgundy at the End of the Middle Ages* (London: Duckworth, 1981); Léopold Génicot, 'La noblesse médiévale: encore!', *Revue d'Histoire Ecclésiastique*, 88 (1993), 173–201. For Castile, the state of the question in María Concepción Quintanilla Raso, 'La renovación nobiliaria en la Castilla bajomedieval. Entre el debate y la propuesta', in *La nobleza Peninsular en la edad media. VI Congresso de Estudios Medievales* (Ávila: Fundación Sánchez Albornoz, 1999), pp. 286–7.

[173] K. B. MacFarlane, *The Nobility of Later Medieval England* (Oxford: Oxford University Press, 1973), p. 59.

waged outside the kingdom, as was the case in the fourteenth century, with incursions into Castile and, most of all, in the following century in Morocco.

Among the lineages of lesser nobility, from which the majority of servants of the Portuguese kings were recruited, there are those such as the Meira, the Avelar, the Resende and the Barreto families who appear constantly. The Meiras, a Galician family in Portugal from the thirteenth century, witnessed a golden period at court during the following century.[174] I have already referred to their connections with the household and the clients of Leonor Teles, but this position appears to have declined later on and, in the middle of the fifteenth century, it led to a more discreet presence at the court of John I and the Infante Henry. There we find, in the case of the former, the illegitimate line of Fernando's courtier, with Álvaro de Meira and a *morador* of Henry's, João de Meira, who then became part of the entourage of Afonso V.

The Resendes, who were a branch of the Pimentel family that had become independent at the outset of the period being studied, also appear constantly at court from the fourteenth century until the first decades of the fifteenth, although they never reached positions of importance. Those who attended Afonso IV were Vasco Martins de Resende and his son Gil Vasques. The latter, in spite of being judged guilty of involvement in the death of Inês de Castro, appears to have attended the court of Pedro. Fernão Lopes places him in the entourage of Fernando as *aio* to the young Infante Dinis. Meanwhile, his relative Martim Vasques de Resende and his brother Fernão Vasques were in turn close to John I and attended his court. Vasco Martins de Resende II, a descendant of Martim, is documented as being at the court of Duarte.[175] As for the Barretos, they were present in the entourage of Pedro and Fernando, although their continuing presence is less certain, for Gonçalo Nunes Barreto and his son Diogo Gonçalves (who attended the Infante João, the son of Inês de Castro) seem not to have been related to the Barretos who were connected to the Algarve region whom I have placed in the household of Duarte and Afonso V, and were perhaps members of another line.

For some families, service at court shows characteristics which are almost exclusive within the group of their areas of activity, and are more rarely placed in other fields of Portuguese society of the fourteenth and fifteenth centuries. They are thus a true 'serving nobility' of more recent times and are usually connected to the restricted environment of the royal household and its activities. These are families of a very modest situation when compared with the majority of noble lines written of above, about whom areas of regional settlement or problems of articulation among the various spheres of influence are not clearly identified,

174 On the Meira family in Portugal: J. A. Sotto Mayor Pizarro, 'Os patronos do Mosteiro de Grijó' (unpublished master's dissertation, University of Oporto, 1982), p. 121.

175 On the Resendes: Anselmo Braamcamp Freire, *A Honra de Resende*, offprint of *Arquivo Histórico Português* (Lisbon, 1906).

for they lived mostly within the orbit of the court, and were connected to urban environments most visited by the court. In some cases, as with the Teixeiras, the Pessanhas, the Azambujas and the Coelhos, this service dated from the end of the thirteenth century, which corresponded to a flourishing period in the royal orbit of this level of the minor nobility. Among the magnates of the court of Dinis, the dislike of this type of 'privados' is expressed in some famous *Cantigas de Escárnio*, which generally used the common literary *topos* of material desires and avarice at court. So, Count D. Pedro said of some of these servants of the king and the heir, Afonso:

> seu saber é juntar aver
> e non-no comen nem o dan
> mays posfaçan de quem o dá;
> e, de quanto no reyno ha
> se compre tod'a seu talam.[176]

For example, the Teixeiras did not show disdain for service in the *câmara* at the end of the Middle Ages, and were prominent as clerks and men of letters. Martim Fernandes da Teixeira, a *cavaleiro* in the entourage of Afonso IV, and the bastard João Gonçalves da Teixeira, Fernando's *escrivão da puridade*, are examples of the relative modesty of positions of this family. We find Lopo Teixeira at the court of John I, and the *moradora* of Queen Philippa to whom I have already referred. Perhaps the famous Dr João Teixeira, the man of letters of Afonso V, was related to these royal servants, and also Gonçalo Teixeira, the *escudeiro* of his household during the 1440s.[177] As for the Pessanhas, the power of the post of *almirante* of the kingdom and its Genoese origin, as well as his connections with the mercantile environment, paint a peculiar profile of court ascent stemming from these exclusively urban roots. The connection to the court of Fernando's *almirantes* Lançarote and Manuel, and the other Lançarote Pessanha II during the reign of Afonso V, is well known.

The Azambujas attended the monarchs of the fourteenth century and became connected to the powerful Teles family during the reign of Fernando. With Afonso IV we find João Rodrigues de Azambuja and his nephew, Gonçalo Rodrigues. In turn there is Afonso Esteves de Azambuja, whose connection to the court dated probably from the time of Pedro; he was vassal to João Afonso Telo IV. His son, João Afonso de Azambuja (who is sometimes confused with his paternal uncle, João Esteves), was a prominent member of John's *desembargo*, as we shall see. The family is a good example of this nobility of modest standing,

[176] Vicente Beltrán and Mercedes Brea, *Lírica profana Galego-Portuguesa* (Santiago de Compostela: Xunta de Galicia, 1996), vol. II, pp. 759–60. This *cantiga* would seem to have been particularly for Miguel Vivas and Gomes Lourenço of Beja.

[177] On the Teixeiras in the thirteenth century: Pizarro, 'Os patronos', p. 121; Krus, *A concepção nobiliárquica*, pp. 81–2 and note 109.

although it was entrepreneurial and rose at court during the second half of the fifteenth century.[178]

The difficulties which marked the line of one of the branches of the Coelhos during the reign of Pedro perhaps determined the apparent decline of the family in the court circles, a decline which constantly threatened members of the entourage of the kings from the thirteenth century.[179] Several Coelhos attended Afonso IV and also the young Infante Pedro in the middle of the fourteenth century, among whom were the well-known Pero Esteves Coelho and his brothers. Among members of this family on whom we have information during the reign of Fernando, because of their holding various *alcaidarias* (although there is no proof of his presence in the company of the king), is Egas Coelho, who later became close to the new monarch of the house of Aviz. He was related to the Pachecos, and finally emigrated in 1397 to Castile, where his court progress continued.

In its several facets, this noble presence was, as has been said, the most common characteristic of the entourage of the Portuguese kings. It gives rise to reflections on its coincidence with the episcopal circles of recruitment promoted by royal protection, as was the case with the Britos, who were servants at court and had sprung from a bastard line of bishops connected to the urban aristocracy of Évora. We know of the presence of the bastard Martim Afonso de Brito alongside Afonso IV, and of his descendants, and also João Afonso de Brito II and his son Mem de Brito, who with his brothers Álvaro and Gil de Brito was at the court of the kings of Aviz.[180] This is a similar process to that which later involved the Azambujas, who were connected to the rich region of the Tagus valley and whose participation at court during the fifteenth century favoured the gaining of various dioceses and the fact that one of its members became cardinal following a long career as man of letters of the king. As we shall see, the ecclesiastical career appeared at the end of the Middle Ages as a most effective parallel mechanism of social promotion, and included the petty nobles associated with royal service.

Although one cannot place them at court in the period well before the fourteenth century (as in the cases which I have just cited), the court lines of the Mouras, the Cerveiras, the Abreus and the Távoras are similar in their general aspects. The Mouras, who were members of the entourage of the kings from the reign of Afonso IV, enjoyed with the Coutinhos and the Azambujas (to whom they were also related by marriage) a certain promotion in the world

178 Luciano Cordeiro, 'Diogo de Azambuja', in *Questões Histórico-Colonais*, vol. II (Lisbon: Agência Geral das Colónias, 1936), pp. 92–174.

179 On the status of the Coelhos in the thirteenth century: Mattoso, *Portugal medieval*, pp. 409–35.

180 On the origin of the Britos: Krus, *A concepção nobiliárquica*, p. 107 and notes 202 and 203. See also the charter of institution of the entitlement of the bishop D. João Afonso de Brito, in which it is stated that the family was 'da feitura' of the kings of Portugal: *CDA*, vol. II, p. 73. In the fourteenth century, they were related to the de Beja family (who also were distinguished in court service).

of the fifteenth-century court: Gonçalo Vasques de Moura, who according to the fifteenth-century chronicles was *guarda-mor* to Afonso IV, attended the court of that king with his son Álvaro Gonçalves, who was a member of the royal council. The latter was also part of the entourage of Pedro and Fernando, and took part in various diplomatic missions in the 1370s. The women of this family, as has already been seen, were members of the households of the queens. With the monarchs of Aviz we find the descendants of Álvaro Gonçalves, Lopo Gonçalves de Moura and his sons, Álvaro de Moura and Pedro de Moura, as well as Fernão de Moura.

The Cerveiras and Abreus retained the modesty of their origins and occupied various posts specifically in the service of the *câmara* and the *repostaria* at the end of the Middle Ages. The first of these perhaps had two different lines: in the fourteenth century the Cerveiras who were at court such as Martim Fernandes da Cerveira must have come from the north. In the following century, however, the branch of the family with connections in Santarém was prominent, with Mem Cerveira at the court of John I, while his son Rui Mendes da Cerveira was *aposentador-mor* and Álvaro Mendes da Cerveira *escudeiro* to Afonso V. As for the Abreus, Vasco Gomes de Abreu and Diogo Gomes de Abreu are mentioned as being with Pedro and Fernando, while Queen Philippa's *reposteiro-mor* was Fernão Lopes de Abreu, whose family was at the court of John. In addition Pero Gomes de Abreu and his brother Vasco Gomes were at the court of Duarte and Afonso V. The same connection to the service of the royal household occurred with the Távoras, from which family a large number of the servants of the *repostarias* of the monarchs of Aviz were recruited: their presence at court was during the reign of Pedro. At the end of the fourteenth century we find Lourenço Peres de Távora with this monarch. Fernão Lopes placed his son Pero Lourenço at the court of Fernando; later he was *reposteiro-mor* to John I between 1385 and 1421. The post of *reposteiro* was handed down in this family until the reign of Afonso V.

Some generic problems can be found through an analysis of the lines of this group of noble families. An obviously important phenomenon is the existence of client relationships connecting this minor or more recent nobility to the important families who have been studied earlier, who appear to be a means of probable access to royal service. According to each case and depending above all on the duties and positions occupied at court, this service did not always retain exclusive characteristics, and proximity to the entourage was also common in successive generations, with the descendants of a client of the important nobility assuming at court positions of greater importance relative to how well the family was putting down its roots there. These client relationships, which in the case of the royal army could be relationships of vassaldom, connected other families such as the Ataídes, the Góis, the Meiras or the Azambujas to the Teles family. The Camelos, in turn, appear connected to the Pereiras, as were the Coelhos to the Pachecos. This all suggests that, in the origins of proximity of the Melos in the thirteenth century at the court of the kings, there also lies a connection to the old noble family of Riba de Vizela.

I have already mentioned that the service of the kings tended to structure the line of these families in an almost exclusive manner, and because of this we can consider them as representatives of a status which was based to a greater or lesser extent upon military and even administrative and lettered functions, rather than being based on ascendancy or blood. It is not by chance that we find among these families a claim in a more clear and systematic manner than among the magnates to a hereditary succession in duties and offices which were, in a certain manner, considered as part of their 'status', and a possible object of patrimonial appropriation. Among the later nobles, court duties have a far greater importance in genealogical narrative than the origins, which are at times relatively obscure, of many of these lineages. Which are the areas of service to the monarchs that are particularly prominent in these cases? I have already mentioned the importance of the army, which appears to be connected in the main to the promotion and fortune of the Azevedos and Freires of the fourteenth century, but also the Coutinho, the Fonseca, the Melo and the Avelar families. The sphere of the *câmara*, which is that of the 'purity' of the kings, is the area of choice of the Freires in the fifteenth century, as well as that of the Góis, the Teixeiras, the Cerveiras and Abreus, the two last of whom were frequently to be found in the *repostaria*. During the fifteenth century, the status of the Melos was associated in particular to the service of the *copa* of the kings. Some families in this group developed important connections with the Church of the time, as was the case with the Britos and the Azambujas. These connections were in a large part determined, as we shall see, by the patronage of the monarchs themselves. Royal protection did not merely play an important part in access and promotion to ecclesiastical positions, but facilitated noble status for the descendancy, which on many occasions was illegitimate, of these servants. In turn, for many the Church showed itself as an important source of material prosperity. Considered globally, the nobility in service seems to demonstrate fewer episodes of withdrawal from court resulting from political conflicts during the fourteenth and fifteenth centuries, leading one to conclude that the instability of positions to which I have referred regarding important court nobles played a lesser part in this case. When this instability is found, it can almost always be related to links of clientship uniting these two facets of nobility at court in certain particular cases.

Ruptures and mutations

Besides the motive of continuity, which has been explored thus far, there are other contrasting modes of presence of the nobility at the court of the fourteenth and fifteenth centuries, which are generically characterised by the brevity of their passage and which on many occasions do not survive for more than one or at the most two consecutive or close generations. A systematic study such as that which serves as a basis for my analysis allowed the identification of family lines that are more fleeting as well as for an equation of the problems related to ruptures and changes which also contribute to the representation of court nobility in Portugal.

In the first place, there are the lines of the Castilian and Galician exiles who, particularly between 1360 and 1380, fled to the Portuguese court and formed a precise, confined group whose integration in this sphere was short-lived. Then I shall come to the group of noble families whose line was interrupted during the fourteenth century and who did not manage to overcome this period of instability and conflict at the end of the century for a variety of reasons which cannot always be clearly discovered – their characteristics do not differ, in essence, from the group of families of nobles in service described above. Finally, I shall analyse the rise in the fifteenth century of a 'new' nobility at the heart of the court which encompassed families of varying origins who usually emerged from relative obscurity and had no antecedents connecting them to this position, which was a phenomenon whose importance must be related to the reconstruction of a panorama of mutations at the Portuguese court at the end of the Middle Ages. These different situations, which are in contrast to that of the nobility described so far because of the shorter duration of their presence near the king, show themselves in fact to have few elements in common. Because of this I shall deal with each separately.

The permeability of the Portuguese court with regard to the nobles who came from other regions of the Iberian Peninsula and even more distant areas must, because of the values of the age, be understood as a clear expression of the prestige and autonomy of the Portuguese kings. On this matter, the reply sent in 1451 by Afonso V to the Count of Benavente (who was, by the way, a descendant of the Pimentel family who had been in exile in Castile) is significant when he failed to understand his greeting: 'nos entendemos teer em ello aquella maneira que ssempre em ssemelhantes cassos teuerom nossos amteçesores', the king said. 'A qual he aos ssenhores e fidalguos estramgeiros quamdo per algũas neçesidades a nossos rregnos veessem rreçeberem de nos henparo homrra e merçee em todo aquello que bem possamos *como a liberdade de nosso rreall estado perteemçe*.'[181] The phenomenon which is very common during the fourteenth and fifteenth centuries is well known in other neighbouring medieval European kingdoms, as in the case of the attraction of continental nobles to the service of the English kings or the French nobility who were at the court of the Iberian kings. The endemic state of war that prevailed during this troubled time also forcefully contributed towards this mobility of the nobility.

[181] *MH*, vol. XI, p. 57 (my italics).

There was also in Portugal a tradition of immigration, particularly among those nobles who came from around Galicia, and this can be seen as a long-lasting phenomenon dating from the origins of the kingdom. According to Garcia Oro, the continuity of this preference for immigration of Galician nobility to Portugal must be related to their relative indifference to the Andalusian conquests, which formed a sphere of privileged expansion for other members of the nobility of the western regions of the Peninsula.[182] However, not always did this migratory movement lead the nobles to become part of the entourage of the Portuguese monarchs, or even to place themselves systematically in their service, either through a relationship based on vassaldom through the gaining of a tenancy or palace position[183] or, later, by belonging to the royal army and receiving fief-rente (or 'quantia') in payment for military or diplomatic services. This second type of relationship, which was more common in the later Middle Ages for the nobles who were not connected to the monarch by the ties of 'natureza', can be proved only for a restricted number of individuals from other Iberian regions who settled in Portugal.[184] However, it is essential to prove this if we wish to study the presence and eventual influence of these nobles at the Portuguese court, for it is a valuable indicator of a truly significant interaction, rather than a presence which is merely episodic, alongside the Portuguese kings and queens. For some of the more important noble families of the court, such as the Castros, the Meneses or the Albuquerques, I have called to mind the better-known examples of trajectories in the origin of which we recognise the figure of the noble refugee or of one who increased his area of influence in Portugal by living close to the king and placing himself at his service. On many occasions, these nobles settled in Portugal without necessarily abandoning their positions and patrimonies in other areas of the Peninsula or their connections, even though these may have been secondary, with the regions of origin and networks of families and alliances.

It is the 1370s and 1380s that stand out in this generic panorama of mobility and opportunity which can still be seen to exist at the end of the Middle Ages because of the intensity and importance of migratory movement. The number of nobles who went to Portugal from the neighbouring kingdom was large during this period and in the majority of cases these families sought refuge from the instability and violence that marked the civil war in Castile and the subsequent triumph of the bastard Henry of Trastâmara over Pedro the Cruel. Clearly not all would have attended the Portuguese court, although the majority

182 Garcia Oro, *La nobleza Gallega*, p. 10.

183 An aspect analysed at length for the period prior to the fourteenth century by Mattoso, *Ricos-homens, infanções e cavaleiros*, pp. 122–31 and 137–8.

184 On the ties of vassalage and 'natureza' in the west of the Peninsula and the eventual contradiction which may have existed between them: Hilda Grassotti, *Las instituciones feudo-vasalláticas en León y Castilla* (Spoleto: Centro Italiano de Studi sull'Alto Medioevo, 1969), vol. II, pp. 1036–7.

did place themselves in the service of Fernando in the war. The Portuguese monarch also became involved in the conflict with Trastâmara and, from 1369, was linked, although somewhat equivocally and irregularly, with the group of supporters of the legitimist cause. Among the many individuals (many of whom have been identified by Peter Russell and Maria José Ferro) whose movement in Portugal can be reconstructed through references in documents from the reign of Fernando and mention made of them by Fernão Lopes, it is possible to sketch some distinctions which may eventually contribute to an explanation of the characteristics of their differing proximity to the court.

We thus have some Galician nobles in the service of Fernando who in the main played a part in his army, as was the case with several members of the Andeiro, Bolaño, Lira and Parada families. Many of them were connected to the Castros, particularly Fernando Peres de Castro, who headed Pedro's cause and who, as already seen, fled temporarily to Portugal. Some of these Galician who had come at the end of the 1360s, such as members of the Ambia, Novoa, Seabra, Sotomayor and Turrichão families, found branches of their families already established in Portugal, although these had little access to court circles: this was petty nobility connected to the frontier of the Minho or Trás os Montes regions who became prominent in Fernando's army or in obtaining *alcaidarias*.[185]

The situation of the several Castilian and Galician nobles who can be connected to the Military Orders appears different, both in Portugal and in Castile. This is the case with some members of the Campos, Giron and Castel families (all of whom were associated with the Order of Alcântara), the Cordobas (the Order of Calatrava) and the Meiras (the Order of Hospitallers). The mobility of the knights of the Orders was quite accentuated during the entire fourteenth century, which explains the existence of Galician masters in Portugal such as Nuno de Andrade, who has already been mentioned, or the Portuguese masters in Castile, such as Pedro Esteves Carpinteiro. This indicates traditions of recruitment which would make the presence of these nobles in both kingdoms natural.[186] Some, as was the case with the Meira family, had also had relatives in Portugal since the previous century, including some who were connected to the court, as already seen. The majority of these *cavaleiros* were in the pay of the Portuguese king and fought for him, with only a small proportion of those about whom information is available taking part in the court circle.

Finally, we have the group which was more strongly represented at court, made up of the political 'refugees'. The majority of these were Castilian and

[185] For example the Turrichão family (or Churrichão, as appears at times in Portuguese documents) were among the known clients of the Castros, and some of their members are once again documented in Galicia after 1382, where they lived with the Count of Trastâmara, Pedro Henriques de Castro. It should be noted that all these families are referred to in the *Livro de Linhagens* of D. Pedro. On the gaining of *alcaidarias* in Portugal, see Tavares, 'A nobreza no reinado de D. Fernando'.

[186] *LL Conde*, 34Q5; Díaz Martín, *Los Oficiales de Pedro I*, pp. 148 and 151–2.

during the decades prior to 1360 held posts in the household and court of Pedro the Cruel. These were members of the Burgos, Cáceres, Carvajal, Palenzuela, Terraza, Villega and de Aza families. We therefore find among others in Portugal the *alcaide* of the court (and the 'merino mayor' of Burgos), Alfonso Fernández de Burgos; the *chanceler* and *ouvidor* of the audience of the Castilian king, Diaz Sánchez de Terrazas; or the family of the *escrivão da puridade* to Pedro the Cruel, Mateos Fernández de Cáceres, as well as the family of the *camareiro*, Alfonso Gonzalez de Carvajal. The Palenzuelas (Palenzol or 'Palaçoilo' in Portuguese documents) were connected to the Castilian king's treasury, while the Villegas (in Portuguese documents Vilhegas) and de Azas (Daça in Portugal) were connected to several departments of the household and court of Peter. In the case of the de Azas, some of those who were present at the Portuguese court had come from earlier exile in England. These were trusted men of the Castilian king, usually of modest origins, and formed a 'nobility in service' of lower standing than the magnates. Their promotion was a main cause of the violent revolt of the nobility against Peter's government, as Salvador de Moxó reminds us.[187]

The fierce battle between the 'emperogilados' (or 'perjurados', as Fernão Lopes called them) and those who followed Trastâmara, or the 'anricados', as they were called at the Portuguese court, seems also to have been reflected in exile. This is the most probable interpretation which must be given to some of the confiscations of goods made by Fernando during the last two decades of his reign. For example, the noble Galician Juan Rodriguez de Biedma (or Bema) had his goods confiscated in 1369, the year when Pedro's supporters went to Portugal following the events of Montiel. Juan de Biedma had, from the 1350s, been one of the most prominent followers of Henry who had earlier on sought refuge in Portugal.[188] The entourage of Fernando would therefore have been seen as being involved in a political scenario of larger proportions, as Peter Russell has so clearly pointed out. The influence of the Castilian and Galician nobles at the court was, therefore, a factor that cannot be ignored in the analysis of conflict in palace circles during this period, to which I have already referred.

Of all this varied contingent of the immigrant nobility, integration at the court of Fernando can only be confirmed for a handful of individuals whose careers are better known. Among the Galicians, there is João Fernandes Andeiro, an adventurer and agent of Richard II of England during the 1370s who, in Portugal, became Count of Ourém and *mordomo* of the infante heir in the following

[187] Salvador de Moxó, 'La nobleza Castellana en el siglo XIV', *Anuario de Estudio Medievales*, 7 (1970–71), 493–511.

[188] This noble of Galician origin would have been *copeiro-mor* to Pedro of Castile before 1353, and Mem Rodriguez de Biedma (perhaps his brother) was *guarda-mor* of this king until at least 1361: Díaz Martín, *Los oficiales*, p. 79. Juan Rodriguez, who adhered to the cause of the revolt of the bastard Henry *c.* 1353, fled to Portugal after this date. On the confiscation of his possessions (which were later given to Álvares Peres de Castro): ANTT, *Ch. D. Fernando*, 1, f. 46; ANTT, drawer III, batch 11, 8; *CR João I*, vol. I, p. 201.

decade.[189] There were also exiled Galicians such as the cousins Aires Peres and Vasco Peres de Camões who were at court; Paio Rodrigues Marinho; the previous *merino mayor* of Galicia, Soeiro Anes de Parada; and the captain of Fernando's fleet, Gonçalo Tenreiro, who was connected to the Master of Christ, Nuno de Andrade. The court career of the Andalucian Juan Alfonso de Baeza (called João Afonso de Beça by the Portuguese) was parallel to that of Andeiro. He too had been in England between 1373 and 1381, when he took his chance in the entourage of the Portuguese king, although he was less successful than Andeiro. Among the Castilians at court were certainly Alfonso Fernández de Burgos and Alfonso Rodríguez de Cordoba, who were Fernando's diplomatic agents; Fernando Alvares de Queiroz, who was a trusted man of João Afonso Telo IV; João Fozin (or Foçim), captain of Fernando's fleet; and Fernando Afonso de Zamora, who also came from England, where he had been between 1373 and 1381.

In some cases, the stay of these nobles in Portugal continued into the reign of John I,[190] but their integration at court at the end of the fourteenth century was usually characterised by the precarious nature of the positions they had acquired. The rare number of occasions on which they were granted a court position is very clear, as are their marriage alliances, which only exceptionally brought them into this circle. It was a transitory presence, but still important for the evaluation of the period at the end of the reign of Fernando which was marked, at court, by the double influence of the exiled followers of Pedro and of the English. The new version of the 'Livro de Linhagens do Conde D. Pedro', dating between 1380 and 1383, shows particularly clearly the reaction of one part of Fernando's nobility to the presence of these exiles, in particular the Galicians. As Luis Krus found, through a careful analysis of genealogical narrative, in these texts there is clear opposition between those lineages already rooted in Portugal, such as the Pereiras, and the 'new' Galicians cavalry, who were 'ready to excite internal and external discord to prosper and grow wealthy by them'.[191] The old noble and feudal Galicia, where the great families liked to claim their roots and ascendancy, was not part of the argument, for these combined the motive for the foundation of the Portuguese kingdom with the independent disposition of the nobility of the westernmost Peninsula and with the fighting

[189] Among the nobles whom the chronicler Lopes places in the circle of Andeiro are: Martim Gonçalves de Ataíde, João Afonso Pimentel, Pero Rodrigues da Fonseca and Fernando Afonso de Miranda. On his stay in England and several trips to Portugal between 1371 and 1380: Peter E. Russell, 'João Fernandes Andeiro at the court of John of Lancaster', *Revista da Universidade de Coimbra*, 14 (1940), 20–30.

[190] João Afonso de Baeza (or Beça) went on to serve the Master of Aviz in 1383, and in the following year he became a member of his council. However, his presence cannot have lasted beyond 1384. Gomes Garcia de Hoyos (Foios) was also in the campaigns of 1384 and 1387, possibly in the pay of the new king. In his turn, the son of Álvaro de Cáceres, Luis Mendes, was with John I at the beginning of his reign.

[191] Krus, *A concepção nobiliárquica*, pp. 274–88 and esp. p. 276.

values attributed to them. What was in question was, as Krus states, a dark vision of a time characterised by 'contamination and a continuously degraded nobility' associated with the Galician influx, in open criticism of the protection which the Portuguese king granted the exiles.

A varied group of questions would be, as stated above, that which makes one note the apparent inconsistency in the participation of a certain number of noble families at the Portuguese court when analysed during this secular period, since in the early fourteenth century we find this presence in the entourage of the king, while signs of this presence are more or less definitively lost by the end of the century. It must be emphasised that, with the knowledge we have at present, this group of families appears to be highly heterogeneous. The variation of available sources is not a relevant factor in the explanation of their dying out, for these sources increase in quantity and are more widely available for the fifteenth century and in general improve the quality of data available.

The Portocarreiro and Cogominho families found growing prosperity at court during the fourteenth century, although their presence is not noteworthy during the fifteenth. The first of these families also played a part in the Castilian court of the fourteenth century during the reigns of Alfonso XI and Pedro the Cruel through the activities of other, Portuguese, branches of the family.[192] We find the Portocarreiros in Portugal with Afonso IV, but we know that the representatives of the lineage in the entourage of Fernando went into exile with the events of 1383–85, when they continued to serve Queen Beatriz (the daughter of Fernando) and prospered at the court of John II of Castile. Their eclipse in Portugal seems to be due essentially to reasons of a political nature, although in the 1460s we find descendants of the exiled family included, for example, in the entourage of Count D. Pedro. Is this perhaps an indication of a possible return to the sphere of the Portuguese court?[193]

The Cogominhos are the best example of ascent in court service during the fourteenth century of families having connections with urban areas in the south of the country. Fernão Gonçalves Cogominho, the *copeiro-mor* to Afonso IV, also served the king as his *meirinho-mor*. The presence of the family is seen at the end of the reign of Dinis, in circles close to the monarch, with the *almirante* Nuno Fernandes Cogominho, who was the uncle of Fernão Gonçalves.[194] In the court of Afonso, the success of Fernão Gonçalves was accompanied by an expansion of his influence in the Alentejo, and there is every indication of accumulation

192 Krus, *A concepção nobiliárquica*, pp. 191–2 and note 444.

193 Luis Adão da Fonseca, *O Condestável D. Pedro de Portugal* (Oporto: INIC, 1982), p. 350. As Dias Dinis emphasised, John I continued to be in contact with the descendants of the exiled João Rodrigues, and in particular communicated to his son Martim the conquest of Ceuta in a letter of which Zurara writes: *MH*, vol. II, pp. 204–6 and note.

194 *DP*, vol. I, pp. 26–7. It is known that Fernão Gonçalves was the son of the canon of Lisbon, Gonçalo Fernandes Cogominho, a contemporary of the admiral: *LL Conde*, 30AW5–6. Carolina Michaëlis de Vasconcelos says they are brothers: *Cancioneiro da Ajuda*, vol. II, pp. 555–6.

of a considerable fortune. An analogy is found with well-known examples of some servants of the king in the thirteenth century, such as the court career of D. João de Aboim or de Portel, to whom Cogominho was loosely connected. The descendants of Fernão Lopes Cogominho, João Fernandes, the canon Fernão Fernandes and even the bastard Nuno Fernandes, were connected to Évora. During the reign of Pedro they seem to have lived mostly in the Alentejo, and are not found at court. Added to this, the continuity of the line was threatened following this generation. I have already said that Leonor Teles married one of the exiled Galicians, Paio Marinho, to the widow of João Fernandes, perhaps in an attempt to attract or keep this family as prosperous servants in the orbit of the court. With the exile of Paio Marinho and the subsequent confiscation of his wealth, the Cogominhos seem to have withdrawn from the Portuguese court. The position of the female line of the family must have been weakened, and at least one of them returned to Castile during the reign of Duarte.

Among an inferior nobility whose roots are found at the court of Dinis, those who stand out are the lines of the Bugalho and the Buval families. The Bugalhos, who appear to have been descendants of the king's falconers, are documented as being at the court of Afonso IV and Pedro, and then to fall into obscurity.[195] The Buval family, whose relationship with servants of Queen Beatriz of Castile has already been referred to, appears associated with other families of 'nobility in service' of the fourteenth century, such as the Avelar, Portocarreiro and Cogominho families. They acquired positions of standing at court in the reigns of Pedro and Fernando, including the position of *guarda-mor*, but are not mentioned in the following century.

The inferior standing of this nobility and its decline or eclipse at court during the later phase of the period studied here can also be found for the Ribeiro,[196] Alvim, Barroso, Briteiro, Zote and Rego families. Especially connected to the Military Orders, we also find the Leitão family (the Orders of Christ and Aviz) and the Carvalhos (the Order of Santiago), who were more obviously a part of the retinue of the kings and queens in the fourteenth century. It is hard to discover for any of these the vicissitudes of the diverse family histories which led to their presence at or withdrawal from court. What must be emphasised, however, is the fact that their integration in this circle appears to be far less significant in the general context of my reconstruction, although it must be admitted that some element or other of these family nuclei is to be found among many other

[195] C. M. Baeta Neves, *Subsídios para a história da falcoaria em Portugal*, offprint of *Boletim da Sociedade de Geografia de Lisboa* (Lisbon, 1984). The fortune of the Bugalhos as falconers is referred to by the Castilian infante, D. Juan Manuel, in his *Libro de la Caza* (which can be dated *c.* 1325–28); on the cultivation of this art among the 'caualleros de Portogal': José Manuel Blecua (ed.), *Obras completas* (Madrid: Gredos, 1982), vol. I, p. 527.

[196] As Braamcamp Freire explained, the Ribeiros of the fifteenth- and sixteenth-century court are a branch of the Vasconcelos family: *Brasões*, vol. I, pp. 366–8. See the reconstruction of the genealogy of the Ribeiros of the fourteenth century in Pizarro, Patronos family tree VII.

individuals (usually occupying the more modest posts) identified in sources merely by their first name and patronymic, without family name.

Finally I shall move to the discussion of a phenomenon frequently mentioned regarding this last stage of the Middle Ages, which is the rise of a 'new nobility' with the Aviz dynasty. This 'new nobility' will be represented, in this description, by about twenty families who were prominent in the court social circle of the fifteenth century. In many cases, their origins still remain obscure. However, the hypothesis that they represent secondary branches of the old nobility seems to be given the lie, with rare exceptions which I shall clarify through the peculiar panorama of available sources for the study of this mutation in the world of the nobility. Neither the growing genealogical literature, particularly the *Livro de Linhagens* which was added to and reproduced at the end of the fourteenth century and the *Nobiliário* of the sixteenth century, nor the historiographic production of the fifteenth century, repudiates this prestigious connection with the older families or whether it could be established beyond doubt. On the contrary, it must be stated that a solid panorama marked by continuity is particularly emphasised by these sources, and there is an attempt to place the majority of nobles present at the royal court at the end of the medieval era among the old nobility, whose charisma was to be transmitted to successive generations which were related one to the other. Besides this, the careful use and criticism of biographical data obtained solely from the chronicles and genealogical accounts is a fundamental aspect of my research, for I have sought always to bear in mind that among the objectives of the conscious programme presiding in the elaboration of this type of text is also to be found the legitimisation of the elite of the age through the invention of family and linear memory.

Bearing in mind this particular effect in the construction of my data, the presence of the group of families and lineages which was to occupy me from then on is, as a consequence, a still more important fact. Its impact on the group of the nobility of the Portuguese court lies, essentially, in a renewal and reorganisation of hierarchic relations existing during the final period of the fourteenth century through its integration, which can be seen as rapid because of the practice of matrimonial alliances favoured by royal patronage. Among the nobles in evidence at court in the fifteenth century, those who remained there for several generations in the royal service were always more numerous and were those families whose connections to the king dated at least to the fourteenth century or still earlier. But these welcomed new men of more obscure origin, and the effects of a social mobility which seems to have been accentuated at this time of change and which forms the more generally related aspect in this revival become obvious. Let us now analyse more closely some cases allowed by prosopographic research.

Proximity to the young Master of Aviz, John, seems to have been the principal reason for the presence of some nobles at court following his accession to the throne, and this situation seems to lie in the origins of the presence of the

Almeidas and the Sás in the court environment and, very probably, that of other families such as the Borges, the Barros or the Albergarias. These were all a modest nobility connected to the Military Orders, like the actual Master, who became king as John I. Their access to the court thus represents the experience of a generation which was also that of Nuno Álvares Pereira and John I himself.

Fernão Álvares de Almeida is a fine example of ascent through 'privança' of the new king. Connected to the Order of Aviz, where he held the knighthood of Juromenha, he had served John as *vedor* of his household when he was Master of the Order and continued to serve him when he was king, both as *vedor* and as part of his royal council, as well as being the *aio* of the infantes. His numerous illegitimate descendants remained in the service of the monarchs of the fifteenth century, in particular his son Diogo Fernandes de Almeida, the *reposteiro-mor* of Duarte and *vedor da fazenda*, and his grandson Lopo de Almeida, who was also *vedor da fazenda* and counsellor, as well as being the famous author of an interesting group of letters sent from Italy to Afonso V in 1451–52. Other members of the family who were contemporaries of Fernão Álvares were Martim Lourenço de Almeida, the *reposteiro* of John I and his sons, one of whom served as Duarte's *almotacé-mor*. The Almeidas, who were connected to the household of the king and the *fazenda*, represented a 'nobility in service' which rose with the new dynasty from one particular person through the trust shown him by its founder king. In the same way, the Sás who were at the court were descended from João Rodrigues 'das Galés', the *comendador-mor* of the Order of Christ, who was *camareiro-mor* to the new monarch and his *privado*, perhaps continuing the relationship he had with John I, which dated from the reign of Fernando. Several of his successors also attended the courts of Duarte and Afonso V, and particularly important was the son of João Rodrigues and also the *camareiro* Fernão de Sá and his descendants, João Rodrigues de Sá II and Diogo da Cunha (also known as Sá).

We find the families of *escudeiro*s who served at court in an inferior hierarchic position also descended in many cases from individuals connected to the Military Orders in the reigns of Fernando and John. The Borges and Barros, of whom there were many in the entourage of John I, were for example distinguished in the *puridade* of John's successors, the monarchs of Aviz, either in the *guarda-roupa* or in the service of the *ucharia*. Finally, there are the Albergarias, a branch of the Figueiredos, who were already connected to important courtiers of the reign of Fernando. Gonçalo Garcia de Figueiredo was *aio* to the Infante João, and his cousin Diogo Afonso de Figueiredo was *vedor* of the household of the infante, whom he accompanied into exile. A descendant of Gonçalo, Aires Gonçalves de Figueiredo, was in turn 'aio e governador' to Gonçalo Telo, according to Fernão Lopes, and is perhaps the same person who appears as a famous *monteiro* and *caçador* in the 'Livro de Montaria'. The Albergarias were also in evidence at the courts of John I, Duarte and Afonso V as servants close to the king within the *fazenda*. We find families such as the Furtados preferentially placed in the military sphere of the royal retinue of the fifteenth century. They stemmed from a famous captain of the wars during the reign of Fernando and successively held the post of *anadel-mor* until the reign of Afonso V. More ephemeral is the presence of the Filipes at the court of Aviz, whose origins stemmed from the clients of the Meneses at the end of the fourteenth century.

Regarding this last group of family nuclei, the central problem which arises is, of course, that of their modest standing, which justifies the question: is one in fact dealing with the nobility? The fact that it is not possible to follow at the time the ascendancy of these families beyond the final decades of the fourteenth century makes a definitive reply as to the problem of their origins very difficult. However, the diverse sources used are clear as to their standing: their status was similar to that of the other 'nobility in service', even though we are dealing with a promotion in status considered recent and with a nobility of inferior standing. It is certain that, at least within the ambit of this social circle, these individuals enjoyed the privileges and led the life of the nobility at the beginning of the fifteenth century, while forming a less illustrious stratum and being more dependent upon the king. The same can be said of other servants of the monarchs of Aviz who, in the heart of court society, approached this more modest nobility, which was perhaps not translated into undisputed acceptance of their noble standing in other fields of social activity. Since they were on the fringes of the nobility the problems which their status led to are particularly interesting, and there are naturally important differences of status in relation to the grand nobility or the older families, even those who were by now in relative decline in the court world.

Fernão Lopes spoke in particular in his account of those who had urban origins and became connected to the *fazenda* of the king in the first decades of the century, and we find various members of the Lisbon families of Faria and Valente, or those such as the Freitas and the Sampaios who came from the north of the kingdom.[197] Among the 'new nobility' from the cities who accompanied the Portuguese kings in the fifteenth century there are, however, some families representing large fortunes, such as the Almadas and the Lemos, and with regard to these we can speak of an elimination of hierarchical differences so far referred to, in spite of their burgher roots.[198]

[197] On the chapel of these members of the Freitas family in the church of the Collegiate of Guimarães (and whose construction goes on to 1419): M. A. Pereira Morães, 'Capelas vinculadas na Colegiada de Nossa Senhora da Oliveira', in *Actas do Congresso Histórico de Guimarães e sua Colegiada*, vol. II (Guimarães, 1981), pp. 451–80. The Sampaios, who at the beginning of the fifteenth century were also related to the Freitas family by marriage, were at the court of John and Duarte.

[198] A. S. Costa Lobo, *História da sociedade em Portugal no século XV* (Lisbon: Editora História Crítica, 1979), p. 487; Carlos Riley, 'A Inglaterra como espaço de projecção da memória e imaginário linhagísticos da família Almada', in *Actas do Colóquio Comemorativo do VI Centenário do Tratado de Windsor* (Oporto: Faculdade de Letras, 1988), pp. 161–72.

The first known member of the Almadas was an official of the *fazenda*, and several members of this family (as was the case of the Lemos) were involved in the government of Lisbon. They had been burghers, in the medieval sense of the word, that is members of the merchant elite of the cities who took part in local government oligarchies. In the case of the Almadas, there are the well-known figures of João Vaz de Almada and his son Álvaro Vasques, Count of Avranches; this is a rare case of rise to titular nobility, in this case a title certainly granted by a foreign king. Both were *capitães-mores* during the reigns of John I and Duarte, and their success uniquely illustrates the mobility, as well as the rapid process of the ennoblement of this city elite who were involved in maritime commerce. The path of the Lemos family is analogous. This family with Lisbon origins descended from Gomes Martins, 'criado' of the new monarch of Aviz, and chosen as *aio* to his bastard son D. Afonso. It is probable that the marriage of Gomes Martins to the heiress of the Góis, which took place in 1399, was also due to the protection of the Master. Some years later, Gomes received from John I the ship in which he had gone in 'company' with the Count of Barcelos to Ceuta, and this is a clear indication of his maritime activities. Mécia de Góis, who was by now a widow, used the Medici bank, and lent large sums to the Infante Henry. So we are able to gather many indications of material prosperity of this family during the first decades of the fifteenth century, which tallies with the declaration made by the Lemos family in 1461 that their predecessors 'pesuirom mujtos bens mouees e de rraiz e eram muyto rricos'.[199] Several generations of the Lemos family took part in the royal court of the fifteenth century and, for example, Fernão Gomes de Góis (also Lemos – and note the common preferred use of the more prestigious surname, although it was inherited through the female line) was prominent as *camareiro* to John I. This family rose rapidly, although they did not enjoy the importance of the Almadas, which was to a large degree based on their connections with the English court.

Finally, the actual service of the monarchs at court, in particular in the *desembargo*, the *fazenda* and the positions of clerks, is found in the origin of ascent to the nobility of some families in the fifteenth century who form a small nucleus of what we might call 'nobility of the robe' at the end of the medieval period. These families were able to rise in the royal service during the reigns of Afonso IV and Pedro, as was the case of the Nogueiras, the Lobatos or the do Sem family. In the fifteenth century, the Fogaças, the Gomides and the Castelo Brancos and, more modestly, the Cotrim family and the Gouveias, are shown to have risen up the ladder. I shall deal later in detail with this promotion to noble status of royal officers, which seems directly related to the process of bureaucratisation which I have detected within the court organisation during this period and referred to in the outline sketched above of the configuration of their principal posts in the fifteenth century. While the presence of these families in

[199] *MH*, vol. XIV, p. 148.

the company of the Portuguese monarchs can be proved for the earlier era, it was in the fifteenth century that the officials came to occupy a position of note and prestige in the social heart of the court which eventually led them to various levels of the nobility. From this point of view the Portuguese situation can also be compared with that of other European situations, for example that evoked by Françoise Autrand for the French kingdom, when she concludes that one cannot properly speak of a 'noblesse de robe' before 1400, since it was only during the fifteenth century that ennoblement appears clearly connected to royal service in the judicial and administrative spheres.[200] As we shall see, in Portugal it was frequently through the intermediate step of adoption of the status of *cavaleiro* and through matrimonial alliances favoured by the kings that officials attained a promotion of a similar order, which was progressively confirmed throughout that century.

We witness in the first decades of the fifteenth century this renewal of the nobility at court, be it by the attraction of nobles of inferior standing or through a recruitment which was increasingly broadened within the group of king's servants, clearly favoured by a variety of factors. I shall stress first the well-known movement of emigration which removed to Castile a part of the nobility who occupied important positions at the court of Fernando in two successive waves: 1383–85 and 1396–98. This factor of change is traditionally declared as decisive – the 'new nobility' would result from the withdrawal of a large part of the 'old' – and today this can be more precisely defined. José Mattoso suggested some fifteen years ago the hypothesis that it would have been most of all the heads of the noble lines who abandoned Portugal, while the second sons and more distant relatives, the 'social basis of support of the Master of Aviz', began a rise to more prominent positions with the new dynasty. This thesis has more recently been the subject of reappraisal by Mattoso, with a view to studies being undertaken on practices of succession found throughout the fourteenth century which appear not to be as inegalitarian as he had previously suggested, so making it less probable that there was a connection between the political instability of the nobility and the evolution of family structures.[201] My research also tends to uncover some lines of indisputable continuity among the entourage of Fernando and John I, contributing to a clearer design of the limits of change and recognising that the 'new nobility' was, in every sense, a small minority of families at court. We must put into perspective in a less radical manner the interpretation of the effects of dynastic change in the 'renewal' of the Portuguese nobility, which in reality continues to be poorly studied for

200 Françoise Autrand, *Naissance d'un grand corps d'état: les gens du Parlement de Paris, 1345–1454* (Paris: Publications de la Sorbonne, 1981), esp. p. 297.

201 José Mattoso, 'A nobreza e a revolução de 1383', in *Portugal medieval: novas Interpretações* (Lisbon: Imprensa Nacional–Casa da Moeda, 1992), pp. 277–93; José Mattoso, 'Lección inaugural. A nobreza medieval Portuguesa (séculos X a XIV)', in *La nobleza peninsular en la edad media*, p. 25.

the fourteenth century. From the point of view of its family composition, the nobility at court during the fifteenth century is not very distinct, as we have just seen, from the panorama of the previous century.

Fernão Lopes appears to state the contrary in a well-known passage in his *Crónica de D. João I*, where he mentions this 'new world' and 'new generation of people' who triumphantly appeared with the Aviz dynasty:

> porque filhos dhomeens de tam baixa comdiçom que nom compre de dizer, per seu boom serviço e trabalho, neste tempo forom feitos cavalleiros, chamandosse logo de novas linhagens e apellidos. Outros se apegarom aas amtiigas fidallguias, de que ja nom era memoria, de guisa que per dignidades e homrras e offiçios do reeino em que os este Senhor seemdo Meestre, e despois que foi Rei, pôs, montarom tamto ao deamte, que seus deçendentes oje em dia se chamam doões, e som theudos em gram conta.[202]

The influence of this text on modern historiography is enormous. There often follows an overliteral reading which does not pay attention to its inclusion within a complex of ideas formed by Lopes in the trilogy of chronicles, which suggests a 'refoundation' of the kingdom to which the chronicler attaches the reason for the arrival of the new dynasty, consequently emphasising the 'novelties' of the times which would above all, in this text, be the evident signs of the coming of the 'seventh age' suggested by his millenary scheme.[203] Another present-day historiographic tendency replaces this vision, which stresses the ruptures resulting from the crisis with hypotheses which concede to the mutations of the nobility a decisive role in the interpretation of the actual political crisis of 1383–85. However, the political changes cannot always be made to coincide clearly with the deeper social mutations. The processes of change found in the configuration of the nobility at the court of the kings, and the instability of their political behaviour at the end of the Middle Ages, can reappear in many aspects during the second half of the fourteenth century, while others (as is the case of the growing wealth of many families) are connected to the fifteenth-century expansion and to the new social roles created or proposed within its ambit. And while, for the eleventh and twelfth centuries, we can talk of a disappearance of the magnates who dominate the politics of the old County of Portucale and a subsequent predominance of younger lines connected to the claim for autonomy of the first king of Portugal, it is necessary to recognise that analogous processes of change are not so clearly detectable in the political crisis of 1383–85. Nor is it necessary for them to be so if we abandon the illusion of 'refoundation' so successfully constructed by the fifteenth-century chronicler. It may be said that my perspective is partial, since it is taken solely from the point of view of the court. It cannot be doubted, though, that this was also the point of view of Fernão Lopes.

[202] *CR João I*, vol. I, p. 308.

[203] Luis de Sousa Rebelo, *A concepção do poder em Fernão Lopes* (Lisbon: Livros Horizonte, 1983).

When placed within their precise context, the movements of social ascent must be analysed case by case. For example one must consider, at the level of the process of social promotion, the intensification of the practice of making some royal servants *cavaleiros*, which is amply mentioned by the contemporary chronicles and to which one must pay renewed attention. In the accounts of the great military feats, such as Aljubarrota or Ceuta, there appear lists of *cavaleiros* where we find, respectively, the Almadas, Charnecas, Lobatos, Farias, Castelo Brancos (at Aljubarrota) or then the Almadas, Silveiras, Almeidas, Castelo Brancos, Albergarias (at Ceuta).[204] As is already known, the chivalric ideology was an active, catalytic complex of ideas at the Portuguese court at the end of the Middle Ages, particularly in the fifteenth century.[205] From the reign of Fernando until the middle of the fifteenth century, which corresponds to the period of the entire rule of Afonso V, this would have been a process which was amply used in order to cultivate the splendour of the 'new nobility' which, in many cases, comprised descendants of individuals whom the king distinguished from among the servants in his entourage.[206]

Another factor to consider in this integration of the various sectors of the elite which occurs at the court of the time is the general enrichment of those who benefited from their proximity to the king, all the more notable when this was related to the various initiatives and movements leading to the fifteenth-century expansion in Morocco, on the African coast and in the Atlantic islands – and other opportunities to obtain the material resources which allowed them to 'live nobly'.[207] In this way, the permeability of the noble group seems to have increased in court circles through the relative assimilation of lifestyles allowed by wealth. This assimilation however was not without problems, and led to critical contradictory appreciations by contemporaries. A comparison of noble values suggested by the poetry of the first decades of the fourteenth century, for example by the Conde D. Pedro de Barcelos, with the complex web of arguments of the 'Virtuosa Benfeitoria' (written between 1418 and 1425), suggests similarities and differences in positions. In both cases, these values are based upon a contradiction between 'giving' and 'receiving' in their expressly material meaning. 'Power' and 'gain' are associated in the critical vision of

204 *CR João I*, vol. II, pp. 88–9; *CR Ceuta*, p. 212 *et passim*.

205 For a synthesis on the relationship between the knighthood and the nobility at the end of the Middle Ages: Maurice Keen, *Chivalry* (New Haven: Yale University Press, 1984), pp. 148–53. For Portugal: José Mattoso, 'Cavalaria', in *Dicionário da literatura medieval Galega e Portuguesa*, pp. 152–4.

206 For a comparison, showing how investitures were performed more and more within the court in Castile: Nelly Porro Girardi, *La investidura de armas en Castilla, del Rey Sabio a los Católicos* (Valladolid: Junta de Castilla y León, 1998).

207 Vitorino Magalhães Godinho, *A expansão quatrocentista Portuguesa: problemas das origens e das linhas de evolução* (Lisbon: Empresa Contemporânea de Edições, 1944), in particular pp. 47–9 and 98. See also for a renewed perspective Vitorino Magalhães Godinho, *Mito e mercadoria: Utopia e prática de navegar. Séculos XII–XVIII* (Lisbon: Difel, 1990), pp. 95–6.

the court evoked by the poetry of the old count: 'd'estes privados non sey novelar/ se nom que lhes vejo muy gran poder/ e grandes rendas, casas gaanhar [...] ca os nom vejo dar nen despender/ ante os vejo tomar e pedir'.[208] The fifteenth-century infante cannot resist observing in his translation of Seneca's texts that 'estão cheias as vontades dos Cortesãos, ainda que se louvem de grande fidalguia' with 'autos de comprar e vender', distinguishing clearly the transaction from which stems material gain (which he does not openly condemn) of pure liberality, from the gift which grants prestige and connects men with a new, political tie. This suggests a new vision of this value of liberality which the nobility must have traditionally cultivated, whether in the light of 'giving' or that of 'receiving'.[209] The same dynamic picture of values and ideas also appears in discourses in the parliaments, which were usually based upon the concepts of order of the nobility and which cultivated a rhetoric of exaltation of royal authority, which would be exclusively rivalled by noble 'giving' or 'doing'. In the general chapters 'da Casa e da Fazenda' presented to the Cortes of 1472–73, the representatives of the cities allowed for the existence of three different types of nobles at the court of Afonso V. On the one hand, there were those who were nobles 'de seu próprio naçimento e sangue'. On a par with these was a large group 'dos que vosa merçe faaz de bemfeitoria'; and then a third group, composed of those 'que de sy mesmos tomam estados de fidalgos sem lhos vos primeiro dardes'.[210] Naturally, it was in this third type that the *procuradores* of the cities saw the roots of disorder and subversion of the hierarchies. These hierarchies, in their express opinion, would find in the monarch himself a final guarantor. Wealth as a route to promotion in status appears in this discourse as a common phenomenon, and the 'status of fidalgo' – a concept which we must take in the simultaneously broader and legally more precise sense than the modern concept of 'status'[211] – appears to be a more easily attainable reality for those individuals who resided with the king.

To conclude briefly the analysis of court nobility, there seem to appear through the history of these hundred families some concomitant and complementary processes of the movement towards the making of court life in medieval Portugal which started new modalities of relationships between the monarchs and the nobility and contributed strongly to the definition and transformation of the latter. What appears beyond doubt is the existence at court of an *aristocratisation* of the nobility, or perhaps a diffusion of cultural models

208 Beltrán and Brea, *Lírica profana*, vol. II, p. 762.

209 Infante D. Pedro, *O Livro da Virtuosa Benfeitoria*; M. Lopes de Almeida, *Obras dos príncipes de Avis* (Oporto: Lello, 1981), p. 575. I am indebted to Vitorino Magalhães Godinho for having drawn my attention to this text: '"Entender la praxis de los negocios". Esboço de modelo para a economia dos séculos XV e XVI', in *História das Ilhas Atlânticas* (Funchal: Centro de Estudos de História do Atlântico, 1997), vol. I, pp. 13–39 and in particular 18.

210 ANTT, Cortes, M 2, 14, ff. 65–65v.

211 Kaminski, 'Estate, nobility and the exhibition of estate', p. 689.

which are linked to the reproduction of family traditions, creating a common memory, with the institution of given political relations (as occurred in the case of families of royal blood or the important families) and with material wealth connected to the demonstration of individual and family status.[212] On the other hand, we can speak also of an *ennoblement*, as mentioned regarding the highest echelons of court hierarchy, the relatives of the kings, when they adopted family models of lineage and were granted lordships which made them close in status to other important families at court. However, we can also speak of a process of ennoblement in the case of promotion which took place at the opposite end of the scale, that of the more modest families in the noble world of the court who in some cases had been present for several generations in court service until this promotion could finally take place, either through individual promotion or through recourse to important matrimonial alliances. A third process which I believe essential is that of the valuing of *service* to the king, or the fact of 'ministerialising' (the notion of 'ministerialist' still being genetically connected to specific forms of dependence, which will be discussed in the following chapter) which appears in the Portuguese context as a clearly defined social area, while closely associated with the experience of the nobility and with determined noble values which the court propagated, such as obedience to the king or seeking personal ties to the monarch as a form of distinction. The fact that one of the essential modalities of royal service was the exercise of war cannot, however, conceal the growing importance which other spheres of activity were acquiring and which, in the case of the nobility, constantly encompassed more duties of a bureaucratic, financial and administrative order and social roles which were related to the functioning of state institutions.

THE ECCLESIASTICS

The ecclesiastical presence at court, while in a minority *vis-à-vis* the numerical predominance of the laity surrounding the monarchs in the fourteenth and fifteenth centuries is, however, no less important for a correct understanding of this social world. In the global reconstruction which I am attempting, this presence was a challenge in itself, not merely because of the problematic character of an actual definition of what was an ecclesiastic at the end of the Middle Ages. Naturally I shall not return to the minute codification of the canonical notion of *status vitae*, although this is one of the most relevant aspects of the reflection of the age upon the difference between clergy/laity and another type of social classification of medieval society. Its incidence in three central factors of

[212] Stephen Weinberger, 'The ennoblement of the aristocracy in medieval Provence', *Medievalia et Humanistica*, 20 (1994), 1–14; Kate Mertes, 'Aristocracy', in Rosemary Horrox (ed.), *Fifteenth-Century Attitudes: Perceptions of Society in Late Medieval England* (Cambridge: Cambridge University Press, 1994), pp. 42–60.

understanding of the clerical state – adherence to an *ordo* (with implications of judicial and fiscal privileges); service to the sacred; a distinctive way of life – is perfectly well known and merely draws a normative picture more or less distant from the extraordinary variety of concrete experiences.[213]

The disciplining we witness of this variety in the period following the Middle Ages, particularly in the context of the Reformation, with the construction of diverse structures based on more rigid distinctions regarding the role to be performed by the clergy in society must not lead us to forget that, as emphasised by, among others, Lucien Febvre, the final years of medieval Christianity were, rather, times of normative proliferation and growth, times of turbulence in the search for new solutions. These movements were above all reflected in the worlds of the 'men of the Church' and in their extraordinary expansion and internal differentiation. The evolution of the Church institution during this period, seen by its contemporaries as a period of crisis and change, thus came to influence the way in which the clerical condition was defined and equated within the social context of the era. This evolution appears to be marked by successive ruptures in the leadership of the Church and by a process of laification and temporalisation – inevitable consequences of the way in which the ecclesiastics became involved at the time in almost all aspects of community and individual life. This all contributed, in diverse contexts, to the displacement of the limits that clarity of the juridic norm rationally placed between the clergy, the laity and the religious orders.

It is, for example, beyond doubt that the practice of gifts and the complex mechanisms of the system of benefices which were fully developing at the time[214] linked a considerable number of beneficiaries with the new bureaucracies which surrounded the European monarchs. This was even though these were not clerics in the definitive sense, nor in the traditional distinctions of their mode of life, even though they abandoned to a large extent the effective practice of any religious office. This process was particularly in evidence at the royal court. Some historians do not hesitate to speak of an actual appropriation of income associated with ecclesiastical positions by the monarchs and of the consequent inclusion of this income, in practice, in the mechanism of remuneration for their performance and, most of all, in the financing of their scholastic training during the fourteenth and fifteenth centuries.[215] The apparent equivalence of beneficiary and cleric must therefore be carefully studied in each case

[213] For a global exposition of the system in his 'classical' period: Gabriel Le Bras, 'Institutions ecclésiastiques de la Chrétienté mediévale', in A. Fliche and V. Martin (eds.), *Histoire de l'église depuis les origines jusqu'à nos jours, XIV* (Paris: Blond and Gay, 1959–64), pp. 150–71.

[214] A general vision can be found in R. Naz (ed.), *Dictionnaire de droit canonique* (Paris: Letoyzey et Ané, 1935–65), pp. 239–48.

[215] Hélène Millet, 'La place des clercs dans l'appareil d'état en France à la fin du moyen âge', in Jean-Philippe Genet and Bernard Vincent (eds.), *Etat et église dans la genèse de l'état moderne* (Madrid: Casa de Velázquez, 1982), pp. 239–48.

in the light of biographical data available, for fear of removing this important aspect, and the greatest care must be taken where data are lacking. Even when adopting a fairly broad acceptance of the condition of ecclesiastics, encompassing all who enjoyed the privileges of the order, the perception of this group becomes difficult in the grouping of court society if we do not pay attention to other, simultaneous criteria of belonging to which, besides, contemporaries attributed no less importance, such as the practice of celibacy or the performance of sacred functions. As in the case of the nobility, it is important to discover how the distinctions and hierarchies which contributed to making the clerical condition both definable and concrete were configured.

Having said this, I shall start by observing that the most important poles of attraction for the men of the Church were, essentially, the royal chapel, the *câmara* and, in a more varied manner, the *desembargo* and the council. As will be seen, the laity had to share with the multiform presence of the clergy some of the central places of life and activity of the medieval court. It often occurs quite unexpectedly that there is reference to their participation in other areas and structures of the royal service, but these, as we shall see, are less characteristic examples. For all this, I believe that my description should, in this case, remain on firmer ground for the more problematic areas of identification of this clerical presence. In view of the fact that the functions of rite and religious ministry are the essential aspect of the ecclesiastical office, I shall naturally start with the chapel.

The chapel and its members

The existence of a chapel of the Portuguese kings from the era prior to the fourteenth century has already been the subject of some consideration in my introductory chapter. It is now of interest to analyse the problems of its internal composition, taking it as the clerical organism *par excellence* that accompanied the court. By taking the name of 'chapel' merely in one of its restricted meanings – the group of clerics who were involved in the religious practice of the royal entourage – I shall start by noting the relatively modest size of this group in the fourteenth century.

Some papal documentation, comprising petitions and papal bulls, mentions important aspects of its organisation: the bull *Sincere devotionis*, dated 1325, granted to Afonso IV ample gifts for ten ecclesiastics who served him and again, in 1360 and 1361, Pedro asked for papal authorisation that twelve clerics in his service chosen by him should receive the fruits of all benefices without being obliged to live in them.[216] The majority, if not the entire number of clerics

[216] *Quadro*, vol. IX, p. 335. The exemptions refer to the receipt of the fruits of the benefices of ten of the king's clerics, but the power of personal dignities or benefices with a curate for six of them are excepted. See also *MPV*, vol. I, pp. 362–3 and 388–9.

referred to, had to serve in the royal chapel, as is expressly recognised by similar documents granted successively to several kings. Among them are the petition of Fernando to Clement VII in 1380, the several petitions granted at the request of Leonor and the regent D. Pedro in 1439–40 and the bulls of Nicholas V and Calisto III in 1452 and 1456.[217]

Since this mechanism of recruitment was systematically used by the Portuguese monarchs in their chapel, it is not surprising that the available data up to the middle of the fifteenth century point to an effective number of chaplains, and this does not contradict the ruling: in general the royal chapels did not exceed much more than twenty, with a maximum of thirty ecclesiastical servants referred to during each reign. The list of *moradores* at the court of John I correctly mentions fifteen chaplains and choristers as well as seven servers. During the reign of Afonso V, this seems to have been increased, owing in the main to the number of choristers, which rose to fifteen identified individuals,[218] but the list of those mentioned merely as chaplains remains within the appointed size: there is information for twenty clerics up to the 1480s. Both in size and in the practice of payment of the servants through use of profits from a variety of benefices, the Portuguese organic is close to that known for other medieval chapels of kings and princes.[219]

In a ruling of Duarte's in the notes to his *Livro dos Conselhos* we see that this king was preoccupied while still infante with instituting periods of service in his chapel, a fact which must be related not only to a preoccupation in limiting the size and expenses of his entourage but, most of all, to probable 'reforming' intentions as to the state of the Church, which so impassioned the ecclesiastical elite and the princes of his time. Thus, 'deseJando ... ser seruido de seus capelães e sua capela ser honrrada per eles aos tempos necesarios e que outrosy seus benefiçios seJam seruidos e regidos por eles',[220] the infante determined that there should be two-monthly rotations for his chaplains but also ensured their presence for important annual feasts. Once released from duties at court, the clerics could effectively take up their ecclesiastical offices during the remaining time. In my research I could not confirm obedience to this ruling but, at least following Duarte's accession to the throne, there is every indication that this practice never occurred systematically and that the 'reforming' intentions

[217] *CUP*, vol. II, p. 74; vol. VI, p. 26; *MPV*, vol. II, pp. clxxx–clxxxi. See also the book of register of several Bulls and papal documents granted to the Portuguese monarchs to 1452: ANTT, drawer XIV, M 6, 30.

[218] These are: Afonso Anes (1439), Antão Gonçalves (1442), Vicente Fernandes (1445), Gabriel Gil (1449–59), Estevão Anes (1444–75), Álvaro Anes (1451), Pero de Penela (1452–56), Pero Vasques (1454), Pero Anes (1455), Rodrigo Afonso (1450–72), Nuno Álvares (1462), Estevão Afonso (1463), Guilherme Afonso (1470s) and Clemente Afonso (1480s): F. M. Sousa Viterbo, *Subsídios para a história da música em Portugal* (Coimbra: Imprensa da Universidade, 1932).

[219] J. Fleckestein and others, 'Hofkapelle', *Lexicon des Mittelalters* (Zurich and Munich, 1990–91), cols. 70–3.

[220] *Livro dos Conselhos*, pp. 213–14.

of the monarch did not have any lasting consequence. On the contrary, in a ruling instituted in 1474 by Afonso V and recorded in his *Livro Vermelho*, it is established that the chaplains and choristers 'se nom devem partir pera nenhũa parte sem de nós averem licença, e leixarem outros que pera taes oficios sejam pertencentes, e nos comtente de nos de taes pesoas servirmos'.[221]

The initial period of Afonso's reign under the regency of the Infante Pedro was also marked by a preoccupation with the restructuring of the royal chapel, whose ceremonial and liturgical aspects will be of interest to us in the second part of this study. At the request of the Portuguese court, the dean of the English royal chapel, William Say, wrote a ruling, the *Liber Regie Capelle*, which included the description of the various rituals practised in England and also, which is of interest to this study, the detailed description of the internal hierarchy and the organisation of this chapel – comprising a dean, thirty choristers (of whom half would have taken holy orders), two priests, a choirmaster, a master of grammar, ten choirboys and four laymen, or a total of forty-nine individuals.[222]

The manuscript of this work of 1449 which is to be found in Portugal remained largely unknown in studies of Portuguese historiography, since it was considered that the ruling must never have been used in Portugal. For obvious lack of data, it was not possible for its modern editor to reconstruct the vicissitudes as to why this unique manuscript would have been overlooked, or to prove its use in Portugal. It is important to mention on this matter the new data which I have investigated as to its presence in the collection of books of King Manuel pointing towards the possibility of the use of this ruling within the Portuguese court at least until the sixteenth century.[223] One element which is no less relevant to the discussion of the problem lies in the influence which the English ruling apparently had in the actual structure of the Portuguese chapel and curiously there appears in royal documentation of the period of the regency (and even before 1449) the first known mention of a dean of the chapel.[224] In any case, what is beyond doubt is the greater complexity and size of the royal chapel in Portugal after 1450 and, in spite of multiple aspects common to other chapels which we can find – the English, the Aragonese, and even the papal – it can be said that its structure, in essence, was retained during the final years of the Middle Ages, in particular: access to benefices under royal protection by the chaplains and choristers; their selection by the monarch; and their permanent appointment.

What can we discover about the diverse clerics who made up this court organism? Their mention in royal documents, although only occasional, in particular the prosopographic research made by the conjunction of this data

[221] *Livro Vermelho*, p. 484.

[222] *Liber Regie Capelle. A manuscript in the Biblioteca Pública, Évora*, ed. by Walter Ullmann (London: Henry Bradshaw Society, 1961), pp. 15 and 56–7.

[223] ANTT, *NA*, p. 798, f. 92 ('hũu liuro da coroação del Rey d ymgraterra').

[224] ANTT, *Ch. D. Afonso V*, 5, f. 75v. (in a royal charter of 1446). In England a large part of the duties of the *capellanus maior* or the *archicapellanus* of the continental courts fell to the dean of the chapel: Ullmann, *Liber Regie Capelle*, p. 8.

with that supplied by the papal petitions, leads to some apposite questions. Since these reveal something of the respective ecclesiastical careers, I shall conclude that, in this last aspect, participation in the service of the royal chapel was not particularly remunerative for the clergy, especially when compared with that of *desembargo* or positions more closely linked to the 'secrecy' of the monarch. Certainly, royal favour allowed access to great profits through the accumulation of benefices, as can be proved in the case of several chaplains from the time of Afonso IV, the majority of whom were secular clerics. However, there was not the rapid access to high positions in the structure of the Church, contrary to that which occurred in the case of clerics who were present in other organisms of the court.

The presence in the chapel of some members of religious orders is also found at the end of the Middle Ages, as in the example of the observant canon of Santa Cruz, João Lourenço do Porto, the *capelão-mor* to John I between 1402 and 1417; or the Augustinian hermit, Fr. Lourenço Afonso, who succeeded him as *capelão-mor* until 1429. The importance of the presence of the Benedictines at the court of John I at the turn of the fifteenth century must be critically evaluated in the light of the desertion and abandonment which we know was the situation of monasteries of the order at the time.[225] Among the chaplains to John I in the first decade of his reign there appears one Afonso Martins, the abbot of Pendorada, and also the abbot of Rendufe of the same name. The first of these was prominent during the reign of Fernando as leader of the monastic community in the Minho, and the building of a new cloister in the monastery in 1382 was, according to a contemporary inscription, due to his initiative.[226] Another Afonso Martins, the abbot of Pombeiro, at times performed functions of *escrivão da puridade* to John I.[227] It is of course possible that under this homonym there is concealed a reference to the same person, in which case his influence was carried on from the court of Fernando to that of his successor. Another example of the continuity of the presence of the Benedictine abbots at the palace is the case of the chaplain to Duarte, Soeiro Gomes, who was the abbot of Tibães and then of Santo Tirso.[228] Although the monastic chroniclers

225 José Marques, *A Arquidiocese de Braga no século XV* (Lisbon: Imprensa Nacional–Casa da Moeda, 1988), in particular pp. 640–99.

226 His leadership of the monastery would have begun in 1367. The master of the contemporaneous work of Nossa Senhora da Oliveira at Guimarães worked in this cloister: *DHDA*, vol. I, p. 411. It is possible that the connection of this monk to the court dates from the middle of the century if we identify him as Afonso Martins, the monastic prior of Pendorada, who is the subject of the supplication presented by King Pedro in 1359, where he appears as 'dicti regis quamplurimum dilectus': *MPV*, vol. I, p. 349.

227 *Desembargo*, pp. 271–2 (which attributes to him activity between 1383 and 1391). Note also on this subject the ecclesiastical presence connected to the Benedictine monasteries, since the chaplain to Philippa of Lancaster was also Lopo Dias, who was successive abbot of Pombeiro: Fr. Leão de S. Tomás, *Beneditina Lusitana*, ed. José Mattoso (Lisbon: Imprensa Nacional–Casa da Moeda, 1974), vol. II, p. 73.

228 Armindo de Sousa, 'O mosteiro de Santo Tirso no século XV', *Estudos Medievais*, 1 (1981), 141–3, quoting documents of the archives of S. Tirso.

do not include these men in the list of commendatory abbots, I believe that the process of absenteeism and the appropriation of the possessions of the monasteries characteristic of the system of *commenda* must have started with these abbots who integrated the royal entourage.[229] In the neighbouring kingdom of Castile, the typology of abbeys *in commendam* discussed in the Cortes during the 1390s distinguished those which originated (a) in royal foundations; (b) in the privileged relationship of the monasteries with patron families; and finally (c) in those which were the result of 'obeniencias e cunposiciones' of the communities themselves (or agreements made at the initiative of the monks) with protectors whom they did not usually meet.[230] This third type resembles most the relationship between these 'court' abbots and the monasteries in decline, where theoretically they should live continuously. From the beginning of the fifteenth century the granting of various Benedictine and Cistercian monasteries to clerics at court *in commendam* appears in the logical sequence of earlier and contemporary practices which also continued in a growing dissociation between the religious houses and their leaders.

While one seeks to find a career in the royal chapel which would culminate in a bishopric or in the Curia, or which would extend beyond the sphere of the chapel, an example is not easily found. One of the few cases of certain fortune is the career of Fernão Álvares Cardoso, whom we find as chaplain to Duarte from at least 1435. A Bachelor of Arts and Medicine at that date, he had been a 'familiar' of the Castilian cardinal of St Peter *in vincula*, but the main essence of his services seems to have developed as a doctor, successively to Duarte and Afonso V, and as confessor to the latter from 1450. He was a rare case among those who had been chaplains, and took part in the king's council, gaining various favours and benefices.[231] The main factor in explaining this relative modesty of an ecclesiastical and even a political career among the overwhelming majority of royal chaplains at the end of the Middle Ages lay certainly in the specialised, almost professional character of the services they

229 The introduction of the beneficiaries in general occurred in Portugal throughout the fifteenth century. On Rendufe: José Mattos, 'O mosteiro de Rendufe (1090–1570)', in *Religião e cultura na Idade média Portuguesa* (Lisbon: Imprensa Nacional–Casa da Moeda, 1997). On Pendorada: *Beneditina Lusitana*, vol. II, p. 230. On Pombeiro: Fr. António de Assunção Meireles, *Memórias do Mosteiro de Pombeiro*, ed. A. Baião (Lisbon: Academia Portuguesa da História, 1942), pp. 29–30.

230 José Luis Santos Díez, *La encomienda de monasterios en la Corona de Castilla, siglos X–XV* (Rome and Madrid: Instituto Juridico Español, 1961), p. 159.

231 A. D. Sousa Costa suggests João de Cervantes, who was made a cardinal in 1426, as the dignitary whose *familia* requested this cleric: *MPV*, vol. IV, p. 275 and note. On the importance such a connection might carry: E. Pásztor, 'Funzione politico-culturale di una struttura della chiesa: il cardinalato', in *Aspetti culturali della società Italiana nel periodo del papato Avignonese* (Todi: University of Perugia, 1981), pp. 199–226; *CUP*, vol. IV, pp. 97, 119–22, 226; vol. V, p. 253. *MH*, vol. X, pp. 108–10, 200; vol. XI, p. iii; vol. XII, pp. 133, 146; *DCH*, vol. II, pp. 53, 87, 89, 103, 136 *et passim*. See also the privileges of 1444 and 1453: ANTT, *Ch. D. Afonso V*, 5, f. 87v; 4, f. 24.

performed; in other words it eventually resided in the growing importance of the chapel from the point of view of religious and court ceremonies. This aspect, which has already been noted in other contexts, must also have contributed to the creation of a certain *esprit de corps* among the members of the royal chapel, so that their careers were extended in time and on occasions they moved from one monarch to his successor. This logic of the community very early on affected the group of choristers of the chapel who from the beginning of the fifteenth century formed a true 'schola' with their head chorister and choirmaster.[232] In Duarte's appointments in the 'Ordenança' of the chapel, completed when he was king, we read: 'Estes quatro som muyto neçesareos pera a capela *scilicet* capelam mor e mestre da capella e tenor e mestre dos moços.'[233] The recruitment of the choristers was, according to the suggestions of this monarch, in the main from among the servers, although because of the education they had received some servers may also have achieved an ecclesiastical career and taken orders. Their apprenticeship took place within the chapel itself, and led to careers which would have lasted for decades. The same can be said in relation to the 'tangedores de órgão', who were members of the chapel and whose position was similar to that of the choristers.[234]

Duarte referred to these facts indirectly when the Castilian court succeeded in attracting a chorister from his chapel, which led to a letter of protest to the neighbouring king in 1434: 'Reçebemos uosa carta pola qual nos fizestes saber como filhareis aluaro fernandez nosso cantor e organista . . . auemos direita tençom em nos desprazer ele ser asy per uos filhado uysto como ele he criado e natural noso, e todo o mais que sabe de Cantar e tanger auer aprendido em nosa casa.' Later in the same letter the monarch mentions the constant pressures from the neighbouring court 'sentindo alteração em nosos capelães por engalhamentos que de uosa corte lhe erom feitos', inducements in which Álvaro Fernandes would himself have been involved, which 'nos engalhou pera a dita raynha [of Castile] tres capelães nosos e os pos em tal alteração que por hũ tempo reçebemos deles pouco seruiço'.[235] This is a curious musical competition between the Peninsular royal chapels, evoking battles as hotly disputed by the choristers as those known in other medieval European courts. Although many

232 See the supplication of Dinis Dias, 'in capella domini Regis Portugalie cantor', in 1430: *MPV*, vol. IV, p. 551. Among the masters who served in the chapel of Afonso V are Álvaro Afonso (1452), Gomes Anes (1454) and João de Lisboa (1476): Viterbo, *Subsídios*, pp. 5–7, 76 and 314–15.

233 *Livro dos Conselhos*, p. 212.

234 There is also information for the reign of D. Afonso V of a 'Mestre dos horgos', Manuel Pires Rombo, and of the 'tangedor' of the organ, Fr. Afonso: Viterbo, *Subsídios*, pp. 5 and 454–5. I shall refer later to the musicians of the Sala. An important comparison can be made with the court of Aragon, all the more since we know of the arrival of musicians of the Aragonese court in Portugal in the first half of the fifteenth century: Alan Atlas, *Music in the Aragonese Court of Naples* (Cambridge: Cambridge University Press, 1985).

235 *Livro dos Conselhos*, pp. 90–1.

choristers were probably simply tonsured, as suggested in available documents which say that some had married, almost all the fifteenth-century tenors I have been able to identify received various ecclesiastical benefices. For example in papal petitions there are Antão Gonçalves and Afonso Anes, who were tenors who moved from the chapel of Duarte to that of Afonso V, and the tenors who were in the service of Afonso such as Guilherme Afonso or Rodrigo Afonso.

The entire complex structure of the chapel was under the supervision of the *capelão-mor*. His functions made him a prestigious cleric with most effective powers, both in the ecclesiastical sphere, particularly in the areas connected to royal patronage, and in the court sphere itself. The evolution we can detect throughout the period studied and the institution, already mentioned, of a dean of the chapel with the duties of coordination and leadership of its members reveal a broadening of the sphere of activity of the *capelão-mor* which made his relationship with the actual chapel less direct and exclusive and brought the duty closer to that of a dignity with an importance in the Portuguese reality of the Church of the time.

Until the end of the fourteenth century, the *capelães-mores* on whom we have information were usually secular clerics, as was the case with the preceptor of Lisbon, Vasco Lourenço, who served during the reign of Fernando. With John I we are able to see in the succession of the *capelães-mores* – Martim Lourenço, João Lourenço do Porto and Fr. Lourenço Afonso (of whom I have already spoken), and Afonso Anes – an alternation with some members of religious orders but, above all, the characteristic association of episcopal dignity to this court duty, which was to become a constant during the fifteenth century. The figure of the Augustinian, Fr. Lourenço, master of theology, non-resident bishop of Mégara and abbot of Pendorada, deserves particular mention. He served as *capelão-mor* throughout the 1420s and was the first example of a characteristic common to all the *capelães-mores* of the fifteenth century, that is a clear indication that his role as head of the chapel was a position of great importance. From the point of view of active liturgical service during the fifteenth century, it is legitimate to doubt that all these men had daily duties, and they must have performed their duties only on particularly solemn occasions; I shall have an opportunity to study these later. Besides, in the ruling of Duarte it is stated: 'Quando vierem algũas festas espeçiães o capelão mor *ou quem seu lugar tyuer* deue perguntar ao senhor onde e como quer ouuyr o ofiçio e os corregimentos de que se auera em ela de serujr, [etc.].'[236]

According to several mentions made by the chroniclers, the *capelão-mor* of this monarch was the Franciscan Fr. Aimaro de Aurillac, who had served Philippa of Lancaster and who was also made bishop of Ceuta and headed the monastery of Pombeiro. During the regency period of D. Pedro, we have information as to the parallel existence of a dean of the chapel and a *capelão-mor*

[236] *Livro dos Conselhos*, pp. 211–12.

who, following the death of Fr. Aimaro in 1444, was chosen from among Duarte's chaplains, a promotion made within the organism itself.[237] The presence of the bishops in this position occurred once again, for it was then performed first by the Carmelite bishop of Ceuta and Guarda, Fr. João Manuel, and then until the 1470s by the bishop of Lamego, the Franciscan Rodrigo de Noronha.[238]

With an analysis of the list of *capelães-mores* we approach in some way the complex problem of honorary chaplains, or the royal appointment of chaplains who were 'nas honras', although they did not perform any effective function in the royal chapel. Several examples of letters of appointment registered in the *chancelaria* of Afonso V from 1450 make clear the use of extending to clerics and members of religious orders the privileges owed 'aos nossos outro capellaeens familliares e presemtes asy nossos como papaees', exempting them from the jurisdiction of the ordinary. This is a use whose beginnings I have not been able to date precisely, owing to the absence of similar registers in the chanceries prior to this reign.[239] Some sparse information does at least show during the reign of John I examples of honorary concessions, but these related to certain ranks or entire communities as, for example, the abbots of Pendorada, or the prior and head of Nossa Senhora da Oliveira in Guimarães, who had the privileges of the royal chapel. It is only perhaps in the later period that these honorary distinctions were granted to particular individuals, for it is certain that, in the papal court, there existed at the beginning of the fourteenth century 'honorary chaplains' with privileges granted individually.[240] Even so, it is important to state that the beneficiaries of these concessions of a personal nature were usually known and named by the office which they performed, the honorary title being merely subsidiary, clarifying their position.

It appears necessary to move on to the distinction between the royal chapel itself and the several chaplaincies instituted by the Portuguese monarchs in various of their residences. Many of these were under the invocation of St Michael, as was the case of the royal chaplaincies at Alcáçovas in Lisbon, Santarém, Coimbra and Évora, which were the oldest residences of the monarchs in these

[237] This concerned Luis Peres, chaplain to Duarte: ANTT, *Ch. D. Duarte*, 3, f. 37, also quoted in the *Livro dos Conselhos*, p. 20. See also *MPV*, vol. II, pp. clxxiv (note 407) and clxxxi, which demonstrates his activities in the curia in 1439. On his position as *capelão-mor* to D. Afonso V, see ANTT, *Ch. D. Afonso V*, 5, f. 41; *MH*, vol. IX, pp. 201 and 300 (note 4).

[238] Fr. João was *capelão-mor* at least between 1443 and 1465. As to D. Rodrigo, this bishop of noble parentage, also under royal protection, held the post of prior of Santa Cruz at Coimbra. In 1465 he was dean of the royal chapel, and during the period 1468–77 he was *capelão-mor*. For a biography of this prelate: A. D. Sousa Costa, 'Bispos de Lamego e de Viseu no século XV', *Itinerarium*, 34 (1988), 232–73.

[239] On the evolution of the Portuguese *chancelaria* relating its organic to diplomatic typology: Armando Luis Carvalho Homem, *Para uma abordagem da burocracia régia: Portugal, séculos XIII–XV*, offprint of *Revista Portuguesa de História* (Coimbra, 1996); Maria Helena Coelho and A. L. Carvalho Homem, 'Origines et évolution du registre de la Chancellerie royale portugaise (XIIIe–Xve siècles)', *Revista da Faculdade de Letras*, 12 (Oporto, 1995), 47–74.

[240] Paravicini-Bagliani, *La Cour des Papes*, p. 70.

places. These sites of religious rite, to which there was usually attached a restricted number of clerics (one, and a maximum of two chaplains with their assistants), were, in the main, founded in the thirteenth century and were, together with the chapels instituted by the queens in their palaces, a sign of the importance of the liturgical activity as an expression of the devotion of the royal family.[241] Unlike the members of the royal chapel, the chaplains who served and prayed in these 'pelo estado do rei reinante e pelos outros seus antecessores' always retained a well-defined and unequivocal relationship with the area. The possessions and incomes associated with these places in each case transformed the chapels – which in everything else resembled any other lay chapel, including their perpetual nature – into something very similar to an ecclesiastical benefice.[242]

As institutors, the monarchs naturally had the right of naming the clerics who served in them, which explains why it is common to find, in the royal chanceries, letters of appointment of chaplains for these places, showing that these same chaplaincies could be given (although this rarely occurred) to members of the royal chapel itself who had generally been 'retired' from effective service of the king. It is important to note that, certainly in the case of S. Miguel in Lisbon and S. Miguel in Santarém, the documents of institution of these chaplaincies which are still available specify that the cleric appointed for each must serve personally and himself celebrate the liturgical offices. By these means it was sought to preserve the dignity and guarantee the permanence of the rite which, with time, naturally tended to deteriorate if the service could be performed by third parties.[243] The connection with one place and the certain, previously determined obligations clearly distinguished these chaplains from the profile given above for the members of the actual royal chapel, who had multiple duties and accompanied the monarch in his itinerances. It approximates the former to the situation of chaplains associated with the various burial sites of the medieval monarchs (as was the case for example at the monastery of Batalha). The history of the chaplaincies is, besides, closely connected to the destiny of the actual royal residence, on which I shall speak more broadly in another part of this study.

It is important to note that for the period at the end of the Middle Ages indications increase as to the decline of some of these chaplaincies, either because

[241] There is information on the old foundations of the queens in Torres Vedras and Óbidos, for example, which continued to exist in the fourteenth and fifteenth centuries: ANTT, *LN*, Reis, 1, ff. 111–111v; *Ch. D. Afonso V*, 13, f. 25; 23, f. 25v.

[242] 'That which distinguishes in essence the manual or lay chaplaincies from the ecclesiastical benefices is that they remain the property of the founder, be he lay or ecclesiastic; they are not, however, ecclesiastical possessions': *Dictionnaire de droit canonique*, vol. II, pp. 528–30.

[243] In the words of the royal charter of 1299 instituting the chapel of S. Miguel de Lisboa: 'que a dita Capela aia capelam seu proprio pera todo sempre que seruha y pessoalmente e faça y continuadamente Residença . . . E contra esto nom lhy ualha nenhũaa despensaçom nem de bispo nem de nenhũu outro prelado': ANTT, drawer 1, M 6, 9. This, however, dealt with a sacerdotal chaplaincy. For the same concept, regarding S. Miguel de Santarém: ANTT, *LN*, Reis, 1, ff. 114v–115.

of the inevitable depreciation in the income granted by the founder, or because of the preference given by the kings of the period to other initiatives within the religious ambit. Thus, when referring to the chapel of S. Miguel in Lisbon in 1437, Duarte recognised that 'a dicta capeella nom se cantava como deuja e per el [his ancestor, Dinis], fora hordenado e que o mantijmento que el hordenara que ouuese o capellam que a cantase era pagado em dinheiro e nom era a rrespeito da moeda que ora corre tal que razoadamente se pudese manteer',[244] proceeding, therefore, to a revision of the sums set down at the end of the thirteenth century. Likewise in 1462, and again in 1469, Afonso V had to provide for the chaplaincy of S. Miguel at Coimbra, for there had been no chaplain there since the death of the Infante Pedro.[245] It is also the case, on the other hand, that the monarchs persisted in adding chaplaincies to their new residences, and became preoccupied in granting them gifts and providing them with clerics: thus, at the palaces of John I in Almeirim there was, in the first decade of the fifteenth century, a new chaplaincy for which the monarch obtained the annexation of various incomes through papal authority.[246] Through an analysis of the regulations relating to this case we also discover that the chaplaincies annexed to the residences of the monarchs were under the authority of the *capelão-mor*, which contributed also to a constant expansion of his influence throughout the fifteenth century because of the growing number of clerics under him.[247] The connection with the royal chapel itself, however, was restricted to this fact, contrary to what is written by the majority of authors who have studied this subject. As with the honorary chaplains, those who served in both the funeral chaplaincies or those attached to the residences supported by the kings were not seen in the Portuguese ruling of the time as effective members of the royal chapel, nor did they share in its specific activities. This apparently lesser problem must be clarified, for historiographic tradition relating to the royal chapel has, since the eighteenth century, attributed the sharp decline of certain residential chaplaincies mentioned in some documents to the royal chapel as an entirety, so creating a false concept of a 'decadence' of this organism at the end of the Middle Ages. This is then repeated without criticism by present-day historians.[248] While, to the contrary, the royal chapel was, as we have seen, in a

244 *MH*, vol. VI, pp. 30–2. 245 ANTT, *Ch. D. Afonso I*, 1, f. 34; 31, f. 89.

246 See supplications of 1427 and 1429: *MPV*, vol. IV, pp. 178–9, 421–2. But also the later sentence on the matter in 1432: ANTT, drawer 1, M 1, 16; also the letter from the bishop of Évora to the archbishop and chapter of Lisbon: ANTT, drawer 1, M 6, 9 or *LN*, extras, ff. 204–206v.

247 On the extension of the duties of the *capelão-mor* during the sixteenth century, see the Bulls summarised by Joaquim Santos Abranches, *Fontes do Direito Ecclesiastico Portuguez* (Coimbra: França Amado, 1895), numbered 480, 571, 572 and 644. Also the *Apontamentos do bispo da Guarda sobre as concessões ao capelão-mor*, a manuscript dated 1537 which can be attributed to D. Jorge de Melo: ANTT, drawer XIV, M 21, 21.

248 The work of the Oratorian (and member of the seventeenth-century Academia Real das Ciências) António Pereira de Figueiredo in his *Memória sobre a antiga origem da capela real dos Senhores Reys de Portugal*, which remains in manuscript form, is prominent: BNL, Res, Fundo Geral, Cód. 10982. The essence of his statements on the medieval chapel was taken up by João

full phase of expansion in the fifteenth century and its famous choristers were being wooed by neighbouring sovereigns, nevertheless the decline of certain residential chaplaincies continued to be felt up to the sixteenth century.[249] Recent authors have also approximated the royal chapel to the chaplaincies and religious foundations instituted by nobles, ignoring its diverse nature from the point of view of concepts of the age. This diversity is clearly present in the norms of canon law and was also expressed in the connection which this organism had at the end of the Middle Ages and in the early modern era with the complex of traditions and doctrines relative to royalty, and consequently in its ceremonial and liturgical activity.[250]

Also included in the medieval organic of the Portuguese royal chapel was the service of the almoners. These agents were few in number, and were never more than four or five individuals throughout one reign. They were under the authority of the *esmoler-mor*. The characteristics and recruitment of those ecclesiastics who performed this court service, and who were always connected to the monastery of Alcobaça, attest to the survival during the fourteenth and fifteenth centuries of a parallelism with the court of Aragon, to which I have already referred. Recourse to the Cistercian monks, which occurred in Aragon at least from the beginning of the thirteenth century, was the most important and original aspect of the organisation of the Aragonese royal chapel. In the various statutes of the chapel of Aragon of the end of the Middle Ages – in particular the 'Ordenacions' of Pedro IV – it was stated that the abbot of Santa Cruz (the *capelão-mor*) and the abbot of Poblet (the *esmoler-mor*) could not accompany the king permanently. However, their authority was to be directly exercised over the servants who attended daily, who were in turn members of the respective communities, and the personal service is mentioned for the abbots at important feasts and whenever they were present at court. Both Peninsular chapels – that of Portugal and that of Aragon – thus appear in apparent contrast with the evolution of their contemporaries connected to alms in other medieval European courts, such as for example that of the kings of France,[251] the Angevin

António Rebello, *Capella Real Portugueza: sua origem, progresso, esplendor, decadencia e estado actual* (Lisbon: Tip. Minerva, 1878). This text is, in turn, a good example of the function of the early chapel in the construction of a record of the institution which the royal chapel of the nineteenth century would demand, and served as a basis for later bibliography. I must thank Diogo Ramada Curto for having suggested Figueiredo's text, and his agreement to discuss some aspects of this problem.

249 Only the chapels of the palaces of Torres Vedras and Alcaçova in Lisbon are mentioned in the sixteenth-century lists of chaplaincies under royal patronage: Joaquim Veríssimo Serão (ed.), *Livro das igrejas e capelas do padroado dos Reis de Portugal 1574* (Paris: Fondation Calouste Gulbenkian, 1971), pp. 54–5.

250 Diogo Ramada Curto, 'A Capela Real: um espaço de conflitos (séculos XVI a XVIII), *Espiritualidade e corte em Portugal, séculos XVI–XVIII*, Appendices to *Revista da Faculdade de Letras* 5 (Oporto, 1993), 146 and 148.

251 Xavier de la Selle, 'La confession et l'aumône: confesseurs et aumôniers des rois de France', *Journal des Savants*, 2 (1993), 255–86.

chapel of Naples,[252] the chapel in England,[253] or even, as far as can be seen, that of the neighbouring Castilian court.[254]

The reasons leading to the Cistercian influence, which in Portugal was restricted merely to the service of alms, are not easy to explain, for in truth the problem has not been studied by specialists of the history of Alcobaça. One strong hypothesis of a general nature is that which states that the model of economic rationality which Cistercians represented, and which has been related to the initiative of their important 'cluster of innovations' of a technological nature, was accompanied by a sharp understanding of the new conceptions of time, which were subjacent to the argument for economic foresight cultivated by the monks. This argument explains not only their success in agricultural markets, but also the financial transactions of the Cistercians[255] and the sophisticated alms provision for which they became so famous in each of their abbeys.[256] The connection of the Templars (who, it should be noted, also followed the Cistercian rules) to the medieval kings developed in an analogous form, and several Templar almoners were known at the English court in the twelfth century (in particular with Henry II and Henry III), but also for their financial activities at the court of Anjou in Sicily and for the pope, as well as their connection with the alms of Philip Augustus and the well-known fact that they had headed the administration of the 'ordinary' finances of Philip the Fair of France.[257] It could be felt that, in earlier ages, this decisive incursion by the White Friars into the agricultural market and their position as major producers, with large reserves of food, determined their preferential choice as almoners to the Iberian monarchs because of the ability they possessed for effectively organising the supply of

[252] Anna Maria Voci, 'La cappella di corte dei primi sovrani Angioini de Napoli', *L'Etat angevin: pouvoir, culture et société entre XIIIe et XIVe siècle* (Rome: Istituto Storico per il Medio Evo, 1998), pp. 447–67.

[253] The service of alms was the duty of the 'King's Almoner', a cleric who was not a member of the chapel. On the expenses and function of this post in the fifteenth century: A. R. Myers, *The Household of Edward IV: The Black Book and the Ordinance of 1478* (Manchester: Manchester University Press, 1959), p. 205. See also Given-Wilson, *The Royal Household*, pp. 69–70.

[254] José Manuel Nieto Soria, 'La Capilla Real Castellano-Leonesa en el siglo XV: constituciones, nombramientos y quitaciones', *Archivos Leoneses*, 43 (1989), 7–54. See also Eloy Benito Ruano (ed.), *El Libro del Limosnero de Isabel la Católica*, 2 vols. (Madrid: CSIC, 1990); José Garcia Oro, 'Las constituciones de los Reyes Católicos para la Capilla Real de España', *Bibliotheca Pontificii Athenaei Antoniani*, 24 (1985), 283–326.

[255] 'The monasteries had become not only sources for extraordinary revenues and convenient collateral for loans, but also royal and papal treasuries or depositories. While the Templars and Hospitallers carried on financial operations on an international scale, the Cistercian abbeys in England functioned for the same banking purposes': James Eugene Madden, 'Business monks, banker monks, bankrupt monks: the English Cistercians in the thirteenth century', *The Catholic Historical Review*, 49 (1963–64), 341–64.

[256] Louis Lekai, *The Cistercians: Ideals and Reality* (Kent, OH: Kent State University Press, 1977), pp. 383–4.

[257] Alain Demurger, *Vie et mort de l'Ordre du Temple* (Paris: Seuil, 1989), pp. 255–9. On the Templars as almoners of the kings of France: Selle, *La Confession et l'aumône*, p. 257.

royal alms. This supply had to be made at certain prescribed times of the year, although in different areas, and could, as was the case with the distribution of alms in the Cistercian abbeys of the twelfth and thirteenth centuries, encompass large quantities of rations for the poor. In the era studied here, the service of Portuguese royal alms-giving was largely in monetary form, particularly in the management of monetary fines from which was taken the basis of their income, called the 'arca da piedade'. In a continuation of a venerable tradition, which in Alcobaça claimed its beginnings in the origins of the kingdom, the *esmoleres* regulated these financial resources and proceeded to the distribution of alms at court.[258]

The duty of chief almoner, which was exercised by successive abbots of Alcobaça, presents a similar evolution to that shown by the *capelão-mor* at the end of the Middle Ages. His presence at court, where he actively performed the functions attached to the management and distribution of alms, was naturally conditional upon the position of the abbot in charge of the monastic community, and was restricted to the more solemn occasions of the ceremonial cycle and, clearly, to the choice and appointment of the almoners and servants who accompanied the king. Whatever the method, it should be noted that the abbots of the fourteenth and fifteenth centuries were very close to the court of the Portuguese monarchs, and this appears to have occurred particularly with Fr. Vicente Geraldes (1349–69) during the reign of Pedro,[259] Fr. Martinho (1369–81) in Fernando's reign,[260] and Fr. Estevão de Aguiar (1431–46)[261] and Fr. Gonçalo Ferreira (1446–60) during the fifteenth century,[262] when the choice of the abbot of Alcobaça was made under the more or less direct influence of the monarch. The occasional performance of ceremonial functions must not, therefore, have meant major problems for these prelates who, as far as can be seen, attended the court of the Portuguese kings relatively frequently, and it

258 A fact which is amply referred to by the chroniclers of this monastery: Fr. Bernardo de Brito, *Primeira Parte da Chronica de Cister* (Lisbon: Pascoal da Silva, 1720), p. 333. See also the *Apontamentos sobre a Esmollaria-mor* by Fr. Manuel de Figueiredo: BNL, Fundo Geral, Cód. 1482, ff. 130–3. And Paulo Drumond Braga, *Esmoler mor e esmoler menor do reino*, offprint of *Itinerarium* (Lisbon, 1995).

259 *CDP*, pp. 124–7 and 540–1 on the important privileges granted to Alcobaça, where this abbot is mentioned. Also Fr. Manuel dos Santos, *Alcobaça illustrada* (Coimbra: Bento Ferreira, 1710), p. 178.

260 Fr. Martinho moved to the curia and to Castile as Fernando's ambassador. See the Bull *Accedit Nobis*: *DP*, vol. I, p. 150. Also Santos, *Alcobaça illustrada*, pp. 200–1.

261 On the protection of the Infanta D. Isabel and John I of Estevão de Aguiar from the 1420s: ANTT, CE, box 32, 47 and BLAU, Ash 1792, I, fasc. VII, 19. His appointment meant triumph for the royal will following a serious conflict with the previous abbot, who was suspended at the request of John I. On the activity of Fr. Estevão during the regency (when he was a member of the royal council) and in the conflict of Alfarrobeira: Santos, *Alcobaça illustrada*, pp. 261–5; Fr. Fortunato de São Boaventura, *Historia chronologica e critica da Real Abadia de Alcobaça* (Lisbon: Impressão Régia, 1827), pp. xlii–xliii and 179; Virginia Rau, *Estudos de história medieval* (Lisbon: Presença, 1985), pp. 81–7.

262 See for example ANTT, *Ch. D. Afonso V*, 5, f. 28; *MH*, vol. XIII, p. 189.

is known that there were numerous occasions when the monarch visited the abbey.

The sparse information relative to the various almoners allows us to assert on the other hand that these duties were performed by members of the community of Alcobaça or its branches. In the reign of Fernando, the almoner Fr. João de Ornelas later owed his choice as abbot of Alcobaça to the protection of the king,[263] just as the successive monks who were almoners during the fifteenth century obtained various privileges in recognition of their services. At the court of Afonso V, we find the presence of the almoners Fr. Rodrigo and Fr. Gil and also Fr. Vasco Tinoco, the abbot of Boiro (a community annexed to Alcobaça), who served during the 1450s as almoner. As was the case in Aragon, the monks who were almoners had assistants, but it was they who personally accompanied the royal entourage.[264]

One of the most important positions for the ecclesiastics at court was, by the nature of its functions, that of confessor, because of the particular proximity to the monarch. It is constantly stated that the freedom of the king (as also that of the queen and the infantes) in the choice of confessor resulted from papal concessions which recognised formally the complete emancipation of the medieval monarchs regarding the local structures of the Church. The existence of the royal chapel expresses this freedom and separation. As has been suggested already by some historians of the ecclesiastical institutions, this autonomy concerning religious practices of the medieval monarchs, which in the period beyond the thirteenth century was to extend to a large part of the entourage, functioned from a juridic aspect almost as a 'personal diocese', an analogy which reinforced in a certain way the systematic choice of individuals with episcopal dignity to be the *capelães-mores*, to which I have already referred.[265] Similar principles to those of the recruitment of the clerics of the chapel governed the relationship between the monarch and his confessor, which was characterised by a fluidity and submission to the royal decision, which was its only basis.

The succession of confessors to the kings during this era demonstrates beyond doubt a preference for the mendicant friars for this position which, since of necessity it fell to a man of the Church, was performed within the sphere of 'secrecy'. However, not always was this familiarity with the kings well viewed by some of the more severe spirits of the same orders; men such as the Franciscan Fr. Álvaro Pais, for example, who did not conceal his criticism of the monarchs of his time: 'e confessam-se a seus confessores, aduladores que

[263] ANTT, *Ch. D. Fernando*, 4, f. 21v. Also the Bull *Divine Retributionis Premium* of 1382: *Quadro*, vol. IX, p. 380. On this abbot, see also *CR João I*, vol. I, p. 340; Santos, *Alcobaça illustrada*, pp. 204–23.

[264] Agustí Altisent, *L'almoina reial a la cort de Pere el Ceremoniós: estudi i edició dels mansucrits de l'almoiner Fra Guillem Deudé Monjo de Poblet (1378–1385)* (Poblet: Abbadia de Poblet, 1969), p. xxvii.

[265] Selle, *La Confession et l'aumône*, pp. 261–2.

não lhes exprobram os pecados, antes os acarinham, lisonjeiam e dissimulam, em parte por cegueira, em parte por ignorância, em parte por medo, e em parte por complacência, para que os elevem em honras'.[266] The relationship of the Franciscans with political power was never unanimously accepted or free of suspicion, although it was an integral part of the friars' progress dating from the earliest days of the order.

The systematic choice of mendicants has been seen as of great importance in the evaluation of Portuguese court society, even beyond the strictly religious aspect. Historians such as Jaime Cortesão, for example, considered the 'Franciscan spirit' an essential factor in the evaluation of the intellectual atmosphere in which the monarch and princes of the time moved, and in his proposed synthesis he presents this as an element for the explanation of the birth of the Portuguese discoveries.[267] To this interpretation we can also add, on a highly generic plane such as that used by Cortesão, the preferential connection of the friars with the reflection upon penitence and the practice of hearing confessions which made them not only the preferred confessors of the kings and princes but also of enormous sections of the society of the age, particularly in urban areas. The Franciscan doctrine managed, for example, to establish itself within the core of one of the most important questions relating to the change in ways of life generated by new professional occupations and monetary commerce.[268] In Portuguese society at the end of the Middle Ages, where the market as an economic and social reality had growing importance, we cannot be surprised at the success of the friars within the court circle which, as already pointed out at times, bears much evidence of the development of many commercial activities.[269] On the other hand, the importance of verbal persuasion in the mendicant tradition is directly related to the use made of preaching at court, not only with the idea of religious propagation of the doctrine but also for dynastic exaltation and as a means of political communication.[270]

It is absolutely necessary to recognise that, in spite of the fact that so much has been said generically on the influence of the mendicants upon the Portuguese kings, particularly that exercised by their confessors, little is known as to the concrete make-up of these men, of their intellectual and scholastic progress, or even the ways in which they were connected to the 'puridade' of the kings.

[266] Pais, *Espelho dos reis*, pp. 290–1.

[267] Jaime Cortesão, *História dos descobrimentos Portugueses* (Lisbon: Livros Horizonte/Círculo de Leitores, 1978), vol. I, pp. 63–70, 151–8. In a perspective of religious history: Mário Martins, *O ciclo Franciscano na nossa espiritualidade medieval*, offprint of *Biblos* (Coimbra, 1952).

[268] Lester K. Little, *Religious Poverty and the Profit Economy in Medieval Europe* (Ithaca, NY: Cornell University Press, 1994), pp. 181–3.

[269] G. Todeschini, 'Oeconomica franciscana. Proposte di una nuova lettura delle fonti dell'etica economica medievale', *Rivista de Storia e Letteratura Religiosa*, 13 (1977), 461–94.

[270] Armindo de Sousa, *A morte de D. João I (um tema de propaganda dinástica)* (Oporto: Centro de Estudos Humanísticos, 1984).

During the fourteenth century, the Franciscans appear to have monopolised this function. The identity of three of Afonso IV's confessors, Fr. Francisco, Fr. Estevão da Veiga and Fr. Diogo, is known, and two of these were certainly Franciscans. We also find a Franciscan confessor, Fr. Vicente Amado, with Pedro.[271] During the reign of Fernando, there are many references to the connection of the Franciscans, and the provincial of Santiago, Fr. Fernando de Astorga, was confessor to this king, as was Fr. Gomes, who was also most probably a Franciscan.[272]

Coinciding with a certain crisis of the ecclesiastical government institutions caused by the Schism, a phenomenon which in the case of the Iberian Peninsula contributed decisively to a growing 'regionalisation' of the institutions, we find that the Franciscan Province of Portugal obeyed to the Roman General and not to that of Avignon, so affirming its independence in the Iberian context under the aegis of the provincial of Portugal, Fr. Fernando de Astorga. From then on, a large number of the Franciscan provincials were royal confessors, at times simultaneously with other members of religious orders. This was the case with Fr. Afonso de Alprão (confessor to John I),[273] Fr. Vasco Pereira (confessor to Duarte)[274] and Fr. Gil Lobo or 'de Tavira' (confessor to both Duarte and Afonso V). The last of these withdrew from the post of provincial because of his unavailability for matters relating to the order, which may mean that he was highly active at court.[275]

The list of royal confessors in the fifteenth century shows more clearly than that of the previous century the alternation or the sharing of this position between the Franciscans and the Dominicans. Therefore, in the reign of John I, along with Fr. Fernando de Astorga (who appears to have been confessor both to

[271] *CR 1419*, 204 and 338; *Provas*, vol. I, pp. 342 and 409.

[272] ANTT, *Ch. D. Fernando*, 3, f. 61v; 4, f. 5v. See also the will of the king: Arnaut, *A crise nacional*, pp. 291–5.

[273] To the documents referred to by Fr. Manuel da Esperança, *História Serafica da Ordem dos Frades Menores de S. Francisco*, second part (Lisbon: A. Craesbeck de Carvalho, 1666), 561, can be added the several references to this confessor in papal documentation: A. D. Sousa Costa, *Portugueses no Colégio de S. Clemente e Universidade de Bolonha durante o século XV* (Bologna: Real Colegio de España, 1990), vol. II, pp. 687–9. Having studied in Italy, Fr. Afonso compiled the *Ars Praedicandi* at the beginning of the fifteenth century: Albert Hauf, 'El *Ars Praedicandi* de Fr. Afonso d'Alprão, O.F.M. Aportación de la teoría de la predicación en la Península Ibérica', *Archivum Franciscanum Historicum*, 72 (1979), 233–329.

[274] Fr. Vasco was confessor to D. Duarte from at least 1405: *MH*, vol. I, p. 286 and ANTT, *Ch. D. João I*, 3, f. 130. See also *MPV*, vol. IV, pp. 327–8 and also ANTT, *Ch. D. Duarte*, 3, ff. 15, 13 and 50v. I am not aware of the basis upon which Zurara says he was confessor to John I: *CR Ceuta*, p. 31.

[275] The presence of Fr. Gil alongside D. Duarte dates from the 1420s: *MH*, vol. IV, pp. 260–1 (ambassador to Aragon in 1429). He is frequently quoted in texts of Duarte's reign, such as the *Livro dos Conselhos*, pp. 239 or 288. Through a later supplication we know that 'o dito frei Gil desde a infância foi criado na Ordem de S. Francisco', and that he would have studied theology in Toulouse. In 1442, the Franciscans elected a replacement, since Fr. Gil, 'não se ocupava nem se ocupa' in his post of provincial: *CUP*, vol. IV, pp. 349, 368 and 376–7.

Fernando and to the new monarch of Aviz),[276] Fr. Afonso de Alprão and Fr. João Xira, who was also a Franciscan,[277] we find the Dominicans Fr. Lourenço 'Lampreia'[278] and Fr. Vicente de Lisboa.[279] In the first half of the fifteenth century, the presence of the preaching friars was equally evident alongside the princes and the queen; to name just those who are best known there are the confessors to Henry, the Infante Pedro and Leonor of Aragon.[280] The majority of these men had studied at university and possessed a strong theological education, so that they were also responsible for preaching at court on solemn occasions. This is well documented in the reports of the chroniclers, for example in the case of the confessors Fr. João Xira and Fr. Gil Lobo.[281]

The connection of the fifteenth-century court to the movements of monastic reform, and, in particular in the case of the friars, to the movements of observance, seems to explain why some individuals associated with these movements and possessing particular charisma were also from the first quarter of the fifteenth century appointed confessors to the kings.[282] Thus the monarchs

276 Fernão Lopes says he was confessor to John I in a text relating to 1386: *CR João I*, vol. II, p. 156. I have not found this to be confirmed by the documentation of the chancery of this monarch, for example ANTT, *Ch. D. João I*, 1, f. 49v.

277 ANTT, *Ch. D. João I*, 3, f. 190; *CUP*, vol. II, pp. x–xi. Fr. João would have studied at university financed by the city of Oporto in the final decade of the fourteenth century: António Cruz, *Santa Cruz de Coimbra na cultura Portuguesa* (Oporto: Biblioteca Pública Municipal, 1964), p. 211 (and note 31).

278 Fr. Lourenço was the first prior of Batalha. See the will of the monarch: *GTT*, vol. VI, pp. 2–9 (and in particular 3). Also the statement of the chronicler of the order: Fr. Luís de Sousa, *História de São Domingos*, ed. M. Lopes de Almeida (Oporto: Lello, 1977), vol. I, p. 969. Fr. António do Rosário, *Letrados Dominicanos em Portugal nos séculos XIII–XV*, offprint of *Repertorio de las Ciencias Eclesiásticas* (Salamanca, 1979), p. 584.

279 Fr. Vicente had been Spanish provincial, obeying the pro-Roman general: Fr. Luis de Sousa, *História de São Domingos*, vol. I, pp. 812 and 830–2; Fr. António do Rosário, *Letrados Dominicanos*, p. 597.

280 Fr. Afonso de Beneavente and the observant, Fr. João de S. Estevão, were connected to D. Leonor: *MH*, vol. XIV, pp. 229–30 and Fr. Luís de Sousa, *História de São Domingos*, vol. I, p. 979. On D. Pedro's confessor, the well-known Fr. João Verba: *CUP*, vol. III, pp. 144, 245, 246, 247 and 248 and Dias Dinis, 'Ainda sobre a identidade de Frei João Verba', *Itinerarium*, 3 (1957), 486–90. We also find Fr. Afonso Velho and Fr. Pedro de Sousa alongside Henry: *MH*, vol. III, p. 411 and vol. VIII, pp. 246–7; *CUP*, vol. V, p. 193 and vol. VI, pp. 8 and 12. For an important comparison, the selection of A. López, 'Confesores de la familia real de Castilla', *Archivo Ibero-Americano*, 31 (1929), 6–75.

281 Curiously, nothing is stated in the contemporary chronicles of the actual sermons of the theoretician Fr. Afonso de Alprão: Joaquim de Carvalho, *Obras completas* (Lisbon: Fundação Calouste Gulbenkian, 1978–89), vol. IV, pp. 341–6. On the sermons of Fr. Gil Lobo: *CR Duarte*, p. 500 and also *Livro dos Conselhos*, p. 239. In a general perspective: Roberto Rusconi, 'De la prédication à la confession. Transmission et contrôle de modèles de comportement', in *Faire croire: modalités de la diffusion et de la réception des messages religieux du XIIe au XVe siècle* (Rome: Ecole Française de Rome, 1981), pp. 62–87.

282 A. D. Sousa Costa, 'D. Gomes, reformador da Abadia de Florença, e as tentativas de reforma dos mosteiros Portugueses no século XV', *Studia Monastica*, 5 (1963), 123–60. Also J. A. Freitas de Carvalho, 'Nas origens dos Jerónimos na Península Ibérica: do Franciscanismo à Ordem de S. Jerónimo', *Línguas e Literaturas*, 1 (1984), 11–131.

related directly to their actual person men who were admired for their virtues, although the little we know for certain about their activities, cloaked as they are by the seventeenth-century chroniclers in the fantastic mantle of hagiography, does not show them to be constant attendants in the royal entourage. In the middle of the fifteenth century, emulation among the monarchs and important lords of the kingdom was, in this matter, extremely significant to the prestige of the more scrupulous friars who, however, succeeded in achieving the decision of Duarte and Afonso I to found small 'exemplary' communities such as those of the Dominicans in Azeitão, the Franciscans of S. Maria das Virtudes (in the Tagus valley) and those of Varatojo.[283]

The success of the observant religious was perhaps related at the court of Afonso V to the presence of secular confessors with theological training, which was a significant novelty in the face of the general panorama of the dominance of the mendicants already sketched. During the period of regency of the Infante Pedro, Fr. Gil Lobo, who had been confessor to Duarte, continued with the young king as his 'meestre e confessor e pregador'.[284] Following Alfarrobeira, however, the physician and previous chaplain Fernão Álvares Cardoso, dean of Évora, succeeded him,[285] and then Jorge Martins, who had studied theology and who was also selected as confessor to the sisters of the monarch, and who was identified with the future, celebrated cardinal of Alpedrinha, Jorge da Costa.[286] Meanwhile, the chroniclers of the Seraphic Order named Fr. Dinis as confessor to Afonso; he was vicar of the observant Franciscans, and his presence at court is not recorded. It is only for the decade following 1460 that we find once again numerous references to the presence of Fr. João de S. Mamede, a Franciscan confessor to the monarch.[287]

283 See the reports of Fr. João da Póvoa, confessor to John II: Fr. João da Póvoa, *Memórias soltas e inventários do Oratório de S. Clemente das Penhas e do Mosteiro de N. Sra da Conceição de Masosinhos dos séculos XIV e XV*, ed. A. Magalhães Basto (Oporto: Marânus, 1940), in particular p. 46, on Varatojo. Also *DHDA*, vol. II, pp. 506–7.

284 See the Bull of Eugenius IV granting him in commendation the monastery of Pendorada, at the request of the regent: *CUP*, vol. IV, pp. 317 and 368. Also his function as confessor is much referred to between 1442 and 1446: *DCH*, vol. I, pp. 263, 285, 287, 540 and 582. In 1449 he was still alive: *MH*, vol. X, pp. 115–16.

285 In fact, it is only after 1450 that Fernão Álvares is mentioned as confessor: ANTT, *Ch. D. Afonso V*, 5, f. 87v; 4, f. 24; *MH*, vol. X, p. 200.

286 Jorge da Costa was a highly active ambassador of the Portuguese king in the 1450s and 1460s: *MH*, vol. XIV, pp. 1071–1108; *CUP*, vol. V, pp. 388–9; vol. VI, pp. 239–40; *FAZ*, vol. XII, pp. 80–1. Following this hypothesis of identification suggested some time ago by Manuel Lopes de Almeida and António Domingues de Sousa Costa, it is not surprising that the Infanta Catarina, for example, should have translated the spiritual treatises, influenced by Jorge da Costa, since he would have been her confessor. For a statement of the question on the cardinal: S. D. Chambers, 'What made a Renaissance Cardinal respectable: the case of Cardinal Costa of Lisbon', *Renaissance Studies*, 2 (1998), 87–108.

287 *MH*, vol. XIV, pp. 173–4; *FAZ*, vol. XII, p. 82. See also the will of the monarch: *GTT*, vol. XI, p. 175.

The clerical presence

The evocation of royal confessors encompasses in the detailed perspective the study of ecclesiastical participation at court which is of a less problematic character and corresponds to the performance of well-determined functions of rites and religious ministry and, on the other hand, to a definite, enduring presence in the royal entourage. The presence of the more notable prelates of the kingdom alongside the monarchs was another aspect which was completely different from the clerical experience at court, and this cannot be overlooked in this analysis. Evidently, as in the different situations so far described, the presence of these powerful prelates did not have the same characteristics of duration nor, more importantly, did it correspond to the performance of functions which were exclusive to men of the Church. But this should not impose an anachronistic vision of the place in society and the activity of the important lords of the time who were bishops, abbots of the principal monasteries and holders of higher ecclesiastical positions of the kingdom, since this vision is fragmented in several areas according to the distinctions which at the time were unknown or little used.

This is because of the many references we have as to the participation in the life of the court in the fourteenth and fifteenth centuries of many prelates as members of the successive royal councils, such as nuncios or ambassadors, and also as holders of high offices at court where their legal education and political experience found an appropriate area of activity. Throughout the late-medieval period, an entire doctrinal tradition relative to the ordering of society constantly defended the presence of men of the Church alongside the monarchs as participants in the many duties of government and control of the kingdom in the name of assistance owed to the kings, a fact which the Church did not tire of advocating and theorising upon. It was through recourse to this figure of 'aid to the monarchs' that the popes at the end of the Middle Ages justified expenditure and privileges which were given generously to the clerics who were servants of royal power in more diverse spheres. Many dignitaries who accompanied the kings and infantes in the fourteenth and fifteenth centuries also certainly thought of this, at times with great assiduity, placing themselves at their service not only in the examples already analysed, as chaplains or clerics, but also in bureaucratic and political functions. As will be seen through several examples, in the context of the court the frontiers of status connected to juridic standing and to the identity of the clerics were also permeable, suggesting the possibility of a dynamic reformulation on the part of individuals.

In the case of the bishops a global vision of the problem of the clerical experience at court can be sketched. Although no complete studies have been made on the Portuguese episcopacy of the time, we do know that a number of them were within the circles close to the monarchs, and that they attended court as officials, men of letters and physicians to the kings and queens, and only later rose to the position of bishop. Cases which are known of precisely are those of the cleric Miguel Vivas, who was *chanceler* to Afonso IV and later bishop of Viseu between 1330 and 1345, and the physician, also to Afonso IV, Afonso Dinis, who was successively bishop of Guarda and of Évora between 1346 and 1352.[288] During the reign of John I, the ecclesiastical careers of the servants of the monarch attained a particular relevance with bishops such as Vasco Peres de Elvas and, more still, João Afonso da Azambuja and Martim Afonso da Charneca, who have already been mentioned regarding the Azambuja and Miranda families who were among the court circles.

João Afonso da Azambuja was a member of the *desembargo* of the new king between 1384 and 1395, and was particularly prominent during the first years of the reign. After studying Canon Law he was promoted to the episcopacy, and successively occupied the dioceses of Silves (1387–90), Oporto (1390–98), Coimbra (1398–1402) and Lisbon (1402–15), while throughout being a member of the royal council. He was made a cardinal in 1411, and from that time divided his activities between the kingdom and the curia, and died outside Portugal.[289] As for Martim Afonso da Charneca, who was also a descendant of the servants of the court of Fernando, he had graduated in Bologna during the last decade of the fourteenth century and served John I from the first moments of his reign, when already bishop of Coimbra; he too played an active part in the *desembargo* and the king's council. His presence at court originated, as already noted, from the first generation of descendants of the family who were fully members of the court nobility. After the bishopric of Coimbra he succeeded in 1398 to the archbishopric of Braga, which he held until his death in 1416.[290] For the period after the death of Duarte, we find a further similar case in the career of Álvaro Afonso, who was also a doctor of law and *escrivão da puridade* to the Infante Pedro, as well as acting in the *desembargo* during the regency. His progress in the Portuguese court was interrupted at Alfarrobeira, but his ecclesiastical career and his enormous intellectual and artistic interests progressed in Italy, where he went with the son of the regent, Cardinal D. Jaime.[291] He acted on

[288] *Desembargo*, pp. 369–70 and 391; *MPV*, vol. I, pp. 65–6 and 102–4; *GTT*, vol. VII, pp. 282–3. See also F. Xavier da Serra Crasbeck, 'Catálogo dos Abbades do Antigo Mosteiro de Sta. Maria de Guimarães e Real Collegiada de N. Sra. De Oliveira', *Collecção de Documentos e Memórias da Academia Real da História, IV*, 30 (Lisbon: 1726). A. D. Sousa Costa, 'Mestre Afonso Dinis, médico e secretário de D. Afonso IV, professor da Universidade de Paris', *Itinerarium*, 3 (1957), 310–47 and 510–607.

[289] *Desembargo*, pp. 330–1 and A. D. Sousa Costa, 'D. João Afonso da Azambuja, cortesão, bispo, arcebispo, cardeal e fundador do Convento das Dominicanas do Salvador de Lisboa', *Arquivo Histórico Domínicano Português*, 4 (1989), 1–150.

[290] *Desembargo*, p. 365. See also the biographical sketch of A. Dias Dinis, 'Quem foi o bispo de Coimbra nos anos de 1386 a 1398?', *Colectânea de Estudos*, 3 (1952), 67–109. On his studies in Bologna: Costa, *Portugueses no Colégio de S. Clemente*, vol. I, pp. 268–70.

[291] *CR Afonso V*, pp. 730, 733. On this prelate, see *MH*, vol. XII, pp. 212–15 *et passim*; Costa, *Portugueses no Colégio de S. Clemente*, vol. II, pp. 716–31; C. Martial de Witte, *Les Bulles pontificales et l'expansion portugaise*, offprint of *Revue d'Histoire Ecclésiastique* (Louvain,

Jaime's behalf in the administration of the archbishopric of Lisbon, and later in the construction of the famous funeral chapel of San Miniato al Monte in Florence. Although he became bishop of Silves in 1454 and of Évora in 1468, he resided at the curia from the 1450s.[292]

It can be said that for these prelates the court remained familiar territory, even when new positions in the ecclesiastical structure prevented or made less relevant participation in this environment through the actual performance of duties for the king. The main indication of the common characteristics of their progress resides, beyond doubt, in the protection of the monarchs, which was an essential element in accession to various high positions to which they rose. Everything related them to court circles – their predominant activity as men of letters in the royal service, their position as counsellors, and in not a few cases their family origins. For this reason, it can be considered that these bishops who 'left' the court, even though their presence became less constant later, from the point of view which is of interest to this work continued to play a part at court, for they represented its cultural environment. In spite of their importance and visibility, these prelates who had transferred, let us say, from the court to the Church, did not comprise the majority of the episcopacy. The most frequent case was that of the prelates who were evident through their proximity to the kings in their functions as counsellors and diplomatic agents (the most documented functions throughout the period studied), and this without their ecclesiastical origins or careers connecting them originally to the palace, that is, before their promotion to the episcopacy. Through the accessibility of ecclesiastical recruitment to men of humble origins, the court of the kings was able to become increasingly a site of activity for many whose geographic and social origins were distant from this circle.

These were men of diverse backgrounds who came from a variety of regions of Europe, and their activity as bishops at the Portuguese court naturally varied according to circumstances, although the preference accorded by the kings to certain members of the hierarchy remains largely unexplained. Others, sometimes notable intellectual and administrative figures, opposed the monarchs or

1958), p. 827 and note 1, on his activity at the curia. In a document of the Collegiate of Guimarães dated 1456, it is stated that Álvaro Afonso was 'criado do infante dom Pedro e sua fectura', 'servidor e do Conselho do dicto Ifante como seu leterrado', and the following commentary is also recorded: 'he todo do ssenhor arçesbispo de Bragaa que o recolheo asy quando foy solto da prisom em que foy preso na batalha em que foy com o dicto Ifante e lhe fez merçes e despois em corte de Roma': José Marques, 'A Colegiada de Guimarães no Priorado de D. Afonso Gomes de Lemos (1449–1487)', in *Actas do Congresso Histórico de Guimarães e da sua Colegiada*, vol. II (Guimarães, 1981), p. 254.

292 A recent study considers that this bishop 'was the true patron of the chapel of the cardinal of Portugal, from its conception to its completion': Eric Apfelstadt, 'Bishop and pawn: new documents for the Chapel of the Cardinal of Portugal at S. Miniato al Monte, Florence', in Kate Lowe (ed.), *Cultural Links between Portugal and Italy in the Renaissance* (Oxford: Oxford University Press, 2000), p. 191.

simply seem to have been indifferent to them. The transfer of the papacy to Avignon from the beginning of the fourteenth century is related to the significant number of foreign bishops in Portugal and, in particular, of French prelates during the first half of the century. In the majority of cases, these bishops did not live in, or they came fleetingly to, their Portuguese dioceses, where they installed clerics whom they trusted, their 'familiars', many of whom were foreigners. Along with the Portuguese prelates of noble birth, such as Gonçalo Pereira or João Afonso de Brito,[293] we find in the household of Afonso IV the French bishop Guillaume de la Garde, who was active at court during his short period of residence in the kingdom.[294] In the reign of Pedro there are, equally, the figures of Jean de Cardaillac, an expert in canon law and archbishop of Braga, who attended court until 1361,[295] as well as the bishop of Évora, João Gomes de Chaves, who was particularly prominent during the final period of Pedro's reign.[296] Also present in the royal entourage, although more sporadically, were the bishop of Lisbon, Lourenço Martins, and Gil de Viana, bishop of Guarda.[297]

From the 1370s, and especially during the reign of Fernando, there was a particularly complex period for the bishops, because of the Schism and the political implications of the question of obedience to Rome or to Avignon. The divisions felt in the various structures of the Church were made manifest through the political upheaval of the hierarchy which, for example, led to the exile to Portugal of several bishops and canons from Castilian dioceses.[298] In general, it can be said that the presence at the court of Fernando of prelates who supported Avignon is well documented, and the majority of these came from other Iberian regions. This was the case of the bishop of Silves and

[293] On the archbishop Gonçalo Pereira: *CR 1419*, pp. 275, 283 and 335, and also *GTT*, vol. V, p. 666, referring to his diplomatic missions and his standing as counsellor of the monarch, together with the bishop of Évora.

[294] During the ten years of the episcopacy of Guilherme (between 1349 and 1359), he was only a *morador*, it would appear, between 1354 and 1359. He played an active part, however, in the concordat established between Afonso IV and his son in 1355/56: AHCML, *Liv. Misticos de Reis*, code 3, ff. 40–9. See also Pierre David, 'Français du midi dans les évêchés portugais (1279–1390)', *Bulletin des Etudes Portugaises*, 39 (1942), 18–19.

[295] On João de Cardaillac, author of the *Liber Regalis*: David, 'Français du midi', pp. 19–21 and also *MPV*, vol. II, p. clxi. The sermon written by him for the movement of the body of Inês de Castro (*c*. 1360) can be read in Arnaut, *A crise nacional*, pp. 471–4. The beginning of the same decade was also the date of his exile to Burgos following a probable conflict with the Portuguese king.

[296] The bishop João Gomes de Chaves, who was a witness to the will of the queen mother D. Beatriz, served Pedro in various embassies, particularly Gascony in 1366: *CR Pedro*, pp. 268 and 272.

[297] *MPV*, vol. I, pp. 350, 353 and 394 on Gil de Viana. Lourenço Martins was also *chanceler* to Queen Beatriz and her witness.

[298] The best-known case is that of the archbishop of Toledo, Vasco Fernández, brother of Gutierre Fernández de Toledo, the *reposteiro-mor* to Pedro the Cruel. However, we also find the Sevillian canon Paio de Meira in Portugal, and the successive bishops of Ciudad Rodrigo, for example Afonso and, at the beginning of the reign of John, Rodrigo. It is only in the case of the last of these that there would seem to have been proximity to the court circle.

Lisbon, Martinho, an important individual from Valencia and 'privado' of the king. He was the principal supporter of the popes at Avignon, and maintained his relations with the French curia and its successive nuncios and legates, in particular with the inquisitor, Nicholas Eymerich, and Cardinal Pedro de Luna.[299] However, the successive bishops of Coimbra, the Castilians Pedro Tenorio and Juan Cabeza de Vaca,[300] and the bishop of Guarda, Afonso Correia, were also connected to Avignon and to the Portuguese court.[301] The archbishop of Braga, Lourenço Vicente, who was the principal of the Roman cause in Portugal, became involved in a serious conflict in his diocese, and appears to have had a stormy relationship with the monarch and the court. However, he accompanied the Master of Aviz as one of his main supporters in the hierarchy, as did other prelates who had previously been under the wing of Fernando, such as João de Ornelas, the abbot of Alcobaça.[302]

Within this general panorama, the fifteenth century represented a strengthening of the attraction of court on the principal ecclesiastics of the kingdom in a movement whose several facets are worth distinguishing. We thus have the presence of the bishops who were promoted through their royal service in administration and justice (whose importance was growing in number and influence within the episcopal group), and also the presence of those who, as already mentioned, served as *capelães-mores*. Another phenomenon progressing in the same way as the homogeneity of recruitment is the participation of important Portuguese court nobility in the episcopal hierarchy, which determined the essentially court career of bishops such as Pedro de Noronha or Fernando

[299] Successively bishop of Silves between 1371 and 1378 and of Lisbon between 1379 and 1383, Martinho was Fernando's ambassador in France and Castile: *MPV*, vol. II, p. 394; *CR Fernando*, pp. 301 and 543; *DP*, vol. I, pp. 150–4; Júlio César Baptista, *Portugal e o cisma do Ocidente*, offprint of *Lusitania Sacra* (Lisbon, 1956), pp. 76, 87, 94, 133, 137 and 162. He was a member of the king's council from the 1370s and only withdrew from court, presumably temporarily, in 1381. This bishop was killed in the revolts of Lisbon in 1383, in the famous scene described by Fernão Lopes.

[300] On Pedro Tenório, bishop of Coimbra between 1370 and 1375, see *CR Fernando*, p. 340 and Luis Suárez Fernández, 'Don Pedro Tenorio, arzobispo de Toledo (1375–1399)', in *Estudios Dedicados a Menéndez Pidal* (Valladolid: University of Valladolid 1953), vol. IV, pp. 601–27. During the period mentioned above, this prelate moved to Avignon. His sister, Urraca Tendes Tenório, married the Portuguese courtier Aires Gomes da Silva II, 'o Moço'. On João Cabeza de Vaca, *CR Fernando*, pp. 553 and 575, and Baptista, *Portugal e o cisma*, pp. 142 and 156.

[301] This prelate then served D. Beatriz, daughter of King Fernando, as her *chanceler* when she was queen of Castile: *CR Fernando*, pp. 407, 553 and 575. On her ambassador to Castile in the service of Fernando: *GTT*, vol. VII, pp. 263–70.

[302] Lourenço Vicente studied in France during the 1340s: Joaquim Veríssimo Serrão, *Portugueses no estudo de Toulouse* (Coimbra: University of Coimbra, 1954), pp. 20–3. The conflict which put him in opposition to the monarch in 1377 was rekindled in 1383: ANTT, *Ch. D. Fernando*, 3, ff. 53, 55v. In a diametrically opposed route to that of the bishop D. Martinho, he was called to the court in 1381. According to the chronicler Lopes, his bastard daughter was a member of the entourage of Leonor Teles, as stated above. On his career alongside John I: *CR João I*, vol. I, pp. 48 and 186; vol. II, p. 89. His participation in the council of John is mentioned, for example ANTT, *Ch. D. João I*, 1, f. 12.

da Guerra, whose political activity and influence at court have been carefully studied, since they are essential to an understanding of important events during the middle of the century. This participation, though, also explains the troubled career of Bishop Luis Coutinho and his problems during the regency of the Duke of Coimbra,[303] or in the period following Alfarrobeira the progress, essentially at court, of Rodrigo de Noronha. To this mode of participation at court, which was generally associated to the post of counsellor to the monarchs, and which appears more easily accessed by prelates of noble birth, was also attached the control of some important posts by these men of the Church, such as those of *chanceler-mor* and *regedor* of the *casa da suplicação*, which were held by the archbishop of Braga, Fernando da Guerra, who has been mentioned frequently and who also held the post of *escrivão da puridade*.

Let us look more closely at the progress of some of these men. The principal prelates of the court of John I besides João Afonso da Azambuja, Martim Afonso da Charneca and Fernando da Guerra, whom I have already mentioned, can be grouped in two distinct generations. We therefore find a first group comprising Archbishop Lourenço Vicente, the bishop of Lisbon, João Anes 'Escudeiro', and the bishop of Évora of the same name, João Anes, all of whom were present at decisive moments of the government of the kingdom until the end of the fourteenth century and who also took part in military action and in the more important diplomatic missions.[304] During the 1420s there appear in a second generation the figures of Álvaro de Abreu, bishop of Évora, and the bishop of Viseu, Garcia Rodrigues, both of whom were connected to the Infante Duarte, whose influence in the government of the kingdom was ever increasing. The reign of Duarte was in turn dominated by the figure of the archbishop, Pedro de Noronha, although Álvaro Abreu continued to be prominent, as did the counsellors Luis do Amaral, bishop of Viseu, who was at the Council of Basel, with Antão Martins de Chaves, who was to become a cardinal in 1439. He was the author of a great speech or discourse on royalty written for Duarte which very probably was presented on his accession to the throne.[305]

303 This bishop was prevented from taking over the diocese of Viseu in 1439–40 by the regent, according to H. Baquero Moreno and A. Dias Dinis, owing to the adherence of his family to the cause of Queen Eleanor: *ALF*, vol. II, pp. 789–91 and also *MH*, vol. VII, pp. 119 and 129–30. On his time in Castile in 1445 and 1447: *MH*, vol. VIII, pp. 290–1 and vol. IX, pp. 254–8. Having been successively bishop of Coimbra and archbishop of Lisbon, following Alfarrobeira he was included in the council of Afonso V: ANTT, *Ch. D. Afonso V*, 4, f. 11v.

304 On the war activity of Lourenço Vicente, see the picturesque description by Fernão Lopes: *CR João I*, vol. I, p. 186. On João Anes 'Escudeiro': *CR João I*, vol. I, pp. 277 and 286. On the bishop of Évora, by this time present at the Cortes of Coimbra: *MPV*, vol. II, pp. cxi–cxii and A. L. Carvalho Homem, *Conselho real ou conselheiros do rei? A propósito dos 'privados' de D. João I*, offprint of *Revista da Faculdade de Letras* (Oporto, 1987), p. 56.

305 This text appears attributed to the bishop of Oporto in the *Livro dos Conselhos de El-Rei D. Duarte*, pp. 82–6. The date stated in it (which may be the date of the manuscript copy of the 'oration', and not that of the composition of the text) coincided with the closing, not with

Following the death of Duarte, the palace ecclesiastical circle was clearly more restricted owing to the division of the political society, characterised universally by the regency of Pedro. With the exile of Pedro de Noronha, the death of Álvaro de Abreu and the absence from the curia of Antão Martins, one can speak of a true eclipse at court of the most important prelates of the previous reign.[306] However, it was a propitious moment for Archbishop Fernando da Guerra and the Carmelite Fr. João Manuel, whose careers at court continued trouble-free following Alfarrobeira. The regent had also placed trusted men in important positions relating to the running of the dioceses. Prominent at court at the time, among those 'da sua feitura' were the bishop of Coimbra, Álvaro Ferreira, and also Dr Álvaro Afonso, whom I have already mentioned and who had been promoted to the episcopacy under the patronage of the duke's family, as was the archdeacon of Santarém, the famous man of letters and counsellor to the regent Dr Estevão Afonso, who through Pedro's direct influence was put in charge of the diocese of Lisbon.[307]

Some common aspects of the careers of these bishops, who are seen as zealous servants of the monarchs of Aviz, should be emphasised. In the first place is their education in law at Italian universities, in particular Bologna. Also there was a common experience of the curia in the service of the pope, which frequently meant participation in the governing circles of the great magnates and ecclesiastical patrons of the age who were cardinals, a factor of great cultural importance which has not been sufficiently studied for the fourteenth and fifteenth centuries. Finally is the fact shown by their careers of the opening of a problematic debate as to the fate of the Church through their participation at the Councils of Pisa, Constance, Basel and Ferrara-Florence. As to the first of these points, that is their university education, there is a general tendency towards a predominance of those trained in law among the ecclesiastics present at the courts of the end of the Middle Ages of which the curia itself was an early example; according to Bernard Guillemain, the cardinals of the period of Avignon had, in the main, been trained in law, which tendency was constantly increasing in all groups of the world of the curia from the fourteenth century.[308]

the opening, of the Cortes of Leiria-Santarém. According to Rui de Pina, however, the oration of the 'auto de obediência' to D. Duarte in 1433 must have been made by the bishop of Évora, Álvaro de Abreu, an opinion also taken up by the historian Armindo de Sousa, 'As Cortes de Leiria-Santarém de 1433', *Estudos Medievais*, 2 (1982), 99–100.

306 On the exile of Noronha: *CR Afonso V*, pp. 622–3. The income of the bishopric was 'sequestered' from him by the regent: *MH*, vol. VII, pp. 12–13. Álvaro de Abreu was, however, suggested as 'o prelado que se ha de poer' in 1438 for the council of the regency which arose from the Cortes of Torres Novas: *MH*, vol. VI, p. 270. Two years later he was dead.

307 *CR Afonso V*, p. 636. The texts of the fifteenth-century annual reports of Santa Cruz state of this bishop of Coimbra that 'era criado' of the regent, 'e ele lhe dera o bispado': Cruz, *Santa Cruz de Coimbra*, p. 322. On Doctor Estevão Afonso: *MH*, vol. VII, pp. 145–8, 149 and 187 and Costa, *Portugueses no Colégio de S. Clemente*, vol. I, pp. 519–36.

308 Seventy-one per cent of the total of those who graduated, as opposed to only 28 per cent of those trained in theology and 1 per cent in arts: Bernard Guillemain, *La Cour pontificale d'Avignon, 1309–1376: étude d'une société* (Paris: Ecole Française de Rome, 1962). For an

As to the attraction which the papal court exercised upon the clerics from the Portuguese kingdom, it can be said that this was increased still more in the fifteenth century by the constitution of several cardinalates among the Portuguese, where the most ambitious could prosper and develop their network of connections. On this matter, and evocative of the enthusiasm and brilliant perspectives available for those who went to the curia, is the discourse of the young secretary Lapo da Castiglionchio in his *Dialogus de Curiae Commodis*, written during the extraordinary period of the Council in 1438:

> Be it peace or war, the agreements or the marriages between sovereigns and princes, or the controversies that might arise among them, all of this is granted by the pope, and all is discussed at the papal curia, as if in a public forum. It is necessary, therefore, for one who is in the midst of such a multitude of men and of matters, to see much, to hear much, to learn and to do much. He will take part in the conversations, he will participate in the speeches and in the customs of many uncommon men, he will get to know their habits and their lives, he will be linked to them by friendship and by familiarity. All of this will establish a capacity for judgement, allowing to accept or to reprove many things, to choose or to refuse others, to correct and amend so many cases that any natural talent, even if it is a weak one, provided that he is not negligent, just by the fact of being at the curia will overcome even men of higher natural disposition.[309]

By entrusting to other clerics, in the majority of cases, the effective performance of many of the tasks of government of the dioceses, and by exercising over them a more or less close control, the important prelates at court during the end of the Middle Ages performed an essential role in the structuring of a true clerical circle belonging to the palace alongside the Portuguese kings. This circle was connected through a close-knit network of those dependent upon the ecclesiastical structures and also upon the political society of Iberia (because of their frequent connection with the queens and the relatives of the royal households) and to the even larger strata of ecclesiastical elites which had as their centre the curia. For the period of personal government of Afonso V after 1449, bishops such as João Galvão or Nuno Álvares de Aguiar are well-known examples of this intermediary position and of the extensive political influence exercised at the centre of the political society of the time. João Galvão successively moved in the government of various dioceses but always remained at the royal court as a resident, and held there the important post of *escrivão da puridade* during the 1460s and 1470s.[310] Nuno de Aguiar, who was made

identification of the principal *familiae* of the curia during this period: A. Esch, 'Dal medioevo al Rinascimento: uomini a Roma dal 1350 al 1450', *Archivio della Società Romana di Storia Patria*, 94 (1971), 1–10.

309 Lapo da Castiglionchio, 'Dialogus de Curiae Commodis', in Eugenio Garin (ed.), *Prosatori Latini del Quattrocento* (Milan: Ricciardi, 1952), p. 196.

310 On the studies and court experience of João Rodrigues Galvão: Costa, *Portugueses no Colégio de S. Clemente*, vol. I, pp. 177–81; vol. II, pp. 701–16. Also *DHP*, vol. II, p. 323. In 1483,

non-resident bishop of the Moroccan city of Tangier, accompanied the monarch on his African war expeditions. Once again, the paradoxically traditionalist yet reforming perspective of the debate in the Cortes insisted, in the mid-fifteenth century, on a criticism of this situation, and repeatedly and unsuccessfully exhorted the monarch: 'aos bispos ... deues mandar que desacupem vosa corte e se vam pera seus bispados'.[311]

Even if those prelates of whom I have written never achieved an important role in the structure of the Church, many other clerics were prominent at the Portuguese court of the fourteenth and fifteenth centuries within the ambit of all the posts which demanded some education and, as is very well known, in particular as specialists in law with a university education. In his studies on the *desembargo* of the Portuguese kings, Carvalho Homem detected a certain decline, during the entire fourteenth century and up to the end of the reign of John I, of the ecclesiastical presence among the group of officials who produced the royal charters registered in the *chancelaria*. The 'clérigos d'el-rei' who were predominant during the thirteenth century in bureaucratic, administrative and judicial posts, and who, according to Carvalho Homem, were still represented until about 1340, being about 30 per cent of all the officials who acted in the *desembargo*, appear to have been succeeded by a variety of servants characteristic of the later medieval period. Among them were many lay and tonsured men who were following studies and who later abandoned their ecclesiastical career. This does not mean that in court circles and even directly close to the monarch there did not continue to be some men of the Church in the full sense of the word who visibly combined service to the king with the effective performance of their clerical position, whether in their distinctive way of life (and the question of celibacy here acquires particular importance as the 'sign' of belonging), or in the exercise (although intermittent) of some ecclesiastical office.

Clearly, these distinctions cannot be considered as proof, for we cannot overlook the fact that individuals at court who had received the tonsure could at any moment assert their distinct status and juridical standing. We know that the privilege of ecclesiastical tenancy could be applied to these royal officials, even when in their way of life there was nothing to indicate that they were considered clerics. The example of Dr Gil Martins, who was the object of a petition presented by the monarch to the pope in 1429, allows us to affirm that, even though he had abandoned the major part of his ecclesiastical career, having indeed married and had children, it was still possible (for certain with the important help and protection of the king) to attempt to resume the career which he had interrupted by demanding, by this time a widower, several benefices and

when Galvão was archbishop of Braga, he mentioned to the Cabido the 'grandes e muito largas despesas que fezera depois que el Rey nosso senhor he Rey, andando per sseu mandado e por serviço sseu e destes rregnos sempre em sua corte e nunca della partira': *MPV*, vol. II, p. cccxxvi and note. Afonso V granted him the title of Count of Arganil.

311 General chapters of the Cortes of 1472–73: ANTT, Cortes, M 2, 14, f. 66.

even the episcopal dignity.[312] In fact, in spite of their numbering many and having some influence, the existence at court of this group, some of whom we can call 'quasi-clerics', was one of the most important phenomena of the process of laification of the ecclesiastical structures already referred to above, and a more significant point in the constant negotiation of the statutory limits of servants close to the king. These are individuals whom an historian of the ecclesiastical institutions did not hesitate in calling 'a species of "amphibians" who developed on the margins of the clerical world',[313] who found at the court of the kings one of their preferred styles of life. From the point of view of individuals involved there, the tonsure or the minor orders were merely the inescapable opening to a hypothetical ecclesiastical career, which could be easily exchanged, should circumstances allow, for a beneficial marriage or which could be relegated to the status of a project put on hold because of a burdensome career in the service of the king or of an important noble.

A first group of ecclesiastical servants is prominent among the officials of a bureaucratic and administrative/financial type, as was the case with the successive *vedores da chancelaria* of Afonso IV and Fernando,[314] or with some *vedores* of the household of Pedro, Fernando and John I, all of whom were clerics.[315] Occasionally we also find evidence of some *vedor da fazenda* who was also a member of the clergy. This was an environment where the clerical presence was felt more in the exercise of judicial offices, since their importance in the group of magistrates and judges of the court tribunals remained significant throughout the fourteenth and fifteenth centuries. A career at court could, however, be extremely unstable, for reasons which in many cases are not clear but which are connected to the frequent inconstancy of royal protection. Because of his singular progress, which reveals the vulnerability of court positions, prominent among the various men of letters in the service of the fourteenth-century monarchs is Master Gonçalo das Decretais, a man of the Church who served Pedro and his son, the king, until the 1370s and who then fell into disgrace. During the reign of Fernando, notable careers were also those of the choirmaster of Braga, Vasco Domingues, who was the monarch's ambassador and counsellor, and the dean of Silves and Coimbra, Rui Lourenço de Tavira, who was also a doctor in laws and who participated in several diplomatic missions and meetings of the Council, in particular those relating to the Schism. The

312 *MPV*, vol. IV, pp. 496–7. 313 Le Bras, *Institutions écclésiastiques*, p. 153.

314 This refers to the clerics Vasco Gonçalves and Estevão Gomes, who also served D. Afonso IV as his *ouvidores*, and of the canon of Évora, Martim Gil: *Desembargo*, pp. 387, 295, 366.

315 On Fernando Esteves, cleric and *vedor* of the household of King Pedro: *Desembargo*, p. 472 and *MPV*, vol. I, p. 341. During the reign of Fernando, the ecclesiastic Afonso Martins served in this post in the 1370s and 1380s: *Desembargo*, p. 271; ANTT, *Ch. D. Fernando*, 3, f. 18; *MPV*, vol. II, p. 5. Among the successive *vedores* of the household of John, the dean of Lisbon, Dinis Anes, was also prominent: ANTT, *Ch. D. João I*, 5, f. 86v; *MH*, vol. I, pp. 285 and 317–19; *MPV*, vol. IV, p. 224.

presence of this latter cleric at court continued during the rule of John until the early years of the new century.

Among the officials and lawmakers who were best known in the fifteenth century whose careers progressed as men of the Church we find the choirmaster of Coimbra, Fernão Gonçalves Beleágua at the court of John I,[316] and the dean of Silves and prior of the Collegiate of Guimarães, Afonso Gomes de Lemos, who was protected by Duarte.[317] Dr João Beleágua, dean of Guarda, was *desembargador* at the court of Afonso V during and following the regency of the Infante Pedro,[318] when Dr Estevão Afonso, who has already been mentioned, was prominent as counsellor and trusted man of the regent. Social roles performed by these men and the type of interrelations which define their position at court are entirely similar to those of laymen. Once again, one must emphasise that this relative lack of difference in position and lifestyle of laymen and clerics was the subject of debate and criticism by their contemporaries. For example, the Portuguese André Dias de Escobar, in his translation of about 1435 of Jacopone da Todi's poem 'Pranto da Igreja', included some verses of his own which were intended to lament the development of the times: 'E hu som os doutores plenos de sabedoria / todos os vejo sayr de toda boa vyda / e nom curam de sçiênçia, nem de outra boa doutrina / mays todos trabalham por averem ofiçios / e honrras e benefiçios e muyta pecunya / e pera ajuntarem em requeza e muyto algo.'[319] As in the case of the 'fidalguia', the 'clerezia' are included in his definition for their undisguised quest for material gain.

Closer to the 'purity' of the kings there are some clerics who are prominent as clerks of the *câmara* and secretaries, particularly during the first half of the fifteenth century. With John I there was, as already said, the Benedictine Afonso Martins. But there was also the dean of Lisbon, João Rodrigues, secretary to the then Infante Duarte from the 1420s and agent of the monarch at the curia between 1427 and 1430. A set of nine letters sent to the abbot of Florence D. Gomes by this secretary prove him as such between these years and allow us to define his intellectual profile and to determine his broader professional and cultural interests.[320] João Rodrigues, who saw in Coluccio Salutati a

[316] Having been rector of the college of St Clement in Bologna between 1401 and 1402 this cleric, who was there from the final decade of the previous century, graduated in 1408. The network of his relationships was extensive, and included such prelates as D. Gil Alma, bishop of Oporto and Coimbra, and the well-known doctor Gil do Sem: Sousa Costa, *Portugueses no Colégio de S. Clemente*, vol. I, pp. 25–6 and 271–99; vol. II, pp. 1180–1.

[317] *CUP*, vol. IV, p. 54; *MPV*, vol. II, pp. cclxi–cclxii; *MH*, vol. VI, pp. 144–9. See also *ALF*, vol. II, p. 830 and Marques, 'A Colegiada de Guimarães'.

[318] ANTT, *LN*, Extras, ff. 96v–98. The principal aspects of his scholastic progress in Italy (from 1427) and of his connections with the court circle: Costa, *Portugueses no Colégio de S. Clemente*, vol. I, pp. 627–9 and also *CUP*, vol. IV, p. 43. I have not managed to discover what was the exact family relationship between the Beleáguas.

[319] Mário Martins, *Laudes e cantigas espirituais de Mestre André Dias* (Roriz: Ed. Mosteiro de Singeverga, 1951), p. 23.

[320] Rita Costa Gomes, 'Cartas Portuguesas do século XV. Ensaio de interpretação cultural' (in the foreword).

possible model for his function as secretary, served his master during the 1430s in Portugal, from where he sent a final missive to the abbot and his old protector in Italian lands, telling of the disaster at Tangier.[321] Recourse to clerics as clerks in the *câmara* of the monarchs continues to be found with Afonso V in the case of the canon of Lisbon, Lourenço Abul, his trusted secretary and nuncio,[322] or the clerk of the *câmara*, João Vasques.

Still in the sphere of the 'purity' of the monarchs, there remains to mention the important presence of ecclesiastical doctors in the royal *câmara*, who were among the group of servants of the body of the king, which included the physicians (both Christians and Jews), surgeons, apothecaries and barbers. Some aspects of the activity of the physicians connected to the rulings of the medical profession in the kingdom by the practice of public examinations for the issue of *licentiae praticandi* have been studied by Iria Gonçalves and have contributed to the identification of the majority of clerics connected to this service.[323] We find at the Portuguese court of the fourteenth century some doctors who attended French universities, such as Master Afonso Dinis or, possibly, Master Martinho do Rosmaninhal; this was also the case of Master Lourenço Gomes, doctor to Fernando. At the court of Pedro were Master Gonçalo Vasques and Master João, and during the second half of the century the physicians Master Vicente and Master Gil, all of whom were clerics. The most prominent person at the *câmara* of Fernando, the physician Master Martinho, appeared once again as servant at the court of John with the cleric Lourenço Fogaça. As seen in the case of the confessors, this permanence of the same physicians once again proves an unequivocal continuity between the court of Fernando and John I, a fact which is systematically ignored by modern historiography. In the reign of Afonso V, corresponding to a growing rise of the Jewish physicians within the fifteenth-century court, there is evidence of two converts, Master Afonso Madeira and Master Rodrigo de Lucena, of whose university education we have clear information, at least in the case of the former. This is besides the clerical presence of Fernão Álvares Cardoso, who has already been mentioned several times, and the prior of Óbidos, Master Fernando.[324]

[321] BLAU, Ash 1792 (1716), I, fasc. IV, 10; I, fasc. IV, 12. This last document, which includes a report relative to the doomed expedition to Tangiers, was published by Domingos Maurício Gomes dos Santos, *D. Duarte e as responsabilidades de Tânger (1433–1438)* (Lisbon, Comissão Executiva do V Centenário da Morte do Infante D. Henrique: 1960).

[322] In the successive editions of Rui de Pina, his name was corrupted to Lourenço Abril: *CR Afonso V*, p. 726.

[323] Iria Gonçalves, *Imagens do mundo medieval* (Lisbon: Horizonte, 1988), pp. 9–52.

[324] Numerous data on each of these clerics can be found in the notes of my doctoral thesis. On the Jewish origins of Master Madeira: *CUP*, vol. V, p. 265. Master Rodrigo de Lucena, who also succeeded him as *fisico-mor* was the brother of the famous legist Dr Vasco Fernandes de Lucena, whose conversion is well known: Nuno Espinosa Gomes da Silva, *Humanismo e direito em Portugal no século XVI* (Lisbon: Ed. do Autor, 1964), pp. 114–17 and note 58; H. Baquero Moreno, 'A conspiração contra D. João II', *Arquivos do Centro Cultural Português*, 2 (1970), 56–66. It is possible that the conversion of Master Madeira is related to the possibility

Finally, it can be said that the sphere of the sacred represented merely a small part of the activity of the ecclesiastics in the ambit of the court at the end of the Middle Ages. While members of the 'political body' *par excellence*, the royal council, and while caring for the bodily and spiritual health of the monarchs, but above all as officials and agents of royal power, the men of the Church are revealed as an essential component of the entourage of the monarchs. Theirs was an important role in the execution and even the actual conception of diplomacy of the time, alongside the important nobles and the king's trusted men. We also find in the little remaining to us of their writings a fairly clear notion of the rights and duties of the royal figure and the first formulations of some myths and historiographic constructions relating to the origins of the Portuguese royalty. An example of the first is the speech written for Duarte by the bishop of Oporto, with many quotations from passages of the Bible in support of the idea of a continuity of royalty, not perhaps contingent in view of the recent physical death of his predecessor (*rex in aeternum vive*); a principal and very real theme of this discourse was also a long development supported by Aristotelian authority and by the 'livro do regimento dos príncipes' upon justice as a foundation of government.[325] Significantly, we also find in this 'oration' of 1433 a reminder of a famous episode relating to the Count of Portucale, Henrique, told in the chronicle of 1419, which states exactly how historical ideas contributed to an interpretation of the origins of the Kingdom and of Portuguese royalty in the Portuguese court environment.[326] In this same context, which saw the first formulations of the more famous myth of the foundation of the Portuguese kingdom, is the myth of Ourique, identified by Lindley Cintra in that chronicle.[327] In a similar way, the legendary ascendancy of the Count (and therefore of his son Afonso Henriques) also made its early appearance in the text of the will of Archbishop Lourenço Vicente, the faithful servant of John I whom I have already mentioned and who, in 1391, wanted to be buried 'ali onde jaz o conde D. Henrique filho que foi del rey de Ungria'.[328] These are images of royalty which are combined to establish a lasting mythical and legendary but also doctrinal and political complex whose coherence can be appreciated in the writings of the clerics of the court of the period.

of obtaining the much-desired university doctorate, which was granted him in Salamanca. On this: Cecil Roth, 'The qualification of Jewish physicians in the Middle Ages', *Speculum*, 28 (1953), 834–43.

[325] *Livro dos Conselhos*, pp. 82–6. [326] *Livro dos Conselhos*, p. 84.

[327] Luis Filipe Lindley Cintra, 'Sobre a formação e evolução da lenda de Ourique (até à Crónica de 1419)', *Revista da Faculdade de Letras de Lisboa*, 23 (1957), 168–215.

[328] Published by José Marques, 'O testamento de D. Lourenço Vicente e as suas capelas na Sé de Braga e na Lourinhã', in *Homenagem à Arquidiocese Primaz* (Braga: Academia Portuguesa da História, 1993), p. 203. On the legendary Hungarian rise of Afonso Henriques: Jorge de Sena, 'A família de D. Afonso Henriques', in *Estudos de História e de Cultura* (Lisbon: Revista Ocidente, 1967).

MERCHANTS AND OFFICIALS

Alfonso stated in his *Partidas* that 'de los homes nobles et poderosos non se puede el rey servir en los oficios de cada dia, ca por la nobleza desdenarian el servicio cotidiano et por el poderio atreverse hien mucho aina à facer cosas que tornarien como en dano et en desprecamiento del'.[329] Among the counsels given to his son and collected in the *Libro Enfenido* in the first half of the fourteenth century, Don Juan Manuel also describes the composition of the entourage of an important lord or of a king:

> Vos deuedes saber que los ofiçiales son de muchas guisas: ca vnos ay que por fuerça deuen ser fijos dalgo et los omnes de mayor estado que son en casa de los sennores; asi commo mayordomos et alferes et adelantados mayores et mayorales que tienen la criança de los fijos de los sennores. Otros ay que por fuerça deuen ser fijos dalgo et commo oficiales: esos son los alcaydes que tienen los castiellos. Otros oficiales ay que pueden ser fijos dalgo o omnes onrados, criados de los sennores; asi commo alcalles et alguaziles de las casas de los sennores; et de las sus villas, et chanceller et despensero et camarero et tesorero et recabdador de las rentas de los sennores, tan bien en renta commo en fialdat, et copero, et cauallero et çaquitero et ceuadero, et todos los otros ofiçios de las casas de los sennores que costunbran los sennores de dar a sus criados.[330]

The recruitment of the servants of differing status was in turn during the first decades of the fifteenth century the object of reflection of the Portuguese Infante Pedro in his famous 'Carta de Bruges', which suggests a certain proportionality must be respected between the noble servants and the remainder, condemning the tendency towards overgeneralised class promotion in the service of the kings and lords.[331] Not always were those who served at court recruited from the nobility, according to reflection of the time, and this also depended on the greater or lesser dignity attributed to the various posts or social roles. On the contrary, it is a doctrine constantly restated by the Hispanic texts that a well-organised royal entourage should encompass a hierarchical variety of individuals, and should include men of inferior standing.

This vast group of more humble servants is difficult to evaluate globally and less still can one study it in detail through recourse to the reconstruction of biographies, since there are innumerable obstacles to the identification of individuals. It would seem, however, that those who formed the higher strata can be identified by critical use of the few available facts. Occasionally the progress of some individuals and even at times of entire families stands out. These for some

329 *Las Siete Partidas*, vol. I, p. 58.

330 'Libro enfenido', *Obras completas*,vol. I, pp. 169–70.

331 Artur Moreira de Sá (ed.), *A carta de Bruges do Infante D. Pedro*, offprint of *Biblos* (Coimbra, 1952), p. 19.

reason were noted and escaped anonymity, either because of their connection to the urban elite of the kingdom or through their ennoblement, which occurred after successive generations of faithful service, or through the greater 'visibility' which their functions at court implied. This will be dealt with later.

The presence of merchants alongside the kings at the end of the Middle Ages, although generally ignored, is none the less evidence which places once again within the context of late-medieval society the identification of those who served within the financial sphere of the household and *fazenda* of the monarchs. Let us move on to a careful analysis of the list of successive *tesoureiros* and *reposteiros-mores*, of the *vedores da fazenda* and *vedores da casa* and of the *contadores* (in particular those called the *contador-mores* who, as already stated above, appeared closest to the monarchs, and also the fifteenth-century *contadores da casa*) and also of the later *escrivães da fazenda*. The relative homogeneity from the point of view of social recruitment of these servants who remained at court, leaving aside their active membership of distinct institutions, is a fact which appears to be of great importance. The development of individual progress by crossing between distinct organisms is also not rare, and indeed was common during the period of the Aviz dynasty. This cannot be evaluated by monograph studies of one single organism or institution. It is in the intersection and the dynamic succession of the several roles they performed that a better perception can eventually be obtained of the profile of the merchant officials in the service of the kings.

It appears to have been the Lisbon merchants who were the principal individuals prominent in the *tesouro* and *repostaria* of Afonso IV, where we find the commoner João de Rates serving as *tesoureiro* in the 1330s, or the *reposteiro-mor* João Eanes de Coruche among other, more obscure figures. The activities of the first of these, as well as those of his probable relative Martim de Rates (who received income from sums arising from the customs house of Lisbon in the period between 1336 and 1340), can be evaluated by the supply of various gold objects to the monarch made on the occasion of the marriage of the Infanta Leonor in 1347.[332]

Although from the first half of the fourteenth century we find the tendency for a more rapid replacement of the *tesoureiros* at court, who served for short periods at the time, those servants who moved from one reign to another were not rare, particularly in the sphere of the *repostaria*. It was there that the palace activities of the well-known medieval Lobato family began in the middle of the fourteenth century. The first we find at court is Gonçalo Lobato, who was *reposteiro-mor* to the young Infante Pedro during the lifetime of his father, possibly the same

[332] On the *tesoureiro*: *Desembargo*, p. 348. On the *reposteiro*: *CDA*, vol. I, pp. 169, 364–5 and also Fr. Salvado Martins, *Vida e milagres de S. Isabel*, p. 91. On the Rates family: *DP*, supplement to vol. I, p. 391; *DCA*, vol. II, pp. 80–3; ANTT, *CR*, S. Maria de Aguiar, M 1, 11 (list of objects also published by A. Caetano de Sousa).

who in 1334 married the daughter of the *reposteiro* of the monarch himself, João Eanes de Coruche. Also with Pedro we find Estevão Lobato and, during the reign of Fernando, the best-known, Pedro Anes Lobato, who was a rich vassal of the Count of Barcelos. In the fifteenth century the Lobatos who were connected to the king's *fazenda* were numerous, particularly as *vedores*.[333]

We know little as to the actual functioning of the finances of the king during this period and the fact that we find, as already said, some clerics working with merchants and officials as *contadores* and later as *vedores*, merely confirms indirectly the progressive bureaucratisation of the *fazenda* during the fourteenth century. This process of bureaucratisation was studied by Virginia Rau, in particular through the establishment of a multiplicity of new instances of register and control, such as the 'casa dos contos'. The figure of the merchant and also of the cleric/man of letters serving as a financial official at court is related to the construction of these new instances. Thus, we can speak of the clerics and men of business becoming part of the court as a natural corollary in this growing bureaucratisation of the royal finances. Among the individuals who were prominent in the second half of the fourteenth century we are able to reconstruct the progress, which is notable in every way, of Pero Afonso Mealha, who was the first known *vedor da fazenda*. In the service of Pedro and his son Fernando from 1361 until 1379, Pero Afonso ended by withdrawing from court, probably because of his political standing and not, as most usually occurred among the officials of the *fazenda*, because of debts or financial collapse. A profile of his patrimony and his social circle, which was completed by Lurdes Rosa, demonstrates that he possessed a reasonable fortune in Lisbon around Almada and in the Tagus valley, and that he was the owner of much property which he had gradually accumulated over several decades. Pero Afonso was also related to important families of Lisbon burghers who were close to the court, such as the Palhavãs and the family of Álvaro Pais.[334]

This official lived through the initial stages of the period of clearest predominance of Jewish financiers in the palace circle, which occurred in Portugal in the 1370s and 1380s, corresponding to the time when the *rabi-mor* Judas Aben Menir was *tesoureiro-mor*. This man was the famous 'privado' of Leonor Teles. The withdrawal from court of Pero Afonso may have been connected to the growing importance of Judas Aben Menir, which is a subject still in need of detailed investigation. The activity of the rabbi is found most of all between 1374 and 1383 in the *tesouro* and, at the same time, as *rendeiro* of the king.[335] In this

333 ANTT, drawer XI, M 8, 46; *CDA*, vol. I, pp. 364–5; *CR Pedro*, p. 209. See also *DHEP*, vol. I, p. 393.

334 *Desembargo*, pp. 371–2 and Maria de Lurdes Rosa, *Pero Afonso Mealha, os bens e a gestão de riqueza de um proprietário leigo no século XIV* (Redondo: Patrimonia, 1995).

335 Pedro de Azevedo, 'Culpas de David Negro', *Arquivo Histórico Português*, 1 (1903), 53–7; Maria José Ferro Tavares, 'As minorias religiosas no reinado de D. Fernando e em 1383–1385', in *Actas das Jornadas sobre Portugal Medieval* (Leiria, 1986), pp. 469–77.

financial sphere there seem at the time to have coexisted as officials both Christians and Jews, if we study the information available on the Christian *tesoureiros* and scribes of the *tesouro*, who worked alongside a Jewish *despenseiro* serving at court in the final period of the reign. Although they always remained strongly connected to the royal finances during the entire fifteenth century, particularly as *rendeiros* and also as counsellors to the monarchs on financial matters, we do not continue to find so obvious a Jewish presence at court in this specific sphere of activity as was the case, particularly through the direct control of the palace officials, during the reign of Fernando. Also regarding this aspect perhaps the influence of the supporters of the Castilian legitimist cause was felt, for Pedro the Cruel, in the middle of the century, was accused by propagandists of Henry of Trastâmara of placing the finances of Castile in the hands of favoured Jews.

The situation of the merchants and officials at court appears more clearly still during the fifteenth century, where it is possible to reconstruct actual family networks developing in this sphere of royal finances in direct contact with the monarch and the court. A family group that appears very clearly is that which encompassed, for example, members of the Alenquer family, who were close to the famous *vedor* João Afonso, and the Sardinhas, Lisbon burghers during the reign of John I.[336]

Pedro Afonso Sardinha, the representative of the *homens-bons* of Lisbon who handed the throne to the Master of Aviz at the famous Cortes of Coimbra, was *tesoureiro-mor* to the king at the beginning of the 1390s. He was the father of the *vedor da fazenda* Diogo Afonso Sardinha, whose activity dates back to the first decade of the new century and who was also connected to the government of the city. In the following generation, the Sardinhas made a matrimonial alliance with the English Paim family who had accompanied Philippa of Lancaster and settled in Portugal.[337] João de Alenquer married the widow of Diogo Afonso Sardinha. He is the celebrated individual spoken of in the 'Crónica da Conquista de Ceuta' who, following the interpretative historio-sociological study by the modern thinker António Sérgio, has been considered as the representative of a bourgeoisie which was intensely interested in Portugal's maritime expansion.[338] João Afonso was hypothetically connected to Nuno Álvares Pereira, but was without doubt close to the king and was his official from at least 1395 – first as *contador* and, from 1400, as *vedor* and counsellor. During this final period several close relatives of João Afonso served in the *casa dos contos*: his brother Luis Gomes, who was appointed *contador* at his request in 1418, and his sons

336 The concrete data upon which my studies of these families are based can be found in the notes of my doctoral thesis, to be found in Portuguese public libraries.

337 On the Paim family: W. J. Entwistle and P. E. Russell, 'A rainha D. Felipa e a sua corte', in *Congresso do Mundo Português* (Lisbon: Commissão Executiva dos Centenários, 1940), vol. II, p. 336; Mário Martins, *Dum poema inglês de John Gower e sua tradução do Português para o castelhano*, offprint of *Didaskalia* (Lisbon, 1979).

338 'João Afonso', in *DHP*, vol. I, pp. 50–1.

Rodrigo Afonso and Vicente Anes. If we note the earliest and latest dates given, we see that from the 1390s until the 1420s there was always some member of the Sardinha and Alenquer families in an important position in the management of the royal *fazenda* and close to the court.

We can also add to this example the family of the da Maias, whose influence was felt from the final years of the reign of Fernando until the 1430s. Martim da Maia, *contador* to Fernando, served the new monarch of Aviz and Queen Philippa as *vedor da fazenda* and *contador* at least until 1397. His relative Álvaro Gonçalves da Maia, who performed duties as *escrivão da câmara* between 1407 and 1414, also played a part in various diplomatic missions to Castile and Aragon (and he fleetingly appears as *vedor da casa* of the monarch). After 1415 he was prominent as *vedor da fazenda*, a position he still held at the beginning of Duarte's reign.

The Malafaias, in turn, came from the circles of the royal bureaucracy, where we find Gonçalo Peres, who had served as clerk of Fernando's *chancelaria*, and who later headed the *casa do cível* for the Aviz monarch and was a member of his council. The sons of Gonçalo Peres appear in some sources of the first half of the fifteenth century as *cavaleiros*, as was the case with Pero Gonçalves Malafaia, who served as *vedor da fazenda* between 1416 and 1433. With his brother Luis he also took part in various diplomatic missions at the end of John's reign. Pero Gonçalves became part of the council of Duarte, to whom he must earlier have been close, for his name appears associated with the financial arrangements for the prince's marriage. His brother, Luis Gonçalves Malafaia, also had an important court career, and served as *vedor da fazenda* during the regency of the Infante Pedro and as counsellor and ambassador of the young king Afonso V following Alfarrobeira.

I have already referred to the appearance with the new dynasty of various individuals of the petty nobility in the central nucleus of the *fazenda*. This process was particularly apparent in the reign of John, and there are several examples: the families of the Albergarias and the Távoras in their connection to the *tesouro* and the *repostaria* and the Freitas family, known as *vedores da fazenda* and the *vedor da casa*. Are these perhaps the 'gente nova' of whom Fernão Lopes speaks in his chronicle? A particular case was that of the Monterroios who from the period of the conquest of Ceuta were prominent in the *tesouro* and at court, where Fernão Gil de Monterroio served during the reigns of John and Duarte (until *c.* 1450), followed by his relatives Álvaro Fernandes Monterroio and Afonso Anes Monterroio, successive *tesoureiros-mores* in the rule of Afonso V.[339]

[339] The Monterroios appear to have descended from a branch of the Azevedos who were in exile in Castile at the end of the fourteenth century: Eugénio de Castro, 'Os meus Vasconcelos', *Biblos*, 8 (1932), 24–8. His return to the Portuguese court must date from the period of the conquest of Ceuta.

Because an important part of what I have called the 'nobility in service' and even some of the high nobility traditionally present at court did not show disdain for the control of these financial offices (although as we shall see this did not always mean the effective performance by the holders of the posts), it can be said that during the first half of the fifteenth century this group which materialised around the royal *fazenda* was slowly losing the exclusively mercantile profile which had been so visible during the previous century. We are indeed at the genesis of what Vitorino Magalhães Godinho termed the role of the Portuguese 'knight-merchant', an *idealtypus* in which the historian sought to summarise the main features of a figure he finds in the court social milieu at the end of the Middle Ages, and which was one of his most pertinent horizons of application. In the ideal synchronicity of the characteristics of his status, marked by the tension between two ways of life which were seen as simultaneously conflicting, we can see a crucial aspect of so many cases of social promotion such as that of the Almada and Lemos families, and also of the multiplicity of concrete situations of court society of the fifteenth century, when the noble condition appeared most of all as individual status and did not always result in the social promotion of an entire family group. From the point of view of social classifications of the time, the retention of a dual position could not be exempt from benefits for the respective family group, besides being an expression of the value previously adopted by individual ambitions, as the historian observed: 'we used to speak of the knight-merchant; but among his family some are merchants, others state officials, others nobles or *cavaleiros*, so that individual promotion is facilitated and the individual is more lord of his own destiny'.[340] Making nobles of some but also making merchants of others – these appear to be the two complementary sides of the coin which are always implied in the process of construction of court hierarchies, a construction which is accompanied by the diffusion of cultural models and ways of life which are common but which can be variously shared within the court, at times even within the same families. Commercial activities appear to be connected to the demands made by new lifestyles, requiring expenditure and emulation in wealth, while ennoblement increasingly comprised concrete forms of distinction conferred through proximity to the monarch and the royal family, so promoting in status those dedicated to royal service.

The same connection of court society to the urban elite of the kingdom is established through an analysis of servants within the administrative and judicial spheres of the court, for whom I shall adopt the generic name of 'officials', using the ambiguity and functional sense of the term as used at the time. In the passage of his 'Leal Conselheiro' dedicated to the government of society, Duarte listed the elements of this 'Fourth Estate', 'em que se entendem os

[340] Vitorino Magalhães Godinho, *Mito e mercadoria: Utopia e prática de navegar. Séculos XII–XVIII* (Lisbon: Divel, 1990), p. 578.

mais principaaes consselheiros, juizes, regedores, veedores, scrivaaes e semelhantes, os quaaes boos, leaaes, entendidos, sollicitos, tementes a deos devem seer scolhidos'.[341] The royal court was, in the fourteenth and fifteenth centuries, a place of privileged concentration of many of these social roles, owing to the process of bureaucratisation already mentioned of the structures which found their epicentre within it, or which developed at its centre, with duties connected to the actual survival of the monarch and his entourage also becoming more complex and specialised. During these centuries there was no department or body of service in the household of the king and queen where there was not a quantity of *escrivães*, *vedores*, *recebedores* and *tesoureiros*, not to mention the tribunal which accompanied the monarch, the royal council, the officials of the *desembargo* and finances of the kingdom who were connected more closely to the purity of the monarchs. Regarding the specific case of those connected to the *fazenda*, which I have just analysed, I would say that this larger group of officials was characterised above all by their education and, in spite of the growing laification of the royal servants, by a proximity to the clerical state which many practised in their youth. It is also possible in this case to follow some family progressions which are an excellent counterpoint to my study of the nobility, and which simultaneously illustrate one of the most interesting processes of its renewal and redefinition in the final period of the Middle Ages.

Two particularly significant examples of permanence at court are those of the Nogueira and do Sem families, whom we find accompanying the Portuguese kings from the beginning of the fourteenth century. A Master João 'das Leis' who had perhaps in his youth been a man of the Church was the earliest predecessor of the Nogueiras to be found at the palace, and had been an important individual of the *desembargo* and counsellor of Afonso IV. We find him again at the beginning of the reign of Fernando enjoying some importance alongside the king, but it was without doubt in the subsequent generation that the family confirmed its noble standing at court. Among the descendants of Master João are his daughters Branca, who married Dr Gil do Sem, and Constança, a maid of honour in 1358 in the household of the Queen Mother, Beatriz. Afonso Anes Nogueira (or 'das Leis'), who was a *criado* of Fernando, like so many others became part of the body of vassals of João Afonso Telo IV, the Count of Barcelos, and then held the *alcaidaria* of Lisbon.

The adherence of this last man to the cause of the Master of Aviz was a decisive factor in the continuing influence of this recent lineage at the fifteenth-century court, since Afonso took part in John's council and passed on the position of *alcaide-mor* to his descendants. Also to be noted, as a fine indication of the web of relations established among the various families of servants at court in close hierarchical positions, are the matrimonial alliances of the

[341] 'Leal Conselheiro', in *Obras dos Príncipes de Avis*, p. 247.

Nogueiras at the beginning of the new century. Afonso Anes married Joana Vaz de Almada, of the Lisbon family of whom I have spoken on several occasions, and his daughters Violante, Maria, Teresa and Constança married João Afonso de Brito, Vasco Martins de Albergaria, Diogo Fernandes de Almeida and Duarte Furtado, all courtiers of John I. The most important marriage was that of his first son, Rui Nogueira, who married a bastard daughter of Pedro de Meneses. This alliance also suggests that the first sons of the Nogueiras were strongly connected by protection and vassaldom to the Meneses through successive generations. Also prominent among the male line of Afonso Nogueira are Álvaro Afonso Nogueira, a *cavaleiro* of the court who went with John I's ambassadors to the Council of Pisa, as well as his brother, Gomes Nogueira, assistant to the *feitor* of the king of Portugal at the Tyrrhenian port. He was a young *cavaleiro* whose mercantile activity is confirmed by correspondence from 1426/27 which still survives. We must also mention the bishop of Coimbra and archbishop of Lisbon, Afonso Nogueira, who survived his brothers and was close to the court until the 1460s. Several Nogueiras were members of the entourage of Afonso V, in particular the *fidalgo* Afonso Nogueira and his son, Rui Nogueira II.

Related to the Nogueiras and also resident in urban areas of the south of the kingdom, in this case in Santarém, were the do Sem family, whose presence at court was also a constant throughout the entire period.

Pero do Sem was *chanceler* to Afonso IV and his ambassador to the curia. He was one of the most important royal officials in the first half of the fourteenth century. During this period his probable relative João do Sem distinguished himself as papal chaplain. The grandson of the *chanceler*, Gil do Sem, who was a doctor of law, was Fernando's ambassador in 1371 and 1380 and was a member of the royal council at the end of the reign. He also served the new king of Aviz during the initial period of his reign until his own death in 1387. In the 1390s his son, Martim Gil, studied in Italy, graduating in Pavia in 1398. He too was a member of the council of John I, in whose court he was prominent as legist and ambassador. Dr Martim Gil do Sem married a descendant of the *alferes* Gil Vasques da Cunha, to whom I have already referred, in a progress of alliance with court nobility which was totally parallel to that of the Nogueiras. At the end of his life Martim accompanied the Infante Duarte, and served as his *chanceler* and *tesoureiro* in the 1420s until Duarte's accession to the throne. A nephew, João do Sem, took over the leadership of the family name and also followed a career parallel to that of the legist: study at Italian universities, *chanceler* and 'privado' to Duarte, during whose reign he also became a member of the royal council; he attempted to retain his position at court at the beginning of the regency of the Infante Pedro. Because of the early death of this *chanceler* in 1441, the family found itself in a position of relative obscurity when Afonso V took personal control of the country. However, during the 1460s we find once again a descendant of his, António do Sem, who became a member of the royal entourage.

By electing for a route through military service in the royal army or through the *fazenda*, as in the case of the Nogueiras, or by maintaining their connections with the *desembargo* and the *chancelaria*, as was the case with the do Sem family, the officials of the upper hierarchy at the court of the time thus constructed routes to family promotion which demonstrate the highly prestigious significance seen in service to the king. Their rise up the court status ladder in the fifteenth century to the positions of *escudeiro*s and *cavaleiros* is perfectly clear; they shared these positions with families of traditional nobility. At the Portuguese court we find a significant group of individuals whose social position depended essentially on the retention and transmission of bureaucratic/administrative offices, as well as financial and judicial posts, with several generations of relatives succeeding in the service of the monarchs, corresponding to the typical progress of those whom an English historian called 'gentleman-bureaucrats'.[342] The English name of 'gentleman' can be compared with that of 'cavaleiro' in the Portuguese court, and was the name generally chosen by these officials for inscription on their tombs, as was the case on several monuments of members of the do Sem family in churches of Santarém.[343]

Let us examine some more examples whose reconstruction allows us to equate the different problem of the proximity of these individuals in relation to the ecclesiastical world. We find men of the Church in the origins of the Fogaça family, who were servants of the Portuguese kings at the end of the Middle Ages. João Fogaça, a cleric from Lisbon who studied medicine in Paris, practised in the household of Queen Branca of Castile in the middle of the fourteenth century. This is a period for which there are the first references to Lourenço Anes Fogaça, and these suggest the granting of shares in several Portuguese churches during this time. There is every indication that this concerned very close relatives. Lourenço Anes is found at the court of Fernando as *chanceler* and untiring diplomat to the monarch, and between 1374 and 1380 he moved to Castile, the curia, France and England. Following the death of the king, of whose will he was an executor, Lourenço Anes served Leonor Teles, whose entourage he left to assist the Master of Aviz. He destroyed the seals in his safekeeping and a little later left on a new diplomatic mission to the English court. He was one of the most notable adherents of Fernando's officials to join John I's supporters, a move which was highly fruitful for the *chanceler* and his descendants.

At the court of John I, Fogaça, whom we have already seen married to Leonor Rodrigues 'da Pedra Alçada',[344] once again acted as *chanceler* between

342 Cecil H. Clough (ed.), *Profession, Vocation and Culture in Later Medieval England* (Liverpool: Liverpool University Press, 1982), p. 92.

343 On the tombs of the do Sém family in Santarém and their inscriptions: Vergílio Correia, *Três túmulos: uma arca tumular do museu de Santarém*.

344 On his marriage: ANTT, *Ch. D. João I*, 2, ff. 6v, 69v; ANTT, *Ch. D. Afonso V*, 35, f. 94 (Leonor was still alive in 1448). The so-called 'Pedra Alçada' family, who were rich landowners from the area of Santarém, were also close to the court from the mid-fourteenth century.

1399 and 1440, and received numerous benefits. I have already referred to the presence at the court of John I of the son of João Fogaça, Lourenço Anes Fogaça II (his relative of the same name), who was a doctor at court who had studied in Bologna at the beginning of the century. Among the descendants of the *chanceler*, a prominent member is João Fogaça II, who also served as a royal official. Fernão Fogaça, in turn, moved from the court of John, where he received a *moradia* as an *escudeiro* in the service of Duarte, during whose short reign he was evident, in the wake of his father, as *chanceler-mor* and royal counsellor. At the court of Afonso V we find Diogo Fogaça, who appears to have been a relative, and who between 1449 and 1451 was *despenseiro*.

The figure of the married cleric also meant a simultaneous presence in the institutional ecclesiastical sphere while holding some benefice which did not demand the effective practice of priestly functions, and this is particularly evident among the growing group of court legislators. The figure of Dr João das Regras has been much studied because of the protagonism given him in Fernão Lopes's chronicle. This man's social origins lie in the Lisbon urban elite of the end of the fourteenth century.[345] His mother's second marriage had been to the *vedor* of Fernando's court, Álvaro Pais, who served in the *casa do cível* between 1362 and 1366 and who was *vedor da chancelaria* between 1369 and 1372; the chronicler attributed to him an important role in the rebellion of the Master of Aviz. At the court of John I and Duarte we also find descendants of Álvaro Pais.[346]

João das Regras studied in Bologna (where he graduated in 1378), and his progress is largely similar to that of Martim Afonso da Charneca. Charneca, as we have seen, had elected for an ecclesiastical career, and rose to the episcopacy. In spite of having opted for the prestigious and wealthy marriage with Leonor da Cunha, the daughter of the nobleman Martim Vasques da Cunha II, João das Regras was still prior of the collegiate of Guimarães between 1383 and 1388, and at the same time served as *chanceler* to the new king between 1385 and 1386 and as one of his principal counsellors until 1404, when he died.

345 Nuno Espinosa Gomes da Silva, *João das Regras e outros juristas Portugueses da Universidade de Lisboa (1378–1412)*, offprint of *Revista da Faculdade de Direito* (Lisbon, 1960); A. D. Sousa Costa, 'O célebre conselheiro e chanceler régio Doutor João Regras, clérigo conjugado e prior da Colegiada de Santa Maria da Oliveira de Guimarães', *Itinerarium*, 18 (1972), 232–59; Nuno Espinosa Gomes da Silva, *O chanceler João das Regras. Prior da Igreja da Oliveira em Guimarães*, offprint of *Revista da Faculdade de Direito* (Lisbon, 1974); Luis Gonzaga de Lencastre e Távora, 'Mestre João Afonso, chanceler do rei D. João I', *Arquivos de Cascais*, 1 (1980), 91–120; A. L. Carvalho Homem, 'O Doutor João das Regras no Desembargo e no Conselho régios (1384–1404). Breves notas', in *Estudos de História de Portugal: Homenagem a A. H. de Oliveira Marques* (Lisbon: Estampa, 1982), vol. I, pp. 241–53.

346 Particularly with Diogo Álvares, who can be identified as the *vedor* of the household of Philippa of Lancaster. But also with the son of Álvaro Pais, Luis Álvares, *mestre-sala* of the court: ANTT, *Ch. D. João I*, 4, f. 73v and drawer XI, M 10, 5; *MH*, vol. I, p. 209. See also ANTT, *Ch. D. Duarte*, 3, f. 31; *Ch. D. Afonso I*, 18, f. 84v. For the reconstruction of the line: *LL*, pp. 351–2.

The importance of his marriage in 1398 seems to be clear: in 1397 Leonor had inherited from her father Martim Vasques, a political enemy of the new king, and the 'infamy' incurred by the family when he went to Castile (the usual financial consequence of this 'infamy' would have been the permanent loss of all possessions) was in effect lifted. A large part of the patrimony of this branch of the Cunha family was transferred to the hands of the legist who had assisted the Master of Aviz in taking the throne. The marriage of the doctor and his aristocratic lifestyle must also be connected to the purchase he made in 1390 of the estates 'with their surroundings' near S. Marinha de Lisboa, which had belonged to the court magnate Álvaro Peres de Castro.

The legists of the beginning of the fifteenth century who represent an easily defined group of important officials at court were in many cases, as seen by these examples, immersed in the clerical world for some part of their lives, as was the case with João das Regras. It was also the case with Lançarote Esteves, secretary to John I, the 'brother doctors' Gil Martins Lourenço and Diogo Martins, and the well-known Dr Diogo Afonso Mangancha, who accompanied Duarte.[347] These *clerici uxorati* shared their sphere of activity either with the other ecclesiastics whose presence I have already analysed, or with a growing number of laymen who, from the middle of the century, played an important part in that sphere. Their connections to the urban elite of the kingdom did not prevent their alliance, through marriage, to nobility traditionally found at court, although these alliances were not always made with the more famous lines or the more powerful families, besides the highly individual case of João das Regras. There are other, rare examples among the officials and legists such as Gil do Sem, who also married a Cunha, or Pedro Gonçalves Malafaia, who married a Silva. All this contributed, as I have already said, to a growing similarity in lifestyles of these men and the laity. This does not, however, mean that in the interpretation of their position at court we should overlook the familiarity which they clearly had with the clerical and, in this case, with the university world.

Thus, in the first quarter of the fifteenth century the possession of ecclesiastical rents was associated with the position as official servant of the monarchs, which the secretary to Duarte, Rui Galvão, wrote of in 1437 in a letter to the Abbot D. Gomes:

> desy por eu seer homem de boo linhajem entendia dante a sua muj grande santidade [i.e. the Pope] açeptar perrogatiuas per que poses auer algũa denjdade benefiçios ou rendas da jgreia per que me bem e honrradamente podese manteer nom seendo casado como som como per os santos padres seus anteçesores

[347] On Lançarote: Silva, *João das Regras e outros juristas*, pp. 25–6; A. D. Sousa Costa, 'O Doutoramento em Bolonha do secretário de D. João I – Dr. Lançarote, Conde Palatino e embaixador ao Concílio de Pisa', *Itinerarium*, 3 (1957), 202–20; Costa, *Portugueses no Colégio de S. Clemente*, vol. I, pp. 385–93. On Doctor Mangancha: *DHP*, vol. II, pp. 902–3.

> E per ell senpre foi e he fecto aos ofiçiaaes dos Rex e prinçipes semelhantes de mim. Por ende visto como nosso senhor deus fez primeiro a hordem do casamento que outra nenhũa E os que neella bem vjuem mereçem seer acreçantados E auer grandes perrogatiuas E que ell por sua merçee hordenou de tall guissa que eu som desta hordem E a ella tenho fecta minha profissom em a quall da sua santidade eu de Razom posso e deuo seer proueudo d algũa Renda neestes Regnos em encomenda que aazada fosse pera ajuda e gouernança de minha vida.

In other words, what this clerk of the king's *câmara* was requesting from the Pope was the rent from Campo Maior which belonged to the bishopric of Badajoz and which was then in the hands of an ecclesiastical administrator who, besides, was his father-in-law. Certainly, his secular position was a major obstacle:

> a meu parecer esto nom he coussa em que o santo padre deua de poer duueda visto como esto nom he denjdade nem benefiçio de cura jntitolado mais he administraçom de beens que pessoa sagrall bem pode auer e gouernar que a sua santidade sabera que o papa martinho seu anteçesor proueeo a alguas pessoas leigas de Jgreias e moiesteiros que oje em dia teem emtitolados e de cura em encomenda que he muito mais graue coussa que esta que eu Requeiro.[348]

Among the 'pessoas sagrais' and those who were clerics the differences tended to recede, and indeed the principal differentiating factor, in the words of the secretary, was above all being 'oficial dos reis e prinçipes'.[349]

From when can we speak of the formation of this specific group of Portuguese court society, possessing the characteristics demonstrated by the various examples of merchants and officials in the royal entourage – general enrichment, a slight, 'amphibious' connection with the ecclesiastical circles and ennoblement during the later period studied? In Castile, the process of formation of a similar nucleus of families associated to palace service and the privileged position which they occupied in the heart of Castilian cities has been the subject of important investigations by historians such as Salvador de Moxó, Angus MacKay and Adeline Rucquoi, with an important number of changes centred on the fourteenth century. Moxó revealed for the first decades of the century the mechanism of enlargement of the spatial sphere of influence of some officers of the king's court (from cities such as Ávila, Valladolid, Cuenca and Toledo). This influence ceased to progress at a purely local level and so came closer to the profile of court nobility whose circles of political activity and alliance extended

348 BLAU, Ash 1792 (1719), I, fasc. V, 10. See also two further letters with a similar theme: I, fasc. VII, 2; I, fasc. VII, 9.

349 A parallel should be made between this text and those analysed by Maravall, 'Los "hombres de saber" ', pp. 333–62.

well beyond their patrimonial lands.[350] Rucquoi clarified the process of the contemporaneous formation of urban 'cavaleiros' in a closed group, who were organised by lineage and retained for themselves exclusively the government of the cities and established that this group rarely included servants of the king within the sphere of the palace.[351] This is a 'specific method of organisation' of the city nobility of Castile also studied by MacKay,[352] which process was to establish an important 'internal frontier' in urban society where many nobles were once again establishing their power and siting part of their patrimony at the end of the Middle Ages.[353]

In Portugal, information points towards a similar process of enrichment of the officials, visible for example in the building of some fortunes associated with service to the king, and this can also be seen in the first half of the fourteenth century. This was the period during which a few families of merchants and officials were becoming established at the court. In the main these families were from Lisbon and Santarém, or were connected to urban life in the south of the country. In the fifteenth century, to this group was added a number of families from Évora. Little is known, though, as to the structure of local elites at the time, particularly in the larger cities, or as to an eventual rigidity in their recruitment, which does not seem as accentuated in the Portuguese case according to studies made by Oliveira Marques or Ângela Beirante.[354] The image which appears in Portugal is, to the contrary, that of a greater fluidity in urban society which, curiously, increased with the changes analysed through the different lines of families connected to the court of the monarchs. In the case of Lisbon and Évora, as already seen, these court families were able during the fifteenth century to continue to be connected to the government of the cities.

One particularly surprising observation is the involvement of many of these men in war, which contradicts an overspecialised vision of their activities, both in the 'bureaucratic' sphere and in commerce and finance. Would their activity

[350] Salvador de Moxó, 'La promoción política y social de los "letrados" en la corte de Alfonso XI', *Hispania*, 35 (1975), 5–20; Salvador de Moxó, 'El auge de la nobleza urbana de Castilla y su proyección en el ámbito administrativo y rural a comienzos de la baja edad media', *Boletín de la Real Academia de la Historia*, 178 (1981), 407–510, in particular 488.

[351] Adeline Rucquoi, 'Noblesse urbaine de Castille (XIIIe–XVe siècles)', in *Les Pays de la Méditerranée occidentale au moyen âge. 106e Congrès national des sociétés savantes* (Paris: Comité des Travaux Historiques et Scientifiques, 1983), pp. 35–47.

[352] Angus MacKay, 'The lesser nobility in the kingdom of Castile', in *Society, Economy and Religion in Late Medieval Castile* (Aldershot: Variorum, 1987), [IV], pp. 159–80.

[353] Armand Arrianza, 'Le statut nobiliaire adapté à la bourgeoisie: mobilité des statuts en Castille à la fin du moyen âge', *Le Moyen Age*, 100 (1994), 413–38.

[354] A. H. Oliveira Marques, *As cidades Portuguesas nos finais da idade média*, offprint of *Penélope* (Lisbon, 1992); Maria Ângela Beirante, *Évora na idade média* (Lisbon: Fundação Calouste Gulbenkian, 1995), pp. 560–8. I have attempted an initial approach to this problem for the specific case of the cities of Beira: Rita Costa Gomes, 'As elites urbanas no final da idade média: três pequenas cidades do interior', in *Estudos e ensaios em homenagem a Vitorino Magalhães Godinho* (Lisbon: Sá da Costa, 1988), pp. 229–37.

in this field be merely one of organisation, or would they have taken part in the battles of the time, as the chroniclers appear to suggest? We know that Álvaro Pais organised a company which was 'in the king's pay' during the wars of Fernando's reign. This is expressly recognised by the monarch in a letter dated 1372, in which he states: 'somos obrigados em hũa contia de dinheiros que lhe devemos de soldo que de nos auia dauer por que nos serujo com certos homens de caualo per algũus tempos em quanto durou a guerra que aujamos com dom anrrique de que no ouue paga mais que de quatro meses'.[355] Likewise, the ex-*chanceler*, João 'das Leis' received from Fernando at the beginning of his reign a sum which must have been in payment for the provision of a certain number of lancers for military service.[356] The bestowal of *alcaidarias* to well-known legists such as João das Regras or the *chanceler* Lourenço Anes Fogaça during this same period at the turn of the century was part of this general movement of functions related to the exercise of war becoming more prestigious, even though there is every indication that in practice the performance of the duties of *alcaide* fell to recruited members of the petty nobility.[357] I have already noted that several members of the do Sem family had their names inscribed on their tombs (as can still be seen in Santarém) not merely with a book, but also with their swords, and mentioning in their epitaphs their status as *cavaleiro*. This, by all indications, was not merely an honorary title. All these facts lead one to interpret less metaphorically than has up to now been the case the participation, which is widely described by the chroniclers, of some of the better-known men of letters and royal officials in various war actions, as in the case of Gil do Sem, Martim Afonso and João das Regras at Aljubarrota, mentioned by Fernão Lopes. Less well-known men, like Martim Simões, the *escrivão do paço* during the reign of John, or Duarte's *escrivão da fazenda*, Paio Rodrigues, also served on other occasions as men at arms. It must not be forgotten that the royal army, which was still a temporary body, encompassed the court 'at arms', of which many played a part in time of war. Later, we know that a legist such as Dr Rui Gomes de Alvarenga, for example, took part at Alfarrobeira in the king's army with his own 'company'.[358]

What appears undeniable, on the other hand, is the interest we find in this group in all forms of enrichment. They would turn to innovative businesses, particularly the agricultural and industrial improvement of their properties, on which there remains some information of privileges obtained from the

[355] ANTT, *Ch. D. Fernando*, 1, f. 90. In the following year, the monarch gave him some houses in Lisbon 'em pago do que lhe deuja em pago de seu soldo': ANTT, *Ch. D. Fernando*, 1, f. 136.

[356] ANTT, *Ch. D. Fernando*, 1, f. 13v (charter dated 1367).

[357] The former held the *alcaidaria* of Castelo Rodrigo in 1396: ANTT, *Ch. D. João I*, 2, f. 102. The *alcaidaria* of Lisbon was also temporarily granted to Lourenço Anes: ANTT, *Ch. D. João I*, 2, ff. 9v and 172. On the functions of the *alcaides*: João Gouveia Monteiro, *Os castelos Portugueses dos finais da idade média* (Coimbra: Colibri, 1999), pp. 284–96.

[358] ANTT, *Ch. D. Afonso V*, 20, f. 43.

monarchs. The *escrivão da puridade* to John I, Gonçalo Lourenço de Gomide, was responsible for the building of several water mills on the Tagus between Alhandra and Alverca, for cultivation of a wilderness near Alcoentre, where he had a 'quintã', for the construction of tidal mills downstream on the Tagus, and other 'moynhos, artefiçios e engenhos de fazer ferro e serra madeira e pisar burel e fazer papel ou outras algũas cousas que se façam com arteficio d agoa', near Leiria.[359] To evaluate the importance from a patrimonial and architectural point of view of a 'quintã' during the fifteenth and sixteenth centuries, it is sufficient to consider the important drawings that the Portuguese Francisco de Holanda made in Italy, where he uses the word 'quintã' to name the famous Renaissance villas which he visited and painted.[360] The interest in this type of enterprise was not exclusive to officials, for even high nobility and the more traditional families put capital and interest into such work, as with the Count of Ourém, who also ordered the construction of water mills and other 'artificios de água' on the river Alviela.[361] There are other examples of enterprises of officials and servants close to the king besides Gomide: Álvaro Gonçalves da Maia, *escrivão da câmara* and *vedor da fazenda*, ordered the construction of tidal mills near Aldeia Galega do Ribatejo, and some years later he exploited salt flats near Caminha, with the full approval of the king, as well as fishing areas on the Douro.[362] The approving attitude of the monarch is well exemplified in the words of a charter granted to the *escrivão da chancelaria*, Pedro Anes, who in 1414 claimed possession of some land which he had cultivated: 'he hũ daquelles que se trabalhou e trabalha d aproueitar aquello que lhe de seu padre aconteceo e nom soomente o seu mais ainda o que a el nom pertencia e a outrem nom aproueitaua assy como fez em a nossa villa de santarem em hũa boa quintãa que muito afremosenta a dicta villa'.[363] According to the contents of the royal charter, the actual profit and use of the 'coisa pública' were associated in these initiatives emerging among the circle of officials who attended court.

While, particularly during the period prior to the reign of Fernando, the fourteenth century was mainly characterised by a greater accessibility of palace society to officials and merchants who tended to be succeeded by several directly related generations working for the king, it can in general be said that the fifteenth century was the moment of increasing ennoblement of these royal servants. Because of this, I have already spoken of the formation of a 'nobility

359 ANTT, *Ch. D. João I*, 2, f. 199v; 3, ff. 131, 87 and 127v.

360 Francisco de Holanda, *Desenhos das Antigualhas*, facsimile edition (Lisbon, 1989).

361 ANTT, *LN*, Místicos, 2, f. 223v. At the end of the fifteenth century, the *reguengo* of Alviela was still held by the Braganzas.

362 There is information on these activities, respectively in 1405, 1411 and 1421; ANTT, *Ch. D. João I*, 3, ff. 53 and 139; 4, f. 46v. According to Carvalho Homem, da Maia, as *vedor da fazenda*, was strongly connected to Oporto and its region from 1420: *Desembargo*, 281.

363 ANTT, *Ch. D. João I*, 3, f. 174v.

of robes', to which the Nogueira, the do Sem, the Lobato and the Fogaça families belonged, but which also included other families who were to have a brilliant future at the courts of Afonso V and John II, and whose presence in palace circles in some cases continued through to the Manueline period. It would be fair to say that their fortune was founded upon the interior of court society at the end of the Middle Ages. Some of these families were eventually to form the true 'nobility of service' of the sixteenth century who were boldly despatched during the maritime expansion to the four corners of the discovered world in the name of the king.

In the particular sphere of the *escrivães da câmara* and of the secretaries, the Gomides, the Cotrim and the Galvão families all made their progress.[364] Gonçalo Lourenço de Gomide was of an Évora family, and began his career as *escrivão da câmara* of Fernando. From the beginning of the reign of John I, Gonçalo Lourenço was *escrivão da puridade*, and was a member of the royal council as well as taking part in various missions of trust, in particular on the occasion of the marriage of the daughter of the monarch, Beatriz, in England. His son, João Gonçalves, succeeded him in this position after 1422, and also served during the reign of Duarte. During this period the progress of the line was interrupted for obscure reasons related to the punishment and execution of the clerk, who was accused of falsifying documents relating to Fernando's reign. This led to the abandonment of the surname of Gomide, and the family claimed to be members of the more prestigious Albuquerque family through the female line.[365] The descendants of the condemned clerk, such as João de Albuquerque and Dr Lopo Gonçalves, remained at the court of Afonso, and started new court lines.[366]

A group of individuals who used the surname Cotrim are to be found in the *câmara* and court of John, and these were also originally from Évora.[367] The

[364] For a comparison with the profile of the secretaries at other courts: Robert-Henri Bautier, 'Les notaires et secrétaires du roi, des origines au milieu du XVIe siècle', in A. Lapeyre and R. Scheurer (eds.), *Les Notaires et secrétaires du roi sous les règnes de Louis XI, Charles VIII et Louis XII* (Paris: Bibliothèque Nationale, 1978), vol. I, pp. ix–xxxix; A. Arago Cabanas, 'La escribanía de Juan I', *VII Congreso de la Corona de Aragón* (Valencia, 1970), vol. II, pp. 193–269; J. L. Bermejo Cabrero, 'Los primeros secretarios de los reyes', *Anuario de Historia del Derecho Español*, 47 (1979), 187–296.

[365] As should be expected, the explanations gained through genealogical literature are utterly diverse. This tradition of family origin collected by Braamcamp Freire (*Brasões*, vol. II, p. 198) is given the lie by the royal charter of 1437: ANTT, *Ch. D. Duarte*, 1, f. 148v. See also ANTT, *Ch. D. Afonso V*, 4, f. 61.

[366] On the Albuquerques, see above. Dr Lopo Gonçalves served at court as *juiz dos feitos* of the king from the period prior to Alfarrobeira. He was 'curador' of the Infanta D. Joana, sister of the young King Afonso V and future queen of Castile following her marriage to Henry IV.

[367] Fernão Lopes names Martim Cotrim among the 'fidalgos' of Évora who assisted the master: *CR João I*, vol. I, p. 301. Beirante does not consider the family as important in the local context: Beirante, *Évora na idade média*, p. 200.

process of their progress towards nobility was not, however, as spectacular as was the case of the Gomides and some others. Martim Afonso Cotrim was in the mission for the negotiations with Castile in 1392 and we find his relatives Álvaro and Rui Cotrim among the *escudeiro*s resident at the court of John I. Álvares Peres Cotrim, who was also at the court of Duarte, was *escrivão da câmara*. The surname of this family was later to be connected to a coin of the time of Afonso V, the 'cotrim', which suggests that they were connected in some way to its issue.[368]

Likewise, the court progress of the Galvão family began with Rui Galvão, who was the son of a cleric of Évora and who, according to his own testimony, was a *criado* in the *câmara* of Duarte and acted as secretary and on various diplomatic missions. We know that Rui Galvão was an enemy of the regent Pedro, for in his letter to the Count of Arraiolos following his withdrawal from court he commented on the animosity of the secretary towards his person and on the withdrawal of Lopo Afonso, the *escrivão da puridade* to the young king, so that this post might be given to Rui Galvão.[369] Galvão's rise to the status of *cavaleiro* would date from this point, and his career progressed well in the entourage of the new monarch, of whose council he was a member in the middle of the 1450s. Among his direct descendants should be noted the bishop, João Rodrigues Galvão (of whom I have already spoken), and the famous Duarte Galvão, a cleric who later married and who was the secretary-chronicler of the Portuguese kings in the middle of the fifteenth century.[370] Also present at the court of Afonso was the *cavaleiro* Pedro Rodrigues Galvão, who was connected to the Order of Aviz, and the younger Jorge Galvão.

Families whose presence beside the king is found only in the fifteenth century are those of the Castelo Brancos and the Gouveias, who appear to have been connected to petty nobility on the peripheries and who were related to officials of the *fazenda*; they were also in the palace department related to hunting. The Castelo Brancos were present in the entourage of John I, where Lopo Vasques held the office of *monteiro-mor*, while Nuno Vasques de Castelo Branco accompanied the infante heir as *vedor da fazenda* from the 1420s, as did Diogo Gonçalves and Rui Gonçalves, who were possibly closely related. Rui Gonçalves was later Duarte's *vedor da casa* and *tesoureiro* of the Lisbon mint. This family held the hereditary position at the palace of *monteiro-mor* which was handed down from Lopo Vasques I to Nuno

368 On this family, see Costa Lobo's statement, *História da Sociedade*, p. 325.

369 *MH*, vol. XI, p. 351.

370 See, beside the classic work of F. M. Sousa Viterbo, *Duarte Galvão e a sua família*, offprint of *História e Memórias da Academia Real das Ciências* (Lisbon, 1905), the observation of Costa, *Portugueses no Colégio de S. Clemente*, vol. II, p. 724; 'Duarte Galvão', *Dicionário da literatura medieval Galega e Portuguesa*, pp. 225–6.

Vasques II and Lopo Vasques II, and also the post of *almotacé-mor*, which was handed down by Gonçalo Vasques II to his son Pedro Vasques; they also intermittently held several positions as *vedor* in the *fazenda* and Lisbon mint.

We also find the Gouveias most certainly at the court of Duarte, where João Gouveia and his relatives Vasco and Fernando de Gouveia also lived.[371] These last two established themselves from the end of the 1430s at the court of Alfonso V of Aragon, where they held important court positions, while João Gouveia himself was absent from the Portuguese court during the regency of the Infante Pedro. In the case of Vasco de Gouveia, who was *monteiro-mor* to the king of Naples and his counsellor at the middle of the century, we know that he went as ambassador to the Portuguese court on at least four separate missions between 1440 and 1455. His presence in the entourage of Alfonso V of Aragon must also be related to the construction of the important venatic library of the Aragonese king and to the intense practice at the Neapolitan court of the various methods of hunting in which the Castilian head falconer Iñigo d'Avalos, who was a contemporary of the Portuguese, and like him a diplomatic agent, played a prominent part.[372] A well-known treatise on falconry was at the time in the hands of a relative of Vasco, the bishop of Lamego João da Costa, and this perhaps explains the circulation of this treatise between Naples and Portugal.[373] The Gouveias demonstrate a progress parallel to that of the Castelo Brancos, although it developed among several European courts, while the family had a continued presence at the court of the Portuguese king in the second half of the fifteenth century.

I shall end with an evocation of two families, the Silveiras and the Alvarengas, both of which had a great number of legists. In the first case, the large Silveira family, who were also from Évora, were represented at court at the beginning of the fifteenth century by Fernando Afonso, a lay doctor of law whose place of study has not been ascertained.[374] He served in John's *desembargo* in a career which culminated with the retention of the office of *chanceler-mor* in the final phase of the reign. Meanwhile, his brother Nuno Fernandes da Silveira was, at least from 1416, *escrivão da puridade* to the infante heir Duarte and his trusted

371 Vasco Fernandes de Gouveia, 'o moço', the origin of this line, was a contemporary of John I, but it is not known for certain whether he was a member of his entourage. By 1436 he was dead. Vasco de Gouveia and Fernando de Gouveia were related to each other and to João de Gouveia.

372 Antonio Lupis, 'Per una storia della caccia Aragonese', *Quaderni Medievali*, 2 (1981), 86–101.

373 João da Costa was bishop of Lamego between 1446 and 1456. A. P. Sousa Leite, 'O bispo de Lamego D. João da Costa e a sua compilação de livros de cetraria no manuscrito Sloane 821 do Museu Britânico', *Boletim da Academia Portuguesa de Ex-Libris*, 12 (1967), 18–30.

374 The connection of the family to Évora was to last throughout the fifteenth century: Beirante, *Évora na idade média*, pp. 526–8. On the genealogy of the Silveiras: *LL*, pp. 300–6 and *Brasões*, vol. III, pp. 300–10. A biographical reconstruction of Nuno Martins and his children, particularly of the eldest, is to be found in Rosa, *O morgadio em Portugal*, pp. 132–56.

servant, being involved on various diplomatic missions in the complex Castilian negotiations of 1429–30. Connected as they were to the two complementary positions in the *desembargo* during the final phase of John I's reign, which corresponded to the supremacy of officials and nobles closest to the Infante Duarte in the government of the country at the time, the Silveiras made solid court progress in the following decades. Among the descendants of Dr Fernando Afonso we find in the service of Afonso V the legislator João Fernandes da Silveira. He was originally connected to the *chancelaria*, where in 1443 he acted as *vice-chanceler* 'por D. Fernando da Guerra'. The essential part of his career, however, was in the high tribunals of the *casa do cível* and the *casa da suplicação*, where he served during the regency of the Infante Pedro and occasionally acted as *chanceler* in the *casa do cível* and *regedor* in the *casa da suplicação*. João Fernandes da Silveira, a court legislator, was successively the king's ambassador to the court of Naples, to the emperor and to the curia, and played an important part in the negotiations of the marriage of the king's sister. Afonso V gave him the new title of baron in 1475.

Nuno Martins and his children also managed to increase their spheres of activity in the court organisation, in spite of the difficult circumstances caused by their withdrawal from court following the death of Duarte and the regency of the Duke of Coimbra. Nuno Martins had been one of the more important 'privados' of Duarte, as shown clearly in the famous ruling on the hours to be devoted to his duties in the 'Livro dos Conselhos': during public audiences held on Saturdays, 'Nuno martinz estara connosco pera reçeber as jnformações e tera hũ escrivão pera lhes por, se cumprir, os desembargos ou repostas', but this trusted official was also to work with the king on Thursdays after dinner, and Mondays and Wednesdays after sleeping.[375] As well as this daily appearance at Duarte's *câmara* he took part in the royal council following his return to court after Alfarrobeira, when he held the offices of *coudel-mor* and overseer of the works of Afonso V. The duty of *escrivão da puridade* was passed on to his son Diogo da Silveira after his death in 1454 and the youngest descendant, Fernão da Silveira, was to be the famous *coudel-mor* and court poet, as well as being a member of some important diplomatic missions in the middle of the century.

The progress of the Alvarengas started with the lay legislator, Dr Gomes Martins, who was a judge at the court of John I and whom we find in John's service from 1396 until the final decade of the reign.[376] His son, Rui Gomes de Alvarenga, who studied at Bologna in 1436, also became famous as a doctor of law. He served in the *desembargo* during the regency of Pedro, in particular as

[375] *Livro dos Conselhos*, pp. 12–13.

[376] The Alvarengas were, it would seem, originally from the town of Torres Vedras: Ana Maria Rodrigues, *Torres Vedras: a vila e o termo nos finais da idade média* (Lisbon: Fundação Calouste Gulbenkian, 1995), p. 456.

vice-chancellor under Fernando da Guerra, but he became decisively supportive of the cause of the young king Afonso V. Following the civil war he was given the supervision of the *chancelaria* of the kingdom, which he shared with other court lawyers such as Pero Lobato, Nuno Gonçalves and João Fernandes da Silveira. Dr Rui de Alvarenga held the presidency of the *casa da suplicação* from 1452. Several descendants of this important official continued to attend the court of Afonso, from then on using the more prestigious name of Melo. Following in the footsteps of his father, Afonso Rodrigues studied under royal protection in Bologna, Perugia and Ferrara in the second half of the fifteenth century.

This examination could continue with respect to the integration of numerous officials of the court nobility with an analysis of further individual and group progressions. I believe, however, that I have related the essential aspects of this process which is interesting to evaluate through families whose reconstruction was possible, allowing us to consider the court of the Portuguese kings as a social environment of a certain plasticity, in a constant state of reorganisation owing to the possibility of rising up the hierarchy through a series of factors to be analysed in the next chapter. The main problem posed by this analysis is the position of officials and merchants at court and, without doubt, the *limits* of ennoblement as the principal mechanism of integration in court society. Although there is no lack of examples of spectacular promotion in status of some individuals, which is repeated in the social standing of their descendants, this ennoblement did not always survive harmoniously with the necessary specialisation of a profile of activities and with the set of diverse roles performed by these men. In some cases, the retention of some direct involvement in commercial activities was related to the material wealth of the family or to the affirmation of individual destiny, while in other cases we find the attempt to harmonise the 'lettered' status with the position of *cavaleiro* through a withdrawal from certain lifestyles and an involvement in the clerical world. Following the adoption of typically noble values and forms of family organisation, the descendants of these men of modest origins, on many occasions enriched in the service of the kings, reverted whenever possible to the use of prestigious family names, usually the result of matrimonial alliances with court 'nobility of service' or, more rarely, with important noble families. Consequently, the inclusion of many of these families who descended from officials and the urban elite among the sixteenth-century nobility must be noted, for these constitute, around 1450, about half the noble lines described.

Finally, the marked preference seen among these families for the new mechanism of patrimonial succession, that is entailment, must be emphasised. From the middle of the fourteenth century, families such as the Azambujas, the Britos, the Gomides, the Almadas, the Castelo Brancos and the Silveiras began to form entailments, which were not only intended to avoid the dispersal of a patrimony, which at times had been acquired at great cost through successive generations of royal ministry, but which were seen most of all as forms of symbolic investment in the family's identity – 'house'.[377] This created a founding logic and one of intergenerational cohesion in these recent lines, whose roots from then on were to be found in the concrete place, that is the 'quintãs' and 'solares' which had by definition to be handed down according to the wishes of the founders of the respective 'houses'. As observed by Lurdes Rosa, 'the entailments created with possessions of the crown after Duarte were subject to a regime where the desire of the founder was no longer the one law. Any family transaction demanded royal authorisation.'[378] We can also say that the inexorable logic of the process of belonging at court was translated during the fifteenth century by different degrees of freedom or of interdependence of the nobility at court in relation to the king, including the fundamental dominion of patrimonial transmission. This process and interdependence would be all the stronger should this patrimony be recent and the result of royal favour – factors generally to be found in the case of the officials and merchants who were moving towards nobility, as well as for many of those families belonging to the 'nobility of service'.

THE WORLD OF THE PROFESSIONS

Integration in the royal entourage with a certain constancy was without doubt an experience common to men and women of modest origins whose relative obscurity prevents a true unravelling of the probable modalities and causes of their presence alongside the monarch. One of the more important reasons for this presence was the exercise of a profession or art, made necessary by the concentration of several hundreds of individuals in an itinerant organism which was, above all, a centre of consumption. This dimension of the court is usually relegated to a secondary level, although it was fundamental not only from the economic point of view but because it modelled forcefully the physiognomy of court society.[379] There was to be found there a specific collection of men and women given to highly specialised activities, such as the world of bureaucracy so often referred to here, which were not found in other contexts of late medieval society. The important group of individuals whom we can term in their entirety

[377] Jean-Pierre Molénat, 'La volonté de durer: majorats et chapellenies dans la pratique tolédane des XIIIe–XVe siècles', in *En la España medieval V: estudios en memoria de Claudio Sánchez-Albornoz* (Madrid: Universidad Complutense, 1986), vol. II, pp. 683–96.

[378] Maria de Lurdes Rosa, 'O morgadio em Portugal, séculos XIV–XV', in *Modelos e práticas de comportamento linhagístico* (Lisbon: Estampa, 1995), p. 257.

[379] On this, see the observations of Marcello Fantoni, 'L'economia dello splendore. La corte medicea fra Cinque e Seicento', in Maurice Aymard and Marzio Romani (eds.), *La Cour comme institution économique* (Paris: Maison des Sciences de l'Homme, 1998), pp. 115–24.

as servants connected to the material life of the court play a part within it in a variety of ways. The most important distinction would be between on the one hand those who held a court 'office' which was institutionalised, consigned to certain hierarchies and systems of payment – a good example would be the court cook or the falconer – and, on the other hand, the professionals and artisans whose presence did not assume these formal aspects, and which therefore had a more precarious character. The court was a place of attraction for all these men, owing to the great possibility of exercising those arts which the entourage of the kings demanded: it is sufficient to think of the important monetary activity in the creation of arsenals and the complex world of professions necessary in the army, in the construction of residences and of every type of ephemeral or permanent architectural device related to the royal presence, in the involvement of the kings in industries, in navigation and in technological innovations of a different type which formed the specific atmosphere in which engineering of the first renaissance developed. As Lynn White remarked, this climate of technological innovation in the fifteenth century was due not to a systematic application of scientific theories or to the stimulus of a renewed discovery of textual traditions of antiquity, but fundamentally to the rapid expansion of a commercial society and to the action of monarchs 'eager to increase not only their armed might but also the prosperity of their realms'.[380]

The presence of artisans and professionals connected to life at court is better known and documented, and I shall stress three nuclei which are particularly visible in the Portuguese case. First, the group of artisans connected to clothing and adornment of the body and of court spaces; second, a small nucleus of professionals connected to mechanical arts, such as building and metal working; finally, the large groups of servants in the spheres of itinerance and hunting. Supplies for the court, as we shall see, implied distinct areas of activity where we find the presence of a large number of professionals.

The first group comprised several artisans whose presence was required by the kings in the thirteenth century. These were artisans related most of all to the making of clothes and to leather working, particularly the court tailor and shoemaker. It is only in the fifteenth century that we find more frequent identification of these individuals, which allows us to state that a group of Christian and Jewish officials worked in this service, and that the making up of clothes at court implied growing specialisation, for there is information as to a group of artisans including the embroiderer and the furrier, with the tailor, all of whose names can be found from the reign of John. The complexity of the confection of costly articles of clothing at the end of the Middle Ages determined the need to make use of these services on a permanent basis. Not

[380] Lynn White, Jr, 'The flavor of Early Renaissance technology', in Bernard Levy (ed.), *Developments in the Early Renaissance* (Albany: State University of New York Press, 1972), pp. 36–57.

only was the cutting and creation of clothing the duty of these artists, but also the making of vestments and every type of adornment involving materials to be used in the *câmara* and the chapel or on saddled animals.[381] Their elaborateness called for precious materials (gold, silver, pearls, etc.) or those which were expensive ('feathers', furs of various types), on articles of clothing made by specialised artisans who also inscribed mottoes and distinctive markings on clothes intended for distribution to the entourage.[382] Studies of other courts at the end of the Middle Ages, particularly that of Burgundy, have shown the relatively rigid method by which the court hierarchies were moulded in their ways of dress, as well as the inclusion of items of clothing periodically offered by the monarchs as a method of payment to the servants of the court.[383] In spite of the tendency towards financial payments, which will be studied later, in Portugal items of clothing also remained a last resort of payment in kind (which as already mentioned was originally a type of prebendary), owing to this use of clothing as a system of social significance.[384] At the end of the Middle Ages clothing acquired a central emblematic value within the specific context of the court, and became a method of demonstrating membership of given hierarchical strata. At the same time, the adoption of devices and mottoes at the fifteenth-century Portuguese court, often embroidered on the clothes of the courtiers, inscribed on their bodies the logic of interpersonal relationship which connected them to their lord or patron, be he the king, a prince or a court grandee, so becoming a language which signalled membership of a group and a differentiation within the groups themselves,[385] a language whose use, much like other emblematic systems such as coats of arms, demanded forms of specific adaptation and apprenticeship.

As to the king's shoemaker, whose curious ceremonial functions in the Hispanic sphere will be studied later, he had the specific task of creating footwear for the monarch and the royal family. His activity at court must have been particularly profitable, since all the pieces made under him would be,

381 A. H. Oliveira Marques, *A sociedade medieval Portuguesa* (Lisbon: Sá da Costa, 1981), pp. 23–62. For an evaluation of the complexity of the duties of the officials connected to the making of clothing and accoutrements of the court: Françoise Pipponier, *Costume et vie sociale: la cour d'Anjou, XIVe–XVe siècles* (Paris: Ecole des Hautes Etudes, 1970), pp. 123–32. See for example the *cartas de quitação* of the king's tailor: ANTT, *Ch. D. João I*, 5, ff. 13v and 46.

382 On the use of livery at the Portuguese court: *CR Fernando*, p. 166; *CR Ceuta*, pp. 72–3. And the listing of liveries in ANTT, *Ch. D. João I*, 4, f. 71. In the will of the infante Fernando in 1437, there is reference to the distribution of liveries to the members of his entourage: *Provas*, vol. I, p. 211. Also the Count of Ourém, on his entrance to Basel, was accompanied by his servants who were dressed in his livery: *Provas*, vol. V, p. 278.

383 Michèle Beaulieu and Jeanne Baylé, *Le Costume en Bourgogne, de Philippe le Hardi à la mort de Charles le Téméraire* (Paris: PUF, 1956).

384 Philip Hersch and others, 'The semiology of dress in late medieval and early modern Spain', *Razo*, 7 (1987), 95–100.

385 Georg Simmel, 'La différentiation sociale', in *Sociologie et Epistémologie* (Paris: PUF, 1981), pp. 217–18.

according to the regulation of prices at the court of Afonso, more expensive than those made by any other master-artisan in the place where the court was.[386] Close to the privileged position of this artist were the saddler of the royal household and the harness maker, both related to the work of the leather harnesses necessary for the horses. For an evaluation of the wealth and importance of the work they did, it suffices to quote the constant description of the royal saddle in the laws of Afonso of 1340, 'dourada com ouro e prata, e com seda e cordas', whose use was reserved solely to the king, his sons, and the *ricos-homens* and Masters of the Orders. In this case the court hierarchy also rested, as we shall see, upon the number, quality and methods of adornment of the mounts.[387]

We can also include within the sphere of activities connected to bodily adornment and to the making of objects to be used at court the goldsmiths who accompanied the Portuguese monarchs. As we shall see, they were predominantly Jews, and their activity was not only within the entourage of the kings but also outside the court. So the list of privileges granted to the goldsmith to Queen Leonor Teles tell us: when they moved throughout the kingdom in the service of the queen, they must be housed, fed and mounted with 'homens de cauallo e de pee que o ponham em saluo'. Above all, their activity could be carried out wherever they felt it most convenient for the service of the queen: 'que costrangedes esses mesteiraaes ourivyzes que uos ell diser pera lhe ajudarem a fazer lauores da dicta Raynha. Outrosy lhj constrangede ferreyros que lhj façam sa ferramenta por seus dinheiros para o dicto ofiçio E fazedelhi dar caruam por seus dinheiros Aquell que lhy compridoyro for per guissa que esses lauores sse nom leixem de fazer per mingoa delle.'[388] Fernão Lopes tells us of the excellence and the value of the treasures of this queen, and relates that the king of Castile ordered the *aia* of Leonor Teles to be 'pôr tormento' until she revealed the place where the widow queen had hidden her jewels. An analysis of the privileges of the goldsmith of the court shows that in spite of this being a market which was relatively open to urban economic realities of the places where he stayed, the logic of protection and importance of the court artisan in relation to the realities of local production must have been a powerful factor of attraction for the professionals of the various arts.

A second group is composed of artisans in building, painting and metal working, whose presence at the Portuguese court frequently has a merely temporary character, especially in the case of builders, who depended essentially on the various royal residences whose building operations will be referred to later. It is certainly the case that there is evidence of successive carpenters and stonemasons at court in the service of the Portuguese kings, besides some others

386 The monarch justified these privileges 'por o trabalho que levam em nos seguir, e despesas que fazem em carretos de seu fato, e outras despesas semelhantes, e de ferragem, e courama, e cousas que pertençem a seus ofiçios': *Livro Vermelho*, p. 520.

387 *CPA*, p. 107.

388 ANTT, *Ch. D. Fernando*, 4, f. 16.

who worked throughout the kingdom for the monarchs. In the first of these cases, there were Gonçalo Domingues, João Óbidos and Master João de Landim, who were in the service of John I and Duarte. Also in the fifteenth-century household were some masters 'of stonemasonry', such as the Castilian Master Pedro or, in the reign of Afonso, Master João dc Alverca. The construction of a large Portuguese building of the time, for example the monastery at Batalha, demonstrates that every work of royal initiative had its own hierarchy of the master and a precise group of artisans, although we know that the presence of some individuals might be necessary in several places, and this certainly occurred in the royal entourage.[389] The case of the painters is particularly interesting, since at the time their activity was far from being favoured with the prestige which has later been associated with this profession. The painter was an 'official' who was a dependant of the monarch, just as were the barber and the tailor: his presence at the fifteenth-century court has not yet been studied in this perspective, even in the case of a Gonçalo Anes or a Nuno Gonçalves. As Martin Warnke suggests, the inclusion of the painters in the court hierarchy through the bestowal of titles of 'cavaleiro' and 'escudeiro' represented promotion and favoured a growing freedom in relation to the mechanisms of corporative artistic framework.[390] The 'illuminators' who worked for example on the books of Afonso V in the production of manuscripts for the royal collection seem to have held a similar position.[391]

Artists in metalwork represent another group known to have been at the Portuguese court, and many of these were foreigners. The first official armourers and metal specialists identified in the service of Pedro and Fernando seem, however, to have been nationals. Later there is the figure of Alberte, a German armourer who worked for Fernando and made numerous pieces in the context of the wars of the end of the fourteenth century. He then joined the service of John I, where he remained at least until the last years of the century. João Anes was to succeed him, and was armourer to John until the 1430s, and is to be found again in the service of Duarte. An entry by this monarch shows that the opinion of this armourer and that of the *vedor* João Afonso was taken into account by the royal *contador* in the commissioning of specialists for the determination of the value of several metals which could be used for coinage.[392] This once again alerts us to the connection between the several mechanical arts which

389 Saul António Gomes, *O mosteiro de Santa Maria da Vitória no século XV* (Coimbra: Universidade de Coimbra, 1990).

390 Martin Warnke, *The Court Artist: On the Ancestry of the Modern Artist* (Cambridge: Cambridge University Press, 1993), esp. p. 11.

391 F. M. Sousa Viterbo, *A livraria real, especialmente no reinado de D. Manuel*, offprint of *Memórias da Academia das Ciências de Lisboa* (Lisbon, 1901); F. M. Sousa Viterbo, *Calígrafos e iluminadores Portugueses* (Coimbra: Universidade de Coimbra, 1916), p. 20; also ANTT, *Ch. Afonso V*, 13, f. 170v.

392 *Livro dos Conselhos*, pp. 139–41.

existed in the court sphere, in this case between the minting of coinage and the manufacture of arms and other metal objects. For the following decade we find the Milanese Cristóvão as king's armourer, and the number of artists known increases significantly for the reign of Afonso V.[393] Jews formed an important presence during the fifteenth century among the artisans of this group, as will be explained later. Finally, we cannot ignore the presence of the masters of the new art of artillery who, by order of Afonso V in 1449, were not from then on to be considered as members of court with rights to a *moradia*, except with the express authorisation of the *vedor da casa*. This is an indication of the probable withdrawal of a type of presence at court which until then had been similar to that analysed regarding other professions, such as the armourers.[394]

Of those privileged servants who accompanied the entourage of the kings, a relatively restricted group can, as already said, be related to the itinerance and to hunting. In the service of the fourteenth-century *estrebaria* we find an extremely curious Moorish preponderance, beginning with the holding of the office of *estrabeiro-mor* to Afonso IV by a certain Master Ali. Master Ali became known as a horse-breeder, and contributed decisively to the success of the royal army. This is proved by the fact that he was known by the chronicler of Alfonso XI of Castile, who does not forget to mention him among the entourage of the Portuguese in the context of military victories.[395] To promote horse-breeding in his stables, Afonso IV acquired an estate owned by the monastery of Alcobaça in Muge, which was granted on loan to Master Ali, where he must 'criar sas Eguas e potros e seus gaados'.[396] This is a unique case known with certainty to exist in Portugal of a mechanism of adding a property specifically to a palace duty, although it is probable that it was also used for the *monteiros* and falconers. In fact we know that this same 'quintã' at Muge, which was situated in one of the richest agricultural regions of the country, was later successively under Pedro's *estrabeiro* (probably also a Moor, as suggested by his name of Master Brafeme) and of Fernando, although his certain identity is not known. The royal preoccupation with the quality and promotion of horse-breeding can be seen as

393 The traditional view of accentuated mobility of this type of artist must, according to more recent research, be reconsidered for the end of the Middle Ages. Far more common, as occurs in the Portuguese case, are the 'sedentary' careers, lasting a lifetime in the service of a prince: Philippe Braunstein, 'Les techniciens et le pouvoir à la fin du moyen âge: une directon de recherche', in Fr. Autrand (ed.), *Prosopographie et genèse de l'état moderne* (Paris: Ecole Normale Supérieure de Jeunes Filles, 1982), p. 228. On the presence of Germans: A. H. Oliveira Marques, *Hansa e Portugal na idade média* (Lisbon: Presença, 1993), pp. 101, 108 and note 90.

394 See the 'Regimento dado ao vedor-mor das artelharias': *DP*, vol. I, p. 468.

395 *CRO Alfonso XI*, vol. II, p. 191.

396 *CDA*, vol. II, p. 166 (doc. Of 1337). On the function of the royal and noble stables of the Middle Ages, profitable use may be made of the old monograph by E. Picard, 'L'écurie de Philippe le Hardi, Duc de Bourgogne', *Mémoires de l'Académie des Sciences, Arts et Belles-Lettres de Dijon*, 10 (1905–6), as well as Henri Lemoine, 'Les écuries royales sous Charles VI et Charles VII', *Bulletin Philologique et Historique* (1928–29), 130–7.

a constant throughout the late Middle Ages. The subject received considered recommendations from the Infante Pedro in his 'carta de Bruges', as well as in several legislative measures in the second half of the fifteenth century.[397] The relatively high number of mounts which the removal and functioning of court demanded justified the presence of the 'king's farrier', who also had his dependants, totalling four on the list of *moradores*, among whom are also mentioned 'alveitares', or horse veterinarians.[398] Although little is known about these, beyond their privileged position and the eventual indication of one or other name, everything leads to the belief that this was an area where services of quality were highly regarded because of the importance (including economic) of the animals of the king's household.[399]

This relative success, which was clear in the fourteenth century, of the royal stable in the promotion of horse-breeding must in my opinion be related to the social context in which Portuguese technical literature flourished at the end of the Middle Ages. In his well-known treatise on 'montaria' John I mentions exactly the separation and the implicit hierarchy between the 'liberal arts' and the 'mechanical arts', and also suggests a course of apprenticeship for the courtier who should consider and harmonise the two areas – and particularly in the case of the former, arts of the trivium such as grammar and rhetoric and in the latter such disciplines as physics, medicine and veterinary medicine or falconry. So there appears a Portuguese context of explicit re-evaluation of the mechanical arts which, although they appeared particularly in the writings of the princes of Aviz, are certainly not absent in the fourteenth-century treatises or the environment of Fernando's court. This was in contrast with the medieval traditions of devaluation of these arts, as is particularly clear in clerical writings. As Allard reminds us, the reception of the Augustinian doctrine competed powerfully and created a 'topos' which related the 'mechanical arts' to the exterior man, making them a part of the order of the conventional and the acquired, contrary to the liberal arts, which were more fully human.[400] This devaluation can also be found in another way in scholastics, which organised man's actions hierarchically, placing at the head theoretical knowledge, followed by moral actions, and relegating to a lowly position the activities of 'doing' – the indignity of the mechanical arts made these deserve the common classification

397 Moreira de Sá, *A carta de Bruges*, p. 21; also the list of places drawn up in 1485: Álvaro Lopes de Chaves, *Livro de apontamentos* (1438–89), ed. by A. M. Salgado and A. J. Salgado (Lisbon: Imprensa Nacional, 1984), pp. 274–5.

398 In a *carta de quitação* to Afonso's farrier there are mentioned the 'Reçeptas de mezinhas que lhe deuia e nam era dellas paguo as quaaes despemdeo em cura das minhas bestas que foram doemtes': ANTT, *LN*, Extras, ff. 21v–22.

399 Yves Renouard, 'Un sujet de recherches: l'exportation de chevaux de la Péninsule ibérique en France et en Angleterre au moyen-âge', in *Homenaje a Jaume Vicens Vives* (Barcelona: Universidad de Barcelona, 1965), vol. I, pp. 571–7.

400 Guy H. Allard, 'Les arts mécaniques aux yeux de l'idéologie médiévale', in *Les Arts mécaniques au moyen âge* (Montreal: Vrin, 1982), pp. 13–31.

of 'adulterine' which Hugo de São Vitor gave them in the twelfth century. This dominant intellectualism, Allard reminds us, was directly related to the social preconceptions of some clerics and intellectuals of the time, who were the authors of a fiery criticism of the *curialisation* of the time of the nobility and of the principal ecclesiastics associated with greed for money and material goods particularly related to the cultivation of practical and mechanical knowledge. So in the writings of John of Salisbury for example, in both his *Metalogicon* and his *Policraticus*, he condemned the 'low and degrading' activities of the arts of healing, or the court knowledge of hunting and fishing. In this general portrait we find some significant ruptures occurring in the fourteenth century, which was the period of the first flowering of technical literature in Portugal and Castile. In his *Convivio*, for example, Dante had related the 'arts of doing' to ethics, in the way of the ancients, and even for certain university intellectuals such as Roger Bacon the general and speculative sciences ceded their hierarchically dominant position when confronted with specific knowledge, both particular and utilitarian, as were the mechanical arts. However, what must be emphasised is that, through the symmetry imposed with the organisation of the liberal arts, the mechanical arts were also, in the late Middle Ages, an organised system of knowledge, which in the time of John I was widespread, and which distinguished the seven distinct areas or 'disciplines'. The best known of these are *opificio*, *armatura*, *navigatio*, *agricultura* and *venatio*, but there are also the healing arts and finally the 'courtly arts' (or *Hofkünste*, as suggested by Eis), at times also called *theatrica* and among which we find, for example, the arts of jousting, combat, chess, carving and serving, as well as the art of horse riding.[401] Both the works of John I and the writings of Duarte show a perfect knowledge of this disciplinary architecture and a creative and reflective ability through the interior of this cultural universe which is proper to the medieval courts, and which was the place from where the first theories on the mechanical arts such as specific forms of *sondersprache* or technical language connected to them emerged. These arts flowered at the Portuguese court, since the monarchs cultivated them themselves, besides promoting the dissemination of writings and compilations composed by professionals in their service.

It is equally important to ascertain the presence of the horse as the object of a sphere of knowledge or distinct 'arts', since they occupied different places in the disciplinary ordering of the mechanical arts. This knowledge was related for example to hunting (not so much to agriculture, as the Roman tradition preferred) and through treatises and prescriptions for the treatment of horses and to courtly arts through equine arts.[402] Portuguese writings on treatment of horses appeared early on at the Portuguese court during the first decades

[401] Gerhard Eis, *Mittelalterlische Fachliteratur* (Stuttgart: Sammlung Metzler, 1967).

[402] Charles Homer Haskins, 'The Latin literature of sport', in *Studies in Medieval Culture* (Oxford: Clarendon Press, 1929), pp. 105–23.

of the fourteenth century, and were usually written by educated professionals, such as the physicians.[403] While, as Guy Beaujouan found in the case of the Iberian Peninsula, Hispanic technical literature was particularly abundant in this discipline of the treatment of horses or veterinary studies ('alveitaria' being, importantly, a word of Arab origin), it was however seen as greatly indebted to sources beyond the Pyrenees, in particular the Italians (Giordano Rufo, Teodorico Borgognone and Lorenzo Rusio).[404] However, the same is not the case with horsemanship, or 'the art of horse riding', where the treatise by the Portuguese king, Duarte, shows in its originality the fruit of the multifaceted culture of the king and a fine interest in these useful arts which is clear in agricultural books on falconry and horsemanship, or in the treatise on leprosy to be found in his library, as well as a collection of numerous recipes in his 'livro de conselhos'.[405] His contemporary, the Castilian Marquis de Villena, also produced several treatises which demonstrate a similar breadth of interests, particularly with his 'Arte cisoria', a treatise on carving and serving, or his now lost script on 'engenhos', or war machines. The existence of these treatises written by princes and important lords which handed down in ordered (and at times speculative) form specific knowledge regarding the activities of hunting and riding must be placed on an equal footing with the search for knowledge on war,[406] associating the writing of these texts to the sphere of war and charismatic power which was still a fundamental element of the aristocratic culture of the late Middle Ages. Whether on the art of the tourney or jousting, or whether on the 'cunning' of battle, these are found in important references in the 'livro do cavalgar' by Duarte, for they were adjacent and complementary knowledge to the disciplines of court in the system of classification referred to. Other forms of technical writings which were equally valued in the Portuguese context were treatment of horses and falconry, which were connected to the professionals of the stable and the hunt.

We know something as to the identity of those connected to hunting, particularly the hawskmen and falconers, and also the *monteiros* and the boys of the hunt, whose activities are fully described in hunting literature.[407] I have already

[403] This is what occurred with Master Giraldo, who was physician to D. Dinis and drew up his compilation at the request of the king in 1318: 'Livro de Alveitaria de Mestre Giraldo', and 'Tratado de Alveitaria', in *Dicionário da literatura medieval Galega e Portuguesa*, pp. 405–6 and 635.

[404] Guy Beaujouan, *La Science en Espagne aux XIVe et XVe siècles* (Paris: Université de Paris, 1967); Yvonne Poulle-Drieux, 'L'hippiatrie dans l'Occident latin du XIIIe au XVe siècle', in Guy Beaujouan and Y. Poulle-Drieux (eds.), *Médecine humaine et vétérinaire à la fin du moyen âge* (Geneva: Droz, 1966), pp. 9–172.

[405] Isabel Dias, *A arte de ser bom cavaleiro* (Lisbon: Estampa, 1997).

[406] João Gouveia Monteiro, 'A cultura militar da nobreza na primeira metade de Quatrocentos. Fontes e modelos literários', *Revista de História das Ideias*, 19 (1998), 195–227.

[407] Gerhard Eis, 'Die stellung der Jadg im mittelalterlichen System der Wissenschaften', in *Forshungen zur Fachprosa, Ausgewhälte Beiträge* (Berne and Munich: Francke, 1971), pp. 260–4.

mentioned the tendency to ennoble the royal servants in those positions which were hierarchically superior in this department of the court related to hunting from the earliest period studied here; this was the case of the Bugalho family, who were descendants of royal falconers. In the fifteenth century, the court nobility began to occupy powerful positions in this area of activity, so showing the prestige related to these activities and the knowledge itself of the man at court. However, in essence the servants of the *caça* and the *montaria* comprised individuals who were apparently more humble, who performed their duties for long periods, at times for life. Among the successive fourteenth-century falconers who were probably connected to the golden period of this type of hunting in Portugal, the prominent names are Luis Anes and Geraldo Fernandes, who served Pedro and Fernando as hawksmen and falconers. In a later generation there are also Gil Gomes, João Gonçalves and the famous Pero Menino. The last of these was the author of a treatise on the art of falconry which was later used as a direct source by Pedro López de Ayala in his *Libro de la Caza de las Aves*, as well as in later treatises of the Castilian court of Juan II.[408] All these falconers moved from the service of Fernando to the new dynasty, and were important in the royal service in the reign of John I. The *escudeiro*s Vasco d'Arval and Gil Martins d'Outel, as well as the 'grande monteiro' and hunting companion of the monarch, Aires Gonçalves de Figueiredo, were all connected to this hunting king as *monteiros* in his entourage. There is also information that the Portuguese queens, particularly Leonor Teles, had their own *monteiros*. Hunting was also practised by the women of the nobility, particularly at the end of the Middle Ages, and this was always connected in the texts of fifteenth-century chronicles to royal sovereignty, particularly in the description of the figures of King Pedro and, somewhat ambivalently, that of his descendant, the Infante João, son of Inês de Castro.[409] This information gives a new meaning to the 'speech' attributed by Fernão Lopes to Leonor Teles in the *Crónica de D. Fernando* following the death of her husband: 'a mim nom compre andar pella terra a montes e a caças, como têm em costume de fazer os rreis, mas tenho voontade de tomar assessego nos logares que dissestes [Santarém and Coimbra] e nesta cidade [Lisbon] e despender meu tempo com meus officiaaes e rreger e assessegar o rregno em verdadeira e dereita justiça'.[410]

408 'Livro de falcoaria', 'Livro da cetraria', 'Tratado de cetraria do Rei Dancus', in *Dicionário da literatura medieval Galega e Portuguesa*, pp. 408–9, 399 and 636.

409 On this, see the statement of Evelyne Patlagean, 'De la chasse et du souverain', *Dumbarton Oaks Papers*, 46 (1992), 257–63.

410 *CR Fernando*, p. 599. See also the statement in the Portuguese version of Christine de Pisan on the 'desenfadamentos' of the princesses when 'jr a caça de ribeira, dançar ou fazer outros jogos': Dorothee Carstens-Grokenberger, *Christine de Pisan Buch von den drei Tugenden in Portugiesischer Übersetzung* (Münster: Aschendorff, 1961), p. 60. For women hunting: J. Verdon, 'Recherches sur la chasse en Occident', *Revue Belge de Philologie et d'Histoire*, 56 (1978), 805–29.

Because of their complete integration in the system of the court officials, these professionals whom I have just described contrast with those who were related to supplies, who usually were not counted among the residents of the king. For example, there was a variable number of small merchants who accompanied the royal entourage, the 'regatães de corte'. There were also those who were specialists, such as the spice and grocery suppliers.[411] Contrary to the merchants of large resources, who were involved in the business of the leasing of royal rights and in the distribution of produce of greater importance whose presence at the royal court among the financial officials has already been mentioned, these more modest individuals presented characteristic mobility and instability, and would move with the royal entourage according to their suitability, trying always to profit from the privileges and exemptions which the kings used to attract their presence.[412] Yet again, the picture drawn is one of privilege and access in relation to the highly regulated world of the local markets, whose rigidity possibly had made problematic the flow of goods necessary for supplying a concentration of people as represented by the court. A slightly more structured profile is that which can be sketched of the meat supplier, who was another fundamental individual in the king's entourage whose profession connected him, in this case, to the supply of a basic food. The presence of a meat supplier at court, to which was also attached the payment of a *moradia*, sought to guarantee an abundance of meats, and also took into account the payment of rations to those who had a right to these. One practice which it seems Fernando tried to reform, which he explained to the people at the Cortes of 1371, was that he wished to cease having a meat supplier at court, since 'nom auemos por que o trazer [the court meat supplier] porque damos raçom de carne em dinheiros e tragemos nosa carne dos nosos gaados que temos [here is understood for the king's table]'.[413] This proposal cannot have been successful, for at least during the reigns of John I and Duarte we know the identity of the court butcher, Vasco Vicente, for whom the monarch repeatedly exempted any 'searching' or rationing of meats which he cut, 'por quanto anda conosco continoadamente e nos nunca estamos dassessego em hũu logar'.[414]

With regard to a general description of the world of the professions at the Portuguese court, we must also consider the Jewish and Moorish presence which has been emphasised by some studies and which is seen as characteristic of the

411 On his privileges for spice and grocery merchants see, for example, ANTT, *Ch. D. Afonso V*, 5, f. 48.

412 From an analysis of the set of royal charters naming successive 'regatães' can be drawn a marked profile for the temporary presence and for the geographical proximity of these men to those places where the court was. For an example, see the series relating to the years 1382–83: ANTT, *Ch. D. Fernando*, 3, ff. 13, 13v; 14, f. 14v; 15, f. 45v. For an example of the complaints of the people relating to the 'regatães' of the court, see the chapter of the Cortes of 1436: ANTT, Suppl. to Cortes, M 2, 19 (bis), ff. 2–2v.

413 *CPF*, p. 20.

414 ANTT, *Ch. D. João I*, 5, f. 84v.

final period of the Middle Ages. This presence had as its foundation the particular relationship of the monarch with the communities which were established throughout the kingdom and organised in several 'communes' under his protection. It could be said that the professionals who came from these minorities found at court a situation of greater assimilation than in other social contexts, for although similar criteria of differentiation were still felt, the activities and modes of life were little different from those of the Christians. The ministry or service to the monarchs was open both to Moors and to Jews, as already seen in the case of the *estrabeiros* and *tesoureiros*.

The particular relationship between the Jews and the king is frequently mentioned by texts of the time, with the statement that they formed part of the royal *câmara*.[415] This shows, on the one hand, their direct relationship with the person of the king and, as a result, their specificity in matters of justice or fiscal matters related to the mechanisms of normal mediation of the king's authority as represented by the royal officials and, on the other hand, that any offence made against them was a serious crime against the person of the monarch.[416] The *câmara* was, as will be shown in detail later, the innermost part of the court, the symbolic centre from which privilege and the monarch's favour were derived, but it was also the place where precious objects and treasure were kept, and the organism of the court was especially conceived for the protection of the body of the king. It seems significant from an anthropological point of view that, even metaphorically, one part of the population of the kingdom that was seen as 'impure' and subject to an enormously complex system of taboos and prohibitions, should be evoked by their proximity to the physical person of the king. In mentioning this aspect of the frequently glossed 'tolerance' (a curious word in the medieval context) of the kings of the age in relation to the Jewish presence in the kingdom and even at court, I do not wish to compare it, as is usual, with the harshness and radicalism of the exclusion of the Jewish population which occurred later. I merely wish to mention specific cultural traits of the age which contribute towards an explanation of the importance of the principal role at the court of the kings which a Jew could obtain, that is the office of Chief Rabbi, who was also connected in a particular manner to the *câmara* and the person of the monarch.

As is already known, all the Jewish communities were directly connected to the king, particularly with regard to justice. However, in the fourteenth and fifteenth centuries, the king rarely personally made judgement, even regarding his Christian subjects. The right which every Jew had to be judged according

[415] In the words of a royal charter of the time of John I, 'elles sempre forom e som da nossa camara e da dos reis que ante Nos forom seendo per nos guardados e defendidos nos corpos e nos aueres': ANTT, *Ch. D. João I*, 4, f. 64v.

[416] See for a general perspective Maria José Ferro Tavares, *Os Judeus em Portugal no século XV*, 2 vols. (Lisbon: Universidade Nova de Lisboa and INIC, 1982 and 1984).

to his own law, which was sanctioned by royal authority, was under the control of the Chief Rabbi, who was close to the monarchs and who would, ideally, be a specialist in law, and who could also more frequently turn to specialists under his authority within the community. As Maria José Ferro pointed out, the structure in Portugal of a hierarchy among the local Jews, the authorities in the communes and the Chief Rabbi, who was called in matters of justice, is parallel in every way to the structure which connected the authorities of the Christian councils with the court *corregedor*. This special relationship of the monarch with the Jewish communities must always be borne in mind in an analysis of the effective power of the Chief Rabbi at the end of the Middle Ages. He was, let us say, the principal mediator between the communities and the king, and dealt with every variety of question, including financial and those concerning an actual fiscal system relating to the Jewish population. We can regard this system, somewhat crudely, as being valid until the 1460s, when it began to demonstrate some important changes. From the fourteenth century, the important role of the Chief Rabbi at the Portuguese court was always in the hands of particularly powerful and rich families.

By his proximity to the monarch and by being the person of his choice (as opposed to the case with local authorities in the communes) the Chief Rabbi was, during the fourteenth and fifteenth centuries, almost always a great merchant and a counsellor to the kings on matters of the *fazenda*. I have already mentioned his importance during the final years of the fourteenth century as *tesoureiro-mor* as well as within the financial organisms of the kingdom and of the court, and have named Jewish officials who held this post. Later, particularly at the courts of the Aviz dynasty, the physical figure of the Chief Rabbi became dominant. This did not mean, it would seem, that the rabbi became merely a man of knowledge. From then on, we might say, he was a professional, a participant in the royal *câmara* in his role as specialist in medicine, sharing with the monarch and with his more intimate circle some specific cultural interests such as a passion for astrology, but always remaining an important official of justice and mediator between the communities and the king. Frequently, as counsellor and man of finance, the Chief Rabbi openly took opportunities for profit which maritime commerce brought, in which the monarch himself was involved, as were the relatives of the royal family and many other courtiers. This was the progress of the Abravanel, Latão, Palaçano and Negro families, to name the main families of Jewish courtiers of the fifteenth century. Throughout the century, the position of Chief Rabbi was handed on in practice to the Negro family.[417]

However, the Jewish presence is not found merely in the case of the richest and most powerful, or in a daily participation in the royal *câmara* through

[417] See the genealogical plans given in Tavares, *Os Judeus em Portugal no século XV*, vol. I, pp. 228–9 and 233–5. On the Negro family, vol. I, pp. 116 and 133.

the physicians. We must also mention the respect and esteem in which the Jewish artisans and artists were held in their particular specialisms. These were to be found in various palace organisms, but particularly in the case of tailors, goldsmiths and armourers.[418] The case of the goldsmiths is well known for their participation in the making of ceremonial objects such as the silverware, liturgical plate and even ornamental jewellery, as was the case with the goldsmith to Leonor Teles, cited above. Some accompanied the king on his itinerances, but others appear also to have had their business houses in Lisbon and other places, and would perhaps travel, as did Leonor's goldsmith, in search of material for their work. As to the Jewish tailors of the Portuguese court, they do not seem to be related solely to the specialised duties necessary for the making of complex garments but to be, most of all, specialised and knowledgeable in materials and costly articles or even as an occasional purveyor who knew how to value and obtain them, at which the Jewish artisan was found to be indispensable.[419] The figure of the court tailor or goldsmith of the fifteenth century seems to correspond best to the picture of the master of his art and the rich official living aristocratically as the gentleman-bureaucrat who did not scorn involvement in wars. José Arame did just this in the service of the Infante Henry, taking part in the conquest of Ceuta and the expedition to Tangier 'com cavalo e armas e dois homens de pé'.[420] There is little evidence in the Portuguese court of the presence of the Moors, with the exception referred to above of the *estrabeiros*. Even so, there is information on several Muslim physicians in the royal *câmara*, as was the case of the physician to Fernando, Master Mafamede. It could be said that, apart from the certainly large presence, already written of in the case of women, of domestic slaves or 'mouras' in the various court organisms, Moorish participation in the Portuguese court was less evident than that of the Jews at the level of documented offices and professions.

The dignity and prestige of the professionals who were at the court of the kings is particularly evident in the methods of hierarchical organisation which are to be found in certain areas of activity. One particular case was, for example, that of the musicians and minstrels of the court, whose performance was required on various festive occasions and, as we shall see, in the cycle of the more common ceremonies of the court. They were not part of the royal chapel, and were at times called 'músicos da sala', in order to be distinguishable from the chapel musicians.[421] We know the identity of several of these professionals

418 On the work of the armourers: Tavares, *Os Judeus em Portugal no século XV*, vol. I, p. 260 and note 67.

419 Such is the image taken from the legislation of the thirteenth century, for example of the group of norms of 1258: 'Mandarom que aia el Rej em sa casa huum boom alfayate que saiba conheçer panos E penas E compra-llos E apreça-llos E que saiba bem fazer seu mester': *OD*, p. 57.

420 *MH*, vol. VII, p. 4.

421 As was the case in other medieval courts, a certain group of minstrels could not receive residences, although they could be contracted sporadically (like the itinerant players, acrobats, mummers, etc.): Andrés Descalzo, 'La música en la corte de Pedro IV "el Ceremonioso"',

in the fifteenth century, and their presence in the service of the monarchs of the fourteenth century is not in doubt, particularly regarding the bugles and shawns, whose traditional use had appeared at least in the century before. Several of these musicians were also foreign, as clearly indicated by their names. One family in the service of Afonso V was, for example, that of 'Copim' and 'Jeanim' de Reste, who played the shawn and came from beyond the Pyrenees. A model of organisation which we might call 'monarchic', because of the strangeness of their titles, ruled the hierarchy of these professionals who were organised in distinctive bodies. Thus, there were at the fifteenth-century court several 'kings' of the shawn and 'kings' of the bugles and minstrels, all individuals who superintended the activity of these professional musicians, not only at court but throughout the kingdom, including the musicians who were dependants of the infantes and important lords, 'em salas reais, como em batalhas e em quaisquer outros lugares'.[422] The analogy with the group of heraldic officials, who were also ruled by a 'King of Arms', seems pertinent. In a certain manner it is to the same model that Olivier de la Marche refers ironically when describing the cook at the court of Burgundy as a monarch, seated in his high chair, 'between the buffet and the fireplace', holding in his hand, like an insignia, an enormous wooden spoon which served two purposes – tasting the food and punishing the boys.[423]

Forming the centre of society of the Portuguese court at the end of the Middle Ages, the small world of people who surrounded the kings shows itself in this description to be marked entirely by changes in and access to their recruitment. The change is seen, for example, in the succession of the groups of women who remained with the queen, who split up and re-formed in each case according to the nationality of the queen, her connections and the vicissitudes of her life. There is also the mutable panorama of the families of the court nobility, which I have attempted here to evoke in some detail. Then again there is the plasticity of the line which at the end of the Middle Ages divided the court clerics who were entirely immersed in a life of profanity from the position of the laity. Despite all these changes, there are some fundamental tendencies which characterise this social environment as a whole.

Looking at matters from the point of view of the nobility, we could say that the essential process resided in the constitution of a local court society, which was granted its own autonomy and dynamic and which, in my opinion, could only be clearly found during the fifteenth century, reaching its full maturity in the reign of Afonso V. Until the end of the fourteenth century, one can perhaps speak of a court nobility which existed on a Peninsular scale, marked by pendular

Acta Historica et Archeologica Mediaevalia, 11–12 (1990–91), 401–19; Constance Bullock-Davies, *Menestrellorum Multitudo: Minstrels at a Royal Feast* (Cardiff: University of Wales Press, 1978), pp. 15–16 and 26.

422 F. M. Sousa Viterbo, *O rei dos Charamelas e os Charamelas-mores*, offprint of *Arte Musical* (Lisbon, 1912); Viterbo, *Subsídios para a história da música*, p. 25.

423 Olivier de la Marche, *L'Estat de la maison du Duc Charles*, p. 50.

movements of the various families and their relatives between Galicia, Portugal and Castile, and which found one of its fundamental sites of activity in the company of the Portuguese kings. The concrete promotion of a small number of these families, who accompanied the advent of the new dynasty of Aviz after 1385, have been somewhat overvalued by modern historiography, concealing the larger process of local implementation and independence which also occurs, as we have seen, with other concomitant and interrelated processes as a formation of a 'nobility of service' dependent on the monarchs, whose origins appeared in many cases in the thirteenth century, or the accentuated integration of the diverse noble strata arising at court. The structure of the nobility in lineages which was clearly visible from the twelfth century had shown itself to be compatible with a tendency towards mobility associated with becoming a member of court and with the obvious movement between the various Peninsular courts. But there was in the fourteenth century a new laying of roots of the nobility, either through their connection to urban areas or in the growing practice of patrimonial transmission through entailment, which was favoured and even promoted by the monarchs. Is this a 'new' nobility at the court of the monarchs of Aviz? The reply is in the affirmative, if we consider that the novelty lies in great part in the court itself. Or, better still, in the diverse rhythms with which this small society renewed itself in the fifteenth century, which in the case of the nobility occurred not only through the process of setting roots, which is also an indication of a growing dependence on the profits which the monarch offered, but also by a small number of episodes of individual and family ascent. These episodes of social promotion reveal positions of power and wealth achieved by people who until then had been obscure, but who did not, in the end, represent anything other than a small part of the court nobility, which I have attempted to define precisely for the first time.

Some aspects of this research which are relative to the remaining groups who figure in the society of the court contribute to the reinforcement of an image of a growing attraction and centrality of the organism surrounding the monarchs in the context of Portuguese society. Thus, the evolutive tendency which we found earlier in the organisation of the court as the central point of an institutional system in development seems decisively to influence the internal diversity of this environment because of the importance vested in it by the presence of the functionary, the merchant and the professional in general (be he a musician, physician, clerk or artisan). From what can be seen, the servants of the monarchs came from various regions of the country, but with a certain preference for urban nuclei which, as we shall see, were more often visited by the royal itinerances. This is, therefore, a world which is wide open to the exterior, which does not prevent the formation of family lines of service through the succession of generations in the service of the kings and queens and which denotes the existence of specific mechanisms of recruitment.

At this point of my journey, the detailed description of court society will therefore have to give way to another complex of problems formed around the mechanisms of constitution and of internal cohesion of this environment. We now have a more or less precise idea as to the identity of the Portuguese courtier of the fourteenth and fifteenth centuries. What is now of interest is an analysis of what takes him to the court and what keeps him there.

3. Criação *and service*

What are the overall characteristics of the presence of this group of men and women alongside the Portuguese monarchs who, as stated above, shared the same material and symbolic spaces? How were they integrated in these spaces, and what relationship did they build among themselves, and with the monarchs? In an attempt to answer these questions, medieval sources once again respond with a diverse panorama, so giving rise to further questions. In the first analysis, we find that this was a matter of a constant presence in some cases and of a more precarious duration in others; paid in some cases, in others not, according to the way in which the individuals (or even certain groups) made use of the complex group of roles and functions at court. In my opinion, the identification and study of these characteristic forms of participation are an indispensable, empirical basis for the study of the court as a social configuration of the past. In fact, whether it is theoretical proposals of the sociology of configuration which are adopted, the abstract perspective of the theory of systems, or the more restricted optic of the theory of social exchange, I believe it to be beyond doubt that the understanding of court society requires to be nurtured directly with the wealth resulting from the actual process of construction of historical sources, with new data and new theories arising which present a greater degree of coherence and explanatory capacity of the cultural reality of pre-modern societies in their variety and specificity.[1]

As a point of departure, I particularly kept in mind the relationships which were woven between the man of court and the monarch himself, at the

[1] 'The construction of models by the historian through the actual sources is, without doubt, one of the responses... Note, however, that when I spoke of the construction of notions, of logical operations through an analysis of sources, I set off from a presupposition that is also not confirmed: that there are sources which are given which I used as a point of departure for the historical work. However, sources are never given to us. There are no sources upon which I built facts so that I might then safely define the relationships which interlink them. The sources are constructed relative to the construction of the facts themselves.' Vitorino Magalhães Godinho, *A construção de modelos para as economias pré-estatísticas*, offprint of *Revista de História Económica e Social* (Lisbon, 1985).

interconnection of a study of the terminology of these relations with their characterisation in texts of the age. As a result of this analysis, the court appears to be an arrangement or particular disposition of these relationships, from which there result forms of interdependence and a global design of hierarchy, and through which the heterogeneity of the individuals and of the groups was resolved within a given order of importance and distinction. The problem of the relationships within this order, and, in a general manner, between the 'social form' which the court represents and global society, certainly posited by the work of Norbert Elias, seemed to me equally essential to the construction of my subject.

TERMINOLOGY

A first route of research lies in the study of the group of terms which, in the contemporary texts, are applied to the individuals who became integrated in the royal entourage, and by an attempt to penetrate their diverse meanings. This route is cloaked in some difficulties, essentially owing on the one hand to the impossibility of reconstructing in an entire, coherent manner the distinct semantic fields within which these sets of meanings are grouped and, on the other, to the secular time in which we are moving, and to the historicity of these same relationships between words and things, whose mutation implies the possibility that the same terms might have distinctive meanings with changes in time. Having said this, my analysis sought some exploratory routes, turning to several types of texts of the age, and keeping in mind the deciphering of terms applied to those who attended court, generically evoked by expressions such as: 'those who live with the king' or 'those in his favour'. Three words occur particularly frequently in Portuguese sources, without which the spectre of concrete situations to which they allude within court society would not have been studied in due depth; these are *criado*, *morador*, *vassalo*. What these have in common is only the reference of a dyadic relationship between the individuals and the monarch. Each of these words opened up for me a fascinating field of study in the light of texts of the fourteenth and fifteenth centuries.

What is understood at the time by *criado*, or the individual among the *criação do rei*, seems totally different from the present meanings of the term. Once again, we return to the juridic/encyclopaedic nature of Alfonso's work, for example the *Espéculo* as a point of departure: 'Mucho tenemos que deuen sseer guardados los de criazón del rrey, ca el nombre lo demuestra que lo deuen sseer; ca tanto quiere dezir de criazón commo criado de casa del rrey o gouernado después por su bienffecho e por esto tenemos por bien que ssean onrrados e guardados.'[2] The association, in this text, of living together from

[2] *Leyes de Alfonso X*, vol. I, *Espéculo*, p. 161.

infancy in the king's household under his protection or 'benfeitoria', constitutes a recurring fact in the texts of the late Middle Ages in Portugal: the observations of Fernão Lopes serve as an example, when he speaks of the 'muitos criados da Rainha, assi per criaçom come per benfeitoria e offiçios que lhe dera',[3] or the commentary of Rui de Pina on the political action of the Ataídes, who 'forom como ingratos aa sua criaçam e benfeitoria', refusing to accompany their master on the eve of the battle of Alfarrobeira.[4] *Criação* constitutes, as deduced from the group of references made, a terrain which is propitious to the development of relationships of particular proximity; thus the epithet 'criado' can be grouped with an enormous variety of situations as to the court occupation of the individuals and even their social standing. This is applied to the members of the great families of the nobility and to ecclesiastics or modest servants of the kings.

The history of this concept is perhaps related to the older term of 'homens de criação', which in texts prior to the thirteenth century we see applied to the dependent smallholders of the great lords whose condition cannot, by all indications, be considered free. Of the relative variety in the juridic situation of the diverse components of *familiae* of the magnates of the eleventh and twelfth centuries, it was possible to isolate these 'homens de criação' as a group which is hypothetically connected to the lord through specific personal ties of dependence moulded within the household.[5] In the kingdom of Leon, for instance, we find another form of dependence in the *homines de benefactoria* who could, according to Estepa Diez, correspond with lower groups of the nobility or even to villein *cavaleiro*s who lived in the sphere of a magnate, and cover a type of relationship current in the central and western zones of the Peninsula at the end of the eleventh century.[6] The relationship of the *criados* of whom we speak with these more archaic figures is, however, problematic and remote in the light of available studies, although without doubt there exists a significant common nucleus which is formed by the domestic context and by the fundamental asymmetry of the relationship to which they allude. In addition, it could be said that the juridic historiography, which makes use of the multiple references occurring in the sources of the westernmost region of the Peninsula, attempted to transform these 'homens de criação' and the 'homens de benfeitoria' into categories which were perhaps excessively rigorous from the point of view of social classifications, corresponding in each case to a personal, precise and exclusive standing. Now, as I have observed them, the 'criados' of the kings during the later period were individuals of highly varied social status, who only had in common the fact of being included in the household and the entourage of the Portuguese monarchs, in a way analogous to the old 'homens

[3] *CR João I*, vol. I, pp. 36–7. [4] *CR Afonso V*, p. 712. [5] *DHP*, vol. II, pp. 446–7.

[6] Carlos Estepa Díez, 'Formación y consolidación', in *En torno al feudalismo Hispánico* (Ávila: Fundación Sánchez-Albornoz, 1989), p. 226.

de criação', as members of their *familia* and their dependants, without this fact implying a specific, well-defined juridic condition. As was the case with the old concept of 'benefactoria', the protection granted to the 'criados' did not always have as its target members of the nobility.

The connection thus established therefore refers to an interpersonal dependence of a peculiar kind, whose material remuneration was transitory while being, however, an extremely lasting relationship in other aspects, and it also refers to a special proximity to the court, since it implied a more or less prolonged social intercourse with the king – his 'agasalho' (Germanic *gasalia*, member of a company).[7] The chroniclers of the age studied here have all been preoccupied with emphasising this subtle tie which related these men throughout their lives to those by whom they had been 'criado', with the majority perforce being the monarchs. Fernando was, according to the chronicler Lopes, 'gram criador de fidallgos e muito companheiro com elles'.[8] In a 'fala' attributed by the chronicler to this king, the king eulogises his faithful servant Nuno Álvares Pereira: 'de tam bom criado como eu em vós fiz nom podia sahir senom tall obra e outras melhores'.[9] *Criação* could be placed above actual consanguinity, in a certain measure reinforcing it or even replacing it with this binding tie. In this sense, the 'Vida' of St Isabel declares that the queen was 'criada' by her grandfather, James of Aragon,[10] just as the several bishops of the first half of the fourteenth century (such as João Martins de Soalhães or João Afonso de Brito) named their biological descendants 'criados' in the documents in which they established the inheritance of their possessions.[11] The same occurred with Master Álvaro Gonçalves Pereira, but only in relation to some of his many children, whom he called 'seus criados' in some documents, probably because they had lived in his household.[12]

A distinctive factor of this relationship of 'criação', even during the final stages of the Middle Ages, was the fact that it could not be easily broken or renegotiated in a lifetime. Once established, this was an enduring, even an almost indissoluble relationship, in spite of living together and material protection resulting from its having finally been interrupted. For this reason in the Castilian

[7] 'It should be noted, however, that *geselle*, companion, is not merely someone who lives or goes with us on an equal footing; it is also one who "accompanies" the leader or patron, who is a member of his company... it is for this reason that in several documents there is reference to this or that person "*com seus gasalianes*"': Paulo Merêa, '*Gasalianes*', in *Para um glossário do nosso Latim medieval*, offprint of *Biblos* (Coimbra, 1940), pp. 5–7.

[8] *CR Fernando*, p. 3.

[9] The chronicler is repeating in this passage the text set out in the anonymous 'Crónica' relating to the *condestável: CR Nuno*, p. 23.

[10] *Vida e milagres de D. Isabel*, pp. 19–20.

[11] See respectively ANTT, Arquivo da Casa de Abrantes, book 6 G, Doc. 1279 (Soalhães) and ANTT, *LN*, Guadiana, 8, ff. 38–40 (Brito). I am grateful to Lurdes Rosa for having supplied me with this information.

[12] *CR Pedro*, p. 222.

Fuero Viejo, compiled *c.* 1350, which can be said to be a most important source for the study of the Hispanic feudal ideology, it was established that the 'rico-homem' who was exiled from his homeland would always be accompanied by the vassals whom he 'criara'. These 'deven aguardar suo Señor, e non se deven tirar de él, mientra que estovir fuera de la tierra', while it was permissible for all others not to follow their lord into exile.[13] The tie to which this designation makes reference therefore demonstrated special characteristics as to its origin, duration and nature.

Did this word retain the same semantic relationship with the social environment of the monarch and the 'benfeitoria' during the entire period studied here? This is a difficult question to answer definitively without proceeding to further research beyond the context of the court, and beyond my limits. By simply taking as a target the social court circle, we can say this relationship was preserved in that circle particularly clearly, which does not mean that the broadening of the meaning of this term does not occur in certain cases in documents of the mid-fifteenth century, with the epithet 'criado' being applied to numerous individuals whose inclusion in the court cannot always be proved for an earlier moment of their lives.

In its association with the domestic sphere, which remains as the significant nucleus, the word 'criação' also has a history which continues beyond the period studied here, through its spread from the Hispanic usage into other linguistic areas, such as the Italian. In usage of the sixteenth century in Italy, the Italian 'creanza' (from Spanish *crianza*) came to mean generically all relationships established within the domestic community, by this time illustrating an important extension of the field of the word in relation to the uses found for Portuguese and Castilian societies of the final centuries of the Middle Ages.[14] The term is also to be found fairly well studied in the several contexts of Spanish society of the so-called 'Siglo de Oro'.[15] In France, too, it began to be equated generically with the neologism 'créatures' from the second half of the sixteenth century for the dependants and familiars of important nobles, being an epithet which encompassed both their clients and the members of their household.[16]

The second word in my list, *morador*, seems the most easy to interpret, since in it we find an allusion to the physical presence of the individuals alongside the monarchs in a situation of complete integration at the court as an itinerant

[13] Jordan de Asso (ed.), *El Fuero Viejo de Castilla* (Madrid: Joaquín Ibarra, 1771), pp. 15–16.

[14] Elide Casali, 'Economica e "creanza" cristiana', *Quaderni Storici*, 41 (1979), 555–83.

[15] José Antonio Maravall, 'Relaciones de dependencia e integración social: criados, graciosos y pícaros', *Ideologies and Literature*, 1 (1977), 3–32.

[16] Arlette Jouanna, 'Des réseaux d'amitié aux clientèles centralisées: les provinces et la cour (France, XVIe–XVIIe siècles)', in Charles Giry-Deloison and Roger Mettam (eds.), *Patronage et clientélismes, 1550–1750 (France, Angleterre, Espagne, Italie)* (Villeneuve d'Ascq: Centre d'Histoire de la Région du Nord et de l'Europe du Nord-Ouest/Institut Français du Royaume-Uni, 1995), p. 29.

organism, with a determined continuity. Not all who played a part in this circle could in truth count themselves among the *moradores* of the king. This word was reserved for those who were 'de cote', as Fernão Lopes said; that is for those who were present on a daily basis and who were also, during the fifteenth century, known as 'contínuos'. The main characteristic of the *moradores* was that they were sustained by the king (or the lord), or they were those who, as stated in Alfonsine sources, 'han ración para si e para sus bestias'. This conclusion would seem to be confirmed also by Portuguese legislation in the second half of the thirteenth century,[17] where the 'moradores do rei' by then found an entire group of judicial privileges to be the norm, and at times referred to the 'rações' which they received.

The *moradores* of the king tended, however, to become transformed almost exclusively into a status group with an internal hierarchy at the fifteenth-century court, which is a dynamic to which I shall refer later. In this case, it could be said that the dyadic nature of the relationship diminishes, becoming hypothetically less personal and close to the monarch, to the same degree as the court grew in size.[18] This evolution was also accompanied by profound changes in the nature and methods of payment relating to the support of the *moradores*. In spite of these changes, it could be said that physical presence at court remained, until the end of the Middle Ages, as its main distinction. Contrary to that which occurred with the *criados*, the relationship which the *moradores* established with the monarch, while more institutionalised, was of indeterminate duration, being only conditional upon this physical presence in the royal entourage. The transitory and fluid nature of this tie thus constitutes an essential aspect which must be borne in mind.

As to the word *vassalo*, its multiple meanings in the social and juridic lexicon of late-medieval society present a complex problem. However, it is a word commonly used to mean those who were integrated in the king's entourage, particularly in the case of nobles. Naturally I do not intend to revert needlessly to listing here the entire, vast group of questions which the interpretation of this word gives rise to, particularly when it refers to the existence of personal ties of a feudo-vassal character in Portugal, along with others of a general nature, which connected the inhabitants of the kingdom to their 'natural' lord, the king. In both cases, the word 'vassal' was used in the fourteenth and fifteenth centuries, and rightly makes one cautious as to the nature of the tie which connected each specific individual to the king. In essence, it is entirely the converse problem of

[17] For example in the *Ordenação* of 1258: *OD*, p. 55.

[18] 'A dyadic relationship is a direct relationship . . . *direct* connotes personal attachment. It distinguishes a dyadic relationship from a relationship in which two actors are connected with each other indirectly as a consequence of the fact that they occupy offices or positions which are interconnected, or because they are members of the same group': Carl H. Landé, 'The dyadic basis of clientelism', in Steffen W. Schmidt *et al.* (eds.), *Friends, Followers and Factions* (Berkeley: University of California Press, 1977), pp. xiii–xiv.

the forms of later feudalism in Portuguese medieval society to be confronted, and which I shall turn to later, concerning payments made to the nobility.

For now, I shall say that the chronology and the context of the numerous references analysed would appear to allow for the statement that some instances in sources of the fourteenth and fifteenth centuries refer to individual nobles connected to the king by a particular and personal tie of vassalage whose counterpart, with regard to the vassal, consisted in the rendering of military service and actual service at court. The transformations experienced by the fact of these vassals' duties, relating to military service, have been well established in the westernmost region of the Peninsula, since they have been studied for Castile by Hilda Grassotti and for Portugal, though in less depth, by José Mattoso, and with regard to the final stages of the Middle Ages by João Gouveia Monteiro. In a general manner, these transformations appear to be a generalisation of the monetary remuneration and revenue paid to the noble vassals, as will be seen.

Very little is known, on the other hand, for both the western Portuguese kingdom and that of Castile on the 'serviço de corte' which I have already mentioned and the methods of performance of this service by the royal vassals from the thirteenth century. One of the traditional areas of their activity, which consisted in a periodic presence at solemn moments for participation in the councils or feudal courts, was also undergoing a profound change in the period studied here. On this point, the institutional organic which developed from the late medieval court tended to create new ties, including in a fairly flexible body of permanent counsellors only a part of the *vassalos*; that is the 'privados', who were from then on accompanied by other members of the direct entourage of the king, particularly those expert in law and finance.[19] All this led to the royal council becoming an increasingly technical and governmental organ, and not simply a periodic organism whose duty it was to create assents, substantially modifying the context in which the vassals could, or should, render the so-called 'serviço de corte'. This transformation, which is well identified in the institutional sphere, also alludes in my opinion to other important changes which the court brought to the mechanisms of political communication and interchange between the nobility and the king.

From the point of view of the nobility, the attraction of the court at this period takes on new meanings, which now tend to consider the portion of the royal presence more as a distinction to be aspired to than as a strict duty of vassalage. This aspect of the 'process of curialisation' of the lay and ecclesiastical aristocracy occurring in the Hispanic societies at the end of the Middle Ages can be studied in detail through the presence of its protagonists at court to whom

[19] Salustiano de Dios, *El Consejo Real de Castilla (1385–1522)* (Madrid: Centro de Estudios Constitucionales, 1982), pp. 34–40 and 57. For the Portuguese case, see A. L. Carvalho Homem, *Conselho real ou conselheiros do rei? A propósito dos 'privados' de D. João I*, offprint of *Revista da Faculdade de Letras* (Oporto, 1987), pp. 26–30.

I referred in the previous chapter. We might recall here, in order to remember the growing *distance* separating the noble vassals from the monarch, the figure of the poor knight of Toledo of Pero López de Ayala's 'Rimado de Palacio', to whom the king's *porteiro* refused access to his lord exclaiming,

> Estad alla, ca ya non puede ser!
> Esta el rrey en consejo sobre fechos granados,
> e non dos o tres priuados;
> e a todos mando que non fuesen osados
> de llegar a la puerta, aunque sean onrrados.[20]

The current medieval topic is clear here: that of the motive of royal isolation as a factor of misgovernment, a motive which is directly complementary to the image of the monarchs being accessible to the people which, returning to the same topic, the Spanish chronicler developed.[21] However, we also see the development of the clear perception of the differentiating function of the 'privança' and its association with the new institutional mechanisms which developed within the court of the kings.

It is a plausible hypothesis that the feudo-vassalic tie which developed for the nobility from this period becomes less significant as a determining factor of social intercourse with the monarchs, there being other, extremely diverse, ways of life in the relationship which do not have recourse to the formality and solemnity characteristic of the feudal world. The actual relationships of vassalage always presented in the westernmost Hispanic societies less constancy and a more precarious character, for they were easily established through the simple ritual of hand-kissing and, by all indications, no less easily dissolved.[22] On the other hand, the Castilian and Portuguese monarchs had systematically used, from the end of the thirteenth century, the tie of 'natureza' which connected them to the nobles of the kingdom, placing it above the personal and retractable character of the tie of vassalage. Several significant factors certainly thus became associated, under the aegis of the doctrinal influence of Aristotelian naturalism, which mutually reinforced each other in this new term of 'natural vassal'. The earlier concept of *naturalis*, including within the semantic field that of vassalage, already referred to obligations determined by birth, 'naturalising', as one might say, the political tie of subordination in relation to the 'senhor rei'. However, we

20 Pero López de Ayala, *Rimado de Palacio*, ed. by Germán Orduna (Pisa: Giardini, 1981), vol. I, p. 213.

21 František Graus, 'Littérature et mentalité médiévales: le roi et le peuple', *Historica*, 16 (1969), 5–79.

22 On this see the classic texts of Luis García de Valdeavellano, 'Las instituciones feudales in España' [1963] and 'Sobre la cuestión del feudalismo hispánico' [1978], in *El feudalismo hispánico y otros estudios de historia medieval* (Barcelona: Ariel, 1981), pp. 63–132, 7–62. Also Salvador de Moxó, 'Feudalismo europeo y feudalismo español' [1964] and 'Sociedad, estado y feudalismo' [1972], in *Feudalismo, señorío y nobleza en la Castilla medieval* (Madrid: Real Academia de la Historia, 2000), pp. 59–72 and 13–58.

also have reference to a 'law of nature' which generically tied all countrymen to the land in which they were born.[23]

This complex of notions was also clearly formed in Portugal at the end of the fourteenth century, for example during the revolt against King Fernando by his half-brother, the Infante João, during the episode of his 'desnaturamento' which occurred in 1381. According to an important feudal lord such as the Castilian Infante Don Juan Manuel, it was legal for a vassal to 'desnaturar-se', by symbolically performing one of three actions forbidden to a 'natural' vassal: not to wound or kill his lord in battle, not to oppose him or attack town or castle, and not to set fire to his land.[24] By this time in exile João was, according to the witnesses of the time, 'fazendo guerra e pondo logo fogo por sua mão', at the border lands of Portugal, so breaking his connection with his king and 'senhor natural', that is Fernando. What seems significant is that this public act of 'desnaturamento', performed in the full understanding of the vassals' code of behaviour set out by Don Juan Manuel, would have been yet another weighty argument invoked in the context of the Cortes of Coimbra four years later used to invalidate the pretensions of the son of Inês de Castro to the Portuguese throne; his action had also had consequences in his relationship with the kingdom itself, and not only with his personal relationships with his brother, the monarch.[25] While the tie of vassalage, in the strict meaning of the term, became more intermittent in its archaic invariability and even tended, as we shall see, to become overlooked in many social contexts owing to other forms of contractual relationships among individuals, the tie of 'natureza', on the other hand, assumed a growing stability and a collective meaning in this new, more complex acceptance. In the beautiful metaphor suggested by the Infante Pedro *c.* 1420, combining the traditional patriarchal image of royalty with a concept of 'natureza' connected to the land, the princes were to be 'padres dos seus proprios subditos, os quaaes elles geeram como naturaaes marydos com a terra que he seu senhorio'.[26]

To summarise, all these changes lead us to consider the mention of 'vassals' in the context of the royal court with some care, recognising that any interpretation is not always safe and unambiguous. When, for instance, the word is applied to the holders of the so-called 'cargos maiores' of the court, it can be considered that 'vassal' in this case alluded to a type of personal tie of the monarch to some courtiers, from whom was demanded a swearing of allegiance which in many cases was intended to emphasise the specific duties connected to the particular

23 Jacques Krynen, '"Naturel". Essai sur l'argument de la nature dans la pensée politique française de la fin du moyen âge', *Journal des Savants*, 2 (1982), 169–90; Ernst Kantorowicz, '*Pro Patria Mori* in medieval political thought', in *Selected Studies* (New York: Augustin, 1965), pp. 308–24.

24 Don Juan Manuel, *Obras completas*, ed. by José Manuel Blecua (Madrid: Gredos, 1982), vol. I, p. 378).

25 See the testimony of Diogo Lopes Pacheco in 1385: ANTT, drawer XIII, M 3, 8.

26 Infante D. Pedro, 'O livro da Virtuosa Benfeitoria', in *Obras dos Príncipes de Avis*, ed. M. Lopes de Almeida (Oporto: Lello, 1981), p. 578.

posts. One of the main duties was that of obedience, which was the subject of an express vow, for example made by an admiral or military commander.[27] In this sphere, which was hierarchically superior in the court organic and permeated with solemnity and tradition, values contradictory to the feudal world were to take more time in being included in a specific form, even in the modern period. I particularly refer to a certain 'professionalisation' of some palace posts which appears in a rudimentary form in the sixteenth- and seventeenth-century treatises on the *mordomo da casa*, the carver and the *mestre-sala*, which were to develop in the European sphere and whose usage in Portugal, however, has never been studied.[28] This resistance to the absorption of new values was, in a large way, due to the ennobling character of these court roles related to the personal service of the king and previously clearly conjoined with the sphere of vassaldom and traditionally opposed to any overexplicit notion of material remuneration.

A nobleman would on several successive occasions be included in the entourage of the king as his 'vassal', with duties as a military escort or connected to the activity of the royal guard, particularly throughout the fourteenth century, and this I feel can be included in the same accepted meaning close to the feudo-vassalic relationship to which I have referred regarding the 'cargos maiores' of the court. While during the fifteenth century, however, I suggest the unifying mantle of the tie of 'natureza', this makes progressively more unclear the number of vassals because of the vulgarisation of the term in numerous discursive spheres. The word also appears to be less used in an individual sense in the royal entourage and appears to assume connotations of group status in the context of the late medieval juridic ordinance, particularly in its fiscal aspects.

My reflection as to the names used more commonly for the members of the royal court thus allows for an initial evaluation of the diversity of the network of relationships in which individuals found themselves in the specific optic of their tie with the monarchs. Not one of the three words analysed can be considered exclusively, for there is no lack of examples of courtiers named simultaneously or successively in a variety of ways: as 'criados', as 'moradores', and as 'vassalos'. Between the two opposite poles evoked by *criação* and by vassalage we therefore find three distinct types of situation. With *criação* we find a lasting relationship which assumes the characteristics of a true form of pseudo-blood relationship.[29] The medieval texts which reflect on the proximity

[27] On the testimony of the admiral: *OA*, vol. I, p. 324. In the chronicle of Nuno Álvares Pereira, for example, it is mentioned that once he was king, John I 'fez logo seu conde estabre a Nun Alvrez, fazendo lhe suas cirimonias segundo ao officio pertence, muy honradamente': *CR Nuno*, p. 99.

[28] A short bibliography of this treatise: Sergio Bertelli *et al.* (eds.), *Le corti Italiane del Rinascimento* (Milan: Mondadori, 1985), p. 271.

[29] On this concept: Julian Pitt-Rivers, 'Pseudo-kinship', in David Sills (ed.), *International Encyclopedia of Social Sciences* (New York: Macmillan, 1968), pp. 7, 408–13. The importance of the forms of pseudo-kinship at the Portuguese court of the thirteenth century is emphasised by Leontina Ventura, 'A nobreza de corte de Afonso III', vol. I, p. 174 and esp. pp. 240–1 and 247.

between biological relationship and *criação* are numerous, such as, for example, in the speech attributed to Sancho IV: 'E para mientes quand muy fuerte cosa es la criança que el omne faze, que el fijo que es ajeno por la criança que le faze aquel que le cria, le ama e lo tiene bien asi commo si fuese su fijo. E muchas vegadas acaesce que le quiere el omne mas que sy fuese su fijo.'[30] The complex of affection and the obligations thus instituted was known as 'amor de dívedo', a recurring concept in fifteenth-century Portuguese texts referred to, for example, by Duarte in numerous passages of his works. The argument between the different texts of the late Middle Ages, in which the variety of human relations is reflected and classified, alluding frequently to ties of relationship, of marriage or of affection within a vast semantic field around the concept of 'love' is informative on this matter. Don Juan Manuel, for example, talks of fifteen distinct modes or 'maneras de amor' in his *Libro Enfenido* (written *c.* 1340), and defines 'amor de debdo, quando un omne a recebido algun bien de otro, como criança o casamiento o heredamiento, o quel ocorrio en algun grant mester o otras cosas semejantes destas. Este es tenudo de amar aquella persona por aquel debdo.'[31] This specific connotation of obligation can also be found in the Portuguese Duarte, who in his *Leal Conselheiro* distinguishes between the diverse causes and 'maneiras de amar', the 'dívido', for example, of the 'benfeitoria', which, as we shall see, did not have the same character of obligation.[32] To summarise, it would seem that 'criação' and the 'dívido' associated with it refer to a tie which was not easily negotiable between individuals and the monarch and which, once begun, tended to remain as the structuring link of the entire life of the 'criado'.

Another different situation was that of living together, which might be merely temporary, to which the epithet *morador* alludes. To live at court appears in these texts as a more effective manner of access to something which, at first sight, was similar to a type of royal patronage. The relationship of the *morador* with the monarch was, in fact, the actual terrain for the establishment of certain specific exchanges: of economic aid and food on the part of the king, and of dependence and service on the part of the courtier, whose figure was, at times, like that of a true client. As we shall see, a reflection of the fourteenth-century Portuguese texts concerning these modes of interchange and of relationship is very rich in suggestions and in new problems which defy an overstrict interpretation of this client figure. To live at court could also, for many men and women, be the simple condition for the exercise of a concrete office or profession. We should not forget that these also were called 'moradores', although their social standing was at

30 Agapito Rey (ed.), *Castigos e documentos para bien vivir ordenados por el Rey don Sancho* (Bloomington: Indiana University Press, 1952), p. 57.

31 *Obras completas*, Vol. I, p. 184; Ian R. Macpherson, '*Amor* and Don Juan Manuel', *Hispanic Review*, 39 (1971), 167–82.

32 *Leal Conselheiro*, in *Obras dos Príncipes de Avis*, p. 238.

times modest and the roles they performed restricted. Considered in its entirety, this appears to be a somewhat more diffuse relationship which, although it bore certain formal characteristics corresponding clearly to a concrete set of roles at court, included a large heterogeneity of situations, demonstrating several degrees of transitoriness.

At the opposite end of the scale, we find the type of highly formalised tie referred to by *vassalage*, related to a precise group of values and assuming all the aspects of a conscious action which solemnly stipulated a set of reciprocal obligations. In a word, we find ourselves on a totally contractual sphere of negotiation and revocability of contracted ties.[33] Dealing with a defining relationship of a notion of service which was, simultaneously, a central value for the vision of the world of medieval nobility, the word and the forms related to this relationship tended to penetrate the several spheres of court life. This diffusion was, however, far from being uniform, and there was never an unambiguous meaning since it depended strongly on the perception and the solidity with which the social standing of each was constructed, through multiple signs and material and symbolic positionings. Vassalage continued to be fundamentally connected to noble status, while at the same time it expressed an alliance and a lack of symmetry of positions between the king and his vassal.

However, in order better to understand the characteristics of the diverse social relationships at court, studying more closely this perhaps overschematic vision, we should now consider the problem of payments made by the king to the members of his entourage.

THE QUESTION OF REMUNERATION

The variety of payments which the monarchs of the fourteenth and fifteenth centuries made involving the same people upon whom my prosopographic study was made was yet another important indicator for the study of the characteristic forms of court society. In my research I sought to relate the payments systematically with the way in which the various individuals are named in the sources so that, in this way, I might reconstruct the logics which were eventually subjacent to these payments made by the king.

One of the best-known payments related to attendance at the Portuguese court is the 'moradia' which, as its name suggests, was paid to those who lived at court, be they or not the king's 'criados' or vassals. Besides this, the most precise

[33] A fundamental aspect which Barthélemy recently raised regarding the analogy of vassaldom with 'pseudo-kinship' previously suggested by Marc Bloch: 'Entre parenté et vassalité, il faut sans doute faire quelque rapprochement, rituel ou fonctionnel; mais j'inclinerais à ne pas aller trop loin, car entre des parents n'existent tout de même ni dissymétrie, ni rétribution spécifique, ni automaticité de l'aide': Dominique Barthélemy, 'Fiefs et vassaux au moyen âge', *Annales HSS*, 52 (1997), 328–9.

method, one could say that 'moradia' was usually paid to those 'da criação' of the king until these had reached adulthood and, in a general manner, to all those included in the entourage for the performance of any office or specific duty while this performance implied their actual presence. This distinction appears somewhat more important since it alludes to the specific dynamic of several types of exchange which can be detected within the court circle. The position of the 'criados' was that of receiving protection and 'benfeitoria' from the king, although in this case the 'moradia' was not truly remunatory, while it could be seen, as indeed it was, as a payment for services performed in the most varied of ambits, by many of the other 'moradores'.

What, therefore, was the 'moradia', and from what time did this payment exist at the Portuguese court? The first documented references known appear in the mid-fourteenth century, particularly in the agreements established between Afonso IV and his son, Pedro.[34] Already at the time at the Portuguese court, 'moradias' were paid, possibly as a result of the transformation into money of some part of remuneration to those who accompanied the king, of which there is evidence for the thirteenth century. These payments continued, however, to be mentioned until the middle of the fifteenth century by the association of 'rações', 'cevada' and 'vestir'. In the first of these, it would have been a payment in cereal, wine and other products for the sustenance of the 'morador' himself, similar to that seen for the examples analysed in other medieval courts. In the will of King Pedro, the 'rações' are distinguishable from the 'quitações'[35] although it is not known whether this should be attributed to the practice of a mixed remuneration in kind and money, as occurred later at the Castilian court[36] or whether by 'quitação' should be understood simply an alternative name for the 'moradia' itself. The calculation of these payments was, as is clear from the numerous examples of the fifteenth century, based on monthly sums. From the list of 'moradores' of 1405 we learn that there also existed an equivalence between the daily 'rações' and the total of monthly 'moradias': the ration of four loaves of bread was equal to 500 *libras* at the time, while seven loaves equalled 900 *libras*. An analysis of those in receipt of these quantities – 'moços' of the

[34] Among the clauses of the agreements established in 1355/56 is stated the reintegration of the nobles who had sworn allegiance, 'com os officyos *e moradeas* que dElRej teuerem': AHCML, *Livros Misticos de Reis*, Code 3, f. 45. Also in legislation attributed to the reign of Pedro reference is made to the 'moradias e vestiarias' paid by the monarch: *OA*, vol. II, pp. 314–15.

[35] *Provas*, vol. I, p. 408. On 'rações' of wine and meat paid at the fourteenth-century court: *CPA*, p. 97; *CPP*, p. 7; *CPF*, p. 20.

[36] Alicia Gómez Izquierdo, *Cargos de la casa y corte de Juan II de Castilla* (Valladolid: University of Valladolid, Cuadernos de la Cátedra de Paleografía y Diplomática, 1968); also A. de la Torre, *La Casa de Isabel la Católica* (Madrid: CSIC, 1954). Regarding the 'quitaciones' as a monthly payment in number made to the members of the Castilian court, it should be noted that the lists of Sancho IV allow us to to examine it at least to the end of the thirteenth century: 'Libro de diferentes cuentas de Don Sancho IV (1293–1294)', ed. Gaibros de Ballesteros, pp. c, cii, *et passim*.

stable and the *câmara*, 'mulheres' of the *câmara*, *reposteiros* and 'homens' of the *aposentador* – suggested that these rations were lower in quantity.[37]

On the other hand, the 'cevada' was intended for the feeding of horses, and was calculated daily, corresponding to the number of animals to which the 'morador' had a right, and the amounts varied enormously. A rare example which allows one to see how this payment was calculated is the charter relating to a musician at the court of Afonso V; in 1451 he received a total of 1080 *reais* a year 'em preço de sua cevada', at a rate of a half *alqueire* a day at six *reais* an *alqueire* – so that he received the equivalent of 360 days of ration for his mounts.[38] During this later period we are far from the practice of the thirteenth century, which consisted in the payment of different quantities of barley, depending upon whether the court was 'em estada' or 'em andada', as established in legislation of 1261.[39] Finally, 'vestir' probably consisted in the giving once or twice a year of cloth and/or made-up clothing and also, in Portugal, remained the last form of payment in kind to the 'moradores', due no doubt to the distinctive meaning lying in the consumption of certain types of material and to the generalisation during the fifteenth century of the emblematic system of court livery.[40]

The 'moradia' was, according to the first occurrences to be found, fundamentally a payment in money and could, during the fifteenth century, be accompanied for example by 'cevada' and 'vestir' and also a 'ração'. While a change was in progress from all other forms of payment to payment in money to the 'morador', the term 'moradia' tended however to include the entirety of these forms, and became a global sum whose main characteristic was its direct relationship with a physical presence of the individual at court. The earliest history of the 'moradias' as a sum paid by the king is very obscure both in Portugal and in the other Iberian kingdoms. The most probable hypothesis is that it resulted, as already said, from a fixing of the highly varied payments made by the Portuguese monarchs of the first dynasty, based upon the standing of the position or of the individual, to the members of their entourage. I have already spoken, in the first chapter, of the existence of a 'mixed' regime of payment at the courts of the High Middle Ages known to us, which was formed by the association of 'prebend' and 'benefice', the first of which was related to the sustenance of the courtier while the second corresponded on many occasions to the holding of certain palace posts (to which there corresponded concession of land). The Portuguese 'moradia' in the fourteenth century represents a significantly more

37 *MH*, vol. I, pp. 290–1 and 293. 38 ANTT, *Ch. D. Afonso V*, 11, f. 88v.

39 *OD*, p. 59.

40 Françoise Pipponier, *Costume et vie sociale: la Cour d'Anjou, XIVe–XVe siècles* (Paris: Ecole des Hautes Etudes en Sciences Sociales, 1970), pp. 243–53; Colette Beaune, 'Costume et pouvoir en France à la fin du moyen âge: les devises royales vers 1400', *Revue des Sciences Humaines (Lille III)*, 4 (1981), 125–46; J. M. W. Bean, *From Lord to Patron: Lordship in Late Medieval England* (Manchester: Manchester University Press, 1989), pp. 20–2.

structured system which, in the final analysis, is explained by the growing importance of monetary payments and by the diffusion of new economic practices at the medieval court. We see early on the enormous range of this monetarisation of the 'moradias' from the point of view of the internal classification of the 'moradores' at court, whom we find organised in three large hierarchical categories at the beginning of the fifteenth century, and these correspond to a scale of payments which was variable within certain limits. A system which appears with such clarity and coherence cannot have appeared suddenly. There are few significant occurrences of the word in royal documents of the following century to reinforce my hypothesis that the 'moradia' results from the transformation of the system of payments existing in the thirteenth century, although they always talk either of a social category or of a duty of the beneficiary. With the growing importance of the court as a system of sociability whose model was imposed on noble and ecclesiastical houses, there are also in Portuguese documentation by the fifteenth century several mentions of 'moradias' paid by important lords, and not merely by the king and queen.[41]

I have said above that the 'criação' of the king was not a paid relationship, but it could imply the payment of the 'moradia' while living alongside the monarch continued. In fact, a large number of the 'criados' were nobles destined, by their respective families, for life at court, either through the desire for royal patronage, through family tradition or even through demands of the king himself in the case of the young or children whose handing over served as a guarantee in political or judicial agreements. In the majority, these were to receive 'moradias' of a fixed amount. Also, as a result of prosopographic analysis of contemporary rolls, however, there were included in the category 'dos de criação' – descendants of other 'moradores' at court who were not identified as nobles and who performed highly varied duties – and in this case the bestowal of 'moradias' of the lowest sum would seem to cover simply a section of the young who were of more modest standing.

The payment which best characterises the peculiar situation of the 'criados' was, in truth, 'casamento'. While still young, the monarch wished to exercise a form of patriarchal protection to which 'criação' refers through a dowry and the choice of the matrimonial partner, and this lies in the origin of this other type of royal favour, which is 'casamento'. Also listed according to the standing of each individual, payment of 'casamentos' at the Portuguese court is also proved for the fourteenth century, as I have also had the opportunity to analyse when mentioning the young women who accompanied the queens. The development observed in the forms and nature of this payment during the final stages of the

[41] See for the well-known case of the infantes, the 'reform' of 1408: *MH*, vol. I, pp. 316–19. This fact can be found simply through an analysis of the wills of the Infantes Fernando and Henry, sons of John I, and in the 'Regimento' of the Infante Pedro contained in the *Livro dos Conselhos de El-Rei D. Duarte*, pp. 153–4.

Middle Ages is highly complex, as can be seen a little later when I analyse some actual cases. Because of the impossibility of effecting the handing over of such sums, the increase in the sums paid and, by all indications, the total number of 'casamentos' to be performed led the monarchs to the granting of incomes to their beneficiaries *in pignus*, a practice found in Portugal at least from the first decades of the fifteenth century. In a parallel form to that occurring with the 'moradias', the quantitative differences of the 'casamentos' were altered in a most important code of hierarchic significance at the Portuguese court. In the records of royal dowries during the fifteenth century there appears yet another form of payment, which must be distinguished from the 'casamento' resulting from the 'criação' at court to which I have referred, which is 'ajuda de casamento', by which the king added to the sum given to a young noble couple by their respective families, even though these were not individuals who were connected to the monarch or the queen by the specific ties referred to.

Finally, it is necessary to consider a little the difference between these royal concessions and payments made to so many courtiers of the Portuguese monarchs and payment of actual services performed in the ambit of the royal entourage. For, as in the case of what has just been said, neither 'moradias' nor 'casamentos' can be strictly considered as payment for specific duties – the former are related merely to *presence* at court, for whatever reason, and the latter to *criação*, in the exact meaning I have attempted to give. Regarding payments which can be considered as true remuneration to men and women of the court, a distinction should be made between the nobles, the officials and the ecclesiastics, since the problem of payments, as also the nature of service performed, can naturally be totally different.

Payments involving the nobility connected to the king in the fourteenth and fifteenth centuries can occasionally be related in a concrete manner to service at court. By being a part of the royal entourage the nobles appear, as already seen, to be called in general 'vassals' of the monarch, and my initial hypothesis was that the tie of vassalage could be related to some of the payments on which there is information. The importance of the performance of military services by the nobility of the Peninsula also determined, in Portugal, that forms analogous to the varieties of 'fief-rente' existing in other European regions be generalised from the twelfth century. The specific question which I now wish to clarify is whether these forms of payment would also have been used at court, bearing in mind that many nobles who lived there were known as 'vassals' of the king, and whether these payments can be related to the 'service' which the nobility performed for the king outside times of war.

In her investigations relating to the Castilian situation, Grassotti was able to establish the main lines of an evolution which immediately preceded the period studied here, analysing the payment of vassals in the western zone of the Iberian Peninsula from the earliest times of the Asturian-Leonese monarchy until the middle of the fourteenth century. The most marked sign of this evolution is the early appearance of payments in money (*soldadas*) which still played an enormous part in Iberian societies, whether or not their origins were connected to the actual influence of Peninsular Muslim practices, as this author would wish.[42] The growing availability of coined metal established by the reconquest, through the system of *parias* at the hands of the Leonese and Castilian monarchs, emphasised still more this use of monetary payments from the twelfth century, leading to the generalisation of the vassalage *soldadas* and that of the *tierras* or *maravedies* paid in money by the Hispanic monarchs. The situation at the end of the thirteenth century, which is so well theorised by the Alfonsine texts, was that of a progressive lack of distinction between these diverse beneficiary payments, affirming 'a unique reality of the character of wages in the different sums received by a vassal'.[43]

What would seem to be unquestionable, according to Grassotti, is that whether this is about sums in money directly paid by the royal treasury or fixed incomes arising from certain crown lands, in Castile the vassalage payments at the time implied the establishment of a personal tie of a specific nature, with the sums in money being true beneficiary concessions subject to the rules of the feudal system, particularly in that which refers to reciprocal rights and duties of lord and vassal. This institution of vassalage 'soldadas' and 'maravedies', which existed in Leon and Castile in the twelfth and thirteenth centuries, is very similar to that known as 'fief-rente' so much used in Europe at the same period, and studied in the main for the cases of England, France and the Low Countries.[44]

By turning to fief-rente, which has been studied in depth by Bryce Lyon, the feudal monarchs sought to strengthen the complex web of fidelity which tied them to the nobility, or which attracted magnates and simple *cavaleiro*s to the contingent of their vassals from neighbouring kingdoms, as was the case with the kings of France when they wished to secure military services from the Hispanic *cavaleiro*s, or the kings of Castile in the fourteenth century, when they attracted French knights or even members of the well-known troops of the monarchs of England in order to increase the number of their continental vassals.[45] The importance of the fief-rente lay essentially on the one hand in the flexibility it brought to the feudal system, disconnecting it from the bidding of concrete territories and, on the other, in the increase in the number of individuals involved in the system, overcoming the natural limits to its growth formed by the

[42] Hilda Grassotti, *Las instituciones feudo-vasalláticas en León y Castilla* (Spoleto: Centro Italiano di Studi sull'Alto Medioevo, 1969), vol. II, pp. 729 and 733–4.
[43] Grassotti, *Las instituciones*, vol. II, p. 827.
[44] Bryce Dale Lyon, *From Fief to Indenture: The Transition from Feudal to Non-Feudal Contract in Western Europe* (Cambridge, MA: Harvard University Press, 1957).
[45] Lyon, *From Fief to Indenture*, pp. 158–9, 179 and 210; Grassotti, *Las instituciones*, vol. II, p. 857.

territories available for granting in fief. For many monarchs, its frequent practice meant, on the other hand, the beginning of recurring financial difficulties and the constant search for monetary resources. Such was, according to Grassotti, the case of the Castilian monarchs from the thirteenth century.

What is the main difference between the fiefs comprising lands and the fief-rentes? To quote Bryce Lyon:

> if a vassal received possession of land producing his annual income he became responsible for getting out of it what it was supposedly worth and so came to hold an ordinary fief. When a lord, however, assigned an annual income on his own lands without handing over possession to the vassal, then a *fief-rente* had come into being. The lord retained possession of the land and remained responsible for its producing the amount to pay the fief. The vassal had no need to concern himself with the land and probably never even saw it; he cared little whether the money came directly from land, a treasury, or a revenue as long as he received payment every year.[46]

Representing a characteristic institution of a more intensely monetarised economy, the fief-rente of the thirteenth century fell slowly into disuse in non-Peninsular Europe at the end of the Middle Ages. It was to be replaced by other, non-feudal forms of contract, also involving stipendiary payments which had developed in particular in the military sphere, and by other mechanisms which did not take on a purely personal value like vassalage in the political sphere. This is a development which, in both spheres, whether military or political, was accentuated by the Hundred Years War.[47]

From a comparative point of view, the Hispanic tradition of an early monetarisation of benefice and the instability and fluidity of the actual feudo-vassalic relationship seems in Castile to have determined an easy transition from the feudal contract to forms which one can consider as more evolved, such as the 'cuantias' and 'acostamientos', both characteristic of the fourteenth and fifteenth centuries. In the first of these, a sum to be paid was established which might or might not have been in direct relation to a given piece of land or royal income, but which tended above all to correspond to a type of military service which was far more regulated than in the past, and which led to a proportionality between payment made by the king and the number of men at arms ('lanzas') to be given by the vassal. Definitively regulated by Alfonso XI in the *Ordenamiento de Alcalá* (1348), this quantitative principle in a certain sense distanced the 'cuantias' of the fourteenth century from the more archaic

[46] Lyon, *From Fief to Indenture*, p. 134.

[47] See the classic article by K. B. McFarlane, 'Bastard feudalism', in *England in the Fifteenth Century: Collected Essays* (London: Hambledon Press, 1981), pp. 23–43, and more recently P. R. Coss, 'Bastard feudalism revised', *Past and Present*, 125 (1989), 27–64; David Crouch *et al.*, 'Debate: bastard feudalism revised', *Past and Present*, 131 (1991), 165–203; Michael Hickes, *Bastard Feudalism* (New York: Longman, 1995), advocating a most ample definition of 'bastard feudalism'.

'fief-rente' or 'fief de bourse', whose main objective for the kings lay far more in the political usefulness of the tie of vassaldom than in its military consequences.[48] This was the reason why service to be performed in this ambit of military obligations was only stipulated generically in the fief-rente, while the 'cuantia' came to regulate that aspect more rigorously. The 'cuantia' of the fourteenth century arises, like the system of indenture, from the important need to have available predetermined military contingents to be included in the royal armies. On the other hand, it is certain that many Castilian 'cuantias' implied the establishment of relationships of vassalage, as minutely detailed by Grassotti, and in this sense it approximated true feudal contracts while having essentially military ends.

In turn, the 'acostamiento' would appear to mean something very close to true non-feudal contracts similar to *indenture*, since no relationship of vassalage between the king and the man at arms to whom 'costa' was paid was envisaged in this case, with him making use of his service in a more-or-less pre-established manner, as opposed to the payment of an annuity. This type of non-feudal contract appears in the Alfonsine *Espéculo* – 'los que llaman acostados, tienen tierra o maravedis de algunos *non siendo sus vasallos*'[49] – thus proving that the early-established Iberian stipendiary payment mentioned by Grassotti was accompanied by a large variety of contractual practices in respect of military services, even in the period prior to the fourteenth century. The growing importance of these methods of non-feudal contract in the military sphere in fifteenth-century Castile has been stressed by several authors.[50] It should also be said, for greater clarity in my exposition, that all these payments – *soldadas*, *cuantias* and *acostamientos* – were accompanied by yet another type of payment during campaigns (calculated, however, on the function of the effective duration of the campaign and not on an annual basis), which payments I shall not refer to here, as from the perspective of this book they are a marginal aspect.

When compared with what has just been demonstrated, the Portuguese situation appears to be very close to that of Castile, as shown by recent investigations by Gouveia Monteiro. Some authors such as Paulo Merêa and Costa Veiga have not hesitated, from the 1930s, in recognising in the 'contias' or the Portuguese 'quantias' the same basic characteristics shown for the Castilian case – it dealt with annual payments made by the king, for which the vassal served in the royal army with a determined number of 'lances' or units of combat.[51]

48 Lyon, *From Fief to Indenture*, pp. 240–1 and 243.

49 *Espéculo*, p. 155. On the reform in 1390 of the 'acostamientos' paid by the king of Castile: Grassotti, *Las instituciones*, vol. II, p. 701 and note 489.

50 For example Marie-Claude Gerbet, *La Noblesse dans le royaume de Castille: étude sur ses structures sociales en Estrémadoure de 1454 à 1516* (Paris: Sorbonne, 1979), p. 137.

51 Damião Peres (ed.), *História de Portugal* (Barcelos: Ed. Portucalense, 1928–37), vol. II, p. 452; A. Botelho da Costa Veiga, *Estudos de história militar Portuguesa* (Lisbon, 1936), vol. I, pp. 12–15.

The 'soldadas' and 'maravedis', which were also common in Portugal during the thirteenth century and which, according to the most recent suggestion by Mattoso, clearly refer to forms of feudal contract, become more rarely referred to in royal documentation of the fourteenth century. It would then appear to be related to the growing recourse of the monarchs from 1300 to gifts of land and rents 'em contia', whose feudal nature is most probable, although extremely difficult to establish for certain, since the actual existence of a tie of vassalage is not always mentioned.[52] In the various circumstances of Portuguese society of the fourteenth century, the reign of Fernando appears to have constituted a moment of particular incidence of this form of relationship, although already in the previous period there are some rare references to 'quantias'.[53] There is to hand, in fact, an important group of about a hundred charters of gift of 'quantias' recorded in the *chancelaria* of that monarch, many of which were attributed, as already referred to in detail, to noble courtiers and Galegan and Castilian exiles. Of the total of 115 charters of gift referring to 'quantias' or 'maravedis', about a half (fifty-seven) date between 1372 and 1373, which corresponds to the second war with Castile, and about twenty to the period 1382–83. As Braamcamp Freire has already remarked, a systematic analysis of this series is made difficult because of the many occurrences of abbreviated records ('em ementa').[54] According to several equivalences suggested by the actual charters,[55] the contingents varied between fifty to a hundred lances supplied, exceptionally, by the Teles family in 1372 and 1383, and the two or three by a vassal, whose quota is far more common.[56]

In a legislation of this same monarch, Fernando, and contained in the Afonsine Ordinations, we find that some principles of the *Ordenamiento de Alcalá* were also in use in Portugal in 1374, particularly through death and the confiscation of possessions in the case of a unilateral breaking of an agreement, or its non-compliance by a vassal.[57] Stranger, though, is another aspect of Fernando's

[52] José Mattoso, *Fragmentos de uma composição medieval* (Lisbon: Estampa, 1987), pp. 115–23 and esp. p. 117. A. H. de Oliveira Marques speaks in the same way, in *Portugal na crise dos séculos XIV e XV*, p. 249 and note. The great nineteenth-century Portuguese historian equated 'quantias' with the 'forma feudal': Alexandre Herculano, *Opúsculos* (Lisbon: Tavares Cardoso, 1897), vol. VI, pp. 299–300. In fact we find in a document of 1355 the exact expression 'quantia de vassalagem': AHCML, *Livros Misticos de Reis*, Code 3, ff. 43v–44.

[53] An example dated 1338 of royal grant including express clauses on providing military service: *CDA*, vol. II, pp. 211–12.

[54] *Brasões*, vol. II, pp. 288–9.

[55] In 1372 each lance corresponded to 150 *libras* given and in 1383 this would have been 100 *libras*: ANTT, *Ch. D. Fernando*, 1, f. 112v and 3, f. 56.

[56] Monteiro, *A guerra em Portugal nos finais da idade média*, vol. I, pp. 28–9. This author underlines as the main conclusion of his analysis the relatively reduced size of the 'mesnadas' of the overwhelming majority of Portuguese nobles.

[57] *OA*, vol. IV, pp. 118–19. Significantly, at the end of this chapter of the *Ordenações* an addition in the fifteenth century substituted the death sentence 'por sua aspereza' with exile to Ceuta for two years (*ibid.*, p. 22). See also the commentary by Grassotti on these sanctions: *Las instituciones*, vol. II, pp. 1063–4.

legislation, which instituted the loss of privileges of the nobility for those who refused to attach themselves to the king or the infantes and 'vassalos maiores' through the tie established by the 'quantia', so determining a compulsory aspect of this type of contract, while still close to the fief-rente, for all the nobles of the kingdom.[58] It is extremely doubtful, in my opinion, that the tie instituted by the 'quantia' was, in truth, obligatory and that *all* the nobles of the kingdom should receive this type of gift, as can be swiftly deduced from this legal precept and from the explanation of Fernão Lopes in several passages of his chronicles.[59] An overliteral interpretation of the statements of the chronicler – and it should not be forgotten that, while he was writing, the fief-rente was already a fossilised institution and on the way to disappearing – would lead us to attribute perhaps too much importance to the institutions of late feudalism and to the generalised practice at the end of the fourteenth century of this type of military contribution of vassalic service, proportionately calculated on the amount granted by the king.[60] In fact, 'quantias' or fief-rente and other non-feudal forms of contracting military service appear to have already coexisted during Fernando's wars, in the interregnum, and at the beginning of the reign of John, in a similar manner to that which occurred in the rest of the Peninsula, as well as in France and England. In this sense, the much-mentioned English influence, through the presence of the contingents of Edmund of Cambridge in Portugal in 1381 and of his relative, the Duke of Lancaster, in 1386–87, certainly contributed to making systems such as indenture (with the payment of annuities to 'captains' and the detailed mention in written contracts of the type of services contracted and their remuneration) familiar to the Portuguese and the Castilians. The study made by Gouveia Monteiro of military contingents accompanying Nuno Álvaro Pereira in the war against Castile illustrates exactly this contractual variety.[61]

Thus, while Fernando had contracted many nobles for his wars through 'quantias', the 210 'lances' which the council of Lisbon sent to the Minho in 1386 were a true company of indenture,[62] and Fernão Lopes specifies that

58 *OA*, vol. IV, pp. 120–1.

59 *CR João I*, vol. II, pp. 166–7 and 267. A literal interpretation of the chronicler appears to have served as a basis for the synthesis suggested by Henrique de Gama Barros in his influential *História da administração pública nos séculos XII a XV* (Lisbon: Sá da Costa, 1945–54), vol. II, pp. 378–81.

60 This is the interpretation of Armando de Castro, by which: (1) all the nobles without exception received 'quantias'; (2) the fact of military service in the royal army was simply a 'formal basis' invoked in order to justify the 'distribution of royal receipts among the noble classes'. This author thus ignores the personal and voluntary nature of the fief-rente contract and the reciprocal obligations it established. See the article 'Quantias' in *DHP*, vol. III, pp. 505–6. On the Hispanic feudal contract: Grassotti, *Las instituciones*, vol. I, p. 5 and Paulo Merêa, *Introdução ao problema do feudalismo em Portugal* (Coimbra: França Amado, 1912), esp. p. 97.

61 *A guerra em Portugal*, pp. 38–41.

62 In the description given us by the chronicler there is no lack of the mention of the use of livery by the combatants: *CR João I*, vol. II, pp. 157–8.

many of the fighters who served John I during these years 'não eram vassallos d'el-rey', but they fought 'a soldo'.[63] In the same way, we know that the council of Oporto granted at the same time sums of money for payment of military service by nobles who fought at the battle of Trancoso and, although the type of agreement to which these payments refer cannot be specified, their temporary nature indicates that this must have been some similar type of temporary 'company'.[64] In the same decade, more precisely in 1389, the Portuguese galleons which were sent to England under the command of Afonso Furtado were the subject of an indenture whose written clauses are still to be found in English archives.[65]

Throughout the fifteenth century there are frequent mentions of 'acostamento' in a context which also associates this to military action. It is certain that the number of meanings of this word in fifteenth-century Portuguese gives rise to some problems that are difficult to resolve. While modern historiography usually interprets the word as being close to 'encostar' (to be near to or approach someone), or as alluding to an imprecise relationship of generic clientele (which would seem to be allowed by certain contemporary uses of the verb 'acostar')[66] it can also be shown that its oldest meaning still existed, as mentioned in the *Partidas*: to receive 'costa' or support from someone in exchange for military service. That is, it was not a generic relationship of protection of a patron for a client but an actual, specific paid relationship of service. This seems to be the meaning Rui de Pina refers to, for example, when he says that some of the men of the 'company' of the Duke of Braganza in Alfarrobeira, 'vinham acostados a elle por aquella jornada somente'.[67] Whatever the case, this Castilian word and others (cf. 'apaniguado') appear in documentation of Fernando's reign referring to the entourages of nobles, although it becomes more common only in fifteenth-century texts.[68]

At the end of the Portuguese Middle Ages the 'quantias' appear as a process of payment whose importance was decreasing. The constantly mentioned 'reform' of John I, which can perhaps be dated to the beginning of the 1390s, was already receding before its fall into disuse. Instituted in the reform was a new register of the royal 'vassalos' who received this type of gift and either the

63 *CR João I*, vol. II, p. 167. Among the vocabulary used to designate remuneration for military service in the chronicles of Fernando and John we find 'gajas' (from *gages*, Fr.?) and 'estados', 'soldo' and 'serviço'.

64 Salvador Dias Arnau, *A Batalho de Trancoso* (Coimbra: Universidade de Coimbra, 1967), pp. 34, 71 and 109.

65 Russell, pp. 527–8 and note.

66 See for example A. S. Costa Lobo, *História da sociedade em Portugal no século XV* (Lisbon: Ed. História Crítica, 1979), p. 427.

67 *CR Afonso V*, pp. 714–15. On the changes to 'acostamento' in the second half of the fifteenth century, see the important General Chapter of the Cortes of 1475: ANTT, Cortes, M 2, f. 129v.

68 An example: ANTT, *Ch. D. Fernando*, 3, f. 59v (original register). See also the mention of the 'acostadiços' at the Cortes of 1385: Caetano, *A crise nacional*, p. 111.

restriction of annual payment to adult individuals or, possibly, the transmission of the tie through primogeniture was regulated.[69] This record of the vassals to whom 'quantias' were paid was drawn up in books for the purpose which were held in the monarch's *câmara*, and was executed by the 'escrivão dos maravedis'; unfortunately no example remains.[70] In the neighbouring kingdom of Castile there was a similar attempt at regulation at the Cortes of Briviesca in 1387 and later in the reform of the royal guard of 1390, inspired by the magnates of the high nobility and the masters of the Military Orders.[71] In the Portuguese Ordination relating to the fleet going to Ceuta in 1415, it is seen that the precepts adopted in Fernando's legislation referred to above were no longer practised and that the freedom of the military contracts of an exclusively stipendiary type was becoming the dominating principle.[72] As Oliveira Marques says, 'the new characteristics of the fifteenth-century armies' imposed this, becoming increasingly dependent upon other methods of recruitment and exercise of war.[73]

This entire excursion into the evolution of remuneration of the Portuguese nobility in the primordial sphere of their military activity, although shorter than the subject deserves, has as its object merely a reminder of the residual role which the forms of feudal contract tended to adopt in this field as we progress in time, either as a mechanism of ties to the king or as a mechanism of recruitment of military forces. Several hypotheses can be advanced for an explanation of this more restricted role of the contract of vassalage in the military sphere, particularly through the transformations which have been detected in the recruitment and forces of the royal army, or through reasons connected to the evolution of war. However, it must not be forgotten, both in Lyon's explanation and in the suggestion, for the English case by McFarlane, that this type of contractual connection or formal tie of vassalage had wider functions and was used not only to connect the nobility to the monarchs but also the various strata of the nobility among themselves, grouping around magnates for primarily political ends. As McFarlane has stated, these feudal contracts which were so characteristic of the fourteenth century also became less common later on, 'because they failed to buy the *exclusive* loyalty which was their principal

69 In this sense, it cannot be said that the text of the 'Artigos' on the Lei Mental, when the monarch refers to the 'quantias' and other 'terras' granted, is clear: *MH*, vol. V, pp. 9–10. On his interpretation on this point: Paulo Merêa, 'Génese da lei mental (algumas notas)', *Boletim da Faculdade de Direito da Universidade de Coimbra*, 10 (1926–28), 1–15.

70 For the register of vassals, see: ANTT, *Ch. D. Duarte*, 3, f. 60; 1, f. 68.

71 Luis Suárez Fernández, *Juan I, Rey de Castilla (1379–1390)* (Madrid: CSIC, 1955). For a new interpretation of these reforms: Hilda Grassotti, 'Apostillas a "El Prestimonio" de Valdeavellano', in *Estudios medievales Españoles* (Madrid: Fundación Universitaria Española, 1981), pp. 133–58.

72 *MH*, vol. II, pp. 218–22.

73 Marques, *Portugal na crise*, p. 250.

object'.[74] It could be said that this regulatory role of the feudo-vassalic tie in relation to the fidelity of the nobility tended, in turn, to become residual in the ambit of the court in the specific perspective of the king – although, as seen in various actual cases quoted in the previous chapter, it was used at the end of the fourteenth century by some important court families such as the Teleses in their relations with other lineages of lower standing. It is my belief that the attraction of the court, with the grouping of the nobility around the sharing of the king's favour, went on to perform a primordial and alternative function, as a conjoining principle of the political society of the fourteenth and fifteenth centuries. The type of associations and interdependencies created between the nobility and the kings could be of a diverse nature, not exclusively expressed by the sphere of fief-rente, and were to be found in growing differentiation in relation to the order outside the court universe. Not that this 'process of curialisation' of the nobles, if we adopt yet again the concept of Elias, was *a priori* incompatible with the survival, either of the actual feudo-vassalic institutions in their western Hispanic form, or of feudalism as a system of values. However, it would certainly grant them a different relevance, characteristic of the new times, particularly through the mutation it introduced in the actual concept of service, just as monetarisation of the feudal contract, whose end was obtaining military service, had introduced important changes in the feudo-vassalic institutions. As a golden period of the royal courts also in the Iberian Peninsula, the fifteenth century was, for the Portuguese nobility, the age of court 'service', significantly evoked by Harris with the following words:

> service was personal and honourable, rather than public and political ... service brought rewards, either gains of war or grants of land, offices, annuities and feudal profits. But service was more important to the great magnate than the rewards he received, for these were merely the manifestations of the crown's favour and good lordship on which his own repute and influence was based.[75]

The obtaining of royal favour therefore became an objective in itself, around which the existence of large sectors of the nobility became organised, and the court was the place where this contest took place.

It can be stated once again with fair certainty from the more specific point of view of payments made to courtiers that, in the court organisation, the type of payment to the nobles which was merely stipendiary was early confirmed as predominant during the fifteenth century, as we have also seen in the military sphere. That is, although similar merely in appearance to the fief-rente, as referred to above, because of the indifference of whoever received it as to the

[74] K. B. McFarlane, *The Nobility of Later Medieval England* (Oxford: Clarendon Press, 1973), p. xxxii.
[75] G. L. Harris, in an introduction to McFarlane, *England in the Fifteenth Century*, p. xxiv.

origin of the income (land, rent, money), the payment of the noble courtier now appears distinct from the old vassal's payment, since it did not present a bilateral character and depended simply, as far as can be detected through an analysis of hundreds of examples, on two concrete factors – presence at court and the retention of palace positions. However, in the final analysis it depended above all on the arbitrary nature and the preference of the monarch, who was the determining factor in the variation in granting a specific position in the scale of court hierarchies. This crucial transformation is, in a certain manner, concealed beneath a contemporary process whose evidence is obvious when we go on to study payments relating to individuals within the royal entourage: the progressive disappearance of the mention of the distinct methods of payment in favour of the designation and the unique mechanism of 'tença'. From the beginning of the fifteenth century, this type of donation by the king became predominant, while the financial mechanism which gave rise to concrete payment, generally in the form of an annuity, was accentuated to the detriment of clarification of the type of payment which lay in its origin.

A history of the Portuguese 'tença' as a royal payment arising from the medieval financial system has still to be carried out.[76] The etymological meaning of the term appears to point towards the importance of the *precarious* and *revocable* character of the concession, although there is no lack of examples at the end of the Middle Ages regarding long-lasting grants, which were not merely for an indeterminate length of time. A global analysis of the records of the *chancelaria* of the second half of the fourteenth century (for which, as is known, there is an abundance of copies including many listed grants, although no texts of original records) allows for the detection of innumerable examples of concessions of land and rents 'em tença', although it is not possible easily to distinguish the concrete methods of appropriation by the beneficiaries of the incomes given. This expression already appears in the legislation of 1340 with the meaning of the grant of a certain quantity in income.[77] In the specific context of the court, the 'tenças' served, throughout the century, for the remuneration of some servants such as *falcoeiros*, *camareiras* and *covilheiras*. The word was also much used for revenues associated with the *alcaidarias*, which were granted to nobles with their respective castles.[78]

In many charters relating to the nobility the granting of lands and their respective revenues 'em tença' is expressly associated with the 'préstamo', perhaps

76 The form 'teença' appears in Portuguese documentation of the thirteenth century. See César Oro, 'Las formas del verbo Galaico-Portugués *teer* según los textos, siglos XII y XIII', *Cuadernos de Estudios Gallegos*, 31 (1978–80), 293–328.

77 A. H. Oliveira Marques, 'A Pragmática de 1340', in *Ensaios da história medieval Portuguesa* (Lisbon: Vega, 1980), p. 113 (Art. 11).

78 On an analogous evolution in Castile: María Concepción Quintanilla Raso, 'La tenencia de fortalezas en Castilla durante la baja edad media', in *En la España medieval IV: estudios en memoria del Profesor Claudio Sánchez-Albornoz* (Madrid: Universidad Complutense, 1986), vol. II, pp. 861–97.

because this also consisted, in many cases, in the granting of royal rights over a determined locality.[79] Whatever the case, this variety of situations suggests that the name 'tença' was applied from the fourteenth century to distinct types of concession, having in common in many cases merely the fact of its relating to revenues owed to the king in a determined place or in a precise fiscal organism. This aspect appears to me central in the later evolution of this type of royal grant of polyvalent meaning. In practice, it became more and more close to a simple mechanism of consignment of rents, or free concession or sale to someone having the right to receive determined dues on land or a source of income. As is known, this was a much used method during the medieval period for financial transactions.[80] This characteristic is prevalent in the fifteenth century, and the common mechanism of the royal 'tença' of the fifteenth century consisted in attributing the quantity to be paid to a given source of royal income (*almoxarifado*, customs, etc.). The history of the 'tença' is, therefore, at the end of the Middle Ages inseparable from the study of the evolution of the actual system of public finances.

The situation we find during the fifteenth century is, for the aspect of interest to us, that of the use of 'tenças' for repaying actual services in the ambit of the court, such as that of the men of letters of the *casa da suplicação* or even the actual chaplains and also as a substitute for 'casamentos' or as a form of paying 'moradias'.[81] Regarding the 'moradias' which, as already seen, related to monthly sums, the 'tenças' were usually given in several payments ('aos quartéis do ano'). Certain 'tenças', as was the case with the 'casamentos', covered in particular a regime of periodic sums in which the various amounts given were partially or entirely discounted from the amount granted. However, at the same time there is no lack of examples showing that, through the king's favour, this discount was not made, and the payment became perpetual. The variety and the accumulation of the 'tenças' was a phenomenon of greatest importance during this period studied, which general phenomenon did not occur merely in the royal court but also in many other sectors of Portuguese society, since this mechanism allowed for any regular payments made to individuals or to collective bodies and also came to be adopted in place of the military 'quantias'.[82] The 'tenças' were subject to commercial transaction between individuals from at least the first quarter of the fifteenth century.

79 See two explicit examples: ANTT, *Ch. D. Fernando*, 2, ff. 14 and 36v. The two types of 'tenças' paid by the king – 'tenças dos alcaides' and 'tenças dos vassalos' – appear mentioned at the Cortes of 1371–72: *CPF*, pp. 33 and 87. For a definition of the 'préstamo', see Herculano, *Opúsculos*, vol. VII, pp. 245–6 and also Barros, *História da administração pública*, vol. XI, p. 45.

80 On the importance of the model of 'autonomia da renda' from the juridic point of view: Mário Júlio de Almeida Costa, *Raízes do censo consignativo: para a história do crédito medieval Português* (Coimbra: Atlântida, 1961).

81 Examples: ANTT, *Ch. D. Afonso V*, 14, f. 46v (appointment of a *desembargador*) or *MH*, vol. X, pp. 108–10.

82 An aspect emphasised by Lobo, *História da sociedade*, p. 495.

The constant mention of favour and the royal decision which were the origin of many 'tenças' paid by the monarch and of their sums makes somewhat difficult the distinction among court payments within the larger group of benefits to which many had access. Through 'tença', the payments made by the king in the second half of the fifteenth century became in practice indistinct for modern interpretation, even in the ambit of the court social circle. In 1460 they appear grouped merely in two broad categories of 'tenças obrigatórias' and 'tenças graciosas', expressing the point of view of the payer (i.e. the king), in which types were included generically every sort of grant of annual sums which were the duty of the royal finances, regarding which the Cortes took vehemently critical positions. The situation was already one of intense debt, and Afonso V was well aware of this since he recognised in a general request in 1460 the need for more than double the 34.5 million *reais* granted him that year solely to cope with the 'tenças obrigatórias'.[83] As is known, this debt led later to the transformation of the 'tença' into a financial instrument for consolidating the debt by the sale of 'juros', to which the Portuguese kings turned from the sixteenth century.[84] However, this subject would take us far from our objective, which continues to be that of equating the problem of payments made to the members of the court. The generalisation of the 'tença' led to the alteration, as can be concluded, of the panorama shown above for the payments made to the members of the court, particularly with regard to the possibility of demonstrating the diverse characteristics of concessions which lay in their origin – which does not, however, mean that at the time this distinction was no more clear for those affected than sources would today appear to suggest.

Finally it remains to mention yet another type of payment associated with the actual performance of duties and offices within the court, which introduces a different logic in this reconstruction. This is the so-called 'mantimentos', which were calculated as a monthly or daily sum and associated with the performance of some 'oficio' but, also, there is yet another different type of dues with other names, at times directly received by the actual servants of the king in the exercise of their functions. These payments are little recorded, but they had in common the fact that they were a little more like our understanding of modern salaries because of the relationship to specific duties performed and even at times the amount of work carried out. Their importance in the restricted world of bureaucratic, judicial and financial posts and also of the servants within the area of the material court life and artisan activities and those related to supplies is, of course, far greater than that of the case of the nobles and ecclesiastics.

[83] Iria Gonçalves, *Pedidos e empréstimos públicos em Portugal durante a idade média* (Lisbon: Ministério das Finanças, 1964), pp. 166–7.

[84] The best description of this mechanism is still that of José da Costa Gomes, *Collecção de Leis da Dívida Pública Portugueza*, vol. I (Lisbon: Imprensa Nacional, 1883), in particular pp. 13–28.

The main difficulty in studying this last type of payment is due on the one hand to the fact that, as with the 'ração' and 'vestir' of many courtiers, on many occasions it appears as a payment of a prebendary type, intended to sustain the king's servant. On the other hand, it could also concern payments originating from privileges connected to posts on which I have no systematic information. A good example of the first case was 'mantimento e vestir' paid to the several *escrivães*, *recebedores*, *tesoureiros* and officials of justice and also to the *físicos*, *camareiros*, *barbeiros* and servants in the kitchen and stable. In the second group are included, I believe, certain rights such as the 'avantagium' which the king's purveyor received for example each time he completed the acquisition of cloth for the royal *câmara*, through the custom of his being freely given some pieces.[85] It is probable that this type of indirect payment took on a growing role as one goes down in the hierarchy of the servants in the royal entourage.

CRIAÇÃO AND ADMITTANCE TO COURT

One of the main routes of access to the royal court at the end of the Middle Ages was, without doubt, integration through a tie of particular dependence implied by *criação*. This integration could at the time take place at a relatively young age for present-day patterns and created within the royal entourage a more or less numerous group of children and adolescents who, as has already been observed for the women, performed an essential role in court society. It is therefore not surprising that with regard to a court as well attended as that of Afonso V the *procuradores* at the Cortes complained at the inclusion of increasingly young nobles: 'tamto que estes sam de seys ou sete annos loguo os tomaaes e trazeis em vosa corte e lhes daaes cassa e moradia de homeens, e deles nam vem outro proueito senão sobeja despesa e pejo de pousadas'. They therefore suggested to the monarch that the young children 'non tragam Ayos nem azemalas com cama nem outra maneira de casa, vosa alteza lhes mande dar de comer em sala e seu vestir e calçar onesto sem pano de seda nem outra maneira custosa. E podera vosa merçee hordenarlhes como apremdam a ler e a escreuer e gramatiqua segumdo se custumaua nos tempos delRey voso avoo e padre.'[86]

In this text there are outlined some major indications as to the situation of those who were included in the royal entourage before reaching adulthood, which was a situation not exclusive to the nobility: fed and housed at court, they there acquired the essence of their upbringing. The *criação* was, however,

[85] ANTT, *LN*, Extras, ff. 61–62v. In a measure registered in the *Livro Vermelho*, in 1473 Afonso V removes the rights of *tesoureiros* and *recebedores* to a piece of cloth received as was the custom 'nos tempos pasados': *Livro Vermelho*, pp. 478–9.

[86] ANTT, Cortes, M 2, 14, f. 64v. We indeed find in 1451 mention of Pedro Álvares, bachelor, 'que enssyna os moços fidalgos de ssua cassa': *CUP*, vol. V, p. 228.

related to the problem of the cycles of court life, and was a first experience which, since it was not a privilege enjoyed by all, was nevertheless seen at the time as an important distinguishing factor. An eloquent text on the subject is the letter dated 1437 sent by the king's secretary, Rui Galvão, to the abbot D. Gomes, in which he broadly speaks of his own life: 'o Rej meu Senhor de Jdade de xj anos me criou senpre em sua camera dormindo em ella seruindoo depois que em tall Jdade fuy comtinoadamente em meu ofiçio'. The secretary applied to this early cohabitation 'hua especialidade de fiança' in him by Duarte, 'tam chegada Como vos Senhor dom abade bem vistes e sentistes, em este tempo que em sua corte andastes'.[87]

The difference thus established between the young and the adults within the court world naturally has had a distinct meaning according to the social standing of each. For all, however, the king performed an almost parental function, as suggested by the recurring 'fatherly' metaphor in medieval texts. According to Fernão Lopes, Fernando 'era tam amavioso de todollos que com elle viviam que nom chorava menos por hũu seu escudeiro quando morria come sse fosse seu filho'.[88] The importance of the phenomenon of *criação* contributed to a large extent towards the explanation of the relative continuity in recruitment within the same groups observed in my prosopographic research, when analysing the family lines and the diverse court family ties.

The specific position of the younger members of the royal entourage determined that an entire group of occupations be reserved for them, in which their apprenticeship or education, to which I make reference, was completed. We find them there under the generic term 'moços' connected to the several departments and organisms of the court: in the chapel and the *câmara*, in the *repostaria* and the *copa*, in *caça* and *montaria*, and in the *estrebaria*. For those of noble standing, or 'moços fidalgos' as they were called in the fifteenth century, were perhaps reserved less specific occupations, since we do not find them connected particularly to any palace department. Once they had reached puberty, many were promoted to the status of 'escudeiros'. The numbers of this young component of the royal entourage can be broadly evaluated for the first half of the fifteenth century through some global lists of servants and also from the rolls of *moradias*. It must, for example, have reached about 35 per cent of the number of servants in the entourage of the infantes of the house of Aviz during the first decade of the fifteenth century.[89] This was an order of magnitude still existing in the 1470s as an ideal to be achieved in the *Ordenança* which was intended to reform Afonso's court as well as that of the heir, D. João.[90] One could say that this dealt merely with an ideal since, in contrast to the twenty 'moços fidalgos'

[87] BLAU, Ash 1792 (1716), I, fasc. VI, 10. [88] *CR Fernando*, p. 3.

[89] *Livro dos Conselhos*, pp. 179–80. According to A. Dias Dinis, this text can be dated 1408: *MH*, vol. VI, pp. 134–5.

[90] *Livro Vermelho*, p. 477.

suggested, there were actually to be some sixty named in the monarch's lists. Even with service performed in rotation, the number of those actually included in this category was more than the numbers given in the *Ordenança*.

The largest group was always that of the grooms of the *câmara* and stable, closely followed by the grooms of *monte* and *caça*, whose members oscillated between twenty and thirty. Less numerous were those who served in the *copa* and the chapel, who rarely numbered more than twelve in each. Among those who received 'moradias' as fidalgos, the 'moços' represented about 20 per cent of the total number of named individuals in the middle of the fifteenth century.[91] Unfortunately, the image drawn from these numbers (which cannot be extrapolated for earlier periods because of the total absence of data of this type) showing the number of 'moços' at the royal palace of the fifteenth century is not accompanied by an equal wealth of information on their actual occupations. Even so, I have already referred to the musical and liturgical activities of the 'moços da Capela' who accompanied the monarch and were included in the body of ecclesiastical servants whose noisy dawn presence was evoked by Duarte in such clear form in his 'Livro dos Conselhos'.[92] The 'moços' were also much referred to by John in the hunting treatise he wrote; among these were those who 'andam ao monte', learning the crude exercises of *montaria* and care of the king's dogs: 'ca sabudo he . . . os moços do monte sahirem escudeiros, e auerem bõos casamentos, per que ueem a seer honrados, e ricos'.[93]

Their experiences were not restricted to occupations of hunting or the stable, since these young men were also given delicate missions and were of great diplomatic importance. In 1370 Fernando sent an ambassador to the king of Granada with rich presents for him given by 'sete moços do monte', and to this example can be added many others, such as the departure of Afonso V's 'moço das esporas' for Naples in 1452, or the numerous journeys of 'moços de estribeira' to the papal court as carriers of missives and diverse gifts.[94] The 'moços de câmara' accompanied the officials of this palace organism and carried messages from the monarch and his closest collaborators within the court and also outside it, for example to the *casa dos contos*. In the fifteenth century they included a large variety of young men, and there was a certain preference for this position among the descendants of higher officials of the court and men of letters to whom Afonso V began to grant, in some cases, 'tença para estudo'.[95]

[91] Calculations made through lists published in the eighteenth century by A. Caetano de Sousa in *Provas*, vol. II, pp. 28–57.

[92] *Livro dos Conselhos*, pp. 209–10.

[93] M. Lopes de Almeida (ed.), 'Livro da Montaria', in *Obras dos Príncipes de Avis*, p. 26.

[94] *CR Fernando*, p. 142 or MH, vol. XI, pp. 155–6 and vol. XIV, p. 201.

[95] This was the case of Nuno Gonçalves, son of the *tesoureiro-mor* to Duarte, or Lopo Soares, son of Dr Rui Gomes de Alvarenga, both *moços de câmara* to Afonso V: *CUP*, vol. V, p. 183; vol. VI, pp. 430 and 473.

The protection by the monarch of these members of his court with whom he had formed such an important tie was, as already stated, changed materially by the granting of 'casamentos'. The generic principle that the decision, which was followed absolutely at varying levels, of the choice of the matrimonial partner of the young growing up at court also fell to the king appears from the outset to have encountered numerous obstacles. We cannot otherwise interpret the successive statements of the monarchs from the thirteenth century, including in legal texts,[96] when they declare themselves to be opposed to the constraint on their servants in matters of matrimonial choice, which was a principle successively reiterated in the Cortes by Pedro, Fernando and John I.[97] The royal influence was, however, doubly exercised as far as can be confirmed in many cases. On the one hand, determining the choice of women in the royal entourage and, on the other, removing others from the court to marry their servants and *criados*, which are facts most commonly referred to by narrative sources rather than by genealogies of the period.

In his *Crónica de D. João I*, Fernão Lopes tells with certain detail of some conflicts which the 'interventionist' policy of this monarch regarding matrimony led to and he tells, in a short exemplary story, of his extreme reaction (he who, as has been seen, had married some of the lettered men and 'capitães' of his entourage to heiresses of important noble families) when violently condemning the alliance between Beatriz, the daughter of the magnate Álvaro Peres de Castro and the royal *camareiro* who was the brother of his *vedor da fazenda*, João Afonso. This *camareiro* would, for this, have been publicly executed.[98] Personal initiative in this matter and, more still, opposition to royal designs regarding given matrimonial choices seem, therefore, to have been fiercely prevented through the most stringent means. For this reason I would not believe to be correct, without actually examining these fundamental aspects, the interpretation of matrimonial alliances of the court nobility as a simple result of actual 'strategies' (or rational actions that were necessarily conscious and clearly discernible by the individual) as proposed means of aggrandisement and alliance through marriage. These actions are exclusively attributed by modern historians to the initiative of lineages and individuals in the fourteenth and fifteenth centuries. The necessarily limited character and the inevitable predetermination of

[96] The oldest example known is the law attributed to Afonso II which states that 'os matrimonyos deuem ser liures . . . que nos nem os nosos soçesores nom costrangam nenhuum pera fazer matrimonyo': *OD*, p. 51. On the practice at the court of Afonso III: Ventura, 'A nobreza de corte de Afonso III', vol. I, p. 229.

[97] The subject was mentioned at the Cortes of 1361, 1371, 1372 and 1385 and then sporadically in some Cortes of the fifteenth century: *CPP*, p. 75; *CPF*, pp. 93 and 130; Caetano, *A crise nacional* (Cortes of 1385) and *OD*, p. 637.

[98] *CR Fernando*, pp. 559–60; *CR João I*, vol. I, p. 133 and vol. II, pp. 270 and 284–7. These occurrences would have been in 1389, and in 1390 we see the lady sell the 'paços' of her father in Lisbon to Dr João das Regras: ANTT, *Ch. D. João I*, 2, f. 49v.

data resulting from an exclusive use of the genealogical reconstruction for the study of matrimonial practices demand, on the contrary, the establishment of other conditions on which these decisions were based, some of them unknown or of little relevance in our contemporary societies (where the individual assumes an indisputable autonomy in this matter). We should take note of the data indicating the sphere of freedom or of coaction, which are highly variable in this case and which two individuals of the same line or even of the same family might at times confront, as well as a variability which did not solely depend on the order of birth.[99] Biological relationship must be seen as only a latent order, since we find in many cases that it is not the determining factor of marriage choices in the face of the imperatives of pseudo-kinship and of other forms of dependency which the genealogical narrative does not record, but which had a proven role in the formation of matrimonial alliances, even in the case of the nobility.[100]

Given that court marriages to which I have referred were contracted, in the majority of cases, following royal intervention, the *criado* received a gift of a variable amount according to his standing and the functions he performed. For a calculation of the 'casamentos' of those who received *moradias*, the respective sums of these were taken into account and multiplied by the number of years served. With regard to members of the court who were not nobles, the young men 'de pequeno estado' as they were called at the time, this amount was calculated in a complex manner according to two essential criteria recommended by Duarte: the time that each had served, 'e algũus seruiços especiais se os fez'.[101] He also stated that certain pieces of cloth or clothing be given to the young married man, which were eventually replaced by a quantity in money. For example, through a *quitação* granted in 1403 to the king's tailor, we know that several quantities of material and adornments were used at the time 'pera Roupas que talhou e ffez pera nos e pera a Rajnha e pera os Iffantes; *e pera noyuos e noivas que casarom em nossa casa*, e pera jograres e outras pesoas'.[102] These gifts

99 Karl Schmid, 'The structure of the nobility', in Timothy Reuter (ed.), *The Medieval Nobility* (Amsterdam: North Holland, 1979), p. 54; Anita Guerreau-Jalabert, 'El sistema de parentesco medieval: sus formas (real/espiritual) y su dependencia con respeto a la organización del espacio', in Reyna Pastor (ed.), *Relaciones de poder, de producción y de parentesco en la edad media* (Madrid: CSIC, 1990), pp. 85–105.

100 See for example observations by Ronald Weissman, 'Reconstructing Renaissance sociology', in *Persons in Groups: Social Behavior and Identity Formation in Medieval and Renaissance Europe* (Binghampton: Center for Medieval and Early Renaissance Studies, 1985), pp. 39–45; also Miri Rubin, 'Small groups: identity and solidarity in the late Middle Ages', in *Enterprise and Individuals in Fifteenth-Century England* (Stroud: Alan Sutton, 1991), pp. 132–50.

101 *Livro dos Conselhos*, pp. 154 and 178. For an actual example of 'casamento' granted to a *reposteiro*: ANTT, *Ch. D. Duarte*, 3, f. 80v. A list of 'casamentos' of the Portuguese court relative to the end of the fifteenth century: BL, Manuscripts, Add. 20958, ff. 15–16.

102 ANTT, *Ch. D. Duarte*, 3, f. 80 (an example of a gift in number); ANTT, *Ch. D. João I*, 5, f. 46 (quitação).

were granted whether the royal servant remained at court or whether he later abandoned it.[103]

In the specific case of the nobility we find that, at the end of the Middle Ages, contributions by the king to the young members of the most powerful families when they 'tomaram sua casa' are a valuable indicator of the intervention of the sovereign in the intermeshing of matrimonial relationships and alliances among the distinct groups of court nobility. I have already examined in some depth this process perceived through the reconstruction of the respective lineages and family groups. In practice, the monarchs made use of various means for their execution. In the fourteenth century, we know of several examples to which I have specifically alluded in the previous chapter of concession of lands and incomes to nobles 'em casamento'. We know through the will of Queen Beatriz of Castile, for example, that women in the middle of the fourteenth century received determined sums according to their status, which were indicated in currency (*libras*), and that these could vary from one sum to its double (500–1000 *libras*). The granting of lands and rent by the king could, in theory, lie in the actual method of preventing these payments due to a woman of the court's female household but it could also be the case that the king would add to these sums as a simple sign of royal favour, by which goods were not granted to the women of the court but to noble *criados* who married outside court. The traditional practice seemed unjust to Afonso V, who stated at the Cortes of 1472, in justification of certain favours he was performing, 'que lhe nom pareçe cousa Resoada que os fidalguos e outros que com ele viuem, por casarem com molheres de ssua casa, nom ajam outro casamento senam o que as molheres se daa, e asy fiquem sem gualardão de seu seruiço . . . como quer que os Reis damte ele o nunqua fizesem que as molheres somente se desem casamentos'.[104]

The system is better known for the fifteenth century, when we find the granting of variable sums, also calculated in coinage (gold crowns and *dobras*), in the form of either property and rent, dues or even sums of money, or the increasing practice from 1420 in 'tenças' to be paid in some fiscal organism of the kingdom. Thus, still in 1393 Fernão Gonçalves de Figueiredo and Catarina Albergaria received their 'casamento' in land, as did Estevão Soares de Melo and Teresa Novais in 1413.[105] On his marriage to Inês Leitoa in 1411, the *escrivão da puridade*, Gonçalo Lourenço de Gomide, received the sum of Pedro Afonso Sardinha's dues to the monarch.[106] There is no lack of examples of gifts of rents: Diogo Fernandes de Almeida and Maria de Sousa were in 1430 granted a certain sum of rents from royal property in Abrantes, and in 1425 the *camareiro*

103 Thus, for example, in 1437 'prestações' for his marriage were paid to Nuno de Trancoso, who was stable boy to John I: *DCH*, vol. I, p. 335.

104 ANTT, Cortes, M 2, 14, f. 68.

105 ANTT, *Ch. D. João* I, 2, f. 84v; 3, f. 164.

106 ANTT, *Ch. D. João I*, 5, f. 82.

Diogo Gonçalves de Macedo also received part of the rents of the king in Braga; I could continue to cite such examples.[107]

An analysis of the existing information on 'casamentos' performed throughout the reign of John I (in all about thirty are preserved in his *chancelaria*) allows us to conclude that the most common sums of these gifts were between 1000 and 5000 crowns, although in the case of relatives of the royal house, such as D. Fernando de Noronha, these could amount to the extraordinary sum of 16,000 crowns.[108] The gifts to Diogo Borges and Genebra de Andrade or to João de Gouveia and Leonor Gonçalves, who married at the court of King John, are examples of 1000 crowns.[109] Very close to this sum are the numerous 'casamentos' of 2000 and 2500 crowns given, for example, to Diogo Pereira and Maria de Resende, to João Freire and Catarina de Sousa, to Fernão de Góis and Leonor da Cunha, to Luís Álvares de Sousa and Filipa Coutinho, and certainly to many others.[110] Up to 5000 crowns is found in documented examples of Rui Nogueira and Aldonça de Meneses, Álvaro Peres de Távora and Leonor da Cunha, and Rui Vasques Ribeiro and the 'relative of the king' Ana Afonso.[111]

This scale of 'casamentos', which centred on sums usually between 2000 and 4000 crowns, continues to be found in about fifteen alliances studied of noble *criados* of the king during the reign of Duarte and the period of the regency of the Duke of Coimbra. Notable are the cases of Fernando 'das Alcáçovas' and Branca de Lemos, or of Rui Mendes da Cerveira and Isabel de Gomide, and further of Vasco de Gouveia and Filipa de Vasoncelos during Duarte's reign. The most obvious sum, however, was that of 8000 crowns given to Duarte de Meneses for his marriage to Isabel de Melo.[112] As for the period of the regency, Gomes Martins de Lemos and Maria de Azevedo received a 'casamento', as did Fernão Gonçalves de Miranda and Branca de Sousa or João de Noronha and Filipa de Ataíde, all of which were between 1000 and 4000 crowns.[113]

In the middle of the fifteenth century, however, there are signs that this system was in a state of crisis, and a certain disorder appears in the sums, to which the difficult situation of the royal finances would perhaps not be alien. According to the 'Regimento' drawn up in the context of the political crises of 1438–39 following the death of Duarte, among the topics to be dealt with at the Cortes were the following matters: 'Jtem, nom dar casamentos a que sejam

[107] ANTT, *Ch. D. João I*, 4, ff. 125 and 85.
[108] ANTT, *Ch. D. João I*, 4, f. 117; *Ch. D. Duarte*, 3, f. 73.
[109] *MH*, vol. XII, pp. 63–5; ANTT, *Ch. D. Afonso V*, 18, f. 56.
[110] ANTT, *Ch. D. Duarte*, 3, f. 23; ANTT, *Ch. D. João I*, 3, f. 194 and *Ch. D. Duarte*, 1, f. 160; ANTT, *Ch. D. Afonso V*, 18, f. 79; ANTT, *Ch. D. João I*, 4, f.111v.
[111] ANTT, *Ch. D. João I*, 4, f. 120; *Ch. D. Duarte*, 1, f. 224v; *DCH*, vol. I, p. 471; ANTT, *Ch. D. João I*, 4, f. 136; ANTT, *Ch. D. João I*, 3, f. 162v.
[112] *MH*, vol. VI, p. 286; *ALF*, vol. II, p. 771; *MH*, vol. XIII, p. 12; *CR Duarte*, pp. 572–3 and also *MH*, vol. VII, pp. 321–3.
[113] ANTT, *Ch. D. Afonso V*, 20, f. 72; 5, f. 18v.

obrigadas tenças; Jtem, nom firmar casamentos delrrej nem de seus irmãaos e irmãas.'[114] Several royal charters of around 1450 allude to an 'Ordenança' decreed by the young Afonso V on the manner of processing these payments, but any concrete evidence is, unfortunately, not known of.[115] What would appear to have contributed to the difficulty of the situation is not only the already mentioned debts resulting from the granting of rents 'em penhor' for payments not made, which started to occur from the beginning of the century, but also the gradual expansion of this type of favour among ever increasing circles beyond those of the court as well as its generalisation within the court itself.

The increase of the 'ajudas de casamento' which I have already mentioned, particularly those granted during John's reign to the young nobles who were *criados* with the infantes, must have an important role: in the case of the followers of the Infante Henry, an example is the gift by the king of 4500 crowns to João da Albuquerque and Catarina Pereira. For the case of the Infante Pedro, a gift of 2000 crowns to Aires Gomes da Silva III and Beatriz de Meneses can be confirmed.[116] In his will of 1426, King John I had ordered,

> por minha alma e da dita rainha mynha molher casem e dem casamentos a quorenta molheres de booa linhagem que seJam mynguoadas e os nom possam aver todos ou gram parte delles Segundo compre a suas comdições e estados as quaaes seiam naturaaes destes regnos e nossas criadas ou filhas de nossos criados damdo lhe cassamentos razoados segundo as pesoas e as comdições e linhagem de que forem e com quem casarem.[117]

The 'tenças por casamento' which from then on became part of the patrimony of many noble families were transacted in the same way as any other possession, were cumulative and were completely dissociated from a particular relationship to the monarch who had originated them.[118] One example among many of this process may be that of the 'tença de casamento' granted to Álvaro Vaz de Almada in 1432 (3500 crowns), which was sold to the Infante Henry who in turn in 1433 granted it to Pedro de Meneses as payment for debts he had contracted with him. It ended up by being handed to the latter's daughter, Leonor, who inherited in 1437.[119] That is, a few years after the first-mentioned marriage, this income was no longer in the hands of its original owner and had passed through various hands, and there was nothing to prevent it from continuing to be handed to others. In the 1470s there was a first attempt at regulating the

[114] *MH*, vol. VI, p. 268.

[115] See the original document in a private registry published in *MH*, vol. X, pp. 315–17.

[116] *MH*, vol. III, p. 199; ANTT, *Ch. D. Afonso V*, 11, f. 32v; BLAU, Ash 1792 (1716), I, fasc. VII, 18.

[117] *GTT*, vol. VI, p. 8.

[118] The connection of dowries with the mechanism of the public debt is marvellously studied for the particular case of Florence by Anthony Molho, *Marriage Alliance in Late Medieval Florence* (Cambridge, MA: Harvard University Press, 1994), in particular pp. 27–79.

[119] *MH*, vol. VII, pp. 172–3.

practices of granting of 'casamentos' through a group of measures which are only of interest to the extent that they clarify a little the earlier situation which is often referred to.

Thus, as a result of the Cortes the monarch determined in 1473 that only a number of those servants who were not nobles should receive 'casamentos', and he no longer paid them to many. The explanation supplied deserves consideration: 'porque hũs deles sam oficiaes, que ham grandes ganços de seus oficios, e outros que nom sam realmente nosos oficiais moradores, porque sam servidores de oficiaes nosos, e outros sam como assoldadados'. In spite of many of them receiving *moradia* and *rações*, the monarch did not consider that all these members of the court were 'de calidade que sam os outros nosos moradores e os outros nosos oficiaes, que per ordenança costume e rezam ouveram sempre casamentos'. From then on the royal functionaries (officials and *desembargadores* 'da Relação') and the corps of artisans of the royal entourage (carpenters, gunsmiths, goldsmiths, blacksmiths, shoemakers, candle makers, tanners, tailors, embroiderers and furriers), as well as other professionals such as physicians, surgeons and apothecaries, were to remain excluded. What appears significant is that many of these were also paid in 'mantimentos' and by a payment for objects made or services given, thus being close to the type of tie which the king referred to when saying that they were 'como assoldadados' (somewhat like those whom today we would call 'salaried'). On the other hand, the officials of arms (master of arms, heralds poursuivant) and the court musicians (minstrels and players, but 'que nom sejam escudeiros, ou cantores') were also excluded. Besides these, the king no longer dealt with 'casamentos' for the vast panoply of servants of inferior hierarchy of the distinct court departments (e.g. *mantearia*, *copa*, *repostaria*, *requeixaria*, *saquitaria* and *forno*) and also the working women (sweepers, washerwomen and bread makers), doubtless because he considered that they were on many occasions included among the 'servidores de nossos oficiais' or that among these lower levels of the palace organisation were employees of the holders of the respective offices who were not themselves directly connected to the monarch.[120]

Through the ruling that I have analysed, there was an attempt to return to the uses 'dos reis dante nos', as Afonso V said when reaffirming the specific character of the relationship which had led to this type of favour while on the other hand recognising the novelty of many contemporary situations. The court, by all indications, was growing during this second half of the fifteenth century both in size and in complexity and, as we shall see, the performance of many offices was altered. It was important to restrict the old uses so that new situations would not be embarked upon indiscriminately. As to the members of the aristocracy,

[120] ANTT, Cortes, M 2, 14, ff. 67–9 (several general chapters of the Cortes of 1472–73). Some 'ordenações e determinações' recorded in the *Livro Vermelho* appear in the direct sequence of the positions taken by the monarch at these Cortes: *Livro Vermelho*, pp. 479–81.

the *criação* of the monarch revealed itself to be a prestigious and profitable connection. Because of this the nobility of the fifteenth century showed itself to be interested, even if not able to be present within the royal entourage, in obtaining this form of favour which had its origins in the court. As Afonso V recognised, 'ajudas' and 'tenças' had been granted to many through their marriages, 'asy como se fosem nosos moradores', which caused a privilege which, in the time of his ancestors, was applied exclusively to the young members of their entourages, to extend beyond the court boundaries.[121] The situation from then on was financially ruinous for the monarchs, although on the other hand it also meant the recognition of the court as a hegemonous centre of the world of the nobility for part of large sectors of the nobility, and alerts us to the fact that royal intervention in the matrimonial sphere was considered from then on the norm for a growing number of noble families.

Once this important stage of the life of the 'criado' with his 'casamento' was closed, would there then follow departure from court? There is no lack of examples showing that this happened from the beginning of the period studied here. In fact, in the fifteenth century it was assumed that following this occurrence the payment of the 'moradia' to whoever received it would cease.[122] Those 'da criação' of the king were, in general, a contingent of trusted men whom the successive monarchs used in numerous areas of activity outside the palace universe, with particular importance for those bodies of judicial and financial officials throughout the kingdom – judges and inquisitors, *almoxarifes* and *contadores*, holders of innumerable offices of royal appointment in a variety of situations of which the charters of appointment of officials and local documentation give ample information.[123] However, 'casamento' for many meant merely a more or less significant passage of progress of men and women of the court, implying a change in their way of life, but not a simple and definitive departure from court. This change could for the young noble imply an increased responsibility owing to a multiplicity of fields of activity imposed upon him once he assumed the direction of his 'casa', while not being compelled to abandon living at court as a resident *fidalgo* or a counsellor. The change for the

121 *Livro Vermelho*, p. 481. A few years later his son John determined at the Cortes that 'A nenhũa molher que em casa de seu pay estee, tiramdo aquelas que o ja tem outorgado, se nam de casamento nem ajuda pera casamento nem mantimento algũ per a casa do dito seu pay, posto que a tomada tenha por sua, e nam aja algũa das sobreditas cousas saluo quamdo amdar comtinuadamente no paço morador': ANTT, Cortes, M 2, 14, f. 69.

122 A norm recalled at the Cortes of 1465 (*Livro Vermelho*, pp. 395–6), reaffirmed at the Cortes of 1472–73, and which is known to have been observed in practice until the middle of the century: see documents of 1409 and 1450 in *MH*, vol. I, pp. 323–4; vol. X, pp. 202–4 and vol. XII, pp. 310–11. From the exact month when the marriage took place payment of the *tença de casamento* started and the *moradia* ceased.

123 At the Cortes of the fifteenth century the subject was a recurring one among the complaints of the people. See for example the chapter of the Cortes of 1433: Armindo de Sousa, 'As Cortes de Leiria-Santarém de 1433', *Estudos Medievais*, 2 (1982), 171.

women either was translated into the possibility of performing a role of greater authority and power alongside the queens or infantas, as we have seen was the case of the *donas* (in particular the widows), or, in the case of the more modest servants, this change consisted in assuming entitlement to a determined position for the official and domestic servant who continued to perform duties personal to himself alongside the monarch, since as the kings constantly recalled at the Cortes, he was not able to be easily replaced, for the abilities which on many occasions he would have acquired in the palace could not be overlooked.[124]

By assuming a court duty simultaneously with or even after having 'tomado sua casa', the nobleman who, according to beliefs of the age, assumed adulthood on his marriage, frequently went on to take responsibility, although perhaps indirectly, for the function of complex organisms which demanded his more or less constant presence in the entourage of the king and queen.[125] By assuming a position or office, the 'moços' and 'escudeiros', by now married, could in turn be 'acrescentados', or promoted on the court ladder to the rung immediately above, as demanded at times by the post entrusted to them. In spite of the constant complaints resounding against its existence in the chapters of the Cortes of the fifteenth century, the 'moradores casados' were an enduring reality at the court of the kings during the period studied here, and came to constitute a good number of those who lived there.

THE *MORADORES*

We have already seen in some detail that the generic term 'morador', when attributed to the members of the court of the fourteenth and fifteenth centuries, covered a large variety of situations, be these social standing, occupation, sex and age and also regarding the relationship with the monarch or the queen who maintained the individuals in question. The *moradores* were in fact the main body of the court, its most permanent nucleus let us say, to which many other individuals could then attach themselves in a transient or irregular manner. The *moradores* are, for this reason, one of the more important subjects of prosopographic study of court society, since they show us the individual interacting with others (and with the king) in a set of concrete, social roles. Unfortunately, it is

124 An example is the king's reply to the people at the Cortes of 1472 in which Afonso V stated, regarding the married officials, that 'nom poderia peruemtura asy bem achar outros tam autos e pertemçemtes': ANTT, Cortes, M 2, 14, f. 65v.

125 On the importance of marriage as the commencement of adult life, particularly in the case of the nobility: Georges Duby, *La Société chevaleresque* (Paris: Flammarion, 1988), pp. 129–42; Erich Köhler, 'Senso e funzione del termine *joven*', in *Sociologia della fin'amor: saggi trobadorici* (Padua: Liviana, 1976), pp. 233–56. On the condition of the young at court from the thirteenth century, observations by J. M. W. Bean, '*Bachelor* and retainer', *Medievalia et Humanistica*, 3 (1972), 117–31. For the Iberian Peninsula, Susana Belmartino, 'Estructura de la familia y "edades sociales" en la aristocracia de León y Castilla según las fuentes literarias e historiográficas', *Cuadernos de Historia de España*, 47–8 (1968), 256–328.

only for the beginning of the fifteenth century, more precisely around 1405, that we have the first roll of names of *moradores* at the Portuguese court which can be compared in its global numbers (though this should be done with caution) with a similar roll relating to the court of Afonso V in 1462.[126] An analysis of this allows us to establish some generic characteristics of the *moradores* for the first half of the fifteenth century.

The first assessment is that of the process of growth that this stable nucleus of the court underwent at the time. If we compare simply those who received *moradia* as *fidalgos*, following the 130 individuals listed in 1405 we see a total number of 265 in 1462: that is, the number has doubled. In my opinion, this must mean that the group of *moradores* is that which increased most, which means that this record is perhaps not applicable to the remaining global numbers of the lists. In the entirety of the 390 persons to whom *moradia* was paid at the court of John in 1405 there are in fact some bodies of servants who are not listed by name, such as the servants of *caça* and *montaria* (thirty *moços do monte* and twenty-two *caçadores*), the many messengers and servants (ten footmen and fifteen couriers), and the various personnel connected to the stables (ten muleteers, five stable boys and four farriers and blacksmiths) or even servants of several departments of the royal household (two men of the *dispensaria*, one of the *repostaria* and three of the *copa*), all of whom received the lowest sums. Since the list of 1462 omits this type of *morador*, it will not be possible to state for certain whether their number increased throughout the century to such a significant extent.

Several indications relating to the reign of Afonso, in particular the 'Ordenança' of 1472 included in the *Livro Vermelho*, would appear to suggest that these numbers at the beginning of the century were considered to be relatively balanced but that, in practice, they had been considerably exceeded. The same can be said of the 'oficiais da relação' (*chanceler*, *corregedor*, *ouvidores*, *porteiros* and respective servants) and of the officials connected to the performance of justice at court, both of which are mentioned only in the list of 1405. By a comparison with the fifteenth-century description of the *casa da suplicação* (dated *c.* 1433–36), we can see that a certain stability of the number of *moradores* connected to these organisms was foreseen, and that this number varied little thirty years later, with the exception of the *escrivães* working at court, whose increase is exponential.[127] We can also broaden this general hypothesis of growth for the case of the chapel, which has already been discussed in the previous chapter, and for a hypothetical reconstruction of the

[126] The rolls of 'moradores' were first published in the eighteenth century, those of John I by Soares da Silva in 1734 and those of Afonso V by Caetano de Sousa in 1748. There are new and better versions of the first at *MH*, but no other versions of the latter.

[127] Martim de Albuquerque (ed.), *O Regimento Quatrocentista da Casa da Suplicação* (Paris: Fundação Calouste Gulbenkian, 1980).

global dimension of the monarch's *câmara*, both of which organisms we see increasing significantly in size during the fifteenth century.

This tendency towards growth, as also the dimension suggested by the global numbers of 1405, is entirely similar to that known for other European courts. The approximate size of the Castile/Leon court of the twelfth century was about 226 individuals,[128] while at the end of the fifteenth century it reached an estimated minimum of 400 *moradores*.[129] Rolls analogous to the Portuguese indicate in the French case that in 1291 there were more than 165 persons having a right to 'ração', which corresponded to about 260–270 *moradores* in the middle of the fourteenth century, while for the 318 names shown in 1490 there was a corresponding number of about 400 *moradores*, this not including the queen's entourage.[130] However, a later growth is notable since in 1538 there were 622 individuals named in similar rolls with rights to the 'ração' (*bouche de cour*).[131] For England, Given-Wilson suggests a general evolution which went from 150 individuals present at the turn of the thirteenth century to between 400 and 700 at the end of the fourteenth (depending upon whether the king was at war or not).[132] The English rolls of 1438–39 contain 523 names, but those of 1448–49 contain 875, and the number of the household of the king and queen may have reached 1200 in 1449.[133] The household of the court of Burgundy, for its part, between 1426 and 1474 went from 234 listed to 1030, and reached the greatest number in war time.[134] In these three last cases, which are perhaps the best documented for the late-medieval European context, we find, as in the Portuguese kingdom, that the fifteenth century represented a most important moment of change and vitality of the court organism.

Forming as they did one of the numerous groups of medieval society which were legally differentiated, and by enjoying the distinctive privileges and prestige due to their proximity to the monarchy, the household of the court retained

128 A number suggested by Bernard Reilly and accepted by Simon Barton, *The Aristocracy of Twelfth-Century León and Castile* (Cambridge: Cambridge University Press, 1997), p. 145.

129 Miguel Angel Ladero Quesada, 'Casa y corte. L'hôtel du roi et la cour comme institutions économiques au temps des Rois catholiques', in Maurice Aymard and Marzio Romani (eds.), *La Cour comme institution économique* (Paris: Maison des Sciences de l'Homme, 1998), p. 47.

130 Lot and Fawtier, *Institutions royales*, p. 70; M. L. Douet d'Arcq (ed.), *Comptes de l'hôtel des rois de France aux XIVe et XVe siècles: les états* (Paris: PUF, 1971), pp. 148–9.

131 R. J. Knecht, 'The Court of Francis I', *European Studies Review*, 8 (1978), 1–22; Jacqueline Boucher, *La Cour de Henri III* (Rennes: Ouest-France, 1986), p. 40.

132 Given-Wilson, *The Royal Household and the King's Affinity*, p. 259. See also the detailed discussion of the several lists whose overall sums are published (*ibid.*, pp. 39–41 and 278–9).

133 D. A. L. Morgan, 'The house of policy: the political role of the late Plantagenet household, 1422–1485', in David Starkey (ed.), *The English Court from the Wars of the Roses to the Civil War* (London: Longman, 1987), p. 41.

134 Werner Paravicini, 'The Court of the Dukes of Burgundy. A model for Europe?', in R. G. Asch and A. Bircke (eds.), *Princes, Patronage and Nobility* (London: Oxford University Press, 1991), p. 76.

certain global characteristics throughout the fourteenth and fifteenth centuries. At the fourteenth-century court they shared a group of legal and fiscal privileges which we see instituted in royal legislation from the previous century, particularly that of their being judged only at the court itself and their ability in some hierarchically superior positions to call their opponents to court.[135] From the fiscal point of view, the benefits of inclusion in the royal entourage as a *morador* are made clear, for example in the ruling of 1418 relating to the payment of one of the many 'pedidos' or extraordinary taxes of the reign of John I. We find here that all those 'que andam contenuadamente' with the king were exempt and for this matter they were seen as equal to the noble vassals.[136] This privilege led also to the attempt at deception of the treasury by some of the more modest servants such as, for example, the 'homens dos meirinhos', who merely to obtain this exemption placed themselves temporarily in the service of the court.[137]

All those who lived with the king and queen had to make these distinctions clear, in particular by compulsorily departing on horseback, according to Portuguese legislation of the end of the fourteenth century. The sole exceptions allowed to this practice were the clerics (bishops and members of the chapel), the physicians and the Jews, to whom during the reign of Afonso V were added doctors of law and members of the clerical entourages of the ecclesiastical magnates.[138] Besides this, of course, were the women and children. This ruling was to be successively reaffirmed throughout the fifteenth century and was added to by the prohibition of using other mounts for those vassals who went from court within a radius of three leagues from the place where the king was. Not only dignity and the distinctive marks of status of the *morador* were disrespected should the contrary occur, for the court itself could also be affected in its magnificence and this determined that, at several moments of the reign of Afonso, there was a threat of suspension of payment of *moradias* to anyone who did not comply with this obligation.[139]

The *moradores* of the Portuguese court were, however, far from constituting a homogenous body, and were distributed in distinct categories of differing status. This fact perhaps has its roots in the distinctions among the members of the royal entourage of which we have information as early as the thirteenth

135 The first and second aspects are contemplated in legislation of Afonso III and Dinis which would later be included in the 'Ordenações do reino'. As to the privileges of the 'oficios maiores', of being able in litigation to bring his opponents to court, this was successively restricted through measures dating from the reign of Afonso VI: *LP*, pp. 328 and 404.

136 *MH*, vol. II, pp. 289–98, in particular p. 291.

137 As the ruling states, 'algũus se uam e outros sse uem por se escusarem dalgũs emcarregos': *MH*, vol. II, p. 296.

138 *OA*, vol. V, pp. 398–400 and 403–4.

139 See the decrees aimed at the *moradores* in 1478 and 1480 and registered in the *Livro Vermelho*, pp. 510 and 532. From the point of view of court culture, as I have already shown, the relation with the horse is of great importance.

century. While for these earlier periods the palace hierarchy is not revealed in the different numbers of *moradias*, whose exact amounts are not known, we find it expressed, for example, in the number of servants to which the *morador* had a right according to his standing as *rico-homem*, *cavaleiro* or *escudeiro*. The court status ladder was composed of three main groups in the fifteenth century: that of the counsellors of the monarch, that of the *cavaleiro*s and that of the *escudeiro*s.

The most important positions, and the most desired, were of course those of *morador/conselheiro*, which were reserved to the most important nobility of the kingdom and to the holders of high palace positions. The roll of 1405 was most probably connected to a project of reform of the court of King John, and foresaw the simultaneous presence of merely four noble counsellors, who would receive the largest *moradia* of 100,000 *libras*. The data relative to this monarch's council, however, indicate the true size of this organism, which must have been still larger, since the number of counsellors who were definitely working during the reign oscillated between eleven and fifteen, the majority of whom were nobles.[140] In the short period of Duarte's reign there are twenty-three individuals named as counsellors of the king, although some would only have held the post in an 'epistolary' or honorary function, and were only sporadically present at court.[141] A clear example of the first of these cases is that of the abbot D. Gomes, who was at the time in Florence, but who maintained a large correspondence with the monarch in his position as counsellor. A similar position would perhaps be that of the captain of Ceuta, D. Pedro de Meneses, and later his son, Duarte.[142]

The many mentions of the counsellors in 1405 therefore seem intentional, as they probably related to the use of payment of such high *moradias* to those 'of the council' who expressly went to the court and who only did so at this time. This theory is reinforced by my prosopographic research since I have found some counsellors who were, *de facto*, employed by John and who were included in other categories of the 1405 roll. Similarly, in the 'Regimento' proposed by the regency of the kingdom in 1438, it was suggested that the royal council should function in rotation, and always include only nine people to whom a *moradia* of 200,000 *libras* would be paid in the case of a bishop, 150,000 that of a fidalgo and 100,000 that of a citizen.[143] This arrangement

140 Homem, 'Conselho real ou conselheiros do rei?', p. 65.

141 More precisely four clerics, eight holders of the most important palace duties (*vedores da fazenda, chanceleres, mordomo-mor, camareiro-mor, meirinho-mor, escrivão da puridade*), and a further eleven nobles, according to my prosopographic research.

142 An example of this type of written relationship between Afonso V and his counsellor D. Fernando da Guerra in 1460: *MH*, vol. XIV, pp. 110–14.

143 *MH*, vol. VI, pp. 265 and 270. On the presence of the 'citizen' in the royal council during the period of the regency: *MH*, vol. VII, pp. 86–9 and the observations of Marcelo Caetano, *A administração municipal de Lisboa durante a 1a dinastia (1179–1383)* (Lisbon: Academia Portuguesa da História, 1981), pp. 481–2.

did not last long, however. In the roll of 1462 there are fourteen individuals named among the high nobility who received a counsellor's *moradia*, while the number of those named during the initial period of this monarch's reign in the royal council was far higher if we then include the ecclesiastics and men of letters who certainly held a seat on the council.[144] Even if we consider that the number is underestimated in the available lists of *moradores*, this higher stratum of the court hierarchy is shown as still in the minority and also one in which were included individuals whose presence at court may not have been permanent, as opposed to that which tended to occur in the other cases.

An interpretation of the distinction made at court between *cavaleiro*s and *escudeiro*s leads to far more complex problems, in the first place because the number of the respective *moradias* is not shown in clear, regular stages, and also because many *escudeiro*s received higher sums than the *cavaleiro*s. This is not to speak of the 'moços-fidalgos' who appear for the first time in the list of 1462 with *moradias* which, in the majority of cases, are higher than those of the *escudeiro*s.[145] In the list of 1405 there is also the category of the 'great', which includes merely twenty individuals, who, I believe, correspond to those whom Duarte called 'cavaleiros de grande conta', that is those who formed a higher stratum of the *cavaleiro*s and received the highest *moradias*.[146]

We are able to discern varied factors in the formation of these successive distinctions of status. In the first place, of course, is the social standing of the individual, particularly in the case of the nobles, for whom as I have already suggested the sum of the respective *moradias* does not appear as important for their economic aspect as it is for the possibility of distinction conferred. Several specific references in the first half of the century to the existence of *escudeiro*s of the court who were not of noble birth suggest that, on the other hand, the lowest sums were reserved for these, and were naturally lower than those of the young *fidalgos*.[147] However, as I have explained at length, there is no lack of cases in which members of the same noble lineage or family were 'distributed'

144 Thus just for the period 1438–49 we find in the council three ecclesiastics, ten holders of high positions (*mordomo-mor*, *vedores da fazenda*, *chanceleres* and *regedor da casa do cível*) and nine nobles. The total number of nobles who could be counted among the 'cavaleiros do conselho' exceeds the above fourteen by a small amount.

145 Thus in 1405 the *moradias* of higher amounts swung between 27,000 and 5000 *libras*, but the most usual sum is close to 8000, and the *moradias* of the *escudeiros* between 7000 and 1200 *libras*, of which almost half in this group were on the lowest sum and the remainder almost all concentrated around 2000 *libras*. In 1462 the *moradias* oscillated between 8572 and 4226 *reais* in the case of *cavaleiros* of the council, between 4500 and 500 *reais* for the *cavaleiros*, between 1800 and 600 *reais* for the *escudeiros* and between 4000 and 700 *reais* for the grooms.

146 On those 'de grande conta', see the important law of 1436 compiled in *OD*, p. 647.

147 Thus in 'Soma da gente que cada hũdos jfantes trazia', a text which can be dated to the reign of John and after 1408 it was stated: 'Caualeiros e escudeiros daquella conta biij . . . Doutros escudeiros çento, e destes açerqua o terço d homens fidalgos *e as duas partes doutros de mais pequena conta*': *Livro dos Conselhos*, p. 179.

in the distinct categories of the lists of fifteenth-century *moradores*, which is a clear demonstration that this factor is not the only one to be regarded. As we have seen, it was also dependent upon the age group in which the individual was to be found.

The differences in status to which I have referred and the complex system of calculation of the sums for the *moradias* could also be related to the actual palace duties, as can be drawn from a few, rare indications in Portuguese sources. Thus, Afonso V was much criticised by the Cortes for granting far too easily certain posts whose tenure implied promotion to their holders:

> vossa merçe nam deue fazer escudeiros de moços destribeira porteiros moços de monte reposteiros e homeens d offiçios pois os tomais de tam baixa maneira E em outros ofiçios de Casa nom de comta d escudeiros os pode Vossa merçee acreçentar ataa que casem e quamdo casarem seremlhe desembarguados seus casamentos segumdo a comta em que amdarem e aa tomada de sua casa lhe podereis dar nome d escudeiros pera maior homrra sua.[148]

The representatives of the cities are alluding in this text to a hierarchy of duties which would be 'to the account' of *escudeiro*s or *cavaleiro*s.[149] By applying this criterion of distinction among the posts to the lists of 1405, we find that certain offices such as those of *copeiro*, *mantieiro*, *uchão*, *reposteiro*, *despenseiro* and *comprador*, and also the *regueifeiras*, the *boticário* and the *barbeiro* and various *escrivães* and cooks enjoyed *moradias* approximately equal in value to that of the *escudeiro*s on the same list. The same can be seen for the *porteiros da câmara* and to the body of *besteiros de câmara*, which must also have been reserved for the *escudeiro*s. Thus, one is led to conclude that the granting of status to the *morador* (and of the respective *moradia*) was made through a complex evaluation through a balanced correspondence between the standing and the social origins of the individual, the dignity of the post which he held and the favour of the king, which was the dynamic factor of variation and lay above all others.[150]

This hierarchical order, in the final instance ever subject to alteration at the will of the sovereign, was a fundamental structure of court society. While criticising its vitality and expansion at the end of the reign of John I, in his famous 'Carta de Bruges' Pedro approached his brother, the heir to the throne, in these terms:

> nenhum se contenta de aprender d ofiçio que seu padre auja, nem de serujr outros senhores senão lançaremse à corte em esperança de serem escudeyros del rey ou uosos ou de cada hum de uosos jrmãos. E ajnda por ysto eu vy

[148] ANTT, Cortes, M 2, 14, f. 69.

[149] This distinction between the duties is also mentioned in a ruling of 1431 made for his own house by the Infante Pedro: *Livro dos Conselhos*, p. 154.

[150] For a comparison relating to the case of Burgundy: Paravicini, 'The Court of the Dukes of Burgundy', p. 87.

algũa vez ao senhor rey e a uos tam gastados que ajnda que queseseis fazer bem e merçes a alguns outros a que ereis theudos, ou fazer algũa outra boa obra, não tynheis tal geyto pera o fazer.'[151]

and the position each individual occupied at court, which was expressed through the *moradia* he received, could thus become a sure indication of royal favour or disfavour if interpreted with other important facts in mind, such as individual merits, family origins and the age group. A complete deciphering of this system of signals is unfortunately denied to the historian in the majority of cases. It would probably be a greater exercise of that art 'of meticulous evaluation of interpersonal relationship' which, according to Norbert Elias, characterised the man at court.[152]

What significance, though, can in turn be attributed beyond this particular social context to these names of 'escudeiro' and 'cavaleiro'? I have already referred to this problem when alluding to the processes of ennoblement which took place within the context of the Portuguese court, in particular in the fifteenth century. In general, I would say that the granting of a place on this court ladder cannot be considered on its own as a sure indication of the social status of the individual nor, as a result, of his being made a noble. The fact that many appear as 'fidalgos da casa' of the king and queen, receiving *moradias* as *cavaleiro*s or *escudeiro*s, can be combined with fairly modest social origins in many cases, being itself affirmed in the other contexts of the society of the age as a prestigious personal status associated with the privileges and above all the proximity of the centre of power which the court represented. In addition, when dealing with a movable scale on which the individual could be promoted throughout his life, it would be extremely debatable in my opinion to attribute to these classifications any other value which is not relative to the fourteenth and fifteenth centuries. What is observed for the sixteenth and seventeenth centuries cannot be used anachronistically for previous periods. At the end of the Middle Ages tradition demanded the effective presence at court of the *moradores*. It was status obtained according to non-hereditary, situational criteria and it will be seen that the monarchs had difficulty in enforcing any other understanding of this characteristic. The *moradores* were, as has already been said, a status group formed upon the prestige which the society of the age attributed to those who served the monarch, sharing in his life. Because of this they tended to be modelled to a particular way of life, which was heavily marked by the traditional values and behaviour of the nobility and which distinguished them from the rest. The titles given to the diverse *moradores* of 'cavaleiro' and 'escudeiro' were meant above all to demand this prestige for the servants of the king, simultaneously establishing given expectations as to conduct and bringing

[151] A. Moreira de Sá (ed.), *A carta de Bruges do Infante D. Pedro*, offprint of *Biblos* (Coimbra, 1952), p. 19.

[152] Norbert Elias, *The Court Society* (Oxford: Blackwell, 1983), pp. 90–1.

to them a set of obligations. In Portugal it is only for the modern period, in particular in legislation of the 1570s, that a direct and unequivocal relationship appears in the inscription of the 'Livros de Moradias' of the royal court and the automatic attribution of the legal status of the nobility. This inscription was at the time transmissible through heredity, according to personal and family criteria. It is this later reality which came to be the subject of comment and historical explanation by the principal writers of treatises of the seventeenth century when writing on the nobility: these included António de Vilas Boas and Sampaio, who recalled the origin of this system, specifically during the reign of Afonso V while, however, ignoring the entire medieval past of the *moradores*.[153]

The medieval *morador* included in any one of the distinct categories I have analysed was fundamentally characterised by his presence at court. This was a presence to which, as we have seen, there corresponded the granting of diverse sums of money, although we know little about the effectiveness or regularity of its payment. It could be said that, in a general manner, recourse to the mechanism of the 'tenças' in the fifteenth century represented a force for making payments more secure, although the growing intricacy of the 'obrigações' and 'assentamentos' established throughout the fifteenth century in the diverse fiscal organisms implied, it would seem, that this could not always improve matters for everyone. Hypothetically its effectiveness would be the greater the less was the sum of the *moradia*, and the majority were small amounts, although in general an absence of indications relating to lack of payment would seem to indicate that the *moradias* were paid sufficiently regularly. This regularity would have been accentuated by the practice of contracting out this important responsibility of the royal finances from the middle of the century to Jewish and foreign financiers. The first known contract appears in the period 1446–54 and is at once followed by others, and included members of the powerful Jewish Abravanel and Latão families, with participation of the Genoese Lomellinis and João Dias Beleágua.[154]

There is no lack of indications however that, regarding also the regime of granting of *moradias*, the growth of the court circle in the mid-fifteenth century was expressed by some changes. We know that Afonso V granted some 'tenças' of a new type during the 1450s and 1460s, described by the Cortes as 'por quamto hy ha muitos a que as Moradias que auiam amdamdo na corte sam dadas e postas em Temça em ssua casa, alguus parte delas e allgus todas, e asy

153 The publication of the oldest known Portuguese rolls of 'moradores' both for John I and Afonso V was due only to academics of the eighteenth century such as José Soares da Silva (in 1734) and António Caetano de Sousa (1739–48). See on the importance of sixteenth-century legislation, Sérgio Cunha Soares, 'Nobreza e arquétipo fidalgo. A propósito de um livro de matrículas de filhamentos (1641–1724)', *Revista de História das Ideias*, 19 (1997), pp. 433–5.

154 Tavares, *Os Judeus em Portugal no século XV*, vol. I, pp. 283, 327–8 and 347.

na realidade nam leixão de ser moradores posto que na corte nam amdem'.[155] With this type of measure, which the monarch recognised as being new and even as faulty because of the financial inconvenience, the traditional tie which connected the *morador* to the royal entourage became weakened and his status was transformed into a mere title granted by the monarch, which according to the *procuradores* to the Cortes was granted as though it were any other form of favour. These favours would, however, have remained exceptional, as the king accepted in his reply to the Cortes, so reaffirming the general norm of the validity of the old connection between the *moradia* and physical presence at court.

In the same way, some of the ordinations recorded in the *Livro Vermelho* which can also be dated to the reign of Afonso V reinforce the obligatory nature of this presence, particularly in the case of the *moradores* 'que tem oficio', be this performed in the chapel or in the body of musicians of the hall and officials at arms, or in the *câmara* (for example surgeons and physicians), or further still in the various offices. The norm adopted by many *fidalgos* 'de guamçarem a moradia do mes por servirem os quimze dias' would not have been extended to all these servants, who had to be alongside the monarch 'todo o mees em cheo'.[156] This is confirmation that at the court of this monarch there had already been introduced, in the case of the *fidalgos*, one of the main characteristics of the 'usos de Borgonha', that is service by rotation. It is possible, also, that the Cortes referred to this in the text mentioned in the previous paragraph, when they described the nobles as receiving *moradias* 'em suas casas', without going to court. This method of court service was, as we have seen, clearly described by the fourteenth-century 'Ordenacions' of Aragon, which Duarte appears to have had in his library, but it also seems to be explained in other Portuguese texts, in particular in the report of the journey of the Count of Ourém to the Council of Basel.[157] With the change in the performance of many offices in the court ambit, as I shall show later, the situation of the *morador* tended also to change, since both aspects were interrelated. The intervention of the monarch recorded in this mid-fifteenth-century Ordination was, however, based yet again on the normative meaning of respect through traditional logic of court distinctions and payments, which the royal authority would wish still to be valid during these times of change.

The sole, significant exception to this paid presence of the *moradores* – which was duly regulated – consisted in the 'passagem aos lugares d'alem', which many *escudeiros* and *cavaleiros* of the royal entourage undertook throughout the fifteenth century with royal permission. The departure to Ceuta in fact was, during the first half of the century, a mode of service which the monarch expressly contemplated, and he considered it analogous to so many other missions

155 ANTT, Cortes, M 2, 14, f. 67v (Cortes of 1472–73).
156 *Livro Vermelho*, pp. 484–5. 157 *Provas*, vol. V, part II, p. 276.

of longer or shorter durations which the various members of the entourage performed outside the court organism, to which they would later return. During the reign of Duarte, participation of the *moradores* of the court in military expeditions to Morocco in the defence of Ceuta, in obedience to the orders of the monarch, led to an initial regulation of stipends to be paid, according to which the courtiers received pay and supplies for themselves and those who accompanied them, as well as horses and arms. During the time they were there, however, they did not receive a *moradia*, a decision which was constantly debated in council, against the express intentions of the monarch.[158]

During the reign of Afonso we find that, on the contrary, *moradias* to these *moradores* of the king were paid 'asy como se as servisem em sua corte' during their absence in Morocco, as was a part of food in the form of wheat.[159] The practical application of these norms can be confirmed through analysis of some *cartas de quitação*, particularly in a charter granted to the *tesoureiro-mor* on matters of Ceuta relating to the years 1453 and 1454, which shows that some thirty *escudeiro*s and *cavaleiro*s of the royal household received varying sums in wheat, wine and money in 'mantimento' relating to periods spent in Ceuta of between one and four months.[160] In general, these *moradores* were, as *escudeiro*s and *cavaleiro*s, accompanied by two or three men at arms and archers, or in the case of several 'moços de câmara', by just one individual who would assist them. The small nucleus of fighters made up of the courtier and his men could increase in size in the case of *fidalgos* who held important posts, such as the *mordomo-mor* Álvaro de Sousa or the *camareiro-mor* Álvaro de Castro, forming true 'companies' made up of dozens of *escudeiro*s, archers and footmen, as well as numerous horses. Their 'feitos' and prowess were related in detail by Zurara, the same royal chronicler who inserted in a 'fala' of John I the declaration as to the usefulness of this experience for the Portuguese courtier: 'quamdo me alguus pedem liçença pera hir fazerem armas a França ou a Ingraterra, he neçessario que os correja e lhe faça merçee pera sua viagem, com menos da quall dispesa os eu posso correger e os enviar a esta cidade [Ceuta]'.[161] Since, as I have already stated, the members of the royal entourage were an important part of the royal army and since the defence of Ceuta assumed all the characteristics of a 'frontier' war, it was important for

[158] *Livro dos Conselhos*, pp. 169–70. It is confirmed that this appointment served as a basis for the description by Rui de Pina: *CR Duarte*, pp. 521–2.

[159] *Livro Vermelho*, p. 460. On the other hand, the royal servants charged with diplomatic missions or 'embaixadas' were not to receive *moradias* while these missions lasted: *ibid.*, p. 469.

[160] *DCH*, vol. II, pp. 669–709. Besides this document, see also the references to the years 1450 and 1451: *DCH*, vol. II, pp. 10–11, 67–8, 232–3, 346, 362 and 363.

[161] Gomes Eanes de Zurara, *Crónica da Tomada de Ceuta*, ed. F. M. Esteves Peireira (Lisbon: Academia das Ciências, 1915), pp. 258–9 and *Crónica do Conde D. Pedro de Meneses*, ed. José Adriano Freitas de Carvalho (Oporto, 1988), pp. 228–9. This presence of the 'moradores' had already been noted by Robert Ricard, *Les Portugais au Maroc de 1495 à 1521* (Rabat, 1937).

the monarch to authorise and even to promote the 'Moroccan experience' of the *moradores* of the court.

FUNCTIONARIES AND COURTIERS

Evocation of the medieval and modern court has on many occasions been made simply by the construction of a dichotomy between two different social types. On the one hand would be the bureaucrats, men who were in the main of modest origins and who were indispensable to the function of the embryo of the state 'machinery' which was to develop in the interstices of this old scene which was always ready to crumble and give way to the formidable architecture of the 'modern state'. On the other hand would be the courtier, in the main a nobleman, who was relegated to a merely decorative and parasitic function, and whose existence would personify the 'dissipation' and the 'sumptuous' character of those societies according to the modern criteria of economic and organisational rationality.[162]

Much of what has been stated since the nineteenth century on the basis of this dichotomy arises from arguments which in truth go back to the theory of the Renaissance of the court in its normative and even apologetic decline, which provide a stereotyped image that does not depart from the analysis of specific historical realities. In particular the idea of the uselessness of the noble courtier clearly assumes the critical and satirical sense of that literature. One of the most influential texts in the fifteenth-century debate on the 'vices' of court life was *De Curialium Miseriis* by Aeneas Silvius Piccolomini, but in reality the arguments found in it are deeply rooted in European culture, since some of its themes are already to be found in the anti-court and anti-clerical literature of the twelfth century produced at the Plantagenet court.[163] This is the case of the criticism of the cupidity and impiety of the man of the court, which were themes which the Renaissance came to add to, particularly the reflection on the corrupting capacity of power and the theme of the courtier as 'parasite'.[164]

[162] Cesare Mozzarelli and Giuseppe Olmi (eds.), *La corte nella cultura e nella storiografia: immagini e posizioni tra Otto e Novecento* (Rome: Bulzoni, 1983), pp. 9–33.

[163] Egbert Türk, *Nugae Curialium: le règne d'Henri II Plantagenêt et l'éthique politique* (Geneva: Droz, 1977); C. Stephen Jaeger, *The Origins of Courtliness: Civilizing Trends and the Formation of Courtly Ideals, 939–1210* (Philadelphia: University of Pennsylvania Press, 1985), pp. 176–94; Thomas Szabó, 'Der mittelalterliche Hof zwischen Kritik und Idealisierung', in J. Fleckenstein (ed.), *Curialitas: Studien zu Grundfragen der höfischen-rittelichen Kultur* (Göttingen: Vandenhoeck and Ruprecht, 1990), pp. 350–91.

[164] Specifically on Piccolomini and the anti-court texts of the Renaissance, the essay by Eugenio Garin remains valid, *La cultura filosofica del Rinascimento Italiano* (Florence: Sansoni, 1979), pp. 38–59. On the criticism of Machiavelli: Aldo Scaglione, *Knights at Court: Courtliness, Chivalry and Courtesy from Ottonian Germany to the Italian Renaissance* (Berkeley: University of California Press, 1991), pp. 242–7.

Throughout my progress on this book, I have advanced some elements towards a questioning of this method of examination and towards a critical vision of these stereotypes, attempting to analyse the specific realities of the fourteenth and fifteenth centuries, both from the point of view of organisational practices of the court and through the reconstruction of biographies of the holders of various posts. Certainly, the descriptions and diverse rulings of this period, including of course the fragmentary Portuguese sources, allow the detection of a process of effective bureaucratisation of many groups of duties associated with offices whose field of action was centred on the royal entourage. Also, on the other hand, these sources allow one to confirm that the 'domestic' and patriarchal aspect was present in the relationship with the king, even for offices of the earliest specialisation. Particularly in the case of the fifteenth-century court, I felt I detected a tendency towards the ennoblement of many bureaucrats and men of letters, which was a movement concomitant with their growing laicisation, leading to some questions pertinent to that dichotomy. On the other hand, as I have shown, one cannot underestimate the malleability and initiative of the court nobility, even the most traditional – that is, that nobility whose family roots can be found at the Portuguese court of the end of the thirteenth century – as to the organisational changes of the court itself and the rise of new duties and offices.

It is important, therefore, to return to my initial reflections on the functional evolution of the Portuguese court and the vast complexity of the various strata of its organisation, which comprised many posts which were retained from the thirteenth century, alongside others which were successively introduced. Independent of their sphere of activity, of their temporary or permanent character, of their spatial ambit or power – or lack of power – of jurisdiction, all were known as 'offices', for according to the theory of the *Partidas*, 'oficio tanto quiere dezir, como seruizio señalado', or simply a service which corresponded to a predetermined sphere of activity.[165] We thus see at the court of the end of the Middle Ages the persistence of an archaic group of 'offices' represented by the panoply of various posts which were formed according to the tripartite hall/chamber/chapel. In the stratum which is traditionally associated with the 'household' of the king and queen, there existed at least from the middle of the fourteenth century, if not before, a hierarchy of 'oficios maiores' and 'oficios baixos', corresponding to a differentiation of the respective prerogatives and, probably, of their payment. It is in relation to these duties, particularly in their hierarchically superior sphere, that there are found more clearly two phenomena

[165] The medieval concept of 'office' cannot be simply considered as equivalent to the concept of Weber's influence to which the majority of modern authors refer. For a discussion on this problem: J. M. García Marín, *El oficio público en Castilla durante la baja edad media* (Seville: Universidad de Sevilla, 1974), p. 27. I place the word in inverted commas when referring to the medieval concept.

characteristic of the period studied here: the tendency towards their becoming a patrimony (with the concomitant overvaluation of the *dignitas* in relation to the *officium*) and the twofold situation of their holders (simultaneously 'moradores' and 'oficiais').

Another diverse group is that of the 'offices' whose performance implies a characteristic specialisation, whether or not they had duties of a jurisdictional type acting as delegates of the monarch – these are the *vedores*, the higher officers of justice or the *chancelaria* and the *fazenda*. The medieval doctrine on the 'oficios' produced the embryo of some bases for the transformation of the method of examining the relationship between the king and this new type of servants, emphasising the impersonal aspects and the immobility of the holders in relation to their duties, 'conceived as abstract centres of competence which were entirely independent of personal characteristics and their holders'.[166] The development of the diverse institutional organisms whose central nuclei were to be found in the royal court by the multiplication of the number of agents involved in them tended also towards the creation of a restricted area of higher offices in a dominant hierarchical position. These were possibly in contact with the monarch and his close collaborators, and performed the necessary mediation between distinct organisational levels (cf. the *contador-mor* and the *chanceler-mor*). Also in this case the situation we find for the fifteenth century tends in a certain way to remove the monarch from the direct control of these duties of a more specialised type, through the changes occurring in the sphere of the official/office relationship through dissociation of the title of these offices and their performance. Although the presence of these officials in the royal entourage is certainly proven, they do not always appear as 'moradores' of the king, and were paid either directly or indirectly in other ways.

A third case is that of the officials whose effective functions were not those of permanent practice or, in normal times, were reduced to short performances of a ceremonial type and the maintenance of some unimportant mechanisms which allowed their virtual activity. This occurred in a fairly specific manner with the duties of the army, usually granted to courtiers of the highest status and social standing. Here also an analysis of the list of the successive *condestáveis* and *almirantes*, *capitães* and *marechals* from the reign of Fernando, as was already being predicted in an analysis of the *alferes* of the fourteenth century, demonstrates an accentuated aristocratisation in the recruitment of these offices, whose highest point at the middle of the fifteenth century was worthy of close relatives of the kings. It could be said that, during the greater part of the time, in this case the position of member of court exceeded and was superior to that of the actual 'official'.

[166] García Marín, *El oficio público*, pp. 29–30; in a general perspective see Otto Gierke, *Political Theories of the Middle Ages* (Cambridge: Cambridge University Press, 1987), pp. 99 and 344.

In relation to many of these duties whose normal sphere of activity was centred at the court of the kings, what should be stated is their honorary nature for the period at the end of the Middle Ages, contrasting it with a hypothetical effect of these duties during the period prior to the middle of the fourteenth century. So that we might consider a given post as merely honorary, we must verify a certain number of actual changes, stating for example the total removal of the specific functions to which the term makes reference corresponding in general to an absence of payment. It is in this sense that, at the Byzantine court, certain posts of the Low Empire which corresponded merely to a title with ceremonial importance were considered as honorary[167] or that, during the final period of the Middle Ages, some imperial titles such as that of count palatine were granted in profusion to many notable men of different kingdoms.[168] Some court posts whose existence implies a functional duplication can be seen *à la limite* as honorary, and this was the case of the Portuguese *alferes*. That is, associated to a single group of duties are two or more individuals, one of whom merely had the right to the title while the concrete functions were performed by another, whose position was at times given a different title. For the second of these there was usually a respective payment, and this was a process of duplication common, for example, at the papal court.

In my opinion, this type of phenomenon does not clearly occur at the Portuguese court of the fourteenth and up to the mid-fifteenth centuries, owing perhaps to the incipient character of the regime of the posts. Nor can the situation in this aspect be compared with that of the earlier periods on which, besides, little can be known as to the actual performance of the duties, except as to their titular nature. Many offices which were to arise in the thirteenth century appear to suggest the already mentioned duplication of functions, but I do not find that any of the traditional duties, with the exception of *alferes*, was entirely depleted of its characteristics, so corresponding to a mere title and lacking any form of remuneration, as was the case in the examples quoted for other contexts. What does appear to have occurred with relative certainty from the fourteenth century at the court of the Portuguese kings was a process of a growing *distancing* or *dissociation* among the group of concrete duties falling to offices and holders of those offices, which process did not always culminate in an honorary title or which was restricted to a mere categorisation of prestigious roles.

One of the aspects attached to this process of transformation is that the offices became patrimonial, a process to which I have already referred, especially for

[167] On the Byzantine distinction between the officials *agentes*, *vacantes* and *honorarii*: Giorgio Ravegnani, *La Corte de Giustiniano* (Rome: Jouvence, 1989), pp. 43–5.

[168] On the honorary use of titles of the imperial court: Robert Folz, 'Le régime monocratique en Allemagne (XIe–XVe siècles)', in *La Monocratie*, Recueils de la Société Jean Bodin 21 (Brussels: Université Libre, 1969), vol. II, pp. 306–7.

some 'higher' duties at the Portuguese court. Still in the middle of the fourteenth century it cannot be stated for certain that the majority of the higher offices of the *câmara* and the hall (in particular that of *camareiro*, *reposteiro*, *guarda* or *copeiro*) were by this time for life, as had been the case with the *alferes* since the previous century. Mentions of the holders of such offices are too few to allow for definitive conclusions, although in some cases several servants are known of for the same reign.[169] The panorama of references only becomes a little more enlightening for the reign of Fernando, but in this situation the conflicting nature of court society to which I have referred on several occasions led to some changes in the title of posts, as for example that of the *guarda-mor*, the *copeiro* and the *escanção* of this monarch. Hereditary transmission of corresponding duties in the French and German cases was made from a very early period, and was assured in Castile and in many duties of the English court in particular during the fourteenth century.

In relation to the important office of *mordomo-mor* (as also to the queen's *mordomo*) there seems to have been some instability throughout the fourteenth century. Of the several individuals on whom certain information is available who would have performed this function alongside the kings Afonso IV, Pedro and Fernando, there only appears the figure of the magnate João Afonso Telo III as a possible lifelong holder of the post. It is not even certain whether Telo served in the post in two successive reigns until his death. Therefore only the lifelong character of the majority of offices connected to the household and the royal guard at the Portuguese court in the fifteenth century can be proved, although it is highly probable during the earlier period. This uncertainty is no less symptomatic of a fairly fluid state of the regime or the rules of granting of offices, in contrast to what is known of other contemporary European courts, including that of Castile. The significance of this instability has served as an argument both for the defenders of a strong authority, or of personal charisma, of certain Portuguese monarchs (such as Pedro), and for the diagnostic of progressive weakening of the political autonomy of other monarchs (such as Fernando).

A characteristic of the fifteenth-century court was the progressive connection of court duties to a determined family line. In a more irregular manner, this connection is found regarding the *camareiro-mor* (successively granted to the

[169] Leontina Ventura considers for the twelfth and thirteenth centuries the effectiveness of a formation of patrimony of duties in the Portuguese case, 'forming of patrimony which, on allowing a right of succession in the exercise of power, demonstrated the genealogical organisation of family ties': 'Portugal em definição de fronteiras', pp. 208–9. This somewhat circular reasoning seems to be contradicted for court duties, however, by earlier investigation by the author herself, who several times refers to the non-existence of hereditary transmission, for example of the post of *alferes* ('A nobreza de corte', vol. I, p. 86), which duty only becomes lifelong with Afonso III (*ibid.*, p. 88), and she herself establishes that the duty of *mordomo* to the Portuguese kings was occupied until 1248 by seven different families (*ibid.*, p. 82).

Sá, Noronha and Castro families); in the reign of John, João Rodrigues de Sá served from 1385 to 1396, and from 1425 to 1429 it was his son Fernão de Sá. However, with Duarte's succession to the throne, the post reverted to Fernando de Noronha, who had been his *camareiro* when Duarte was infante. After the departure of the Noronhas, marked by the regency of the Duke of Coimbra, Álvaro de Castro IV served in this post and was then replaced *c.* 1458 by Lopo de Albuquerque, who served until the 1470s. This connection was, however, clearer for the post of *mordomo-mor*, which fell to the Sousas, who were always ready to remind one of the old family glory and tradition related to palace duties. Although the *condestável* Nuno Álvares Pereira had also taken on this office, the *mordomo* of the Infante Duarte, Diogo Lopes de Sousa, succeeded him, and he in turn was succeeded by his son Álvaro de Sousa (1450–71), followed by Diogo Lopes de Sousa II in the 1470s.

However, transmission through the same family is above all clearly assumed regarding the offices of *almirante* (the Pessanhas, and then passing to a branch of the Melos), of *marechal* (the Coutinhos) and of *capitão-mor* (the Almadas), the *guarda-mor* (the Melos) and the *copeiro-mor* (another branch of the Melos); all these are well enough known as being hereditarily transmitted and have already been analysed in detail. I have already mentioned the tendency towards granting certain positions of the household and *fazenda* of the monarchs of Aviz to members of the same families, such as the Almeidas, the Borges and the Távoras in the sphere of the *guarda-roupa* and the *repostaria*; the Castelo Branco family in the service of the *montaria*; the Monterroios in the *tesouro*, etc. However, one cannot strictly speak of hereditary transmission for all these, even for the reign of Afonso V during its early stages. The game of informal reproduction of court society perhaps favoured, for the *criação* and apprentices at the palace, the circulation of duties within the same families, a phenomenon which sixteenth- and seventeenth-century genealogical literature would perhaps have transformed into a family prerogative.

An analysis of the rare data we have on their performance suggests that the importance of the 'higher offices' during the fifteenth century stemmed, fundamentally, from the dignity associated with them, but this dignity could not easily subsist without concrete duties of the office. The example of the *copeiro-mor* demonstrates that to him fell the profits related to the exercise of traditional functions and that he held authority over the servants of the respective department (*copeiros* and men of the *copa*), although in the reign of Afonso V it came to be assumed that the holder of the 'higher office' could place another man of his choice 'que por ele sirva continuadamente', while remaining responsible for all under his authority.[170] Likewise, the organisation and authority over the respective servants (*camareiros* and *moços*) fell

[170] See the description of the characteristics of this post in two charters of appointment dated 1450 and 1471: ANTT, *Ch. D. Afonso V*, 34, f. 135; ANTT, *LN*, Extras, ff. 38v–39.

to the *camareiro-mor*, as did the appointment to the *guarda-roupa*, according to a sketch of a ruling contained in the Afonsine Ordinations.[171] The observation could be extended for the remaining fifteenth-century 'offices' of the 'household', which were at the vertex of more or less complex organisations regarding which, from at least a normative point of view, they retained broad autonomy of activity and whose servants were hierarchically connected to the 'higher officials' to whom they swore allegiance. In emphasising this pre-eminence, Afonso V granted successive 'tenças graciosas' of varying sums to the *mordomo-mor*, the *reposteiro-mor*, the *cevadeiro-mor*, the *almotacé-mor* and the *guarda-roupa-mor*, in an attempt to associate other income with these duties besides those of 'foros, próis e costumes' which were occasionally mentioned in royal charters and, naturally, of the *moradia* from which their holders profited.[172]

The process of actual duties of an office being performed by a third party, or at least its day-to-day characteristics, is not only found regarding the 'high offices' of the *câmara* and the hall, for there are also signs that there was recourse to the mechanism of 'logoteentes' or substitutes at lower levels of the palace organisation and in many duties of the bureaucratic and financial spheres. It was said at the time that the official 'placed another' in his place, while he remained the holder of the title of the office and received, by all indications, the respective remuneration. This mechanism was known and much practised at the Portuguese court from the beginning of the fifteenth century, and became more and more used throughout the century; thus, occasional information relating to the *câmara* of John I and Duarte shows that an *escrivão da câmara* could 'have written' the charters by someone else, or that the *escrivão dos maravedis* had his own deputy to write the registers for which he was responsible. Likewise, from a *quitação* granted to the *tesoureiro-mor* we find that the *despenseiro* of the 1420s and 1430s had a man who 'served in his place', which also occurred with the *escrivão do tesouro*.[173] In the *repostaria* of Duarte and that of Afonso V, almost no *reposteiro-mor* held the position without its 'being served' by a man whom he trusted, whose existence is shown in successive *cartas de quitação*.[174] In the case of the bureaucratic and justiciary 'offices', the institution of *in loco tenens* was highly common, as Carvalho Homem showed with regard to the *chanceleres-mores* of the fifteenth century,[175] to which can be added very many further examples, in particular that of the *corregedor* of the court, João Mendes

171 *OA*, vol. I, pp. 337–40.

172 Jorge Faro (ed.), *Receitas e despesas da fazenda real de 1384 a 1481 (subsídios documentais)* (Lisbon: Instituto Nacional de Estatística, 1965), p. 116.

173 ANTT, *Ch. D. Duarte*, 2, ff. 16–18v (in particular f. 17).

174 ANTT, *LN*, Extras, ff. 38–38v, ff. 40v–41, ff. 45v–46, ff. 91–91v.

175 *Desembargo*, pp. 354 and 299, particularly for the case of D. Fernando da Guerra. On Dr João do Sem, see ANTT, *Ch. D. Duarte*, 2, f. 35v; *CUP*, vol. IV, p. 145 and vol. VII, p. 200.

(whose role as compiler of the Ordenações is well known), or of the *escrivão da chancelaria* during the reign of Afonso V.[176]

In the origins of this mechanism of substitution or sharing of the performance of offices, put into practice through temporary incapacity of the office holder or in order to allow the accumulation of several offices by the same title holder, this was a personal agreement between the official and his deputy, and we find on many occasions that even he is a person close to the court circle. It was clearly of interest to the monarch that the actual servant was a person of ability whom he liked so that, in several passages in the Ordenações compiled in Afonso V's *Livro Vermelho*, mention is made of the necessary agreement of the king that he perform this duty, at least regarding those servants closest to his person. In the *Livro de Recebimentos* of the *chancelaria da câmara* of Afonso V, there is an invaluable manuscript in which we find records of many charters which do not appear in the other documentary series, and several clauses relating to authorisations granted to 'officials' of the household are included where they may be replaced by others for short periods.[177] Thus it is shown that in a period a little later than that studied here, the king granted express authorisation for the holders of offices to have substitutes.

This institution of *in loco tenens* retained its original characteristics, however, and was more or less exceptional and intended to be of limited duration, not changing in any manner the entitlement to the offices. As I have already said, legislation of the thirteenth century foresaw the possibility of the *mordomo*, the *alferes* and the *chanceler* being replaced at times of incapacity or, if they did not do so themselves, that the monarch himself could designate someone to serve in their place. The increasingly frequent recourse to 'logoteentes' and its generalisation in the fifteenth century in the two main groups of offices already mentioned (with the exception of the *vedores*, which I believe is yet another sign of their differing nature) suggests a growing flexibility in the regime of the performance of the various duties. This exercise could be interrupted or performed by the intermediary, although the title holder did not renounce the respective profits or any form of control of the actions of his substitute, and above all he maintained the prestige and privileges of the associated title.

In turn, this flexibility certainly favoured the process of accumulation of offices at the lower hierarchical levels of the court organism during the fifteenth century, and this process is obvious in the retention of numerous offices, *recebedorias*, *tesourarias* and *portarias* of the various organisms, be they temporary or more or less permanent, by 'oficiais menores' of the household or the *fazenda* and members of the royal chapel. We thus find several *porteiros*

[176] *MH*, vol. XI, p. 170 and also ANTT, *Ch. D. Afonso V*, 1, f. 129v. On the actions of the *escrivão na chancelaria*: ANTT, Cortes, M 2, 14, ff. 9v–10.

[177] *O Livro de Recebimentos de 1470 da Chancelaria da Câmara*, ed. Damião Peres (Lisbon: Academia Portuguesa da História, 1974), pp. 52, 57, 80, 85 *et passim*.

da câmara of John I, for example, holding offices in the *casa dos contos* or connected to the works of the king;[178] or the musician of the hall who was, simultaneously, performer of the office of *reposteiro*;[179] in the decades from the 1440s several choristers of the chapel were holders of offices of the kitchen and the stable,[180] such as Afonso's *cevadeiro-mor* who was simultaneously one of the *camareiros* of the monarch,[181] etc. All these indications converge towards the establishment of one fact, which seems to me of greatest importance: the constitution during the final moments of the Middle Ages of a particular social medium comprising a variety of individuals who shared among themselves entitlement to the distinct 'offices' within the court, whether or not able to perform personally the diverse duties associated with these offices.

Recourse to the practices to which I have referred allows the continuity in the court circle of the patrimonial aspect which still marked the system of medieval offices, emphasising the personal character of the relationship between the monarch and the official, which was materialised in the granting of individual favours, in this case in the form of various posts which were also a source of profit. However, other consequences of these practices of substitution must also be mentioned. In fact, the growing dissociation between title and performance tended to create a network of connections between the holders of the offices and those who effectively performed them, while the monarch remained, in part, excluded from these connections which subversively invaded the ambit of court functions. This exclusion did not always occur with the better-known and regulated process of *resignatio in favorem*, which is a known indicator of practices of venality and alienation of offices, since through the faculty of confirming the new holder of the post, the kings themselves attempted to take control of these same practices.[182] In this last case, Federico Chabod has also alerted us to the probable meaning of the interference of the monarchs in the transaction of the posts, not only for financial motives, but also as a form of controlling the clientships grouping round important officials and courtiers.[183] It was at the heart of this atmosphere marked by the relationship of interdependence among

[178] ANTT, *Ch. D. João I*, 5, f. 136v; *Ch. D. Duarte*, 3, f. 50v.

[179] This concerns the bugler Afonso Anes, who served as *reposteiro* in 1405; *MH*, vol. I, p. 287.

[180] F. M. Sousa Viterbo, *Subsídios para a história da música em Portugal* (Coimbra: Imprensa da Universidade, 1932), pp. 49, 215–16 and 314–15.

[181] ANTT, *LN*, Extras, ff. 12–12v and 19–20.

[182] The origins of this practice of *resignatio* appear in Portugal in the fifteenth century, as shown by Judite Gonçalves de Freitas, *A burocracia do 'Eloquente' (1433–1438): os textos, as normas, as gentes* (Cascais: Patrimonia, 1996).

[183] Federico Chabod, 'Esiste uno stato del Rinascimento?', in *Scritti sul Rinascimento* (Turin: Einaudi, 1967), pp. 593–623; Roland Mousnier, *La Vénalité des offices sous Henri IV et Louis XIII* (Paris: PUF, 1971). For the case of Castile: Francisco Tomás y Valiente, 'Origen bajomedieval de la patrimonalización y la enajenación de oficios públicos en Castilla', in *Actas del I Symposium de Historia de la Administración* (Madrid: Instituto de Estudio Administrativos, 1970), pp. 123–59.

officials that not only possible clientships were forged, but also true professional and serving traditions, to which higher office holders appear not to have been entirely foreign, contrary to what defenders of their exclusively 'honorary' nature appear to admit to.

Let us look, with the assistance of the results of some studies in the catalogue of royal charters, at how this sharing of actual functions was processed in the tribunals of the court and in the *chancelaria* during the first two decades of the reign of Afonso V.[184] In my opinion this shows clearly the consistency of the circle to which I refer, in this case essentially comprising men of letters. Between 1450 and 1460 the ecclesiastical magnate D. Fernando da Guerra and the man of letters, the courtier Dr Rui Gomes de Alvarenga, were successively holders of the office of *chanceler-mor* and *regedor* of the *casa da suplicação*.[185] As a dependant of the *chanceler-mor*, we find the new title of *vice-chanceler*, a title introduced in the period of the regency of D. Pedro, and to this post probably fell the actual superintendence of the *chancelaria*, similar to that which occurred in the Pontifical court.[186] In 1443 this office was performed by João Fernandes da Silveira and in the following year by the already mentioned Rui Gomes de Alvarenga, who in 1450 was followed by Dr Pedro Lobato. All three were well-known men of letters of the court. However, we also find that for brief periods which at times lasted for less than three months there were various members of the *casa da suplicação* 'having the duty' of the *chancelaria*: the *ouvidores* Luis Afonso and Duarte Afonso; the *procurador dos feitos do rei*, Dr Álvaro Peres de Guimarães; Dr Lopo Vasques de Serpa; the *corregedor* of the court Álvaro Peres Vicira; Dr Nuno Gonçalves, etc. That is, we always find in the sphere of the exercise of the higher bureaucratic offices the same group of individuals who, as holders of only one post, in practice circulated in a system which brings to mind the contemporary service in rotation in other court environments for various positions of importance in the bureaucratic organisms whose centre was at court. The same is seen in this period regarding some offices in the sphere of justice, such as the *corregedor* of the court. Dr Gonçalo Fernandes and Álvaro Peres Vieira successively held the position, while other members of the *casa da suplicação* such as Dr Lopo Vasques de Serpa and the *ouvidor* João Rodrigues

[184] Research carried out in: ANTT, *Ch. D. Afonso V*, 1, 2, 5, 27 and 34 and in documents published in *MH*. I also return to the works published by A. Braamcamp Freire, 'A Chancelaria de D. Afonso V', *Arquivo Histórico Português*, 2 (1904), 479–87. This general view does not appear to be contradicted by the detailed research in the unpublished work of Armando Carvalho Borlido, 'A Chancelaria Régia e os seus oficiais em 1463', unpublished Masters dissertation (University of Oporto, 1996). I should like to thank the author for allowing me access to his useful prosopographic study.

[185] José Marques, *A arquidioces de Braga no século XV* (Lisbon: INCM, 1988), pp. 48–50; *ALF*, vol. II, pp. 710–11.

[186] Niccolò Del Re, *La Curia Romana: lineamenti storici-giuridici* (Rome: Ed. di Storia e Letteratura, 1970), p. 23. As we have seen, some papal practices relating to the chapel were also adopted following the 1440s.

Malheiro successively 'are charged with organising the tribunal' according to royal charters.

The importance of the effectiveness of payment to this body of servants is mentioned at several moments as the express preoccupation of the fifteenth-century monarchs. Thus in the 'Regimento' of 1438 which I have already mentioned there is the recommendation 'ao que teuer carrego da justiça . . . A ele sera entregado certas rrendas, pera as moradias dos desenbargadores e corregedor e meirinho da corte; e nom dos de fora, porque som aseentadas por ho aseentamento, e deuem dauer suas pagas nas comarquas honde husarem de seus ofiçios.' From a *carta de quitação* of 1470 we know that in the period 1453–58, similar to that found for the *moradias*, the payment 'dos mantimentos e solairo' to the *casa da suplicação* had been contracted out.[187] The higher co-ordination of this complex structure which could almost be termed collegiate fell to such men as D. Fernando da Guerra and Dr Alvarenga, both powerful men whose activity in their multiple facets (political, intellectual and diplomatic) has already been mentioned. Everything suggests that their role at court as holders of offices of the king was not limited to a corresponding demand for titular honours but that they combined their experience and knowledge in order to intervene in the establishment of this sharing of positions and in how the respective departments were organised.

FORMS OF INTERDEPENDENCE

The various angles of analysis which I have successively adopted for the Portuguese royal court allow us to evaluate up to what point the medieval court should be observed not as a simple aggregate of individuals corresponding to a delimitation of a spatial or geographical type, but as a result of a specific arrangement and of its own dynamic of social relationships. These multiple perspectives reveal the mutually articulated action of agents who structure and form this field of relationships, with the movements of some conditioning those of others. The social dynamic of the court creates given roles which are only defined through these movements, sustains specific social positions and aggregates individuals and groups in a characteristic way. Office and salary, benefice and payment, favour and distinction – the different realities designated by this set of fundamental concepts all appear to be included in the actual interdependencies of court society. The heterogeneity and pluralism of these relationships cannot be easily reduced to one sole explanatory paradigm.

The complexity of the forms of interaction at the heart of the old courts cannot be seen merely in the light of exchange and interchange between individuals, giving a dominant or exclusive role to the theory of patronage and of client

[187] *MH*, vol. VI, p. 266. ANTT, *LN*, Extras, ff. 96v–98.

relationships as an explanatory paradigm of court society. Several historians, particularly from the 1970s, have suggested an analysis of the behaviour of the courtier particularly in the light of this theory, although some reservations can be formed as to its pertinence, not only regarding the empirical analysis attempted above relative, for example, to the forms of dyadic relationship with the king or to the methods of payment of the courtiers, but also with regard to the values and doctrinal thought of the age, which cannot simply be ignored or considered as 'smoke screens' intended to conceal the true nature of social relations as though the values were not an integral part of the activity of the protagonists.[188]

As the comparative research of the sociologist Eisenstadt and his collaborators shows, relationships of patronage and clientship were important and abundant in past societies.[189] To prove their existence at the court studied here, we can point to the example I have already mentioned of the ecclesiastics and many court officials. In the first of these, we saw that the clerics were interrelated in a variety of ways with, for example, ties with the king being prominent and constituting a 'vertical' type of pattern which gave rise to the institutionalisation of the actual sphere of activity of the chaplains – and it should be remembered that these men served the person of the monarch and for such they obtained specific privileges connected to this function – while, on the other hand, there remained a 'horizontal' type of relationship which connected the members of the chapel to one another and the 'moços' to the chaplains, leading to the formation of gifted groups and to a certain common dynamic within the court. Client relationships, which were essential to the progress of ecclesiastical careers dependent upon the papal court and possibly to the mechanisms of recruitment of the royal chapels, became combined with this network of interdependence and were clearly distinguished by their informal, non-institutionalised character, although this was neither strongly concealed nor illicit. That the king acted as a patron watching over the progress of 'his' clerics and chaplains in their ecclesiastical career or that these men maintained client relationships among themselves is beyond doubt, but it cannot be considered that the theory

188 Recently Jeroen Duindam suggested once again 'patronage' as a 'typical' form of power in the *ancien régime*, a paradigm which could be a clear alternative to the sociological theory of Norbert Elias: *Myths of Power*, pp. 78–80. A general vision of the present state of this discussion can also be found in Ronald Asch, 'Introduction', in Asch and Birke (eds.), *Princes, Patronage and the Nobility*, pp. 16–19. Among specialists of the modern period, I should emphasise the importance of the works of Sharon Kettering, Orest Ranum and Arlette Jouanna for the attention they give to the necessary confrontation of the languages and concepts of the period and modern sociological theory.

189 Schmuel N. Eisenstadt and L. Roniger (eds.), *Patrons, Clients and Friends: Interpersonal Relations and the Structure of Trust in Society* (Cambridge: Cambridge University Press, 1984); Antoni Maczak (ed.), *Klientelsystem im Europa der frühen Neuzeit* (Munich: Oldenbourg, 1988) (see in particular the contribution of Anthony Molho in which he reminds us 'the institution of patronage is ubiquitous', pp. 23–42).

of patronage strictly explains the actual grouping of clerics at court or their relationship with the monarch.

Similarly we see that the fifteenth-century monarchs had in mind the development of client relationships among the 'officials' of the court, particularly regarding the process of dissociation of a title and its performance which many offices of the bureaucratic and domestic spheres underwent at the end of the Middle Ages and also regarding the underlying generalisation of the practice of offices held 'being performed' by others. The opportunities of protection and exchange of favours thus became multiplied at court to the extent that the offices themselves were seen as important sources of material gain and the process of bureaucratisation increased their number. In the words of an historian of the modern age, however, 'it was the nature of court brokerage to limit access to the source of the distribution of offices and dignities. The broker then used these opportunities to strengthen his position at court itself and, indirectly, his influence in the country.'[190] Thus it was this process of exclusion of prestige, of material resources and of forms of authority associated with the royal offices in relation to a growing number of individuals having the required abilities that naturally began to favour the multiplication of client relationships in court circles.

Although for the fourteenth and fifteenth centuries we have no access to the greater number of private sources which proliferate for the sixteenth and seventeenth centuries (particularly correspondence of courtiers and politicians) allowing for the study of these modes of exclusion and clientele, some indications have been suggested above which allow for the detection of the existence of similar forms of interchange at the Portuguese court. In these, the client relationship was characteristically instrumental and purely informal, and the patron appears as an intermediary regarding the client's objective. At the court analysed here it could be said that these client networks of the 'patron-brokerage'[191] type, inasmuch as they are available to us to prove through a careful research of sources, remained dispersed, being neither interrelated nor related to the normative court system, and led to short, relatively simple chains of transaction. The client relationship is above all perceptible in this particularistic mode in which emphasis is placed on the short term leading to limited, temporary cycles, and, as Norbert Elias emphasised, one cannot conceive in what way it could, on its own, lead to lasting, relatively solid complexes such as the court configuration in which generations of men and women succeeded each other, so reproducing the same positions and constructing characteristic balances of power and the

[190] Antoni Maczak, 'From aristocratic household to princely court. Restructuring patronage in the sixteenth and seventeenth centuries', in Asch and Birke (eds.), *Princes, Patronage and the Nobility*, pp. 320–1.

[191] For a definition of 'patron brokerage' see Eisenstadt and Roniger, *Patrons, Clients and Friends*, p. 244.

same pattern of relationship. Although the concentration at the royal court of routes of access to offices and to profits visibly performs a role in the multiplication of these client relationships, this does not mean that all forms of court interdependency can be characterised merely as modes of patronage.[192]

The actual theory of social exchange and interchange certainly contributes to a better understanding of late-medieval court society, allowing an evaluation in a more abstract manner of the relationship between the monarch and the members of the court, with the analyses attempted earlier in this chapter in mind. From a dyadic point of view this relationship is certainly characterised by the instability and uncertainty which sources grant to the royal favour and by its profoundly asymmetric nature. However, the king does not appear, except marginally, to be connected to the courtier by the characteristic form of reciprocity existing in client relationships, nor can he be attributed merely with a function of mediation similar to that to which I have just referred. Thus, as Polanyi, Barth and Sahlins have suggested, it is necessary to distinguish the coexistence of various types of exchange and interaction in the medieval court.[193] Also to be emphasised, though, are two facts to be observed in the court configuration: in the first place, that exchange of a symmetric type could not be applied, according to values of the age, to the relationship with the monarch; and second, that some measure of centrality and unidirection appears necessary to the formation of networks of court interchange, which were not usually of an indiscriminate type or of generalised exchange.

Coherence of the dominant relationships constructed in the court environment does not appear to derive from the generalisation of reciprocity of a patron–client type but, according to the theorisation of the age, it was the product of a common submission to the seat of all distinction and benefice which resided in the monarch. By following the suggestions of Polanyi and Barth, we can conceive a theoretical model in which at least three ideal types of situation

192 I thus distance myself from the suggestion by McFarlane and English historians of 'bastard feudalism' when they refer to the existence of a 'royal patronage' over the nobility, but in which the concept of 'patronage' does not have a complete definition from the point of view of sociological theory, and only appears as a relationship of generic protection (according to the definition of this word contained for example in the *Oxford English Dictionary*). Neither the feudal contract as traditionally considered nor the new methods of written contract as 'indenture' of the Low Middle Ages is explained historically through a simple classification as 'types of patronage' or even of 'patron–client relations': Coss, 'Bastard feudalism revised', in particular pp. 36–7 *et passim*; J. Russell Major, 'Vertical ties through time', *French Historical Studies*, 17 (1992), 63–71. Some studies on England of the modern period, in turn, consider the existence of an interrelated 'crown, patron and client' triad, also using the concept of 'court patronage' in order to characterise the forms of court interaction: Linda L. Peck, *Court Patronage and Corruption in Early Stuart England* (London: Unwin, 1990).

193 Karl Polanyi, *The Great Transformation* (New York: Rinehart, 1944); Marshall Sahlins, 'On the sociology of primitive exchange', in *Stone Age Economics* (London: Routledge, 1972), pp. 185–275; Frederic Barth, *Models of Social Organisation* (London: Royal Anthropological Institute, 1971); and, further, Alvin Gouldner, 'The norm of reciprocity: a preliminary statement', *American Sociological Review*, 25 (1960), 161–78.

can be distinguished – one in which 'incorporation' exists, that is gain for all those involved; a second of the 'interchange' type, where sequences of interaction are governed in a systematic form by reciprocity (becoming in some way predictable);[194] and finally a type in which a constant loss of a focal point and intermittent gain of all the remaining parts exists. One could therefore say that the relationships of the courtiers with the king were above all similar to a model of the third, that is redistributive, type. At the medieval court there existed a concentration of resources in the person of the king with a continuous dissemination of resources to all the remainder through this focal point of the system.

Royal grace and favour were always conceived in texts of the age as acting according to a redistributive modality, while the fact that this could not be predicted and its gratuitous nature were emphasised. The temporal figure thus drawn is based on an idea of a continuous and unlimited flux of resources and favours through the person of the king, rather than on a repetition of times marked by the realisation of limited and reciprocal services or, as Simmel states, in a succession of acts in which 'to give and to receive are reciprocally conditioned'.[195] In giving continuously, the monarch did not allow for conditions, and related the recipient to his own person in an individual and also a positional manner in a process of constant reinforcement of ties of interdependence. The stated indifference of the monarch regarding what could be offered to him in exchange for benefices granted is a condition of structural and necessary independence, a central element of the court 'moral economy' which can be seen not only as one of the implicit aspects in the theory of the medieval royal sovereignty, but also as a presupposition amply shared by court society.

This reflection is dictated to a large extent by a confrontation between the data of archival research relative to the Portuguese courtiers and an analysis of the theorisation of the later period of the Middle Ages, be this Portuguese, Iberian or European (although circulating in the Iberian Peninsula and in Portugal). In these writings of moral and political doctrine we find essential concepts and values relating to royalty or to the nobility and to their position and functions in the society of the age, which manifestly appear as involved in the expectations and reasons giving direction to the activity of men and women of the court. In the first case, or through a discussion about royalty, there arises the extraordinary reflection of the Infante Pedro of Portugal in his treatise *Da Virtuosa Benfeitoria*, produced *c.* 1418–25. This book can be considered as a translation,

[194] 'One may call transactions those sequences of interaction which are governed by reciprocity. Each and every case of interaction does not have these characteristics. It is possible to define a relationship of incorporation as an analytical opposition to a transactional relationship – one where a value optimum, probably for a restricted range of values, is sought for the sum of the partners, and not for a single party': Barth, *Models of Social Organisation*, p. 4.

[195] George Simmel, 'Exchange', in *On Individuality and Social Forms: Selected Writings* (Chicago: University of Chicago Press, 1971), pp. 43–69.

with comments, of Seneca, in particular of his work *De Beneficiis*, in which the Portuguese author attempts to make relevant and accessible to his contemporaries the essence of Stoic social doctrine through examples of a theoretical reelaboration, in which concepts of other ancient and medieval authors can be used, so constructing a version of that doctrine which is deeply rooted in his fifteenth-century vision of the world.[196]

The fundamental theme of *Virtuosa Benfeitoria*, as I have argued in another text, is a reflection on the gift, or 'benefice', as a mechanism of cohesion of human groups. Throughout the treatise, in its systematic division of arguments there runs a preoccupation in emphasising that 'benefice' is neither the consequence of service to one lord nor its cause; that is, there is no concept of an obligatory connection between the granting of this benefice and the benevolence or number of services performed or to be performed by the recipient. The vision suggested by the author could be said to be a bipolar, active and passive vision of the benefice, that is, in which this is separately seen first in the perspective of the giver and then in that of the recipient, which perspectives thus complement each other. However, there is no suggestion in the text of a reciprocal conditioning of both the benefactor and the beneficiary.[197] For Pedro, the virtue of 'granting benefice' lies in an act of pure will of the king or the lord and is a liberality which is not related to specific obligations and is certainly not compensation owed for or corresponding to a counter-service: 'Porque o que diz aquesto darey e aquesto rreçeberey, mais faz mercadarya, que benffeyturya', the infante repeats.[198] Similarly, serving well forms a basis for the expectation of the giver, but is not the basis for a right he possesses, nor can it ever be seen as the equivalent of what is received: 'o recebimento da benfeyturia nunca he quite, ainda que se pague'.[199] The constant circulation of the gift, which emphasises its free nature, thus envisages a type of 'homeostasis' of the group through this constant flow of benefits, resulting from the disposition to give, which is at the core of the actual person of the prince. It is this disposition in itself which is virtuous, this inclination which must be as though second nature in the monarchs, a propitious terrain in which service, loyalty, *amicitia* and even harmonious family relationships might flourish, and which constitutes the true subject of the treatise *Virtuosa Benfeitoria*.

[196] See what I have said in Rita Costa Gomes, 'Virtuosa Benfeitoria', in Giulia Lanciani and Giuseppe Tavani (eds.), *Dicionário da literatura medieval Galega e Portuguesa* (Lisbon: Caminho, 1993), pp. 681–3. The important article by Luis de Sousa Rebelo should be added to the bibliography shown: 'A alegoria final do Livro da Virtusoa Benfeitoria', *Biblos*, 69 (1993), 367–79.

[197] My reading of this text diverges on this point from that suggested by Giuseppe Papagno, 'Virtuosa Bemfeitoria', in Mozzarelli (ed.), *'Familia' del Principe e famiglia aristocratica* (Rome: Bulzoni, 1988), vol. I, pp. 181–212.

[198] Infante D. Pedro, *O Livro da Virtuosa Benfeitoria*, p. 642.

[199] *Virtuosa Benfeitoria*, p. 691.

The inspiration of Seneca's doctrine is the basis of the treatise of the Infante Pedro, even in the essentially paradoxical structure of his concept of benefice.[200] According to Brad Inwood's comments on his rereading of *De Beneficiis*, in the original text the philosopher defends a radical dissociation between the materiality and the intentional aspect of the gift and of social exchanges, considering it as the *gaudium*, or the typical Stoic response to the manifestation of virtue as a true objective of the act of giving and receiving. Material exchange would, eventually, be merely a simulacrum of this spiritual reality, with Seneca using his moral doctrine in this way in the reinforcement of social and political ties of the real world, justifying the obstacles to the practice of the gift through reason, and particularly envisaging 'the encouragement to give freely despite the likelihood of ungrateful recipients and the reassurance to recipients that one can be indebted with confidence and dignity'.[201] Thus, according to the Stoic philosophy, is the essential opposition analysed by the anthropologist Peristiany in diverse cultural contexts, among which is that which is 'rational, foreseeable, calculated, and binding', and the unjustified gratuity of 'grace' could be cultivated.[202] What appears to me central in the argument of the Portuguese fifteenth-century treatise is its insistence on the political value of this doctrine based on Seneca for the society of the age and the explicit connection of this concept of 'benefice', understood as free 'grace', to the status of the lords and kings.

Acceptance of the Stoic language, which is merely one of the languages used by late-medieval Hispanic and Portuguese political theory, came to reinforce the tradition of a royalty which took a large part of its authority from the scrupulous performance of duty, and what was right and just, as suggested by Isidore of Seville in the famous texts of the *Etimologies* and the *Sentences*, rather than from ties of blood or belonging to a race.[203] This traditional doctrine of royalty appears, in the treatise of the Infante Pedro, to be

200 For a general appreciation of the influence of Seneca: Karl Alfred Blüher, *Séneca en España: investigaciones sobre la recepción de Séneca en España desde el siglo XIII hasta el siglo XVII* (Madrid: Gredos, 1983), in particular pp. 156–230 (where, however, there is no reference to the work of D. Pedro).

201 Brad Inwood, 'Politics and paradox in Seneca's *De Beneficiis*', in André Lacks and Malcolm Schofield (eds.), *Justice and Generosity: Studies in Hellenistic Social and Political Philosophy* (Cambridge: Cambridge University Press, 1995), pp. 241–65; François-Régis Chaumartin, *Le De Beneficiis de Sénèque: sa signification philosophique, politique et sociale* (Paris: Les Belles Lettres, 1985).

202 John G. Peristiany and Julian Pitt-Rivers, *Honor and Grace in Anthropology* (Cambridge: Cambridge University Press, 1992). It should be noted that in classical Latin *gratia* means free benefice as well as payment in return due to someone, which means that in the semantic field of politics it meant both gratuity and reciprocity, and it was only in the later period through Christian influence that it came to take on a religious meaning which definitively accentuated the first semantic sphere at the same time as the word disappeared in the political field (where words meaning a larger complexity in every form of interchange and relationships were to multiply): Claude Moussy, *Gratia et sa famille* (Paris: PUF, 1966), maxims 475–8.

203 Maurice Reydellet, *La Royauté dans la littérature latine, de Sidoine Apollinaire à Isidore de Séville* (Rome: Ecole Française de Rome, 1981), pp. 24–5 and 575–8.

associated with the virtue of liberality, and in this same association it also had an enormous influence on other authors of the fifteenth-century Portuguese court, in particular that of Duarte, coming to be expressed above all in the diverse pronouncements of Afonso V – be this in the Cortes, in the prologues developed in many public documents (at times quoting the *Virtuosa Benfeitoria*); be it in texts written by the monarch himself (particularly his correspondence); be it even through historiographic texts produced at his direct order (especially in the work of Zurara). In the treatises of John of Salisbury, of Aegidius of Rome or in the didactic poem of John Gower, all texts whose acceptance at the Portuguese court has recently been analysed by Ana Isabel Buescu,[204] this figure, which is so close to Christian Stoicism, of the wise king governing by the example of virtue, seems to gain new life through an idea of magnanimity associated with the constant distribution of favours and benefices.[205]

The influence of these concepts in the creation of values which had a real impact on the activity of Portuguese courtiers and monarchs can also be analysed in the optic of discussions regarding the nobility, and gains a new meaning in the face of the process of court life which I have analysed in this book. As has been noted by many authors in the Portuguese and Castilian debate on the nobility, the Aristotelian influence was combined during the fifteenth century with the Hispanic acceptance of Seneca's theory already referred to,[206] in a synthesis which is not lacking in contradictory aspects in which the valuing of political activity and of service to the king appear, however, as a source of ennoblement and also of a 'moralisation' of the aristocracy through the virtue of 'service'. The translation and commentary of ancient authors, as also those of the medieval authorities, which had in mind the new public developing outside the clerical sphere, came thus to allow a contemporary formulation of doctrines which justified dependence and asymmetry in the relationships between the nobles and the monarchs, while remaining in opposition to other discursive spheres in which the mythical independence and autonomy of a nobility transmittable through blood were, in turn, the object of reaffirmation.

These fifteenth-century ideas found their sustenance equally in the sphere of juridic discourse and in particular in the well-known influence of Bartholism

[204] Ana Isabel Buescu, *Imagens do príncipe: discurso normativo e representação (1525–1549)* (Lisbon: Cosmos, 1996), pp. 46–52.

[205] Michel Sénellart, *Les Arts de gouverner: du régimen médiéval au concept de gouvernement* (Paris: Seuil, 1995), pp. 90–2.

[206] On this doctrinal synthesis, which was not uniquely Hispanic: Gérard Verbecke, *The Presence of Stoicism in Medieval Thought* (Washington, DC: Catholic University Press, 1983), p. 70. The diffusion of Aristotelian moral doctrine in the Portuguese court circles of the fifteenth century was directly made through translations of *The Nichomachean Ethics* and *The Secret of Secrets* and indirectly through Gower's *Confessio Amantis* and Aegidius of Rome's *De Regimine Principum*, among other texts whose influence is found firmly established at the court.

through an emphasis based on a concept of 'common good' of society,[207] and also finding there, as Maurice Keen observed, a new justification for the service of the nobles to the monarchs through the suggestion of the supremacy of a 'civil nobility', distinct from the natural nobility through the necessary recognition which would be granted by the prince.[208] Royal favour and benefice could thus appear as an unequivocal demonstration of superiority within the actual sphere of the nobility, expressing the consensus and legal recognition of noble virtue through constituted authority. In turn, in Gower we read that 'kingship was the maintenance of common profit through liberality' (book VII), the virtue of the prince residing ideally in moderation envisaging a certain proportionality between the recipient of the benefice, his virtues and actions, and the grace or favour granted him, so exercising the discretion of the ruler in avoiding the dissipation of resources by an excessive practice of undeserved gifts.[209] There was an expression of lively interest in the exemplariness then imputed to Roman history (in particular the age of the consulate and the empire), so there circulated in Portugal during the first half of the fifteenth century in the court society Portuguese versions of 'Caesar's deeds' or the 'Panegyric to Trajan' of Pliny the Younger, and equally there was a known preference for the reading of Valerius Maximus. These are texts in which an apprenticeship through exemplary episodes could lead to reflection on the limits of dependency in relation to the prince and his ideal magnanimity.[210]

All these paradigms are found to be mobilised by the known reflection of Diego de Valera, the Castilian author who has been translated into other European languages who also retained his ties to the Portuguese court, shown by the correspondence he maintained with the Portuguese king, Afonso V, to whom he dedicated one of his treatises.[211] According to Maurice Keen's comparative analysis, we owe to Diego de Valera in his *Espejo de verdadera nobleza* one of the clearest statements of the supremacy of the authority of the prince over the nobility in Europe of the late Middle Ages, expressed in an ideal of mutual understanding and also in controversial statements, according to which, 'without the prince, the nobility had neither power nor virtue', or the aristocrat

[207] Nuno Espinosa Gomes da Silva, *Bártolo na história do direito Português*, offprint of *Revista da Faculdade de Direito* (Lisbon, 1960).

[208] Maurice Keen, 'Some late medieval ideas about nobility', in *Nobles, Knights and Men-at-Arms in the Middle Ages* (London: Hambledon Press, 1996), pp. 187–207.

[209] Russell A. Peck, *Kingship and Common Profit in Gower's Confessio Amantis* (London: Southern Illinois University Press, 1978), pp. 187–207.

[210] On the 'Feitos de César': Maria Helena Mira Mateus, *Vida e feitos de Júlio César*: *edição crítica de versão Portuguesa quatrocentista de 'Li Fet des Romains'* (Lisbon: Fundação Calouste Gulbenkian, 1983), vol. II, pp. 185–340.

[211] Diego de Valera, 'Prologue to "Tratado de las Armas" ', in Mario Penna (ed.), *Prosistas Castellanos del siglo XV* (Madrid: Biblioteca de Autores Españoles, 1959), pp. 117–18.

would be 'all the more noble the closer he was to the royal crown'.[212] Like the Infante Pedro, Diego de Valera formulated his doctrine with the monarchy and its contemporary nobility in mind, drawing between the two a picture of necessary relationships organised according to a hierarchical principle, existing in a political society in which there must be clearly stated a redistributing centre of benefices and distinctions.[213] It was in the optic of this centre, that is in the optic of the actual court society, that Valera attempted to justify the reasons for the possibility of granting noble status through the simple royal will or the advantages, for the nobility, of an assumed dependence based upon an acceptance of the hierarchical principle as a result or as a function of royalty.

As this focal point of the court of which the contemporary authors speak weakened, the court forms of interdependence between the kings and the nobles tended also to weaken, since the actions of the agents were also a function of the dynamic of the whole, and not solely of the (more or less consciously sought) interests or characteristics of the individuals. The circumstances of the regency of the Infante Pedro, as will be analysed later, are a Portuguese example in which it is possible to observe precisely a process of weakening of the attractive power of the court through the destructuring of the previously constructed balance between groups. This was due, in large part, to the weak position of a young monarch placed under a guardian. The suggestion of interpretation advanced by Norbert Elias of the dynamic of court society as a true field of relations which can be observed in the diachrony[214] allows for a consideration of this field, which is polarised and organised according to unstable balances of power, encompassing a diversity of forms of interaction with different degrees of institutionalisation and/or of coherence or juridic definition. By analysing the medieval contrast between the modes of the feudal contract and *moradia* at court, for example, I have explored this diversity in the modes of court interaction. It is also possible to distinguish, according to the categories of the age used by sources, the ties created by royal 'grace', for example, of the more coercive nature of forms of pseudo-kinship relating to the domestic sphere. On the other hand, Elias's suggestion also allows for an understanding as to how this human configuration could absorb or express different degrees of antagonism and conflict, as well as different degrees of co-operation between royalty and the nobility. In all cases, however, the actual form of the court configuration, which favours the multiplication of connections between individuals and

212 Diego de Valera, 'Espejo de verdadera nobleza', in *Prosistas Castellanos del siglo XV*, pp. 89–116.

213 For a discussion of the concept of hierarchy: Louis Dumont, 'Vers une théorie de la hiérarchie', in *Homo hierarchicus: le système des castes et ses implications* (Paris: Gallimard, 1995), pp. 396–403; Arjun Appadurai, 'Is homo hierarchicus?', *American Ethnologist*, 13 (1986), 757–61.

214 For a definition of 'relational field', besides the work of Elias see also Kurt Lewin, *Field Theory in Social Science: Selected Theoretical Papers* (New York: Harper, 1951).

groups, established around the monarchs a characteristic density of relationships which is indispensable to the creation of lasting forms of interaction and to the actual perception of the court as a centre of society. It is to this centrality that the several thinkers of the late Middle Ages, whom I have mentioned, referred using the language and concepts of the age.

The final problem which I should like to formulate at this point of my study is that of the autonomy or self-sufficiency of the court when considered as a specific social form. As we have seen, certain processes of difference in status had their origin in the court, and I have attempted to clarify their validity for the Portuguese case, in particular by studying the distinctions between certain categories of status at court, such as those of *cavaleiro*, *escudeiro* or *moço*. We have also seen that the regime of reward and payment made to the courtiers arose at least from the thirteenth century from the possibilities of internal formation of the hierarchy of the group, which process is concomitant with (and favoured by) the simultaneous monetarisation of those rewards. The rise of this specific hierarchy has been seen by some recent authors as the product of a self-reference of a systemic type.[215]

One of the main criticisms made of the theoretical construction of Norbert Elias lies, in fact, in the necessary differentiation of the court in relation to its exterior context, instituting not only characteristically exclusive modalities and behavioural codes, but also the hierarchic order to which I have referred. The emerging order of interactions which can be observed in the ancient and medieval courts would show a distinctive hierarchy, as well as the minimum degree of centrality to which I have earlier referred; both are aspects which could be included and explained through a functional analysis of pre-modern societies. The application of the theory of systems (influenced by the sociology of Talcott Parsons and Niklas Luhmann) to the interpretation of this order in the courts of antiquity and the medieval period has been characterised essentially by the application of this new terminology to a reconstruction of social realities of the past based on traditional heuristic methods.[216]

Thus, the rigour and the high degree of abstraction of the theory of systems proposed by Luhmann become especially attractive for the description of the court based on analysis of determined sources, such as lists of payments or normative sources connected to the historic constitution of the formal court regime.

[215] For a definition of these concepts of 'system' and 'self-reference': Nicolas Luhmann, *The Differentiation of Society* (New York: Columbia University Press, 1982); 'The autopoiesis of social systems', in *Essays on Self-Reference* (New York: Columbia University Press, 1990), pp. 1–20.

[216] Jan Hirschbiegel, 'Der Hof als soziales System', *Mitteilungen der Residenzen-Kommission der Akademie der Wissenschaften zu Göttingen*, 3(1) (1993), 11–25; 3(2), 15–19; Jan Hirschbiegel, 'Gabentaush als soziales System? Einige theoretische Überlungen', in *Ordnunsformen des Hofes*, *Mitteilungen der Residenzen-Kommission der Akademie der Wissenschaften zu Göttingen*, 2 (1997), 44–55.

However, these sources must be seen as cultural works and are themselves constructed by the historian in a necessary conjunction with texts arising from other discursive universes of the age, and not merely with concepts arising from modern social sciences. In their attempts at a functional analysis, the emphasis of the historians tends naturally to give supremacy through these sources to the reconstruction of norms which of itself could result in difficulty in exploring other historical realities which are not included in normative processes existing in court society. As Luhmann observes when taking up the distinctions of Durkheim, with medieval societies being less differentiated and less integrated than our contemporary modern societies the difficulties of this functional analysis form a formidable obstacle and perhaps require new conceptualisations, which is a problem avoided by works which make use of the theory of systems through a deductive, ahistorical methodology of analysis, coupled with a highly generic and strictly evolutionist vision of European history. In fact, this would seem also to be true for medieval European societies, and taking up the words of Barth in relation to extra-European societies, 'what we need is not a deductive theory of what these systems will [or would] be but the exploratory procedures to discover what they are [or were]; what degree of order and form they show in each particular situation in question. This needs to be discovered and described, not defined and assumed, and each system and its context should be specified in a way that will reveal the contingencies that have shaped it.'[217]

Because of its high level of generalisation, the image which results from a systemic analysis of the ancient and medieval courts appears fundamentally applicable to any context, and in this sense is not satisfactory either from the historic point of view or from the theory of systems, as Luhmann himself has indeed recently warned.[218] It is also an image which grants to the court a type of multi-secular fixity, since the concept of 'process' with which one is working defines it merely as conceivable within the system itself, expressing a one-and-only possible temporal modality (before/after or *Vorher/Nacher Differenz*), and abstraction which is itself related to Luhmann's hypotheses of self-selectivity of the specific temporal horizons of each system.[219] In the perspective I have adopted in this work, I was not interested in analysing abstractly the system of

[217] Frederic Barth, 'Towards greater naturalism in conceptualizing societies', in A. Kuper (ed.), *Conceptualizing Society* (London: Routledge, 1992), pp. 23–4.

[218] In an observation published on the paper by Hirschbiegel, Luhmann states that it is necessary to go beyond the simple adoption of the terminology, leading to a greater degree of abstraction in historical analysis: 'the only way one can show that by performing a functional system analysis one can finally see more than by just doing an interpretation close to the sources, which then has to be embellished into a bigger painting, using narrative and daring causal assumptions' (*Mitteilungen der Residenzen-Kommission der Akademie der Wissenschaften zu Göttingen* 3(2) (1993), 18–19).

[219] For a criticism of these concepts of temporal and processual construction: Rolf Petri, 'Pamphlet per il tempo storico', in *Velocità storiche: miti di fondazione e percezione del tempo nella cultura e nella politica del mondo contemporaneo* (Rome: Carocci, 1999), esp. pp. 60–1.

the royal court or in considering merely the institutions studied on a normative basis, but I sought also to study the empirical groups of individuals which formed them throughout two centuries and whose behaviour appears more random, erratic and variously conditioned than the descriptions of court, using the system theory, allow us to deduce or to predict. My initial questions on their empirical simplicity (who was related to whom; how these relationships were formed and broken, etc.) allowed me to detect, on the exploratory level to which Barth refers, how it is that the heterogeneity in positions and in social status of the individuals was resolved effectively in hierarchy, as well as detecting actual historic processes by which this hierarchy was not only formed but could also become destructured, change in meaning and be either incomprehensible or useless.

The virtualities of the concepts of 'configuration' or of 'constellations of forces' also allow for effective criticism and overradical affirmation of autarchy in the court hierarchic order. I found that this order at the end of the Middle Ages was constantly undermined in its autonomy by the need to elaborate complex codes of equivalence in relation to the outside world. As has been seen, the determination of status at court was connected, for example, to the actual definition of relevant social categories for society as a whole (such as the nobility), and this connection was formed in some cases positively and in others merely conditionally or even negatively. We can thus observe a tendency for this order to filter beyond the court of the kings. One distinction which seems to me of the greatest methodological relevance then becomes possible, not only between the study of domestic order of the monarchs (the household) and the study of the royal court (as explained in the first chapter of this book), but also between the study of the royal court and the study of 'court society' itself, in Elias's meaning of the concept. By considering 'court society' as a human configuration or a relational field, we shall be able to see how at the end of the Middle Ages it included other social circles beyond that of the court of the monarchs.

A PLURAL COURT?

Although the court of the monarchs was the most important structure of this type existing in fourteenth- and fifteenth-century Portuguese society, it was certainly not unique. One can find a large number of similarities with other like organisms grouped around important magnates of the nobility and the church, or the close relatives of the royal family, in relation to which the royal court at the time was seen as a model to be imitated and followed, at least in some of its aspects. The most important of these organisms for a study of the court as a particular social configuration are the entourages of the queens and the infantes which, although they have never presented the internal complexity of the royal court and, most importantly, they are not seen as the central place of the government of the kingdom and the converging knot of diverse institutions, nevertheless raise some interesting problems because of the partial homology of their organisational configurations and because of the participation of a number of their members in the entourages of the monarchs. A global image of these relationships can be sketched for Portugal at the end of the medieval period, always bearing in mind the evolution which for almost two centuries carefully modified the balance and the relative weight of this type of congenerous organism in court society, in particular of the households of the infantes and other close relatives of the king.

A first period is detected in the fourteenth century, encompassing the period from 1325 until the major part of the reign of Fernando, that is until the 1380s. These some sixty years are marked by the intense conflicts of the 1350s, by a notable continuity in the recruitment of a large number of the courtiers who surrounded the monarchs – in particular of the nobles – and by the importance of the involvement of the court in the Peninsular political scenario which was accentuated in the last two decades and of which the wars of the reign of Fernando, and even those which marked the interregnum, form a natural extension. Data are scarce for this period relative to the construction of the entourages of the infantes in their dynamic relationship with the court. Even so, from the mention of the actual servants and the resources granted to their households, it can be established that the Portuguese infantes had their own entourages from a relatively young age, and that these were more or less organised at the end of their boyhood, at around the age of six or seven, becoming fully autonomous once they reached adolescence at about fourteen or fifteen, when they 'took their households'. During the first years of life, as I have already suggested, the protection of the infantes usually remained linked to the women of the court.

These practices seem to be fairly similar to those seen for the English and French monarchs, known for example through studies made regarding Henry, the first-born child of Edward I of England (1274–1307), or of the young Philip the Fair of France before his accession to the throne in 1286. At only five years old, the first of these young princes had an entourage with several departments (*coquina*, *camera*, *stabulum*, etc.), comprising about thirty to forty adults and an armed guard of several knights. His household depended almost entirely, from the financial viewpoint, on the English monarch.[220] The French prince also had his own entourage and resources, particularly following the early death of his elder brother, Louis.[221] Some differences can also be found in the Portuguese

220 Hilda Johnstone, 'The wardrobe and household of Henry son of Edward I', *Bulletin of John Rylands Library*, 7 (1922–23), 384–420.

221 Elisabeth A. R. Brown, 'The Prince is father of the King: the character and childhood of Philip the Fair of France', in *The Monarchy of Capetian France and Royal Ceremonial* (London: Variorum, 1991), [II], pp. 316–27.

case between the entourage of the first-born heirs and the other children of the monarchs.

During the reign of Afonso IV, the only survivors were the first-born, D. Pedro, and two sisters, both of whom married young (at fifteen and nineteen). From the first years of the reign, when the infante was six years old, there are occasional indications as to his personal entourage, in particular to his guard Domingos Anes and his *reposteiro* Afonso Domingues.[222] Pedro's *aio* was the magnate Lopo Fernandes Pacheco, who also appears as *mordomo* of his household from 1335 to 1338.[223] However, the most prominent figure in his entourage during his adult life in a second phase whose beginning can be dated 1340 (when he married Constança Manuel) was that of João Afonso Telo III who, in the 1350s, was his close counsellor.[224] This is of course besides the influence of the Castros, which has so frequently been referred to in the previous chapter.

The conflicts following the execution of Inês de Castro which were only brought to an end in 1355 and the first months of the following year (leading to several agreements between the monarch and the rebellious infante) formed an episode which was in some way parallel to the uprising of Afonso IV himself against his own father during his old age. The recurrence of these conflicts was greatly facilitated by the formation of retinues of nobles and *cavaleiro*s surrounding the successors to the throne. The image gained of the relationship existing between the court of the king and the group accompanying Pedro in the mid-fourteenth century is that of a separation and incompatibility of both entourages.[225] In a mechanism which probably appeared in earlier ages, the 'colhcitas' of the kingdom were shared between the monarch and his heir, so granting him royal dignity, and certain basic essentials for the itinerance of the royal court and of the infante with his company were provided separately.[226] On the other hand, there is some information as to the granting of lands and rents to the infantes in the form of 'quantias', in particular regarding Afonso

222 Respectively, in 1326 and 1327: *CUP*, vol. I, p. 90; *CDA*, vol. I, p. 105.

223 In his charter of restitution of possessions to the Pachecos, Fernando still referred in 1367 to 'criaçam e serviço que Lopo ferrnandez e dona maria sua molher fezerom a elrrey meu padre et dos diujdos grandes que na sua mercee tijnham'. ANTT, *Ch. D. Fernando*, 1, f. 2.

224 In a supplication to the pope dated 1353, Pedro calls him 'dilectus et fidelis consiliarius suus': *MPV*, vol. I, p. 281. And in the important accords of 1355 and 1356 Telo still appears heading the list of the Infante's vassals.

225 AHCML, *Livros Místicos de Reis*, cod. 3, ff. 39–49v. This important document comprising eight varied decrees written between December 1355 and January 1356 and including the various accords passed by the king and Pedro is now the sole example known of, although documents similar in kind would have been sent to other councils of the kingdom, such as Évora. See on this subject the description of the lost original of the archive of that city: *DEV*, vol. I, p. 101.

226 ANTT, *Ch. D. João I*, 5, f. 78v (two sequential documents). See also António Caetano do Amaral, *Memória para a história da legislação e costumes de Portugal* (Oporto: Civilização, [1945]), p. 92 and note, and also the considerations of João Pedro Ribeiro, *Reflexões históricas* (Coimbra: Imprensa da Universidade, 1835), vol. I, pp. 63–4.

IV to his son, which suggests that the group of vassals related to them were subject to serve in the royal army under the command of the infante, their lord.[227]

The most particular circumstances of this troubled period of the 1350s hinder a clear evaluation of the situation of the sons of Pedro. The first-born, D. Fernando, who by some indications is connected during his infancy to his grandmother, D. Beatriz, had his own *porteiro* in 1351, and from 1357 he appears associated with his *aio*, Aires Gomes da Silva, 'o Moço'.[228] An important indication of the autonomy of his household is the dispensation obtained for several ecclesiastical servants to form a small chapel when the infante was sixteen years old.[229] However, the situation of the remainder of Pedro's descendants, in particular Inês de Castro's eldest son João, appears much like that of the heir to the throne. In the treaties of 1356, Pedro had claimed the county of Barcelos for João, who was still a child, 'com dez mil libras em quantya das quaes as cinque mill libras seJam pera mantimento seu e pera o al que lhy comprir e as outras çinque mill libras pera mordomo e alferez e vassalos que sejam do huso do iffante quaes Elrrey scolher'.[230] This arrangement, whose formation the count, in his *Livro de Linhagens*, lays at the door of the prior of the hospital, Álvaro Gonçalves Pereira, must have remained until João reached the age of fourteen and fundamentally allowed for the formation of an important entourage surrounding the illegitimate infante. This was besides granting him a vast hereditary patrimony rather than one only for the duration of his life, through the concession of the county of Barcelos, which already belonged to the bastard son of Dinis. The formation of more or less important lordships around the descendants of the monarchs is seen as an irreversible tendency from the middle of the thirteenth century not only in Portugal, but also in the neighbouring kingdom of Castile.[231] In the case of the infante son of Inês de

227 On Afonso IV there is the mention in a document of 1388 of the land of Resende and Cádima ('seendo elrey dom afonso nosso auoo que deus perdoe Jffante e teendo a dicta terra em sua conthia'): ANTT, *Ch. D. João I*, 2, f. 9. In August 1355, Pedro asked when seeking the intercession of Queen Beatriz, 'que ElRej nom reteuess nen enbargasse nem a Rajnha outrossj ao dicto Senhor Iffante rem da sua quantja nen do que del tijnha pera seu mantjmento', AHCML, *Livros Misticos de Reis*, cod. 3, f. 42v *in fine*. In the *Crónica Geral* of 1344 there is also mention of a 'contia' of D. Pedro corresponding to 30,000 *libras* 'em terras e dinheiros', which would have been settled by his grandfather Dinis from his birth: *CR 1344*, vol. IV, p. 255.

228 ANTT, *NA*, p. 315, f. 56; *CPD*, pp. 60, 362 and 563. In the same copy of the register of charters of this king, Inês Rodrigues Pimentel, who died in 1364, appears as his *aia*, and in the *Livro de Linhagens* it is stated that she married Mem Gonçalves Camelo: *CDP*, p. 428 and *LL Conde*, 55J2, 55L3. Fernando's grandfather only died in 1359, but at that date the Infante would already have been handed over to his *aio*.

229 *MPV*, vol. I, pp. 362–3 and 388–9.

230 Arnaut, *A crise nacional*, p. 75 (I have followed the reading suggested by this author).

231 Isabel Beceiro Pita, 'Los dominios de la familia real Castellana (1250–1350)', in *Génesis medieval del estado moderno: Castilla y Navarra (1250–1370)* (Valladolid: Ambito, 1987), pp. 79–106 and in particular p. 98. For a comparison where the Iberian singularity emerges:

Castro, we know that the county was never granted to him, but in 1357 and 1358 there is occasional reference respectively to a vassal and 'homem de sua câmara', and in 1359 to his physician, which would appear to point towards the formation of his own retinue.[232]

At this same precise time during which the chapel of Fernando was organised, that is at the time of the Cortes of Elvas of 1361, whose importance has been so emphasised regarding the actual government of the kingdom,[233] numerous parcels of land and rent were given to João and this formed the patrimonial basis of his household, as also the more modest one of his brother, D. Dinis. Dias Arnaut's hypothesis is that João and D. Dinis were close from infancy, and it was their separation after the events of 1372 which determined the withdrawal of the latter from court. This hypothesis cannot be entirely refuted, for one thing because of lack of certain data, but I feel it is somewhat unnecessary in view of documented connections of the individuals, which do not in any way agree. Thus, João appears close to the prior of the hospital and the Castros, and was connected to his uncle, Álvaro Peres, and to the widow of Fernão Peres de Castro. In contrast, D. Dinis appears connected to his *aio* Gil Vasques de Resende, an individual mentioned in Conde Pedro's *Livro de Linhagens* as one of those responsible for the death of Inês de Castro (he was then pardoned by the king), and also to Diogo Lopes Pacheco, whose counsel the infante was to follow and who retreated to Castile. There is nothing to contradict the hypothesis that the infantes were associated to different factions of the court nobility and that before the 1370s they lived less closely associated than the historian suggests.[234]

From that same year, 1361, there is a succession of references to the several officials of the heir, D. Fernando, who had a *vedor* of his household and also his own vassals.[235] During the 1360s there would thus seem to have been organised at least two important organisms of this type around the Infantes Fernando and João, whose relationship with the court of Pedro, however, remains highly obscure. In mentioning the embarrassing visit to Portugal of Pedro of Castile in 1366, the chronicler Fernão Lopes states that the king 'mandou chamar o iffante dom Fernando seu filho, que nom era hi, e com elle e com seus privados

Bernard Guenée, 'Le roi, ses parents et son royaume en France au XIVe siècle', *Bullettino dell'Istituto Storico Italiano per il Medio Evo e Archivio Muratoriano*, 94 (1988), 439–470.

232 *CDP*, vol. I, pp. 157 and 590.

233 A. L. Carvalho Homem, *Subsídios para o estudo da administração central no reinado de D. Pedro I*, offprint of *Revista de História* (Oporto, 1978), pp. 34–9. On the presence of the Infantes at the same Cortes: *CPP*, p. 13.

234 For an analysis of available documents: Arnaut, *A crise nacional*, in particular pp. 104 and 116.

235 *CDP*, pp. 347 and 563–4. Among the *cavaleiros* and vassals of his entourage are Gonçalo Esteves and Pero Esteves (*CDP*, pp. 260 and 516 and ANTT, *Ch. D. Duarte*, 1, f. 122). On the several clerics of his household, see his supplications to the pope: *MPV*, vol. I, pp. 430 and 485–6.

ouve conselho sobre este feito', which suggests that Fernando's retinue did not accompany the court.[236]

However this may have been, the reign of Fernando can be seen in relative contrast regarding the household of the infantes in relation to earlier practice. This change was certainly contributed to by the troubled political situation which was felt particularly intensely at court and which directly involved several members of the royal family. Before his exile in 1380, the Infante João attended the Portuguese court, as was the case with his other siblings, Dinis and Beatriz (who had in turn earlier been in exile in Castile for about eight years), and one can even speak of a relative participation of their entourages at the court of the monarch, as I have analysed in detail through prosopographic research. Fernando had only one surviving descendant besides an illegitimate daughter, who was married as a result of the peace of 1373 to a descendant of the Castilian Henry II (cf. reference above to the Henriques family).

It is in relation to the heir D. Beatriz that there are interesting problems, because of the adoption of some new practices which were perhaps not strange to the consecutive matrimonial alliances negotiated for her. At only a few months, in the first year of her life, the city of Lisbon was forced to grant her for three years the revenue of *sisas*, 'per razam da criaçam da iffante . . . que a queriam criar aas despesas desse concelho'.[237] After this period, with notable signs of precocity and at only three years of age, the infanta witnessed the creation of a patrimony for the maintenance of her household, and at the same time she was emancipated from the control of her father, the monarch.[238] All indicates, however, that she was always associated with her mother, Leonor Teles, and this is not only frequently referred to by Fernão Lopes but is also indirectly confirmed by information available on the several women who accompanied both mother and daughter.[239] When the infanta was eleven years old, according to the chronicler, she was given as officials of her household some influential individuals of Fernando's court, in particular the Galegan João Fernandes Andeiro, her *mordomo-mor*, and Vasco Martins de Melo, her *copeiro-mor*, whose wife served as the infanta's *camareira-mor*. The peculiar political situation of the

236 *CR Pedro*, p. 256. 237 ANTT, *Ch. D. Fernando*, 1, f. 135.

238 ANTT, drawer III, M 2, 8. I believe that the 'carta de emancipação' of 1376 was intended to free the Infanta from the *potestas* of her father, and not from that of Leonor Teles as suggested by J. Montalvão Machado, *Alguns acontecimentos esquecidos do tempo do rei D. Fernando*, offprint of *Anais da Academia Portuguesa da História* (Lisbon, 1982), p. 18. On the act of emancipation from the historical/juridical point of view: A. Otero, 'La patria potestad en el Derecho Histórico Español', *Anuario de Historia del Derecho Español*, 26 (1956), 208–41. The grant of numerous territories comprising a large patrimony to the same Infanta was dated the day following the instrument of emancipation: ANTT, *Ch. D. Fernando*, 1, f. 189v.

239 Particularly her *ama*, Constança Martins Botelha and her *covilheira* Urraca Anes, who had died in 1383. The *aia* Violante Afonso, widow of Diogo Gomes de Abreu, is also mentioned with Teresa de Meira by Fernão Lopes.

time explains to a large extent the adoption of this group of measures, which established a certain contrast with the situation of earlier descendants of the monarchs, in particular the females.[240]

A second period then opens up, in the perspective of interest here, between 1408–9 and 1449–50, demonstrating different characteristics regarding the relationship between the court and the households of the infantes. Behind this period lay some twenty-eight years of agitation due to the events of the civil war and conflict with the neighbouring country, during which period the founder of the new dynasty organised his court and the entourages of his sons, who were born from the end of the 1380s, in a manner apparently similar to that which I have just analysed. In about 1405 the situation of the respective servants is mentioned in detail in the roll of the *moradores* of the court. Only the eldest, D. Duarte, who was aged about fourteen, had a relatively important group of officials, in particular servants of the kitchen, the *copa* and the *ucharia* (cook and *regueifeira*), the *estrebaria* and *montaria*. It would appear that he shared with his siblings the services of a *comprador*, which may be a sign of some dependency on the same sources of income. He also had a barber and his boy, two *reposteiros* and at least one *porteiro*. As well he had his own confessor, Vasco Pereira. In contrast, his siblings, Pedro, Isabel and João, had few servants, the majority being grooms of the *câmara* and stable.[241]

A different situation arose, however, following the Cortes of Évora of 1408, when John I decided upon the constitution of several households for his children, which would involve the granting of their own resources and equivalent dignity in the new age of peace which was then becoming established with the neighbouring country.[242] The main trait of this new period will be seen as the growing autonomy and social and political importance of the entourages of the households of the monarch's children, in particular the three eldest, Duarte, Pedro and Henry. This phenomenon lacked precedent, in contrast with the more modest establishments of the infantes of the fourteenth century, and it

240 On the other members of the household: *MPV*, vol. II, p. 301; ANTT, *Ch. D. João I*, 5, f. 68v; 2, f. 36v.

241 *MH*, vol. I, p. 291 (a general description) and also p. 290 (mention of the same servants) and p. 287 (on the *porteiros* and the Infantes' *ucharia*). In accord with this document, Pedro was to have three *moços de câmara* and two *de estrebaria*, possibly sharing the services of two *reposteiros* with his elder brother. D. Isabel would have had two *moços de câmara*, two *de estrebaria* and one *reposteiro* for herself as well as several *moças*. Henry would also have three *moços de câmara* and two *de estrebaria* and João only two of each. The number of servants decreased with age.

242 The main document, dated April 1408, regarding these measures relating to the households of the Infantes is published in *MH*, vol. I, pp. 316–19. However, in December 1407, according to other, later, information, John I went on to reform the financial mechanism for his court and household, involving the action of the *vedores da fazenda* and *vedores da casa*, the *reposteiro* and the *despenseiro* in an attempt to control his own and the queen's expenditure: ANTT, *Ch. D. João I*, 5, f. 72.

did not cease to increase and evolve for some forty years separating this event and the date of Alfarrobeira.

A careful analysis of the group of measures recommended in 1408 allows us to see how John I planned at this date the foundations for the establishment of his children's households. Autonomy of resources would be obtained by the granting of pre-planned annual subsidies to which would be added the creation of vast patrimonies in land which the infantes were to 'inherit' and which would be bought throughout the kingdom for this purpose. The necessary money for every one of these expenses was to be obtained through *sisas* taken by the districts corresponding to a third of the entire sum they earned. The financial basis for this group of measures was solid, but already there were foreseen a certain tardiness and lack of certainty in the constitution of the patrimonial foundation of the households, for the 'land and inheritance' were to be bought as and when 'they might become available for sale', a process which, it was realised, would take at least 'three, four or five years'. In effect, according to available studies, the year 1411 seems to have been the crucial moment in the constitution of the patrimonial nuclei of Henry and Pedro, which were later to witness notable increase.[243]

Two aspects appear of importance in this initial programme of John I: first, the enlargement and the systematisation of a recourse which was already being set in motion during the reign of Fernando, which was the use of the income from the *sisas* for the support of the monarch's children; then, the formation of patrimonies through their own possessions and not through the granting for life of lands belonging to the royal family since, as has been emphasised by several authors, these were scarce owing to the generosity of the monarch during the first years of his rule. Besides this 'internal' problem of availability, there must be noted John's project with the European horizons in which the sovereign saw himself placed and with the conflicting situations to which similar concessions to the descendants of the kings led and which were visible to all. In fact, this initial project was only partially realised and was consecutively altered throughout John's reign, and in spite of everything the double origin of the incomes of the infantes was certainly retained: on the one hand, the 'assentamentos' (an important tax instituted in the royal income) and, on the other, the patrimonies. To this double source the infantes were to add at their own initiative a more or less large group of resources of a varying nature, as is well known.

[243] See A. Dias Dinis, *Estudos Henriquinos* (Coimbra: Universidade de Coimbra, 1960), vol. I, pp. 15–24, whose main conclusions were taken up by João Silva de Sousa, *A casa senhorial do Infante D. Henrique* (Lisbon: Horizonte, 1991), pp. 85–97. Also on Henry and his men, see the most recent work of Peter Russell, *Prince Henry the Navigator: A Life* (New Haven: Yale University Press, 2000). On the origins of D. Pedro's patrimony, which Dias Dinis states in *MH*, vol. XIV, pp. 176–7 (note).

The most important alteration in John's plan lay in fact in the granting of vast lordships which accompanied the establishment of the dukedoms of Viseu and Coimbra after 1415, and the households of the eldest infantes set root in more or less compact areas in certain regions of the kingdom. On the other hand, the control of the important patrimonies of the Military Orders, for which there was a true diplomatic offensive in the curia, in which Duarte also played an important part, meant also that granting of gifts to the infantes made it difficult to make equal, within the Portuguese kingdom, the level of resources to which the sons of the king had access during this period. Study of these organisms which originated around the infantes of the house of Aviz has not yet produced significant results from the point of view of a structural comparison which would allow for a detailed evaluation of the influence of the model of the royal court in its organisation. In occasional mentions of the officials of the households of the infantes we find that this influence reached the levels of a true parallelism, not only concerning the conventional tripartition between hall, chamber and chapel but also in the case of the eldest infantes regarding the centrality of certain institutional mechanisms which made the government of the respective territories converge in the figure of the dukes.[244] As to the size of the group of the respective *moradores*, it was also relatively close to the actual court of the king, for the 390 individuals mentioned in the list of 1405 are not greatly different from the 374 indicated for the household of the infantes a little after 1408.[245]

Similar phenomena of parallelism are, besides, a characteristic mark of the growth of court society in several European contexts of the last stages of the Middle Ages. It is customary to mention the English example, which would have more directly influenced John I, in particular in the adoption of the title of duke for his sons, which until then was unknown in Portugal. The eldest infantes had visited England in 1405 and were in direct contact with English royalty. It is important, however, to remember that the studies available on John of Gaunt, for example, point to a global dimension of the house of Lancaster to the extent that it is known, and this did not even reach half the size of the English royal court. This relative modesty has been compared by English historians with the examples closer in size to the royal court to be found among the French dukes, for example the Duke of Berry or the Duke of Burgundy, which situations, from this point of view, were closer (naturally on a relative scale) to the Portuguese situation.[246]

244 Some elements for the prosopography of the respective households can be found: for D. Pedro, in *ALF*, in particular vol. II, and for Henry in Silva de Sousa, *A casa senhorial do Infante D. Henrique* and in the many notes of *Monumenta Henricina*. The principal data and conclusions on Henry have been included in the above work of Peter Russell.

245 *Livro dos Conselho*, pp. 179–80 and also *MH*, vol. VI, p. 133 and note. See also for an evaluation of the size of the Infante Pedro's household: Maria Helena da Cruz Coelho, *O baixo mondego nos finais da idade média* (Coimbra: Faculdade de Letras, 1983), vol. I, pp. 563–6.

246 Simon Walker, *The Lancastrian Affinity, 1361–1399* (Oxford: Oxford University Press, 1990), p. 13.

In fact, from the point of view of relative size we are also not far from the panorama of the French monarchy and even of fifteenth-century Italy, with regard to the multiplication of small seigneurial courts of a similar size and marked by the analogy of their structure. The validity of an evolutionary model of explanation suggested by authors such as Cattini and Romani, which through the Italian case would be hypothetically valid for the other European courts, in turn is faced with important obstacles in its application, not only for the Iberian case. This proposal, which is formulated through a disputable generalisation of the example of the evolution of the seigneurial courts of the north of the Italian peninsula would lead to a 'seigneurial' state succeeding the 'consorziali' courts, finally culminating in the 'bureaucratic and ritual' court of the early modern age.[247] By separating according to a temporal vector the various vertents of the late-medieval court which, in my opinion, beyond the particular Italian context coexist in the majority of cases from the High Middle Ages, this analytical suggestion does not relate the court genetically with the cultural complex of royalty (including so many institutional aspects as well as doctrinal and ritual ones), so ignoring the virtuality of the interpretative proposal of Norbert Elias. Comparison between the Portuguese example and studies made for other kingdoms of the Low Middle Ages seems to suggest a variety of cases which challenge the vision of a linear evolution. There must be recognised, in the majority of kingdoms studied for the Europe of the Low Middle Ages, the existence of a court society in Elias's meaning of the term, which does not grow at this period only in the limited environment of the royal courts, but which increasingly includes within its network a larger range of human groups extending outside that environment. That is, it will be necessary to distinguish 'court society' in the meaning attributed by Elias to this 'social form' as a specific disposition of social relationships from the actual royal court, which is the centre of this configuration or larger social field, but which is a centre that also has peripheries and can have other realities subordinate to itself. This is what appears to have occurred in fifteenth-century Portugal. An important indicator of this diffusion of values of the royal court as central values, and therefore of the constitution and complexity of this relational field which, in Elias's wake, we would call 'court society' of Portugal, is formed by the adoption of remuneratory systems such as that of *moradias* or of a similar hierarchy of status at the 'households of the infantes'.

What is of particular interest for continuing this analysis of the Portuguese situation is the consideration of the problem of the household of the eldest, D. Duarte, and the ways it was related to the court of John. It is an example

[247] Marco Cattini and Marzio Romani, 'Le corti parallelle: per una tipologia delle corti padane dal XIII al XVI secolo', in *La corte e lo spazio: Ferrara estense* (Rome: Bulzoni, 1982), vol. I, pp. 47–82; a more recent suggestion taken up in exactly the same terms by Maurice Aymard and Marzio Romani, 'La cour comme institution économique. Introduction', in *La Cour comme institution économique* (Paris: Maison des Sciences de l'Homme, 1998), pp. 3–5.

which illustrates the variety of the process of configuration referred to above. As was the case in Portugal in the period prior to 1390, the heir presumptive to the throne was distinguished from his brothers by the greater importance of his entourage and, in this case, by the higher value of resources available to him for his household which emanated from income from the kingdom. The 'assentamento' of this infante (without doubt larger, as had been planned in 1408, than that of his brothers) supported an important group of his own servants, whose organisation seems in 1420 to have achieved its more-or-less definitive format.[248] We thus find from the first decade of the century mention of the *vedor* of his household, Nuno Gonçalves de Ataíde, and his *mordomo-mor*, Diogo Lopes de Sousa, as well as his *camareiro-mor*, Fernando de Noronha, his *reposteiro-mor*, Diogo Fernandes de Almeida, his *escrivão da puridade*, Nuno Martins da Silveira, and several *escrivães da câmara* (in particular Rui Galvão and João Vasques), as well as an important group of servants within the *fazenda*, such as the *tesoureiro-mor*, *vedores da fazenda* and *contador*. The continuing presence of the infante heir alongside the monarch appears to have been characteristic of the two final decades of John's reign.[249] Until John's death, we are able to see the existence of a type of 'bicephalism' at the Portuguese court comprising followers of the old monarch and also of Duarte, which characteristic came to be reinforced by Duarte's marriage in 1428 and the formation of the household of Leonor of Aragon.

The underlying equivalence between the royal figure and his successor, both members of the royal *dignitas*, was sustained by the political and juridic doctrine of the age, as Kantorowicz mentions:

> In these cases, the fiction of law was actually supported by the philosophers – Aristotle and, in his wake, Aquinas – according to whose biogenetic doctrines the 'form' (*eidos*) of the begetter and the begotten were the same owing to the seed's active power, which derived from the soul of the father and impressed itself upon the son. Legal and philosophical doctrines then were combined with other arguments which were supposed to prove that a king's first-born son was even more than other sons the equal of his ruling father because he was, while the father still was living, one with the father in the royal dignity. Again the jurists could refer to the *Decretum*, where the king's son was called *rex iuvenis* and where the prerogatives of the first-born were enumerated, for instance, the privilege of sitting at the right hand of his father.[250]

[248] I do not wish by this to state that Duarte's household was richer than that of the other Infantes, but simply that the fixed amount of income of the kingdom granted him was higher. In fact, in 1408 the annual sum granted to Duarte had been eight *contos* and to his brothers only five: ANTT, *Ch. D. João I*, 4, f. 77.

[249] The ruling activity of Duarte from the period after 1415, but in particular in the 1420s and 1430s, has left important signs in *Desembargo*: Freitas, *A burocracia do 'Eloquente'*, pp. 26–8 and figure VII, 126.

[250] Kantorowicz, *The King's Two Bodies*, p. 392.

In the Portuguese case, Duarte appears associated with the official ruling of the kingdom in 1421–22 and in particular with the central sphere of justice and the royal council, where his 'privados' emerged together at the same time.[251] His entourage also appears, during the lifetime of his father, to have assumed a dimension and an importance at the interior of the royal court never attained during the previous century by the heirs to the throne.

It can be noted besides that the composition of the entourages of the infantes of the house of Aviz and the courts of John and Duarte appear to a large part homogenous, which is particularly visible regarding the nobility. Detailed analysis of some families for the 1420s and 1430s to which I shall move on demonstrates this fact well. Thus, for example, among the Castros should be considered the descendancy of Álvaro de Castro II, where Pedro and Álvaro appear connected to the Infante Henry, while Fradique was alongside the Infante Pedro and the youngest, Fernando 'Cegonho' and Diogo, were present in the royal entourage as *moradores*.[252] In the other branch of the Castros analysed, Fernando de Castro was an important figure in Henry's entourage, as already stated, while his son Henrique was also very close to this infante.[253] In the innumerable lines of the Cunhas, there can be found a sharing of similar positions. For example, of the descendants of Vasco Martins da Cunha II, the prior of Guimarães, Rui Vasques was a familiar of the Infante Pedro, while his brother Martim Vasques III remained at the royal court, as did his descendants.[254] Of the sons of Gil Vasques, João Pereira was 'escudeiro e criado' of the Infante Henry, while his brother Fernão Vasques early joined the entourage of Duarte.[255] In analysing the two consecutive generations of the Silvas connected to this process, we find that of the several sons of Gonçalo Gomes da Silva, João Gomes da Silva II was at John's court while his brother Diogo Gomes was with the household of the Infante Henry, and the son of João Gomes, Aires Gomes da Silva III, was a central personage in the household of Pedro.[256]

Among the court families of the Azevedos, the Ataídes and the Coutinhos, equivalent processes can be detected, and I shall only name the best-known cases

251 A. Dias Dinis, *À volta do casamento do Infante D. Duarte (1409–1428)*, offprint of *Revista Portuguesa de História* (Coimbra, 1974), esp. 14; Homem, *Conselho real ou conselheiros do rei*, pp. 36–6.

252 *Brasões*, vol. I, pp. 146–7. On Pedro and Álvaro, *MH*, vol. XIII, p. 209 and vol. XIV, p. 103; on 'Cegonho', *LL*, p. 91 and *MH*, vol. XIV, p. 274; on Diogo, *Provas*, vol. II, p. 28 and on Fradique the biography in *ALF*, vol. II, pp. 765–7.

253 On Fernando de Castro in Henry's entourage: ANTT, *Ch. D. Duarte*, 1, f. 67; *CR Duarte*, p. 652; *MH*, vol. III, pp. 69–70 and note. On the activities of Henrique de Castro during the regency: *ALF*, vol. I, p. 95.

254 On Martim, *MH*, vol. I, p. 282; on Rui Vasques, *ALF*, vol. II, pp. 1031–2.

255 On João Pereira, ANTT, *Ch. D. João I*, 4, f. 6 and *MH*, vol. II, p. 267 and note; on Fernão Vasques, ANTT, *Ch. D. Duarte*, 1, f. 166v.

256 On João Gomes da Silva II, *alferes* to John I, ANTT, *Ch. D. João I*, 2, f. 182v; 3, f. 136; on Diogo and his connections with the Infante Henry, *MH*, vol. XV, pp. 420 and 426; on Aires Gomes da Silva, *ALF*, vol. II, pp. 1063–71.

in the composition of the entourage of the infantes of Aviz. Thus, Pero Lopes de Azevedo accompanied John's court, while his brother Fernão Lopes was *comendador-mor* of Christ and close to the Infante Henry, and another of the brothers, Luis de Azevedo, was in the retinue of the Infante Pedro.[257] Among the Ataídes, we find the *governador* of the household of the Infante Pedro, Álvaro Gonçalves de Ataíde, and his brother Vasco Fernandes, connected to the Infante Henry.[258] In another branch of the family, Nuno Gonçalves de Ataíde was *vedor da casa* of the Infante Duarte, as said a little earlier, and his son Gonçalo followed the Infante Pedro.[259] As for the Coutinhos, I have already mentioned Duarte's marshal, Vasco Fernandes, and his brother the bishop, Luis Coutinho, both members of the king's court, although the son of the first Conde de Marialva, Gonçalo Vasques, appears close to the Infante Pedro.[260] Some hypotheses should also be sketched as to other families of more modest standing, such as the Gorizos and the Fogaças, to whom I have already referred.[261] This continuity from the point of view of its social composition suggests some interesting questions as to the possibilities of successive combination and participation of the same individuals or groups of close relatives in several of these organisms, which questions cannot be safely answered because of a lack of studies based upon a systematic identification of the members of the various entourages of the infantes of the house of Aviz. What is interesting is the development of forms of interdependence between the infantes and their followers, which in all are seen as similar to those organised around the kings, instituting a court society in the meaning of the term given by Elias, which as I have said above spread far from the actual royal court.

The situation during the short reign of Duarte regarding the forms of coexistence between the royal court and the organisms which developed around the infantes seems to have been fairly delicate. In truth, as António José Saraiva has written, 'these important seigneurial houses were transformed into authentic principalities, with their own court and great political, administrative and even cultural autonomy'.[262] The presence of the infantes at the royal court was, by all indications, fairly constant and there are even those who suggest, as does the Conde de Arraiolos in 1433, that they 'repartissem certos tempos do ano que andassem com o rei em tal guisa que a corte nunca fosse sem algum deles',[263]

[257] On Fernão, *MH*, vol. I, p. 283 and *CR Duarte*, p. 546; On Luis, *ALF*, vol. II, pp. 1017–18.

[258] *ALF*, vol. II, pp. 720–6 and *MH*, vol. II, p. 198.

[259] ANTT, *Ch. D. Duarte*, 1, f. 71v; *MH*, vol. VI, p. 211 and *CR Duarte*, p. 588.

[260] *ALF*, vol. II, pp. 792–5 and 784–8.

[261] The brothers Martim Afonso Gorizo and João Gorizo became connected respectively to the Infantes João and Henry: ANTT, *Ch. D. João I*, 4, f. 72v; *MH*, vol. III, pp. 76–8 and vol. IX, p. 156 and note. João Fogaça II was in the household of the Infante João while Fernão Fogaça was close to the heir Duarte.

[262] António José Saraiva, *História da cultura em Portugal*, vol. I (Lisbon: Jornal do Foro, 1955), p. 414.

[263] *Livro dos Conselhos*, p. 64.

which process, according to the chronicler Rui de Pina, Duarte would have followed strategically, instituting a system of rotation 'aos quartéis do ano'.[264] In this way, the personal government of this monarch would have made the existence of a plural court prevail where in an ideally ordered form the infantes and important lords, accompanied by their own retinues, would participate. This is perhaps an excessively harmonious image which the later chronicler has given, but the concrete data relative to the prosopography of the counsellors of this monarch (among whom are individuals close to his brothers, the dukes) seem in part to corroborate this, pointing at least towards a regular participation of the entourage of these individuals at the court of Duarte.[265] It was a precarious situation, as shown by the difficulty in adoption of the measures proposed in the Cortes following the unexpected death of Duarte, which gave rise to the grave political crisis of 1438–39, bringing to light the distinct factions already permeating court society.

In fact in 1438, through the constitution of a Council of Regency organised in rotation, participation at court and in the governance of the distinct groups was planned, and what could be considered as a 'political legate' for Duarte continued in a certain form. In the body of counsellors the majority were individuals favouring the widow-queen Leonor, such as the Conde de Barcelos, D. Afonso, Duarte de Meneses, Fernando de Cascais, Diogo Fernandes de Almeida, Gonçalo Pereira, Sancho de Noronha, Dr João do Sem, Nuno Martins da Silveira, Vasco Fernandes Coutinho and Pero Anes Lobato. Also, however, there were elements close to the Infante Pedro, such as Álvaro Vasques de Almada, Fernando de Meneses, Aires Gomes da Silva and Álvaro Gonçalves de Ataíde, and then courtiers who favoured Henry, among whom were Fernando de Castro and Álvaro de Castro, and some close to the Infante João, such as Luis Gonçalves Malafaia.[266] This group of heterogeneous individuals succeeded each other every three months at court, and were supported by various officials of Duarte's court whose political position is hard to discover, but they would have permanently accompanied the two regents, the queen and the Infante Pedro.

The rupture which was precipitated a little later between these diverse factions, as well as the systematic withdrawal of one of these (that which surrounded the queen) from sharing of palace positions after 1439 appears as

264 *CR Duarte*, pp. 504 and 514. This chronicle takes up the text of the Conde de Arraiolos, to which I referred in the previous note, for it is known that the *Livro dos Conselhos* is the direct source of many passages in Rui de Pina: Domingos Maurício Gomes dos Santos, *D. Duarte e as responsabilidades de Tânger (1433–1438)* (Lisbon, 1960) and also *MH*, vol. VI, p. 123.

265 We find among Duarte's counsellors D. Fernando de Castro, a powerful figure in Henry's household (ANTT, *Ch. D. Duarte*, 1, f. 67 and *MH*, vol. X, pp. 1–8) and also individuals connected to D. Pedro, such as Aires Gomes da Silva (*MH*, vol. X, pp. 156–7) and Luis de Azevedo (*MH*, vol. VI, p. 253).

266 For the identification of the various factions see the suggestions in Rui de Pina: *CR Afonso V*, in particular pp. 629–30 and 711–12.

a foreseeable consequence of the new political situation existing during the regency of the Duke of Coimbra. The complex network of contradictory solidarities caused by the system of coexistence among the clients of the infantes and the royal court did not seem destined to last. The new court which was organised in 1439 around the heir, the future Afonso V, was marked by the absolute predominance of the faction of the Duke of Coimbra, and appears to have been fatal to his ability to attract other followers and to the viability of a project of possible synthesis in the diversity of the court clients. Once again, an analysis of the body of counsellors of the monarch is elucidating. Before Alfarrobeira, a majority of individuals close to the regent were a part of this body; these included Aires Gomes da Silva, Álvaro Gonçalves de Ataíde (who was given the function of *aio* to the young king),[267] men of letters such as Dr Diogo Mangancha and the archdeacon Estevão Afonso,[268] and also some men who were close to the Infante Henry, such as Pedro de Castro.[269] A new situation in the late 1440s became unfavourable to the Infante Pedro, and was detectable in the presence of men such as Gonçalo Pereira and Dr Rui Fernandes in the council of the young monarch from 1446.[270]

With the court of Afonso V during the 1450s and 1460s, there came a new time in which the court system seems to have reached full maturity with the affirmation of the royal court as the indisputable centre of the social configuration analysed here. Because of its characteristics, this court appears to me suited to a monographic study of great interest, particularly when examining the alterations it introduced to the court organism of the end of the Middle Ages described here (which alterations can be found at an organisational level) and also of practices in payments and even in the financial and institutional regime. I shall emphasise three factors which, in my opinion, contributed greatly to the beginning of this undisputed supremacy and centrality of the royal court, which was typical of the situation after 1460 and also contributed to the disappearance of a tendency towards policentralism seen in the Portuguese court society of the first half of the fifteenth century. First, there existed an important ceremonial investment, an analysis of which will be made later, keeping some of the uses current in earlier courts, with a view to a systematic 'invention' of a Portuguese tradition solidly rooted in the Iberian and European context. Then was the actual opening to the outside world, represented by the Moroccan adventure, which would continue to play a most important role in the life cycle of the Portuguese courtier of the second half of the fifteenth century and which increased and institutionalised new modes of service alongside the later aesthetic diffusion

[267] ANTT, *Ch. D. Duarte*, 2, f. 35v; ANTT, *Ch. D. Afonso V*, 5, f. 18v.
[268] *MH*, vol. VII, pp. 77–8, 145–8, 149 and 187.
[269] ANTT, *Ch. D. Afonso V*, 5, f. 69; *MH*, vol. VIII, pp. 102–3. Also Rui de Pina: *CR Afonso V*, p. 743.
[270] *MH*, vol. IX, p. 201 and respectively pp. 206 and 351.

of the culture of chivalry. Finally, there was the creation of internal demarcations at the heart of the nobility which had a preferential field of affirmation at court and a resort to the granting of noble titles (such as marquis and baron) which, until then, had not been used in Portugal,[271] and which were hierarchically articulated through their own rules of etiquette. In 1448 in the famous charter which the rejected Infante Pedro wrote to his nephew, the count of Arraiolos, Pedro referred to the 'practicas e deferenças e modos nom acustumados em Portugal que sse tem na corte'.[272] The final episodes in the pluralist period referred to above were formed in 1460 by the final absorption into the royal entourage of numerous elements of the household of the deceased Infante Henry and also of some of the old Duke of Braganza, which brought to a close in a highly significant manner the experience of a generation.[273] In this way there culminated on another plane which is of necessity more complex both on the level of a normative regime and of practices, the logic towards a domestic and ever-more disrupted time of court sociability, making the servants of the major households of the infantes move to the court of the king following their death. Yet another demonstration of this central force which made the court of Afonso V the point of arrival and of departure of individuals and groups and which distinguishes it from the plural court of the last medieval sovereigns.

Criação and service – here lies the fundamental explanatory bond which connects the mechanisms of recruitment at court to the essential stability of its physiognomy in each particular reign. Also, from the point of view of a longer period, it is a bond which I propose as the main factor in the explanation of the lines of continuity and the peculiar autonomy of the retinue of the kings where, as has been seen, we find the same families in recurring form. *Criação* clearly influenced court sociability in its relations with the continuity of a patriarchal image of royalty and also through the important presence of the young in the royal entourage. This was a process of living together and a mechanism of patronage which was more or less complex, and constituted the fertile ground where so many other aspects of this sociability were cultivated. Service, with connotations of feudal values, although in many ambits of court society to a great degree independent of the feudo-vassalic relationship, was the main reason for the presence of the courtier alongside the monarch. There is a highly varied spread of actual activities to which this 'court service' refers, whether we look at it in the specific optic of the functions, of remunerations or even of hierarchies which it helped to construct. I should stress the difficulties which appeared in my research regarding the detection of a specific regime in the transmission of

[271] *DHP*, vol. III, pp. 149–52. [272] *MH*, vol. IX, p. 353.

[273] On the destiny of many of Henry's servants following his death: Dias Dinis, *Estudos Henriquinos* and also Sousa, *A casa senhorial do Infante*, pp. 269–79. In the roll of *moradores* of 1462, several names are given with the denomination 'do infante', showing that they previously accompanied Henry. The subject was also referred to at the Cortes of 1472–73: ANTT, Cortes, M 2, 14, f. 69v.

duties which, in the Portuguese court, appeared very late. Some essential aspects of this regime, such as hereditary succession to the principal offices, appear only in the fifteenth century, as we have seen, which is yet another important indicator of the tendency analysed in the previous chapter of a weakness in the structuring of a 'Portuguese court society' in comparison with the importance of its Peninsular forms until the end of the fourteenth century. Contrasting this late structure of the regime of offices we find, however, an internal hierarchy at the court of the kings which in various ways is found from the end of the thirteenth century with relative force, imposing the traditionality of its norms on the variegated court social circle.

Finally, I emphasise that the court of the kings in Portugal was constructed in relation to other similar organisms with which it competed and from which it sought to differentiate itself in a process of constant reaffirmation of its dominant position. 'Court society' in Portugal, although it has as its centre, let me repeat, the entourage of the monarchs, involved in its network many other human circles in a plurality of highly marked units, both in its organisation and in its ways of life and specific forms of interdependence discussed here, through the direct influence of the court of the monarchs.

4. *The court and space*

The court of the kings during the medieval period was conceived to a large extent as a spatial entity. As an organism of variable dimension and complexity, moving in the physical space of the kingdom with the incessant removals of the monarch, from its beginnings the court also represented a particular, highly characteristic mode of life through this itinerance. Removals and stops of the royal retinue caused degrees of apprehension in the space of the kingdom and, simultaneously, structured events of court life. It is in this dual dimension that I shall analyse these. In relating the places visited by the monarchs of the late Middle Ages and, also, those where their stays were more prolonged, with the network of the diverse royal residences I found some indications of the process of a tendency towards setting down of roots of the Portuguese court in the physical space of the kingdom. This route of research led me not only to reflect upon the actual relationship existing between the court and the sites of its lifestyle, but also to consider the court as a relatively complex spatial universe. That is, a conceived, actual spatial universe with the concepts of the age (in particular the known territorial projection of medieval juridic pluralism) in mind, but a universe which establishes a specific connection having multiple aspects with the various places where the court moves for the creation of intermittent areas of supply and economic influence, and also of jurisdictional spheres which could temporarily transform the most modest of towns into the centre of the entire kingdom.

THE ITINERANCE

In spite of the fact that it has been much referred to in the historiography of the nineteenth century, the constant movement of the medieval monarchs throughout the actual physical spaces over which they exercised power forms a phenomenon which is still enigmatic, both in its actual forms and in its meaning. The most current explanation for this removal was that the itinerance was for essentially economic reasons, and there was seen in it the expression of dependence for their support by the sovereigns of the earliest periods of the High Middle Ages on resources facilitated by the diverse territories and, on the other hand, the fruit of a supremacy which was entirely theoretical (and even, as Marc Bloch has emphasised, theoretically inadequate because of its *a priori* reasoning) of a 'natural' economy.[1] In an echo of this argument which became commonplace in all the manuals, although it enunciated some important and acute reservations as to the monetary practices of Portuguese society of the twelfth and thirteenth centuries, Lúcio de Azevedo even conceded in 1929 in his *Épocas de Portugal económico* that when they removed, the first Portuguese sovereigns had to consume locally the possessions and *colheitas* owing to them by the entire kingdom; this statement later came to be mechanically repeated by many others.[2] However, it is a theory which deserves some critical attention in the face of what is also known of medieval royalty leading one to stress, as a counterpart statement, the essentially political meaning of the royal itinerance. Nor, in ages as early as the Merovingian period, as definitively established by Carlrichard Brühl in the 1960s, could the removal of the monarchs have as its reason merely the consumption of dues owed, for to the contrary, there was a demand for far more complicated mechanisms than until then supposed for the concentration of these products in precise, given places ('palaces', abbeys or bishoprics) and even the transaction of these products or the administration of their consumption in a manner which would allow that the sovereign and the royal entourage had access to them.[3] That is, the traditional argument that the itinerance was the result of the necessity for the monarch to consume locally the tributes due to him appears to have no foundation, even for the earliest periods which would be characterised by a supremacy of the 'natural economy', and instead to be emphasised is the antiquity in the diverse European territories of France, Germany and Italy of a complex system of services dating from the sixth and seventh centuries which came to be called *servitium regis* or *gistum*, and which were destined to make possible the movement of the kings throughout their kingdoms. Contrary to what was believed to be the traditional explanation, the royal objective was indeed the itinerance, and the eventual consumption of goods provided in the areas

[1] Marc Bloch, 'Economie-nature ou économie-argent: un pseudo-dilemme', *Annales d'Histoire Social*, 1 (1939), 7–16. For a present-day discussion: Joel Kaye, *Economy and Nature in the Fourteenth Century: Money, Market Exchange, and the Emergence of Scientific Thought* (Cambridge: Cambridge University Press, 1998).

[2] João Lúcio de Azevedo, *Épocas de Portugal económico: esboços de história* (Lisbon: Clássica, 1973), pp. 30–1, 35 and 41. On the use of the concept of 'natural economy' by Lúcio de Azevedo (a careful reader of Werner Sombart), see the texts on 'economic organisation' of the history of Portugal (Barcelos), now united in João Lúcio de Azevedo, *Elementos para a história económica de Portugal, séculos XII a XVIII* (Lisbon: Inapa, 1990), in particular pp. 71–4.

[3] Carlrichard Brühl, *Fodrum, Gistum, Servitium Regis*, 2 vols. (Cologne: Böhlau, 1968). A developed summary of the main conclusions of this erudite work can be found in F. Vercauteren, 'L'Hôtel du Roi (à propos d'un livre récent)', *Le Moyen Age*, 74 (1968), 577–97.

was a means which made it possible, and was an end in itself. Thus one can establish a certain contrast between the royalty of western Europe, where they were more connected to the physical presence of the monarchs as they moved, and the more sedentary character of the Byzantine sovereign for example who, however, also made substantially diffused the imperial image throughout the several provinces.[4] According to Millar when writing on the Low Empire (of the third and fourth centuries), it would seem that a growing mobility of the court existed which was related to the actual transformation of imperial authority, and in this lay the roots of this long-lasting political structure.[5] In his initial reflection, the Muslim historian Ibn Khaldun observed in the fourteenth century that the power of any sedentary dynasty would weaken in the furthermost regions, and that to take its centre would mean having power over its heart and vital spirit, so provoking the dissolution of that power.[6] This fundamentally political understanding of the value of itinerance is characteristic of the predominant perspective during the Middle Ages to which I refer. Medieval societies attributed much meaning to the presence of the king in the different parts of the territory, and mobility was a characteristic and a way of life strictly related to the condition of royalty. This political and cultural reality persisted in the later period analysed here, in spite of the indubitable progress towards a better understanding and control of the territory by the royal power, which made itinerance, from a strictly administrative viewpoint, increasingly less necessary in the fourteenth and fifteenth centuries. The same could be said regarding the mechanisms of perception and administration of tributes by the kingdom, and the final period of the Middle Ages witnessed the emergence of an innovative royal fiscality whose evolution progressed at the time largely at the margin of the traditional practice of royal itinerance and even in a certain way ignored it, since it was ever more based on tributes of an 'extraordinary' or indirect character.[7]

For societies such as those of the Iberian Peninsula of the thirteenth to fifteenth centuries, with an economy which was seen in many areas as intensely

[4] Sabine MacCormack, *Art and Ceremony in Late Antiquity* (Berkeley: University of California Press, 1981), in particular pp. 73–84 on the *adventus* of imperial images, and also the statement of Wallace-Hadrill, *The Long-Haired Kings*, pp. 181–2.

[5] Fergus Millar, *The Emperor in the Roman World* (Ithaca: Cornell University Press, 1977), pp. 28–40.

[6] *The Muqaddimah*, pp. 128–9.

[7] 'C'est parce que les charges publiques dépassent de beaucoup le volume des revenus ordinaires, même lorsque ceux-ci sont les revenus d'un domaine royal, que les finances publiques trouvent, dans le recours à une fiscalité extraordinaire comme dans l'usage d'expédients fondés sur l'exploitation de la puissance publique, leur caractère le plus original': Jean Favier, *Finance et fiscalité au bas moyen âge* (Paris: SEVPEN, 1971), p. 71; Iria Gonçalves, 'Estado moderno, finanças públicas e fiscalidade permanente', in Maria Helena da Cruz Coelho and Armando Luís de Carvalho Homem (eds.), *A génese do estado moderno no Portugal tardo-medievo (séculos XIII–XV)* (Lisbon: Universidade Autónoma, 1999), pp. 95–110.

monetarised when compared with the general European context,[8] the idea of an itinerance caused by the need for a systematic consumption in places by the kings of gifts in kind paid by the population is truly hard to accept. The problem of the complexity of supply to the royal entourage, which has in a way been concealed by this traditional explanation, will be studied in detail later. It is enough to remember, for the moment, that the gifts which in the Portuguese as in the Castilian case were intended for the sustenance of the monarch, and were known as 'colheitas' or 'jantares' from the end of the thirteenth century were beginning to be given in money.[9] If we compare the accounts of the Portuguese king, Afonso III, to which I have referred elsewhere in this book, where there is also reference to produce resulting from 'colheitas', with the later 'cartas de quitação' for officials such as the purveyor or the *uchão* whose duty was the provisioning of the court, we find in effect the disappearance of this type of collection and a systematic recourse to the buying of produce and victuals of every type.[10] The Hispanic evolution is found in the general panorama known to us, for Brühl determined that in Italy the *fodrum* was calculated (and on many occasions paid) in money very early on, from the eleventh century, just as the *gistum* in France was to be in the following century, while in the German instance the *servitia* owed to the emperor were settled in coinage from the thirteenth century.

On the other hand, it should be emphasised that many of these gifts were specifically destined for the royal table and not that of the entire court, and the food for the monarch, as I have already stated several times, was the subject of a most particular symbolic and ceremonial investment, not only in its preparation and production but also in its origin. Supplies for the court, though, formed a far greater problem which must, I believe, be distinguished from this. According to norms recorded in the Aragonese *Ordenacions* of Pedro IV, for example, it was up to the court official, the 'comprador', to proceed to the acquisition of food intended for the king, but he also had to receive tributes in 'cena' (equivalent to the Castilian 'yantar' and the Portuguese 'jantar') which he was obliged to use for the supply of the royal table, even though these were by now paid in number, and this currency had to be 'converted' into kind.[11] This is yet another example, alongside so many others which Marc Bloch has suggested, of the use

8 A. H. de Oliveira Marques, 'A moeda Portuguesa durante a idade média', *Ensaios de história medieval Portuguesa* (Lisbon: Vega, 1980), pp. 195–220 and in particular pp. 196–7.

9 *DHP*, vol. I, p. 615 (s.v. 'colheita'); Nilda Guglielmi, 'Posada y yantar. Contribución al estudio del léxico de las instituciones medievales', *Hispania*, 26 (1966), 5–40 and 165–219.

10 Besides *quitações* for the *uchão* already mentioned, see for example the series relating to the king's *comprador* for the years 1438–40, 1441–51, 1450–61 and 1472–75: ANTT, *LN*, Extras, ff. 240, 118–19, 43–4 and 32v–33.

11 'totes les cenes que en diners seran pagadores, aquells diners convertesca en la provisio del nostre menjar': 'Ordenacions' (ed. Bofarull y Mascarò), pp. 46–7. Iria Gonçalves pronounced in a similar meaning for the Portuguese case: 'the basic products could continue to be present and would reappear at the time of each payment to have a value according to the prices then

at the time of the monetary instrument as a simple means of deferring the consumption of a particular product. However, in my opinion the text shows more than anything the understanding which existed of the specific relationship of this tribute with the body of the king: the various communities of the kingdom were symbolically connected to each other by common obedience, which was expressed by this function of feeding the king. Thus we find the possible retention of the original meaning of this giving of 'jantares' in the mid-fourteenth century, in spite of the transformations undergone in the actual methods of collection and administration of these tributes at the end of the Middle Ages. This is a meaning to which the doctrine of the Castilian *Fuero Viejo* referred in its enumeration of royal prerogative, in which it saw the 'jantares', alongside the minting of coinage, as an exclusive attribute of the monarchs.

In Castile from the fourteenth century, and certainly in Portugal from the middle of the same century, the *colheitas* or *jantares* already had the characteristics of a fixed gift which was not subject to the fact of the monarch's visit, this at least in the regions of the country where this tribute was paid by the districts.[12] In the Portuguese instance, we still find in the fifteenth century how the evolution of this tribute had a certain complexity, and how it varied according to the territories. North of the Douro, for example, as was the case in Galicia, there continued to be mention of payment of *colheitas* resulting from a visit by the king, and even of the payment of *colheitas* in accumulation either to the king or to the heir to the throne (the sum due on the visit of the former was usually double that paid for a visit of the infante).[13] However, in the Alentejo area, south of the river Roxo, and in the territories of the Order of St James, the problem was seen in differing ways, as can be deduced from conflicts following the visit of the king to Beja in 1444–45, when payment of the *colheitas* was difficult, since the tribute had previously been transferred by John I during the

in use or, what is more curious, to be preferable to money. There are various examples of this fact, arising from the fourteenth and fifteenth centuries': 'Estado moderno, finanças públicas e fiscalidade permanente', p. 102.

12 Guglielmi, 'Posada y yantar', pp. 203–4; Iria Gonçalves, *Alguns aspectos da visita régia ao Entre Cávado e Minho, no século XIII*, offprint of *Estudos Medievais* (Oporto, 1993). The change in methods of payment, by all appearances, was discussed at the Castile/Leon court *c.* 1286, and recognised in a curious cantiga ('tensão de escárneo') on the subject: Aurora Juarez Blanquer, 'El tributo del "yantar" en el siglo XII. Una tenson de Payo Gomez Charinho', *Cuadernos de Estudios Medievales*, 12–13 (1984), 109–17. On the Castilian evolution, see also Miguel Angel Ladero Quesada, *Fiscalidad y poder real en Castilla (1252–1369)* (Madrid: Editoria Complutense, 1993), pp. 37–40.

13 According to a royal document of the 1450s, the royal *colheita* was due 'por nossa chegada a alguns certos lugares ou por passagem dalgũs rios cabedaes ou ribeiras ou por quaesquer outras certas divissoens honde per obrigaçom e direito nos ajam com ellas d acudir': ANTT, *Ch. D. Afonso V*, 4, f. 63v. On the crossing of the Douro: José Marques, *A Arquidiocese de Braga no século XV* (Lisbon: INCM, 1988), p. 682. An example of what I have said on the king and heir can be found for example in documentation of the Minho Paço de Sousa monastery archives: João Luis Fontes, 'Fr. João Álvares e a tentativa de reforma do Mosteiro de S. Salvador de Paço de Sousa', *Lusitania Sacra*, 10 (1998), 240–1.

difficult times of the beginning of his reign in favour of the Order.[14] That is, the space of the medieval kingdom cannot be seen as a homogeneous reality even from the viewpoint of the monarch, and in many aspects it is far from modern notions of abstract and atopical space, which are wrongly and easily extrapolated from our own times and which continue to be implicit in the interpretation of many historians.[15] This territorial diversity has not been entirely explored in its possible relationship with the travels of the Portuguese monarchs as yet another factor in the explanation of the global pattern of royal itinerance of the fourteenth and fifteenth centuries. There are also many examples in the Portuguese instance from the middle of the fourteenth century of the giving of *colheitas* or *jantares* in an unspecified form to nobles or kings' officials, apparently regarding this tribute as being yet another revenue in number due to the monarchs, which could have diverse destinations. Yet again, investigations on the evolution of fiscality and medieval royal finances are seen as essential if we wish to advance in clarifying this complex question.

Leaving aside for the moment the material and organisational aspects of the itinerance, and once its profound need is established, as well as the central value it assumed as a constitutive element of the royal power,[16] it is important to analyse globally how it was included in the physical space in the actual case of the Portuguese kingdom. For this, we have to hand an important group of data collected for the establishment of the itineraries of the medieval monarchs from the brief initial period between 1325 and 1342 (which corresponds to a part only of the reign of Afonso IV) and continuing almost uninterrupted after 1360 until the period of the regency of the Infante Pedro, which comes to an end in 1448.[17] What value can be attributed to this data series, when considering the reconstruction of the movements of the kings and the court? Beyond the problem of the lacunae detected in the series (corresponding to the less-recorded period

[14] ANTT, *Ch. D. Afonso V*, 5, f. 59v. See also several sentences relating to this post in Beira and the Alentejo: ANTT, drawer XV, M 10, 17; drawer XI, M 8, 32; drawer XI, M 3, 16; drawer XI, M 6, 29.

[15] Rita Costa Gomes, 'Monarquia e território: residências reais Portuguesas (séculos XIV a XVI)', in Rita Costa Gomes and Gérard Sabatier (eds.), *Lugares de poder/Lieux de pouvoir/Places of Power* (Lisbon: Fundação Calouste Gulbenkian, 1998), pp. 85–105.

[16] See the observations of Clifford Geertz, 'Centers, kings and charisma: reflections on the symbolic of power', in J. Ben-David and T. Nicols Clark (eds.), *Culture and Its Creators: Essays in Honour of Edward Shils* (Chicago: University of Chicago Press, 1977).

[17] Pedro de Azevedo, 'A Chancelaria de D. Afonso IV', *Boletim da Segunda Classe da Academia das Ciências de Lisboa*, 4 (1912), 180–99; Maria Teresa Campos Rodrigues, 'O itinerário de D. Pedro I, 1357–1367', *Ocidente* (ns), 82 (1972), 147–76; Maria Teresa Campos Rodrigues, *Itinerário de D. Fernando, 1367–1383*', offprint of *Bracara Augusta*, 1978; Humberto Baquero Moreno, *Itinerários de El-Rei D. João I* (Lisbon: Institute de Cultura e Lingua Portuguesa, 1988); Humberto Baquero Moreno, *Os itinerários de El-Rei Dom Duarte (1433–1448)* (Lisbon: Academia Portuguesa de Histórico, 1976); Humberto Baquero Moreno, *Os itinerários do Infante D. Pedro (1438–1448)*, offprint of *Revista de Ciências do Homem da Universidade de Lourenço Marques* (1968).

of documentation of the Portuguese monarchs in the 1350s), and considering also the specific case of a possible divergence of movements between the regent and the infante heir in the period 1438–48, some generic observations must be made as to the limits of this type of collation, whose methodology also presents a certain variation of criteria depending on the historians who reconstructed these itineraries.

Generally resulting from the chronologically ordered list of the places cited in the catalogue of royal documents recorded in the chancery, the itineraries first pose the question of the simultaneous nature of the movements of the king in relation to those of his *desembargo* – a multifaceted instance involving various institutions including the chancery, which is responsible for the production of these documents. This is a problem which acquires a greater importance for the fourteenth and fifteenth centuries, as Carvalho Homem demonstrated, for we have available several indications on the spatial dissociation of the various components of the *desembargo*, for example between the monarch and the chancery.[18] There are no existing records of the documentary production of the bureaucratic instance (his chamber) closest to the king during this period. The conflict between the series obtained through this and the reconstructed series based on the records of the chancery would reveal for certain some variation in the respective data.

One of the most predictable aspects of these discrepancies results from full removals of the monarch, who would not always be accompanied by the officials most indirectly related to him. This fact perhaps explains, in the opinion advanced by editors of the itineraries, certain discrepancies seen in the chronological list of localities. It is thus important to keep in mind that even when the so-called royal chancery allows for documentation of a large part of the chronological span of the several reigns, the removals which it reveals can only be a clumsy sketch of the royal itinerance of the monarch, more or less coincident with him and perhaps approximating more to an itinerance of the court in its broader expression – that is, of the most numerous and larger part of the entourage which would follow at its own pace, 'in the steps' of the monarch.

Another problem which cannot be avoided is the unequal value which from an heuristic point of view the diverse 'chanceries' which have reached us possess, and through which the royal itineraries are reconstructed. In its present state, this source comprises in the main, in the case of all the reigns from Afonso IV to Duarte, later-fifteenth-century copies, which are more or less partial and abbreviated, of the original group of recorded documents in the chancery itself, which was destroyed. In the face of this problem we can detect a diversity in the method followed by various authors, since the itineraries reconstructed for the fourteenth century (of Pedro and Fernando) are limited to data obtained through

[18] *Desembargo*, pp. 155–63.

the remains of actual archival collections called 'chancery', respecting in a certain way the singularity and the present state of this source which largely comprises copies of original records, while the itineraries of the fifteenth-century sovereigns (John I, Duarte and the regent Pedro) are based on an attempt at a construction of a documentary *corpus* from a variety of sources which, although in the main dependent upon the same type of copies of the 'chancery', seeks to fill in lacunae by referring to other sources. For an interpretation and commentary of the data obtained, we can also refer to the contemporary chronicles of Fernão Lopes and the later ones of Rui de Pina, and seek to contrast them with data from royal documentation. The principle, which is hard to contradict, of having to hand all information available arising from documents produced in the name of the kings reveals itself as a unifying method regarding a plurality of sources whose reports, from the point of view of royal diplomatics, are not clarified.

For the reasons I have just listed, it is my opinion that data collected for the royal itineraries can be treated globally while adhering to my objective, which is the study of the relationship between the court and the space of the kingdom, in particular collating data relative to several reigns in order to obtain the most expressive possible image of the royal itinerance – while we know that treatment on the smallest scale of this series, for example through annual cycles, would be seen anyway as a hypothetical construction which merely evokes an approximation as to the removal of the king and the court, or of a part of it, by referring to data of highly unequal quality. Added to this, the variation in such short cycles would not be pertinent to my analysis, nor would a reconstruction of the geographical itineraries themselves, that is, the actual spatial journeys as deduced hypothetically from the succession of localities where the kings had decrees published and relating these journeys or not to the little which is known of the most utilised medieval routes. I have, to the contrary, centred my attention on two sets of information which can be obtained through the study of the frequency of the itineraries: the probable number of times that the kings visited the various places on the one hand, and the length of stay in these places, characterised in their temporal length and in seasonal distribution.[19]

[19] See on the treatment of this series and the possibilities of graphic representation of the data obtained: Júlia Galego et al., *Os itinerários de D. Dinis, D. Pedro e D. Fernando: interpretação gráfica* (Lisbon: Centro de Estudos Geográficos, 1988). The proceedings I have used are closest to those already recognised by this excellent work: *visita* is considered the entire presence documented on a non-consecutive day in a given location, and preceded by a different location; *estada* is the time included in the number of consecutive days of presence, including the occasions of only one day. In this case, although there are chronological discrepancies, or where for the same date there are documents attributed to two different locations, I have taken into account both places mentioned (for it is most probable that the monarch had been in both). On the other hand, the documents dated 'do arraial' of certain places were not taken into account for the evaluation of the stops in these places, since the kings were outside them, attempting their military conquest.

Always bearing in mind the relatively approximate character of these data for a precise spatial-temporal localisation of the court of the end of the Middle Ages, I consider that the relationships of the court with the diverse localities of the kingdom are reasonably evoked by the two vectors of the itinerance, that is, the frequency of the royal visit and its duration. The actual reasons for the removals of the monarchs can be most varied. Among the most important are the exercise of war, solemn and ceremonial occasions, the hunt, the meeting of the Cortes, plague and the actual time of the year, which would determine a certain tendency for seasonal removal among the most visited localities. These weather-related reasons are always hard to assess, and have been noted for some monarchs whose mobility seems more accentuated, as for example is the case of Pedro.

As can be seen from maps I have reproduced,[20] where the places visited by the kings of the fourteenth and fifteenth centuries are shown, itinerance covered in a different way the distinct spaces of the kingdom (Maps 1 and 2). The presence of the monarchs certainly occurred in almost all Portuguese regions, with the exception of some zones known to be less populated, such as the coast of the Alentejo and the Beira Baixa, as also the frontier region of Trás os Montes. The most frequently travelled regions, where we find the greatest spatial density of places visited, do not however correspond to the most populated zones of the country, which would be Entre Douro e Minho and the Beira, but they do correspond to the central and littoral regions. On the other hand, the maps show clearly the tendency towards reduction in spatial amplitude of the removals in the case of the fifteenth-century monarchs, who overall visited fewer places than their antecedents, and who were almost unseen in the Algarve and very little in the frontier region of the Alentejo and areas of Beira.[21] Thus we see that, in the period studied, there is a propensity towards favouring the regions of the centre of the country, and it can be concluded that this is characteristic of the royalty of the final stages of the Middle Ages.

20 The following localities are not included on the maps either because their location is uncertain or because they are too close to others and therefore would prejudice their clarity. Map 1: Comba (Coimbra), Mora (Santarém), Porto das Mestras (Coruche), Póvoa dos Cortiços (Alcobaça), Avelar, Homem, Queiras, Coles, Acoa (Rio Coa?), Égua, Momportom (?), Bembelide (?), Franceira and Sazes. Map 2: Póvoa de S. Catarina (Coimbra), Aldeia do Outeiro (Coimbra), Freches (Trancoso), Vale de Paraíso (Aveiras), Segadães, Soza (Viseu?), Quintã do Monte Olivete and Camarate (Lisbon), Água dos Peixes (Alvito) and S. Domingos da Ordem (Évora). In all cases, these are places of little import in the totality of the data. I have also ignored the rare removals of the monarchs outside the territory of the kingdom: for example those of Afonso IV to the extreme south of Andalucia, or those of Fernando to Galicia, and then in the case of John I to Galicia and the Leonese Estremadura, and, of course, to Ceuta. Because of their connection with wars, their specifity is somewhat distant from the problem studied here, although connected to the usual ways of life of court society.

21 It should be noted that the locations shown on Map 2 in Trás os Montes and the Beira interior correspond to the military campaigns of the first years of John's reign and that, once forced into obedience, they were not visited again by the monarchs until the reign of Afonso V.

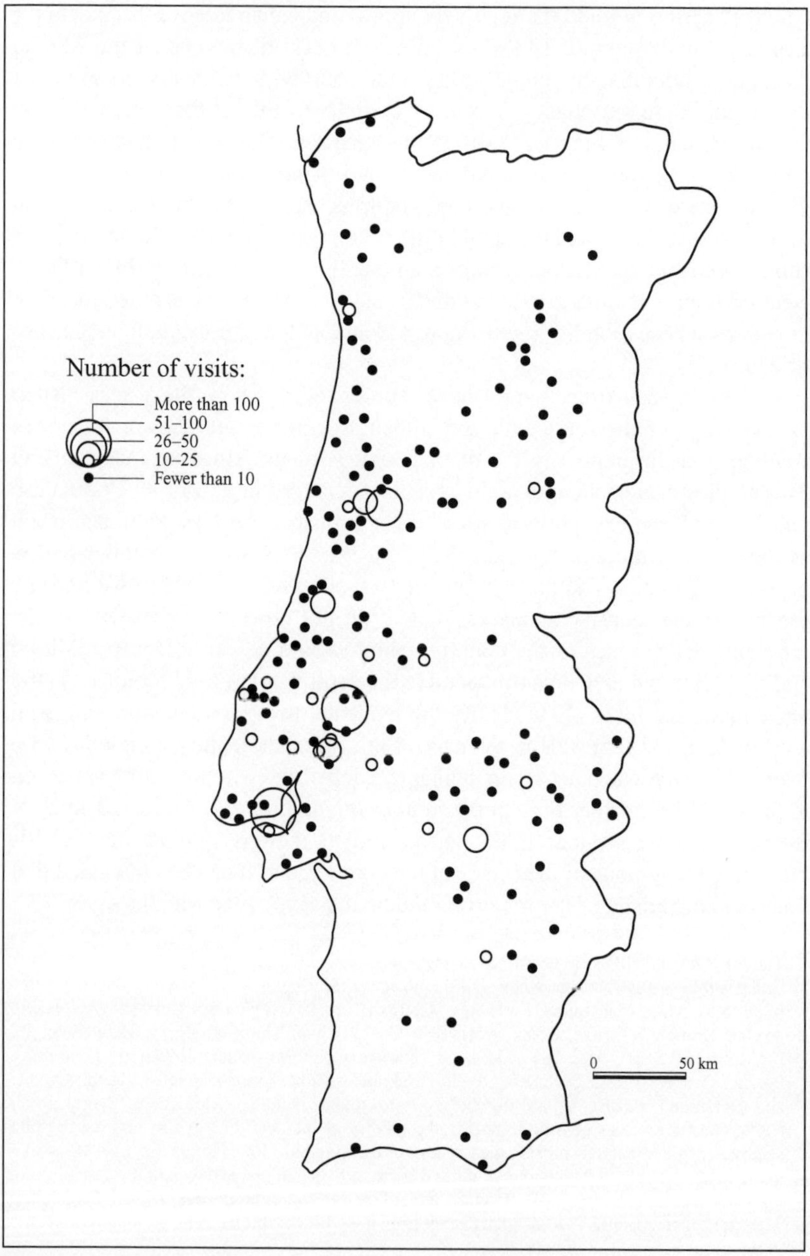

Map 1 Places visited according to the royal itineraries (1325–42 and 1360–83)

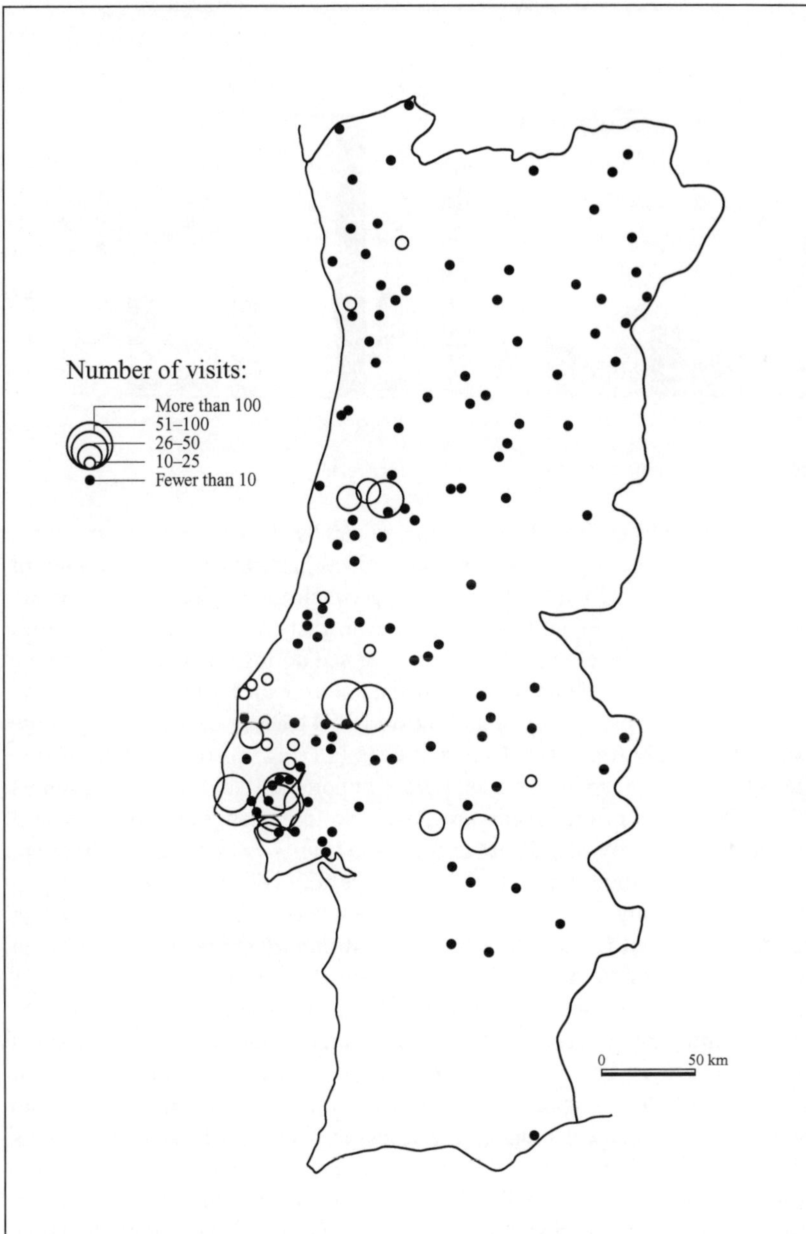

Map 2 Places visited according to the royal itineraries (1385–1438)

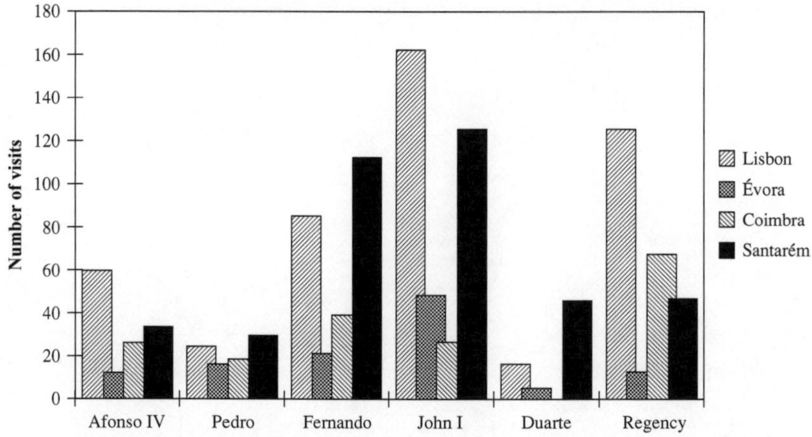

Fig. 6 Number of visits to the four main cities in each reign

Among the places visited most by the monarchs, the principal urban centres of the kingdom hold an important place since in themselves they represent a high percentage of the total days during which the stages of the court are known to us in each reign (Fig. 6). However, Lisbon and Coimbra are cities whose relative political importance was reversed during the period prior to the fourteenth century. Lisbon was in the ascendant from the thirteenth century, and represented the most important and most visited locality of the country at the end of the Middle Ages. The decline of Coimbra (Fig. 7) continued during the fifteenth century, in spite of the temporary importance which the city assumed during the period of the regency of Pedro (so influencing the prominence it appears to have in my Map 2). As to Santarém (Fig. 8), which was an important nucleus of population during the medieval period, being as it was accessible by river and having a central position in a rich agricultural region, it could be said that it rivalled Évora as the second most important locality for the royal itinerances, with little difference from Lisbon (Fig. 9) both in the number of visits and in the duration of stays spent there. As has recently been observed through cartographic reconstruction of the journeys begun from there, carried out for some royal itineraries of the fourteenth century, Santarém was the most central locality, topographically speaking, of this court geography, since the monarch was in an ideal situation for access to his most frequent destinations when setting off from there.[22] In turn, the importance which Évora (Fig. 10) progressively attained and which becomes most clear in the fifteenth century also corresponds to a period during which, as has already been said, the kings removed less, and to places less distant from the central coastal line to the south

[22] Galego *et al.*, *Os Itinerários*, 37 (maps in fig. 14A) and 48 (fig. 19).

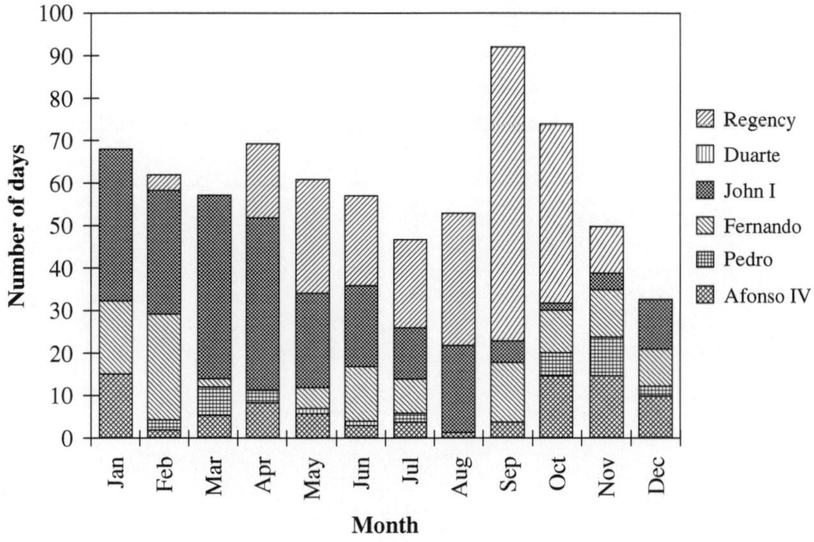

Fig. 7 Seasonal distribution of royal stays in Coimbra

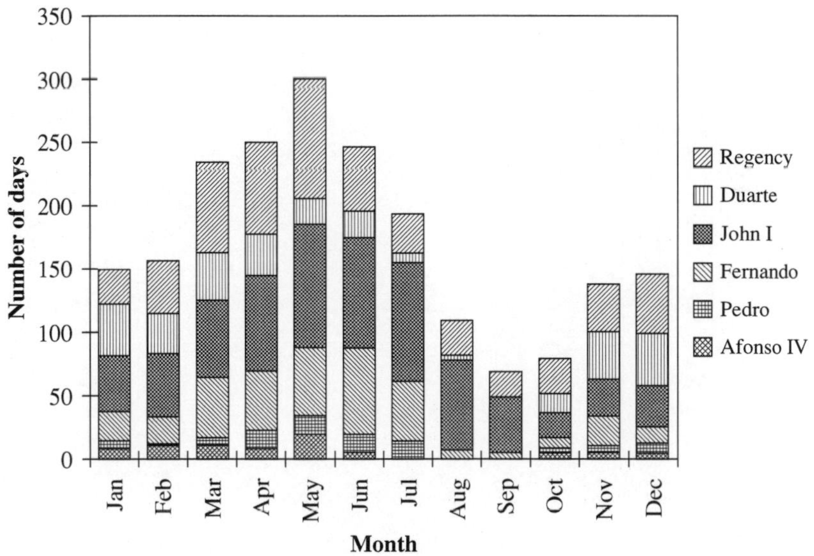

Fig. 8 Seasonal distribution of royal stays in Santarém

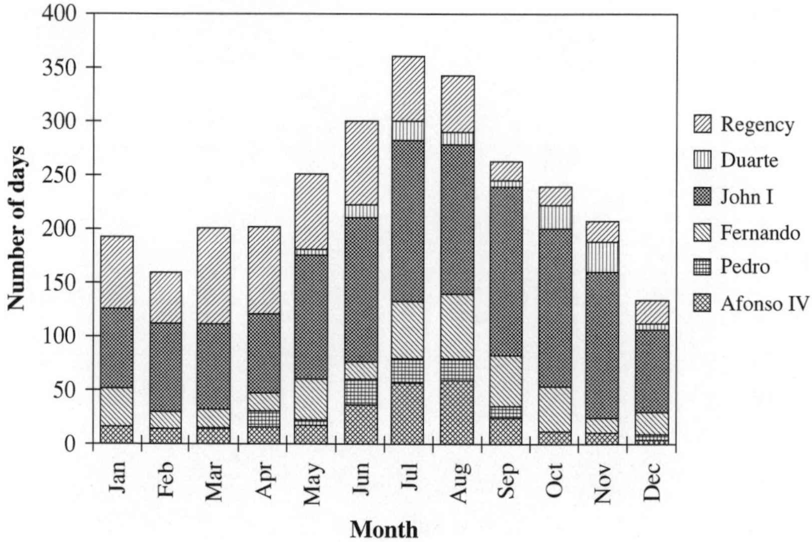

Fig. 9 Seasonal distribution of royal stays in Lisbon

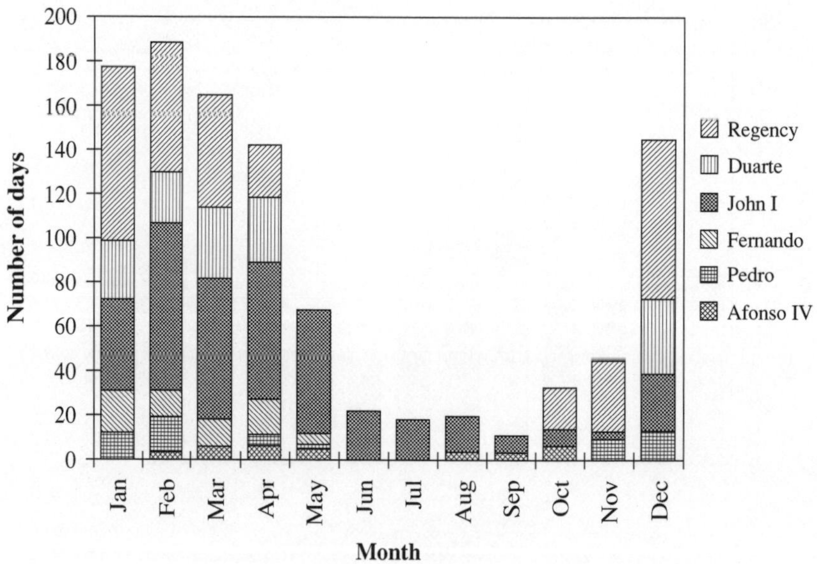

Fig. 10 Seasonal distribution of royal stays in Évora

of Coimbra, which remained the most usual scenario for royal itinerance, and became polarised in Lisbon and Santarém. Maps 1 and 2 show the total number of visits to each locality, and the global importance of Lisbon can be compared with Santarém, for example, with their importance reversed visibly only during the reigns of Fernando and Duarte, or the numbers attained by Coimbra during the regency of the Infante Pedro, in comparison with the earlier tendency.

An analysis of the places most frequently visited by the monarch must be made, in turn, bearing in mind the enormous weight of these four main poles in the travels of the court. Thus, certain localities appear to have held great importance because of their position, being situated along the possible routes connecting them to the royal cities, in particular Montemor-o-Novo, between Lisbon and Évora (but which, as can be seen on Map 3, was also the heart of an important hunting zone, the Coutada Velha) and, to a lesser degree, Coruche;[23] or as was also the case of certain localities close to Lisbon, such as Sacavém (on the route of the Tagus valley) or Almada (which remained connected to the crossing of the river estuary). A similar observation can be made for other, lesser places which were much visited but where royal stops never lasted long, such as Teixoso during the fourteenth century, because of its specific position on the route from the Estrela mountain. By comparing Maps 1 and 2, we see that the role played by the localities of the Alentejo, apart from Évora, diminished a little for the fifteenth century and disappeared totally in the case of Beja. To the south of the Tagus, the episcopal city (Évora) was to be confirmed from then on as the undisputed centre of court itinerances. In contrast, the region of the Minho seems to have reached particular importance during, almost exclusively, the reign of John, and this was polarised in the towns of Oporto and Guimarães (although here the data appear very distorted owing to the lacunae of the first half of the fourteenth century, which possibly would reveal more northerly itineraries for Afonso IV).

Corresponding to these two indisputable facts – the importance of the centre and the littoral of the kingdom; more frequent departures to Lisbon, Santarém, Évora and Coimbra – I would emphasise a network of places habitually visited by the kings of the end of the medieval period which were organised upon three principal nuclei. In the region of the Estremadura from the fourteenth century, Rio Maior, Torres Novas, Óbidos, Atouguia and Torres Vedras were much visited and, to the extreme north, Leiria; in the fifteenth century to these were added places such as Aldeia Galega, Bombarral and Arruda dos Vinhos. A natural limit to the south of this space was the Tagus valley, which formed an easily travelled region where, as we shall see, there were numerous royal residences, and this determined the frequent visits to Alenquer, Vila Nova da

23 Suzanne Daveau, 'Géographie historique du site de Coruche, étape sur les itinéraires entre Évora et le Ribatejo', *Revista da Faculdade de Letras*, 5th series, 2 (1984), 115–35.

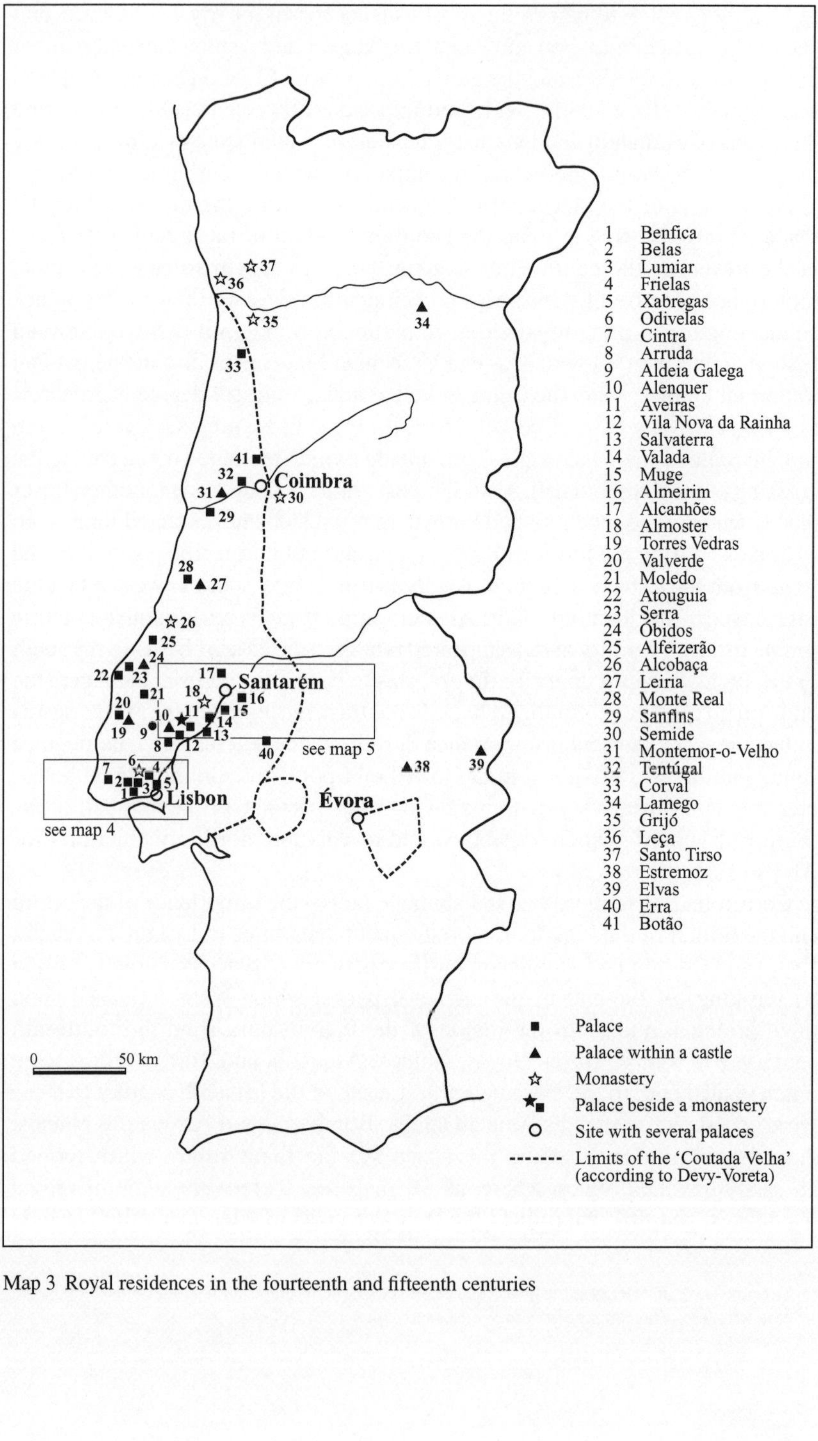

Map 3 Royal residences in the fourteenth and fifteenth centuries

Rainha, Salvaterra and Valada in the fourteenth century, but above all it explains the importance achieved by Almeirim in the following century. Next to Lisbon, for similar reasons, Cintra stands out because of the appreciable number of visits of the fifteenth-century monarchs. Finally, reference must be made to the group formed by the places where the kings moved which lay in the Mondego valley, a short distance from Coimbra: Montemor-o-Velho and Tentúgal, which also owed a large number of visits to the existence of a residence of the king. With the exception of Évora, which was in a less populated region, the four localities most visited by the monarchs appear surrounded by an appreciable number of places of lesser importance, where the court frequently stopped, and which can be considered as being within the spatial orbit of the others – a phenomenon which is particularly visible in the case of Lisbon and Santarém. In conclusion, the spatial pattern which arises from this analysis comprises the larger and more frequently visited localities (associated with the group of places lying a short distance around them), and by a network of places of an intermediary nature, the majority being situated in the central region of the kingdom. We must, however, interpret these data and the clumsy evaluation they allow while noting the information on the stops of the monarchs in the various places.

In this other aspect we see that the Portuguese kings spent a significant part of their reigns in the same cities – Lisbon, Santarém, Évora and Coimbra. With greater or lesser frequency of interruption, the stays in these localities are the most significant, both from an absolute and from an average point of view. For the fourteenth century, the total number of proven days of the kings' stays in each locality presents the most significant values immediately following these four principal cities as being the localities of Estremadura and the Mondego valley. In the following century, stays were also relevant in Oporto which, however, is not among the most frequently visited places, and also Cintra and Almeirim where, as we shall see, the principal country palaces of the fifteenth century were.

When considering the importance achieved by the four principal places, should we concede that the itinerance of the monarch was somewhat in decline, residual and of less importance than the settling of the court suggested by the number of stays in each of the cities? From the point of view of interest to us, that is the study of relationships between the court and the space of the kingdom, recognition must undoubtedly be made of the characteristic fact of the fourteenth and fifteenth centuries, that is their preferential association with the urban areas.[24]

Multiple aspects analysed here of the evolution of the court organism are linked to this generic tendency. The growing organisational complexity, for

[24] For a pertinent comparison: Jocelyne Dahklia, 'Dans la mouvance du prince: la symbolique du pouvoir itinérant au Maghreb', *Annales ESC*, 43 (1988), 735–60.

example, is traditionally placed in relation to the predominance of these centres in the itinerances, in particular of Lisbon, since many royal organisations tended to become permanently installed there, and the monarch appeared not to have given up frequent if indirect contact with them through recourse to the numerous agents who accompanied him. From the point of view of the composition of court society, I also found the presence of many members of the royal entourage connected, at times continuously throughout several generations, to the cities mentioned. It would seem, however, that the growing importance of these urban centres does not represent an unequivocal tendency towards the creation of a headquarters of the court, although it does become manifest through the creation of specific forms of itinerance which were organised around these places. These forms can be characterised by the frequency of small removals and the reproduction of seasonal cycles when the progress of the monarchs took place, alternating stays in an urban location with removal to many other places of lesser importance, where they might even remain for many days; these would include Cintra and Almeirim for the fifteenth century and Salvaterra for the previous century.

The diagrams relating to seasonal distribution of stays in the four main localities, which I shall analyse later, represent clearly the importance of this phenomenon. Thus, if we compare the distribution of the days of stay in Lisbon and Évora, we find that in the latter city there appears a visible preference for the winter months, with stays between the months of May and October being almost non-existent. This tendency becomes reversed in the case of Lisbon, in which city the king installed himself for longer periods during the summer, particularly in June, July and August. In a less accentuated manner, stays in Santarém were longer during spring, and they were less significant during summer, in a probable attempt to avoid the unhealthy humidity of the valleys of the large rivers, which I also feel can be seen for Coimbra, particularly if we ignore the figures relative to the period of the regency of the duke, Pedro. In summary, if the differing seasonal incidence of the stays of the kings in the four main localities is taken into account, there emerges a second pattern which characterises the itinerance of the medieval monarchs – their cyclical aspect, when they sought different destinations according to the seasons of the year. For a partial explanation of this phenomenon, it would be necessary to go along with other factors of the physical and social reality of the kingdom, in particular to refer to a history of the medieval travels and routes which might contribute to a specificity of the removals of relatively large groups of individuals, such as the retinues of the monarchs. It is important at the moment to confront this seasonality generically as something which grants a characteristic physiognomy to the court life of the space, which had its places of preference in the cities but which changed frequently so that it is difficult to discern initially the distinct centres where it was going to remain at given moments of the year.

With its great complexity, the itinerance of the king and the court was, however, an historical fact of the greatest importance in the Portuguese case, which I shall characterise in synthesis through an analysis of the itineraries based upon the following lines. First, because of the tendency to reduce the size of the progresses to the global scale of the kingdom. This aspect appears interrelated with the second global characteristic, which is the predominance of the central/littoral region of the kingdom in the network of places of power of the medieval monarchy. A third characteristic is the attraction found in relation to the urban nuclei. Finally, in fourth place, I also found a seasonal character in the stays of the kings in the most significant locations of the itinerances.

In this way the itinerance appears as a structuring factor of court society which I believe must not only relate it to its forms of life but also reflect on its effects on the dimensions of the court, in the light of the natural limits of its growth, dictated by frequent movement in space. In his studies on the influence of economic activities and spatial patterns related to these activities in the morphology of societies, the anthropologist Goodenough observed that, while in societies organised in semi-nomadic groups around centres of exchange or ceremonies, communities usually reached sizes of about 250 individuals, they could be larger when the organisation was based in settled towns, but rarely numbered more than fifty in the case of migratory bands.[25] This is a generic observation which it seems to me should be taken into account in the analysis of the values we have available for an estimation of the dimension of the courts.

In the first place, in relating its growth which, as I have already mentioned, characterised the passage of the medieval period to the modern age (the sixteenth to eighteenth centuries), with the contemporaneous process, more or less effective for the various monarchs, of forming headquarters, the court is seen to be more numerous and, concomitantly, less mobile if not entirely fixed, from the sixteenth century. On the other hand, lists of *moradores* available for the several courts of the end of the Middle Ages tell us in general of more modest sizes than those observed once the court is installed in a given place. How, for example, should we examine the some 400 *moradores* of the Portuguese court enumerated in the lists of the beginning of the century and relate this number to the statement of Duarte in his *Leal Conselheiro*, that there could be up to 3000 persons at court?[26] Certainly these sizes altered according to the spatial situation of this organism, tending to grow when the monarch remained in places, that is with the court 'em estada', and becoming restricted owing to itinerance when the court was 'em andada'. These two differing facets of the reality studied here directly arising from royal mobility allow us to state that, being a space defined by the presence of the king, the court was a true spatio-temporal complex with its own dynamism and was of variable dimensions.

[25] W. H. Goodenough, *Basic Economy and the Society* (New Haven: Yale University Press, 1941).
[26] M. Lopes de Almeida, *Obras dos Príncipes de Avis* (Oporto: Lello, 1981), p. 358.

THE ROYAL RESIDENCES

The mobility of the court naturally demanded a highly varied group of material conditions, among which the royal residences are prominent. Whether, as we have seen, one is dealing with the least significant expression of a reduced personal entourage or of removal and, above all, of the stay of the court with all its elements (including, eventually, the entourages of the queen and the infantes), the decision relating to the main stages of the itinerance of the monarch was mindful, more than anything, of the existence of places appropriate to the residence of the king. It therefore seemed to me that the identification and study of these places would constitute an important factor in the explanation of the way in which the progresses of the court were configured.

There is sparse information on the variety of residences of the medieval Portuguese monarchs spread across distinct regions of the country. By 'residences' I take as the point of departure for my research any material structure where there is reference to the king's being installed there, be this his property or not. When looked at more closely, and above all in an attempt to follow the evolution of some of these residences throughout several reigns, a most common characteristic immediately becomes clear, which is their relative precariousness: there are places which are no longer visited or which were abandoned by successive monarchs and which at times in the short space of one or two generations fell into complete ruin. Confronted with this diverse and relatively uncertain panorama, from the point of view of the actual architecture of buildings or constructions of whose existence we at times have little information, I centred my attention exclusively on the residences which were effectively visited by the several monarchs of the fourteenth and the first half of the following century.[27] Other medieval royal residences certainly existed. However, since apparently the court did not visit them during this period, it seemed to me that their importance for this research into the court space is, in a way, secondary.

One of the principal difficulties for the study of this network of residential places lies in the almost total absence of descriptions and of material remains which, in the majority of cases, could serve as a basis. However, a global typology allows us to distinguish their diversity. In the first place, we have the royal castles, which were generally associated with the fortresses in nuclei of larger or, more rarely, isolated populations, and which form one of the oldest types of royal residence. The tradition of Muslim urbanisation related the space delineated by the walls of the fortress to the residence of power, and this distinction was to remain in the Hispanic cities until the end of the medieval period.[28] Naturally, the urban evolution of the principal localities of the

[27] I considered for this mentions in the catalogue of royal documentation and also references of the various chronicles.

[28] In the Mediterranean context, this connection was of pre-Islamic tradition: M. O. Carver, 'Transition to Islam: urban roles in the East and South Mediterranean, fifth to tenth centuries A.D.',

kingdom, as is the case with Évora, Santarém and even Lisbon, would create some problems for this ancient spatial characteristic which, however, tended to be reproduced when the layout of the populational nucleus allowed, at times leading to important architectural developments. No less important too was the association of the royal residence with the religious space, particularly that of the monasteries and convents of the kingdom, which constituted a recognised tradition in the entire Iberian Peninsula, and whose roots are to be found in the medieval period.[29] Finally, we have the residences belonging to royalty which appear more or less individualised, whether in a completely urban environment such as Santarém or in peri-urban environments such as Benfica or Lumiar, whether in rural spaces and even associated with moors or woods where there would be cynegetic activities. In this case, when contrasted with a more or less precise group of constructions whose exclusive use was the residence of the monarch, there appears the generic name of 'paço' (from *palatium*).

It is not always possible to reconstruct clearly what was, in each case, the concrete group of constructions corresponding to the 'paço', but there are some data which allow us to establish with certainty that in many cases this did not concern buildings of monumental appearance. In their interior, in spite of the recognised difficulty in discerning a functional distribution of spaces which seems not to have existed in a fixed manner in the medieval period – the interior divisions could be recreated and adjusted according to need for each use – there appears frequently the mention of the hall, the chamber and the chapel and also, occasionally, of the *reposte*, the *guarda-roupa* and the kitchen. Clearly, I am dealing now not with the distinct court departments which up to now I have considered, comprising a variable number of servants, but with the physical spaces associated with them, sketching an internal complexity of the prince's or royal residence which is much like other buildings for community use in medieval civilisation. I speak of buildings for community use since the royal palaces were in fact used as spaces of everyday life and activity for a variety of individuals, and not only for the monarchs. As we shall see in the following chapter, one of the principal normative regimes which formed the different uses of these spaces (and which contributed decisively towards the origin of this distinction of interior space in the palace) was the ceremonial regime. We have available now some elements relating to the Portuguese, Aragonese and Castilian palaces of the later Middle Ages which show the existence of a common pattern of internal organisation based largely upon the parallelism

in N. Christie and S. T. Loseby (eds.), *Towns in Transition: Urban Evolution in Late Antiquity and the Early Middle Ages* (London, 1996), pp. 184–212. For the Iberian Peninsula: Leopoldo Torres Balbás, *Resumen histórico del urbanismo en España* (Madrid: Instituto de Estudios de Administración Local, 1954); A. H. Oliveira Marques, *Introdução à história da cidade medieval Portuguesa*, offprint of *Bracara Augusta*, 1981.

29 Fernando Cueca Goitia, *Casas reales en monasterios y conventos Españoles* ([Bilbao]: Xarait, 1982).

of the respective ceremonial uses to which I shall refer. The main structuring distinction of these interior spaces was, without doubt, that of the *sala* in relation to the *câmara* or, more and more frequently, to the plural, *câmaras*, which came into use at the end of the Middle Ages. This was a distinction whose roots lay in the archetypal value bestowed by the medieval monarchic tradition on the imperial residences of the Roman period.[30] The Portuguese king Duarte described particularly eloquently in a passage of the *Leal Conselheiro* the way in which there was conceived a distinction between the various chambers whose roots lay in the ceremonial rules of proximity, and which has been remarked upon by Vieira da Silva. In this the monarch used the palace for the construction of the metaphor of the human heart:

> eu conssiiro no coraçom de cada huu de nos cynquo casas, assy ordenadas como custumam senhores. Prymeira, salla, em que entram todolloos de seu senhorio que omyzyados nom som, e assy os estrangeiros que a ella querem vir. Segunda, camara de paramento, ou ante-camara, em que custumam estar seus moradores e algũs outros notavees do reyno. Terceira, camara de dormyr, que os mayores e mais chegados de casa devem ter entrada. Quarta, trescamara, onde sse custumam vestir, que pera mais speciaaes pessoas pera ello perteencentes se devem apropriar. Quinta, oratorio, em que os senhores soos algũas vezes cada dia he bem de sse apartarem pera rezar, leer per boos livros, e penssar em virtuosos cuidados.[31]

This description of the 1430s amply emphasises the uses granted to the distinct spaces and the community aspect to which I have referred. Having in view the maintenance of this structure represented by the group of royal palaces, the monarchs handed the guarding of the palaces to officers specifically deputed to the post, to whom were given the name 'paçeiros'. During the reign of Afonso V their number rose to fifteen, while the annual costs for the monarch were estimated at 24,000 *reais* for 'treze paçeiros de todos os paços'.[32]

However, before dealing in any detail with this variety of royal residences, it is important to analyse their spatial distribution in the kingdom, which is directly related to the problem of the itinerance shown earlier. In Map 3, I show the various residences which the Portuguese monarchs visited in the final period

[30] Birgitta Tamm, *Auditorium and Palatium: A Study on Assembly-Rooms in Royal Palaces during the 1st Century BC and the 1st Century AD* (Stockholm: Almqvist & Wiksell, 1963); Alain Labbé, *L'Architecture des palais et des jardins dans les Chansons de Geste: essai sur le thème du Roi en Majesté* (Paris: Champion, 1987).

[31] José Custódio Vieira da Silva, *Paços medievais Portugueses* (Lisbon: IPPAR, 1995), pp. 27–9. This distinction between various spaces of the 'câmara' or 'cubículo' type is mentioned for the papal palaces from the earliest periods, in particular for the Lateran palace in texts of the twelfth century: Gary M. Radke, 'Form and function in the thirteenth-century papal palaces', in Jean Guillaume (ed.), *Architecture et vie sociale: l'organisation intérieure des grandes demeures à la fin du moyen âge et à la Renaissance* (Paris: Picard, 1994), pp. 18–20. It is not, however, a creation of the Renaissance or yet another fruit of the omni-explanatory 'ceremonial of Burgundy'.

[32] Faro, *Receitas e despesas da fazenda real*, p. 100.

of the Middle Ages, and at once it is clear from the itineraries that they were located in the zone of the kingdom most frequently visited by the court. The delimitation of the territorial area of the so-called 'Coutada Velha' is informative, where the woodland, at the time cleared in many regions of the country because of the pressure of agricultural use, was protected from intensive exploitation and devastation by fire and indiscriminate felling of trees and was the usual territory for royal hunts.[33] Within this there were, during the medieval period, areas enclosed by the king for capture of the principal species, in particular wild boar and deer but also smaller game such as rabbits, and partridges and other birds (such as doves, martins and aquatic birds).[34] This territory included some of the most important hunting areas of the kingdom, many of which were humid, marsh areas lying beside strips of water or even along the coast – ideal countryside for falconry – and there were more intensely forested areas which became more and more restricted by cultivation of the countryside and the continuing clearing of woods for a variety of uses by sections of the population.

Because of its connection to the complex of royal residences, the entire mountain area of Santarém is prominent, including zones on the left bank of the Tagus (with the game preserves of Muge and Salvaterra) whose natural extension was formed by the barren lands of Coruche and Benavente. On both banks of the Tagus there were abundant marshes, which also lay along the left bank of the river Ulme and in a continuous line on the other bank from Alviela and Alcanhões as far as the marshland of Asseca. The reserved area also included the zone of olive groves of Santarém and the moors towards Azambuja, and continued to the north to the limits of Abrantes up to Sardoal and Torres Novas.[35] In Alenquer and Ota was more of the king's parkland bordering that already spoken of, all of which lay around the Tagus valley.[36] Near Lisbon the importance of the hunt at Cintra is well known, where from the end of the thirteenth century the monarchs had systematically protected the woodland from pressure of cultivators of crown land in the surrounding

[33] Nicole Devy-Vareta, 'Para uma geografia histórica da floresta Portuguesa', *Revista da Faculdade de Letras – Geografia*, 1 (1985), 47–67: 2 (1986), 5–39. See in particular the maps in vol. I, p. 61 and vol. II, p. 21, where the headquarters of the several *montarias* are shown.

[34] These prohibitions varied, of course, with time and place. On small-game hunting, which was cultivated by the monarch in numerous places to some degree throughout the country, see the general norm in *Livro Vermelho*, pp. 499–501. On rabbits, the abundant documentation collected in *HFAC*, for example: vol. I, pp. 197–8 (Peniche) and 206 (Setúbal); vol. II, pp. 192–3 (Coimbra and Buarcos). On partridges: vol. I, pp. 197–8 (Peniche) and vol. II, pp. 13–14 (Montemor-o-Novo), 162 (Avis), 166 (Torres Vedras), 168 (Évora), 184 and 208 (Elvas), 199 (the Lisbon boundaries), 212 (Azambuja), etc. On the left bank of the Tagus there were special measures of protection for 'aves que se caçam com falcão': *Livro Vermelho*, p. 501.

[35] On the area and limits of the *montaria* of Santarém: *Livro Vermelho*, pp. 486–91. Specifically on the reserve of Muge: *HFAC*, vol. II, p. 49. The listing of reserves in Paúis and Ribeiras do Tejo in 1407: *HFAC*, vol. I, p. 195.

[36] *Livro Vermelho*, pp. 492–3; *HFAC*, vol. I, p. 261.

areas.[37] Travelling in a northerly direction we find other territory of intense cynegetic use under the control of the hunting authorities of Óbidos, where there were the several enclosures of Atouguia, Lourinhã and Óbidos (the two last, for example, in 1434 having an important group of thirty-one huntsmen).[38] In the particular coastal zone north of Coimbra must be mentioned the enclosures of Mira and Gândaras (Aveiro),[39] and in the interior of the territory, but relatively closer to the city, were the woodlands of Botão, whose existence appeared in the thirteenth century, and included the slopes of the Buçaco range.[40] The majority of residences simply called 'paços' were included in these protected zones, and in many cases were isolated or associated with small settlements; this was the case of the palaces of Muge and Erra, Valverde and Moledo, Atouguia and Botão. Even the palaces which were not located specifically in these areas were still relatively close to them.

Another observation which arises when analysing the locality of the kings' residences is the partial coincidence of this with the territories of the crown land ('reguengo'), that is, their property which formed an important component of the royal domain. In this case, the term 'paço' seems to be applied most appropriately during this final period of the Middle Ages to some type of construction situated in a place which had possibly always been associated with the royal residence, and to the payment of the various sums due to the sovereign. The use of buildings which, at the end of the Middle Ages, were located in association with crown land, the authentic *palatia* in the most archaic meaning of the word,[41] indicates that the royal itinerance preserved in its progress, which seems apparently random, a link with the distinct enclaves of the fragmented royal domain. Thus, among the palaces in the region close to Lisbon, we know of the existence of that of Frielas, which was destroyed at the end of the fourteenth century, and which was situated beside the crown land of the same name. Near Santarém, there were the famous palaces of Valada whose existence certainly appears at the beginning of the fourteenth century; these were surrounded by the property of the king and formed the crown land called 'Reguengo de Valada', beside the countryside of the fens of Galego and

[37] On the relationships with the *reguengos*: *HFAC*, vol. I, pp. 28–9. The evocation of the 'montes e caças' by Duarte in a prologue to a charter to the residents of Cintra: *HFAC*, vol. I, p. 271.

[38] *Livro Vermelho*, pp. 496–9; *HFAC*, vol. I, pp. 197–8 and 292–3.

[39] *Livro Vermelho*, pp. 494–5.

[40] These wooded reserves, as well as the royal estate lying beside them, called 'das Terras Galegas' were beside the land of the monastery of Lorvão: *HFAC*, vol. I, pp. 29–31, 31–6 on the forests and 256–7 on the royal estate. As to the locality of the latter: Coelho, *O baixo mondego nos finais da idade média*, vol. I, pp. 121 and 126–7.

[41] Du Cange, *Glossarium Mediae et Infimae Latinitatis*, vol. VI, pp. 98–107 (s.v. 'palatium'). On the notion of 'palatium' in the territories of the north of Portugal in the period prior to the thirteenth century: Alberto Sampaio, *As vilas do norte de Portugal* (Lisbon: Vega, 1979), pp. 165–7.

Atalaia.[42] North of the same locality of Santarém was the palace of Alcanhões, which was frequently visited by Fernando, at the interior of one of the several nuclei which in the fourteenth century formed the crown land called 'Reguengo dos Bairros'.[43] Near Leiria the palaces of Monte Real were on the crown land called 'Reguengo da Camarinha', in a place where we know that in 1310 there existed a settlement of cultivators on the king's land.[44] Further north, on one of the most important pieces of crown land near Coimbra, we know of the palaces of Tentúgal where the several monarchs whose removals I have followed spent time on many occasions.[45] Also the palaces of Botão, already referred to above, were possibly related to the crown land called 'Reguengo das Terras Galegas'. Finally, the residence on royal property situated further north in the extensive area of the 'Coutada Velha', the palaces of Corval, were in Terra de Santa Maria, in an area lying beside the estuary of the Vouga, not far from the much-travelled route of Avenca which ran alongside the coast, within the area of the crown land called 'Reguengo de Figueiredo'.[46] Spread out in a more or less unequal manner throughout the central/littoral territory of the kingdom with greater concentration beside the Tagus, the location of royal residences (in particular the palaces) is seen to be connected above all to hunting on the one hand and to lands which were the property of the monarchs on the other.

Other than the region of the 'Coutada Velha', there is only recorded in royal documents recourse at the end of the Middle Ages to the fortresses of Lamego, Estremoz and Elvas as kings' residences, and to the monasteries of the region of Oporto – Grijó, Leça and Santo Tirso – and, near Coimbra, the monastery of Semide. Where would the sovereigns have stayed during their removals to the other regions of the kingdom? In the majority of cases, they would certainly turn to the various castles and monasteries or to episcopal residences and, more rarely, to those of lay lords, although there does not appear to be any actual mention of solutions adopted in any of the cases. Even in the localities

42 Pedro de Azevedo, *Os reguengos da Estremadura na 1a dinastia*, offprint of *Miscelânea de Estudos em Honra de D. Carolina Michaëlis de Vasconcelos* (Coimbra: Universidade de Coimbra, 1930).

43 The place was already included in the royal estates at the beginning of the fourteenth century: Azevedo, *Os reguengos da Estremadura*, p. 40.

44 Azevedo, *Os reguengos da Estremadura*, p. 43: royal charter of Dinis 'a todolos pobradores da mha pobra que chaman MonReal'. See also Manuel Heleno, *Antiguidades de Monte Real* (Lisbon: Imprensa Nacional, 1922) and 'Antiguidades de Monte Real (Aditamentos)', *O Arqueólogo Português*, 26 (1924), 331–45.

45 On the royal estate: Coelho, *O baixo mondego nos finais da idade média*, vol. I, pp. 123–4 and also vol. II, figure 4. Mention of the palace: ANTT, *NA*, p. 287, f. 62.

46 Regarding the location of this palace: João Pedro Ribeiro, *Reflexões históricas* (Coimbra: Imprensa da Universidade, 1835–36), vol. I, p. 64 and note c). In the text of the *Inquirições* of 1284, however, the 'paço' associated with this place is not mentioned: José Mattoso *et al.* (eds.), *A Terra de Santa Maria no século XII: problemas e documentos* (n.p.: Comissão de Vigilância do Castelo de Santa Maria da Feira, 1993), p. 209.

where they had use of their own residences, the monarchs at times settled in palaces belonging to other individuals: among several examples should be noted the stays of John I in the palace of the archbishop João Esteves de Azambuja, on the outskirts of Santarém, or the estate of his *guarda-mor* Martim Afonso de Melo III in Água de Peixes (Alvito).[47] Or we have the example of the visits of Duarte to the palaces of his brothers, the Infantes João (Belas) and Henry (Tomar). Besides this, of course, are the many references to the use of the episcopal residences by the Portuguese kings, as at Oporto and Évora.

While locating the royal residences appears a relatively simple task, the same cannot be said for a detailed study of each of them, grouped in the several types to which I have referred. For example the analysis of the processes of adaptation to city topography which led to the tendency, already referred to, of the frequent and prolonged stay of the monarchs of the fourteenth and fifteenth centuries in Lisbon, Santarém, Évora and to a lesser degree Coimbra is of indubitable interest for the study of relationships between the court and space. In all these cases, it could be said that the general tendency of this more or less complex adaptation to the urban organism was the progressive turning from the fortresses, which were more archaic residential spaces, to the use of other palaces which the monarchs built, leading to a multiplication or a development of possible places of residence. It is only in Lisbon that this process is certainly seen to be belated, perhaps because of the extraordinary conditions of topography of the fortress and the medieval castle, and this only commenced in the sixteenth century with the construction of the Paço da Ribeira alongside the Tagus.[48]

In the principal city of the kingdom during the fourteenth century until the middle of the fifteenth, the kings made use of two distinct residences: the palaces of the castle, within the precincts of the fortress, and the palaces of S. Martinho, which lay in front of the parish church of the same name within the first walls of the city.[49] The existence of both appears in the period prior to 1300. Their relative importance seems besides to have been retained throughout the period studied here, since the second palace is always seen as somewhat secondary in contrast with the complexity and supremacy of the residence lying beside the Moorish castle at the hill's summit. Owing to the later abandonment by the monarchs of the fortress as a residence, which abandonment was definitive following the seventeenth century,[50] and most of all owing to the destruction by

47 ANTT, drawer XI, M 3, 15 or John I's *chancelaria*, 4, f. 30v.

48 Costa Gomes, 'Monarquia e território'.

49 A. H. de Oliveira Marques, *A sociedade medieval Portuguesa* (Lisbon: Sá da Costa, 1981), pp. 68–9. A. H. Oliveira Marques, 'Depois da Reconquista. A cidade na baixa idade média', in Irisalva Moita (ed.), *O Livro de Lisboa* (Lisbon: Horizonte, 1994), pp. 89–113.

50 Pedro de Azevedo, 'O Castelo de S. Jorge', *O Arqueólogo Português*, 13 (1908), 98–116.

the earthquake of 1755, it is difficult to form a precise idea of these palaces of the Lisbon castle and of their architectural structure. Like so many medieval palaces known of for other Hispanic and European regions, there was a diversified group of buildings whose construction dated from various periods and which, as indicated by later iconography, perhaps communicated with various structures of the systems of fortifications surrounding the entire group, in particular the towers of the fortress walls. Some of these towers would have been used to guard the royal treasures and the archives of the king.[51] According to Oliveira Marques, the total area occupied exceeded that of the main building which followed the old royal palace, and perhaps reached some 8000 m^2 at its largest. Several essential elements in the composition of an important medieval royal residence are to be found in the palace of the castle, in particular in the chapel (which, as we have seen, was named after St Michael), the hall and several royal chambers. The approximate dimensions of the principal hall of the palace from the sixteenth century would have been 480 m^2 according to indications from a visitor of the period. An appreciable size, if we note that the halls of the several medieval royal palaces would have been considerably smaller: in the palaces of Etampes and Gand they were, respectively, 77 m^2 and 176 m^2, although in Poitiers the hall was the more impressive size of 800 m^2. The larger palace halls of the medieval west appear to have been Westminster and the royal palace of Paris, which was about 1500 m^2.[52] No less important in the functional organisation of this group of principal rooms would be the courtyard of the palace, which is much referred to in narrative and documents of the period,[53] and the kitchens, of whose existence there are signs in the toponymy of the area.[54]

In the final period of the Middle Ages the Portuguese monarchs collected some wild and exotic animals in their residences such as lions. The Lisbon lions must have been fed through contributions from the Jewish community, at least from the beginning of the fifteenth century, and in the space of the fortress,

[51] A. Vieira da Silva, *O Castelo de S. Jorge em Lisboa* (Lisbon: Empresa Nacional de Publicidade, 1937). As this author has definitively clarified, the palaces and the actual castle (*castelejo*) were distinct although contiguous. See for example in the sixteenth-century iconography of Lisbon the method as to how they are represented in great detail in a famous panorama preserved in the library of Leiden: *Lisboa Quinhentista: as imagens e a vida da cidade*, Catalogue of the Exhibition (Lisbon: Câmara Municipal, 1983), no. 45.

[52] P. Héliot, 'Sur les résidences princières bâties en France du Xe au XIIe siècle', *Le Moyen Age*, 61 (1955), 27–61 and 291–317. See also H. M. Colvin (ed.),*The History of the King's Works*, vol. I, *The Middle Ages* (London: Her Majesty's Stationery Office, 1963), in particular the various plans of the palace halls collected in vol. I, p. 44.

[53] *CR João I*, vol. I, pp. 283 and 285. In a document relating to the declaration of John II, the entrance by the Alcáçova gate is described and then the gates of the palace and the ceremony which was 'dentro no currall', and finally the gates of the castle (*castelejo*): Eduardo Freire de Oliveira, *Elementos para a história do município de Lisboa* (Lisbon: Imprensa da Casa Real, 1887), vol. I, pp. 343–44.

[54] Silva, *O Castelo de S. Jorge em Lisboa*, p. 124.

alongside the palace, was the place where they were kept in captivity.[55] The custom of the monarchs of keeping wild animals in the residences was much practised in the Iberian Peninsula of the period: the king of Navarre kept in his palace of Olite a pair of lions, a camel, an ostrich and a monkey and likewise in the fifteenth century the report of the journey of the count of Ourém to Basel records that the king of Aragon had a palace in Valencia, outside the gates, and 'em estes Paços andão leoens, e tres cervos, e tres hemas muito grandes'.[56] This is an important element in the definition of the royal palaces, both in the Christian tradition and in the Islamic, and is the result of an ancient custom related to the belief in a king's ability to pacify both nature and animals, surrounded as he was by *serenitas* and realising the biblical prophecy of the domestication of the wild.[57]

Returning to the case of Lisbon, we have information in the thirteenth and fourteenth centuries of other buildings alongside the actual royal palace, forming a natural prolongation: there were for example the 'casas da escançaria',[58] and the 'casas da reposte',[59] which were successively reoccupied and used for other purposes and whose exterior in relation to the palace is an indication of the fact that in the fortress itself the entire complex in a space alongside the church of Santa Cruz connected to the palace services, both of the royal palace and the episcopal palace which lay close to the former, must have held great importance.[60] The principal periods of construction of the Alcáçova palace would have been, besides during a primitive nucleus which seems to have arisen in the thirteenth century, during the reign of Fernando[61] and, above all, the period of John I.[62] With the personal rule of Afonso V, however, once again there is information on work carried out in the fortress palace, and for this period there is also

55 In the report of the journey by Jerónimo Münzer, relating to the years 1495–96 there is mention of a visit to the Lisbon castle where they were shown 'dois formosos leões': García Mercadal (ed.), *Viajes de extranjeros por España y Portugal* (Madrid: Aguilar, 1952), p. 379. See also Silva, *O Castelo de S. Jorge em Lisboa*, p. 59 and Tavares, *Os Judeus em Portugal no século XV*, vol. I, p. 192.

56 *Provas*, vol. V, part II, p. 240; Javier Zabalo Zabalegui, *La administración del Reino de Navarra en el siglo XIV* (Pamplona: Universidad de Navarra, 1973), pp. 80–1; Anna Adroer, 'Animals exotics als palaus reials de Barcelona', *Medievalia*, 8 (1988), 9–22.

57 Heinrich Fichtenau, *Living in the Tenth Century* (Chicago: University of Chicago Press, 1991), p. 163; Franco Cardini, 'Teomimesi e cosmomimesi. Il giardino come nuovo Eden', *Micrologus*, vol. IV, *Il Teatro della Natura* (1996), 331–54.

58 ANTT, *LN*, Direitos Reais, 2, f. 83: a document of Dinis mentioning the 'escançaria' which was 'ante a porta do seu paaço'.

59 In 1373 Fernando made a gift to Mestre Martinho, his physician, of some houses 'na alcaceua de lixboa que chamam as casas da reposte': ANTT, *Ch. D. Fernando*, 1, f. 121.

60 On the episcopal palaces: Silva, *Castelo de S. Jorge em Lisboa*, and also Ferreira de Andrade, *A Freguesia de Santa Cruz da Alcáçova de Lisboa* (Lisbon: Câmara Municipal, 1954), pp. 92–3. Rui de Pina mentions them: *CR Afonso V*, pp. 622–3.

61 Mention of the 'camara nova dos paços': *CR Fernando*, p. 460.

62 Silva, *Castelo de S. Jorge em Lisboa*. See also the main texts available on the castle published by A. Vieira da Silva, *Dispersos* (Lisbon: Câmara Municipal, 1968–70), in particular vol. I, pp. 25–31, 377–92 and vol. III, pp. 171–7.

a generic description of the chapel, whose size, according to the calculations of Augusto Vieira da Silva, must have been about 135 m^2 – which approximates it, for example, to the English palaces of Clarendon and Westminster in the thirteenth and fourteenth centuries.[63]

As for the palace of S. Martinho in Lisbon, knowledge of its material structure is also very incomplete.[64] The oldest iconography of Lisbon seems to suggest on the site of this palace a constructed mass whose compact character created a certain contrast with the varied profile of the buildings of the fortress referred to above. The existence has been suggested of a royal residence in S. Martinho (approximately at the present site of Limoeiro) for certain from the period of Afonso III, whose interest for Lisbon was in every way notable, or perhaps even in the previous period.[65] It is known that this second palace was used in the fourteenth century, particularly during Fernando's reign, either by the monarch or by the queen.[66] During the first decades of the fifteenth century Duarte used it as his Lisbon residence, where he had his own chamber and a 'casa' for the judicial activities of the 'Relação',[67] and in the middle of the fifteenth century we find the sisters of Afonso V installed in this palace.[68] Intermittently these buildings would have been used as (or were close to) sites for minting of coinage, for which reason they are also known in medieval texts as 'Paços da Moeda' or 'Paços dos Infantes'.

The second of the most important localities of the royal itineraries at the end of the Middle Ages was, as we have seen, Santarém. Owing perhaps to the relative difficulty of access to the precipitous fortress or to the unstable geological characteristics of the formidable mound on which it was built, it could be said that the process of construction of a second royal residence was fairly early in Santarém, for at the beginning of the fourteenth century we have information as to the existence of the palaces known as 'do Chão da Feira'.[69] These were built exactly opposite the fortress at the other end of the large principal urban

63 On the important works carried out in the palaces of the castle in 1448–52, there is a valuable *carta de quitação* whose existence was revealed by Viterbo: ANTT, *Ch. D. Afonso V*, 12, f. 42. In this there is mention of large sums for lining the chambers with wood and also the arrangement of the 'casa onde esta a nossa livraria', where two tables were made. On the chapel, see the drawing reproduced in the following chapter (Fig. 12) and also Colvin, *History of the King's Works*, vol. I, pp. 125–6.

64 See Freire de Oliveira, *Elementos*, vol. I, p. 248 and note, and vol. II, pp. 179–80. Also A. Vieira da Silva, *A Cerca Moura de Lisboa: estudo histórico-descritivo* (Lisbon: Câmara Municipal, 1987), vol. II, pp. 169–70.

65 Gérard Pradalié, *Lisboa, da Reconquista ao fim do século XIII* (Lisbon: Palas, 1975), pp. 28–30.

66 *CR Fernando*, pp. 259 and 593; *CR João I*, 1, pp. 17–23 and 29.

67 *MH*, vol. III, pp. 293–4 and *CR Duarte*, p. 499.

68 A. Augusto do Nascimento (ed.), *Leonor de Portugal, Imperatriz da Alemanha: diário de viagem do Embaixador Nicolau Lanckman de Valckenstein* (Lisbon: Cosmos, 1992), p. 33. Leonor's wedding ceremony, however, took place 'no Paço do Duque a S. Cristovão', according to Rui de Pina.

69 These appear in the thirteenth century, very possibly in the reign of Afonso III: Ângela Beirante, *Santarém medieval* (Lisbon: Universidade Nova, 1980), p. 61.

axis which crossed the town, but in direct contact with the 'rossio' outside the walls (*chão da feira*). Next to the Leiria gate, one of the main exits of the town, and built against the wall on its internal face, these palaces would perhaps have had a fortified appearance, since in documentation of the age they are known as 'new fortresses', and the chronicler Fernão Lopes did not hesitate to call them 'castle'.[70] In fact, from Lopes's reports, it would seem at least at the end of Fernando's reign that the palaces communicated directly with the exterior of the walls, so reproducing one of the distinctive characteristics of that type of structure, which was that of the fortresses of Islamic origin. Whatever the case, the frequent stays of the monarchs must have led to the development of this residence in the fourteenth and fifteenth centuries so that in turn the old fortress (Portas do Sol) began an irreversible decline, as did the chapel of S. Miguel which in the thirteenth century was associated with the early royal residence.[71]

Fernando's reign, which was a particularly significant period for the royal presence in Santarém and the surrounding region, witnessed important interventions of that king in the sense of better adapting the palaces of Chão da Feira for installation of the court. The most relevant fact was in the construction of a tribune or high choir in the neighbouring monastery of S. Francisco, which lay at only a short distance but outside the walls, where Fernando ordered his tomb to be placed, as well as that of his mother (whose body was removed from the monastery of S. Domingos), determining that this choir should be used as a chapel royal.[72] Although the association of the residences of the Portuguese monarchs with the Franciscan convents is a fact which may have occurred during the earlier periods, Santarém was one of the first significant examples, alongside S. Clara at Coimbra, in the development of an actual activity of construction of the monarchs which affected decisively the physiognomy of these religious spaces. Associated thus to the mendicant church, although as far as we know these were not buildings which were directly communicating, because of the use to which the palace was put at the end of the fourteenth century the royal palace of 'Chão da Feira' was often visited in the first decades of the fifteenth century,[73] and it became confirmed as an ordering element of the surrounding urban space. Thus, in John's reign, and continuing on to the times of Duarte,

[70] *CR Fernando*, pp. 289–90 and also *CR João I*, 1, pp. 107 and 110–11.

[71] Beirante, *Santarém medieval*, pp. 60–7. See also on the royal chapel: ANTT, *LN*, Reis, 1, ff. 114v–115. Great magnates of the court of Afonso III had lived in the fortress, and the royal prison was also there until the end of the Middle Ages.

[72] Gérard Pradalié, *O Convento de S. Francisco de Santarém* (Santarém: Câmara Municipal, 1992), in particular pp. 99–122. The construction of this important building (which required major alterations to the church) dated from the 1370s (1374–76) according to this author. Pradalié sees a Castilian influence (particularly from Toledo) in this use of the high choir which is perfectly in tune with what is found in other cultural aspects of Fernando's court circle. As we shall see, a wooden tribune was also constructed in the same period in the church beside the palaces of Óbidos.

[73] See among other mentions, ANTT, *Ch. D. João I*, 3, f. 101 and *MH*, vol. VII, pp. 145–8.

there was an important urban development through the destruction of houses lying beside that of the kings, so that the square in front of the palaces might be opened up or enlarged within the enclosure; this probably determined the ordering of a city façade the like of which had not until then existed.[74] Information is available as to the continuity of works in these palaces in the middle of the fifteenth century during the personal rule of Afonso V, as well as of the maintenance of the system of water supply to the building and of the existence of the respective 'paçeiro'.[75] All this indicates that they continued as residences of the monarchs and this led to eventual alterations of their enigmatic construction, which awaits a detailed study from the archaeological and architectural point of view.

In Coimbra, a city whose importance in the royal itineraries can be considered as being in relative decline at the end of the Middle Ages, the available residential spaces were equally formed by a palace in the fortress and by the peri-urban palace beside the female convent of S. Clara, whose origins can be placed at the beginning of the fourteenth century.[76] The oldest palace, which corresponds approximately to the area later occupied by the university, comprised, as did that in Lisbon, several buildings and a spacious courtyard, and had a chapel to St Michael which was still much used during the reign of Afonso V.[77] At its interior, to judge by the state of the locality during the Manueline period, we find the usual hall and chambers for the king and the queen.[78] The palace which Isabel of Aragon ordered to be built beside the Clarist convent on the opposite bank of the Mondego was much used by the monarchs of the late Middle Ages: the Castilian king installed himself there in 1384, accompanied by Leonor Teles, as did Leonor of Aragon in 1428 at the time of her marriage to Duarte, and a *paçeiro* was retained in the area during the reign of Afonso.[79] Leo of Rosmithal, a foreign traveller between 1465 and 1467, mentioned the beauty of the area of S. Clara, 'onde se vêem muitos ciprestes e formosos jardins'.[80]

Parallel to the evolution detected in Santarém is that of various residential sites of the kings in the city of Évora. During the first half of the fourteenth

[74] Beirante, *Santarém medieval*, pp. 92 and 103, note 190.

[75] *MH*, vol. XI, pp. 220–1; *DHDA*, vol. III, pp. 165–6.

[76] Vergílio Correia and A. Nogueira Gonçalves, *Inventário artístico de Portugal*, vol. II, *Cidade de Coimbra* (Lisbon: Academia Nacional de Belas Artes, 1947), p. 72. The general description of the complex can be found in Amorim Girão *et al. Coimbra e Arredores* (Coimbra: Universidade de Coimbra, 1939), pp. 77–82.

[77] On the courtyard or 'curral' of the palaces, see the document of 1367: *CUP*, vol. I, p. 269. On the chapel: ANTT, *Ch. D. Afonso V*, 1, f. 34.

[78] Vergílio Correia, 'O edifício da Universidade. Notas de arte e história', in *Obras* (Coimbra: Universidade de Coimbra, 1946), vol. I, pp. 132–4.

[79] *CR João I*, vol. I, p. 131; *GTT*, vol. VI, p. 529. See the charters of nomination of *paçeiros* in 1439 and 1453, for example: ANTT, *Ch. D. Afonso V*, 19, f. 33 or 4, f. 66.

[80] J. García Mercadal, *Viajes de extranjeros por España y Portugal* (Madrid: Aguilar, 1952), p. 282.

century, in fact, there is information as to the fact that the kings Afonso IV and Pedro used the building of the monastery of S. Francisco for their stops. This monastery was situated outside the oldest walled battlements, and the large convent church had appeared only in the middle of the previous century.[81] The royal residence in the fortress of Évora, in turn, originally comprised buildings of the Muslim period and also included ruins of Roman Évora; it had had a troubled evolution. A recorded donation from Afonso Henriques to the friars of Évora tells us of its existence, but in 1264 the entire area, or part of it, reverted once again to the king. Following that date, there can only have been built in the same place, perhaps by adapting existing structures, a royal residence of fortified appearance which was known at the time as the 'alcácer novo'.[82] Its area of expansion would always have been very restricted, mainly because of the importance of the neighbouring monumental buildings, in particular the episcopal complex organised around the cathedral, with the attached cloister which was built in the fourteenth century.[83] The repeated stays of the fourteenth-century monarchs at S. Francisco can also be connected to all these vicissitudes and even to the inadequacy of the 'alcácer novo'.

At the beginning of the fifteenth century we know that the early walls of the fortress of Évora were in ruins and that the monarchs had granted to the Melo family of the court a section of this walled area or even the fortified palace, which is hard to identify.[84] In a movement similar to that which had occurred in Santarém, of being near to the places most visited in the city and those connected to commercial activities ('rossios'), there began construction of other royal residences in the principal square of the town. The period of installation and enlargement of the sites of the new palace, 'da Praça', seems to have coincided most of all with the short reign of Duarte,[85] but still in the period of the regency during the 1450s Afonso V installed himself there.[86] Little-known reasons which are perhaps related to the growth of the royal entourage of

[81] On the stops by Afonso IV and King Pedro in S. Francisco: *GTT*, vol. VII, pp. 282 and 529–40; *CPD*, p. 204.

[82] Ângela Beirante, *Évora na idade média* (Lisbon: Fundação Calouste Gulbenkian, 1995), pp. 44–6. The chapel of S. Miguel would be associated with this early palace as it was later with the palace of the friars according to André de Resende: Joaquim Caetano and José Alberto de Carvalho, *Frescos quinhentistas do Paço de S. Miguel* (Évora: Fundação Eugénio de Almeida, 1990), pp. 9–11.

[83] Mário Chicó, *A Catedral de Évora na idade média* (Évora: Ed. Nazareth, 1946), pp. 38–9.

[84] 'o nosso castelo velho . . . com suas torres, casas, pardieiros, quintaes e arvores': *DEV*, vol. II, p. 50. See also Beirante, *Évora na idade média*, pp. 529–30.

[85] According to a notice of 1450, Duarte had ordered the destruction of buildings of the older one surrounding the fortress, 'per a pedra e cantaria dellas se fazerem os nossos paços que estam em a praça da dita cidade'. *DEV*, vol. II, p. 74. The fact that probable remains of Muslim buildings survive, most of all the ruins of the forum of Évora in this space, leads to some interesting questions as to the reuse of these materials. As we shall see, materials from other places were also used in Cintra in the fifteenth-century royal palace.

[86] *MH*, vol. IX, pp. 201 and 206 and also ANTT, *Ch. D. Afonso V*, 34, f.141.

Afonso (for the 'estaus' operated in the same place), but most of all to the desire to commence construction works of greater importance and significance in the context of the city itself, led however to the abandonment of this residence by the monarch in the middle of the century. This abandonment was to the benefit of the construction or the enlargement of new palaces in S. Francisco, which also had the relevant traditions of association to the residence of the kings, as has been seen, and whose practical use as their residence is proven during the entire period of the late Middle Ages.[87] The building of these new palaces, whose beginnings can be dated from the reconstruction of convent spaces under the patronage of Afonso V from the 1460s, was essentially to be carried out during the final period of the century. This residence was to become a paradigm of the typology of the royal palace associated with the monastery during the Manueline period in a more or less complex amalgam marked by the use by the palaces of convent spaces, for which reason it can be considered, in its completed form, as being later than the period studied here.[88]

Now that I have made a rapid evocation of the places of residence of the kings in the principal urban nuclei, where they remained for a large part of their lives (although in interrupted stays because of frequent removals), it is important to emphasise some specific characteristics of these examples which distance them in some way from the general panorama of the other royal residences. The problems caused by the royal itinerance, in particular by supplies and lodgings for the entourage, apparently found an easier solution in the cities, all the more because in all these principal cities, in a more or less accentuated way, there is seen the existence of residences belonging to the courtiers, at least in the case of the main noble families. However, it could also be said that the monarchs faced highly complex realities in this urban scenario, be this from the point of view of regulation and organisation of cohabitation between the court and the city, be it from the material point of view of the institution of actual residential spaces. The composition and use of these residential spaces tended to be retained during successive reigns, and so it could be said that the royal residences evolved slowly in the cities.

This panorama contrasts in a certain manner with that of the residences situated outside the urban environment, in general groups of more modest buildings which, on many occasions, were to be found a short distance from the principal

87 John I, for example, installed himself there in 1428 and at the time these were referred to as 'paços de S. Francisco': *GTT*, vol. VI, p. 533. These residences of John's reign comprised 'two chambers' built by the monarch at the beginning of his reign (the first known mention dates from 1387): M. Carvalho Moniz, *O Convento e a Igreja de S. Francisco de Évora*, offprint of *Boletim da Junta da Província do Alto Alentejo* (1959), p. 10. On the vicissitudes of this palace up to the Manueline period: José Custódio Vieira da Silva, *Paços medievais Portugueses* (Lisbon: IPPAR, 1995), pp. 130–6.

88 The fusion of the spaces is well evoked by existing documentation, for example ANTT, drawer XIII, M 6, 11. It was then brought up again by Túlio Espanca, *Palácios Reais de Évora: cadernos de história e arte Eborense*, vol. II (Évora: Edições Nazareth, 1946).

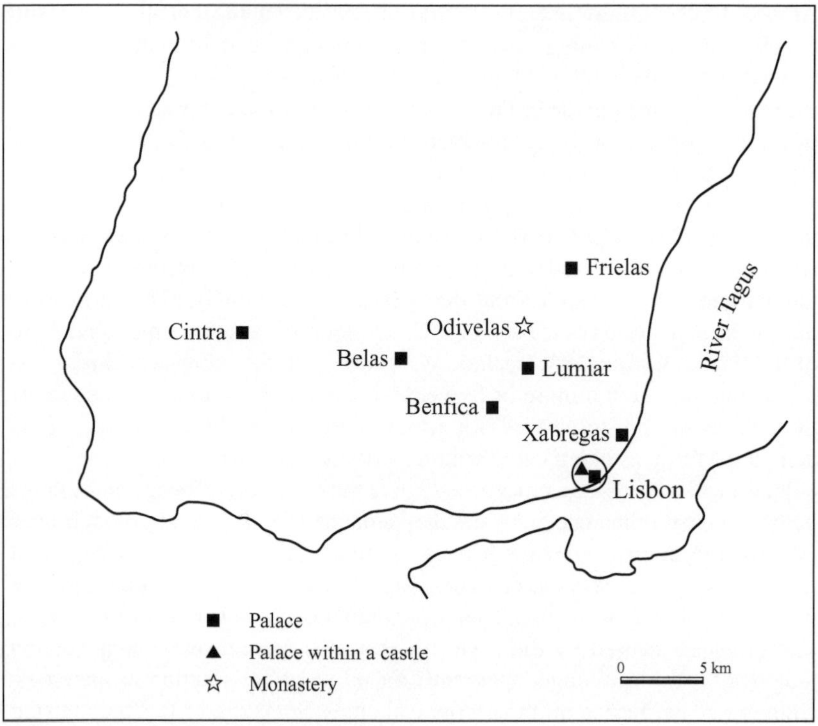

Map 4 Royal residences in the Lisbon region

centres. Here, the changes can be more frequent and more rapid. The role of these small residences is relevant in the explanation of the numerous progresses of lesser size which, as we have seen, were characteristic of the medieval royal itineraries. At times the monarch installed himself there more or less fleetingly prior to a solemn entrance, or at the end of a long journey towards a principal city. The important guests were also lodged there, and they too must be greeted with pomp and ceremony. Also, the proximity of the most important of the localities allowed the kings a country stay which could be interrupted should some matter require their presence in the city, which meant an installation with a more reduced entourage. For all of this, I believe that an analysis of these places must be made in conjunction, with attention being paid to the nexus they reveal with the principal cities.

The monarchs had use of a variety of residences in the Lisbon region, shown in Map 4, all of which were situated within a radius not much larger than 20 kilometres along the banks of the river. Not all of these co-existed in time, for some disappeared and others developed in various circumstances. By examining their localisation I shall distinguish the various examples of small, peri-urban palaces, such as the case of those at Lumiar, Benfica and Xabregas, from those which developed in areas of 'montes e caças', of which the best example is Cintra. The three first-listed palaces already existed in the fourteenth century, and were used by several late medieval monarchs. Afonso IV removed frequently to Benfica, which was also visited by Pedro, while there is at least one stay of Fernando documented at the palaces of Xabregas in 1369.[89] This last residence was destroyed and burnt by the Castilians in 1382 according to Fernão Lopes,[90] and remained totally or partially ruined in the following century; in 1450 it was donated by the monarch for a Franciscan monastery 'perto do mar e da cidade de Lisboa'.[91] These palaces of Xabregas were surrounded by orchards and olive groves and had a large orange grove, a well, a spring and several buildings including a tower. In John's reign the monarch had made a gift to Fr. Estevão de Aguiar of 'toda a pedra e cantaria e argamassa das paredes e arcos e portadas dos nossos paços d enxobrega'; that is, what remained of the old palace of the previous reign, for the construction of another religious building.[92] Because of its privileged situation, this same place was also to be chosen by the sixteenth-century monarchs for the construction of a new royal palace, of which Francisco de Holanda has given us a beautiful sketch.[93] The fourteenth-century palace of Benfica had a parallel destiny. It was here that the Dominicans had settled under the protection of John I, using the buildings of the old royal palace which the king had given them.[94] Prior to the fourteenth century, of these three residences only the palaces of Lumiar (which appear to have originally been a residence of the bastard Infante Afonso Sanches, confiscated by his brother Afonso IV) were apparently used exclusively as a residence, also in the fifteenth century. It appears that they were used in particular by ambassadors to the court, who there awaited the solemn reception being prepared for them.[95] In any case, this transformation of the small palaces near Lisbon into convent buildings is most interesting, since besides denoting

89 Pedro de Azevedo, 'A Chancelaria de D. Afonso IV', *Boletim da Segunda Classe da Academia das Ciências de Lisboa*, 4 (1912), 190 and 191; *CDP*, 412; ANTT, *Ch. D. Duarte*, 1, f. 13.

90 *CR Fernando*, p. 476.

91 ANTT, *LN*, extras, f. 87; *Ch. D. Afonso V*, 9, f. 110v and 15, f. 118v. See also *Brasões*, vol. I, pp. 82–3 and note; *DHDA*, vol. III, pp. 414–15.

92 ANTT, special collection, box 32, 47.

93 On the sixteenth-century palace whose exact location appears not to have been at the same place as the medieval palace (associated, as already seen, with the Franciscan monastery): *DHDA*, particularly vol. II, pp. 525–30. In a general perspective, Ferreira de Andrade, *Palácios Reais de Lisboa* (Lisbon: Vega, 1990), pp. 11–26.

94 ANTT, *Ch. D. João I*, 2, f. 184. On this subject, see also Gabriel Pereira, *Pelos subúrbios e vizinhanças de Lisboa* (Lisbon: Clássica Ed., 1910), p. 27.

95 ANTT, *Ch. D. João I*, 1, f. 53 (mention of the palace 'apar do lumiar'). See also Pereira, *Pelos subúrbios e vizinhanças*, pp. 236 and 237. According to Rui de Pina, the ambassadors from Frederick III waited there for the reception by the court and the city; this is not confirmed, however, in the report of Nicholas of Valckenstein: *CR Afonso V*, p. 760.

a selective investment in initiatives of construction and maintenance of these residences – and the place favoured by the kings of Aviz was, without doubt, Cintra – it also reveals a continuing interest by their visiting these religious centres, since the kings went there seeking the proximity of the friars, as was the case with so many other religious communities of the kingdom and, in this area, also the female convent of Odivelas.[96]

Two other palaces of the Lisbon region visited in the fourteenth century were to undergo important modifications: Frielas and Belas. In the first of these, the little information available indicates that this was a group of buildings of a certain importance during the 1370s, for they were situated in a walled area with their own orchard and a chapel. Fernando gave the entire site to a hermitage for the construction of a convent of St Jerome, but this project appears not to have been carried out.[97] We know that the Castilian destructions of 1382 were also felt here and this determined the later disappearance of this residence during the fifteenth century.[98] The origins of the royal palaces of Belas also occur as a result of confiscation of goods, since they had belonged to Diogo Lopes Pacheco, who had probably inherited them from his father, Lopo Fernandes.[99] Pedro took them over and they were a preferred residence of this monarch, who had important works carried out there, for Fernão Lopes states that he built the palaces.[100] It is probable that the ephemeral reinstallation of Diogo Lopes at the court of Fernando led for the first time to the problem of the destiny of these palaces, regarding the return of his possessions, since this was to occur in 1385. In the charter of 'restituição de bens e fama' of the new monarch of Aviz to this individual, the palaces and estate of Belas are mentioned – 'forom fectos na herdade propria do dicto Diego Lopes' – and they are returned to him, 'com todas suas casarias e pomares e vinhas', and were to form the nucleus of an entailment drawn up by Pacheco some years later.[101] As I have already said, the descendants of Diogo Lopes were also to see their possessions confiscated in 1398 following their exile to Castile, so that once again we find the palaces in

96 In particular during the reign of John, when the queen died at this same place: Baquero Moreno, *Itinerários de El-Rei D. João I*, p. 341; Moreno, *Os itinerários de El-Rei D. Duarte (1433–1439)*, p. 44.

97 ANTT, *Ch. D. Fernando*, 2, f. 31v.

98 *CR Fernando*, p. 476. On the locality of these palaces: J. Montalvão Machado, 'O paço real de Frielas', *Olissipo*, 28 (1965), 187–94.

99 Maria Yolanda Costa, '*Diogo Lopes Pacheco: subsídios para o estudo da acção política de um magnate Português do século XII*', unpublished dissertation, Universidade de Coimbra, 1967, p. 154. Besides these seigneurial palaces the Pachecos owned at the end of the fourteenth century some 'casas com seu vergel' in the district of Santiago in Lisbon which had been bought by Lopo Fernandes, as were some 'paços com seu bairro' in Santarém: ANTT, *Ch. D. João I*, 3, f. 130; 2, f. 143v.

100 *CR Pedro*, p. 112. According to much-cut documentation which remains of the chancery, the earlier visit of the monarch to these palaces was dated 1364.

101 ANTT, *Ch. D. João I*, 1, ff. 85 and 135. On the magnate, see the charter of 1389: ANTT, *Ch. D. João I*, 2, f. 12.

the hands of John I, whose stays in this residence at Belas are shown in 1414 and 1417.[102] Later, that is in the 1420s, the palaces and surrounding property were for a time in the hands of another court family from whom the monarch took them as a gift for his son, the Infante João.[103] While in the hands of this infante, they were to have a royal visit from Duarte in the initial stages of his reign.[104]

However, the residence which most attracted the presence and the building activities of the monarchs near Lisbon was, as is still visible today, that of the palaces of Cintra. Starting from an original nucleus built on a Moorish palace, whose existence is seen at least at the beginning of the fourteenth century, John I and his successors proceeded to a total remodelling of these palaces following a short period when they were in the hands of the magnate D. Henrique Manuel.[105] The art historian José Custódio Vieira da Silva has reconstructed in exemplary form the architectural construction and evolution of the group, without overlooking the data relating to the use of spaces constructed and the evocative description which Duarte made of its interior.[106] Cintra is, in effect, a well-preserved example, in spite of the inevitable transformation it has undergone over the centuries, of a fifteenth-century Portuguese residence situated outside the urban environment. In this case it was also an amalgam of diverse architectural bodies communicating with each other. The rooms which formed it, according to the enumeration and measurements supplied to us by Duarte, were of slightly more modest dimensions than, for example, those of the principal palace of the kings in Lisbon – the large hall of Cintra is only 187 m^2 and the chapel was, to judge by the measurements given and by its present size, a little less than 100 m^2.[107] The monarchs had, however, a reasonable number of distinct, relatively specialised interior spaces: the *guarda-roupa* which varied between 10 and 20 m^2; small oratories of 4 to 6 m^2; the *saquitaria*; diverse 'casas' for *escrivães* and numerous smaller chambers. They also had rooms which would appear to have been state rooms, such as the 'Câmara de Ouro' (some 60 m^2), the 'Câmara das Pegas' (some 100 m^2), and the Casa de Meca (some 160 m^2). From the infante's description there appears a certain duplication of the spaces, suggesting that perhaps the 'bicephalism' of the court referred to above for the period of John's reign, involving the entourages of the king and of the infante heir, has been modelled in a singular manner in the

102 See in particular ANTT, *Ch. D. João I*, 3, ff. 170, 170v, 192.

103 They had possibly been given as a pledge in payment of a 'casamento' to Álvaro Nogueira. The gift to D. João is dated 1424: ANTT, *Ch. D. João I*, 4, f. 92v.

104 Besides the itinerary of this monarch, see also *CR Duarte*, p. 499. A careful interpretation of what remains of these fifteenth-century palaces can be found in Silva, *Paços medievais Portugueses*, pp. 123–7.

105 ANTT, *Ch. D. João I*, 1, f. 164v.

106 *Paços medievais Portugueses*, pp. 201–47. See the description in the *Livro dos Conselhos*, pp. 166–8.

107 According to the hypothesis of Raul Lino, the tribune which is seen in it dates from later than the medieval period, an opinion which the study of Vieira da Silva would appear to corroborate.

internal organisation of this residence, being even a hypothesis for a plausible explanation for the duality of the monumental chimneys, each corresponding perhaps to their own kitchen. Careful examination of the oldest structures of the palace, which later became attached to an important Manueline body, allowed José Custódio Vieira da Silva to ascertain that in Cintra some recovered materials were used, possibly coming from other, destroyed residential buildings. As we have seen, this reuse was frequent in many royal residences of the period. On the other hand, what must be emphasised is the presence around the courtyard situated in front of the main body of the palace of an important group of small, contiguous but individualised buildings which do not exist today but nevertheless are visible in the oldest iconography, that is in the sixteenth-century drawings of Duarte Darmas. Some courtiers appear to have lived ephemerally in these places: in 1426, at a ceremony where the Infantes Duarte, Henry and Fernando were present, 'e peça de ricos-homens, cavaleiros e outros', was celebrated, for example, the marriage by proxy between Beatriz Coutinha and Pedro de Meneses, which took place 'nos paços delrei D. João, na casa em que ora pousa D. Beatriz que é dentro no curral dos ditos paços'.[108] Such a thing was most common in the English royal residences of the same period which were situated a short distance from London, such as Eltham, Sheen and Windsor, where the familiars of the monarch Richard II also had separate lodgings in small buildings contiguous to the royal palace, as was the case, for example, of John of Gaunt, the father of Philippa of Lancaster, or Richard de Vere.[109] From this group of buildings must result an impression of the supremacy of the residential function over the defensive function which made Cintra the best Portuguese example of its type of what we might call the 'country palace' of the late-medieval kings.

Along the length of the pleasant natural route formed by the Tagus during the medieval period there was a second group of palaces, shown on Map 5, whose common characteristics lay precisely in their accessibility by river and in their proximity to one of the localities most visited by the monarchs, such as Santarém. None of these residences has left significant material traces, for which reason we must remain content with information from texts. It appears that the oldest residences of the Portuguese kings in the Tagus valley were, besides the fortress of Santarém and perhaps that of Alenquer,[110] the palaces of Valada and Muge. The first was situated in disputed territory in a highly fertile area which the council of Santarém always claimed as its own during the thirteenth

108 *MH*, vol. III, p. 110.

109 Gervase Mathew, *The Court of Richard II* (London: Murray, 1966), pp. 30–2.

110 Since this town was much visited by the monarchs, as it was constantly given to the queens, they were also able to make use of the important monastery of S. Francisco which from the thirteenth century was the site of a royal residence. The Master of Aviz rested there, for example, when he was attempting to win the castle: *CR João I*, vol. I, p. 91.

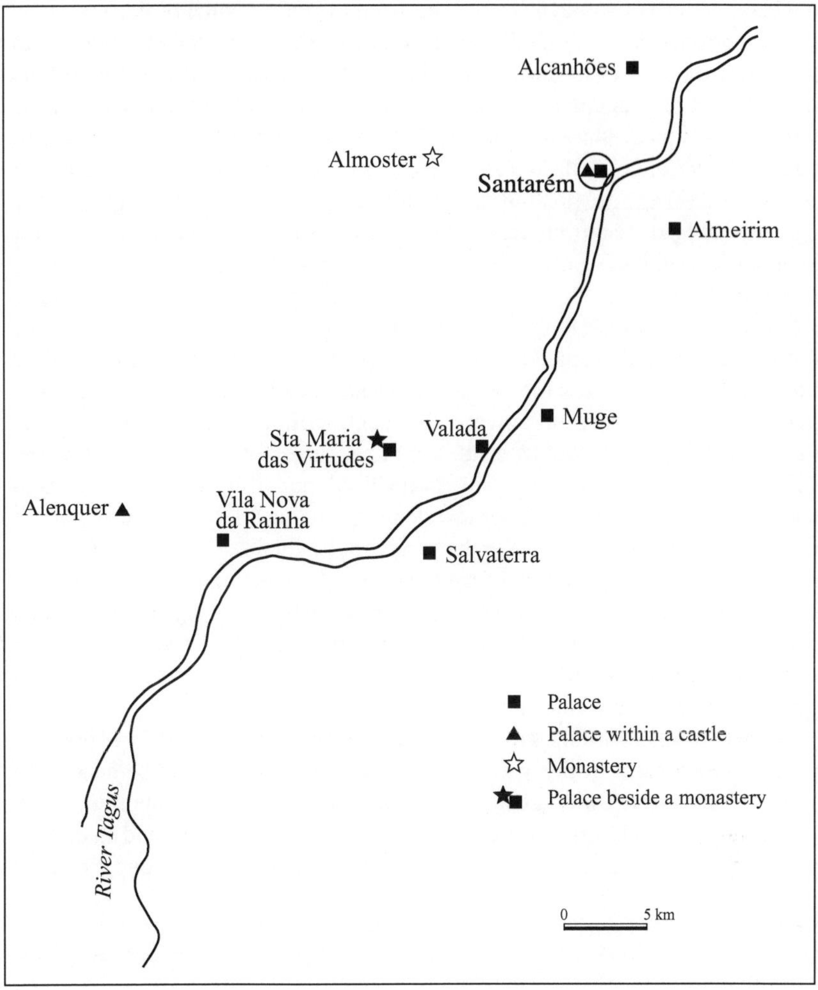

Map 5 Royal residences in the Tagus valley

century, while Dinis however obtained it for himself, and it formed an important piece of crown property. In the first decades of the fourteenth century there is mention of the existence of a palace built in the marshland of Atalaia, which appears during the reign of Dinis.[111] Corresponding or not to those buildings,

[111] *CDA*, vol. II, p. 195. On the conflicts of the monarchs with Santarém: Pedro de Azevedo, *Os reguengos da Estremadura na 1a dinastia*, offprint of *Miscelânea de Estudos em Honra de D. Carolina Michaëlis de Vasconcelos* (Coimbra: Universidade de Coimbra, 1930), and also the codex in which the several documents relating to this conflict are collected: ANTT, *NA*, p. 866.

the Paço de Valada would have perhaps been the most visited of this region by all the medieval monarchs until John I, and was only supplanted by Almeirim in frequency of royal visits during his reign.[112] The palace of Muge also appears to surface at the beginning of the fourteenth century, when the interest of the kings for this place increased. So in 1301 Dinis obtained through exchange of part of the terrain of Valada a farm which had been built by the monastery of Alcobaça. Perhaps the first initiatives of drainage and use of this highly fertile agricultural land are attributable to the Cistercians and this then led to bases for later, more long-lasting human occupation.[113] Indeed there is certain reference in the mid-fourteenth century to a small settlement situated a short distance from the palaces of the king.[114] As already referred to, the monks' farm would in turn have been dedicated to a stud from the time of Afonso IV for breeding horses for the Portuguese monarchs. Information dating from almost a century later allows us to distinguish clearly the locality of the palace from that of the farm of the fourteenth and fifteenth centuries, since it had a distinct structure. The palace was situated in the 'ribeira do Tejo', and also had contiguous land and a ranch 'para as éguas do rei', while the farm must have led to the 'pobra', or small settlement, as was often the case with Cistercian farms.[115] In the mid-fifteenth century a description of the buildings of this royal residence speaks of several rooms within the palace of Muge among which was a ground-floor hall and 'outras casas', as well as 'uma crasta com árvores'.[116] Contrary to what appears to have occurred with the medieval palace of Valada, the residence at Muge survived to the sixteenth century.[117]

A little further south, still on the left bank of the Tagus, we find the palace of Salvaterra, which was much visited during the time of Fernando and John I,[118] and which was situated, like that at Valada, near an important group of marshes.[119] In the fifteenth century it comprised several halls and chambers, and there was 'fora do asentamento dos paços huu lanço de casas que sam antre

112 On the royal visits to the palace of Valada: *CDP*, p. 468 and *CR Pedro*, p. 255. ANTT, *Ch. D. Fernando*, 1, f. 194; 2, f. 27 and *CR Fernando*, pp. 178 and 289–90. See also ANTT, *Ch. D. João I*, 2, f. 177v; 3, f. 13; 4, f. 104v.

113 Vieira Natividade, *As granjas do Mosteiro de Alcobaça*, offprint of *Boletim da Junta da Província da Estremadura* (Lisbon, 1944), p. 14.

114 See the charter of privilege to the residents 'da pobra de muje': *HFAC*, vol. I, pp. 123–5.

115 ANTT, *Ch. D. João I*, 3, f. 93.

116 ANTT, *NA*, p. 335, f. 164v. On the *paçeiro* of Muge: ANTT, *Ch. D. Afonso V*, 30, f. 55.

117 Besides the mention in the chronicles, see the document of 1532: *GTT*, vol. II, pp. 716–20.

118 In 1383 Beatriz and D. João of Castile 'received each other' in the palaces of Salvaterra: Arnauth, *A crise nacional*, pp. 376–9. On John's *paçeiro* at Salvaterra: ANTT, *Ch. D. João I*, 4, f. 43.

119 One of them was the marshland of Albacetim south of Salvaterra. In documentation of Afonso V in particular there is reference to the 'Paços de Albaçotim' which I believe can be identified as the fourteenth-century palace to which I have referred – unless it concerns a new place of residence of the kings in the Tagus valley, which would seem improbable: ANTT, *Ch. D. Afonso V*, 18, f. 93 and 5, f. 39v (nomination of *paçeiros* in 1439 and 1446).

os paços e a pouoraçam de saluaterra', which brings to mind the type of residential association known in Cintra. Next to this group was an occupied property with an orchard and trees, 'valada e çarrada sobre si'.[120] The existence of these palaces is again attested to during the Manueline period.[121] On the opposite bank of the river, in countryside which did not lie far from Valada or Salvaterra, we find another country palace in the fertile land of Vila Nova da Rainha, which was also often visited by the court in the time of Fernando. According to the chronicler Lopes, this palace was sacked and destroyed by the Castilians in 1382, but in this case I have found, for the reign of Afonso V, mention of a *paçeiro* remaining in the area, which suggests that perhaps reconstruction or maintenance of the buildings had begun during the first half of the fifteenth century, and that it was in suitable condition for housing the monarch.[122] To complete my succinct panorama of the fourteenth-century palaces whose use was particularly intense during the reign of Fernando, we have the residence of Alcanhões, which I have already mentioned, in the fertile valley of the same name, north of Santarém.[123] Near this locality are still today sources of thermal springs which were perhaps known and used during the medieval period.[124] The royal palaces fell into decline during the fifteenth century, but ruins of the buildings still existed in the first years of Manuel's reign, with 'casas e pombal derribados' and a large 'ressio' beside them; the group at the time was eloquently named 'Paços Velhos'.[125]

As was the case in the Lisbon region, a residence attracted the late-medieval monarchs in a particular manner, for they remained there frequently, enlarging their material structures throughout successive campaigns of construction. There are the palaces of Almeirim, whose origin can be dated to the first decades of the reign of John, and in the middle of the century they became the most important royal residence in the Tagus valley.[126] Here is the evocation made by the royal functionary who, during the reign of Afonso V, drew up the *tombo* of the properties of the monarch in this region:

120 ANTT, *NA*, p. 335, f. 168.

121 On the palaces in the sixteenth-century period and their later development: José Manuel Silva Correia and Natália Correia Gudes, *O Paço Real de Salvaterra de Magos* (Lisbon: Horizonte, 1989).

122 ANTT, *Ch. D. Fernando*, 2, ff. 38, 39v and 43; *CR Fernando*, p. 476. Also ANTT, *Ch. D. Afonso V*, 18, f. 8.

123 On Fernando's stops: ANTT, *Ch. D. Fernando*, 1, f. 189v and also *CR Fernando*, pp. 8, 254 and 365. Fernão Lopes records the popular saying about this monarch, 'ei-lo vai, ei-lo vem, de Lisboa para Santarém', which could strictly be applied to almost all the kings of the fourteenth and fifteenth centuries. Rui de Pina, for example, mentions regarding Duarte that the king had been 'teer o inverno a Santarem': *CR Duarte*, p. 737.

124 Raul Proença (ed.), *Guia de Portugal* (reprint) (Lisbon: Fundação Calouste Gulbenkian, 1983), vol. II, p. 372.

125 *DHDA*, vol. II, pp. 525–30.

126 There is information on the building activities throughout the fifteenth century for example in 1433, 1453 and 1468: *DHDA*, vol. III. pp. 171–2, 179 and 231–2.

> O muy famoso e da louuada memoria Elrrey dom Joham, avendo achado seus grandes desenfadamentos de caças e montarias na charneca de santarem desejou fazer casas da parte daalem do rryo e dalpiarça pera sua pousentadaria por que muitas vezes embargauam seu desenfadamento as auguas das cheas do Tejo. Auido seu preposito começou logo de executar a grandeza de sua manyficencia que era fundada em fazer sempre grandes obras. Mandou comprar por seus dinheiros todallas terras da Valla que jazem dentro das deuysooens e confrontaçooens que dito avemos. E parte dessas terras ouue per escaymbo por outras que eram da coroa do rreyno, todo esto feito a prazer dos Senhorios aa booa fee e sem engano. Ora tanto que as terras foram suas as mandou cerquar de grossos e altos vallos honde por rrazam dos vallos leuou toda a terra de dentro deles nome a vala e por que a Serra se chama d almeirim lhe poseram o sobrenome a Valla d almeirim asy he chamada atee o presente dija e per este nome yntitollada. Acabado esto fundou o boo rey suas casas de pousentadaria dentro da terra da vala que he huu grande e nobre asentamento de paaços segundo dam delo testemunho seos edificios com grandes salas camaras rretretes varandas e outras muytas casas nos sobrados e terreas. E doos paaços com crastas dentro bem poboradas de larangeiras e outras aruores. E arredor dos paaços huu grande cercoyto de casas E fora do asentamento dos paaços outras casas arredor Todas propeas delrrey . . . Outrosy dentro no asentamento dos paaços hua capeela situada em honrra da Senhora sancta maria. Aa qual capeella ese boo rrey fez enexar e apropiar os dizimos que deus em cada huu anno ha dauer de dentro das deuisooens da valla, confirmado e outorgado per o santo padre. Que uos diremos mais de tam nobre asentamento dalmeirim senam que foy asy como por camara da coroa do rreyno fundado.[127]

The author continues with his description, and we find the palaces surrounded by an important area of cultivated land with vines, an orchard, a kitchen garden 'com palmeiras e outras árvores', and a 'cerrado'. All leads to an emphasis on the architectural importance and the protected countryside which surrounded this residential complex, the only one of the group along the Tagus for which we have certain information of an important structural element – the chapel.[128] During the first half of the fifteenth century Almeirim was a favourite residence of the monarchs, for after Lisbon and Santarém it was the third most visited locality of all for John I and Duarte.

Finally, in my study of the residences of this region of the Tagus, shown on Map 5, I must mention the palaces of Santa Maria das Virtudes, situated close to Aveiras, of whose short-lived existence there is information for the period

[127] ANTT, *NA*, 335, f. 103. According to some internal signs, this collection which I have used dates from the period following 1460.

[128] As I have said, the documentation of ecclesiastical origin relating to the establishment of this chaplaincy dates from 1427–32.

after 1420, which also includes the final decades of the reign of John I. They were visited by Duarte as infante, and by his wife D. Leonor.[129] The importance of these palaces lies in their association with a site of religious rite, where later there was to be a Franciscan convent, for which the monarch granted some already-built parts of his residence in 1431.[130] The place must have continued to be visited by him, however, and in the 1450s Afonso V became involved in the construction of the convent building.[131] Unfortunately, the ruins of what was the convent are now threatened and in a serious state of decay.

As we have seen, the majority of residences of the fourteenth and fifteenth centuries which the Portuguese kings definitely visited were in the variegated countryside of the Estremadura. The area situated furthest south, which we can associate with the typical physiognomy of the countryside of the Alentejo, is that of the palace of Erra which, however, fell into decline during the fifteenth century.[132] Besides these were almost always small palaces which for one reason or another tended to disappear; these were in a modest panorama from which we can only exclude the urban residences and the particular cases of Cintra and Almeirim. A close example to the first of these, in the Estremadura, is the royal palace of the small town of Torres Vedras, which was much visited at the end of the Middle Ages. Also here was the older residence of the kings in the castle, which was abandoned as a residence during the fourteenth century, and the monarchs used as a residence in the final period of the Middle Ages a group of houses situated in the centre of the town outside the walls of the fortress. The origin of these palaces occurred during the thirteenth century at the initiative of the queen, and for this reason they appear under the name of 'Paços da Rainha'.[133] No vestige of them remains. From the impression given by texts, this would have been a royal residence with its own buildings, including a hall and an adjacent chapel.[134] The actual form of the remaining palaces of the

[129] See the mention in the *Livro dos Conselhos*, p. 281.

[130] *MPV*, vol. IV, pp. 340–2; ANTT, drawer 1, M 3, 19; *MH*, vol. III, pp. 343–6.

[131] *DHAD*, vol. IV, pp. 340–2. There is reference to the relative modesty of the convent buildings and the attached palace in Correia, *Obras*, vol. II, p. 115.

[132] This residence was visited most of all during Fernando's reign: ANTT, *Ch. D. Fernando*, 2, f. 96; 3, f. 31. However, during John's reign it was in the ownership of individuals: ANTT, *Ch. D. João I*, 1, f. 36; *LN*, *Odiana*, 2, f. 17v. The same also occurs with other residences on this side of the Tagus on which there is only indirect information. For example, on some palaces beside the Ulme: ANTT, *NA*, 335, f. 142v.

[133] It appears that this second residence would have resulted from the purchase of several houses and a later fusion into one residence: Ana Maria Rodrigues, *Torres Vedras: a vila e o termo nos finais da idade média* (Lisbon: Fundação Calouste Gulbenkian, 1995). According to this author, the hypothesis of the existence of two distinct palaces, that of the king in the castle and that of the queen in the town, should be dropped since only the second was inhabited during this period. See mentions of these palaces, for example, in *CDP*, pp. 473 and 475. On *paceiros*, ANTT, *Ch. D. Afonso V*, 13, f. 107 and 14, f. 97v.

[134] The chronicler Zurara, for example, describes the meeting of John's council 'em hũa salla deamteyra que esta em aquelles paaços de Torres Vedras, homde esta a capella': *CR Duarte*, p. 78. On the chapel, ANTT, *Ch. D. Afonso V*, 13, f. 25.

Estremadura is impossible to reconstruct without recourse to archaeology, but we do know that they existed, and the progress of the monarchs can be found in Arruda[135] and Aldeia Galega,[136] and frequently in the region of Óbidos, Moledo[137] and Atouguia,[138] and even along the coast in Alfeizerão. This last palace, which perhaps corresponded to the site of the small castle of which there still remain vestiges, continued to exist in the fifteenth century, together with a fifteenth-century palace in the locality of Salir of which there is information and which was also situated in the dominial lands of Alcobaça.[139] Closer to Torres Vedras, Fernando built some palaces in Valverde, which the succeeding monarch of Aviz gave to the monastery of Alcobaça.[140] The remains of the palaces of Serra, near Atouguia, suggest that from the structural point of view these were groups of modest buildings associated, in this case, with land surrounded by walls where there were also kept exotic animals such as swans, which became associated with parks, so in favour at the time and of which we have fifteenth-century examples and descriptions in other regions of Europe.[141] Relatively close to Leiria were the palaces of Monte Real, in the countryside near the river

[135] ANTT, drawer XII, M 12, 28; ANTT, *Ch. D. Fernando*, 1, f. 114v. In 1370 this palace was valued at 500 libras: Marques, *Ensaios de história medieval Portuguesa*, p. 130. Among the visits by the fifteenth-century monarchs to this place, those of Duarte have particular importance.

[136] Some court marriages were celebrated at these palaces which were visited several times by John I: ANTT, *Ch. D. João I*, 3, f. 194. See also *Os itinerários de El-Rei D. João I*, pp. 117, 125 and 219.

[137] Palaces visited by Fernando (see for example ANTT, *Ch. D. Fernando*, 2, f. 39) still had their *paçeiro* in the following century, successively appointed in 1443 and 1472 (ANTT, *Ch. D. Afonso V*, 27, f. 138 and 29, f. 110). Beside the buildings there appeared orchards, all taken over by the monarch in 1480: ANTT, *LN*, *Estremadura*, 7, f. 1v.

[138] Visited at least by Fernando and John I: ANTT, *Ch. D. Fernando*, 1, f. 23; ANTT, *Ch. D. João I*, 5, f. 134v. In 1367 Fernando granted privileges to the residents of Atouguia, 'contanto que morem conthinuadamente arredor do paço': ANTT, *Ch. D. Fernando*, 1, f. 23.

[139] On Alfeizerão, a place repeatedly visited by Kings Pedro and Fernando, see also the appointment of a *paçeiro* in 1445: ANTT, *Ch. D. Afonso V*, 25, f. 19. The place had access to the sea, which nowadays cannot be seen, and was a small port used by the Cistercians, where naval construction played an important part. This aspect is referred to in the old maps of Bernadino Rizo (1490): 'un altro luogo a nome el fiume alfisaron che e porto de marea e qui se fano de molte nave e navili per esser di boschi asai'. See D. S. Chamber, 'Venetian perceptions of Portugal c. 1500', in Kate Lowe (ed.), *Cultural Links between Portugal and Italy in the Renaissance* (Oxford: Oxford University Press, 2000), p. 20 and note 15; Gonçalves, *O património do Mosteiro de Alcobaça*. On the small castle there: *DHDA*, vol. I, p. 566 (document of 1538 which mentions that the castle 'estava devasso sem nele morar pesoa algũa'). On the royal palace in Salir, which is however not proved to have been visited by the monarchs (which is why it is not shown on my Map 3): ANTT, *Ch. D. Afonso V*, 13, f. 10v; 26, f. 17v (appointment of *paçeiros*). On Salir: Manuela Santos Silva, 'Salir do Porto: um exemplo dos pequenos portos da Estremadura durante a idade média', in *A região de Óbidos na época medieval: estudos* (Caldas da Rainha: Património Histórico, 1994), pp. 34–43.

[140] ANTT, *Ch. D. João I*, 1, f. 48.

[141] These palaces were the most visited in the Estremadura by all the monarchs from Pedro with the sole exception of Duarte. See *MH*, vol. X, p. 116 and ANTT, *Ch. D. Afonso V*, 10, f. 108 (on the *paceiros*). On the birds which were bred there, *DHDA*, vol. II, p. 530. In the *Livro Vermelho* it was established 'que nehũa pesoa mate cirne na Alaguoa d'Obidos, sob pena de paguar por

Liz,[142] and around Coimbra those of Sanfins and Botão, which I believe were not much different from the more modest palaces listed.[143] As for the palaces of Tentúgal, the residential buildings existing in the fourteenth century were considerably rebuilt or even gave way to a new palace with its own chapel, according to José Custódio Vieira da Silva, at the initiative of the Infante Pedro, who would have built them in the 1420s and 1430s.[144] The palaces of Corval only received visits from Fernando and John I as far as is known, and served as backup on their progresses towards the Minho region, but nothing is known of their construction.[145]

In the first established typology I have distinguished the residences situated in the castles and fortresses from those to which the monarchs turned, essentially in rural environments and which, in the majority of cases, did not coincide with fortified structures – although, as we have seen, they were in fact spaces much used also as more or less temporary residences in the late Middle Ages. It is important, however, to distinguish those where the king lived more or less sporadically from the castles or fortresses where, during this period, there were important initiatives of construction leading to the existence of true 'paços', that is, buildings that were predominantly residential within their interior, with significant alterations to the appearance and functions of some of these structures. Examples closer to the first case are some castles where the royal presence does not seem to have influenced decisively the original appearance of these spaces, which continued most of all to be marked by their original military function, as in the cases of Alenquer, Lamego, Montemor-o-Velho and even the castle of Elvas in the Alentejo.[146] Of the little that is known of their appearance at this time, or from iconographic images and descriptions of the early sixteenth

cada hũa cabeça cem reis': *Livro Vermelho*, p. 496. On the parks of the period, see the works of Jean Chapelot, *Le Château de Vincennes: une résidence royale au moyen âge* (Paris: CNRS, 1994), pp. 40–1; H. M. Colvin, 'Royal gardens in medieval England', in *Essays in English Architectural History* (New Haven: Yale University Press, 1999), pp. 3–4.

142 Fernando stayed there frequently. On the *paceiro* linked to the site in the mid-fifteenth century, ANTT, *Ch. D. Afonso V*, 4, f. 27v. On the present-day ruins of the palace: Gustavo de Matos Sequeira, *Inventário artístico de Portugal* (Lisbon: Academia Nacional de Belas-Artes, 1995), vol. V (District of Leiria), p. 75.

143 On the palaces of Sanfins, not far from Buarcos where the monarchs also frequently went, ANTT, *Ch. D. Fernando*, 1, f. 200v. On Botão, ANTT, *Ch. D. João I*, 2, f. 9v. In Botão there would appear to have been a Manueline palace of which there were still remains in the twentieth century: A. Nogueira Gonçalves, 'O tesouro de D. Catarina de Eça', *O Mundo da Arte*, 12 (1982), 5.

144 Silva, *Paços medievais Portugueses*, pp. 127–9. An argument suggested by me on the reconstruction of the old royal palaces by the Infante is the invocation of the chapel, which, as for all those at the royal palaces of the first dynasty, is to S. Miguel.

145 ANTT, *Ch. D. Fernando*, 1, f. 182; 2, f. 68v; *Ch. D. João* I, 2, ff. 1 and 3.

146 On Lamego, Rui Fernandes, 'Descripção do terreno em roda da cidade de Lamego duas leguas', in Abade Correia da Serra (ed.), *Collecção de ineditos de historia Portugueza dos reinados de D. João I, D. Duarte, D. Affonso V e D. João II* (Lisbon: Academia Real das Ciências, 1926), p. 592. At the beginning of the fifteenth century several visits by John I to this city stand out.

century, it can be deduced that the monarchs made varied use of environments within the fortifications, but that these spaces were characterised, as is the case at Elvas,[147] by their relatively small size, and few more than the royal chamber and its servants could be housed there. We also know of the existence of chapels associated with the castles, for example in Montemor-o-Velho, but we know nothing of their possible use by the Portuguese court in the Middle Ages.

Three palaces located in castles are seen in contrast with this generic evocation: Estremoz, Óbidos and, most of all, Leiria. In the first of these, the royal palaces comprised various bodies of buildings associated with the formidable tower which still exists, and these were visited during the entire fourteenth century and the reign of John, although here (as was the case also in Alenquer and Elvas) the monarchs turned equally to the mendicant convents for their residence, or for that of part of the court.[148] Óbidos was a particular example of architectural development, particularly during Fernando's reign, and the monarchs of the period made use of two distinct residential spaces associated with the fortress: the palaces of the king, at the interior, and the palaces of the queen built against the wall, which as has already been seen included her own chapel.[149] At the end of the fourteenth century, while Óbidos was becoming essentially a palatine town, the principal building of the royal residence communicated with the church situated in the fortress. Thanks to Fernando's initiative, we find in this church a modest wood choir connected directly to the palace. All the monarchs studied here visited this residence regularly and, in the mid-fifteenth century there was to be found there the usual *paçeiro*.[150] Leiria is the example whose remains are the most impressive today because of their

As to Montemor-o-Velho, see Jorge Larcher, *Castelos de Portugal: distrito de Leiria* (Lisbon: Imprensa Nacional, 1933), pp. 273–356, and in particular the plan on p. 291. On Elvas, 'Castelo de Elvas', *Boletim da Direcção Geral dos Edifícios e Monumentos Nacionais* (1948). On the stays of Pedro, Fernando and John I at this castle: *CDP*, p. 234; *CR Fernando*, p. 523; *CR João I*, vol. I, p. 4. In several other places in the kingdom some castles seem to have been included as residences, but there is no express mention that the monarchs studied here stayed in them. For example, the palace in the castle of Montemor-o-Novo is cited by foreign travellers such as Jeronimo Münzer and the secretary to the cardinal of Alexandria.

147 See the plan of the castle at Elvas by Duarte Darmas which is included and analysed in the larger iconographic collection: Francisco Silva Alves and Luzia Afonso, *O castelo de Elvas* (Lisbon: IPPAR, 1991), 21. In the 'aposentamentos sobradados' there is mention of six small rooms and two still smaller and a small walled garden.

148 On the stays of the monarchs at the castle of Estremoz: *GTT*, vol. VIII, p. 477; *CR Fernando*, p. 418; *MH*, vol. III, p. 284. It was in S. Francisco, however, that Pedro wrote his will: *Provas*, vol. I, p. 410. An important revision of the chronology and situation of the castle building can be found in Silva, *Paços medievais Portugueses*, pp. 89–90.

149 See 'Castelo de Óbidos', *Boletim da Direcção Geral dos Monumentos Nacionais* (Lisbon, 1952). And above all Manuela Santos Silva, *Estruturas urbanas e administração concelhia: Óbidos medieval* (Cascais: Patrimonia, 1997). On the chapel of the queens' palaces: ANTT, *Ch. D. Afonso V*, 23, f. 25v.

150 Manuela Santos Silva mentions the building of the tribune which communicated directly with the palace through the tower which overlooked the town. On the *paçeiro*, ANTT, *Ch. D. Afonso V*, 13, f. 95.

monumental character, and it is a singular case of the association of a palace with a system of fortifications which to a large degree already existed. Whether or not in the fortress of Leiria there was some structure built for the residence of the king in the fourteenth century, it was John I who came to realise the most important construction campaigns from which resulted a palace with two towers at the side opening into arches to the panorama of the plain and a small chapel, whose architecture is much like that of the monastery at Batalha.[151] Relatively modest in its total size and having a hall of about 130 m^2 and three chambers on the main floor, the palace of Leiria was a perfect example of residential transformation of an already existing castle, marked by the introduction of certain comforts and amenities which the old fortifications did not generally have. On this point, it is important to speak of the presence of light through newly introduced apertures, of wood panelling (of which vestiges remain, in this case, in the ceilings), and of several fireplaces. To judge by other representations from the drawings we owe to Duarte Darmas, the number of small chimneys in the residences is notable, as is the case at Elvas, but most of all at Cintra.

To finish, let us consider the problem of the use of the monasteries as residential spaces, which in the case of the Portuguese monarchs demonstrates a short-lived nature during this later medieval period, with sporadic but frequent stays. We have already seen how, in localities which were particularly important on the itinerance, use was made almost always of buildings belonging to mendicants (above all the Franciscans). The frequent visit of the kings in certain cases determined the development of residential spaces whose symbiosis with the body of the convent buildings could be translated either by an absorption of the palace by a part of the building, or by the inverse phenomenon, when the royal residence becomes subordinate to the convent building. Not always, however, did this phenomenon of symbiosis occur in relation to the court and the places used by religious communities. A particular case was that of the female monasteries, as I have already had occasion to emphasise with regard to the Portuguese queens, and at times these were connected to the court by the protection of the queens and even through certain aspects of recruitment of the court female household. The Portuguese monarchs thus visited the Cistercian female monasteries at Almoster, Odivelas and Semide,[152] on short stops whose

151 Marques, *A sociedade medieval Portuguesa*, pp. 69–70 and also Ernesto Korrodi, 'A Alcáçova do castelo de Leiria e a sua significação social e política', *Boletim da Academia Nacional de Belas-Artes*, 13 (1944), 12–28. More recently, Silva, *Paços medievais Portugueses*, pp. 120–2 and Saul Gomes, *Introdução à história do castelo de Leiria* (Leiria: Câmara Municipal, 1995).

152 On Odivelas and its relationship with the court, see the important material collected in 'D. Filipa de Odivelas', a dossier put together by Anselmo Braamcamp Freire, Biblioteca Pública de Santarém, manuscript cupboard, shelf 18. On the stays of the kings in Semide: ANTT, *Ch. D. João I*, 2, ff. 74v, 69, 90. On Almoster: ANTT, *Ch. D. Fernando*, 1, f. 123 and *Ch. D. João I*, 5, f. 80. This last monastery was the subject of a monograph study: Francisco Teixeira, 'O Mosteiro de Santa Maria de Almoster', Master's thesis, Universidade Nova, Lisbon, 1992.

organisation and consequences for the life of the community are to a large extent unknown. Alcobaça in this context plays an absolutely unique role, since it is there that are documented stops of all the monarchs with the exception of Afonso IV (whose itinerary, as has already been seen, is incomplete), and these stays were more or less important in relation to their frequency.[153] Two factors seem to me to emphasise the well-known attraction of the Alcobaça abbey for the court of the kings. First, its locality was ideal in relation to the regions of the kingdom most visited by the monarchs. Then there is the involvement of the abbot himself in the structure of court duties, to which I have already referred, and also in the celebrations of anniversaries at the tombs of the royal family during the fifteenth century.[154] The occasional visits of the late-medieval monarchs to another type of religious community are significantly connected to progresses in the northern region which lay off the general pattern of the royal itinerance during this period, such as the convent of the Hospitallers in Leça, in the case of Fernando,[155] or the Augustinian community at Grijó during the first years of the reign of John I or, again, the Benedictines of Santo Tirso who were visited on two different occasions by this monarch.[156] I believe this is in fact a type of connection between the court space and the oldest monasteries which tends to take on a merely residual character in relation to the important function which it would have performed in the period prior to the fourteenth century.

THE COURT, A SPATIAL COMPLEX

When the monarch wished to remove, an entire series of complicated mechanisms was put in motion with a view to planning not only the days, however long, of the journey, but also the installation of the court once it had reached its destination. Two court departments in particular were involved in the royal itinerance: the organisation placed under the authority of the *aposentador*, and also the *estrebaria*. The first had to move some time in advance to the following

[153] The presence of the monarchs in Alcobaça is found in data from the royal chanceries in 1366, 1381, 1385, 1422, 1433, 1434, 1435 and 1439. However, the occasions of the visits must have been more frequent since these records are much cut. On the importance of the visit of the medieval monarchs to the abbeys and their foundation the German example has been particularly studied: John S. Bernhardt, *Itinerant Kingship and Royal Monasteries in Early Medieval Germany* (Cambridge: Cambridge University Press, 1993), in particular pp. 70–5 on the problem of the definition of the 'royal abbeys'. This problem of the definition from the point of view both of the right and of the practices of royal patronage is not sufficiently considered in the study by Chueca Goitia, *Casas reales en monasterios y conventos Españoles*.

[154] On Alcobaça as a burial place of the kings, see Saul Antonio Gomes, 'Percursos em torno do panteão quatrocentista de Avis', *Biblos*, 70 (1994), 197–242.

[155] It should be remembered that the monarch married Leonor Teles there and stayed in the convent building beside the church which still exists.

[156] ANTT, *Ch. D. João I*, 1, ff. 198 and 157; 5, f. 87.

stage in order to co-ordinate with the representatives of the local council the distribution of lodgings for the monarch and his entourage.[157] This was a difficult task, for the regimentation of this use of spaces of private property for the court, which was a characteristic of the medieval period, was a tangle of precepts which had to be respected. Put simply, it concentrated on two orders of reasoning: from the point of view of who was to be lodged, the choice of place appropriate to the status of each one (which for the *aposentador* and his officials meant an overall knowledge of the hierarchy and size of the royal retinue) and, from the point of view of the inhabitants of the place, the record of available places, above all paying attention to the status of their owner. The privileged, who were exempt from supplying this service of hospitality which was a personal obligation, were numerous and highly varied in standing: the clerics and 'vassalos do rei' (a category in which were included many strata of the petty nobility), their widows and also numerous individuals exempt on an individual basis or because of their participation in some organism which granted this mark of distinction. The residences of an important part of the population were, therefore, removed more or less systematically from use by the court. Some spaces at the end of the Middle Ages were also forbidden for use for housing the royal entourage, particularly the areas used for storage, such as wine vaults and barns; places of activity, such as shops and artisans' workshops; buildings for community use, such as hospitals and inns. Wishing to please the population in certain places, the monarchs granted this exemption from lodging the court to the inhabitants of many fortresses, in order to avoid their being abandoned, or to those who lived in important commercial streets, as occurred for example with the principal street in Santarém.[158] The task given to the *aposentadores* of the court was, therefore, somewhat complicated since it demanded an evaluation of this diversity of situations.

As to the *estrebaria*, it fell to it to provide for the transport of persons and much luggage pertaining to the distinct court services, and they had to resort to all methods possible, not only using their own resources but also through inevitable recourse to the hiring or compulsory requisition of animals and services. It was not by chance that, in the majority of European medieval courts whose composition we know in detail, this department appears as the most numerous and certainly one of the most unpopular.[159] The chorus of protest which in the Portuguese case found a hearing at meetings of the Cortes was in the majority of cases due to the lack of payment for carriage and transport and to the state in which the animals used were returned, at times far from the residence of their

[157] See the *regimento* of the *aposentador-mor: OA*, book I, pp. 348–50.

[158] ANTT, *Ch. D. João I*, 1, f. 86.

[159] Given-Wilson, *The Royal Household and the King's Affinity*, p. 58; and above all E. Picard, 'L'écurie de Philippe le Hardi, Duc de Bourgogne', *Mémoires de l'Académie des Sciences, Arts et Belles Lettres de Dijon*, 10 (1905–6), 342–3.

owners.[160] This most general evocation of the duties of the *aposentadoria* and the *estrebaria* which serves as a departure point must, however, be taken as the closest to the abstract situation described for us by normative sources as to the varied practical solutions and even the conflicts of which so many other texts speak. From the analysis I follow through the royal itineraries, it is possible to conclude the enormous diversity of the places where the court was installed, making pertinent the distinction between (1) the more or less improvised stages in occasionally visited places; (2) the network of places where it was possible to remain for some days; and, finally, (3) the urban centres which were undoubtedly the principal places of the court geography. As to the way in which the court in fact moved, occasional indications show that the king could travel separately with his *privata familia* prior to the vast transfer and slow installation of the majority of the court in the locality, or he might remain at the previous stage until the essentials for the conditions of his stay were ready, for his removal was quite often with a fairly reduced retinue, occupied for example in hunting and independent of the situation in which the remainder of his retinue was to be found.[161] The report sent by the spy in the service of the king of Aragon in 1415 serves as an example, from which we discover John I with the queen in Sacavém, while the Infantes Duarte and João were in Camarate and Pedro in Charneca, localities about a league away. However, it seems that it was considered that all were 'at court'.[162] When a place was small or had little suitability for lodging, the king's entourage would be distributed about various close towns, which solution also led to protests.[163] These were different rhythms and places representing many other solutions for the avoidance of the difficult management required for the royal itinerance of men and resources. For the same reason, the spatial limits of the court were configured in a plural regime, as we shall see, leading to a variation in size although always being centred on the physical presence of the king.

The removal of the entourage of the monarch was an event of certain importance, for its installation exercised upon the local community a considerable, though temporary, pressure, owing to the presence of some hundreds of people who created problems of lodging and supply of victuals. The localisation and size of the places, or the existence of residential spaces, were decisive factors however. The use of private residences to house the royal retinue through a system of lodgings was constantly a focus of tension and conflict in late-medieval

[160] See for example chapters of the Cortes of 1361, 1389, 1427 and 1451: *CPP*, p. 66; ANTT, Supplement to the Cortes, M 1, 11; BNL, Res, Cod. 2638, ff. 216v–217; ANTT, Cortes, M 2, 14, f. 11.

[161] Carvalho Homem studied the ruling of Pedro on the activities of the *desembargo* during his absence at the hunt. Also at the Cortes of 1371 the councils mentioned the supply of food to the restricted company of Fernando when he was hunting: *CPF*, p. 44.

[162] *MH*, vol. II, p. 135b.

[163] See for example: BNL, Res, Cod. 2638, ff. 216v–217.

society. The granting of rights and duties in this area was linked, as we have seen, to social representations of the age, and was an important indicator of social standing in the context of the local societies, giving rise to distinctions of fundamental importance whose interpretation, however, was not a matter of consensus. Thus for the municipal communities, as for the monarch, lodging due to the company of the king was a consequence of the situation of the *moradores* of the court, although it expressed the obligation of the population with regard to the royal presence, while many nobles appear to have claimed it in some circumstances as a right inherent to their social status. The translation made in the fourteenth century of the famous 'Penitencial' attributed to Martim Perez mentions the possibility of being lodged whenever they were travelling to the court of the kings as being one of a variety of situations when it was permissible for the nobility to ask the vassals and workers dependent upon them for help and assistance.[164] This seems to have been a demand dear to the Portuguese nobles of the late Middle Ages. In fact, in one of the few known examples of demands presented in the Cortes by the fifteenth-century nobility in the final years of the reign of Afonso V, the nobles attempted to invoke the respect of one of their old privileges of being lodged throughout the kingdom, to which the monarch replied somewhat dryly, denying the legitimacy of the right and its tradition, for 'não acharão que antiguamente aos fidalgos per caminho pousadas sem dinheiro se desem'.[165]

While from the fourteenth century the municipal demands became more insistent, as Mattoso observes, perhaps attesting to the systematic abuse of a service which was only due in law to the lord of the area or to the monarch himself, it can be said that a restrictive interpretation of this obligation had always been defended by royal authority. Thus in the ruling given to the *corregedores* in 1340, the careful evaluation of those 'que querem seer pousados' was recommended: 'ueia o corregedor os foros de cada huu logar pera ueer que onra deuem auer os que forem pousados e segundo no foro for contheudo assy o faça guardar'.[166] In another piece of legislation of the same year, the monarch also ordered the number of the companies of nobles and ecclesiastics who move to court, recommending 'nem lhys dem pousadas hu eu for pera majs companha que a que conpre pera tantos como dito he'.[167] The same restrictive

[164] José Antunes, 'A nobreza no discurso medieval de confissão (séc. XIII a XIV)', *Revista de História das Ideias*, 19 (1997), 169. This assistance due to the nobles who moved in the service of the king is analogous to the services related to the old Roman *cursus*, of which there is mention in the legislation of the Visigoths: F. L. Ganshof, 'La Tractoria. Contribution à l'étude des origines du droit de gîte', *Revue d'Histoire du Droit*, 8 (1927), 69–91.

[165] ANTT, Cortes, M 2, 14, f. 61 (Cortes of 1472–73).

[166] Mattoso, *Identificação de um país*, vol. I, pp. 442–3. On the ruling of the *corregedores*, Caetano, *A administração municipal de Lisboa*, p. 172.

[167] A. H. Oliveira Marques, 'A pragmática de 1340', in *Ensaios de história medieval Portuguesa*, p. 166.

interpretation is also found in Castilian royal documentation of the thirteenth century.[168] The image of this turbulent and predatory band which formed the itinerant court of the kings, generally constructed by medieval sources and originating from towns in order to give foundation to their complaints against the lodgings, often puts in the shade the true reason for their protests, which was a disrespect for the existing ruling, in particular by the nobility. This disdain in general assumed two forms, according to the chapters of the Cortes: the demand for lodging in places and from persons who had no duty to provide this service, and the destruction or abusive use of installations and domestic furniture which were made available to them.

During the final period of the Middle Ages there are however important changes to be found in the provision of the service of lodgings, tending to untie this conflictual knot and in which we can distinguish two different vertents: on the one hand, the change in the relationship between the court and the localities, in particular through the mediating instance *par excellence*, that is the local town council, which had always been connected to the actual process of distributing lodging; on the other hand, the evolution of the provision and distribution of lodging and assistance to the members of the entourage in the actual court organism. Thus, as to the first aspect, there should be emphasised the peculiar development of the problem in the large cities, where recourse to paid hospitality was much recognised and practised from the thirteenth century[169] and also where the town council organisation became collectively responsible for the provision of the service of lodging to the monarch. One is led to believe that the size and diversity of housing of these localities made difficult or unsatisfactory the traditional solutions found for the lodging of the court.

At the end of the fourteenth century there are signs that, in Lisbon, the provision of lodging to the members of the entourage was by then voluntary and corresponded to a payment. This service was given the generic name of 'estau': a 'meio estau' was five beds, and an 'estau inteiro' was ten. As a port city connected to maritime trade, this Lisbon use of a term pointing towards a Mediterranean context is not strange, for the most important merchant communities living in the city came from the Mediterranean area, and in fact this term is close to the Catalan 'hostal' and the Occitan 'ustal' or 'ostau', all words used for the same type of service.[170] In the principal locality of the kingdom the

[168] Nilda Guglielmi, 'Posada y yantar. Contribución al estudio del léxico de las instituciones medievales', *Hispania*, 26 (1966), 14–15 and note 24. On the *regimento* of the *corregedores*: Caetano, *A administração municipal de Lisboa*, p. 172.

[169] Gonçalves, *Imagens do mundo medieval*, pp. 143–55. See also in a comparative perspective Miguel Gual Camarena, 'El hospedaje hispanomedieval. Aportaciones para su estudio', *Anuario de Historia del Derecho Español*, 32 (1962), 527–41.

[170] A. M. Alcover and F. B. Moll (eds.), *Diccionari Català–Valencià–Balear* (Palma de Mallorca: Imp. Alcover, 1930–62), s.v. 'hostal'; M. Sagristà i Artigas (ed.), *Diccionari de la llengua Catalana* (Barcelona: Ed. Enciclopèdia Catalana, 1993), s.v. 'hostal' and 'hostaladge'; Jules Coupier

institutionalisation of mechanisms leading to the transformation of this obligation into a tax of a general character must have been concomitantly processed from this period.[171] Following its brave adherence to the installation of the new dynasty from 1383 to 1385, Lisbon repeatedly attempted to gain exemption from this duty, which it managed to obtain fleetingly from the monarchs of Aviz and, consequently, all lodging was to be paid for; some historians consider this situation was implemented in the middle of the fifteenth century.[172] During the second half of the century, the councils of Santarém and Évora also instituted, as in Lisbon, a certain amount of income obtained from taxes on the consumption of common products and from other sources in order to meet their obligation to the monarch and his retinue when they made use of the availability of local lodging. That is, in these cities too, payment was made to those who provided this service to the *moradores* of the king, according to a table corresponding to a careful regulation of this service.[173]

At the end of this development, we witness the establishment of true contracts between the cities and the lodgers in the final decades of the century which can be considered as characteristic of the situation of the principal localities of the itinerance of the monarchs – Lisbon, Santarém and Évora – and through which the councils turned to the services of a professional intermediary. This professional saw to the furniture and services necessary for the housing of the court in a previously agreed manner, and there was planning for a certain period in order to advise in advance the supplier; this could be between a fortnight and

(ed.), *Dictionnaire Français–Provençal* (s.l.: Edisud, 1995), s.v. 'hôtel – oustau'; M. Cortelazzo and P. Zolli (eds.), *Dizionario etimologico della lingua Italiana* (Bologna: Zanichelli, 1989), s.v. 'òste'. The hypothesis that the Portuguese word could be related to the High German 'stal' as proposed by Cândido de Figueiredo seems less probable than that of its Latin origin. See the general observations of B. E. Vidos, 'Les termes techniques et l'emprunt', in *Prestito, espansione e migrazione dei termini tecnici nelle lingue Romanze e non Romanze* (Florence: Olschki, 1965), pp. 355–78. The Portuguese authors of the fifteenth century had a quite specific notion of what these 'estaus' were, for the report of the journey of the Conde de Ourém mentions their existence in several places outside Portugal such as Chiva (Valencia), Pisa and Strasbourg.

171 Henrique de Gama Barros, *História da administração pública em Portugal nos séculos XII a XV* (Lisbon: Sá da Costa, 1945–54), vol. V, pp. 216–18, 221 and note.

172 In particular Maria Teresa Campos Rodrigues, *Aspectos da administração municipal de Lisboa no século XV*, offprint of *Revista Municipal* (Lisbon, 1968), pp. 120–1.

173 See the ruling of Évora of 1464: *DEV*, part I, pp. 97–103. For Santarém, the ruling is dated the same year: ANTT, *Ch. D. Afonso V*, 8, f. 51v. This system was also published in other places in the second half of the fifteenth century, and its management was usually handed to the *mesterais*. For the example of Setúbal: Paulo Drummond Braga, *O regimento excepcional da aposentadoria da vila de Setúbal de 1471*, offprint of *Boletim dos Trabalhos Históricos* (Guimarães, 1989). The fact of being housed by the court *aposentador* without paying the householder directly did not prevent the payment of tips on departure such as the 'belaxira' mentioned in Portuguese sources; the word is of Franco-English origin: 'a gift to an innkeeper or his servants on departure was known as *bel chere* ('good cheer', later corrupted in English to *belly-cheer*)': C. M. Woolgar, *The Great Household in Late Medieval England* (New Haven: Yale University Press, 1999), p. 26.

a month.[174] For greater surety for the monarch, however, there was also an agreement both in Lisbon and in Évora that the council should organise a list of a considerable number of individuals (up to 500 inhabitants who were not exempt from this duty) to whom they could turn should the arrangement be deemed insufficient to guarantee lodging for the court.[175]

One aspect of the problem, in spite of everything, appeared hard to resolve in these localities, and this was the non-existence of material spaces, of actual buildings sufficiently large to house the numerous retinues which otherwise would have to be distributed among the existing lodgings and in houses which would receive them in small groups, giving rise to the habitual chorus of protestation and argument. For this reason the 'estaus' were created. These were buildings, either royal or private, where men of the court entourage could be installed preferentially (in particular in the first case of royal 'estaus'), where beds, bedding, domestic furnishings and stabling would be made available. The same buildings were, it would seem, open to use by travellers upon payment, and became public spaces of the greatest importance in the Portuguese urban areas of the fifteenth century, directly originating from the presence of the court in the principal cities of the kingdom. Once again, we see a coincidence with the uses of this term for public buildings in other Mediterranean areas, as for example used in Occitan with the 'Oustau de la Mounedo' (Hôtel de la Monnaie) or the 'Ostau de Vèndo' (Hôtel des Ventes).

At the beginning of Duarte's reign in the case of Lisbon there arises the initiative of construction of the king's 'estaus', which were sited near the Rossio in a space contiguous to the important seigneurial palace of the Conde de Ourém. However, it was only during the regency of Pedro that they were completed.[176] These were also in Évora, for we see they functioned in a building in the main square previously used for a while as a royal residence.[177] In Santarém there is no indication, however, of the construction of an actual building, be this because the number of small lodgings was seen as sufficient in this case, or because in Almeirim the kings had use, as we have seen, of plenty of lodgings for the court. During the period of personal rule of Afonso V, this monarch would have attempted to ensure that the residences in Lisbon of the principal nobles of the

[174] An example of a contract relating to Santarém dated 1496: *GTT*, vol. XIV, pp. 189–94. On Lisbon, Rodrigues, *Administração municipal*, p. 121.

[175] See the already quoted *regimento* for Évora, p. 102 and Rodrigues, *Administração municipal, p.* 123.

[176] I. de Vilhena Barbosa, 'Fragmentos de um roteiro de Lisbon (inédito). Paços dos estaos, paços da inquisição', *Archivo Pittoresco*, 6 (1863), 33–4. See also Júlio de Castilho, *Lisboa antiga: os bairros orientais* (Lisbon: Câmara Municipal, 1937), vol. X, pp. 32–49. Important works significantly altered the building to allow for the installation of the Lisbon Inquisition during the reign of John III. See on this *DHDA*, vol. III, p. 222 and also a reproduction of the old plans of the building of the Inquisition in Francisco Bethencourt, *História das Inquisições: Portugal, Espanha e Itália* (Lisbon: Círculo de Leitores, 1994).

[177] Espanca, *Palácios reais de Évora*, pp. 5–14.

court also had their 'estaus' attached, where the respective retinues could be installed, as was already the case with the Infante Henry in Tomar.[178] The interest of the monarch in promoting the expansion of this method of characteristically Mediterranean lodging demonstrates, I believe, that the solution found was considered effective.

The similarity between the actual form of this last building of 'estaus' in Tomar, which can still be reconstructed through the remains to be found, and the form of the little which remains of the royal 'estaus' of Évora suggests that this can be seen as a specific constructive typology where the modular spaces led on from each other but did not intercommunicate internally, rather having archways or porticoes.[179] As has been emphasised in studies of late-medieval urbanism, the fifteenth century witnessed the development of solutions through construction in the principal commercial cities with a view to a collective use, be this temporary or permanent. The case of Venice has been well studied with the construction of residences for poor families (the *marinarezza* or *case-ospizio* which existed from the fourteenth century) or the example of the houses of the canons of St Mark, both being modular, contiguous spaces of small size organised around a central courtyard, but most of all with the construction in the sixteenth century of the famous Fondaco dei Tedeschi in the Rialto, which was based on a similar typology and given a monumental appearance.[180] The Islamic tradition of creating spaces intended as lodging for travellers and merchants was known in the Iberian Peninsula, and there are still important remains of a Nasrid *funduk* with square foundations and a central patio surrounded by lodgings along a gallery, structurally identical to the *maristan* or hospice built in Granada by Muhammad V in 1365–67, with a water reservoir in the centre of the courtyard of which there are some vestiges identified by Torres Balbás.[181] It should be noted, so we are informed by available glossaries, that on occasions the Catalan 'hostal' was also called 'fonda'. Iconography available, for example in the famous marginal illumination dating 1530–40 showing a view of Lisbon in the 'Genealogia dos Reis de Portugal', points to a similar evolution to that of the Fondaco dei Tedeschi in the case of the 'estaus' of Lisbon built in the

[178] José Anastácio de Figueiredo, *Synopsis chronologica de subsidios ainda os mais raros para a historia e estudo crítico da legislação Portugueza* (Lisbon: Academia Real das Ciências, 1790), vol. I, p. 94 (quoting document of 1449 of the collection of the house of Braganza).

[179] On Henry's 'estaus', Eugénio de Figueiredo e Silva, *Os estaus de Tomar*, offprint of *Anais da União dos Amigos dos Monumentos da Ordem de Cristo* (Tomar, 1961). According to Rui de Pina there would also have been 'estaus' in the town of Setúbal, but it is probable that in this case the chronicler is referring to the organisation of lodgings for the court (comprising, as seen above, a particular number of beds) and not to the existence of a particular building: *CR João II*, p. 941.

[180] See the thematic dossier 'Storia dell'urbanistica: le residenze colletive', *Urbanistica*, 42–3 (1965), in particular pp. 7–14 on Venice.

[181] Leopoldo Torres Balbás, *Ciudades Hispanomusulmanas* (Madrid: Instituto Hispano-Árabe de Cultura, 1971), vol. I.

Rossio, which became a truly 'important monument' in the sixteenth-century city, and it was considered such by Damião de Góis.[182]

The solution found with this material structure appears to be particularly satisfactory and exemplary. The 'estaus' could follow on from the older noble 'bairros' of which so many fourteenth- and fifteenth-century texts tell us. These delineated spaces which surrounded the residences of the principal families of the nobility in the important cities such as Lisbon or Santarém were authentic, differentiated territories within the urban space where dependent men or the clientele of the respective lords lived.[183] In Genoa too, the so-called 'consorterie' of the city nobility owned lodgings for the respective retinues and dependants, and from the twelfth and thirteenth centuries use was made of archways favouring the development of urban spaces which were truly 'insular' with an intense life 'sub porticu'.[184] The advantage of the 'estaus' as suggested by the Portuguese monarch and based upon the example of Tomar would, in comparison, be that they were concerned with public spaces and not removed from the jurisdiction of the city through the privileged status of their owners, open to use by other retinues and visitors besides the actual followers of the nobility and the court of the kings – as is shown by the reports of travellers who stayed in the 'estaus' throughout the fifteenth and sixteenth centuries. As for the *moradores* of the king in particular, the existence of buildings for 'estaus' certainly represented for the councils an improvement in conditions of provision of lodgings, since it planned for lodging of a collective type sufficiently large to dispense with private dwellings belonging to the inhabitants, and reduced the impact of the presence of the court in these localities. It was not possible to make use of these buildings, however, except in the indicated populated centres, that is in the principal urban centres of the kingdom, which could be seen as yet another element reinforcing the tendency referred to above for the monarchs from then on to install themselves in the cities in the centre and south of the kingdom.

As to the evolution of the actual court organism mentioned above, this was processed in a manner which restricted and normalised the rights of the *morador* of the king with regard to lodging. As stated in the previous chapter, the court hierarchy of the end of the Middle Ages was constructed with this factor in mind, as were the number of mounts and the support to which each had a right, according to his position on the scale of personal standing. Thus in laws promulgated by Afonso IV in 1340, it was determined that the company of

[182] A reproduction of this 'vista' and its commentary can be found in Marques, 'Depois da Reconquista. A cidade na baixa idade média'.

[183] See the protests made by the councils against the existence of these 'bairros' at the Cortes of 1361: *CPP*, p. 68. In Évora, John prohibited them in the 1390s: *DEV*, part I, p. 101.

[184] Ennio Poleggi, 'Le contrade delle consorterie nobiliari a Genova tra il XII e il XIII secolo', *Urbanistica*, 42–3 (1964), 15–20.

ricos-homens, archbishops and counts could number thirty mounted men having the right to be lodged whenever they were at court, and from then down the number would certainly fall.[185] The magnates naturally made use of their own houses or those of their peers or their family, as occurred in a general manner in the fifteenth century in the larger localities, and if this was not the case they would stay in the best houses at the place where the monarch might be.[186] The number of the company was, however, significantly restricted to those who were most constantly in the royal entourage, including among the many examples of those who received *moradia* only the person of the courtier and his mount.

The young *moradores* of the king, who as already seen formed another significant part of his entourage, received lodgings for themselves and shelter for their animals according to their standing as *escudeiros* or 'homens de pé', as seen in the known ruling relating to the principal cities, which was to serve as a model for the entire country.[187] In 1449, according to a ruling of the local council, the 'cama' of the *escudeiros* of the court in Lisbon comprised various household linens (mats, mattress, cushions, sheets and blankets), and the same number, but in considerably inferior material, corresponded to the lodging of the so-called 'homem de pé'. Also provided were napkins for eating, a skewer, plates and a tankard, salt cellar and bowls, all of which were for the use of the esquire *morador*.[188] 'Bestas de carga, mantimentos, palhas e outras cousas' would be given for those of the same standing. Officials of the tribunals of the court would also have had their 'pousadas e camas', for example, as long as they personally performed their duties.[189] The relative material precariousness of this picture, as well as the physiognomy of the collective space which the 'estaus' comprised as a place for lodging of many courtiers, determined a particular way of life for the majority of the entourage whose gregarious forms and possible discomfort were the subject of a lively and biting evocation of satirical intent composed by a 'cortesão arrependido' and poet of the *Cancioneiro Geral*, included in a curious attempt at explicitly cultivating for the first time in Portugal the theme of opposition between 'corte e aldeia'. It goes thus:

185 Oliveira Marques, *Ensaios de história medieval*, p. 116. In fact, the entourage of an ecclesiastical magnate such as Fernando da Guerra comprised in the 1450s 'trinta de mullas escudeiros, capellães e outra jente que ell quiser': José Marques, *A Arquidiocese de Braga no século XV*, p. 130.

186 The ruling for the *aposentador* stated that there could be demanded from the householder the granting of his own chamber in such cases: *OA*, vol. I, p. 349.

187 See the decisions of the Cortes of 1471–72: ANTT, Cortes, M 2, 14, f. 66.

188 See the text of the contract made with the commune of Lisbon: Tavares, *Os Judeus em Portugal no século XV*, vol. I, pp. 210–11 and note 133 and also ANTT, *LN*, Estremadura, book 10, ff. 93 v–94; J. C. Aires de Campos, 'Antiguidades nacionais. Dos estaos e aposentadorias em 1439', *O Instituto*, 13 (1866), 20–3. In a letter sent to the residents of Cintra in 1436, Duarte specified the obligations for clothing due to the residents of the court: ANTT, *Ch. D. Duarte*, 1, f. 211.

189 ANTT, *LN*, extras, f. 98–98v, clarifying on this point the *regimento* of Évora. On the duty to serve personally in the post: *ibid.*, ff. 127 and 131.

Já nam reçebo pousada
de vosso apousentador
panela nem telhador
espeto, mesa quebrada,
cadeyra desengonçada
e lençoes de mes a mes
ao longo nem oo traves
me nam cobrem a bragada.

Quantas vezes pelejey
comvosco sobola manta,
onde era a pulgua tanta
quanta sabeys que matey.
Quantas vezes jejuey
sem ter muyta deuaçam,
Deos o sabe e vosso yrmãao
com quem ja tambem pousey.[190]

The measures adopted in the fourteenth and fifteenth centuries for establishing recourse to paid lodging for the company of the king must in fact have contributed to an approach to the material conditions of life of the members of the court for those of any other traveller, and this is the basic fabric which can give to this text its entire verisimilitude, upon which is based the practice of satire. More and more these conditions of lodging were to depend, from then on, on the personal wealth of each individual, with the probable threshold of greater comfort being the ability to make use of the individual's own residences, as was the case with courtiers of higher standing.

A fundamental aspect of the functioning of this spatial complex of the court lies in fact in its insertion in the complex of traffic and exchange through the creation of intermittent markets in space and time. The evolution of the problem of lodging of the royal retinue was a significant example of this general problem which has already been stated by Werner Sombart, if we consider the progressive abandonment of the old obligations of seigneurial origin through recourse to the practice of lodging 'por dinheiros'. As I have already stated, the sudden pressure of demand which the presence of the court represented was felt above all in the supply of victuals and lodging. Its effect would, however, be highly diverse according to the size of the locality and the vitality of the network of exchange and the commercial circuits involved in the processes of supply to this same locality, perhaps adopting, according to what is described to us by

190 Garcia de Resende, *Cancioneiro geral*, ed. by A. J. Costa Pimpão and A. Fernandes Dias (Coimbra: Universidade de Coimbra, 1973), vol. I, p. 342. These lines are included in a composition by João Rodrigues de Castelo Branco, a court poet at the turn of the sixteenth century.

some chapters of the Cortes, perturbing aspects in the smaller places or those located outside the major commercial fluxes.

Also in this area the presence of the court was seen as a destabilising factor in the fiercely regulated universe of local markets placed under the control of the local council authorities in essential aspects of their functioning – in weights and measures, in control of places of sale and, above all, in price control. As Duarte said to the residents of Cintra, the presence of the monarch always evoked two contrary but complementary realities: 'por aazo de nossas estadas os moradores da dicta ujlla e seu termo recebem algus nojos e perdas em algũas suas cousas que geralmente se nom podem escusar em pumares e ujnhas E ajnda nas pousadias posto que elles ajam outros proueitos dos mantijmentos que uendem milhor por aazo de nossa estada'.[191] These 'proveitos' or benefices would be all the more visible, I would add, the more structured and dynamic was the local economic space, which naturally occurred in a more accentuated form in the larger localities.

The first problem to be confronted lay, from the point of view of the court organism, in the construction of circuits of supply which were not solely dependent upon this local reality and which, as has been seen, could be highly varied. Thus the court of the fourteenth and fifteenth centuries made use of its own 'regatães' or retail merchants who had to supply basic products to the entourage of the monarch and even of some more specialised merchants such as grocers and spice sellers, as well as butchers and bakers who also accompanied the progress of the monarch. The privileges granted to the spice sellers of the court in 1446 are enlightening as to the hierarchy desired: not only would they be the first to be supplied in the local market, but they would be exempt from duties of circulation (tolls, duties, customs and *dízimas*). However, they could not freely sell products 'para regatar' within five leagues when the court was 'em estada', or one league when it was 'de caminho'.[192] With the intention of giving incentive to the sale of products from outside the localities where he was installed, John I had instituted a total or partial exemption of the *sisa* on basic products – cereal, wine, meat, game and fruit – 'per os da nossa corte averem melhor os mantijmentos E os da nossa terra passarem melhor por nom seerem apremados de nos tragerem mantimentos per constrangimento'.[193] Likewise, in many places of the Estremadura and Alentejo the smallholders within the

[191] ANTT, *Ch. D. Duarte*, 1, f. 211. Also in his treatise the Infante Pedro shows an understanding of the perspective of the populations, defending the strange doctrine by which collections and dinners would originally be voluntary, and only after the communities 'começaram de sentir a despeza que a elles fazia pequeno proveito': *Virtuosa benfeitoria*, p. 562.

[192] ANTT, *Ch. D. Afonso V*, 5, f. 48.

[193] Significantly this exemption which was later to be partially included in the Manueline Ordinations would not be applied to the city of Lisbon: ANTT, *Ch. D. João I*, 5, f. 57v. In Santarém it provoked repeated protests which were taken by representatives to the Cortes of the fifteenth century.

boundaries would be obliged to supply straw in abundance in preparation for the 'wintering' of the court in these regions as well as for the growing needs of the product for the animals.[194]

Regarding an internal regulation of the temporary market which the court gave rise to, particularly revealing is the group of characteristics of certain agents who accompanied the entourage such as the *meirinho* and the *corregedor* of the court[195] or, later, the *almotacé-mor*.[196] One could say that, generically, the principal model for the activity of these officials, particularly in the case of the last of these (whose ruling was only included in the Manueline Ordinations although it adopted earlier precepts), was the urban organism. When there appeared to be a shortage of products it was the duty of these agents of the king to have them brought from more distant locations and to force the traders to supply them (in particular fish traders during the periods of penance or on fasting days), to distribute the produce when scarce in a manner acceptable to the various hierarchical groups, to oversee compliance with the local pricing in the town and to set prices for victuals coming from outside, as well as to control weights and measures used at court, whose transport from place to place was by mule especially used for the purpose.

The multiplicity of the various markets which were thus intended to function in the same place, ideally distinct and controlled by diverse authorities, seems never to have functioned in accord with the standard, that is in a watertight manner. The regulation of prices of products sold to the court entourage, for example, was always contested by the councils in successive Cortes from the middle of the fourteenth century: at the Cortes of 1361 and, in the following decade, the Cortes of Fernando's reign in 1371, and recurring during the fifteenth century until the Cortes of 1468.[197] According to protests of the councils there were those who benefited marvellously from this plurality of rules and markets – including many court officials who 'se faziam mercadores e regatães', negotiating with the citizens the transaction of certain products intended for the supply of the royal retinue, in particular fish.[198] Behind this constant lament could be seen the deception of the local merchants since they could not name their own prices for the court and so the 'proventos' to which Duarte referred increased.

194 *OA*, vol. I, pp. 52–3.

195 See in particular the 'apontamento' of Joane Mendes, the old royal servant telling of the practices of the time of John I: *OD*, pp. 639–40. See also the 'regimento' which follows this in the same source, pp. 640–2.

196 *OA*, vol. I, in particular pp. 48–57 (§26 on), precepts which later came to be included in the 'regimento' of the *almotacé-mor*.

197 *CPP*, p. 58 and again p. 93 (special chapter on Coimbra); *CPF*, p. 33. Also ANTT, Cortes, M 2, 14, f. 51v (Cortes of 1468). As was the case of the *aposentadorias*, the councils related that the nobles wished to impose the same prices on food even when they were outside the court.

198 See the chapters of the Cortes of 1372: *CPF*, p. 130.

The supply for the tables of the palace and the king, which manifestly included only a small number of the company of the court (as we have seen, rations in kind or in money would generally be given to the majority), also included specific commercial markets. There is available a fairly detailed vision of the problem solely for the royal table, thanks to a surviving book of expenses relating to a quarter of the year 1474: here it can be seen that the acquisitions of these fresh products were made once or twice a week at times in a place far from the court (which at the time was staying in Santarém), and the king is seen principally as a consumer on this particular occasion of sea fish (flounder, sole, red mullet) and oysters.[199] Another specific market was, for example, small game and domestic birds – and the 'galinheiros' were, to judge from the protests of the Cortes, particularly detested by the population. The quantity of birds consumed was enormous, as seen in some later receipts: between 1493 and 1497 these show an average of ten hens a day, three cockerels and sixteen eggs, as well as 152 capons a year, about 300 goats and fourteen sucking pigs, six lambs and a hundred web-footed birds.[200] Finally, the supply of wines also, as is well known, gave rise to a large number of complaints against the king's *copeiros* as well as those of the queen and the infantes.

A practice which took time to be imposed appears to have been that of deferment of payments in order to assist the introduction of centralised mechanisms of accountancy. Thus the *galinheiros* and *estrabeiros* of the monarchs of the fourteenth century caused various protests from the population, for they gave them 'senhas talhas de fuste' in exchange for products, then sending them to the town or city to receive sums which were at times very small.[201] This was the well-known process of giving a small wooden stick with cuts which represented the sums owed and which later were settled by compensation with another formal 'tally' from the debtor, with a record made by the respective official. This system was, for example, used in England in royal accountancy from the twelfth century until the dawn of the nineteenth.[202] In Portugal, the system is mentioned in connection with the court by legislation of the thirteenth

199 ANTT, *NA*, p. 783 and the publication of this source by Maria José Azevedo Santos, 'O peixe e a fruta na alimentação da corte de Afonso V', *Brigantia*, 3 (1983), 307–43. For a comparison with the Burgundian court: Monique Sommé, 'L'alimentation quotidienne à la cour de Bourgogne au milieu du XVe siècle', *Bulletin Philologique et Historique*, 1 (1971), plate 3, p. 111.

200 ANTT, *LN*, extras, f. 9. From a clause in another charter relating to 1451 we know that several *alqueires* of corn were used 'pera mantimento das aves que pera nos tijnha nosso gallynheiro': *DCH*, vol. II, p. 352.

201 *CPA*, pp. 15–16 (chapters on Santarém relating to the Cortes of 1325). The citizens of Lisbon complained in the same way in 1371 of the 'talhas e alvaras que nunca som pagadas': *CPF*, p. 34.

202 Hilary Jenkinson, 'Medieval tallies, public and private', *Archaeologia*, 84 (1923–24), 289–351. In this work is the description and analysis of the largest collection known of these 'tallies', that of the Public Record Office. I should like to thank Kate Lowe for having assisted me in accessing this publication.

century, precisely regarding the activity of the king's *porteiro*.[203] Through the use of 'talhas' or written notes there was an anticipation of supplies and there could be a better control of settlement – which, if we believe the complaints of the councils, was made late or never.[204] Contrary to what occurred with debts of the monarch himself, private debts of the courtiers included the taking of pledges and, in view of the protests of the burgers of Évora, Afonso V in 1471 ordered the pledges to be sold should the indebted *fidalgos* not settle their debts within a month and a half.[205]

A final aspect of the court system which must be referred to is better known, and lies in the existence of actual jurisdictional spaces, in particular those attached to the tribunals which had their headquarters there. As is known, all unlawful acts committed within five leagues of the locality were taken to the *casa da suplicação*, which accompanied the monarch, as was trial of crimes committed throughout the kingdom. From the 'internal' point of view, as one might call it, the company of the king remained under the control of the *corregedor* of the court and the *ouvidores*, which seems not to have effectively suppressed petty crime, which at the court of the period was rife. Numerous charters of pardon granted following brawls and insolence attest to the fact that violent conflicts were common. In many cases, we see a lively animosity between the 'vila' and the 'paço', that is between the court and the urban community, for the *moradores* of the court and the inhabitants of the town were involved.[206] The autonomy and specificity of the court space were of greater importance in this jurisdictional aspect, and contributed to the establishment of one of its most important limits.[207]

The spatial entity to which I have referred developed in concentric circles and affirmed its existence by the demarcation of various limits, expressing the formation of 'disciplinary' spaces (in the meaning Foucault gave to the word),

203 In a law of 1211 there is mention of the executions made by the *porteiro*, 'quer com fuste quer com letras': *Leges*, vol. I, p. 128.

204 See for example in the Cortes of 1389, ANTT, supplement of the Cortes, M 1, 11. Or those of 1459, where the councils suggest that the householders be paid at once 'da arca do Concelho', which would then be reimbursed, which the monarch refused: BNL, Res, Cod. 2639, f. 85.

205 This was particularly regarding debts contracted 'na estada da corte': *DEV*, part I, p. 122.

206 An eloquent example in *DCH*, vol. II, pp. 273 and 287–8. Among the useful 'manhas' at the palace, the *coudel-mor* recommended to his nephew, 'Hoos arroydos da uylla acoddyr, ser muy desposto': Garcia de Resende, *Cancioneiro geral*, vol. I, p. 72. I have mentioned these in Rita Costa Gomes, 'La vida en la corte portuguesa', in *La paz y la guerra en la época del Tratado de Tordesillas* (Madrid: Electa, 1994), pp. 46–9.

207 For a comparison with Castile, see the definition of 'corte' and 'rastro': Miguel Angel Pérez de la Canal, 'La justicia de la corte en Castilla durante los siglos XIII al XV', *Historia, Instituciones, Documentos*, 2 (1975), 414–15. According to Alfonso X's *Espéculo*: 'En corte dezimos que están todos aquellos que sson en la çibdat o en la villa o en el logar o es el rrey e tres migeros alderedor a todas partes, que ffazen vna legua. E otrossi tenemos que non sson partidos de la corte aquellos que van fuera destos términos, commo a caçar o a rrecabdar alguna otra cosa que ayan grant meester dexando ssu conpana en la corte para tornarsse y e non ssiendo espedidos del rrey': *Leyes de Alfonso X*, vol. I, *Espéculo*, p. 164.

that is a territorial dynamic based on the inclusion or exclusion of access to determined places and in the control and manipulation of determined spheres of activity.[208] For example, all those in the same locality as the king or in the city and its surroundings to a limit of two leagues were protected by the peace of the court.[209] A space at times confused with this was the 'rastro' which could be increased to four leagues, and was the territory of jurisdiction of the *meirinho* and his men.[210] In cases of exile or banishment from court, the presence of the condemned man was forbidden within ten leagues of the presence of the king. In taking its place as the centre of justice of the entire kingdom, the *casa da suplicação* extended its activity to all judicial spheres within a radius of five leagues from the presence of the king, which limit was also used for the space of supply under the authority of the *corregedor* or the *almotacé*. The latter could eventually cover up to eight leagues when supply was difficult, but he was restricted to a league when the court was 'em andada'. The most important characteristic of this spatial dynamic lay in this case in the fact that there was no known exception in the diverse territories of the kingdom, as John I clarified with regard to conflicts arising in lands belonging to the queen, with the spatial reality of the court being imposed at least in theory on all existing privileges and on the diversity of normative regimes in practice in the kingdom.[211]

All these concentric, interrelated spaces allowed for the regulation of the impact of the court, and were simultaneously spheres of influence where the royal presence resounded, increasing its effects in a certain way. Here should be remembered in this respect the important observations of Paolo Grossi:

> The 'particularism' of the late Middle Ages does not represent a rupture of an eminent unitary order. It is an order itself that has many facets, an order which is a complicated set of autonomies and becomes articulated in a plurality of rules. Medieval law is a universe of autonomies, founded in such a typical and basic notion of 'particularism'. According to this notion, it is easy and almost obvious to assume that at the same place and inside one single political entity there can exist a plurality of regimes, each one having its own specific sphere, and each supposing a respectful coexistence with the others, none of them presuming to expand and to become an encompassing dominant rule.[212]

208 Claude Raffestin, *Pour une Géographie du pouvoir* (Paris: Librairies Techniques, 1980), pp. 134–5; Christopher Tilley, *A Phenomenology of Landscape: Places, Paths and Monuments* (Oxford: Berg, 1994), pp. 26–7.

209 *OD*, pp. 186, 303 and 376–8 (group of laws of the fourteenth century). In a ruling after Fernando's reign, the carrying of arms within these limits is also forbidden: ANTT, *Ch. D. Fernando*, 3, f. 95. The same limit is found in John's legislation included in the *Ordenações Afonsinas*.

210 Although this word is rare in Portuguese documentation it occasionally appears, as can be seen for example in the ruling of John I relating to the treatment of the 'barregueiros': *OA*, vol. V, p. 78.

211 ANTT, *Ch. D. João I*, 4, f. 121v.

212 Paolo Grossi, *L'ordine giuridico medievale* (Bari: Laterza, 1995), p. 226.

It is in this fabric, in which a multiplicity of normative ordinations and regimes are spatially coincident, that the court is decisively seen as a project of dominion of space through a specific articulation of territorial practices existing in the kingdom. The perception of this particular spatial order is subjacent to the definition in the legislative texts of the Hispanic thirteenth century of the court as a 'lugar do rei', so identifying this 'projecto de poder' in constant realisation in space.

Considered as a spatial complex originating from the presence of the monarchs, the court does not however show a fixed or random localisation in the geographic space of the kingdom. According to what is shown in my analysis of the itinerance of the court, the Portuguese monarchs of the end of the Middle Ages appear in fact as connected in a particular way to certain regions of the kingdom and also to the urban centres. By their movement in space, the 'lugares do rei' were interconnected, leading to a spatial network which finally appears as a sophisticated 'map' of the territory, in which certain ties and itineraries were activated, others ignored or demoted. The spatial perception which can result from these practices of the king's itinerance and that of the court would without doubt be connected to a spatial density of this network of places or, as Michel de Certeau said, to a metamorphosis of space created by synecdoche, in which the part was the whole and a restricted number of places, interconnected by the frequent removal of the king, could be conceived as a substitute for the physical totality of the kingdom. Thus the network of places of royal power involved sacred spaces, in particular through visits to monasteries and religious communities where not only proximity and the transforming contact with venerated objects were possible but also the reminder of the hagiographic charisma of certain members of the royal dynasties because of the number of tombs of dead monarchs. A statement of the Infante Henry is therefore helpful towards an understanding of the visit to the tombs of the kings and queens; in a famous letter he wrote to his father telling of the marriage of the infante heir, remembering the virtues of the queen, Saint Isabel, who was associated with the use of the monastery of Santa Clara by the monarchy of Aviz.[213] Also the 'wild' space associated with the exercise of hunting imposed given notions of cosmology, in particular concepts of separation between the human sphere and an animal universe conceived hierarchically, of whose frontier the monarchs showed themselves to be guardians, constantly reinforced by the creation of specific laws against removing given animal species for any use other than the ritual of the hunt and consumption at the royal table. As we shall see later, this cynegetic ritual had a central value in the system of beliefs of medieval royalty and it is important to emphasise that its inclusion in the space of the kingdom through a territorialisation of given norms implied a purposeful and expensive infrastructure. Another space included through the network of places of royal

[213] *MH*, vol. III, p. 258.

power was naturally the territory of the local communities, in particular in the case of urban centres of the kingdom where, as we have seen, the monarchs removed more frequently. I shall also refer to the fulcral significance which certain rites had, such as the royal 'entradas', as vectors of the experiences and perceptions of royalty held by the citizens, precisely in their community dimension which is undoubtedly accentuated at the end of the Middle Ages. Finally, it is also fitting to emphasise the existence of a network of places connected to the spaces owned by the king – the 'reguengos' – and the process of relative decline which I have detected in the importance of these places in the organisation of the itinerance. In fact, the 'reguengos' are a form of countryside 'domesticated' by royalty, and their agricultural use is also connected to the value of the typical feeding function of the tri-functional synthesis associated with the figure of the medieval monarch, but which rationalities of another order in the fifteenth and sixteenth centuries, indicators of a certain 'commodification of the landscape', made more opaque or less significant, bringing with them other perceptions of the territory and determining during the Manueline age the abandonment of many of the countryside residences used in the previous centuries.

It is in the light of these conclusions that there is imposed a final reflection on the overall meaning of the retention of the itinerance as a form of life which, as we have seen, was linked with the charisma of royalty but which demanded substantial expenditure and a heavy and complex organisation, marking the actual forms and dimension of court society with its stamp. In fact, the itinerance of the monarchs should not be seen as an unambiguous sign of dependency, be this of an economic/tributary meaning, as we have seen, or even in a more directly strategic/political meaning, concentrating for example the preferential stay of the kings of the period in an urban environment. For the medieval royalty, on the contrary, the inhabitants of the kingdom ('naturais'), just as the territories themselves and their resources, were means of royal power, and this understanding is imposed on the monarchs as a preconception which made possible the project of affirmation of their authority. For this reason, the itinerance which 'marked' or led to the territory of the kingdom through the institution of a spatial centrality can be seen as a necessary condition or even as proof of the exercise of royal functions, just as certain forms of tribute were an acquisitive activity inherent to royal status. The urban stages, the countryside palaces and the constant and seasonal movement between both are the fundamental material structures which the itinerance implied in the later age I have studied. Is this a tendency towards the establishment of a headquarters of the court, or merely the final compromise of a perpetual movement to which it was seen to be obliged according to the values of that culture, but which was a means of facilitating the installation of a more numerous entourage and its supply? For the reasons given, I shall incline more to the second response.

In its dual reality – the court 'em andada' and the court 'em estada' – the territory which the court instituted varied substantially in its limits. It also influenced diversely the ways of life of men and women because of the variety of interior spaces and solutions to which it was necessary to turn for their lodging, activities and life in common. As was the case in the entire medieval west, the Portuguese retinues also had recourse to tents and lodgings of a temporary type, whenever this was seen to be necessary. More characteristic of the end of the Middle Ages appears to have been, however, the establishment of a dichotomy, moulded into distinct residential structures, between the royal space of the palace and the court spaces. The latter were to find in the 'estaus' their own specific typology, but one which in its precariousness does not appear to be much distinguished from the space of other travellers. Meanwhile the residence of the monarch, in turn, resorted to various architectural structures, all of which were generally given the prestigious name of 'palácio' or 'paço', which tended towards an internal complexity which adapted them to diverse uses and was protagonised by an appreciable number of people for whom the 'paço' was a place of daily activity. The physical move from place to place was, however, a practice leading to an inexorably uprooting effect, and for this reason it can be conceived that the internal rules for the court space were equally intended to reinforce the unity of the multifaceted group which was the royal retinue, giving it some type of permanence, as suggested by Simmel: 'its spatial determinacy was not like that of a substantive object, which one would always find at the same place, but akin to the abstract stability of a pivotal point, which keeps a set of elements in a specific distance, interaction and interdependence'.[214] The royal 'paço', wherever it might be, appears to be a 'pivotal point' of this type.

[214] Georg Simmel, 'The sociology of space', in David Frisby and Mike Featherstone (eds.), *Simmel on Culture: Selected Writings* (London: Sage, 1997), p. 147.

5. *Court times*

In this space defined by the presence of the king which we call 'court' the activities of those whom the modern age came to call 'courtiers', that is the men and women living permanently at court, developed. Although the word is new, in the thirteenth century the *Partidas* distinguished the permanent residents from those who were present at court for reasons other than those of 'daily service'. The word 'courtier' found its first appearance in Portuguese in writings of the princes of the Aviz dynasty such as Duarte and the Infante Pedro, in Zurara's chronicles and in the fifteenth-century Portuguese translation of the pseudo-Aristotelian *Segredo dos Segredos*, while its semantic field was from the outset associated with a daily presence alongside the monarchs and in 'court service'.[1] 'Court service' as referred to by the sources of the age to a large extent comprised ritual activities.

As a result of the main lines of the study I have been outlining, I do not examine this specific way of life of the man at court in isolation. On the contrary, I have emphasised the narrow articulation existing among various juridical, bureaucratic, pragmatic, financial and ritual aspects of the duties and offices of the court. Court life did not solely comprise ceremonies. Having said this, ritual activity was prominent in spite of everything as something fundamental in 'palace life' as seen by the age, and remained the final redoubt of an effective performance of many court 'offices', since it was endowed with enormous importance. A combined vision of these modes of action which took place there thus becomes necessary for an understanding of the court and its functions in the society of the time, not only as an organisation of offices and an ordered group of social roles but also as a specific social configuration with its own cultural practices. In this final aspect, through the succession of occurrences of collective living the ritual was an ordering element of a temporal picture in which characteristic forms of court life developed. It was in this light that I

[1] António Geraldo da Cunha (ed.), *Índice do vocabulário do Português medieval* (Rio de Janeiro: Fundação Casa de Rui Barbosa, 1988), vol. II, p. 112.

attempted to analyse its coherence, so forcing the debate upon the existence of a Portuguese court culture and on the forms which characterise it.

For an understanding of these cultural forms I felt it necessary to investigate the Iberian dimension of court ceremonies and rituals which took place in Portugal. This means exploring a group of problems whose formulation owes itself to a comparison of forms and ceremonial events within a larger environment, which problems would in another way be largely incomprehensible from the historical point of view. It is the actual nature of the rites as historical phenomena to be studied that dictates the need for the comparative methodology and the broader context of my research.

USES AND CEREMONY

The point of departure of my reflection will, as is usual in this book, be the understanding of the several concepts used during the period. In this case the distinction between 'uses' of the court mentioned by the medieval texts and the ceremonies themselves seems to me useful. The former appear as a more or less complex set of practices, more or less structured by ritual activities to which the courtiers were dedicated which was, in each case, recognised as specific and corresponded to a local, identifiable tradition, even though at times it appeared somewhat vague. These 'uses' or 'customs' had, however, as their basis a group of practices common to other courts of the medieval west. These practices were diversely understood and performed not only by each reigning dynasty in each country but also by each monarch within one same kingdom; that is they varied within certain limits according to time and space. The contemporary word 'custom', in turn, points to some common characteristics of ritual activities of the court: its demanded traditionality; its conventional and formalised nature; its undoubted validity in the context of the society of the time.

The Portuguese court, like many of its contemporaries, also had distinct 'uses' at the end of the Middle Ages. However, what occurs is that the court 'uses' are a difficult subject of history since, as their name suggests, they are mostly transmitted by word of mouth and through direct apprenticeship. The word seems to mean not only 'that which was done', but also certain 'methods of doing' or of performing this or that ceremony which were common to other courts but which for us continue to be hard to discern – something which the word 'style', which is more frequently used in the modern age, perhaps evokes more clearly. That is, there is an emphasis on the fact that the contemporary concept of court ceremonial activity implies a certain plasticity and the recognition that a determined margin of variation would be expected within the framework of a broadly common repertory. However, it is necessary for the study of the ceremonial uses or activities of a medieval court to turn to every type of source in order to equate and understand this flexibility which in many cases is intentionally denied by texts:[2] the most usual sources, such as descriptions and narratives of the chronicles or foreign travellers, or doctrinal and juridical sources, but also the less obvious, such as sources emanating from financial practice and from court organisms, iconography, sources of local origin, material objects, legends and myths regarding royalty. Clearly, one must also turn to normative sources *par excellence*, since they are the records of ceremonies or ceremonial-books.

By 'ceremonial' I thus mean two realities in this study. On the one hand is a particular discourse through which the transmission of uses of one particular court was made, but which was included within a normative construction whose enunciation was in general of the responsibility of the monarch himself. A particularly famous example for the High Middle Ages is the compilation of the rites of the Byzantine court attributed to Constantine VII Porphyrogenite. This type of text has its tradition in the medieval west, and since it generally dealt with manuscripts which were little circulated, it is quite rare. A generic comparison of the few known texts points to two explanatory structures which are the most common: either an explanation formed according to ceremonies or ritual acts juxtaposed in the text in a logic of chronology or typology or an explanation based upon court offices and their characteristics, having regard to those involved in these rites.

It could be admitted that certain uses were frequently transmitted from one court to another through these written 'ceremonials', as well as through historiographic descriptions and narratives or even other forms of texts such as correspondence. As an example of the first of these, we have the 'Ordenacions de Cort' of Pedro IV of Aragon (1344), which was the result of a rewritten translation of the *Leges Palatinae* instituted by Jaime III of Majorca (1324–49) of which the Aragonese king sent a copy, for example, to the Castilian monarch in the 1380s.[3] The influence of this ceremonial in the formation of the uses of the several Iberian courts was probably decisive, along with the doctrine relating to the court and its functions in the Castilian legislative work originating at the court of Alfonso X, which also appeared in fourteenth-century versions in Portuguese and Catalan. The second, that is historiographic descriptions and narratives, can be evoked through the text of Olivier de la Marche, which I have already used in my first chapter, which comprised a detailed description of Burgundian uses at the time of Charles the Bold. It could be said that this does not exactly consist of a ceremonial-book. Fifteenth- and sixteenth-century

[2] The rites of the monarchy always claimed tradition, as David Cannadine saw: 'The context, performance and meaning of ritual: the British monarchy and the "invention of tradition" (1820–1977)', in *The Invention of Tradition* (Cambridge: Cambridge University Press, 1983), pp. 101–84.

[3] For a study of the written dissemination of the text of the *Leges Palatinae* and the 'Ordenacions' it is essential to turn to Olivetta Schena, *Le Leggi Palatine de Pietro IV di Aragona* (Cagliari: Istituto sui Rapporti Italo-Iberici, 1983).

copies of this text are to be found in Portuguese and Castilian manuscript collections (now held, for example, in the Torre do Tombo, the Ajuda library and the National Library of Madrid), which were produced for circulation of the text in various Hispanic court spheres from the final quarter of the fifteenth century. We also have the example of the description of 1320 of the uses and structure of the *hôtel* of Louis d'Evreux, the brother of Philip III of France, complete with the indication of the names of holders of each office which, according to modern historians such as Béatrice Leroy or Zabalo Zabalegui, would have served as a pattern for the organisation of the court of Navarre and many of its 'customs' at the end of the Middle Ages.[4] Finally, we might remember among many other examples the letter written in 1480 by the 'Mestresala' of the Catholic sovereigns Ferdinand and Isabella, Diego de Valera, 'sobre la cerimonia de dar la dinidad de marques', which was a record of certain Castilian uses of the time, of which we can find echoes in descriptions in the chronicles and treatises on Hispanic nobility.[5] The royal libraries at the end of the Middle Ages were thus repositories of texts of a varied nature on the uses of the courts both of their own and of neighbouring countries, and the 'ceremonials' were seen as equal to liturgical and devotional works, the classics and their translations into the vulgar vernacular, the treatises on the education of princes, or chronicles and collections of poetry. This was the case, as is well known, in the library of the Portuguese king Duarte, where I believe we find reference to the presence of the Aragonese royal ceremonial.[6]

As a source for the study of the uses and system of ceremonies of a court, it is necessary to note however that the ceremonial-book must, like any other normative source, be an object of careful criticism. It is above all a testimony of a desire to order, to regulate given practices which were considered worthy of appearing in a textual architecture intended to distinguish and enlarge a monarch and his court. Let us remember Michael McCormick's observations regarding the Byzantine ceremonial:

[4] Text published by J. A. Brutails, *Documents des Archives de la Chambre des Comptes de Navarre (1196–1384)* (Paris: Bibliothèque des Hautes Etudes, 1890), pp. 33–6.

[5] Diego de Valera, *Epístolas de Mosen Diego de Valera enbiadas en diversos tiempos e á diversas personas* (Madrid: Sociedad de Bibliófilos Españoles, 1878), pp. 49–54.

[6] As I have already stated, in the list of Duarte's books I have identified this text on the rubric 'Liuro dos offiçios da casa dalgũ rey': *Livro dos Conselhos de El-Rei D. Duarte*, p. 207. Following attempts by Duarte Leite and Joseph Piel at identification of the text, Joaquim de Carvalho suggested that this concerned the *Epistola de Gubernatione Rei Familiaris*, wrongly attributed to St Bernard. This medieval treatise of *Oeconomica* is in fact quoted by Zurara in his *Crónica dos feitos da Guiné*, as well as being mentioned by King Duarte himself in his texts, which proves its dissemination at the Portuguese court. I believe, however, that it concerns two different works, for the *Epistola* does not actually refer to offices, while the Aragonese text is organised in chapters dedicated to each official of the royal court and corresponds better to the descriptive rubric. See Joaquim de Carvalho, *Obra completa*, ed. José V. de Pina Martins (Lisbon: Fundação Calouste Gulbenkian, 1978–89), vol. II, pp. 243–4.

> the prescriptive tone of most of the Ceremony Book, its pervasive present tense and the rarity of explicit dates and personal names may have fostered the illusion of its ahistorical character . . . the false analogy of the relative stability of the Roman Catholic and other traditional liturgies since the advent of the printing press and the Council of Trent may also have undermined modern perceptions of the dynamism in Byzantine ceremonial . . . in fact, imperial ceremonies were subject to the relentless process of historical change no less than other facets of human existence.[7]

If we compare court and royal ceremonials with the type of medieval liturgical text which in a certain way is parallel to them, that is the 'ceremony books' or *ordines*, we shall see that also in this last case it is hard to obtain a reconstruction of the religious ritual, in spite of the eminently pragmatic and laconic register of the liturgical ceremonial books which separates them from the underlying hyperbole of the secular texts. Such a reconstruction is difficult, owing to the prescriptive nature of a cautiously generic type of these texts (showing who must do what and with what, but not always exactly how to perform the rite), intended to allow for the liturgical performance through the construction of a minimal framework of indications.[8] The particular case of compilations of the named papal ceremonies with their incidence in the religious liturgy presents a useful contrast with the secular 'ceremonials', since critical examination of these texts has shown that there is a slow sedimentation of uses from several periods which undergo processes of harmonisation and hybridisation, at the same time as an incomplete emancipation of the contemporary notion of a *disciplina arcani* was including them in an aura of exclusivity, appropriate to collections not intended for the masses.[9]

This leads us to the second meaning of the word 'ceremonial' which I should like to propose, or the systematically organised group of ritual practices of one court. It is not my intention to spend time on the conceptual distinction which could be established between 'rite' and 'ceremony', which is a sufficiently profitable debate in the field of anthropology.[10] Some authors who work essentially upon the notions of Durkheim and Tylor insist on this distinction

[7] Michael McCormick, 'Analyzing imperial ceremonies', *Jahrbuch der Osterreischen Byzantinistik*, 35 (1985), 2.

[8] G. Martimort, *Les Ordines, les ordinaires et les cérémoniaux*, Typologie des Sources du Moyen Âge Occidental 56 (Brepols: Turnhout, 1991).

[9] Cyrille Vogel, *Medieval Liturgy: An Introduction to the Sources* (Washington, DC: The Pastoral Press, 1986), pp. 136–9.

[10] Arnold Van Gennep, *Les Rites de passage* (Paris: E. Nourry, 1909); Victor Turner, *Dramas, Fields and Metaphors: Symbolic Action in Human Society* (Ithaca: Cornell University Press, 1974). As a general introduction to the problem of the rites and their devaluation in western European culture: Mary Douglas, *In the Active Voice* (London: Routledge and Kegan Paul, 1982), pp. 34–8 and also Jack Goody, 'Against ritual: loosely structured thoughts on a loosely defined topic', in S. Moore and B. Myerhoff (eds.), *Secular Ritual* (Amsterdam: Van Gorcun, 1977), pp. 25–35.

which implies, in the case of ritual, the existence of a belief or a form of communication with the supernatural, while the ceremony was to develop within the secular sphere and could not always be articulated with a doctrine or a group of beliefs relating to the sacred.[11] Such rigid conceptual distinction implies a certain narrowness of perspectives, in particular when confronted with an historic semantic of the late-medieval period in which a distinction between 'ceremony', 'rite' and 'cult' is made with some precision in relation to the religious sphere but did not forcefully eliminate a dialogue with the traditions of the sacred associated with the figure of the monarchs; besides, as so well analysed by Schramm and Kantorowicz, this had strongly contributed towards a definition of the actual religious rite of the Christians during late antiquity and the High Middle Ages. As we shall see, this dialogue continued to develop in the case of the inaugural anointing with oil of the kings, which as a religious rite was equally part of the sequence of a royal ceremony, as was the baptism of the infants or, in certain aspects, the funeral rites of the dead kings. The ceremonies of medieval royalty frequently included therefore the sphere of the Christian religion, be this positively, with a sharing of common symbolic languages, or negatively owing to the existence of dynamics of mutual exclusion.

Throughout this study the distinction between rite and ceremony which I propose is more that of relating to the type; that is the court ceremony appears above all as a type of particular rite – a group of procedures being included within a circumscriptive symbolic universe, whose performance takes place in pre-established times and spaces through the action of selected individuals, forming a type of distinctive behaviour. In my research I have, to the contrary, developed an approximation towards that which rite and ceremony have in common rather than that which separates them. It appears to me that the ceremonies performed by the courtiers are an excellent example of what might, by its character, be termed the 'reminiscent' nature of the rite, that is the fact of its including a form of individual and group apprenticeship forming a type of 'work of reflection' on reality. Within this meaning, the ceremonies appear in court society as a tool for the construction of royalty and for the understanding of its specific nature, of the way in which the sacralisation of the royal figure was articulated with other spheres and processes of sacralisation or profanation of collective life, and also as a method of representing symbolically the relationship between the monarch and his predecessors, his relationship with the natural and social order and with his own kingdom.[12]

[11] See for example Jack Goody, 'Religion and ritual: the definitional problem', *British Journal of Sociology*, 12 (1961) and Stephen Lukes, 'Political ritual and social integration', in *Essays in Social Theory* (London: Methuen, 1977), pp. 52–73. A useful résumé of existing theses can be found in Catherine Ball, *Ritual: Perspectives and Dimensions* (New York: Oxford University Press, 1997).

[12] Moore and Myerhoff (eds.), *Secular Ritual*, pp. 7–9. See also David Cannadine, 'Divine rites of kings', in David Cannadine and Simon Price (eds.), *Rituals of Royalty: Power and Ceremony in Traditional Societies* (Cambridge: Cambridge University Press, 1987), pp. 1–19.

Beliefs or even doctrines of the age, constructed on the interconnection of the various languages arising from the theological or juridical sphere, cannot always be clearly related to a system of rites of royalty, that is to a concrete ceremonial, owing also to the frequently ambivalent and precarious character of these forms of symbolic representation.[13] A type of systematic arrangement of rituals centred on the royal figure, provocatively called *religio regis* by some historians, can be seen, rather than as 'a unified system of beliefs and practices relative to sacred things and uniting in a moral community all believers' (Durkheim), as simply a group of rites which can be articulated in a coherent cult of an orthopraxic style in which the correct procedures and ritual performance are more important than beliefs and emotions. A broadening of the comparative sphere of my research, not only in space but also in time, allows the useful adoption of heuristic tools created by historians of antiquity to confront similar problems of cultural interpretation of the forms of cult and religion of the past. As Simon Price states, for example, regarding the imperial cult in Asia Minor, it is necessary to proceed to a radical criticism of Judaeo-Christian notions subjacent to the traditional explanations of the cult of the sovereigns in the Greek and Roman worlds, which explanations frequently 'Christianised' these phenomena uncontrollably, so making it difficult to accept their 'authenticity'.[14] In turn, Versnel suggests the useful concept of 'inconsistency' to characterise certain forms of ancient religion which, like the medieval *religio regis* in its relationship with the Christian religion, can lead to forms of resolution which cause dilemmas, including beliefs which become mutually void from the doctrinal point of view.[15]

These problems cannot bc analysed if we consider the rites as something which imposes itself, which merely 'gives sight of' or 'shows' a pre-existent royalty which, in the final instance, is able to exist without these rites, in opposition to a conception of rites as a modality for the existence of royalty itself, that is an indispensable aspect of its historical reality. For example, it is highly common among today's historians to call upon the theatrical metaphor when speaking of court ceremonies, which in my opinion is somewhat ambiguous.[16] As Ernst Cassirer observed,

> Rites are not originally 'allegorical', they do not merely copy or represent but they are absolutely *real*; they are so woven into the reality of action as to

[13] This problem was clearly stated by the historian Ralph Giesey, 'Modèles de pouvoir dans les rites royaux en France', *Annales ESC*, 41 (1986), 579–99.

[14] Simon Price, *Rituals and Power: The Roman Imperial Cult in Asia Minor* (Cambridge: Cambridge University Press, 1984), pp. 10–11.

[15] See the definition of the concept suggested in H. S. Versnel, *Inconsistencies in Greek and Roman Religion*, vol. I (Leiden: Brill, 1990), p. 4.

[16] On the relationships that can be established between ritual and the theatre: Victor Turner, *From Ritual to Theatre: The Human Seriousness of Play* (New York: Paj Publications, 1982). The use of the 'theatrical metaphor' was highly influential in the social sciences of the 1980s. See on this the observations of Clifford Geertz, 'Blurred genres: the refiguration of social thought', in *Local Knowledge* (New York: Fontana, 1983), pp. 19–35.

> form an indispensable part of it . . . The cult is the true instrument by which man subjects the world, not so much in a spiritual as in a purely physical sense . . . what happens in these rites is no mere imitative portrayal of an event but is the event itself.[17]

This is an observation which proves itself to be entirely valid for an analysis, in this case, of court ceremony. Why is it necessary that the court 'represent' (and for whom?) through this ceremony any order or other message which would be the 'true' content of the ceremonial occasion? The ritual activity was in itself its own object, and its efficacy and its end lay fundamentally in the performance of this activity. I do not wish of course to remove with these observations what anthropological theory calls 'the performative character' of the rite, or if you will its proximity to what would be events of 'staged performance'.[18] Nor do I wish of course to deny the importance of festivity and spectacle in court life, which are areas in which the rite, as we shall see, can also have its place. If we reread medieval texts, however, we find that a perception of that type, where the court and theatre are formed into one sole metaphor, was rare in relation to these occurrences, and this leads us to conclude that it would perhaps be as out of the question in those cultures to speak of a 'theatrical representation of the court' in the court banquet as it would to speak of a 'theatrical representation of the city' in the Corpus Christi procession or of a 'theatrical representation of divinity' in the rite of the mass. When speaking of the court, Iberian authors of the period did not make comparisons with the theatre (as was to occur later, in particular in the early modern age), and preferred other metaphors such as, for example, that of the sea. As with the sea, the court is 'grant e larga', as the *Partidas* say, and 'caben en ella pescados de muchas naturas'.[19] Or, equally suggestively, it was evoked metaphorically as a fair where everything could be exchanged and sold, with the courtier at times choosing to purchase something which did not suit him.[20]

[17] Ernst Cassirer, *La Philosophie des formes symboliques*, vol. II, *La Pensée mythique* (Paris: Minuit, 1972), p. 61.

[18] Stanley Jeyaraga Tambiah, 'A performative approach to ritual', in *Culture, Thought, and Social Action: An Anthropological Perspective* (Cambridge, MA: Harvard University Press, 1985), pp. 123–66.

[19] *Las Siete Partidas*, vol. I, pp. 83–4. This motive which arises from the patristic is also used by the 'Réthoriqueurs', for example Jean Meschinot: 'La cour est une mer dont sourt / vagues d'orgueil, d'envie orage . . . / Malebouche y fait maint dommage, / Ire esmeut débas et oultrage . . . / Qui les nefs gittent souvent bas, / Traïson y fait son personnage: / Nage aultre part pour tes esbas': Pierre Champion, *Histoire poétique du quinzième siècle* (Paris: Champion, 1966 [reprint]), p. 219.

[20] 'La corte del rey es como la feria, que lleuan los omes alla todas las cosas que entienden bien vender; e los omes siguen las maneras del Rey, e sy hay en el muchas buenas maneras e vieren una mala, ante seguiran aquella que las otras buenas': *Libro de los Cien Capítulos*, ed. Agapito Rey (Bloomington: Indiana University Press, 1960), p. 2. This same image, like that of hell, is used in literature of clerical origins, for example the *De Nugis Curialium*: Walter Map, *De Nugis Curialium: Courtier's Trifles*, ed. M. R. James (Oxford: Clarendon Press, 1983), pp. 506–8.

The study of rites in court society following these perspectives led me also to a certain reserve as to the use of the concept of 'propaganda', which is significantly absent in anthropological writings and is rarely considered in sociological theory as applicable to societies where there was no 'public space', that is differentiated societies where politics could be a clearly distinct sphere, for example from religion.[21] Since propaganda is a technique for specific communication with the intention of altering the activities of individuals and groups, it can appear in given circumstances as a 'superimposition of meaning' in a ritualistic sequence, all the more since, as frequently occurs with rite, the propaganda message is characterised by its schematic. However, even in these cases, rite continues to exist as a distinct modality of action. When sufficiently structured so that it forms a perfectly distinct 'type', as is the case for example with the coronation, the ceremony can be the object of metaphrasis, or a transformation and interpretation through specific manipulation of the symbolic language and of given constitutive elements of the ritualistic sequence during its performance, as occurred in the much-debated case known as the 'Farsa de Ávila', or the dethronement of Henry IV of Castile.[22] An excessively broad concept of 'propaganda' applied systematically to all ceremonial occasions would, however, obscure important differences, particularly as to the impossibility of considering sufficiently clearly the entire group of meanings which the rite can configure by establishing that only one single and unequivocal meaning was expressed. Ritualistic activity is frequently a modality of action which, like a type of game, includes all individuals as players, while propaganda has authors and an audience in a structural inequality which does not disappear. The medieval ceremonies of royalty are within their own sphere one of the processes through which royalty exists, but they are neither mimetic nor theatrical representations of political principles and values or of virtues and characteristics of the monarchs whose interpretation is evidently impressed upon people's eyes – the contemporaries' or our own. The eventual perceptions of royalty allowed by ceremony would always be somewhat condensed, simplified, reduced and schematic, not lacking ambiguities or those mysterious elements which remove the experience of the rite from the sphere of events of the everyday profane and rationally determined actions.[23]

21 Paul Veyne, 'Propagande, expression, roi, image, idole, oracle', *L'Homme*, 114 (1990), 7–26. See also the observations of Nancy L. Roelker, 'The impact of the Reformation era on communication and propaganda', in Harold D. Lasswell *et al.* (eds.), *Propaganda and Communication in World History* (Honolulu: University of Hawaii, 1980), vol. II, pp. 41–84.

22 Angus MacKay, 'Ritual and propaganda in fifteenth-century Castile', *Past and Present*, 107 (1985), 3–43.

23 I am reusing some observations formulated in Rita Costa Gomes, 'Cerimónias da realeza nos finais da idade média', *Penélope*, 14 (1994), 129–36; Rita Costa Gomes, 'A realeza: símbolos e ceremonial', in M. H. Cruz Coelho and A. L. Carvalho Homem (eds.), *A génese do estado moderno no Portugal tardo-medievo (séculos XIII–XV)* (Lisbon: Universidade Autónoma, 1999), pp. 201–13.

Having made these distinctions, I should emphasise that the study of uses or customs of a court regarding ceremonies must aim for the most complete reconstruction possible, for ceremonies mutually illuminate themselves because of their tendency, as said above, to form into a system or a group of elements articulated in their entirety by the structural or functional relationship of their constitutive elements. Ideally, each ceremony should be reconstructed and interpreted by itself through a careful reconstruction of ceremonial events and their repetition and variation within actual historical contexts.[24] But this must also be in relation to the totality of the ceremonial, which makes normative sources truly indispensable since they allow us to perceive principles of interrelationship and composition formed in the actual period or, put another way, to the detection of a logic which, in the period, could link the various rites in a coherent whole. On the other hand, the ceremonies have, according to my definition, certain participants who perform within a group of roles. These roles were distributed by the different 'officers' of the court, which leads me to emphasise the importance of the relationship between the organisation of court posts and its ceremonial, between the court as a structured group of duties and the rites which might take place there. Without going as far as to state, like Hocart, that the ritual itself would engender the organisation of the offices, I would say that it powerfully aids the construction of the techniques of power and the sharing of political roles within the heart of the court. Above all, one cannot ignore this relationship between the regime of duties and rite, since it is central for any analysis of the construction of the mutations of the ceremonial. By studying the agents of the rite, we study its configuration and the limits of its flexibility.[25]

The ambit of comparison in this chapter covers, as I have said above, the entire Iberian Peninsula without ignoring a necessary recourse to other examples studied for medieval Europe, although my objective is the study of Portuguese uses and ceremonies. The Peninsula comprised neighbouring societies where the actual monarchic institution demonstrated a parallel evolution and where we find an intensification between 1300 and 1450 of the circulation of individuals and cultural works, and a recognised emulation between the courts and many common signs of their organisational structures. No less important is the recognition of tradition on a common past expressed in the body of myths and

[24] Arthur Hocart, *Kingship* (London: Oxford University Press, 1970), pp. 39–40 and 102–27. See the methodological indications in Sergio Bertelli and G. Crifo (eds.), *Rituale, cerimoniale, etichetta* (Milan: Bompiani, 1985), and also Sergio Bertelli, *Il corpo del re: sacralità del potere nell'Europa medievale e moderna* (Florence: Ponte alle Grazie, 1990) (a new edition in English in press).

[25] 'It is not only the ritual that exhibits a certain structure, but also the society that practices it; for the ritual is a social affair, it requires the cooperation of many, and so society must organize itself for ritual': Arthur Hocart, *Kings and Councillors: An Essay in the Comparative Anatomy of Human Society* (Chicago: University of Chicago Press, 1970), pp. 34–5. See also Hocart, *Kingship*, pp. 39–40 and 102–27.

historiographic narratives spread unequally throughout the Peninsula which the ceremonies constantly reiterated in a certain manner, establishing the present of men and women of the time in the dominion of primordial times. These are processes of which the Iberian monarchs showed themselves to be conscious, and they actively took part in the elaboration of these traditions, seeing themselves once again in the mirror of an archetypal Gothic royalty and in the reiteration of the warring deeds of the reconquest.[26]

We must continue to discuss on this point the existence of a general codification of Portuguese customs in a written ceremonial, relating the uses to the several court offices in a similar way to that suggested in the text of the Aragonese 'Ordenacions'. There is evidence that this Portuguese ceremonial was compiled possibly during the reign of Afonso V. A few years later, in 1481, it was removed from the royal archives, to which it never returned.[27] However, two normative fifteenth-century texts have been preserved, although both are more restricted. The first, which came from abroad, was always considered little relevant as a source for the study of Portuguese ceremonies. Contrary to what has been stated, the compilation of uses at the English royal chapel of Henry VI which led to the *Liber Regie Capelle* had, as already seen, a certain influence on the Portuguese royal chapel, which influence can be proved as far as its organisational aspect from the 1440s. The initiative for the production of this ruling perhaps fell to the regency of the Infante Pedro, for it was then that a member of the Portuguese chapel, the cantor and master of the chapel Álvaro Afonso, obtained the compilation from the English dean William Say between 1446 and 1461.[28] The ceremonies described in this compilation, in particular

[26] On the importance of archetypes, see the enlightening pages of Julio Caro Baroja, 'Sobre la formación y uso de arquétipos en historia, literatura y folklore', in *Ensayos sobre la cultura popular Española* (Madrid: Dosbe, 1979), pp. 95–6. See also Luis Krus, 'Os heróis da Reconquista e a realeza sagrada medieval peninsular: Afonso X e a Primeira Crónica Geral de Hespanha', in *Passado, memória e poder na sociedade medieval Portuguesa* (Redondo: Patrimonia, 1994), pp. 129–42.

[27] A receipt dated 1481 documents that a 'regimento da casa do rei das cerjmonias' was taken out of the royal archives. I assume this to be the one to which I refer: ANTT, Drawer XIV, Maço 1, 1. In 1521, this codex was still missing: José Pessanha, 'Uma reabilitação histórica. Inventários da Torre do Tombo no século XVI', *Arquivo Historico Português*, 3 (1905), 287–303, in particular Document III, p. 298. There are quotations of varying length from this text in other manuscripts which prove its later circulation: British Library, Add 20592, ff. 120–89. The diffusion of other manuscript versions of it (most probably incomplete) is mentioned by Diogo Ramada Curto, 'Ritos e cerimónias da monarquia', pp. 210–11.

[28] On the date and circumstances of the production of this manuscript: Walter Ullmann (ed.), *Liber Regie Capelle: a manuscript in the Biblioteca Pública, Évora* (London: Henry Bradshaw Society, 1961), in particular pp. 9–11 and 44–5; F. M. Sousa Viterbo, 'A cultura intelectual de D. Afonso V', *Arquivo Histórico Português*, 2 (1904), 261–2, whose facts were taken up by António Brásio, 'O problema da sagração dos monarcas Portugueses', *Anais da Academia Portuguesa da História*, 12 (1962), 35–6. More recently the musicologist Manuel Pedro Ferreira critically declared on this subject: 'the dates which have been attributed to the resulting manuscript kept in the Biblioteca Pública at Évora (1439, 1449, 1454) do not rest on any documentary basis nor

the baptism of the princes, the purification of the queens after giving birth, the coronation of the king and queen, the royal funerals, certainly had an influence on the construction of the Portuguese ceremonial. This influence can be seen in each case thanks to the documented practices. The manuscript remained in the hands of the Portuguese kings even after the battle of Alfarrobeira, contrary to what is stated by its editor Ullman, for it is still mentioned in the inventory of the books of Manuel at the beginning of the sixteenth century.[29] The second text to which I refer comprises a collection of internal ordinances and general norms relating to a variety of subjects and known as the *Livro Vermelho*, which was used at the Portuguese court until the sixteenth century. There still exists a copy made *c.* 1531 by the monarch's secretary, as made clear in the prologue, since the original had been damaged.[30] This forms the most important description, although there are lacunae and it lacks systematic purpose, of Portuguese uses at the end of the Middle Ages. The circumstances and reasons for the composition of the *Livro Vermelho* which is attributed to the reign of Afonso V (1438–81) remain obscure, but in its characteristics this collection cannot be said actually to be a written 'ceremonial' of the same type as the Aragonese ordinances, and is closer to a compilation made by court officials for reserved use. A reading concentrating on the first and final parts of the text suggests it is highly probable that this copy, which survived in the sixteenth century following the accident that caused the loss of the original, gives us only a part of the original.

Confronted with this panorama, I have tried to build a whole picture, even though some of its principal elements are lacking, using some similar studies on the ceremonial practices of the other Peninsular courts and an attempt at a general interpretation for the modern period in Portugal for which we must thank Diogo Ramada Curto.[31] As I have said, this was a matter of following two complementary routes – the study of each ceremony (through a simultaneous exploration of the group of sources, textual or otherwise, which it leads to), and also their inclusion in large coherent groups. Rather than what we might call a detached analysis of the Portuguese ceremonies of which there is evidence in the chronicled reports, as has up to now been done, I have concentrated on the study of the organisation of the rites in the hope of including the ceremonial as a whole.

do they correspond to solidly argued hypotheses': Ferreira, 'Da música na história de Portugal', *Revista Portuguesa de Musicologia*, 4–5 (1994–95), 179. I am grateful to the author for having told me of this text.

29 ANTT, *NA*, 789, f. 92 ('hũu liuro da coroação del Rey d ymgraterra').

30 Explained in the first page of the existing version: BGUC, strong safe, *Livro Vermelho de D. Afonso 5°*, 84 sheets, paper (acquired in 1939). A have followed the eighteenth-century edition of this text which is included in the *Inéditos da Academia*, which I found to be generally faithful in the brief comparison I made with the original.

31 Diogo Ramada Curto, 'Ritos e cerimónias da monarquia', in Francisco Bethencourt and Diogo Ramada Curto (eds.), *A memória da nação* (Lisbon: Sá da Costa, 1991), pp. 201–65.

This second route leads in particular to the reconstruction of the ceremonial cycles, that is, it is seen as particularly adapted to the study of periodic rites and leaves aside those I have called occasional rites. As Pierre Smith suggests, the periodic rites are organised along a methodical axis marked by their recurrence and celebrating expected moments such as death or the daily feeding of the king, but occasional rites, which offer a variety of ceremonial responses which only circumstances demand, are organised along a paradigmatic axis in an unpredictable order, as was the case with the activities of the Cortes or the royal entry.[32]

A large part of the ceremonial activity of the medieval courts was, in fact, absorbed by the repetition of the same gestures and words on the same occasions. Two cycles should be studied for the ceremonies of royalty in my opinion. In the first place, the cycle of the reign which was formed by the great ceremonies of the monarchy and which in the Portuguese case is shown, as we shall see, to be weakly structured. This is in relation to some occurrences in the individual existence of the kings, which I shall emphasise: baptisms, marriages, accession to the throne and funerals. This must be distinguished from the daily and annual cycle whose influence in the succession of the diverse court times is a determinant. As already stated, this second ceremonial cycle could even influence the sharing of offices and roles at court in rotation, as occurred in Aragon, Castile and Navarre and, although later, at the Portuguese court.

This ritualisation influenced not only the great occasions but also more common everyday aspects. By modelling individual behaviour, etiquettes (also known simply as 'uses') appear in turn to be closely related to the entirety of the ceremonial system of the court in each one of the vertents of the cycles I have just described. Etiquette determined, for example, what was the specific position of the several titles of the nobility or of the relatives of the king at important ceremonies such as banquets or the royal inauguration, but it also established the rules of living together and of distancing between men and women, between the officials and the other courtiers during the performance of the daily ritual activities of the court. As Norbert Elias has observed, there is a clear relationship between the court hierarchies and the forms of interaction regulated by etiquette, with the latter regulating the former. The tendency to differentiate the roles is also found through these rules, continuously regulating and at the same time recreating silent conflicts, forms of tension and competition inherent to court life, the claiming of authority and superiority of status which were perhaps inevitably connected to the rite for this human configuration which was, as we have seen, marked by a great intensity of relationships and an almost promiscuous proximity among individuals.

32 Pierre Smith, 'Aspects de l'organisation des rites', in M. Izard and P. Smith (eds.), *La Fonction symbolique* (Paris: Gallimard, 1979), pp. 139–70.

THE CYCLE OF IMPORTANT CEREMONIES

With regard to the fundamental cycle of royal ceremonies, Arthur Hocart suggested that three types of ritual should be distinguished and considered as structuring elements: the rites of accession to the throne or consecration, with emphasis on the royal condition being an acquired one, that is that the individual becomes king; the rites of marriage, frequently connected to the fertility of the land; funeral rites, which are related to the problem of succession, or the continuity of royalty.[33] In the context of western societies of the medieval and early modern age, there are available some works which can be regarded as 'classics' relative to some components of this cycle of ceremonies, with which several historians of this century have been occupied.[34] Thus it could be said most succinctly that, thanks to Marc Bloch, what has been made clear is how the rituals of accession to the medieval throne demonstrated from the period of the late Middle Ages the importance of a royalty which had sacerdotal characteristics, assimilated in the figure of the *rex-sacerdos*, through the concrete modalities of the coronation associated with the unction of the monarch or the anointing with holy oils, a ritual of purification that lies in the origins of the magical powers of the English and French kings.[35] In turn, around the death of the king, which is a moment of collective disharmony and insecurity,[36] particular rituals which emphasised the continuation of royalty developed during the Low Middle Ages, forming in some cases the difficult concept of a king who was not subject to the temporal order in his 'political' body, even though, as shown by Kantorowicz, physically he was seen to be vulnerable in his natural body.[37]

As to the Iberian Peninsula in particular, we should remember the debate begun by Teófilo Ruiz in the mid-1980s in an article published in the French review *Annales*, in which he analysed the fact of a ceremony as important as the coronation and consecration of the kings in Castile demonstrating simply occasional characteristics, while in other contexts of Iberian ceremonials, including in Aragon, this appears to have great importance.[38] This historian

[33] Hocart, *Kings and Councillors*. See also for the 'constitutional' implications of this problem in the Middle Ages, Fritz Kern, *Kingship and Law in the Middle Ages* (Oxford: Blackwell, 1939), in particular pp. 20–9 and 34ff.

[34] Marc Bloch, *Les Rois thaumaturges: Etude sur le caractère surnaturel attribué à la puissance royale particulièrement en France et en Angleterre* (Paris: Gallimard, 1983) and Ralph Giesey, *Le Roi ne meurt jamais* (Paris: Flammarion, 1987), on the coronation ceremonies and funeral rites respectively.

[35] According to Robert Folz, a correction must be made to the priority established by Bloch in favour of the French monarchs as to their curing power following the proof of the authenticity of the *Vita Aedwardi* which was rejected by Bloch: Robert Folz, *Les Saints Rois du moyen âge en occident* (Brussels: Société des Bollandistes, 1984), p. 119 and note 7.

[36] See the important research by Bertelli on the interregna and rituals of violence: *Il corpo del re*, pp. 36–54.

[37] See the cited work of Giesey and also Kantorowicz, *The King's Two Bodies*, pp. 419–50.

[38] Teófilo Ruiz, 'Une royauté sans sacre: la monarchie castillane du bas moyen âge', *Annales ESC*, 39 (1984), 429–53; 'Unsacred monarchy: the Kings of Castile in the late Middle Ages',

thus reminded us that the important ceremonies of the medieval monarchy remained little studied in the central and western regions of the Peninsula, and he suggested at the same time its specificity in the face of the sole model which had been reasonably studied, and which is that suggested by Marc Bloch. The Castilian monarchy, according to Ruiz, would not be a royalty of a sacral type since the rites of consecration do not appear to have the importance which, for example, Bloch found in France and England.[39] The resolution of this question in the terms in which it has generally been formulated implied an acceptance of the excessive value placed upon the inaugural rites which become the sole indicators to be borne in mind.[40] Even regarding these rituals, perhaps it is worth remembering some aspects which Bloch helped to establish. For example, that the anointing with oil, which was an invention of the ecclesiastical hierarchies in the High Middle Ages, represents an influence of the Christian liturgy upon the ceremonies of royal inauguration which naturally existed before this. As Janet Nelson reminds us, the principal barbarian royalties used this rite in the middle of the tenth century, and the fact that the sources of the age gave so much importance to the anointing of the kings results above all from the elaboration of an ecclesiastical ritual committed to the written word, analogous to others codified by the clerics, regularising and recording the practices of the time in one and the same movement: 'But such a record by no means included the total process of a king's inauguration – non-clerical procedures were rarely documented . . . If we have to think in terms of a whole process, *consisting of extra and intra-ecclesiastical ritual, constitutive only in its totality*, we also have to distinguish between different observers and different periods in the ritual's evolution' (my italics).[41] The anointment was never in itself a sufficient element of the royal inauguration. It was an ancient element well known in the Iberian

in S. Wilentz (ed.), *Rites of Power: Ritual and Politics since the Middle Ages* (Philadelphia: University of Pennsylvania Press, 1985), pp. 109–44. For Aragon, see Bonifacio Palacios Martin's monograph, *La coronación de los reyes de Aragón, 1240–1410: aportación al estudio de las estructuras políticas medievales* (Valencia: Anubar, 1975); Carmen Orcástegui Gros, 'La coronación de los reyes de Aragón. Evolución político-ideológica y ritual', in *Homenage a Don Antonio Durán Gudiol* (Huesca: Instituto de Estudios Aragoneses, 1995), pp. 633–47.

39 In contrast to Teófilo Ruiz's theory, José Manuel Nieto Soria for example produced 'La monarquía bajomedieval Castellana. ¿Una realeza sagrada?', in *Homenaje al Profesor Juan Torres Fontes*, vol. II (Murcia: University of Murcia, 1987), pp. 1225–37. See also Soria, *Ceremonias de la realeza: propaganda y legitimación en la Castilla Trastámara* (Madrid: Nerea, 1993), and my review of this work: Costa Gomes, 'Cerimónias da realeza nos finais da idade média'.

40 Again regarding the Castilian polemic, there is Peter Linehan's intervention, 'Frontier kingship. Castile 1250–1350', in Alain Boureau and Claudio-Sergio Ingerflom, *La Royauté sacrée dans le monde chrétien* (Paris: Ecole des Hautes Etudes en Sciences Sociales, 1992), pp. 71–9; Adeline Rucquoi, 'De los reyes que no son taumaturgos: los fundamentos de la realeza de España', *Temas Medievales*, 5 (1995), 163–86.

41 Janet Nelson, 'Inauguration rituals', in P. H. Sawyer and I. N. Woods (eds.), *Early Medieval Kingship* (Leeds: Leeds University Press, 1977), pp. 50–71 and particularly p. 56. See also Nelson, 'Symbols in context: ruler's inauguration ritual in Byzantium and the West in the Early Middle Ages', in *Politics and Ritual in Early Medieval Europe* (London: Hambledon Press, 1986), pp. 259–81.

Peninsula (the Visigoths had practised it),[42] but it performed a function which was quite distinct in the several ages and the several ceremonial systems. It became an ordering centre of the royal inauguration in the French or English context which coincided with the coronation and which in the Low Middle Ages remained an indispensable element of a venerated tradition. In the Castilian and Portuguese cases, as Peter Linehan has recently shown when studying closely the Castilian sources from the time of the reconquest, it was assumed that the anointment did not deserve systematic mention by the medieval historians, as also other extra-ecclesiastical elements of the royal inaugurations did not deserve this, even though the anointment would appear, for example, referred to in the title used in the drawing up of decrees. There was a clear knowledge of what it meant in the context of a debate which could be termed political when one considers the fulcral role that clerical participation held within it.[43]

In Portugal José Mattoso took up the question in the 1990s in terms which were a little different from those which António Brásio and Paulo Merêa had brought up some decades earlier, when they discussed in detail the few indications of the possible performance of coronation ceremonies with the anointing of the Portuguese monarchs during the medieval period.[44] The main conclusions of this later evaluation of the problem in the Portuguese context tend to allow for the performance of such ceremonies for the thirteenth century, certainly from the reign of Sancho I to that of Afonso III. There continue to be many doubts regarding the actual modalities which such events would have possessed and their association to a precise locality in the kingdom – Coimbra. Liturgical sources produced by Mattoso to support his thesis significantly placed the Portuguese uses in direct relation with those of Castile and Leon.[45] The theory that the first Portuguese kings used some ritual form of association to the dignity of the canons also points to the same locality, specifically towards a

[42] On the anointment in Visigoth royalty: Pablo C. Diaz and M. R. Valverde, 'The theoretical strength and practical weakness of the Visigothic monarchy of Toledo', in Frans Theuws and Janet L. Nelson (eds.), *Rituals of Power: From Late Antiquity to the Early Middle Ages* (Leiden: Brill, 2000), pp. 59–93.

[43] Peter Linehan, *History and the Historians of Medieval Spain* (Oxford: Oxford University Press, 1993); Linehan, 'The king's touch and the dean's ministrations: aspects of sacral monarchy', in Miri Rubin (ed.), *The Work of Jacques le Goff and the Challenges of Medieval History* (Woodbridge: Boydell and Brewer, 1997), pp. 189–206.

[44] José Mattoso, 'A coroação dos primeiros reis de Portugal', in Bethencourt and Curto, *A memória da nação*, pp. 187–200; Reinhard Elze, 'Ein Krönungsordo aus Portugal', in *Memoria Sanctorum Venerantes: miscellanea in onore di Monsignor Victor Saxer* (Rome: Pontificio Istituto di Archeologia Cristiana, 1992), pp. 323–34; Paulo Merêa, *Sobre a aclamação dos nossos reis*, offprint of *Revista Portuguesa de História* (Coimbra, 1962); António Brásio, 'O problema da sagração dos monarcas Portugueses', *Anais da Academia Portuguesa da História*, 12 (1962), 21–49. See also Caetano, *A crise nacional*, pp. 52–5 (note IV).

[45] For an evaluation of the Castilian context of the fourteenth-century coronations: Peter Linehan, 'The politics of piety: aspects of the Castilian monarch from Alfonso X to Alfonso XI', *Revista Canadiense de Estudios Hispánicos*, 9 (1985), 385–404.

connection with the community of Santa Cruz in Coimbra, for at the beginning of the fifteenth century they were still in receipt of the ration respective to this.[46] Although this documented fact can be simply interpreted as a recognition of the patronage of the monarchs, the fact that the ration was 'tamanha como a de um cónego' is an indication that it must not be overlooked in the light of medieval practices in other contexts. The Germanic emperors of the eleventh and twelfth centuries, for example, were also consecrated as canons of the most important dioceses, shared the profits of the churches and took part in the election of the bishops.[47] This practice also spread to France (for example in St Martin of Tours) and to England. More important, because it can be directly related to the Portuguese context, was the admission of Alfonso VII as *concanonicus* of Santiago de Compostela in 1127, when he received *panem in canonica et ebdomadam in altari et cetera beneficia*.[48] In the description in the fifteenth-century annals of Santa Cruz of the opening of the tomb of Afonso Henriques during the time of King Manuel I, there is a curious report that the king 'staua uestido como conego', a fact in itself improbable although the reference is significant and denotes the existence of a tradition preserved within the community of observant canons that the kings played a part there.[49] From the point of view of the much debated problem of the meaning which should be given to the small or even non-existent importance of rites of anointment in the royal inaugurations, these facts alert us to the attention which should be given to other ceremonial contexts in which royalty of a sacerdotal type could be expressed.

While anointment was only one of the inaugural rites and among the less mentioned both in the Portuguese and the Castilian context, mention must be made of all the others. One of the most quoted rites in the Hispanic context is the elevation or 'raising up' of the king which, in contrast with the anointment,

46 ANTT, *Ch. D. João I*, 3, f. 82v.

47 On the importance of the clerical investiture in the imperial context: Josef Fleckenstein, 'Rex Canonicus. über Entstehung und Bedeutung des mittelalterlichen Königskanonikates', in Peter Classen and Peter Scheibert (eds.), *Festschrift Percy Ernst Schramm*, vol. I (Wiesbaden: Steiner, 1974), pp. 57–71; Manfred Groten, 'Königskanonikat und Krönung', *Deutsches Archiv für Erforschung des Mittelalters*, 48 (1992), 625–9.

48 Michael Borgotte, 'Über Typologie und Chronologie des Königskanonikates im europäischen Mittelalter', *Deutsches Archiv für Erforschung des Mittelalters*, 47 (1991), 19–44 in particular 37–8. On the ceremonies performed by Alfonso VII, see the recent essay by Barton, *The Aristocracy in Twelfth-Century León and Castile*, pp. 140–1.

49 António Cruz, *Santa Cruz de Coimbra na cultura Portuguesa* (Oporto: Biblioteca Pública Municipal, 1964), p. 291. It is important to remember that, as Schramm established, contrary to what occurred in the earlier periods, the medieval kings of the fourteenth and fifteenth centuries were rarely buried with regalia, and frequently used as a sign of humility and devotion to be buried in religious habits. In the French case, the opening of the tombs during the Revolution is a famous example, when corpses after Charles VII were not accompanied with any insignia. Perhaps the annals of Santa Cruz wished to refer to these later uses, mentioning the habit most of all as a sign of Afonso Henriques's protection of the community.

is not a ritual 'of transformation' but rather a type of act of recognition. A first, very similar ancient rite that also appears in association with the *adventus* or triumphal entry is the *anátellon*, which is part of the triumphal sequence and which as a type of 'epiphany' of the king could also appear as a ritual of inauguration.[50] The 'raising' (*levantamento*) was practised in all the Iberian Christian kingdoms. The Portuguese use of the verb 'to raise up', lift or hold up is enlightening. It is around this extra-ecclesiastical rite that other important elements are organised, such as hand-kissing, whose origin lay in the Iberian feudal repertory of gesture and which at the end of the Middle Ages was transformed into a rite of submission to the king by the magnates. Also there is the taking of the oath made by the monarchs which in several European contexts was included in the sequence of the coronation ceremony and which in the Iberian Peninsula could be performed within an extra-ecclesiastical context, as is well known in the paradigmatic cases of Navarre and Portugal. Another element of great importance is the acclamation, 'the customary proclamation Royal, Royal, Royal repeated three times, which is equivalent to the triple *vivat* of some coronation rituals'[51] or the equivalent of the *laudes* described by old ecclesiastical sources but, in the Portuguese case, also performed outside the sacred space. Finally, we have the investiture of arms, although its use in the context of the royal inauguration is rare, and the coronation (placing of the crown), both rites whose adoption has, however, a relevant role in forms of emulation which so contributed towards the development of the Hispanic traditions or 'uses'. By dispensing with parts of the rite of investiture and defining it with religious and vassalic connotations from the thirteenth century, the sovereigns proceeded to auto-investiture of arms: Ferdinand III of Castile did this in 1217, James I of Aragon in 1221 and the kings of Navarre after 1234.[52] It is not by chance that the legend of Afonso Henriques also comes to incorporate this element in the famous episode of Zamora when the founding monarch of the kingdom, refusing any vassaldom to the king of Leon, took arms himself. It would also appear to have spread from Aragon to Castile, when the kings began to crown themselves, an interesting development in view of the Portuguese inaugurations, where this act is never mentioned.[53]

It should be emphasised that in the Portuguese case the chroniclers give us reports which refer systematically and preferentially to two elements: the raising and the acclamation. Both are rituals of recognition of the royal figure, which led Paulo Merêa to admit, in theory, their possible dissolution in other contexts

50 Bertelli, *Il corpo del re*, pp. 63 and 129.

51 Merêa, *Sobre a aclamação dos nossos reis*, p. 9.

52 Bonifacio Palacios Martín, 'Investiduras de armas de los reyes españoles en los siglos XII y XIII', *Gladius* (a special edition, *Las armas en la historia*), (1988), pp. 153–92.

53 Carlrichard Brühl, 'Les auto-couronnements d'empereurs et de rois (XIIIe–XIXe siècles). Remarques sur la fonction sacrementalle de la royauté au moyen âge et à l'époque moderne', *Comptes-Rendus de l'Académie des Inscriptions et Belles-Lettres* (1984), pp. 102–18.

'so that the principle of heredity took root'. In Portugal, to the contrary, these were to become the most important elements of the sequence of inauguration of the monarchs, around which the ceremony was organised. The evolution of the acclamation can be followed in several descriptions by the chroniclers – generally made in the presence of the court, and consisting in the repetition of the formula 'Real, Real, Real' by a number of the heralds and magnates of the kingdom before the new monarch, with the exposition of the royal standard. Its later form is clear in the 'Auto' regarding the acclamation of John II in Lisbon, in which the proclamation was made at several points of the city, with particular importance in the main churches, the castle and the gates of the walled circumference, which constituted a tour with a lustral, renewing meaning.[54] The importance of the raising and acclamation in the construction of a Portuguese tradition at the end of the Middle Ages perhaps results to a large extent from the tendency, in particular in the second case, for these sequences to be transformed into 'civic rites' according to the concept suggested by Richard Trexler, so involving urban communities or the large councils of the kingdom.[55] The raising, in turn, sometimes coincides with the performance of the Cortes and turned into a public act of great importance a rite whose efficacy, however, *does not, it should be emphasised, arise from this fact*, for in no source of the period is it expressed as indispensable, and at times it happened that the raising was also practised outside of parliamentary reunions, without reducing its efficacy.

It is in the face of these relatively early customs, in respect of the codification and elaboration of inaugural ceremonies where the anointment played a marginal or unimportant role, that the efforts of the monarchs of Aviz appear as innovative. When reconsidering the requests of John I and Duarte to the pope which led to the well-known papal bulls of 1428 and 1436 authorising the anointment of the Portuguese kings, Mattoso suggested that what might have been the reason for this initiative of taking up once again a past practice which the monarchs of the fourteenth century had ignored was the bastard status and religious profession of the Master of Aviz, which might be considered as obstacles to a royalty and which anointment could 'purify', one might say, of debatable origins.[56] These were initiatives which were a little surprising in their delayed use (for example, Navarre had obtained the same permission from the pope at the early date of 1257) and in a certain way it is foreign to the tendency which can be seen in the final period of the Middle Ages towards a certain devaluation of the ceremony. This devaluation can be

[54] Eduardo Freire de Oliveira (ed.), *Elementos para a história do município de Lisboa* (Lisbon: Imprensa da Casa Real, 1887), vol. I, pp. 344–5. On the same ceremony in Évora: *DEV*, vol. I, pp. 155–6.

[55] On the concept of 'civic ritual', Richard C. Trexler, *Public Life in Renaissance Florence* (New York: Academic Press, 1980).

[56] The main documents were published by Brásio, 'O problema da sagração dos monarcas Portugueses', and also in *MH*, vol. III, pp. 212–13 and vol. V, pp. 261–5 and 266–9.

seen as a general tendency which was well established in the fifteenth century, in spite of the complex developments which can be seen in kingdoms where the rite existed traditionally, such as in England. As Kantorowicz reminds us, this devaluation of the anointment is due on the one hand to the evolution of the sacramental theory which tended to sublimate the rituals of access to ecclesiastical offices, carefully distinguishing these rites from those of royal anointment, but most of all it is due to the development of juridic concepts of the autonomy of the royal figure, removing it from the old sacerdotal model.[57] The identification with the sacerdotal figure would become less and less necessary to the monarchs after the twelfth century, and its sacralisation 'did not remove the strength from the idea of a *Christus domini*, of the altar, or of the church, but from its own sphere, *sui iuris* and *sui generis*, separate from the ecclesiastical institution', instituting a type of 'secular sacredness' as Kantorowicz calls it, which became translated into a new independence for the monarch and a greater autonomy in the construction of a more direct connection to the sphere of the sacred. John I's requests (through the direct intervention of the Infante Pedro) and those of Duarte appear in a context of global reformulation of the Portuguese ceremonies which should be related to the advent a few years later of the ceremonial of the English royal chapel, and which culminated in the initiative leading to the compilation (which has been lost) of Portuguese ceremonies written in the second half of the century.[58] Although it perhaps was never performed, since there is no strong evidence in the narrative sources of the time besides the actual request to the pope, the anointment as proposed by the papal decrees was intended to ensure greater solemnity among the royalty of Duarte and his descendants, expressing more clearly the intangibility of their persons which the common rites of raising up and acclamation did not emphasise. This rite indeed resulted in a consequence for the anointed which appears to have taken on greater importance in the Portuguese context: untouchability and supernatural protection.[59]

Curiously it was also in relation to the problem of the naming of the heir to the throne and his particular standing in the group of descendants of the monarch that, in the fifteenth century, there developed another type of specific ceremony,

[57] Kantorowicz, *The King's Two Bodies*, pp. 318–24. The first aspect is also much present in the text of the actual pontifical documents published by Brásio. See also Marc Bloch's statement, *Les Rois thaumaturges*, pp. 216–19 and Reinhard Elze, 'Le Consacrazione Regie', in *Segni e riti nella chiesa altomedievale occidentale* (Spoleto: Settimane di Studio del Centro Italiano di Studi sull'Alto Medioevo, 1987), pp. 43–55 and 57–61.

[58] The coronation ritual was only a small part of the *Liber Regie Capelle*, although naturally it is the section of the text to which English historiography has given most importance. The modality of anointment suggested in it differs substantially, as Mattoso emphasises, from the modality related in the pontifical documents. However, at the Portuguese court there were two important textual sources available, both normative, which allowed for a good knowledge of the characteristics and modalities of this rite.

[59] On the untouchable nature of the anointed kings: Bertelli, *Il corpo del re*, pp. 232–48.

the public oath of succession. Gama Barros says that this use can be confirmed in Portugal only from the reign of Afonso IV,[60] and that it evolved during the Aviz dynasty, becoming an essential element of the dynasty's ceremonial. There is certain information as to its occurrence during the first year of life in relation to John I's first-born, the Infante Afonso (who died later aged about ten),[61] and that it also took place in the early years of Duarte's reign with the heir, the future Afonso V.[62] The most complete description available of the sequence of acts and words of which this ceremony consisted is regarding João, the first-born of Afonso V, whose 'oath' was performed in 1455.[63] Contrary to what occurred in the fifteenth century in the other Iberian kingdoms, such as Aragon, Navarre and also Castile, this oath was not necessarily made within the context of the parliaments, but it did involve the cities and towns of the kingdom.[64] From the description of 1455 included in the authentic register we can judge the solemn character of the act, with the royal child in a position of pre-eminence on the lap of his nursemaid and the display of the royal sword as it was raised 'to the said prince'.[65] The essence of the ceremony lay, however, in a succession of solemn oaths weaving a fabric of sworn promises of obedience to the future king which the chief magnates of the kingdom, many of whom were members of the royal family, mutually took. It should be emphasised that this oath was not made directly to the figure of the heir: the guardians of João in 1455, the Infante Henry (uncle of the ruling king) and Fernando (the king's brother), each swore homage on the hands of the other 'not to obey nor receive as king any other' than the royal child. We could say that the Portuguese case was the inverse of the famous oath analysed by Kantorowicz which the English magnates proposed

60 Barros, *História da administração pública em Portugal*, vol. III, p. 310 and note 2. There are no safe sources available on its performance for the other fourteenth-century kingdoms.

61 *CR João I*, vol. II, p. 290 and ANTT, Supl. Cortes, M 4, no. 21. On the same ceremony performed for Duarte, who had just succeeded to the throne, ANTT, drawer XIII, batch 9, no. 25.

62 See the mention made by Rui de Pina: *CR Duarte*, p. 499. See also ANTT, drawer XIII, M 7, no. 3. The chronicler also relates (although the act is not stated in any other source) that in 1438 Fernando, the brother of Afonso V, would have been sworn as heir in a similar ceremony which would have taken place following the death of Duarte and the 'raising' of the first-born Afonso: *CR Duarte*, p. 575. This would mean that no fifteenth-century Portuguese monarch reigned for long without having a 'sworn' successor who could be, for lack of a direct heir, a brother of the king while still a child.

63 *MH*, vol. XII, pp. 145–52.

64 The ritual sequence of swearing of the Castilian heir was reconstructed by Juan Manuel Carretero Zamora, 'Representación política y procesos de legitimación', in J. M. Nieto Soria (ed.), *Orígenes de la monarquía Hispánica: propaganda y legitimación (ca 1400–1520)* (Madrid: Dykinson, 1999), pp. 177–205 (in particular pp. 186–7). For Aragon see Ralph Giesey, *If Not, Not: The Oath of the Aragonese and the Legendary Laws of Sobrarbe* (Princeton: Princeton University Press, 1968), pp. 189–90 and 192–3.

65 On the importance of the insignia in the Hispanic context, Percy Schramm, *Las insignias de la realeza en la edad media Española* (Madrid: Instituto de Estudios Politicos, 1960), pp. 59–61 and also José Mattoso, *Fragmentos de uma composição medieval* (Lisbon: Estampa, 1987), pp. 213–32.

in 1308 should be made 'to the crown' and not to the person of the king. In Portugal, on the contrary, the sacred power of the promissory oath demanded respect for the person.[66]

The same ritualistic sequence appears to have occurred with the 'oath' of Afonso, the son of John I, in which Count Nuno Álvares Pereira and Master Lopo Dias de Sousa took part. These were perhaps the most powerful men of the beginning of John's reign for they controlled a large part of the contingents of the royal army. This was also the case with the oath of Afonso V during his father's lifetime, which was performed by his guardians and uncles, the Infantes Pedro and Henry. Following the taking of the oath, in the most documented case of 1455, the relatives kissed the infante's hand, so recognising his royal standing. In this description there is no mention of the presence of the reigning monarch, and in all probability he was not there. The entire ceremony, which in the fifteenth-century Portuguese court was seen as a rite prior to accession to the throne, was focused in the same way on the protection and guarantee of succession of the heir through use of the powerful 'political sacrament', the solemn oath. Besides this it was a practice subject to lively argument at the time – many authors attempted to analyse the disharmony in the world, the cause of which lay in the abuse of oaths and in the generalisation of perjury, particularly in the political and religious spheres, as shown in the debate on the breaking of the oath and the assassination of the Duke of Orleans in 1407, or on the condemning of Wyclif and Huss at the Council of Constance.[67] This dramatic reaffirmation of the principle of succession in the Portuguese kingdom through use of a specific ritual denotes an investment which is congruent with the difficult political situation of the age which I have earlier termed that of the 'plural court'. This ritual should be related to the new actuality in the initiatives of using anointment in the Portuguese context if we are to accept the explanation suggested by the chronicler Rui de Pina that, in 1435, Duarte attempted 'to order holy oil to be placed on his sons', so wishing to protect their political future.[68]

As a result of this analysis, I believe it to be just to conclude, following the suggestion of Merêa, that the Portuguese inaugural ceremonies expressed a notable focus upon the hereditary mechanism of succession. During the entire fourteenth century the use in Portugal, to which I have already referred in this book, of internal conflicts or 'civil wars' opposing the monarchs and their heirs, with the eventual involvement of other legitimate and illegitimate descendants of the kings, points in the same direction. There does not appear to have been

[66] 'In their well-known declaration of 1308, [the magnates] proclaimed: "Homage and oath of allegiance are more by reason of the crown than by reason of the king's person"... Apparently the barons were prepared to face a desperate alternative: to choose between Crown and King': Kantorowicz, *The King's Two Bodies*, pp. 364–5 and 368.

[67] Paolo Prodi, 'Il sacramento del potere', in *Il giuramento politico nella storia dell'ocidente* (Bologna: Il Mulino, 1992), p. 221 and pp. 224–5.

[68] *CR Duarte*, p. 509.

much argument during the period, and indeed an analysis of the ceremonies reinforces this conclusion as to the virtue or right which royal blood brought with it and which placed the 'infantes' in a position of hypothetical rivalry. The founder of the new dynasty himself, as is known, based the claim of his legitimacy on his descendancy from King Pedro, a figure upon whom the Aviz chronicler Fernão Lopes based in the trilogy of his chronicles the beginnings of an augured 'change of the times'. While the possibility of the performance of anointment was fundamentally confirmed in the fifteenth century as a rite which allowed a compensation for the fragility of the hereditary principle of primogeniture, it was confirmed in perfect parallel with the development of other aspects of the ceremonial cycle of inauguration which were also intended to avoid the disharmony of a contested succession. In this way one must admit that the fabric of public oaths allowed the fifteenth-century monarchs (a rare situation in Portugal during the previous century) to reign almost all the time with a 'sworn successor', eventually turning to the brother of the monarch should there be no direct successor, which suggests that this confirmation of a clear principle of succession reinforced the authority of the actual reigning monarch.[69] The change of dynasty in 1383–85 was thus demonstrated as a time during which the great political effervescence seems to have fomented ritual creativity in complete parallel with other innovative aspects of the political culture of the age. One of the most important was the development of the founding myths of the nation and the kingdom, such as the myth of Ourique, whose first composition in its 'canonic' form is to be found in a text which can be dated 1416, which rooted the archetypal figure of Afonso Henriques in the political imagination of the age,[70] associating this royal archetype with the relative novelty assumed in Portugal by the reception of crusading ideas of the 'holy war'.[71] In spite of this new emphasis placed upon the figure of the warrior king who was the conqueror of the infidel, it must be emphasised that the desire to adopt the ceremony of anointment, with its sacerdotal connotations, continued all the same to retain its fascination for the monarchs of Aviz.

The problem of the funeral rituals can be considered as connected to that of the ceremonies of accession to the throne, and forms a link in an important chain in the successive reigns in the cycle to which I have referred. Also in this case, Portuguese sources are richer only for the fifteenth-century period, whose practices may be reflected in the chroniclers' descriptions regarding the

69 I must thank Carvalho Homem for having drawn my attention to this problem, alerting me to the fact that no fifteenth-century monarch whose inauguration I have attempted to study had acceded to the throne in circumstances of consensus and political tranquillity.

70 Luis Filipe Lindley Cintra, 'A lenda de Afonso I, Rei de Portugal (origens e evolução)', *ICALP-Revista*, 16–17 (1989), 64–78; Ana Isabel Buescu, 'Vínculos da memória: Ourique e a fundação do reino', in Y. Centeno (ed.), *Portugal: mitos revisitados* (Lisbon: Salamandra, 1993), pp. 9–50.

71 On the late reception of the idea of the crusade in Portugal, see Carl Erdmann, *A ideia de cruzada em Portugal* (Coimbra: Instituto Alemão da Universidade, 1940).

fourteenth century, which alerts us to a certain critical caution regarding these narrative sources. There are at least two ritual sequences which are clearly distinguishable in the thirteenth century, one surrounding the funeral rites of the deceased king and the other putting in relation the moment of the death and the inauguration of the new king. This second transition seems to have been performed with relative simplicity during the final period of the Middle Ages, immediately following the death of the predecessor, and it always included a sequence of 'mourning' marked by mourning clothes which were replaced by regal clothes on the day of the 'raising up'.[72] This is what Duarte did on the day following the death of his father, as did Afonso V when still a child, and his successor.[73] In Fernão Lopes's description of the 'raising up' of John of Castile and Beatriz as sovereigns of Portugal, the chronicler coincides the funeral rites of Fernando with the accession to the throne and the acclamation of his daughter in Toledo in a sequence also related by the Castilian chronicler: 'fizeram seu dó, e depois alegrias como é costume'.[74] This would however have been a special case of an unusual delay of the sequence of inauguration in relation to the moment of the physical death of the king, which moments were, as has been said, generally consecutive. It must be said that the simplicity referred to by Fernão Lopes of the funeral ceremonies surrounding the death of Fernando might be intended to avoid greater significance in this unusually long preliminary period.

Contrasting with this brevity, the actual funeral exequies unfolded in several stages, so extending the death of the monarch across the various areas of the kingdom. An initial very simple burial or a prolonged vigil of the body was followed by the actual ceremony of the 'saimento' which took place about a month later, although there was no exact time scale, at which the new monarch and the court played an important role.[75] According to the place chosen for the burial, at times the solemn removal of the body was a process which might considerably

[72] Not only the mourning by the monarch but also that by the entire court is carefully regulated in the *Livro Vermelho*.

[73] Armindo de Sousa, *A morte de D. João I (um tema de propaganda dinástica)* (Oporto: Centro de Estudos Humanísticos, 1984), p. 483. On the raising of Afonso V: Gomes Eanes de Zurara, *Crónica do Conde D. Duarte de Meneses*, ed. Larry King (Lisbon: Universidade Nova, 1978), pp. 108–10; also the reference to the act in the 'Actas das Vereações', *Actas das Vereações do Porto (anos de 1401–1449)*, ed. J. A. Pinto Ferreira (Oporto: Câmara Municipal, 1980), p. 324. For the case of John II, see the 'Livro de Apontamentos' of the secretary Álvaro Chaves: A. M. Salgado and A. J. Salgado (eds.), *Livro de Apontamentos (1438–1489)* (Lisbon: Imprensa Nacional, 1984), pp. 105–9.

[74] This description poses many problems, in particular that of the sources used by Lopes, for the acts reported are not described by Ayala, who is (as Peter Russell established) his main source for the events which occurred in Castile: compare *CR João I*, vol. I, pp. 94–5 (cf. also vol. II, p. 305 on the succession of the same Castilian king) and *CRO* (Ayala), p. 549. In general the succession referred to is alluded to in the Portuguese chronicles through the history of the clothing of the new king – first mourning and then the 'regal garments'.

[75] Although this frequently coincided with the month of the death, it could be delayed for several reasons. See a further document relating to this practice: H. Baquero Moreno, *Novos dados sobre as exéquias solenes de D. Afonso V*, offprint of *Bracara Augusta* (Braga, 1982).

prolong the funeral rites surrounding the royal corpse.[76] The removal of the deceased kings was in the Portuguese case performed with considerable participation of the members of the court, in particular the officials of the deceased king. There are at least five places in Portugal (Arouca, Guimarães, Odivelas, Portela de Azeitão and Silves) which still today have monuments or crosses erected for the occasion of the removal of royal corpses up to the end of the fifteenth century, of which the most interesting is that at Odivelas, which is a simple stone construction much like a covered dais with an arch resembling a niche.[77] These constructions, which were true funeral 'stopping places' where tradition says that the funeral cortèges paused, also evokes the well-known use in France of the fourteenth-century 'montjoies' erected between Saint-Denis and Paris,[78] or for England of the so-called 'Eleanor Crosses' erected for the funeral procession of Eleanor of Castile, who died in 1290.[79]

The rites or 'funeral processions' are seen during the fifteenth century as organised around two of their principal constitutive elements – the funeral lamentations and the breaking of shields. Each of these, states José Mattoso, was an element which had existed in earlier periods.[80] The lamentation, or 'planctus', is represented on a thirteenth-century tomb of a queen preserved at Alcobaça, which is probably that of Urraca, the wife of Afonso II.[81] The top of the dead queen's sarcophagus shows a male figure accompanied by other, smaller figures in a characteristic gesture of despair and ritual weeping.[82] These lamentations occurred during the solemn ceremonies, and during the final period of the Middle Ages always included the use of funereal catafalques ('essas'). This is a custom found from the end of the thirteenth century in the Hispanic sphere not only in Aragon but also, later, in Castile.[83] The relatively well-studied

[76] As for example occurred with John I and Philippa: on the first, Duarte states that 'a trelladaçam prymeira e segunda pera sua capella' was performed in 1435, while the monarch had died in 1433 (*Livro dos Conselhos*, p. 112). On Philippa, compare Zurara's statement with the version of the event given by Mateus Pisano, and also *MH*, vol. II, pp. 166–7.

[77] The monuments of Arouca and Odivelas are shown in Flávio Lopes (ed.), *Património arquitectónico classificado: inventário* (Lisbon: Instituto Português do Património Arquitectónico e Arqueológico, 1993), vols. I and II, sections relating to Lisbon and Aveiro. See also João Barreira, *Arte Portuguesa: as artes decorativas* (Lisbon: Excelsior, 1949), vol. I, pp. 78–80 and 90–8.

[78] A. Lombard-Jourdan, *Mont-Joie et Saint-Denis! Le centre de la Gaule aux origines de Paris et Saint-Denis* (Paris: CNRS, 1989).

[79] See the map locating these crosses in Colvin, *The History of the King's Works*, vol. I, pp. 480–1.

[80] José Mattoso, 'A morte dos reis na cronística pré-afonsina', *Estudos Medievais*, 20 (1993), 79–96; 'O poder e a morte', *Anuario de Estudios Medievales*, 25 (1995), 395–427.

[81] This is found in the catalogue, Maria Antónia Pinto de Matos (ed.), *Nos confins da idade média: arte Portuguesa, séculos XII–XV* (Oporto: Instituto Português de Museus, 1992).

[82] Moshe Barash, *Gestures of Despair in Medieval and Early Renaissance Art* (New York: New York University Press, 1976). See also Ernesto de Martino, *Morte e pianto rituale: dal lamento funebre antico al pianto di Maria* (Turin: Boringhieri, 1975).

[83] Elena Lourie, 'Jewish participation in royal funerary rites: an early use of the *repraesentatio* in Aragon', *Journal of the Warburg and Courtauld Institutes*, 45 (1982), 192–4. See also Denis Menjot, 'Un Chrétien qui meurt toujours. Les funérailles royales en Castile à la fin du moyen

example of the medieval popes shows that the device known as *castrum doloris* ('fortress of sorrows') was also used in the liturgical vigil which took place in the papal chapel.[84] The *Liber Regie Capelle* also proposes its use for the case of the English monarchs in the organisation of the funeral ceremony which was the duty of the royal chapel. The 'essa' (in the English ceremonial 'hersa', in Latin) was a tall structure made of wood which could hold a large number of wax tapers. Placed in a sacred area, the royal corpse was laid in it during the 'saimento'. According to Rui de Pina's description of the removal which took place two months after the death of John I, this was also the device for placing the royal corpse in the churches at each pause along the route taken from the cathedral of Lisbon to the monastery of Batalha, with stops in Odivelas, Vila Franca de Xira, Alcoentre and Alcobaça.[85]

However, the generalised use of this ephemeral construction allowed above all that the religious rites and rites of passage which took place around the mortal remains of the monarch were repeated in numerous places in the kingdom. Outside the royal chapel or the churches in which the royal corpse was physically deposited, this construction was strictly a false bier adorned with symbolic elements of royalty and mourning. As with the acclamation, the royal funeral rites or 'saimentos' tended during the later period to become civic rites, which process has been well studied for the Aragonese case.[86] Thus some material elements can be collected on these facts for the royal family of the fifteenth century in locally produced sources; for example, in a chapter of the Cortes of 1456 the council of Évora reports on the 'saimento' of Queen Isabel that 'four pieces of dyed cloth had already been bought for the said hearse'; this cloth would also serve to make up clothes for the officials of the city to wear during the solemn act. Some years later we know from expenses incurred in Oporto regarding the hearse for Prince Afonso, the son of John II, that it cost 1600

âge', in *La idea y el sentimiento de la muerte en la historia y en el arte de la edad media* (Santiago de Compostela: Universidad de Santiago de Compostela, 1988), pp. 127–38; José Luis Martín, 'El Rey ha muerto. Viva el Rey!', *Hispania*, 51 (1991), 5–39. In a broader chronological perspective, Javier Varela, *La muerte del Rey: el ceremonial funerario de la monarquía Española (1500–1885)* (Madrid: Turner, 1990), in particular pp. 49–50.

84 Reinhard Elze, '*Sic transit gloria mundi*: la morte del papa nel medioevo', *Annali dell'Istituto Storico Italo-Germanico in Trento*, 3 (1977), 23–41; Agostino Paravicini-Bagliani, *The Pope's Body* (Chicago: University of Chicago Press, 2000), pp. 114–17.

85 *CR Duarte*, pp. 491–2 and 499–503. This later source appears to have been somewhat influenced by practices of the time of the writer. Compare it for example with the sixteenth-century description relating to the exequies of King Manuel: Biblioteca Pública de Évora, cod. 75, no. 18.

86 See the excellent monograph by Flocel Sabaté which uses the 'books of ceremonial' of the councils, *Lo Senyor Rei es mort! Actitud i cerimònies dels municipis Catalans baix-medievals davant la mort del monarca* (Lerida: Universitat de Lleida, 1994). The communication of the death of the king could be made by letters sent, in the Aragonese case, from the royal council, from the city of Barcelona or from the monarch's chancellor, but the most important, as in Portugal, was the letter from the successor to the throne which usually contained a eulogy of the deceased and information as to the performance of the exequies.

reais, paid to a carpenter, and the structure was covered in cloth 'of mourning' with a white cross. The 'saimento' that year included unprecedented costs for wax in the same book of accounts.[87] The hearse was the most important material element of the ceremony, beside which the funeral liturgical offices were performed, and it was also the site of the respective lamentations by the local authorities who were expressly advised so that there should be a temporal unity in the performance of the rite.

The 'breaking of the shields' by all indications was performed on the occasion of the death of John I, again locally if we note the instructions made by Duarte in a letter sent to the council of Évora.[88] This practice consisted in accompanying the ritual lament with the destruction of the heraldic devices of the dead man, which were placed upside down during the funeral procession (on shields and standards) until arrival at the church, where the cenotaph or symbolic bier lay.[89] So the entire kingdom allowed, as the word 'saimento' suggests, the physical body of the king to 'depart from' his earthly state, returning it to the sacred spaces and times of the Christian religion. This was a rite by which 'active' royalty, so to say, abandoned the body of the dead monarch, although the memory and periodic remembrance through the liturgical celebration of the day of his death remained as an ideally eternal mark, always to be associated with the corpse which continued to be a royal corpse; for this reason it could be exhumed, removed and inspected and even plundered of its insignias. It is highly probable that the 'breaking of the shields' became more widely used and was contained within the sequence of laments or ritual weeping in the medieval period after the twelfth century when heraldry was instituted as a preferential emblematic language, becoming a practice not exclusive to the Portuguese kingdom. However, it holds particular importance for the Aviz dynasty in the sequence of funeral ceremonies associated with the death of the kings and is symbolically evoked in the reference of the contemporaneous *Livro dos Arautos*, according to which Afonso Henriques's shield in Coimbra fell to the ground every time a Portuguese king died.[90]

Studies available on other Hispanic contexts, particularly Castile, show us that in the thirteenth and fourteenth centuries this was not a rite exclusive to royalty. According to Faustino Menéndez Pidal, the shields (objects) of the

[87] *DEV*, vol. II, p. 78 and Iria Gonçalves, *As finanças do Porto na segunda metade do século XV* (Oporto: Câmara Municipal, 1987), pp. 104–5.

[88] Dated 25 August 1433, a few days following the death of John I, this letter asks those of the council, 'por agora de quebrar escudo nem fazer outro chanto nom vos enbargees ataa os xbij dias do mes doutubro que vos encomendamos que façaaes o saymento e doo por o dito senhor, o mais honradamente que bem poderdes': *DEV*, vol. II, pp. 39–40. See also the 'Capitolo do Pramto' in the Lisbon rulings of 1502: Freire de Oliveira, *Elementos para a história do município de Lisboa*, vol. I, p. 110.

[89] Marquês de São Payo, 'A heráldica nos usos e costumes funerários', *Armas e Troféus*, 6 (1965), 220–30.

[90] Mattoso, *Fragmentos de uma composição medieval*, p. 227.

nobles, as personal emblems, accompanied the dead in the Castilian churches, and this possibly influenced their sculptured representation on the funeral monuments which in a certain way came to replace them. The deafening noise at the breaking of the shields during the funeral processions of the nobility was accompanied, as frequently described in ecclesiastical sources somewhat censoriously, by dreadful cries and the sound of animals who were deliberately wounded for this, such as dogs and horses, whose tails were cut as a sign of 'mourning'. It is important to emphasise that the 'custom' was retained in the case of the monarchs until much later than was the case of the funeral rites of the nobles, who through clerical pressure and the influence of new forms of religious lifestyle upon death abandoned this during the fifteenth and sixteenth centuries. It could even be said that, for royalty, the rite came to assume an exclusive tone since the arms of the kingdom were strictly associated with royal standing. Beyond this ceremonial context, which is quite unique, any attack or destruction of the 'images' of the king and his heraldic signs, be this on coins, shields or any other object, was severely punished, as explained in the Alfonsine 'Fuero Real'. The funeral rite is particularly well represented on the tomb of a Castilian infante, the son of Fernando III, which dates from the end of the thirteenth century, as well as on the miniatures of the famous 'Cantigas' of the Wise King.[91]

Even beyond the Iberian Peninsula it could be said that this ritual use of heraldic devices or inscriptions through their destruction being included in the ceremonies and intended to mark moments of transition was no less familiar to men of the time. In the Venetian republic, as Muir tells us, 'at the death of the Doge two silver emblems were made, one a large one with the name of the deceased on it and a smaller one, which was similar save for the absence of the name. In a simple ceremony, the large emblem was smashed and the smaller one retained to be given to the new Doge after his election.'[92] The funeral ceremonies of the monarch in medieval Poland also included a sequence of ritual destruction of the royal seal, with which, according to Gieysztor, the reign of the deceased monarch symbolically came to an end.[93] In the case of the pope, the rite is well known with which the period called *sede vacante* was begun, when the fisherman's ring was removed from the finger of the dead pontiff and solemnly broken.[94] All these cases not only display a culture

[91] Faustino Menéndez Pidal de Navascués, 'Heráldica funeraria en Castilla', *Hidalguía*, 13 (1965), 133–44.

[92] Edward Muir, *Civic Ritual in Renaissance Venice* (Princeton: Princeton University Press, 1981), p. 272.

[93] A. Gieysztor, 'Gesture in the coronation ceremonies of medieval Poland', in Janos Bak (ed.), *Coronations: Medieval and Early Modern Monarchic Ritual* (Berkeley: University of California Press, 1990), pp. 152–64.

[94] Laurie Nussdorger, 'The vacant see: ritual and protest in early modern Rome', *Sixteenth Century Journal*, 18 (1987), 173–89.

in which the emblems and material signs associated with the functions and offices held enormous importance as mechanisms of representation; in spite of their enormous variety they also express a similar anxiety at the physical disappearance of the rulers, which these rites are able to express in a certain manner. In the Portuguese case, as in the Castilian, it seems entirely logical that the arms of the deceased king be broken and replaced by others displaying the same symbols once the successor had been inaugurated as king, for these were associated with the royal *dignitas*, which would never die.

The conjunction of these two elements – the 'weeping' and the 'breaking of the shields' – thus formed a truly ceremonial aspect of the Portuguese royal funeral rites. The liturgical celebration of the death of the kings naturally proceeded in its own sphere, was solemn and more or less grandiose, but was distinct from the unique ritualistic sequences to which I have referred, whose principal significance seems to reside to a large degree in a symmetry of the court ceremony of mourning with equal manifestations that included the principal communities of the kingdom. The term 'saimento' is also used during this period for the liturgical commemoration of the anniversaries of death which also held great importance in the Aviz dynasty. Not only at the time was a pantheon for the dynastic use of the Portuguese kings in the Dominican monastery of Santa Maria da Vitória or Batalha conceived,[95] but the monarchs also demonstrated a particular attention to the liturgical commemoration of the kings of the previous dynasty. The Annals of Santa Cruz for example relate that Duarte ordered golden cloths to cover the tombs of the first kings (as he also did with the tomb of Queen Isabel of Aragon at S. Clara de Coimbra), at which the prior of the community said masses 'com panos d ouro sobrellos e tochas e cirios seemdo presentes as donas e freires conversos'.[96] Likewise, we know that Afonso V annually celebrated the 'saimento' of Fernando I and John I as well as of his father Duarte, as stated in the list of his expenses.[97]

I shall close this fragmentary analysis of the great ritualistic cycle of the medieval Portuguese royalty with a consideration of the rites connected to the marriage of the king and the birth of his children. In both cases there is a matter of complex ceremonial which is particularly interesting, for it allows us to study what is the function and the place of rites within the festivities of the age, which were events marked by their relatively gratuitous nature, a framework of possibly unpredictable conduct and also collective moments having a plurality

95 Saul António Gomes, 'Percursos em torno do panteão quatrocentista de Avis', *Biblos*, 70 (1994), 197–242.

96 Cruz, *Santa Cruz de Coimbra*, p. 320.

97 Jorge Faro (ed.), *Receitas e despesas da fazenda real de 1384 a 1481 (Subsídios documentais)* (Lisbon: Instituto Nacional de Estatística, 1965), p. 99. For an evaluation of the contents of the annual 'saimento', see what Duarte established for his father in the Lisbon cathedral: ANTT, *Ch. D. Duarte*, 2, f. 20–20v. The positioning of the torches and the participants would be the same as that observed in the royal chapel.

of meanings in which disagreement, an explosion of attitudes and even a quest for non-sense might exist, which contrasts, when viewed within this perspective, with the formalisation and stylisation of the actual royal ceremony. Royal marriage can also be analysed from multiple points of view, particularly as an inaugural ceremony, since for the Portuguese queens it was a true moment of passage and access to the ruling status. We have available interesting facts relating to the matrimonial event of 1428, the marriage of Leonor of Aragon to Duarte during the lifetime of John I. This was a carefully prepared event which followed long negotiations and which is found included within a particularly complex cycle of festivities which lasted some months, and which was studied within its Castilian setting by Teófilo Ruiz.[98] The nuptial ceremony itself took place in Coimbra in September 1428 and is the subject of a description by the Infante Henry in a curious 'familiar letter' sent to the old monarch, his father.[99] The choice of the place, the convent of S. Clara at Coimbra, is the actual church where the tomb of the 'queen saint' Isabel of Aragon was kept, and this merited a significant report from the infante, which makes us realise the importance this choice held for the princes of Aviz. The solemnity of the act, according to the perception of the prince, was clearly associated with the decoration of the church and the altar, which is the subject of particular attention, and also the use of torches and flambeaux (whose use caused the 'accident' of the brief fainting of the bride). Some customary elements of the court festivities associated with matrimony are also to be found, particularly games with bulls and tourneys. As I havc had occasion to observe above, Duarte was linked to the throne as 'rex iuvenes' following this period, which can be related to the actual marriage. From comments from the same letter the decisive function of the consummation of the marriage is clearly stated, following the blessing solemnly made in a church by an episcopal figure. Even in the case of crowned queens, as Carmi Parsons says,

> the rite's purpose was less to confirm her as a ruler than to designate her as the king's legitimate wife and the mother of his lawful heir... as the queen took no oath, she was not established in a defined relationship with the realm, nor was the kingdom obligated to her by oaths of homage. She was anointed with the holy oil, not with chrism, before she received a ring for integrity

[98] Teófilo Ruiz, 'Fiestas, torneos y símbolos de la realeza en la Castilla del siglo XV. Las fiestas de Valladolid de 1428', in A. Rucquoi (ed.), *Realidad e imágenes del poder: España a fines de la edad media* (Valladolid: Ambito, 1988), pp. 249–65. See also the French version of this article: 'Festivités, couleurs et symboles du pouvoir en Castille au XVe siècle. Les célébrations de mai 1428', *Annales ESC*, 46 (1991), 521–46.

[99] An English version of this text was recently published in the final appendix of his biography of this prince by Peter Russell, *Prince Henry the Navigator: A Life* (London and New Haven: Yale University Press, 2000). Information on the passage recorded among the appointments of Duarte, however, allows us to establish that particularly important festivities were planned in Évora associated with his marriage: *Livro dos Conselhos*, p. 52.

of faith and a crown of majesty for honor and dignity, and her first act after investiture was to bow to the king, 'adoring the royal majesty as is fitting'.[100]

The association of the fertility of the queens to the continuity of royalty is expressed perhaps most clearly when we analyse the ceremonies accompanying the birth of the sons of the kings in the Portuguese context. Those which could be called 'of information'[101] are the most well-known ceremonies, when the reigning monarch had a fundamental role, for example taking part in the cities and towns of the realm, but also informing other sovereigns through correspondence on the birth of the descendant. Several of these letters for the sixteenth-century period are to be found in local Portuguese archives, or they are recorded in entries made by the royal secretaries in their note-books. However, rites held at the court itself were performed around the new-born child and the queen. Regarding the queen, there was imposed a period of retreat lasting several weeks following the birth, for which there was the decoration of the several beds, be these the 'bed of state' (to which I shall refer later) or that in which the queen actually slept. This has been studied in detail by Monique Sommé, from the material and financial point of view, and this arrangement surrounded Isabel of Portugal, the Duchess of Burgundy, for example during her three confinements.[102] Although there is no equal amount of detail for the Portuguese case, it is known that the practice of this initial period following the birth was most common, also among the wealthy classes of urban society, for example in Italy, and led to the exchange of presents.[103] This in the case of the queens started a ritual cycle not interrupted by the baptism of the new-born, which the queens did not usually attend, since the desire was to perform this liturgical rite soon after the birth owing to the risk of the children's premature death.

A description available on the baptism of John II, performed twenty days following his birth, mentions some aspects of the ceremonial performed, in

[100] John Carmi Parsons, 'Ritual and symbol in the English medieval queenship to 1500', in Louise Olga Fradenburg (ed.), *Women and Sovereignty* (Edinburgh: University of Edinburgh Press, 1992), pp. 61–2. On the anointment of the queens, see the important study by Janet L. Nelson, 'Early medieval rites of queen-making and the shaping of medieval queenship', in Anne J. Duggan (ed.), *Queens and Queenship in Medieval Europe* (London: Boydell Press, 1997), pp. 301–15. In the Hispanic sphere, see the work of Bonifacio Palacios Martín, *La coronación de los Reyes de Aragón*, where there is reference to the coronation of the queens by the monarchs themselves in the Aragonese ceremonial.

[101] This concerns acts surrounded by a certain solemnity as was also the case with the communication of the death of the king, as already seen, which also led to local ritualistic cycles. On the concept, see Michèle Fogel, *Les Cérémonies de l'information dans la France du XVIe et du milieu du XVIIe siècles* (Paris: Fayard, 1989).

[102] Monique Sommé, 'Le cérémonial de la naissance et de la mort de l'enfant princier à la cour de Bourgogne au XVe siècle', in *Fêtes et cérémonies aux XIVe et XVe siècles: Rencontres de Lausanne, Septembre 1993* (Neuchâtel: Centre Européen d'Etudes Bourguignonnes, 1994). I should like to thank the author for having informed me of her work.

[103] J. M. Musacchio, *The Art and Ritual of Childbirth in Renaissance Italy* (New Haven: Yale University Press, 1999).

particular the procession from the Alcaçova palace to Lisbon cathedral, the use of the canopy under which the child was carried and also the symbolic lighting of candles: 'todolos senhores e povo iam a pé, com tochas por acender, e à tornada, depois de bautizado, todas acesas'.[104] If we study the *Liber Regie Capelle* we find that these rites were described there in detail, and the description directly documents the influence of English customs at the court of the Portuguese kings. According to this ceremonial, the infante was always to be carried under the canopy, including in the church, and was to be accompanied by members of the royal chapel, who supplied the water to be used for the baptism. There was to be a curtain beside the baptismal font where the royal child would be undressed and then dressed again at the end of the liturgical rite. Following the baptism, there would be the lighting and offering of a candle at the high altar on behalf of the child, who was still wrapped in a robe. It was this action which set off the lighting of all the candles of those who accompanied the child as well as the church candles, to the sound of the *Te Deum*. All the elements of the rite which took place within the church are missing in the Portuguese description referred to above, suggesting that its author was not present in the cathedral. The ceremony closed with a solemn procession in which the child was taken back to the queen's chamber in the palace following the celebration of the baptism.[105]

It is highly probable also that the end of this cycle which included the mother and child would be marked by some specific rite as set out by this ceremonial, but this cannot be safely documented for the fifteenth-century Portuguese court. This was the 'solemn purification' of the queen sixty days following the birth. The ceremony would have begun in the chamber with the 'bed of state', enclosed by curtains, on which the queen would lie a little before the arrival of the nobles and members of the chapel. Two noble ladies would then draw the curtains and open the bed, and two nobles would lift her. Accompanied by all, the queen would then go to a church or to the palace chapel where she would be blessed by a cleric of episcopal dignity and once the holy water had been received she would be taken into the holy space by this dignitary. She would attend mass in her oratory which she would only leave to make her offering, and immediately following this mass, if it was the king's pleasure, she would 'hold state' at a solemn meal with her ladies and young women 'with great glory and honour'.[106] As has already been emphasised by John Carmi Parsons, some aspects of this ceremonial, in particular the solemn hymns sung by the members of the chapel during the queen's procession, associated this purification of the queen with the feast of the Purification of the Virgin, a liturgical and iconographic theme which was very common at the end of the Middle Ages. It is of interest to note also

[104] *MH*, vol. XII, p. 133. [105] Ullmann (ed.), *Liber Regie Capelle*, pp. 67–72.
[106] *Liber Regie Capelle*, pp. 72–3.

that the queen's offering at this mass was a particular object: the 'chrismal' or linen cloth soaked in holy oils, possibly the same as that which had been used at the baptism.[107] However, it must be noted that the birth of the infantes led to a specific sequence of ceremonies centred around the mother which we find in Van Gennep's model – separation, an initial or transitional period, readmission – which lasted several weeks in this case and during which, from all indications, the child remained close to the mother in her chamber, as is suggested by the most-studied case of Isabel of Portugal, although as we have seen the child would have been breast-fed and cared for by other women.

This ritual cycle was not incompatible with other festivities to which the birth of the infants gave rise. A particularly interesting aspect in the Portuguese context is the celebrations in which the populace took part, which are documented in the case of the Infante Henry, and everything points to this having occurred during this cycle in which, as we have seen, baptisms were a fundamental element. From accounts held in the archive of the city of Oporto, we find that the baptism of that infante, which would have occurred in 1394, coincided with the performance of 'matinadas'.[108] At least seven individuals were involved in this: a servant of the bishop of Oporto (João Afonso da Azambuja who, as we have seen, was much present at John's court) and the servant of a known burgher of the city, as well as two young men who must have been members of the queen's household: one 'Janin' and a servant of the English chancellor, Adam Davenport, who had accompanied her.

In order for us to understand what the 'matinadas' would have been exactly, it is necessary to study the contemporary meanings of this type of celebration, and for this we have some important witness accounts such as that of Fernão Lopes. The various types of festivities which the chronicler reports in his works are in general classified in two large groups following a social criterion. Thus, the 'popular' and burgher festivities *par excellence*, which usually took place in towns, were the 'jogos' and 'trebelhos' (such as tightrope walking, 'tornos de mesas', the 'royal leap' and dances) and the 'matinadas' which the chronicler associates particularly with the evenings. Fernão Lopes contrasts these festivities with those associated with *fidalgos* and knights, in particular jousts and tourneys. For the 'matinadas' performed on the occasions of the baptism of the infante, the association of the men of the city of Oporto with young men from the court itself as well as the bagpiper seems significant. In old Portuguese texts the acceptance of the 'matinada' as a noise, and especially a noise produced by bagpipes and wind instruments, seems to have been preserved until the sixteenth century, as we are told in authorisations recorded by

[107] According to Guillaume Durand's explanation, 'chrismale dicitur denique vestis candida quae super caput baptizati ponitur': see the important information in Du Cange, *Glossarium Mediae et Infimae Latinitatis*, s.v. 'chrismale'.

[108] *MH*, vol. I, pp. 267–71.

Bluteau.[109] The 'matinadas' were in fact associated in the Mediterranean tradition with the 'charivari', which involved most of the younger people in noisy behaviour, on many occasions occurring at night.[110] Their connection with the propitiatory rites of fertility has been emphasised by many authors, but we also know that these festivities were suppressed by the urban authorities, most of all because they took place at night.[111] In the Portuguese context, what is surprising is the payment to the participants by the municipal authorities, which seems to show not only their acquiescence but also the promotion of such festivities which were explicitly associated with groups of the young and which in other European contexts frequently led to activities seen as contests. Only a more detailed study of these 'matinadas' in Portuguese society of the age would allow for a fair attempt at an interpretation of this event which was certainly cloaked in a particular character and concerned the son of the king. The local festivity, which suggests the effect of a 'gloss' of the ceremonial cycle I have just described, could lose its more common meaning and its restricted sphere when the court was present, and it becomes an important way of enlarging and prolonging the demonstrations which the birth and baptism of the infantes led to within the city organism.

DAILY LIFE

Let us now study in a little more detail the daily and annual cycle, an important part of the court ceremonial. Together with the principles of analysis shown initially, we must relate it to the structure of the offices. As I have repeatedly had occasion to mention, the royal courts of the medieval west demonstrated a fundamental tripartition also to be found in the Peninsular courts: the separation between the Hall, the Chamber and the Chapel. It should first be noted that the rituals of commensality fell to the Hall. To the Chamber were those related to the body of the king – and let us not forget also that 'ordinary' food was served there. Finally, the rites of Christian worship took place in the Chapel, but the king assumed a particular position in these rites, so emphasising his specific relationship with the sphere of the sacred-religious. There are just two observations to be made on this division: on the one hand it assumes other aspects which I have explored here, appearing as a fundamental structure of the court; on the other, the distinction, which has been seen throughout this study,

109 Rafael Bluteau, *Vocabulário Portuguez e Latino* (Coimbra: Colégio das Artes, 1712–28), s.v. 'matinada'.

110 Christiane Klapish-Zuber, 'La *mattinata* médiévale', in *La Maison et le nom: stratégies et rituels dans l'Italie de la Renaissance* (Paris: Ecole des Hautes Etudes en Sciences Sociales, 1990), pp. 229–46.

111 Silvia Mantini, 'Notte in città, notte in campagna tra medioevo ed età moderna', in Mario Sbriccoli (ed.), *La notte: ordine, sicurezza e disciplinamento in età moderna* (Florence: Ponte alle Grazie, 1991), pp. 30–45.

must be maintained between the departments and the bodies of officials to whom I am now referring and the physical spaces which also have the same names but with which they can never hold a variable relationship. The itinerance of the kings implied, as we have seen, that the material spaces where the court was installed were highly diverse in their material characteristics, and frequently during the final period of the Middle Ages they were still few and at times improvised. The various departments of the court to which I have referred were bodies formed by officials who were also, to my mind, agents of the royal ceremonies, preserving and transmitting traditions and 'customs' relative to this sphere of their action. While the important ceremonies (complex events which at times took several days for one and the same ritual sequence) created royalty in a particularly solemn way, appropriate to the unique or extraordinary events which were the death and the raising up of the king, the daily rites re-created it in a permanent form. The repetition of these ritual acts every day re-created and renewed through their recurrence the dynamics of separation and the distinctions necessary for the sacralisation of the royal figure. It is certainly not by chance that the great ceremonies to which I have referred appear more frequently to be a 'transformative' type of rites, while the daily cycle presents other characteristics, on many occasions functioning through the institution of taboos and the forbidden, implying notions of pollution and purity associated with the physical being of the kings, which as is known are fundamental to the distinction between the sacred and the profane. This distinction, as suggested by Van Gennep, is not fixed nor can it be considered as inherent to the nature of the beings or spaces, but it results from the ritual process which indeed instituted it. Through the rites which accompanied the kings and queens, profane aspects of royal daily life can be sacralised, although they are endowed with a special value and their own symbolic effectiveness without necessarily implying, as I have stated above when using the notion of an orthopractical worship, an emotional involvement or a clear perception of theological or religious beliefs and notions. These rites form for the monarchs a type of 'fixed framework' which accompanied them inexorably through their life and helped to model royal behaviour, being centred on the physical reality in the actual body of the king, as Bertelli analysed, and including determined pragmatic activities common to all men – eating, sleeping, dressing and adorning oneself, etc. – which the rites regulated while simultaneously making possible an aesthetic dimension in their performance.[112]

It is therefore fitting to begin with the Hall, a word which as we have seen evokes the meeting of the king with his servants and vassals and which is directly associated with the rites of eating in common. The Aragonese ceremonial teaches us, and could naturally serve as a more complete guide, that the

[112] On the notion of 'fixed framework', see Tambiah, 'A performative approach to ritual', p. 136.

food for the king was carefully separated in its preparation and consumption. There were thus two kitchens at the Peninsular courts, and in Aragon there were two 'panaderias', two 'botillerias', etc., and it must be emphasised that all the officials or servants who worked with or even touched in any manner the food destined for the king had to swear a special oath of fidelity.[113] Everything suggests that these practices, which were intended to emphasise the creation of strong proscriptions concerning food and the act of eating, were older than the actual 'Ordenacions' of 1344. Portuguese documentation of the thirteenth century, as we have seen, mentions the contrast between the 'cozinha d'el-rei de seu corpo' and the 'cozinha do paço', just as in Castile, in particular in the accounts of the court of Sancho IV, the 'cocina del cuerpo del Rey' and 'ambas dos las cocinas' appear distinct. We find this distinction in England in the *Constitutio Domus Regie* of the twelfth century, and in France it was practised at the court of the kings at least from the middle of the thirteenth century. What the 'Ordenacions' allow us to confirm, owing to the careful prescription of the assignment of the foods from their arrival at the palace until their consumption, is that the separation can be found in all circumstances, even when the king ate in public. These prescriptions suggest therefore a set of questions which continue to be very poorly studied, particularly on the possibility of instituting distinctions between the local products intended for the king's table which, as we have seen in the Portuguese case, were associated with the *colheitas*, and the products (even those resulting from the same biological *colheitas*) brought to the court as tributes, or purchased and redistributed as goods for consumption at court, be this in the form of gifts and presents or as food rations. In other words, what these normative sources suggest is the possibility of instituting distinctions between the king's food itself and the food to be ritually distributed by the king, which as we shall see is not a gratuitous distinction when taking into account the hypothesis of interpretation of the rites of commensality. Thus the circulation of consumables within the court and out towards its exterior has various aspects, which in my opinion imply separating the daily food from that of banquets or public meals, as normative and literary sources suggest.

The public meals were special occasions which the Aragonese source terms 'convits solennes' or simply 'convits', and they were those at which the Aragonese monarch ate together with his court or, to be more precise, in front of the court. This concerned ritual occurrences which took place periodically: Pedro IV's list included the four feasts of the year (Christmas, Epiphany, Easter and Pentecost) and also a curious succession of feasts of the saints associated with the various parts of his kingdoms. The Aragonese king must therefore give a 'convit' on the feast of St John the Evangelist in Murcia, on the feast of

113 The list of officials who made an oath 'de boca e mãos' to the monarch thus included apparently modest individuals such as the 'boteller' (*copeiro*), the 'panicer' (baker), the 'coyner' (cook), and the 'moseu' (guard of the king's food), etc.

St Ann in Mallorca, on the feast of the Assumption of the Virgin in Barcelona, on the Adoration of the Cross in Perpignan and on the feast of St Martin in Saragossa, naturally when he happened to be there on those occasions. The importance of the four annual feasts prescribed by this ceremonial is also found for Portugal[114] and for Castile.[115] Beyond those previously established days, however, the king gave a 'convit' whenever he wished, making it known earlier through his *mordomo*. The royal 'convites', as they were called in Portugal, were associated for example with the royal inauguration, marriages and the reception of foreign envoys.

That the fact of eating with the king, of being his *conviva*, was granted a prestigious meaning from the High Middle Ages is well established thanks to the historians of royalty and also to specialists on court literature who, from Theoderic and Charlemagne up to the more recent ages of European feudalism, have analysed the frequent mention of royal banquets in medieval texts.[116] The thirteenth-century *Partidas* outlined in this way the activities of the king in his palace: 'el rey se ayunta con los homes ... en tres maneras, ó para librar los pleytos, ó para comer, ó para fablar en gasajado'.[117] That is, the common meals are placed in parallel with the actual exercise of justice, forming a fundamental aspect of the court way of life. It must be agreed, as Labbé suggests through an analysis of literary sources, that the development of architectural spaces of the Hall is indissolubly associated with ceremonial aspects, in particular with solemn meals. In the case of the Roman imperial residences, we know that certain spaces were associated with ceremonial practices, and were distinguished functionally between *aula* or *auditorium* for meetings or audiences (*consilia*) and pronouncements, determined spaces where greetings (*salutationes*) occurred such as at the entrance, in the vestibule or within the actual walls of the buildings, and spaces for banquets (*convivia*), with a multiplicity of constructive solutions which also corresponded to various distinctions between the types of meal; important for our purpose is the distinction between

114 On the importance of these feasts: João Pedro Ribeiro, *Reflexões históricas*, 2 vols. (Coimbra: Imprensa da Universidade, 1835–36), vol. II, pp. 87–90. Afonso V recommended to the resident musicians that they should present themselves at court 'nas festas do natal e do Reis e da paschoa e pentecoste e Corpo de Deus': Viterbo, *Subsídios para a história da música*, pp. 309–10.

115 Jeanne Allard, 'L'étiquette de table à la cour de Castille au bas moyen âge', *Temas Medievales*, 3 (1993), 5–29.

116 J. Wallace-Hadrill, *Early Germanic Kingship in England and on the Continent* (Oxford: Clarendon Press, 1980), pp. 137–8 and also Ian Wood, 'Kings, kingdom and consent', in P. Sawyer and I. Wood (eds.), *Early Medieval Kingship* (Leeds: Leeds University Press, 1977), pp. 6–29. The pages which Reto Bezzola dedicated to the royal banquet in literature in the High Middle Ages are also important: *Les Origines et la formation de la littérature courtoise en occident, 500–1200*, 5 vols. (Paris: Honoré Champion, 1958–63), in particular vol. I; and more recently Pierre Riché, 'Les représentations du palais dans les textes littéraires du haut moyen âge', *Francia*, 4 (1976), esp. 162. For the Iberian context, see Victor Alonso Troncoso, 'Banquete, hospitalidad y regalo en la poesía épica española', *Hispania*, 51 (1991), 835–74.

117 *Las Siete Partidas*, p. 85.

convivium and *epulum* or public banquet, when there were public distributions of food and drink.[118] Archaeologists have also emphasised the important function of banquets in the so-called 'age of great migrations' which influenced the creation of traditions of commensality inherent to barbarian royalties, but it seems to me that classic heritage plays an extremely relevant role for the age which occupies us here. These classical definitions were well known, not only through generic references of Isidore of Seville in book X of his *Etimologies* but, as Stephen Jaeger observed, the descriptions of the actual banquets written for example by Thomas à Becket follow closely the precepts and distinctions of Macrobius, while in highly influential passages of John of Salisbury we also find the typology of banquets present in the *Saturnalia*.[119] On the other hand, the architecture of the palaces reveals the creation of mechanisms of visibility which, as we shall see, were fundamental for the medieval characterisation of a royal banquet and which are found inherently associated with late-imperial practices. As Tamm shows, the apse in reception halls appears from the first century as 'an architectural variation for the decoration of the back wall', and was always associated with the creation of sacred spaces where the perception of the users was focused. During low antiquity, it became an indispensable element both in the halls used for audiences and in the banqueting halls; as Labbé states,

> the general similitude which appears between the *aula regia* of the low empire and the basilica reveals the existence of a common *étymon* of the architectural form. In both, the apse grants either to the imperial throne or to the altar the prestige of a cosmic symbolism which places palace etiquette such as the liturgy in a larger perspective of a 'mise en ordre' of the universe, centred on a ceremonial 'mise en forme' of a *Presence*, be it sovereign or eucharistic.[120]

To return to the late-medieval Hispanic context, what do the normative sources tell us about the royal banquets known as 'convites'? As the 'Ordenacions' establish, the king was placed at a separate table from the invitees, having 'draps de lana amb istories' (armorial cloths) placed behind him, that is it was intended that his face be seen, reproducing the axial mechanism of the apse which Labbé considers to be the origin of the actual Hall as an architectural concept. Exceptionally, the Aragonese 'Ordenacions' establish that the invitees of the highest standing could be placed at his side; these would be sons of kings, cardinals, bishops whom the monarch wished to honour. The ceremony

118 Birgitta Tamm, *Auditorium and Palatium: A Study on Assembly-Rooms in Roman Palaces during the 1st Century B.C. and the 1st century A.D.* (Stockholm: Almqvist & Wiksell, 1963). See also Inge Nielsen, 'Royal banquets: the development of royal banquets and banqueting halls from Alexander to the Tertrarchs', in I. Nielsen and H. Nielsen (eds.), *Meals in a Social Context: Aspects of the Communal Meal in the Hellenistic and Roman World* (Aarhus: Aarhus University Press, 2000), pp. 102–33.

119 C. Stephen Jaeger, *The Envy of Angels* (Philadelphia: University of Pennyslvania Press, 1994).

120 Labbé, *L'Architecture des palais et des jardins dans les Chansons de Geste*, pp. 370–1.

itself could then begin. In front of the king the table was blessed, trumpets and other instruments 'of the hall' were sounded and a long procession of servants carrying the food moved from the kitchen, flanked by the porters and following the hierarchy of court duties (the text states: 'in such a way that the greater are placed before the lower, as required by the rule of law'.[121] Each servant had to try the food before passing it to the next, and this continued from the kitchen in places not visible to the invitees – the cook would taste what he had cooked, the *copeiro* would try the wine, the *reposteiro* of the fruits the fruit, etc., down to the carrier of water for ablutions, who tasted the water for hand washing. All had to be done in front of the *mordomo*, who carried his rod 'as a sign of authority', and whose duty it was finally to try the food in front of the king. Following its careful check by the physician, the food was cut by the 'escuder davant nos tallar ordenat', that is the Aragonese equivalent of the Castilian and Portuguese carver.

It is sufficient to read carefully the extraordinary text *Arte Cisoria* by Enrique de Villena to find an account of the notable complexity of the duties of the carver and his central role in the rituals of court eating of the late Middle Ages.[122] What should be emphasised is the early date of the codification of this ritual duty in the Hispanic sphere; the English 'Boke of Keruynge' (Book of Carving) seems to date only from the end of the same century, although the Duke of Gloucester's hall porter, John Russell, includes in his treatise 'Boke of Nurture' (*c.* 1447) several chapters on this art of the royal and seigneurial halls.[123] A well-known episode of the medieval legend of Tristan attributes to the art of carving a revelatory function as to the noble identity and court education of the hero, who shows he knows the art when the meat is brought to the table.[124] In fact the division and distribution of the pieces of food – be this meat or fish – was the duty of the carver, as was also that of all kinds of cooked dishes, fruit and vegetables. Thus not only could court hierarchy be based upon the ways of eating but above all the division of foods reflected a homology between certain fragments of food and the royal position.[125] After being sufficiently reduced to a practical size and the less good parts of the food discarded, the food was finally placed in front of the king on his 'carver'.

[121] 'Ordenacions fetes per lo molt Alt Senyor en Pere Terç Rey Darago sobra lo Regiment de tots los officials de la sua cort', in Próspero de Bofarull y Mascaró (ed.), *Colección de documentos inéditos del Archivo General de la Corona de Aragón*, vol. V (Barcelona, 1850), p. 173.

[122] Enrique de Villena, 'Arte Cisoria, arte de trinchar o cortar con cuchillo carnes y demás viandas', in *Obras completas*, vol. I, ed. Pedro M. Cátedra (Madrid: Turner, 1994), pp. 133–218.

[123] Frederick Furnivall (ed.), *Early English Meals and Manners* (London: Early English Text Society, 1868), pp. 147–74 and 1–123 respectively.

[124] Gottfried Von Strassbourg, *Tristan*, trans. A. T. Hatto (Harmondsworth: Penguin, 1960), pp. 78–82. I should like to thank Stephen Nichols for having drawn my attention to this passage.

[125] C. Grottannelli, 'Divisioni delle carni, organizzazione del cosmo, dinamica sociale', *Studi Storici*, 25 (1984), 824–33.

But what then happened to the other participants of the 'convite'? They also ate, for a group of higher and lower servants carried the food for the remaining invitees at the same time as the food was carried for the king – this latter was the only food expressly to be brought in covered. After its preparation – the carving or 'cutting' of meats for example – the food would come in with order and perfection to be placed in front of the others, but not indiscriminately, for the quantities of food appear to have been carefully calculated in the 'Ordenacions', and the king wished that this should be performed for each 'according to the condition of his standing'.[126] On certain days of the year the poor were admitted to the table of the 'palau' (palace) or 'tinell' (a rarer word in the Castilian and Portuguese context), and certain variations of this sequence were performed, to which I shall refer later.

What general significance can be attributed to this order which the Peninsular ceremonial model shows us on this point and which is similar to that known in other European contexts? Why should it be necessary that the royal person, surrounded by every form of alimentary taboo, should eat in front of his household on these occasions open to the presence of many others whom the monarch expressly invited for the occasion? The entire rite clearly underlines that the king was a distinct being, outside the group, who must be protected – as well as a being from whom, as Frazer would say, it was also necessary that the others protect themselves.[127] The Aragonese text states that at least on the four principal feasts of the year, 'on those days all may contemplate the king's joyous face'.[128] This leads us to associate the royal banquets in their periodic modality with the numerous Castilian texts of the thirteenth and fourteenth centuries earlier put together by Jole Ruggieri upon the theme of the 'happiness' of the court, the *gaudium*,[129] which here certainly appears associated with the distribution of food, as well as the contemplation of the monarch while he was eating. In the more or less abundant passages of the Portuguese and Castilian chronicles – think for instance of the banquets of King Pedro described by Fernão Lopes[130] – or in the famous verses of Ayala's *Rimado de Palacio* these ceremonies evidently do not appear reported in such detail. However, there are

126 'Ordenacions fetes per lo molt Alt Senyor', p. 170.

127 James G. Frazer, *The Golden Bough: A Study in Magic and Religion* (abridged edition) (London: Macmillan, 1933), p. 202. For an anthropological perspective, see also the observations made by Laura Makarius, 'Du roi magique au roi divin', *Annales ESC*, 35 (1970) 222–3 and 269. For an interpretation of the rituals of royal eating emphasising the eucharistic image, see Bertelli, *Il corpo del re*, pp. 164–85 and Sergio Bertelli, 'Il drama della monarchia medievale, ovvero: il pranzo del Signore', in Maria Grazia Profeti (ed.), *Codici del gusto* (Milan: Angeli, 1992), pp. 22–41.

128 'als dies aquestes la nostra cara alegra tots hagen facultat de guardar': 'Ordenacions fetes per lo molt Alt Senyor', p. 167.

129 Jole Scudieri Ruggieri, *Cavalleria e cortesia nella vita e nella cultura de Spagna* (Modena: Mucchi, 1980), pp. 38–40.

130 In particular *CR Pedro*, pp. 91 and 143–5.

the essential elements and even at times a clear understanding of the specificity of the royal position, as for example in Ayala:

> Los rreyes e los principes, maguer sean señores / asaz pasan en el mundo de cuitas e dolores; / sufren de cada dia, de todos sus seruidores, / que los ponen en enojo, fasta que vienen sudores . . . / Con el son al comer, todos al derredor / paresçe que alli tienen preso un malfechor / quien trae la vianda o el su tajador / por tal cabo alli llega que no puede peor. / Las gentes y son tantas que non puede allegar, / maguer un ballestero, dice: 'Fazed logar, / tiratuos e arredraduos, e gardatvos del manjar', / mas que una gran peña, non se quieren mudar. / Fisicos e capellanes a la su mesa son; / alli fazen sus sermones e disputan su quistion; / cada uno lo que sabe, ponelo por inquisiçion; / maguer fazen argumentos, ál tienen en coraçon. / El principe, por cierto, deue ser enojado, / que es de tantos ojos asi atormentado / que non puede a la boca, leuar solo un bocado / que de trezientos omnes, non le sea contado. / En muy muchas maneras anda asi perseguido; / el estado es grande, mas sienpre con gemido, / ca cuidado e enojo non le dexan el oluido / que plazer es el tal cuando bien me lo comido![131]

Several examples of the Portuguese 'convites' are found in Portuguese chronicles with mention of the particular arrangement of the spaces, as for example in Fernão Lopes: 'muitas mesas bem corregidas, e tres d'ellas eram principaaes, a d'el-rrei que era travessa e bem levantada como compria, e huua da parte dereita, e outra da parte sestra'.[132] In this chronicler's works we also find reference to a form of service known in Portugal as 'de talho e de copa', that is with the carver and *copeiro*.[133] The monarchs of the Aviz dynasty practised the highly interesting custom of allowing the members of the royal family to perform the main ritual roles at public banquets and other court meals which included the use, as the Infante Henry describes, of 'estrado e pano de estado'. For example, we know that in the sequence of his marriage to Leonor, his brothers served Duarte 'in the palace'; in the words of Henry, 'o Iffante dom Pedro leuaua o pano e eu o confeiteiro e o iffante dom fernando a fruita e o comde o vinho'.[134] Likewise, the ambassadors of Burgundy comment that at the banquet of the wedding of the Infanta Isabel in 1429 the king was served by the infante heir and 'by the other infante lords', which is a practice to which Duarte himself perhaps refers when saying of his father: 'todas cerimonias em seu serviço, por acreçentamento de sua honrra que lhe prazia de receber de nos, muy sem empacho eramos contentes de as fazer'. Later the knight Lalain, on a visit to

131 This poem was composed in the 1380s, apparently while Ayala was imprisoned in the Portuguese kingdom in Óbidos following the Castilian sacking of Aljubarrota. See Pero López de Ayala, *Rimado de Palacio*, ed. Germán Orduna (Pisa: Giardini, 1981), vol. I, pp. 225–7 (lines 477–85).

132 A description of the wedding meal of Beatriz in Badajoz in 1383: *CR Fernando*, p. 571.

133 *CR Fernando*, p. 546 and also *CR João*, vol. II, p. 206 (a 'convite' with the English), and also pp. 201, 209 and 213.

134 *MH*, vol. III, p. 258.

the Portuguese court in 1448, observes that at the solemn banquet which he attended the regent Pedro 'gave water into the hands' of the young King Afonso V.[135]

In these generic remarks in Portuguese sources, the banquet appears frequently to be followed by dancing, music, games or a tourney, leading us to understanding the inclusion of rite in a feast – a feast which could at times last several days, and of which there is just one more element which must be listed.[136] Its character of an extraordinary meal is well noted by the 'Ordenacions', which on this matter is close to other sources (from Castile, Portugal and Navarre): the king also ate without all this apparatus, and the 'tinell' or 'paço' was a meeting of a smaller number of invitees when desired by the monarch or established by custom. In the case of Prince John, the heir of Ferdinand and Isabella, a more restricted group of servants had a right to 'dos tablas al dia',[137] and this could also be the case in the Portuguese palace, in spite of the more usual recourse to the distribution of rations which each individual would eat or use as a form of transaction according to convenience. It must be stated, as already observed within the ambit of the papal curia and particularly in the cardinals' households, that the complexity in the establishment of precedence (as we have seen, this played a fundamental role in the distribution of food) would have been the determining factor in a growing recourse to rations. It must also be remembered that particularly on certain occasions such as royal marriages or inaugurations there would be 'convites' which were open to public participation and became similar to the *epulum* of the Romans.

Thus the distribution of food could be performed in an ordered manner proportional to the standing of each invitee, following the court hierarchical order. But when the feast was open to participation of the citizens, distribution was made indiscriminately as a sign of abundance and waste. That the first aspect had an immensely hierarchical significance is reported anecdotally in a celebrated episode in his chronicle in which Nuno Álvares Pereira, who was a 'criado' of Fernando and a member of his court, expressed his displeasure at seeing the position meant for him at a 'convite' given by the Castilian king already occupied, at which he overturned the table and left the

135 Joaquim de Vasconcelos (ed.), 'Voyage de Jehan Van-Eyck', *Revista de Guimarães*, 14 (1897), 22; M. Lopes de Almeida (ed.), *Obras dos príncipes de Avis* (Oporto: Lello), p. 430; Georges Chastellain, *Chronique de Jacques de Lalain*, ed. J. A. Buchon (Paris: Collection des Chroniques Nationales Françaises, 1825), p. 148.

136 The bibliography on these festivities is extensive today and I have limited myself to two more recent works on Castile, where the analysis of the ritual has a relevant place: Rosana Andrés Díaz, 'Las fiestas de caballería en la Castilla de los Trastámaras', in *En la España medieval: estudios en memoria de Claudio Sánchez Albornoz*, vol. I (Madrid, 1986), pp. 81–108; Teófilo Ruiz, 'Fiestas, torneos y símbolos de la realeza en la Castilla del siglo XV', pp. 249–65.

137 Gonzalo Fernández de Oviedo, *Libro de la Cámara Real del principe Don Juan e offiçios de su casa e serviçio ordinario* (Madrid: Sociedad de Bibliofilos Españoles, 1870), p. 94. On the court of Navarre, Zabalo Zabalegui, *La administración del Reino de Navarra*, pp. 70–1.

hall.[138] As for the second aspect, indiscriminate distribution could also be endowed with ritualistic aspects. The distribution of a particular type of food is related to these medieval royal banquets: oxen, which were roasted whole and for public consumption. The much-quoted passage of the chronicle of King Pedro reports this, when Fernão Lopes describes the distribution of 'whole cows' as the high point of the feasts of that reign. This tradition, which would appear to be of medieval origin, remained alive in Europe at least until the seventeenth century, as shown by the analysis of several iconographic representations made by Bertelli. According to this author, this included ritual foods which were intended to be pillaged by the crowd, in particular on occasions of imperial or royal inauguration, and this complemented the *congiarium* of bread and wine, which was a propitiatory rite of abundance. The oxen might be stuffed with other strange ingredients, in particular a variety of whole animals symbolically associated with royalty (cockerels, ravens, boars, etc.), with the heads protruding from the re-formed, cooked skin following a complex technique of cooking of the whole, also mentioned by some medieval documents. In his treatise, Enrique de Villena refers precisely to this practice, and explains that such meats were not very tasty, perhaps because they were covered, like the famous swans of the main courses of Burgundy,[139] with gold leaf:

> Suele fazer en reales conbites, que dan las terneras asadas enteras e los vientres plenos de capones e otras avez preçiadas, asadas o cochas, por magnifiçençia; e cosida ençima el logar por donde la pusieron. Estonçes ábrese por la costura e sacan las aves. E si quisieran pueden fazer pieças d'ella e cortarla, como dicho es, antes o despues de las aves, segun fuere plazible a los comedores. E si las dan doradas, non se comen sinon los tajos de la cabeça, de ojo, de lengua, de paladares e lo ál déxanlo por magnifiçençia.[140]

The insistence on royal 'magnificence' being shown by the distribution of this particular food, associating 'cocaigne' with the figure of the monarch, suggests that the actual choice of food had ritual aspects, as did its distribution and even the carving or dividing in parts, and that this also contributed to the distinctions which the Hispanic sources refer to between the court banquet or *convivium*, the public banquet and the ordinary meal – all, it should be emphasised, the object of ceremonial.

The monarchs' chamber is a world which unfortunately is not as well known regarding ceremonies as the royal hall. As I have said, the body of the king was its centre. The preservation, the communication with the exterior, the security, the bodily adornment of the monarch were all the final objective of the activities

[138] See chapter 14 of *Estoria de Nun'Alvrez Pereira*.

[139] See Agathe Lafortune-Martel, *Fête noble en Bourgogne au XVe siècle: le banquet du faisan (1454)* (Montreal: Bellarmin-Vrin, 1984).

[140] Villena, 'Arte Cisoria', p. 179.

of the officials who were members of the medieval chamber. Aragonese sources can on this matter be compared with the 'Livro de la Cámara Real' of Castile and the Portuguese *Livro Vermelho*, both of which describe practices from the second half of the fifteenth century. The most important of the ceremonies of the chamber appear to have taken place at the beginning and the end of the day. In the first sequence the *camareiro* performed the main role for the ritual handing over of garments which would be brought from the place where they were kept wrapped in material. The *camareiro* was the first to see the king in his shirt as soon as he had risen from his bed. When he was still barefoot other officials would make their entrance, among whom was the barber (who would shave his lord and do his hair), the shoemaker (who, at least in Castile, would put on the king's shoes), and the physicians, who would talk of the royal digestion and the mood of the monarch, and would carefully observe his urine. A table was available for a meal which took place in this same space or in an adjacent room.[141]

All the Iberian cases I have studied emphasise that these meals, which the king took 'in private', were the responsibility of the chamber officials, who were to prepare the table and serve the food. The same occurred in other medieval European kingdoms, particularly in England.[142] Besides this, the services of these officials were not limited in any way to the physical space of the royal chamber(s) – these continued in all those places where the king might be staying, including outside the palace, for example when hunting or at war. In the Portuguese case there are indications that these meals were occasions of great importance for those who were admitted to this site of special sociability. Fernão Lopes, for example, describes Leonor Teles receiving her 'privados' and her audacious lover in her chamber, where Andeiro would come to her in a familiar manner 'a par da cama honde a rainha estava aa mesa'.[143] Likewise, Rui de Pina states that the Infante Pedro was responsible for the practice of eating 'in public', which the earlier monarchs 'dantes nam faziam, ca pella moor parte sempre comiam retraydos', referring, I believe, only to the meals served in the chamber within this more restricted sphere, and not as has been literally interpreted at all royal meals, since the solemn banquets and 'convites' are confirmed as dating from earlier periods.[144] In the Portuguese context, there

[141] Oviedo, *Libro de la Cámara Real*, pp. 25–7.

[142] 'Whatever its origin, the custom of serving the king's meals in his chamber was clearly well established by Edward II's reign, for the Ordinance of 1318 begins its section on the chamber by describing the "escuier surueour et gardien dez viandez", the "escuier trenchant" and the "esquier pour luy seruire de sa coupe", and designates as a duty of one of the ushers of the chamber that "he shall count the portions of food in the chamber every day"': R. Firth Green, *Poets and Princepleasers*, pp. 35–6.

[143] *CR Fernando*, p. 510.

[144] It is only in this way that the statements of the chronicler can be understood when relating them to the 'ordinary' meals – 'dizendo elle que suas mesas deuyam ser escollas de sua Corte, pera que custumava mandar ler proveitosos lyvros, e ter praticas e disputa, de que so tomava muyto insyno e doutrina', *CR Afonso V*, p. 754. In the several material spaces of the palace mentioned

are also some later indications available on the practice for the queens to eat in their chambers, surrounded by ladies and unmarried girls, in particular for the Manueline period, in a manner entirely parallel to that seen for the kings.

As to ceremonies at the end of the day, these consisted in preparation of the bed and the locking with a key of the space where the king was.[145] The chamber implied a distinct space in all the royal resting places, as is proven in documents in the case of Afonso V.[146] The existence of the ceremonial space has a distant analogy, as we have seen, with the royal ritual of the Byzantine 'Kubukleion'. Alfonso X's *Espéculo* is quite clear on this matter:

> el rey deuen guardar quando yoguier, que ninguno non sse deue atreuer a echar con él en el lecho nin ssin él ssi non gelo mandare, nin assentarsse en su lecho. Otrossí tenemos por grant cosa e por muy grant osadía de ssaltar nin de pasar ssobre ssu lecho e mayormiente quando el rey y joguiesse, ca tenemos que esto es más atreuemiento. Otrossi tenemos que ninguno non deue tomar la rropa de su lecho para echarsse en ella ssi non gela él diere; quanto mas tomárgela de ssuso el rrey y jaziendo.[147]

The use of the two chambers, which was general in the Hispanic sphere in the fourteenth century, was clearly included in this group of proscriptions. In the 'robing chamber' (or, as the Portuguese *Livro Vermelho* calls it more precisely, the 'chamber of the bed of state'[148]) was a bed which remained permanently empty, for the king slept in his 'retrete' (the 'reecambra' of Aragon).[149] As we have seen, in the Portuguese palaces of Cintra and Almeirim there were several 'retretes'. In this actual meaning of retreat and space segregated for the individual use of the monarch, these could also be said to be the direct antecedents of the humanist *studiolo*. The use of separate beds and particularly of the so-called 'bed of state' as a mechanism of representation was also common to other medieval courts, as was shown for example by Paul Binski in the study he dedicated to the 'Painted Chamber' in Westminster, where the English monarchs made use of a bed of this type.[150]

The 'chamber bed of state' was ornately decorated, as required by the Aragonese 'Ordenacions' when mentioning the periodic replacement every

in the *Livro Vermelho* there is a 'casa para comer' next to the 'câmara de estado', in both of which the *porteiro da câmara* served.

145 In the Aragonese 'Ordenacions' one of two *camareiros* who had to sleep in the royal chamber that night had to guard the key carefully: 'Ordenacions fetes per lo molt Alt Senyor', p. 69. See also Oviedo, *Libro de la Cámara*, pp. 24–8 and *Livro Vermelho*, p. 443.

146 'oyto tendas . . . e hũa camara da nossa temda reall': *MH*, vol. XIII, p. 284.

147 G. Martinez Diez (ed.), *Leyes de Alfonso X*, vol. I, *Espéculo* (Avila: Fundación Sánchez-Albornoz, 1985), p. 126.

148 *Livro Vermelho*, p. 442.

149 Oviedo, *Libro de la Cámara*, pp. 53–6; *Livro Vermelho*, pp. 440–2 (where it is called the 'câmara secreta'); 'Ordenacions fetes per lo molt Alt Senyor', p. 69.

150 Paul Binski, *The Painted Chamber at Westminster* (London: Thomas and Hudson 1986), pp. 36–8. See also for the complex example of France: Elisabeth A. R. Brown and Richard C. Famiglietti, *The Lit de Justice: semantics, ceremonial, and the Parliament of Paris, 1300–1600* (Sigmaringen: Thorbecke, 1994), pp. 21–2.

four years of the rich cloths which covered it on which the king's arms were sumptuously represented.[151] In the curious description of the cover of the bed of the 'new chamber' of the Lisbon palaces in the time of Fernando, Fernão Lopes shows that he did not find this practice unusual:

> A cama era bem emparamentada, e a cubricama d'hũu tapete preto com duas grandes figuras de rrei e de rrainha na meatade, todas d'aljofar graado e meaão, segundo rrequeria honde era posto; a bordadura d'arredor era toda d'archetes d'aljofar, e dentro iguaaes feguras d'aljofar brolladas das linhagees de todollos fidallgos de Portugall, com suas armas acerca de ssi.

The ritual of the marriage of the Infanta Beatriz progressed in this setting, and the chronicler goes on to allude to a public act in the actual 'chamber of state'.[152] In his treatise on insignias and coats of arms, the jurist Bartolo de Sassoferrato describes this use, distinguishing between the most common objects bearing the arms (such as shields, horse blankets, standards, etc.) and the bed covers:

> sometimes coats of arms are depicted in bed covers and on similar objects. And in this case, the object on which the coat of arms is to be depicted should be viewed as others are expected to see it. Some parts of the covers lie flat on the bed, and some hang down from it. The part on the section lying flat follows the pattern of a person lying on the bed. On the section hanging down, the design of the coat of arms follows the pattern of a person standing up.[153]

Now, as I have already mentioned for other ceremonial contexts, the royal arms were emblematic elements of the greatest importance, and this leads to the hypothesis that the actual 'bed of state' had developed as a support of this emblem, which would help in an understanding of the system of proscriptions to which I have referred above in the text of the fourteenth-century *Espéculo*, distinguishing the king's bed as a reserved place, even though the monarch did not physically lie on it.

In Aragon, we know that it was in the space of the 'bed of state' that Pedro IV's council met during the day,[154] and in Portugal we know that all the councillors had free access to it.[155] At night, the bed in this chamber was carefully guarded, and in Portuguese sources there is also talk of permanent lighting.[156] The monarch lay in the second chamber, that of 'retrete', which was also closed and in front of which the guards and porters were to sleep[157] – in the curious

151 'Ordenacions fetes per lo molt Alt Senyor', p. 175.

152 *CR Fernando*, p. 460. This rite usually consisted in laying down the bride and groom, with the groom being represented by a proxy, making them cross a leg as a sign of acceptance and symbolic consummation of the marriage.

153 Osvaldo Cavallar *et al.* (eds.), *A Grammar of Signs: Bartolo of Sassoferrato's Tract on Insignia and Coats of Arms* (Berkeley: University of California Press, 1994), p. 120 (Latin text) and p. 156 (English translation which I quote).

154 'Ordenacions fetes per lo molt Alt Senyor', p. 187.

155 *Livro Vermelho*, p. 441.

156 'Ordenacions fetes per lo molt Alt Senyor', pp. 69–70 and *Livro Vermelho*, pp. 442–4.

157 *Livro dos Conselhos*, p. 172 and *Livro Vermelho*, pp. 440–3. In the sixteenth century, chapters of the Cortes refer to the tradition 'que durmão no Paço o Guardamoor, e assi os Moços do monte, como sempre se fez': Ribeiro, *Reflexões históricas*, vol. II, p. 95.

description of the rotation of the chamber guards of the Castilian prince ('prima, modorra, alva'), it is shown that the guards were provided with 'sus ampulletas o rrelox'.[158] In the chamber of the king of Navarre we also know of the presence of a clock in 1390,[159] and at the court of John there was among the residents a 'mestre do relógio' whose function would perhaps be, as at other contemporary courts, to carry and install the clock at each new stop made by the monarch.[160] In the case of Castile and Portugal, only the *camareiro* and the grooms had access to the 'secret' place, which was the chamber where the king slept. The lighting was permanent there too, and the bed where the monarch slept was surrounded by diverse objects. Note should be taken of the enumeration of the Castilian ceremonial, which evokes prescriptively the tranquil and devout nights of the royal infante: holy water, books, scissors, a mirror, water for washing, a bowl for eating, a brazier, a small table with stools, a chess set and writing paper. According to the Iberian sources, the monarch would have remained protected throughout the night, and nothing could be taken into the 'retrete' after his retiring.

This entire group of practices denotes the importance of the rules of proxemics which, as I have emphasised, more or less rigidly structured the organisation of the chamber, be this as to the organism of offices, or as to material space. The 'intimate distance' remained for the royal figure as a true taboo reserved to very few, and the secret chambers were a space where the modalities of 'personal distance' were preferentially organised. In turn, the robing chamber or the state chamber at the time appears invested with practices of interaction expressing 'social distance' and 'public distance'.[161] The control of gradual access to the person of the monarch, which had an extraordinary development in the modern age in royal ceremonies in Europe, determined the concrete solution of occupation and arrangement of the diverse residential spaces and also was

[158] Oviedo, *Libro de la Cámara*, pp. 128–9. We know from the *Livro Vermelho* merely that *porteiros* and *reposteiros* went out at night and would present themselves again the following morning. The guard of the royal body seems to be a very old ceremonial mechanism, and is for example prescribed in the *Libellus de Ceremoniis Aule Imperatoris* of Otto III (ninth century): 'Comes cesariani palatii, qui est supra comites, qui sunt in mundo, et cui palatii cura commissa est, habet sub se duos comites, comitem prime et comitem secunde cohortis. Prima cohors habet milites DLV, qui debent vigilare et custodire imperatorem usque ad mediam noctem. Secunda cohors similiter habet milites DLV, qui similiter vigilant et custodiant imperatorem usque ad diem': P. Schramm, *Kaiser, Rom und Renovatio* (Leipzig: Teubner 1929), vol. II, p. 90. I should like to thank Kate Lowe for helping me to access this text, which is hard to access in Portugal.

[159] Zabalegui, *La administración*, p. 84 and note 241b; see also Béatrice Leroy, 'La cour des rois Charles II et Charles III de Navarre (vers 1350–1425), lieu de rencontre, milieu de gouvernement', in Adeline Rucquoi (ed.), *Realidad e imágenes del poder: España a fines de la edad media* (Valladolid: Ambito, 1988), pp. 233–48.

[160] This is what occurred in Burgundy, where the master of the clock accompanied the 'fourrier': H. David, 'L'Hôtel ducal sous Philippe le Bon. Mœurs et coutumes. Les offices', *Annales de Bourgogne*, 37 (1965), 241–55. The master of the court of John I was perhaps English, as his name, Colim, would seem to indicate: *MH*, vol. I, p. 287.

[161] Edward T. Hall, *The Hidden Dimension* (New York: Doubleday, 1966).

reflected in these rites which, from the Middle Ages, involved the monarch in a human circle which protected him and at the same time distanced him from the common man. Rui de Pina therefore comments regarding the thwarted attempts by Afonso V to travel in France 'incognito' as we would say today: 'porque ElRey por desymullaçam daquelle apartamento, *por não ser por caminhos em alguma deferença conhecido*, nom comia nem dormia apartado, mas com todos familiarmente'.[162]

Some much fragmented indications in the Hispanic contexts inform us of the possibility of other periodic practices connected to the world of the chamber, such as those surrounding the king for his bath, prescribed for certain moments of the year, or the mention of the ritual of the washing of the feet of the poor, which also was performed at the Aragonese chamber and in Castile, although the ceremony has not yet been confirmed at the Portuguese court. In the Aragonese case it is necessary to relate this practice to other moments of contact of the king with the poor, for example their presence at an annual 'convite', and the fact that the king served them water for washing, or the fact of the poor having the right to the leftovers of the royal food. The washing of the feet took place on Maundy Thursday both in Aragon and in the chamber of Isabel of Castile, and there are other examples beyond the Iberian Peninsula, the most famous of which is that of Louis IX of France washing the feet of the poor in his 'garderobe'.[163] The monarch's bath as a ceremony, which developed within the sphere of the chamber, is also a little-known practice. We know from Castilian references that there were common ablutions as well as the bath on important feast days, whose water was the subject of particular care, relating it in my opinion to the equal attention given to other organic waste such as hair and nails, which could be a source of danger according to magical beliefs of the time.[164] Not to be forgotten is the lively Hispanic dissemination of the curious medieval legend on the bathing of the emperor Theoderic as the cause of his madness and the disorder in the kingdom, a theme which Joaquim de Vasconcelos identified particularly clearly on a Portuguese court salver and which appears to point

162 *CR Afonso V*, p. 863.

163 A. de la Torre (ed.), *Cuentas de Gonzalo de Baena, tesorero de Isabel la Católica*, 2 vols. (Madrid: CSIC, 1955–56), vol. II (Año 1494), and Georges Duby (ed.), *Histoire de la vie privée*, vol. II, *De l'Europe féodale à la Renaissance* (Paris: Seuil, 1985), p. 417. See for the case of St Louis, as stated by Jacques Le Goff, *Saint-Louis* (Paris: Gallimard, 1996), pp. 628–9 and fig. 8 which, 'according to tradition, shows the head of St Louis washing the feet of the poor in a fresco in Sainte Chapelle'.

164 Mercedes Gaibros de Ballesteros (ed.), 'Libro de diferentes cuentas de Don Sancho IV (1293–1294)', in *Historia del reinado de Sancho IV de Castilla*, vol. I (Madrid: Tip. Archivos Bibliotecas y Museos, 1922), pp. cv, cxxii, cxxiv and cxxviii. The English *Constitutio Domus Regis* established that the servant named *Aquarius* should receive the extra sum of four pence each time that the king bathed, with the exception of the 'important feasts of the year', which were times when he usually served: Richard Fitz Nagel, *Dialogus de Scaccario: Constitutio Domus Regis*, ed. Charles Johnson *et al.* (Oxford: Clarendon Press, 1983), pp. 129–35.

towards an anxious perception of those moments of royal daily life, as shown in the investigations by François Delpech.[165]

I must bring to an end this examination of the cyclical aspect of the ceremonial with the chapel, which as I have analysed earlier formed the ecclesiastical organism *par excellence* of the court and also the place where the rites of the Christian faith took place. If we look at the triple aspect referred to by Fleckenstein, that is if we consider the chapel as a group of relics and sacred objects, as a group of ecclesiastical servants of the kings and as a material space, we have to recognise that the medieval royal chapels have been studied with a clear predominance being given to the two last vertents, in particular from the point of view of the history of music and of architecture. The relics were a no less important aspect, although they are still very little studied in the Iberian chapels, which must be related to the actual genesis of this organism and even with certain developments of their ceremonial. According to Van den Bosch, in their first appearance the palatine chapels of the eighth century appear early on to have been treasuries of sacred objects, and it was only later that they became sites of religious practice.[166] This aspect also influenced the ceremonial and religious functions of the royal chapels[167] which, as we have seen, were an expression of the freedom of the monarchs in relation to the usual structures of inclusion of believers constructed by the medieval church. Although, as I have already observed, it was opposed to an overliteral interpretation of the sacerdotal image associated with imperial traditions or with certain rites such as the anointment or consecration of the kings, the ecclesiastical institution contributed powerfully to the construction, through this mechanism, of a unique pre-eminence of the royal figure. Analogous problems had already occurred in the Byzantine Church in its relationship with the emperor. But in this case, as Dvornik explained,

> it would be wrong to explain the actual functions [of Emperors in liturgy] by comparing them with those of the deacon and the defensor – deputatus – two minor degrees in the Byzantine system of clerical orders . . . these duties bore no relation to the dignity which the Church intended to bestow on the emperors, who were more than defensors or deacons, even more than bishops and patriarchs: the emperors stood above the hierarchy and outside the

165 On the legend, François Delpech, 'Un souverain, un ange et quelques folies: avatars d'un exemplum médiéval', in Augustin Redondo and André Rochon (eds.), *Visages de la folie (1500–1650)* (Paris: Pub. de la Sorbonne, 1981), pp. 55–65. See also Joaquim de Vasconcelos, *A Ourivesaria Portuguesa* (n.p. [1882]), pp. 60–2 (salver of the collection of the imperial treasury of Vienna).

166 J. van den Bosch, *Basilica, monasterium et le culte de Saint Martin de Tours: étude lexicologique et sémasiologique* (Utrecht: Dekker and Van de Vegt, 1959), pp. 35–50.

167 See for the specific case of France and the role played there by the diffusion of the relics of St Louis, Claudine Billot, *Les Saintes Chapelles royales et princières* (Paris: Editions du Patrimoine, 1998).

ecclesiastical circle as the representatives of God on earth and the leaders of their people to God. Such eminence made them indifferent to the prerogatives of priests or bishops.[168]

The actual responses found at the time were, naturally, different from those of the Roman Church, both from the liturgical point of view and from the ceremonial, but the problem of the presence of the sovereign at religious moments could be said to be common.[169] When Charlemagne built his chapel in Aachen in about 798, with the marble plaques and columns which he had brought from Rome and Ravenna, he demonstrated with this initiative an equal reminiscence both of imperial Byzantine grandeur and of the magnificence of the Eternal City.[170] The construction of their own chapels subsequently became for the medieval monarchs a visible sign of their standing, granting them interesting opportunities for reaffirmation of the dignity of their own function through their association with the religious faith, made possible even by the simple fact of their permanently having to hand members of the clergy in their service. As a specific place or space the chapels of the Low Middle Ages were precisely the principal seat of religious cult in the royal palaces, although one must also note the mentions of profane use of these spaces, as well as the performance of liturgical acts outside them. Just like the servants of the *câmara*, the chaplains of the Low Middle Ages could, for example, celebrate masses in other places in the palaces, using portable altars and, when accompanying the monarchs during their removals, performing religious acts and royal ceremonies in other sacred places, as I have shown above for the baptism of the kings.

In order to analyse the ceremonial activity of the medieval chapels it is fundamental to take note of the specific liturgy performed there.[171] The organisation of times and spaces of the religious faith formed an indispensable ritual setting at the interior of which the monarchs acted directly either through the selection of determined uses to the detriment of others or through the adoption of practices or ceremonies which did not form a part of the actual liturgical repertory in its common acceptance, but that the kings ordered to be performed by their chaplains. In the area of ceremonies related to the chapel, the practices common to the several Iberian courts are more difficult to detect, merely because each royal chapel had its own liturgical uses. The Cistercian uses appear to

168 Francis Dvornick, *Early Christian and Byzantine Political Philosophy* (Washington, DC: Dumbarton Oaks Centre for Byzantine Studies), vol. II, pp. 645–6.

169 On the principal moments of participation of the Byzantine emperors in the religious liturgy, see the description by Otto Treitinger, *Die Oströmische Kaiser- und Reichsidee nach ihrer Gestaltung im höfischen Zeremoniell* (Darmstadt: Geutner, 1956), pp. 136–57 and in particular pp. 145–57 for a comparison with the west.

170 W. Eugene Kleinbauer, 'Charlemagne's Palace Chapel at Aachen and its copies', *Gesta*, 4 (1965), 2–11.

171 Massimo Miglio, 'Liturgia e cerimoniale di corte', in Giovanni Morello and Silva Maddalo (eds.), *Liturgia in figura: Codici Liturgici Rinascimentali della Biblioteca Apostolica Vaticana* (Rome: Biblioteca Apostolica Vaticana/Edizioni De Luca, 1995), pp. 43–50.

have been adopted in the royal chapel from the thirteenth century in the case of Aragon where, as we have seen, the abbot of Santa Creus was the principal chaplain. The fact that the archbishop of Santiago de Compostela was also from the twelfth century the head of the royal chapel in Leon (which is also to be found following the union with Castile) appears to indicate that the uses of the Compostela church appear to have prevailed. However, the initiatives taken by Isabel the Catholic towards regularising the activities of the Castilian chapel allow us to establish that both the Roman and the Toledan rites were performed.[172] In Portugal it is also shown that the Roman use was practised in the royal chapel, with a later adoption of the customs of Salisbury during the fifteenth century.[173] In the final period of the Middle Ages the influence of the Aragonese rulings seems to have been important, particularly in the customs of the other Iberian courts concerning the importance given to certain celebrations in the liturgical calendar and the decoration of the respective chapels, and there are the several fifteenth-century manuscript copies of Pedro IV's 'Ordenacions' circulating in the Iberian Peninsula which contained only the section relating to the chapel. Also decisive was the granting of every form of papal dispensation and authorisation to which I have already referred in the Portuguese case which demonstrated yet another area of emulation for the Iberian courts, as has been made abundantly clear in correspondence of the agents of the monarchs at the curia.[174] From the organisational point of view the fifteenth-century period was characterised by a regulating force and by an entirely parallel institutionalisation, in particular in the Portuguese and Castilian cases. While, as we have seen, the Portuguese court obtained a description and directive from the English royal chapel, John II of Castile also had produced a directive in 1436 for the service of his chaplains which specified their obligations and the internal hierarchy, and allowed for the reconstruction of certain aspects of the ceremonial.[175]

In the Portuguese case, the register made by Duarte of the activities of the chapel which he attended, as well as the investigations made by Solange Corbin into some aspects of the liturgy practised there, allows us to examine carefully

[172] Tess Knighton, 'Ritual and regulations: the organization of the Castilian royal chapel during the reign of the Catholic Monarchs', in *De Musica Hispana et Aliis: miscelánea en honor al Prof. Dr José López-Calo, S. J.* (Santiago de Compostela: University of Santiago de Compostela, 1990), vol. I, p. 310. See also the observations of Rafael Domínguez Casas, *Arte y etiqueta de los Reyes Católicos: artistas, residencias, jardines y bosques* (Madrid: Alpuerto, 1993), pp. 213–23.

[173] Fortunato de Almeida, *História da igreja em Portugal*, vol. I (revised edition, Oporto: Portucalense, 1967), pp. 252 and 471 and most of all Mário Martins, *Estudos de cultura medieval* (Lisbon: Brotéria, 1983), vol. III, pp. 237–52.

[174] A well-documented aspect in the collection of charters preserved by Abbot D. Gomes de Florença and now in the Biblioteca Laurenziana (Ash, 1762 (1716)), vol. I.

[175] José Manuel Nieto Soria, 'La capilla real Castellano-Leonesa en el siglo XV: constituciones, nombramientos y quitaciones', *Archivos Leoneses*, 43 (1989), 31–44 (edition of the text).

certain moments of the temporal calendar such as the four feast days mentioned above with regard to the royal 'convites', and also in a particular manner the feasts of the Easter cycle. Duarte mentioned the following succession of the temporal feasts as moments of participation which for him were fundamental: Christmas, the Purification of the Virgin and the Easter cycle. In this cycle were included Ash Wednesday, mass to Mary on the following Saturday, mass 'de quatro têmporas', Palm Sunday, the Wednesday offices (first, second and third matins), Maundy Thursday and Good Friday 'das Endoenças', all ending on Holy Saturday. Besides these, the eve of Pentecost was to be celebrated in the royal chapel in the presence of the king, while for the remainder of the religious calendar the king only mentions the feast of St Peter, the Assumption and All Saints.[176] This somewhat austere liturgical picture is organised with particular importance being given to the royalty of Christ, for the purification itself, as Kantorowicz says, is associated with the theme of the *saeculum novum* begun by the divine child at his meeting with the old Simeon.[177] Finally, among the high moments of the calendar suggested by Duarte in the 1430s must be emphasised the anniversaries or 'saimentos', in particular commemorating the death of Philippa and John I relating to Duarte's concerns and analysed above, which his successor Afonso V was also to respect. As Mário Martins observed, Duarte effectively added to his Book of Hours two prayers for the souls of his ancestors.[178]

The Portuguese monarch played a part in the religious faith in a variety of ways on these liturgical occasions. One of the modes of participation consisted in the symbolic oblations at the offertory during mass. The regulation of the offering in its connection to the liturgical feasts is particularly interesting: thus, in Portugal as in Navarre the king would offer at Christmas and Epiphany a number of coins equal to the number of years of his reign, so emphasising the relationship between Christ's birth and his own ascent to the throne.[179] Epiphany was a relatively recent feast, introduced only in the ninth century, which throughout the medieval period was increasingly associated with images of royalty. However, the practice of commemorating the *natales* of the sovereign is already to be found in the 'Gothic Breviary', one of the final western testimonies identified for a practice which would tend to disappear in the Latin west.[180] As Jean Leclercq studied, however, the actual image of Christ took on the characteristics of royalty, and this concomitant process was to contribute strongly towards a mutual reinforcement of this association between the

176 *Livro dos Conselhos*, pp. 215–17.
177 Kantorowicz, 'Puer Exoriens', in *Selected Studies*, pp. 25–36.
178 Martins, *Estudos de cultura medieval*, vol. I, pp. 173–9.
179 *Livro dos Conselhos*, p. 219. Zabalegui, *La administración*, p. 78.
180 Kantorowicz, 'The "King's Advent" and the enigmatic panels in the doors of Santa Sabina', in *Selected Studies*, pp. 37–75, in particular p. 67.

monarchs and the liturgical theme of Epiphany.[181] According to the testimony of the Portuguese infante, Pedro, the feasts of the cycle of the 'naçença do Cristo Jesus' were particularly adapted to the exercise of royal generosity, shown by 'dando e recebendo cousas de proveito pequeno e muito praziveis aos que dellas usam em o mes de Ianeyro'.[182]

Other participation by the monarchs in the chapel liturgy took place in particular during the high moment of the Easter cycle of which echoes were to be found at several levels of court life. According to his own testimony, the Portuguese king attended the curious ceremony of the committal of Christ and his 'encerramento' or 'interment' which took place in the chapel in the symbolic form of a host which remained concealed in a 'moimento' (funeral casket) from Good Friday until the office of the Resurrection. As Solange Corbin has explained, both the Peninsular rite and the Roman rite had early on not allowed any liturgy on Good Friday, and the Roman Church proposed that no consecrated host should be kept in the church between Good Friday and Easter Sunday.[183] This fifteenth-century practice, which, it should be emphasised, was not a part of the actual Roman liturgy, was entirely foreign to local Iberian tradition and must have contrasted with the other Peninsular chapels, in particular with the Aragonese practice which was influenced by the Cistercian simplicity. The adoption of this extra-liturgical rite allowed, however, for the creation of a ritual occasion related to the final moment of the Christian religious calendar in the royal chapel's own space-time in which the monarch also took part. This is a practice known in several regions of northern Europe (from France and England to Poland and Hungary) and also in Italy, in particular in Parma, and was celebrated in several dioceses connected to the Salisbury practice which, as I have said, would have been introduced to the Portuguese royal chapel with the new dynasty of Aviz. The ritual sequence is relatively well studied thanks to its links with the development of the liturgical theatre, and forms three distinct moments: the *depositio* or interment on Good Friday, the *elevatio* on Easter morning and finally the celebrated sequence of the *visitatio sepulchri*. Several types of material structure were used for this symbolic 'sepulchre', in particular: the altar itself, a small receptacle or casket surrounded by curtains or covered in veils and placed on an altar, a wooden, fixed structure made specially (which at times was octagonal or round, in imitation of the sepulchre in Jerusalem), placed in the church and, especially in England, a device much like a cenotaph

181 Jean Leclercq, *L'Idée de la royauté du Christ au moyen âge* (Paris: Ed. du Cerf, 1959). See also Jean-Marie Privat, 'Rois mages, images des rois (matériaux pour une recherche)', in Jean Dufournet *et al.* (eds.), *Le Pouvoir monarchique et ses supports idéologiques aux XIVe–XVIIe siècles* (Paris: Sorbonne Nouvelle, 1990), pp. 213–31.

182 *Virtuosa Benfeitoria*, p. 559.

183 Solange Corbin, *La Déposition liturgique du Christ au Vendredi Saint, sa place dans l'histoire des rites et du théâtre religieux (analyse de documents portugais)* (Paris: Les Belles Lettres, 1960).

or funeral 'essa' (called a hearse or coffin), also constructed for the purpose, which would be taken down before Easter mass. There were also times when only the host was 'interred', sometimes just a cross, and others when it was both the host and the cross.[184]

What is certain is that in Castile, following this introduction to the Portuguese chapel, in 1486 the monarchs asked for papal authority to install a 'monument' during Holy Week in their chapel, which attests to the Iberian spread of this ceremony that came from the north and that until then was, it would seem, only practised by the Portuguese kings.[185] The success of this particularly expressive liturgy was later demonstrated by its adoption in dioceses and monastic communities throughout the Portuguese kingdom, in particular in the modern age, and this success owed much, according to Solange Corbin, to its association with other practices leading to the particularly expressive or para-theatrical developments such as the laments (*planctus*) and the slow procession accompanying them.[186] These developments, it would seem, did not take place in the royal chapel as far as can be judged from Duarte's text, although this practice may have given way to signs of devotion in the royal family in the fifteenth century. Thus the Infante Fernando, the youngest brother of the monarch, with whom he was 'criado', according to his biography practised a personal vigil of the sacrament until Easter Day, a statement which may have been the source of other aspects of the ceremonial of the Portuguese royal chapel for the modern age.[187] There is naturally a relationship between the development of this type of rite and the complex of the feast of Corpus Christi, in particular in the elaboration of processions and moments of exposition of the sacrament, following on from visits to the interior of the church towards the 'sepulchre' on Good Friday and from there on Easter Day. It should be noted that the Portuguese practices of the royal chapel, however, seem to grant greatest importance and development to the initial moment of this sequence, that of the *depositio* or 'interment', and not, as was done in other geographical or chronological contexts, to the host (*elevatio*) or the famous 'visitation of the sepulchre', so emphasising the sad moment and death lament which the king attended (Fig. 11).

[184] Neil C. Brooks, *The Sepulchre of Christ in Art and Liturgy* (Urbana: University of Illinois Press, 1921), pp. 30–6 and 73.

[185] Domínguez Casas, *Arte y etiqueta de los Reyes Católicos*, p. 214.

[186] Corbin, *La Déposition liturgique*, in particular pp. 136–52. In parallel, 'popular' forms developed, influenced by this ceremony: the so-called processions 'do Enterro'.

[187] Corbin, *La Déposition liturgique*, p. 135 (where it refers to the Chronicle of Fr. João Álvares). In a later period, according to a manuscript containing uses in the Portuguese court later than the sixteenth century, it says, 'os tres dias que o Santissimo Sacramento estava dezemsserado athe dia de Paschoa Dormião os Reis deste Reino junto do altar sem se despirem e jejuavão estes tres dias a pão, e agua, e na manhãa da Paschoa mandavão fazer huma solemne procissão': BNL, Reservados, Cod. 4426, f. 29v. At the present stage of my research I have not succeeded in determining whether this later practice resulted from the influence of the biography of the 'Infante Santo' which was printed in the seventeenth century, or whether it was already the practice of the fifteenth-century monarchs.

Fig. 11 Miniature of the office of the dead, Book of Hours of King Duarte, fol 323 v. (Arquivo Nacional da Torre do Tombo, Lisbon)

The information from Duarte allows us to reconstruct the essence of the royal calendar, but other indications for the fifteenth-century period also point towards the importance of the daily office. As to daily mass, of which the chroniclers of the period so frequently make mention regarding the royal figure, the Portuguese monarchs attended mass from the interior of a movable structure especially constructed in the space of the chapel which was entirely similar to the Aragonese 'oratori' and which was also known as 'cortina' both in Castile and in Portugal.[188] The use of 'cortinas' for the kings and princes in the chapels was common at the end of the Middle Ages and can be included above all in an older tradition of reserving certain spaces within the churches for the use of the monarchs. Once again we should turn to the example of Santa Sophia, where the emperors made use of a space called the *metatorion* or oratory, which they used during the liturgical service.[189] In the chapel at Aachen, according to Kleinbauer, 'the marble throne of Charlemagne still stands in his loge, but has been much restored. From it the emperor had a direct line of vision to the altars installed below at the eastern periphery of the center space and across this space to the apse of the gallery as well as to the mosaic of the cupola above.'[190] This spatial characteristic was repeated with the Iberian use of the 'cortina' in the three cases mentioned of Aragon, Portugal and Castile – but also in the case of the tribunes used by the English monarchs, for example, which Colvin mentions existed in their principal residences, or in the 'cortina' which is magnificently shown in the Burgundian miniature of the 'Traité de l'Oraison Dominicale' in which one can see Philip the Good (1419–67) reciting the Lord's Prayer in this device, which a servant is removing so that the prince might be seen.[191] In the royal chapel of the French castle of Vincennes, near Paris, Charles V had two beautiful oratories built on each side for the monarch and the queen, which were hidden within the thickness of the walls and allowed them the same position in

188 For a description of the Aragonese 'oratori': 'Ordenacions fetes per lo molt Alt Senyor', p. 97. For the Portuguese chapel, *Livro dos Conselhos*, pp. 209–14 and *Livro Vermelho*, pp. 420–2. The latter contains the illustration shown in my Fig. 12 from the manuscript kept in Coimbra. This leads to a correction to John Adamson's error when he states that this Portuguese use is found 'by the eighteenth century at the latest, and probably long before': *The Princely Courts of Europe: Ritual, Politics and Culture under the Ancien Régime. 1500–1750* (London: Weidenfeld and Nicolson, 1999), p. 29. As can easily be found when consulting a chronology of the Portuguese kings, Afonso V reigned in the fifteenth century, and the cited source is an eighteenth-century edition of a sixteenth-century manuscript copy of this fifteenth-century source, as explained by its editor. This source tells us nothing on the uses of the chapel of the eighteenth century.

189 See the recent contribution by Catherine Jolivet-Lévy, 'Présence et figures du souverain à Sainte-Sophie de Constantinople et à l'église de la Sainte-Croix de Aghtamar', in Maguire (ed.), *Byzantine Court Culture from 829 to 1024*, pp. 231 and 233.

190 'Charlemagne's Palace Chapel', p. 2.

191 Brussels, Royal Library, MS 9092, f. 9r. I should like to thank the Brussels library for having allowed me to make a reproduction of this miniature, which I showed at a public lecture on the Portuguese royal chapel.

relation to the altar, while in the famous example of the Sainte Chapelle in the palace of Paris the monarch had direct access to the 'high chapel' where the service was performed.[192]

The contemporary interpretation of this device is explained by the Alfonsine *Espéculo*, where it states: 'non deue ninguno estar en la iglesia ant él [rey], entrél e el abad, quando estubieren por oyr las oras ssinon fueren aquéllos que las an de dezir'.[193] In this case the rite imposed a spatial hierarchical imperative which, in some way, was inherent to the actual genesis of the chapel space, as shown by the Aachen prototype, particularly if we consider, following the important observations made by David Parkin, that ritual often implies a 'formulaic spatiality' which frequently does not need words.[194] As we have seen, principles of orientation and spatial direction were also observed at royal banquets and could be related to the entire complex linked to the visible manifestation of the royal presence. It is important to say that the use of other reserved spaces such as the high choir or the tribune was not unknown in the Hispanic courts and, as we have seen, particularly at the Portuguese court, and we can find this in several chapels or churches connected to royal residences of the period, such as at Cintra, Óbidos and Santarém. However, in the fifteenth century the 'cortina' was much in use in several European courts. As a device of visibility it allowed, in fact, a multiplicity of uses, in particular the inclusion or display of the royal figure in certain liturgical sequences or at other para-liturgical or even profane ceremonies.[195]

For a better understanding of this multiplicity of uses it is important to say that, as has been seen in the specific case of the 'sepulchre' of Holy Week, there were several 'cortinas' in the churches, and these sequences of concealment and display were particularly familiar to the experience of the medieval religious faith.[196] In this way the particular standing of the monarch was emphasised,

192 Billot, *Les Saintes Chapelles royales et princières.*

193 *Leyes de Alfonso X*, vol. I, *Espéculo*, p. 125.

194 'Ritual is formulaic spatiality carried out by groups of people who are conscious of its imperative or compulsory nature and who may or may not further inform this spatiality with spoken words': David Parkin, 'Ritual as spatial direction and bodily division', in David Coppet (ed.), *Understanding Rituals* (London: Routledge, 1992), p. 18.

195 On the importance of the rituals of 'visible manifestation' of the sovereigns in the medieval Islamic context, see the important research by Jocelyne Dakhlia, *Le Divan des rois, le politique et le religieux dans l'Islam* (Paris: Aubier, 1998). This comparison is particularly relevant for the Iberian societies. Ibn Khaldun says, for example, that among the insignias of power is the 'prayer enclosure' (maqsûrah) in the mosque, a space reserved for the sovereign, and which the Nasrids of Granada would also have used.

196 It is always instructive, on this matter, to read the descriptions of church ornaments by Guillaume Durand, the author of the most important and influential commentary and liturgical essay on the Low Middle Ages: Charles Barthélemy (ed.), *Rationale Divinorum Officiorum* (Paris: Louis Vivès, 1854), 5 vols., in particular vol. I, pp. 41–66. The suggestion of a 'eucharistic prince' put forward by Adamson (*The Princely Courts*, esp. p. 29) appears to be an oversimplification. The monarch was not the object of religious cult in the chapel, although at times he

for he claimed to be a quasi-cleric because of his own spatial positioning in the chapel, making him distinctly and hierarchically superior to the other laity, who touched the book prior to the reading of the Bible, when the *pax* (in the form of a kiss) was given in the 'cortina' at the same time as the ritual kiss between the celebrant and the dean of the chapel.[197] In his *Livro da Montaria* the Portuguese king, John I, demonstrated his understanding of these rites, explaining why a lie cannot enter the king's mouth: 'ca por esto lhe dam a beijar o euangelho, quando ouue a missa, como em juramento, que porque o euangelho he uerdade, que a boca que em elle poem sempre diga verdade'.[198]

More precise as to the use of this device, the Portuguese ceremonial recorded in the *Livro Vermelho* explains to us that the 'cortina' remained closed for the greater part during the offices, although the king could show himself from it to the ambassadors and the court, whose benches are shown turning not towards the altar but towards the royal 'cortina' (Fig. 12).[199] The extra-liturgical use of the 'cortina' is no surprise, given that the chapel was, in the fullest sense, a royal ceremonial space. Recent studies on the uses of the palace chapel in Palermo, for example, state that in the twelfth century it was common, in the Mediterranean environment, also to use this space for receptions, when the monarchs used a raised tribune for liturgical occasions while a throne was placed on the platform of the nave for solemn receptions.[200] This opening of the 'cortina' for the ambassadors in the Portuguese instance can be compared from the ritual point of view with certain Byzantine practices such as the *prokypsis*, as suggested by Kantorowicz, which made the chapel a central place of revelation of the particular nature of the royal person.[201] In such a case this was a wooden tribune surrounded by gold cloths, inside which the emperor showed himself at certain feasts such as Christmas and Epiphany, when he entered it through a side opening and would then have the curtain opened, making an 'epiphanic' appearance which would lead to eulogistic acclamation from the court poets.[202]

was treated as a saint: Andrew Hughes, 'The monarch as the object of liturgical veneration', in Duggan (ed.), *Kings and Kingship in Medieval Europe*, pp. 375–424.

197 On the meaning of this rite: John Bossy, 'The Mass as a social institution, 1200–1700', *Past and Present*, 100 (1983), 52 and 56.

198 *Obras dos Príncipes de Avis*, p. 30; Bertelli, *Il corpo del re*, pp. 130–1.

199 Only the monarch had the seat or 'throne', as was the case in the papal chapel, where it was only the pontiff who did not use the benches. On this hierarchy of seats in Portugal: Paul Teyssier, 'Estrados e cadeiras: estudo de alguns objectos culturais em Gil Vicente e na escola vicentina', in *Studies in Portuguese Literature and History in Honour of Luis de Sousa Rebelo* (London: Thamesis Books, 1992), pp. 63–71.

200 William Tronzo, 'Byzantine court culture from the point of view of Norman Sicily: the case of the Cappella Palatina in Palermo', in Maguire (ed.), *Byzantine Court Culture from 829 to 1204*, pp. 101–14.

201 I should like to thank Sergio Bertelli for having suggested this comparison to me. See also Bertelli, *Il corpo del re*, pp. 130–1.

202 Kantorowicz, 'Dante's "two suns"', in *Selected Studies*, pp. 325–38.

Fig. 12 The royal chapel with the king's curtain in the fifteenth century, *Livro Vermelho de D. Afonso V*, f. 35 (Biblioteca Geral da Universidade de Coimbra)

To return to the Portuguese royal chapel, I should emphasise that although important lords such as the Infante Pedro, or during John's reign the Duke of Viseu, used the 'cortina' in their chapels, there is no evidence of the performance of any ritual of recognition or of their participation on liturgical occasions.[203] An analysis of the ceremonial cycle drawn from this within the actual liturgical cycle seems to indicate the importance of the contested affirmation of the sacerdotal image of royalty, if we study the use of the 'cortina' at given moments of the sequence of preparation of mass (the reading) or communion (the kiss of peace, the ablution). As Marc Bloch reminds us regarding communion in two kinds by the French kings, 'it is obvious that the assimilation between royalty and priesthood was never complete, because it never could be. Yet this did not prevent a considerable approximation between the two'.[204] The chapel was, without doubt, the court organ where this constant tension between the Christian faith and the *religio regis* made itself felt in a more visible form, with the formation of an essential ambiguity of their relationships through the rite. However, on the other hand the chapel ceremonies are also seen as profane or para-liturgical ritual moments taking place alongside the specific spatial-temporal picture of the religious rite relating to it in a different and more direct way than the other court ceremonial occasions such as the 'convite' did. It is in the light of these problems, more than of a simple desire to 'privatise' the faith, that it is necessary to analyse more deeply the ceremonial practices in this important organ of the court.

OCCASIONAL RITES

The group of ceremonies which, in its customary periodicity, was constructing the life of the court, and of royalty itself, can be distinguished, as I have suggested above, from various rites in which the court eventually became involved and which were focused upon the figure of the monarch, but whose performance had no determined times. To these, which we call occasional rites, enormous importance was also given at the time, forming in the optic of the construction of the times of the court true 'movable', though frequent, occasions in the royal calendar which were marked by court ceremonial activity and by the change in the common order of the days. These were no less important than

[203] On the use of the 'cortina' by the Duke of Coimbra: Cruz, *Santa Cruz de Coimbra*, p. 322. On the Duke of Viseu's 'cortina' see the letter of protest from João II, which shows eloquently the importance the kings gave to the use of the 'cortina' by the nobles and how they jealously guarded their prerogatives: *Livro de Apontamentos*, pp. 263–5. The same occurred in other non-Peninsular kingdoms, as analysed by Françoise Robin, 'Les chapelles seigneuriales et royales françaises au temps de Louis XI', in *La France de la fin du XVe siècle: renouveau et apogée* (Paris: CNRS, 1985), pp. 237–52.

[204] Bloch, *Les Rois thaumaturges*, p. 207.

periodical rites, and maintained with these a relationship which is not always easy to explain. Thus, for example, meetings of the Cortes (parliaments) in the Portuguese kingdom, while they did not have a fixed periodicity, occurred during the final stages of the Middle Ages with particular intensity, and sometimes coincided with the inauguration of the monarchs. Here too there is no lack of indications as to the wealth of the Hispanic context, particularly surrounding the two ceremonies which I shall deal with in more detail: the royal entries and the performance of the Cortes (*parlamentos*).

The entries were traditional ceremonies of the Hispanic royalty which are found from the earliest times, since many of their forms appear in the period of the Visigoths.[205] Like the old *adventus*, the medieval entry comprised a ritual sequence in three parts, developing in particular during the Low Middle Ages as a ceremony related to the itinerance of the kings. It had three main elements. The first rite, the *occursus*, included the reception by the city of the royal persons following a graduated process: the further away the greater the dignity. Significantly, in Castile and in Portugal there is frequent mention of the reception two leagues from the place (a limit which, as already seen, holds great importance in the court spatial system), and it could be considered that a lesser distance would mean the coincidence or spatial indistinction between the court and the community being visited. The second rite was the entering of the battlements, usually through the main gate. On the occasion of a triumphant 'taking power' of a conquered city, as analysed by Bertelli, this entrance could be marked by the ritual pulling down of a fragment of the wall, which is a practice that can be confirmed for the Aragonese monarch of the fifteenth century. This crossing of the gate or of the wall might or might not be marked by particular acts related to obedience due to the monarchs (speeches, gifts). Finally there was the glorious progress, usually leading to the royal residence, with the final visit to one or several churches within the city.[206]

As is well known, the medieval royal entry above all increased this essential sequence of rites with the entire complex of gestures and actions associated with the collective organisation of urban life. This implied that, for example, the 'contractual' aspect be emphasised at the time of the meeting at the gate: frequently the king promised to maintain the privileges of the city at that point, as was the case in several Castilian examples of this period.[207] Or through the inclusion of the organisation of the professions, the entry was similar to the entry of other festivities which were immensely popular in these later centuries, such

205 So Kantorowicz records that 'the most elaborate *odines* for the *profectio* of the king (as for his *adventus*) are found in the Visigoth liturgy': The "King's Advent"', note 82.

206 Bertelli, *Il corpo del re*, pp. 55–86.

207 Rosana Andrés Díaz, 'Las entradas reales Castellanas en los siglos XIV y XV, según las crónicas de la época', *En la España Medieval*, 4 (1984), 47–62.

as the urban feast of Corpus Christi.[208] In particular with the use of the canopy which in Portugal is found on several occasions in the fifteenth century,[209] besides a manifestation of symbolic equivalence between the monarch and the sacred object of the procession of the Corpus, the ceremony demonstrated the existence of a common model in the entry or *adventus* of Christ in Jerusalem performed in the manner of a *basileus*.[210] Of particular interest in the Iberian context is the mention of the communities of Jews and Moors, which is included in the tendency already spoken of towards the participation of the citizens at the royal entries, included in the diverse bodies comprising the local society. In the Portuguese case the medieval entry is at times spoken of in the chronicles either merely by the mention of the reception outside the place or through the rapid indication that the king was received 'com as toras' or 'pelos Judeus', or with celebrations 'dos mouros',[211] a fact which does not fail to be mentioned by the majority of foreign travellers as an exotic characteristic of these receptions. Such curiosity is due perhaps to the fact that in other European contexts, as Coulet has established, in particular in the French example or even in the Roman, the Jews would not have been allowed to be admitted to the *occursus*, and would have presented their 'toras' inside the city, usually at the entrance of the areas where they were confined, changing the rite in order to suggest acts of submission and/or with a reaffirmation of the protection of the sovereign towards this religious minority.[212]

For the Portuguese case, it is difficult to determine the frequency of the performance of the entries, even in their less solemn version of 'recebimento' in the period studied here. As is natural, demanding a prior preparation and no small expenditure, and on the other hand being related to given characteristics of the places visited, they did not occur every time that the monarch moved on to a new destination, although they certainly took place several times in each reign, for they were particularly seen during this period as ceremonies for the renewal of the inaugural charisma, especially when they included the principal

208 M. J. Branco Silva, 'A procissão na cidade: reflexões em torno da Festa do Corpo de Deus na idade média Portuguesa', in *Actas das Jornadas Inter e Pluridisciplinares sobre a Cidade* (Lisbon, 1993), vol. I, pp. 195–217.

209 On the use of the canopy by Queen Leonor and Afonso V: *GTT*, vol. XII, p. 153 and *DEV*, part I, p. 110.

210 Kantorowicz, 'The "King's Advent"' and also Bernard Guenée and Françoise Lehoux, *Les Entrées royales françaises, de 1328 à 1515* (Paris: CNRS, 1968) on the adoption of the canopy. See also Lawrence Bryant, 'La cérémonie de l'entrée à Paris au moyen âge', *Annales ESC*, 41 (1980), 514–41; and more recently Gordon Kipling, *Enter the King: Theater, Liturgy, and Ritual in the Medieval Civic Triumph* (Oxford: Clarendon, 1998), a study which does not, unfortunately, mention the kingdoms of the Iberian Peninsula.

211 See for example *CR João I*, vol. I, pp. 54 and 111. On the medieval Portuguese entries: Ana Maria Alves, *Entradas régias Portuguesas: uma visão de conjunto* (Lisbon: Horizonte, 1986), pp. 12–22.

212 Noël Coulet, 'De l'intégration à l'exclusion: la place des Juifs dans les cérémonies d'entrée solennelle au moyen âge', *Annales ESC*, 34 (1979), 672–83.

cities of the kingdom. An example of what I have just said is to be found in the 'recebimento' of Afonso V in Lisbon by the Cortes of 1439, when he was still a child and was under the protection of his uncle who was at the time starting his contested regency in the kingdom.[213] What appears undeniable is the understanding that, in medieval Portugal, there arose a royal ritual from its function. In this way the interesting descriptions of Fernão Lopes regarding the entries of John I are explained – his 'spontaneous' reception in Coimbra before the Cortes which made him king,[214] and his famous entry into Oporto in 1385.[215] The first mention reminds us, following the well-known intention of the chronicler, of the royal standing of the Master of Aviz, whom the city 'recognises' even before the legitimising occurrence, his selection by the Cortes. Great importance has been given by literary criticism to the mention made by the chronicler of the participation of children at this event, which is extremely common in the actual performance of the royal entries of the period and does not result forcefully from specific 'messianic' interpretations of the figure of the master.[216] On the other hand, the description of the entry in Oporto, with all its ingredients, serves to stage the mutual promise, by the city of obedience and aid and, by the king, of protection and defence of the people. From the point of view of the ceremonies described, Lopes turns possibly to practices of his own time, as appears from the comparison between this entry and that of Leonor of Aragon in Lisbon in 1428 as described by the ambassadors of Burgundy.[217]

I cannot fail to mention, finally, perhaps because of the notable frequency of their performance in the fourteenth and fifteenth centuries, the meetings of the Cortes and the public rituals which this led to. In a certain sense, this is an inverse situation of that to which I have just referred of the royal entries. That is, the king called the several communities of the kingdom to an occasion of a meeting which the ceremonies, on the specific plane of ritual activity, also brought about.[218] The *procuradores* of the cities, of nobles and prelates, moved to the royal presence

213 See the report by Rui de Pina: *CR Afonso V*, p. 641. 214 *CR João I*, vol. I, p. 342.

215 *CR João I*, vol. II, pp. 17–19. Certain problems in the chronology of this royal visit were brought up by Salvador Dias Arnaus, when he said that this must have taken place in April and not in May, which is a version which better suits the highly symbolic evocation of the chronicler. This small chronological 'adjustment' brings to the fore the conventional character of the report.

216 The presence of the *pueri hebraeorum* expresses the 'messianic' theme common to all the entries which is even present in the way in which Christ's entry into Jerusalem was reported by tradition: Bertelli, *Il corpo del re*, pp. 73–4.

217 Vasconcelos, 'Voyage de Jean Van Eyck', pp. 16–18 and *GTT*, vol. XII, p. 153.

218 See Armindo de Sousa, *As Cortes medievais Portuguesas (1385–1490)* (Lisbon: INIC, 1990), vol. I, pp. 135–43. For Castile: Wladimiro Piskorski, *Las Cortes de Castilla en el período del tránsito de la edad media a la edad moderna* (Barcelona: El Albir, 1977), pp. 89–90 and also Salustiano de Dios, 'La evolución de las Cortes en Castilla durante el siglo XV', in Rucquoi (ed.), *Realidad e imágenes del poder*, pp. 148–9. I have attempted to study a fulcral occurrence for the construction of a 'Portuguese tradition' relating to these ceremonies: Rita Costa Gomes, 'Um acontecimento: as Cortes de 1481–82', in Diogo Ramada Curto (ed.), *O Tempo de Vasco da Gama* (Lisbon: CNCDP-Expo 98, 1998), pp. 245–64.

and this meeting was solemnly performed at the sessions of the opening of parliament, complex and long ceremonies with great impact on the narrative in the chronicles. There followed long weeks, or even months, of particularly intense and costly bureaucratic activity for the participants coming from the various places of the kingdom. The participation of the court was in this case direct, through a significant part of the officials of the royal entourage who were present at the most important assemblies, when there was also the exposition of an insignia: the sword.[219] The monarch presented himself on a dais, seated on his royal throne. There is little information for Portugal for the period prior to the end of the fifteenth century on the public oaths made by the *procuradores* of the cities at the courts which would allow one to reconstruct the actual sequence of acts performed, contrary to what occurred in Castile, where it is known that these oaths took on a certain solemnity, and the representatives of the cities were paid from early on by the king's chamber. Just as the monarch's counsellors, who as has been seen had their place of activity in the 'câmara de estado' for they were *membra corporis* of the monarch, the *procuradores* of the councils were associated with the court through the ceremony and received their symbolic stipend for as long as the Cortes lasted, and this, too, was paid by the king's chamber.

It was, however, above all the power of the word which had a most important function at these parliamentary ceremonies. Systematically from 1433 the principal solemn act of the Portuguese Cortes which was performed by all was the 'oração' made by an ecclesiastic or man of letters in the name of the monarch. As seemed appropriate to the royal majesty, the fifteenth-century monarch did not speak directly to the Cortes, but used the services of an 'orador'. There then had to be a response to this speech, possibly concerning a more recent ceremonial practice, with a previously prepared speech. The Portuguese monarch recommended in his instructions to the secretary:

> os procuradores das cortes sejam auisados antes de se fazer arengua do que se nella ha de dizer por parte del Rej pera delles terem sua reposta formada alegante de que banda deue ser conforme ha arengua por nom aconteçer a mingua que cada dia passam por nom saberem o que hamde responder o que nos autos pubricos muito he de olhar.[220]

Evidently, the extreme form of this 'ostentatious' eloquence resulted in a joint action in which the purposeful 'tirade' determined the contents of the response. As Maurice Bloch states, in this type of communication, 'rebellion

[219] Sousa, *As Cortes medievais Portuguesas*, vol. I, p. 134. This study reproduces the image of the hall of sessions at the end of the fifteenth century, with the mention of the officials present among whom the royal *alferes* had a relevant ceremonial role along with the *mordomo*, the *chanceler* and the *escrivão da puridade*.

[220] *Livro de Apontamentos*, p. 104.

is impossible... power is all or nothing'.[221] Although this rite of exchange of speeches explicitly wished to reconcile the promised restitution of justice and peace which the Cortes were promising, through the ceremony the position of the sovereign was defined as endowed with the maximum authority and the position of the *procuradores* as expectant and supplicant. But since it is formalised and conventional, would this dialogue be less significant historically if they devoted to it – monarch, court and subjects – such a large part of their days?

Marc Bloch alerted us, in his study on the magic powers of the medieval kings, to the care to be taken in the use of comparison: 'the comparative method is extremely fertile, but in the case of our not departing from the general plane, it cannot serve to reconstruct details'.[222] It was, therefore, outside the realms of possibility to supply an overdetailed vision of the various times of the Portuguese court through an analysis of the ritual activities based on a comparison with Iberian practices. It is, however, possible to draw some generic conclusions. In the first place, the times of the court were centred, as we have seen, on the person of the monarch, both in the broader sense of the importance that relevant facts acquired from his individual existence, and also in the manner as to how the daily and corporeal reality of the king dictated the rhythms of common life and was confirmed as the principal focus of the ritual life of the court. With his death, court time was suspended, with a temporary disappearance of the tie of a 'service' which, in almost all spheres, was still seen to a large extent in relation to the physical person of the monarch, only to re-form itself at once around the new king at the start of the great cycle of court life. The times of court daily life appear solemn and synchronised with the royal gesture and will, based upon the 'reverence' of behaviour in the learning and repetition of a group of gestures and attitudes which always appeared equal. It could be said that this is an overordered image of a world which saw itself as expressing a harmony which united, through the time of the rite, the past with the present, the king with the order of the cosmos, putting into the shade conflicts and cleavages which court society, viewed in other perspectives, revealed to us. In establishing through the rite the spatial picture in which the royal presence could be manifest, the court shows itself to be a mechanism inseparable from medieval royalty, as suggested to us by the medieval texts from which I set off at the beginning of this book.

221 Maurice Bloch (ed.), 'Introduction', in *Political Language and Oratory in Traditional Society* (London: Academic Press, 1975).

222 Bloch, *Les Rois thaumaturges*, p. 53.

Conclusion

When describing the festivities which the Infante Henry held in his city of Viseu during the first decade of the fifteenth century, the chronicler Zurara comments: 'pareçia a algũus estramgeiros que per alli passauam que aquelle ajuntamento nom era senam corte de rre'. Thus he stressed the importance of the court as a mechanism that made apparent the grandeur and magnificence of the monarchs through the 'ajuntamento' or human concentration brought about by their presence. However, the chronicler referred also to a common process of imitation or repetition of this grandeur in the households of the great princes of the age. In order to understand this cultural and political process in the context of the societies of the end of the Middle Ages, I have found that it is useful to maintain a certain distinction between what would on the one hand be the king's household, on the other the royal court and, finally, the actual 'court society' as a human configuration and a specific field of social relationships.

As I believe I have proved in the first chapters of this book, the household of the monarch was merely one part of the medieval royal court; an essential part, without doubt, but one on which a restrictive study does not allow for an evaluation of the diversity of functions to which the medieval concept referred. The court, a human organism which surrounded the kings, included a variety of agents and activities embracing several domestic organisms (for example, alongside the king's household, that of the queen) and above all constantly including a political and territorial dimension which the households of the great nobles and prelates, for example, did not attain. The power or domination of the monarchs extended far beyond the sphere of domestic authority, even though this continued, as has been seen, to have a relevant role in the structure of the court. This power implied during the fourteenth and fifteenth centuries a growing organisational complexity of the court itself which is expressed in the overall increase in its size and also in a variety of processes of institutionalisation and bureaucratisation of some spheres of activity which took their course there. Thus, in the Portuguese case, for a definition of the court not only the existence of the household of the kings and queens is essential, but also that of the royal council and the presence of specific agents connected to the 'state of finance' or to the exercise of justice such as tribunals of the king.

As for the actual 'court society', this could be defined more broadly as a web of interdependencies displayed in distinct spheres of late-medieval society, while remaining centred at the royal court and, in the final instance, in the figure of the monarch himself. I have attempted to analyse the role performed by this human configuration in the dissemination of values connected, for example, to the social classifications of the period, in particular to the definition of the nobility and royalty itself as guarantor of the unity of society and of solidarity among its several parts. The characteristic process of the age of monopolisation of political power by the king led him to become more and more dependent upon a larger number of individuals; that is, according to Elias's formulation, the chains of activities and intermediations (not only bureaucratic) by which this power was constructed tended to be longer and more complex and to include a growing number of people. Many of these chains or concatenations, as we have seen so positively in the Portuguese case, converged at court. As to the nobility and the elites of the kingdom in their turn, the search for influence and balance of power made them, through their participation at court, more dependent upon the monarchs but, more than ever, more dependent upon the relationships of forces opened up within this social field. For this reason, even when absent from the royal court in its strictest sense, the nobles and elites of the kingdom showed themselves, as I have analysed in the Portuguese case, as acting more and more as a function of that field and not merely of local realities or isolated spheres of activity. The centrality which the royal court assumes in relation to society of the end of the Middle Ages, therefore, expresses a level of possible integration of this society and leads to social dynamics which go beyond that reality both in its inter-individual dimension and in the spatial or territorial dimension. It is the whole of these dynamics which ultimately forms 'court society' of the end of the Middle Ages. It is at this third level of analysis that the study of the court of the Portuguese kings was found to be particularly rich, covering a small kingdom strictly related to the other political units of the Iberian Peninsula and culturally participating not only in the complex of ideas and values relative to the western European monarchic tradition but also to a process, concomitant with the other Iberian monarchies, of differentiation and affirmation of a single identity which tends to become confused with that of the nation. The existence of 'court society' contributed powerfully in the Portuguese case towards the diffusing of central values and to directing the political projects upon which the affirmation of the unity of the country and the memory of a common Peninsular past depended, in the face of which a possible identity of the kingdom and the monarchy was defined.

I have studied the Portuguese court in this book essentially through two vectors: as a social organism and in its modes of life. In the first aspect I believe

I have proved that at the court there was a concentration of men and women of the most diverse standing, providing the image of a microcosm endowed with its own hierarchies. In spite of this diversity the most important facets of common man are absent – let us not forget that the medieval court was not, except marginally, a place of production of goods but it was, above all, a centre of consumption. Would the nobility and clergy therefore have been the two principal faces of the identity of the man of the Portuguese court as courtly ideology wished? Throughout this book I have sought to study empirically how these categories were forged and modelled in the social practice of the age, starting from the minute reconstruction of biographies and the systematic identification of the individuals in their fabric of family relationship and of origin, but most of all in their mutual relationships. The court thus appeared as a place, *par excellence*, of 'becoming noble' in late-medieval society through processes which make evident the relativity of social classifications of the age, illuminating the intrinsically ambiguous attitude of the monarch in the face of such an important internal frontier of the society of the time. To grant generously the attributes of the nobility was also to aggrandise the court and, of course, to reinforce his own figure and authority. The clergy, in turn, demonstrated within the court sphere of the time an enormous variety in their physiognomy, not only in the specific sphere of their attributes in the face of the sacred but most of all in so many other profane spheres where they accompanied the lay functionary, the diplomat knight, the noble magnate in the royal council. By lessening the distinction which was fulcral to the formation of his identity, his functions as an intellectual appear constantly less exclusive in the face of the process of laification characteristic of the court culture of the time.

I also attempted through the study of the ceremonial activity of the courtiers to explain the court of the end of the Middle Ages in its spatial dimension, fundamentally moulded by the royal itinerance and also as a ritual organism. On the first aspect, we saw how the itinerance was a natural limit to the growth of the court, determining the variable physiognomy of the spaces that constituted so many other forms which the court took on in the face of a territory which it travelled and subordinated. The Portuguese kings also had their 'small kingdom' which was more intensely travelled, where they sited their residences, their dominions that were distributed in small enclaves throughout the country at the time. Above all they had a clear preference for the network of cities where the court was frequently installed, on occasions for some time. In the double modality of the journey and the stay, the court tended to isolate and separate the courtier from his roots (or relativised them) in a process which accentuated its dependence on the monarchs. For the monarchs, these practices of spatial mobility led to the construction of the territory of the kingdom itself and to its structuring through a hierarchy of places which in the modern age led to the construction of a capital.

In their turn, the ceremonies which surrounded the king were another reason for the existence of the court, structuring forms of life and making clear, within the Hispanic context in which they developed, the mutual circulation and influence of the various uses and customs, of the various images and myths relative to royalty. It thus demonstrated itself, through the detection of a parallelism and of a differentiation of uses, to be a true common culture which could be related to a movement of individuals, which was analysed in detail in the second chapter of this book, and simultaneously facilitated it. The study of these cultural forms and methods of the Portuguese court, like the other Peninsular courts of the age, can only be made when taking into account the incessant movement of men, ideas and things, or comparing them one with the other.

The forms of interdependence between the monarch and the courtiers and of the latter among themselves are the most salient characteristic of the court as a social form of the past, human ties to which the fifteenth-century texts, inspired by humanism, began to refer as forms of servitude and alienation as for example occurs in the Portuguese poetry of the later *cancioneiros*. This is a society which was also structured through an 'ethos' linked to an 'hierarchical' type of solidarity, and according to practices and values which demonstrate a necessary mutual separation and distancing of individuals in the quest for 'fortune'. Both aspects were the subject of reflection of the Infante Pedro in his *Virtuosa Benfeitoria*, which, through his defence of a social cohesion obtained through the circulation of gifts and of the ideal of a royal freedom released from the formal obligation of *quid pro quo*, remains an essential work of the social and political theory of the late medieval age. The king's freedom was a necessity, but it was a freedom which must be related and understood historically within the frame of his possibilities of action, limited by a position which the court constructed through daily rite, isolating him and distinguishing him radically from other men, and also limited by the actual physiognomy of this same human nucleus which served him as an organ of understanding of the complex reality of the kingdom and made real the mechanisms of his power.

Bibliography

I Manuscript sources

1. Arquivo Nacional da Torre do Tombo (ANTT)

Núcleo Antigo
Nos. 274, 287, 314, 315, 335, 783, 789

Drawers
I, Maços 1, 3, 6
II, Maços 1, 2, 5, 8, 11
XI, Maços 3, 6, 8, 10, 11
XII, Maços 7, 12
XIII, Maços 3, 6, 7
XIV, Maços 6, 21
XV, Maço 10

Religious institutions
Santa Maria de Aguiar, Maço 1
São Vicente de Fora, Maço 26
Mosteiro de Santos, Maços 1, 3, 6, 49, 50, 51, 53

Chanceries
Chancelaria de D. Afonso IV, book 4
Chancelaria de D. Fernando, books 1–4
Chancelaria de D. João I, books 1–5
Chancelaria de D. Duarte, books 1–4
Chancelaria de D. Afonso V, books 1, 2, 4, 5, 7–15, 18–23, 25–8, 30–2, 34–7

Leitura Nova
Reis, book 1
Além Douro, book 4
Estremadura, books 7, 10
Odiana, book 2
Direitos Reais, book 2
Extras, book 1

Cortes
Maço 2
Suplemento de Cortes, Maços 1, 2, 4

Special Collection
Box 32

Laws
Maços 1, 2

2. Arquivo Histórico da Câmara Municipal de Lisboa (AHCML)

Livros Místicos de Reis, Códice 3

3. Biblioteca Nacional (BNL)

Reserved, Códices 1482, 2638, 2639, 4426, 10982

4. Biblioteca Geral da Universidade de Coimbra (BGUC)

Strong box, Livro Vermelho do Senhor Rey D. Afonso V
Reserved, Códices 170, 490

5. Biblioteca Pública de Évora (BPE)

Códice 75

6. Biblioteca Pública de Santarém (BPS)

Manuscripts of the estate of Anselmo Braamcamp Freire

7. British Library (BL)

Manuscripts, Cottonian, Nero, B-1
Manuscripts, Add. 6298, 20952, 20958, 33469

8. Biblioteca Medicea-Laurenziana (BLAU)

Ashburnam, 1792 (1716) vols. I and II

9. Biblioteca Nacional de Madrid (BNM)

Manuscripts, 1159, 2420, 3301

II Printed primary sources

Actas das Vereações do Porto (anos de 1401–1449), ed. J. A. Pinto Ferreira, Oporto: Câmara Municipal, 1980.

Actas das Vereações, 1431–1432, ed. João Alberto Machado and Luís Miguel Duarte, Oporto: Câmara Municipal, 1985.

Almeida, Lopo de, *Cartas de Itália*, ed. M. Rodrigues Lapa, Lisbon: Imprensa Nacional, 1935.

Brito, Fr. Bernardo de, *Primeira Parte da Chronica de Cister*, Lisbon: Pascoal da Silva, 1720.

Brutails, J. A. (ed.), *Documents des Archives de la Chambre des Comptes de Navarre (1196–1384)*, Paris: Bibliothèque des Hautes Etudes, 1890.

Cancioneiro da Ajuda, ed. Carolina Michaëlis Vasconcelos, 2 vols. Lisbon: Imprensa Nacional–Casa da Moeda, 1990.

Cantigas d'Escarnheo e de Mal-Dizer dos Cancioneiros Medievais Galego-Portugueses, ed. M. Rodrigues Lapa, Vigo: Galáxia, 1965.

A Carta de Bruges do Infante D. Pedro, ed. A. Moreira de Sá, offprint of *Biblos*, Coimbra, 1952.

Castiglionchio, Lapo da, 'Dialogus de Curiae Commodis', *Prosatori Latini del Quattrocento*, ed. Eugenio Garin, Milan: Ricciardi, 1952, pp. 169–211.

Castigos e documentos para bien vivir ordenados por el Rey don Sancho, ed. Agapito Rey, Bloomington: Indiana University Press, 1952.

Chancelarias Portuguesas: D. Afonso IV, ed. Centro de Estudos Históricos da Universidade Nova de Lisboa, 2 vols., Lisbon: INIC, 1990–92.

Chancelarias Portuguesas: D. Pedro I, ed. Centro de Estudos Históricos da Universidade Nova de Lisboa, Lisbon: INIC, 1984.

Chastellain, Georges, *Chronique de Jacques de Lalain*, ed. J. A. Buchon, Paris: Collection des Chroniques Nationales Françaises, 1825.

Chaves, Álvaro Lopes de, *Livro de Apontamentos (1438–1489)*, ed. A. M. Salgado and A. J. Salgado, Lisbon: Imprensa Nacional, 1984.

Christine de Pisan buch von den drei Tugenden in Portugiesischer Übersetzung, ed. Dorothee Carstens-Grokenberger, Münster, Aschendorff, 1961.

Comptes de l'Hôtel des Rois de France aux XIVe et XVe siècles, ed. M. L. Douet d'Arcq, Paris, Société de l'Histoire de France, 1865.

Cortes Portuguesas: Reinado de D. Afonso IV (1325–1357), ed. Centro de Estudos Históricos da Universidade Nova de Lisboa, Lisbon: INIC, 1982.

Cortes Portuguesas: Reinado de D. Fernando (1367–1383), ed. Centro de Estudos Históricos da Universidade Nova de Lisboa, Lisbon: INIC, 1990.

Cortes Portuguesas: Reinado de D. Pedro I (1357–1367), ed. Centro de Estudos Históricos da Universidade Nova de Lisboa, Lisbon: INIC, 1986.

Crasbeck, F. Xavier da Serra, 'Catálogo dos Abbades do Antigo Mosteiro de Sta. Maria de Guimarães e Real Collegiada de N. Sra. de Oliveira', *Collecção de Documentos e Memórias da Academia Real da História*, Vol. VI, no. 30, Lisbon, 1726.

Crónica Geral de Espanha de 1344, ed. Luis Filipe Lindley Cintra, 4 vols., Lisbon, Imprensa Nacional–Casa da Moeda, 1983–1990.

Crónica dos Sete Primeiros Reis de Portugal, ed. Carlos Silva Tarouca, 3 vols., Lisbon: Academia Portuguesa da História, 1952–53.

Cuentas y Gastos (1292–1294) del Rey D. Sancho IV el Bravo, ed. Asunción López Dapena, Cordoba: Caja de Ahorros, 1984.

Descobrimentos Portugueses. Documentos para a sua História, ed. José Martins da Silva Marques, 5 vols., Lisbon: INIC, 1988.

Documentos das Chancelarias Reais relativos a Marrocos anteriores a 1531, ed. Pedro de Azevedo, 2 vols., Lisbon: Academia das Ciências, 1915–34.

Duarte, King of Portugal, *Livro da Ensinança de Bem Cavalgar*, ed. Joseph Piel, Lisbon: Bertrand, 1944.

Durand, Guillaume, *Rationale Divinorum Officiorum*, 5 vols., ed. Charles Barthélemy, Paris: Louis Vivès, 1854.

Early English Meals and Manners, ed. Frederick Furnivall, London: Early English Text Society, 1868.

Esperança, Fr. Manuel da, *História Seráfica da Ordem dos Frades Menores de S. Francisco*, part II, Lisbon: A. Craesbeck de Carvalho, 1666.

Estória de Dom Nuno Alvrez Pereira, ed. Adelino de Almeida Calado, Coimbra: Imprensa da Universidade, 1991.

Fernandes, Rui, 'Descripção do terreno em roda da cidade de Lamego duas léguas', *Collecção de Livros Inéditos de Historia Portuguesa dos Reinados de D. João I, D. Duarte, D. Afonso V e D. João II*, ed. Abade Correia da Serra, vol. 5, Lisbon: Academia Real das Ciências, 1926 (2nd edn), pp. 546–613.

Fernández de Oviedo, Gonzalo, *Libro de la Cámara Real del Principe Don Juan e offiçios de su Casa e serviçio ordinario*, Madrid: Sociedad de Bibliófilos Españoles, 1870.

Fitz Nagel, Richard, *Dialogus de Scaccario: Constitutio Domus Regis*, ed. Charles Johnson, F. L. Carter and D. E. Greenway, Oxford: Clarendon Press, 1983.

Fontes do Direito Ecclesiástico Portuguez, ed. Joaquim Santos Abranches, Coimbra: França Amado, 1895.

El Fuero Viejo de Castilla, ed. Jordan de Asso, Madrid: Joaquín Ibarra, 1771.

As Gavetas da Torre do Tombo, 12 vols., Lisbon: Centro de Estudos Históricos Ultramarinos, 1960–77.

Gran Crónica de Alfonso XI, ed. Diego Catalán, 2 vols., Madrid: Gredos, 1977.

Hincmar of Reims, *Hincmarus De Ordine Palatii (editio altera)*, ed. Thomas Gross and Rudolf Schieffer, *Monumenta Germaniae Historica. Fontes Iuris Germanici Antiqui in usum scholarum separatim editi*, Hanover: Hahnsche, 1980.

História florestal, aquícola e cinegética, ed. Carlos Manuel Baeta Neves, vols. I–IV, Lisbon: Ministério da Agricultura e Pescas, 1981–83.

Holanda, Francisco de, *Desenhos das Antigualhas*, facsimile edition, Lisbon: 1989.

Ibn Khaldun, *The Muqaddimah*, ed. Franz Rosenthal, Princeton: Princeton University Press, 1967.

'Inventários e contas da casa de D. Dinis (1278–1282)', ed. Anselmo Braamcamp Freire, *Arquivo Histórico Português*, 10 (1916), 41–59.

James III, King of Mallorca, *Leges Palatinae*, facsimile edition, Bloomington: Indiana University Press; Palma de Mallorca: J. J. Olañeta, 1994.

La Marche, Olivier de, *Mémoires*, ed. Henri Beaune and J. D'Arbaumont, Paris: Renouard, 1888.

Leges et Consuetudines. Portugaliae Monumenta Historica a saeculo octavo post Christum usque ad quintum decimum, 2 vols., Lisbon: Academia Real das Ciências, 1856–68.

Leonor de Portugal, Imperatriz da Alemanha. Diário de viagem do embaixador Nicolau Lanckman de Valckenstein, ed. A. Augusto Nascimento, Lisbon: Cosmos, 1992.

Leyes de Alfonso X – I, Espéculo, ed. G. Martínez Díez, Ávila: Fundación Sánchez-Albornoz, 1985.

Liber Regie Capelle. A manuscript in the Biblioteca Pública, Évora, ed. Walter Ullmann, London, Henry Bradshaw Society, 1961.

'Libro de diferentes cuentas de Don Sancho IV (1293–1294)', ed. Mercedes Gaibros de Ballesteros, *Historia del Reinado de Sancho IV de Castilla*, vol. I, Madrid: Tip. Archivos Bibliotecas y Museos, 1922, pp. i–cxlvii.

Libro de los Cien Capítulos, ed. Agapito Rey, Bloomington: Indiana University Press, 1960.

El Libro del Limosnero de Isabel la Católica, ed. Eloy Benito Ruano, 2 vols., Madrid: CSIC, 1990.

Lírica Profana Galego-Portuguesa, ed. Vicente Beltrán and Mercedes Brea, 2 vols., Santiago de Compostela: Xunta de Galicia, 1996.

Le Livre des cérémonies de Constantin VII Porphyrogénète, ed. Albert Vogt, 4 vols, Paris: Les Belles Lettres, 1967.

Livro da Falcoaria de Pero Menino, ed. M. Rodrigues Lapa, Coimbra: Imprensa da Universidade, 1931.

Livro das Fortalezas de Duarte Darmas, facsimile edition, Lisbon: Inapa, 1997.

Livro das Leis e Posturas, ed. Nuno Espinosa Gomes da Silva and Maria Teresa Campos Rodrigues, Lisbon: Faculdade de Direito, 1971.

Livro das Lembranças (Anais Quatrocentistas, Arenga e Memórias Avulsas, III e IV Crónicas Breves), ed. António Cruz, in *Santa Cruz de Coimbra na Cultura Portuguesa da Idade Média*, Oporto, 1964, pp. 305–75.

Livro das Posturas Antigas, ed. Maria Teresa Campos Rodrigues, Lisbon: Câmara Municipal, 1974.

Livro de Arautos (De Ministerio Armorum), ed. A. Augusto Nascimento, Lisbon, 1977.

Livro de Linhagens do século XVI, ed. António Machado de Faria, Lisbon: Academia Portuguesa da História, 1956.

O Livro de Recebimentos de 1470 da Chancelaria da Câmara, ed. Damião Peres, Lisbon: Academia Portuguesa da História, 1974.

Livro dos Conselhos de El-Rei D. Duarte, ed. J. J. Alves Dias and A. H. Oliveira Marques, Lisbon: Estampa, 1982.

Livros Velhos de Linhagens. Livros de Linhagens do Conde D. Pedro, ed. José Mattoso and Joseph M. Piel, *Portugaliae Monumenta Historica a saeculo octavo post Christum usque ad quintum decimum*, Lisbon: Academia das Ciências, 1980.

Livro Vermelho do Senhor Rey D. Afonso V, Collecção de Livros Inéditos de História Portugueza dos reinados de D. João I, D. Duarte, D. Affonso V e D. João II, ed. Abade Correia da Serra, Lisbon: Academia Real das Ciências, 1793, vol. 3.

Lopes, Fernão, *Crónica de D. Pedro I*, ed. Giuliano Macchi, Rome: Edizioni dell'Ateneo, 1966.

Crónica de D. Fernando, ed. Giuliano Macchi, Lisbon: Imprensa Nacional–Casa da Moeda, 1975.

Crónica del Rei D. João I, ed. Anselmo Braamcamp Freire and William Entwistle, 2 vols., Lisbon: Imprensa Nacional–Casa da Moeda, 1977.

López de Ayala, Pero, *Rimado de Palacio*, ed. Germán Orduna, 2 vols., Pisa: Giardini, 1981.

Crónicas, ed. José Luiz Martin, Barcelona: Planeta, 1991.

Corónica del Rey D. Pedro, ed. C. and H. M. Wilkins, Madison: The Hispanic Seminar of Medieval Studies, 1985.

Manuel, Don Juan, *Obras completas*, ed. José Manuel Blecua, 2 vols., Madrid: Gredos, 1982.

Map, Walter, *De Nugis Curialium: Courtier's Trifles*, ed. M. R. James, Oxford: Clarendon Press, 1983.

Martins, Fr. Salvado, *Vida e Milagres de D. Isabel*, ed. J. Joaquim Nunes, Coimbra: Imprensa da Universidade, 1921.

Meireles, Fr. António de Assunção, *Memórias do Mosteiro de Pombeiro*, ed. A. Baião, Lisbon: Academia Portuguesa da História, 1942.

Monumenta Henricina, ed. António Joaquim Dias Dinis, 15 vols., Coimbra: Comissão Executiva das Comemorações do V Centenário da Morte do Infante D. Henrique, 1960–74.

Monumenta Portugaliae Vaticana, ed. António Domingues Sousa Costa, 3 vols. published, Braga and Oporto: Edições Franciscanas, 1968–70.

Obras dos Príncipes de Avis, ed. M. Lopes de Almeida, Oporto: Lello and Irmão, 1981.

Oliveira, Eduardo Freire (ed.), *Elementos para a História do Município de Lisboa*, vol. I, Lisbon: Imprensa da Casa Real, 1887.

'Ordenacions fetes per lo molt Alt Senyor en Pere Terç Rey Darago sobra lo Regiment de tots los officials de la sua cort', *Colección de Documentos Inéditos del Archivo General de la Corona de Aragón*, ed. Próspero de Bofarull y Mascaró, vol. V, Barcelona, 1850.

Ordenações Afonsinas, ed. Mário Júlio de Almeida Costa and Eduardo Borges Nunes, 5 vols., Lisbon: Fundação Calouste Gulbenkian, 1988.

Ordenações de D. Duarte, ed. Martim de Albuquerque and Eduardo Borges Nunes, Lisbon: Fundação Calouste Gulbenkian, 1988.

Pais, Álvaro, *Espelho dos Reis (Speculum Regum)*, ed. Miguel Pinto Meneses, Lisbon: Instituto de Alta Cultura, 1955.

Paravicini, Werner, 'Die Hofordnungen Herzog Philipps des Guten von Burgund. Edition, I–V', *Francia*, 10 (1982), 131–66; 11 (1983), 257–301; 13 (1985), 191–211; 15 (1987), 183–231; 18 (1991), 111–23.

Pereira, Gabriel (ed.), *Documentos históricos da cidade de Évora*, 3 vols., Évora, 1885–91.

Pina, Rui de, *Crónicas*, ed. Manuel Lopes de Almeida, Oporto: Lello and Irmão, 1977.

Póvoa, Fr. João da, *Memórias soltas e inventários do Oratório de S. Clemente das Penhas e do Mosteiro de N. Sra. da Conceição de Matosinhos dos séculos XIV e XV*, ed. A. Magalhães Basto, Oporto: Marânus, 1940.

Prosistas Castellanos del Siglo XV, ed. Mario Penna, Madrid: Biblioteca de Autores Españoles, 1959.

Pulgar, Fernando de, *Claros Varones de Castilla*, ed. Robert B. Tate, Madrid: Taurus, 1985.

Quadro Elementar das Relações Políticas e Diplomáticas de Portugal com as diversas Potências do Mundo, ed. Visconde de Santarém and Luis Augusto Rebelo da Silva, 18 vols., Lisbon: Academia Real das Ciências, 1842–60.

Receitas e Despesas da Fazenda Real de 1384 a 1481 (Subsídios documentais), ed. Jorge Faro, Lisbon: Instituto Nacional de Estatística, 1965.

O Regimento Quatrocentista da Casa da Suplicação, ed. Martim de Albuquerque, Paris: Fondation Calouste Gulbenkian, 1980.

Resende, Garcia de, *Cancioneiro Geral*, ed. A. J. Costa Pimpão and Aida Fernandes Dias, 2 vols., Coimbra: Imprensa da Universidade, 1973.

Sá, A. Moreira de (ed.), *Chartularium Universitatis Portugalensis*, 12 vols., Lisbon: Instituto de Alta Cultura/INIC, 1966–85.

Sampaio, António de Villasboas e, *Nobiliarchia Portugueza. Tratado da Nobreza Hereditaria e Politica*, Lisbon: Oficina de Filipe Sousa Vilela, 1676.

Santos, Fr. Manuel dos, *Alcobaça illustrada*, Coimbra: Bento Ferreira, 1710.

São Boaventura, Fr. Fortunato de, *Historia Chronologica, e Critica da Real Abadia de Alcobaça*, Lisbon: Impressão Régia, 1827.

São Tomás, Fr. Leão de, *Beneditina Lusitana*, ed. José Mattoso, 2 vols., Lisbon: Imprensa Nacional–Casa da Moeda, 1974.

Sassoferrato, Bártolo de, *A Grammar of Signs: Bartolo of Sassoferrato's Tract on Insignia and Coats of Arms*, ed. Osvaldo Cavallar, Susanne Degenring and Julius Kirshner, Berkeley: University of California Press, 1994.

Las Siete Partidas del Rey Alfonso el Sabio, cotejadas con varios Códices antiguos, Madrid: Real Academia de la Historia, 1807.

Silva, José Soares da (ed.), *Collecçam dos Documentos com que se authorizam as Memórias para a Vida delRey Dom João I*, Lisbon: José António da Silva, 1734.

Sousa, António Caetano de (ed.), *Provas da história genealógica da Casa Real Portuguesa*, 12 vols., Coimbra: Atlântida, 1946–54.

Sousa, Fr. Luís de, *História de São Domingos*, ed. M. Lopes de Almeida, 2 vols., Oporto: Lello, 1977.

Suárez Fernández, Luis (ed.), *Relaciones entre Portugal y Castilla en la época del Infante Don Enrique, 1393–1460*, Madrid: Consejo Superior de Investigaciones Científicas, 1960.

Valera, Diego de, *Epístolas de Mosen Diego de Valera enbiadas en diversos tiempos e á diversas personas*, Madrid: Sociedad de Bibliófilos Españoles, 1878.

Vasconcelos, Joaquim de (ed.), 'Voyage de Jehan Van-Eyck', *Revista de Guimarães*, 14 (1897), 5–45, 145–61.

Viajes de Extranjeros por España y Portugal, ed. J. García Mercadal, Madrid: Aguilar, 1952.

Vida e Feitos de Júlio César. Edição crítica da tradução portuguesa de 'Li Fet des Romains', ed. Maria Helena Mira Mateus, Lisbon: Fundação Calouste Gulbenkian, 1970.

Villena, Enrique de, 'Arte Cisoria, arte de trinchar o cortar con cuchillo carnes y demás viandas', *Obras Completas I*, ed. Pedro M. Cátedra, Madrid: Turner, 1994.

Visconde de Santarém, *Memórias e alguns documentos para a história e teoria das Cortes Gerais*, Lisbon: Imprensa de Portugal e Brasil, 1924.

Von Strassbourg, Gottfried, *Tristan*, trans. A. T. Hatto, Harmondsworth: Penguin, 1960.

Zurara, Gomes Eanes de, *Crónica da Tomada de Ceuta*, ed. F. M. Esteves Pereira, Lisbon: Academia das Ciências de Lisboa, 1915.

Crónica do Conde D. Pedro de Meneses, ed. José Adriano Freitas de Carvalho, Oporto: Edições Comemorativas dos Descobrimentos Portugueses, 1988 (facsimile of the 1792 edition).

Crónica do Conde D. Duarte de Meneses, ed. Larry King, Lisbon: Universidade Nova, 1978.

III Secondary sources

Adamson, John (ed.), *The Princely Courts of Europe: Ritual, Politics and Culture under the Ancien Régime, 1500–1750*, London: Weidenfeld and Nicolson, 1999.

Adroer, Anna, 'Animals exotics als palaus reials de Barcelona', *Medievalia*, 8 (1988), 9–22.

Aldea Vaquero, Quintin (ed.), *Diccionario de historia eclesiástica de España*, 4 vols., Madrid: CSIC, 1972.

Allard, Guy (ed.), *Les Arts mécaniques au moyen âge*, Montreal and Paris: Vrin, 1982.

Allard, Jeanne, 'L'étiquette de table à la cour de Castille au bas moyen âge', *Temas Medievales*, 3 (1993), 5–29.

Almeida, Fortunato de, *História da Igreja em Portugal*, new edition, 4 vols., Oporto: Portucalense, 1967.

Alonso Troncoso, Victor, 'Banquete, hospitalidad y regalo en la poesía épica española', *Hispania*, 51 (1991), 835–74.

Altisent, Agustí, *L'almoina reial a la cort de Pere el Cerimoniós: estudi i edició dels manuscrits de l'almoiner Fra Guillem Deudé Monjo de Poblet (1378–1385)*, Poblet: Abadia de Poblet, 1969.

Alves, Ana Maria, *Entradas régias Portuguesas: uma visão de conjunto*, Lisbon: Horizonte, 1986.

Alves, Francisco Silva and Luzia Afonso, *O Castelo de Elvas*, Lisbon: Instituto Português do Património, 1991.

Amaral, António Caetano do, *Memória para a história da legislação e costumes de Portugal*, new edition, Oporto: Civilização, [1945].

Andrade, Ferreira de, *A Freguesia de Santa Cruz da Alcáçova de Lisboa*, Lisbon: Câmara Municipal, 1954.

Palácios reais de Lisboa, new edition, Lisbon: Vega, 1990.

Andrés Díaz, Rosana, 'Las fiestas de caballería en la Castilla de los Trastámaras', in *En la España medieval: estudios en memoria de Claudio Sánchez-Albornoz*, vol. 1, Madrid: 1986, pp. 81–108.

'Las entradas reales castellanas en los siglos XIV y XV, según las crónicas de la época', *En la España Medieval*, 4 (1984), 47–62.

Antunes, José, 'A nobreza no discurso medieval de confissão (séc. XIII a XIV)', *Revista de História das Ideias*, 19 (1997), 157–75.

Antunes, José, António Resende de Oliveira and João Gouveia Monteiro, *Conflitos políticos no reino de Portugal entre a Reconquista e a Expansão*, offprint of *Revista de História das Ideias*, Coimbra, 1984.

Appadurai, Arjun, 'Is homo hierarchicus?', *American Ethnologist*, 13 (1986), 745–61.

Arago Cabanas, A., 'La escribanía de Juan I', *VII Congreso de la Corona de Aragón*, Valencia, 1970, vol. II, pp. 193–269.

Arié, Rachel, *España Musulmana (siglos VIII–XV)*, Manuel Tuñón de Lara (ed.), *Historia de España*, vol. III, Barcelona: Labor, 1984.

Arnaut, Salvador Dias, 'Froissart e João Fernandes Pacheco', *Revista Portuguesa de História*, 3 (1947), 129–59.

A crise nacional dos fins do século XIV. I – A sucessão de D. Fernando, Coimbra: Faculdade de Letras, 1960.

A Batalha de Trancoso, Coimbra: Universidade de Coimbra, 1967.

'Os documentos do Mestre de Avis. Breves notas', *Revista Portuguesa de História*, 17 (1977), 341–9.

Arnold, Benjamin, 'Instruments of power: the profile and profession of *ministeriales* within German aristocratic society, 1050–1225', in Thomas N. Bisson (ed.), *Cultures of Power: Lordship, Status and Process in Twelfth-Century Europe*, Philadelphia: University of Pennsylvania Press, 1995, pp. 36–55.

Arriaza, Armand, 'Le statut nobiliaire adapté à la bourgeoisie: mobilité des statuts en Castille à la fin du moyen âge', *Le Moyen Age*, 100 (1994), 413–38.

Asch, Ronald G. and A. Bircke (eds.), *Princes, Patronage and Nobility*, London: Oxford University Press/The German Historical Institute, 1991.

Atlas, Alan, *Music in the Aragonese Court of Naples*, Cambridge: Cambridge University Press, 1985.

Azevedo, João Lúcio de, *Épocas de Portugal económico: esboços de história*, Lisbon: Clássica, 1973.

Elementos para a história económica de Portugal, séculos XII a XVIII, Lisbon: Inapa, 1990.

Azevedo, Pedro de, 'Culpas de David Negro', *Arquivo Histórico Português*, 1 (1903), 53–7.

'Os de Vasconcelos', *Arquivo Histórico Português*, 2 (1904), 362–80.
'O Castelo de S. Jorge', *O Arqueólogo Português*, 13 (1908), 98–116.
'A Chancelaria de D. Afonso IV', *Boletim da Segunda Classe da Academia das Ciências de Lisboa*, 4 (1912), 180–99.
'O Tesouro de D. Afonso III no Mosteiro de Santa Cruz de Coimbra', *Boletim da Segunda Classe da Academia das Ciências de Lisboa*, 7 (1912–13), 230–63.
Os Reguengos da Estremadura na 1ª Dinastia, offprint of *Miscelânea de Estudos em Honra de D. Carolina Michaëlis de Vasconcelos*, Coimbra: Imprensa da Universidade, 1930.
Azevedo, Rui de, 'Funcionários da corte nos documentos régios', in *Documentos medievais Portugueses: documentos régios*, vol. I, Lisbon: Academia Portuguesa da História, 1958, cxv–cxxvii.
Bák, Janos (ed.), *Coronations: Medieval and Early Modern Monarchic Ritual*, Berkeley and Los Angeles: University of California Press, 1990.
Baldwin, John W., 'The Capetian court at work under Philip Augustus', in Edward R. Haymes (ed.), *The Medieval Court in Europe*, Munich: Fink, 1986, pp. 71–91.
The Government of Philip Augustus: Foundations of French Royal Power in the Middle Ages, Berkeley and Los Angeles: University of California Press, 1986.
Baptista, Júlio César, *Portugal e o Cisma do Ocidente*, offprint of *Lusitania Sacra*, Lisbon, 1956.
Barash, Moshe, *Gestures of Despair in Medieval and Early Renaissance Art*, New York: New York University Press, 1976.
Barbosa, I. de Vilhena, 'Fragmentos de um roteiro de Lisboa (inédito). Paço dos estãos, paços da inquisição', *Archivo Pittoresco*, 6 (1863), 33–5.
Barreira, João, *Arte Portuguesa: as artes decorativas*, Lisbon: Excelsior, 1949.
Barros, Henrique de Gama, *História da administração pública em Portugal nos séculos XII a XV*, 11 vols., Lisbon: Sá da Costa, 1945–54.
Barth, Fredrik, *Models of Social Organisation*, London: Royal Anthropological Institute, 1971.
'Towards greater naturalism in conceptualizing societies', in A. Kuper (ed.), *Conceptualizing Societies*, London and New York: Routledge, 1992, pp. 17–33.
Barthélemy, Dominique, 'Fiefs et vassaux au moyen âge', *Annales HSS*, 52 (1997), 321–41.
Barton, Simon, *The Aristocracy in Twelfth-Century León and Castile*, Cambridge: Cambridge University Press, 1997.
Bautier, Robert-Henri, 'Les notaires et secrétaires du roi, des origines au milieu du XVIe siècle', in A. Lapeyre and R. Scheurer (eds.), *Les Notaires et secrétaires du roi sous les règnes de Louis XI, Charles VIII et Louis XII*, vol. I, Paris: Bibliothèque Nationale, 1978, pp. ix–xxxix.
Bean, J. M. W., '*Bachelor* and retainer', *Medievalia et Humanistica*, 3 (1972), 117–31.
From Lord to Patron: Lordship in Late Medieval England, Manchester: Manchester University Press, 1989.
Beaujouan, Guy, *La Science en Espagne aux XIVe et XVe siècles*, Paris: Presses Universitaires de France, 1967.
Beaujouan, Guy and Yvonne Poulle-Drieux (eds.), *Médecine humaine et vétérinaire à la fin du moyen âge*, Geneva and Paris: Droz, 1966.
Beaulieu, Michèle and Jeanne Baylé, *Le Costume en Bourgogne, de Philippe le Hardi à la mort de Charles le Téméraire*, Paris: PUF, 1956.
Beaune, Colette, 'Costume et pouvoir en France à la fin du moyen âge: les devises royales vers 1400', *Revue des Sciences Humaines* (Lille III), 4 (1981), 125–46.

Beceiro Pita, Isabel, 'Los dominios de la familia real castellana (1250–1350)', in *Génesis medieval del estado moderno: Castilla y Navarra (1250–1370)*, Valladolid: Ambito, 1987, pp. 79–106.

Bedos-Rezak, Brigitte, 'Ritual in the Royal Chancery: text, image, and the representation of kingship in medieval French diplomas (700–1200)', in Heinz Duchhard, Richard D. Jackson and David Sturdy (eds.), *European Monarchy: Its Evolution and Practice from Roman Antiquity to Modern Times*, Stuttgart: Steiner, 1992, pp. 27–40.

Beirante, Maria Ângela, *Santarém medieval*, Lisbon: Universidade Nova, 1980.

Évora na idade média, Lisbon: Fundação Calouste Gulbenkian, 1995.

Bell, Catherine, *Ritual: Perspectives and Dimensions*, New York and London: Oxford University Press, 1997.

Belmartino, Susana, 'Estructura de la familia y "edades sociales" en la aristocracia de León y Castilla según las fuentes literarias e historiográficas', *Cuadernos de Historia de España*, 47–8 (1968), 256–328.

Benevides, Francisco Fonseca, *Rainhas de Portugal*, Lisbon: Tip. Castro e Irmão, 1878–79.

Bermejo Cabrero, J. L., 'Los primeros secretarios de los reyes', *Anuario de Historia del Derecho Español*, 47 (1979), 187–296.

Bernhardt, John W., *Itinerant Kingship and Royal Monasteries in Early Medieval Germany, c. 936–1075*, Cambridge: Cambridge University Press, 1993.

Bertelli, Sergio, 'Il concetto di corte', in J. C. Margolin, D. Bigalli and A. Tenenti (eds.), *Ragione e civilitas: figure del vivere associato nella cultura del 500 europeo*, Milan: Angeli, 1986, pp. 141–50.

Il corpo del re: sacralità del potere nell'Europa medievale e moderna, Florence: Ponte alle Grazie, 1990.

'll drama della monarchia medievale, ovvero: il pranzo del Signore', in Maria Grazia Profeti (ed.), *Codici del Gusto*, Milan: Angeli, 1992, pp. 22–41.

Bertelli, Sergio (ed.), *Velocità storiche: miti di fondazione e percezione del tempo nella cultura e nella politica del mondo contemporaneo*, Rome: Carocci, 1999.

Bertelli, Sergio, Franco Cardini and Elvira Garbero Zorzi (eds.), *Le Corti Italiane del Rinascimento*, Milan: Mondadori, 1985.

Bertelli, Sergio and G. Crifo (eds.), *Rituale, cerimoniale, etichetta*, Milan: Bompiani, 1985.

Bethencourt, Francisco, *História das Inquisições: Portugal, Espanha, Itália*, Lisbon: Círculo de Leitores, 1994.

Bethencourt, Francisco and Diogo Ramada Curto (eds.), *A memória da nação*, Lisbon: Sá da Costa, 1991.

Bezzola, Reto, *Les Origines et la formation de la littérature courtoise en occident, 500–1200*, 5 vols., Paris: Honoré Champion, 1958–63.

Billot, Claudine, *Les Saintes Chapelles royales et princières*, Paris, Editions du Patrimoine, 1998.

Blanco González, Bernardo, *Del cortesano al discreto*, Madrid: Gredos, 1962.

Bloch, Marc, 'Economie-nature ou économie-argent: un pseudo-dilemme', *Annales d'Histoire Sociale*, 1 (1939), 7–16.

Les Rois thaumaturges: étude sur le caractère surnaturel attribué à la puissance royale particulièrement en France et en Angleterre, Paris: Gallimard, 1983.

Bloch, Maurice (ed.), *Political Language and Oratory in Traditional Society*, London: Academic Press, 1975.

Blüher, Karl Alfred, *Séneca en España: investigaciones sobre la recepción de Séneca en España desde el siglo XIII hasta el siglo XVIII*, Madrid: Gredos, 1983.

Bluteau, Rafael, *Vocabulário Portuguez e Latino*, 10 vols., Coimbra: Colégio das Artes, 1712–28.

Bogner, Artur, 'The structure of social processes. A commentary on the sociology of Norbert Elias', *Sociology*, 20 (1986), 387–411.

Borgotte, Michael, 'Über Typologie und Chronologie des Königskanonikates im europäischen Mittelalter', *Deutsches Archiv für Erforschung des Mittelalters*, 47 (1991), 19–44.

Borsi, F. (ed.), *Il potere e lo spazio*, Milan: Electa, 1980.

Bosl, Karl, 'La "familia" come struttura fondamentale della società medievale', in *Modelli di società medievale*, Bologna: Il Mulino, 1981, pp. 131–61.

Bossy, John, 'The Mass as a social institution, 1200–1700', *Past and Present*, 100 (1983), 29–61.

Boucher, Jacqueline, *La Cour de Henri III*, Rennes: Ouest-France, 1986.

Boureau, Alain and Claudio-Sergio Ingerflom, *La Royauté sacrée dans le monde chrétien*, Paris, Ecole des Hautes Etudes en Sciences Sociales, 1992.

Bournazel, Eric, *Le Gouvernement capétien au XIIe siècle, 1108–1180*, Paris: PUF, 1975.

Braga, Paulo Drumond, *O regimento excepcional da aposentadoria da vila de Setúbal de 1471*, offprint of *Boletim de Trabalhos Históricos*, Guimarães, 1989.

Esmoler mor e esmoler menor do reino, offprint of *Itinerarium*, Lisbon, 1995.

Branco, José Castello, *O mordomo do rei*, Lisbon: Academia Real das Ciências, 1851.

Brásio, António, 'O problema da sagração dos monarcas portugueses', *Anais da Academia Portuguesa da História*, 12 (1962), 21–49.

Braunstein, Philippe, 'Les techniciens et le pouvoir à la fin du moyen âge: une direction de recherche', in Fr. Autrand (ed.), *Prosopographie et genèse de l'état moderne*, Paris: Ecole Normale Supérieure de Jeunes Filles, 1986, pp. 223–9.

Broccheri, Fumagalli Beonio, 'Grandi e piccole virtù', in *Le Bugie de Isotta: immagini della mente medievale*, Bari: Laterza, 1987, pp. 49–68.

Brooks, Neil C., *The Sepulchre of Christ in Art and Liturgy*, Urbana: University of Illinois Press, 1921.

Brown, Elisabeth A. R., *The Monarchy of Capetian France and Royal Ceremonial*, London: Variorum, 1991.

Brühl, Carlrichard, *Fodrum, Gistum, Servitium Regis*, 2 vols., Cologne: Böhlau, 1968.

'Les auto-couronnements d'empereurs et de rois (XIIIe–XIXe siècles). Remarques sur la fonction sacrementalle de la royauté au moyen âge et à l'époque moderne', *Comptes-Rendus de l'Académie des Inscriptions et Belles-Lettres* (1984), 102–18.

Brunner, Otto, 'Das "ganze haus" und die alteuropäische ökonomik', *Neue Wege der Verfassung und Sozialgeschichte*, Göttingen (1968), 103–27.

Bryant, Lawrence, 'La cérémonie de l'entrée à Paris au moyen âge', *Annales ESC*, 41 (1980), 514–41.

Buescu, Ana Isabel, *Imagens do príncipe: discurso normativo e representação (1525–1549)*, Lisbon: Cosmos, 1996.

'Vínculos da memória: Ourique e a fundação do reino', in Yvette Centeno (ed.), *Portugal: mitos revisitados*, Lisbon: Salamandra, 1993, pp. 9–50.

Bullock-Davies, Constance, *Menestrellorum Multitudo: Minstrels at a Royal Feast*, Cardiff: University of Wales Press, 1978.

Burke, Peter, *The Fortunes of the Courtier: The European Reception of Castiglione's Cortegiano*, Cambridge: Polity Press, 1995.

Bustos Tovar, José, 'Notas para el léxico de la prosa didáctica del siglo XIII', in *Studia Hispanica in Honorem Rafael Lapesa*, vol. II, Madrid: Gredos, 1974, pp. 149–55.

Cabrol, Fernand and Henri Leclercq (eds.), *Dictionnaire d'archéologie chrétienne et de liturgie*, 15 vols., Paris: Letouzey et Ané, 1903–53.

Caetano, Joaquim and José Alberto Carvalho, *Frescos quinhentistas do Paço de S. Miguel*, Évora, Fundação Eugénio de Almeida, 1990.

Caetano, Marcello, 'O significado das Cortes de Leiria', in *Páginas Inoportunas*, Lisbon: Bertrand, [1959], pp. 93–111.

História do Direito Português, Lisbon: Verbo, 1980.

A administração municipal de Lisboa durante a 1a dinastia (1179–1383), Lisbon: Academia Portuguesa da História, 1981.

A crise nacional de 1383–85, Lisbon: Verbo, [1985].

Cameron, Averil, 'The construction of court ritual: the Byzantine *Book of Ceremonies*', in David Cannadine and Simon Price (eds.), *Rituals of Royalty: Power and Ceremony in Traditional Societies*, Cambridge: Cambridge University Press, 1987, pp. 106–36.

Campos, J. C. Aires de, 'Antiguidades nacionais. Dos estãos e aposentadorias em 1439', *O Instituto*, 13 (1866), 20–3.

Canard, M., 'Le cérémonial fatimide et le cérémonial byzantin: essai de comparaison', *Byzantion*, 21 (1953), 355–420.

Cannadine, David, 'Divine rites of kings', in David Cannadine and Simon Price (eds.), *Rituals of Royalty: Power and Ceremony in Traditional Societies*, Cambridge: Cambridge University Press, 1987, pp. 1–19.

Cardini, Franco, 'Teomimesi e cosmomimesi. Il giardino come nuovo Eden', *Micrologus*, IV: *Il Teatro della Natura* (1996), 331–54.

Caro Baroja, Julio, 'Sobre la formación y uso de Arquétipos en historia, literatura y folklore', in *Ensayos sobre la cultura popular Española*, Madrid: Dosbe, 1979.

Carrasco, Inés, *Los cargos de la Hueste Real en tiempos de Alfonso X: estudio onomasiológico*, Granada: Universidad de Granada, 1992.

Cartellieri, Otto, *The Court of Burgundy: Studies in the History of Civilization*, New York: Haskell, 1970.

Carvalho, Joaquim de, *Obra completa*, ed. José V. de Pina Martins, 9 vols., Lisbon: Fundação Calouste Gulbenkian, 1978–97.

Carvalho, J. A. Freitas de, 'Nas origens dos Jerónimos na Península Ibérica: do Franciscanismo à Ordem de S. Jerónimo', *Línguas e Literaturas*, 1 (1984), 111–31.

Casali, Elide, '*Economica* e "creanza" cristiana', *Quaderni Storici*, 41 (1979), 555–83.

Cassirer, Ernst, *La Philosophie des formes symboliques*, vol. II, *La pensée mythique*, Paris: Minuit, 1972.

'Castelo de Elvas', *Boletim da Direcção Geral dos Edificios e Monumentos Nacionais*, 54 (1948).

'Castelo de Óbidos', *Boletim da Direcção Geral dos Edificios e Monumentos Nacionais*, 68–9 (1952).

Castilho, Júlio de, *Lisboa antiga: os bairros orientais*, Lisbon: Câmara Municipal, 1937, vol. X, pp. 32–49.

Castro, Eugénio de, 'Os meus Vasconcelos', *Biblos*, 8 (1932), 24–8.

Cejador, Julio, *Vocabulario medieval Castellano*, Madrid: Visor, 1990.

Chabod, Federico, 'Esiste uno stato del Rinascimento?', *Scritti sul Rinascimento*, Turin: Einaudi, 1967, pp. 593–623.

Chambers, S. D., 'What made a Renaissance cardinal respectable? The case of Cardinal Costa of Lisbon', *Renaissance Studies*, 12 (1998), 87–108.

Champion, Pierre, *Histoire poétique du quinzième siècle*, reprinted, Paris: Honoré Champion, 1966.

Chapelot, Jean, *Le Château de Vincennes: une résidence royale au moyen âge*, Paris: CNRS, 1994.

Chartier, Roger, 'Préface', in Norbert Elias, *La Société de cour*, Paris: Flammarion, 1985.

Chaumartin, François-Régis, *Le De Beneficiis de Sénèque: sa signification philosophique, politique et sociale*, Paris: Les Belles Lettres, 1985.

Chicó, Mário, *A Catedral de Évora na idade média*, Évora, Edições Nazareth, 1946.

Chueca Goitia, Fernando, *Casas reales en monasterios y conventos Españoles*, [Bilbao]: Xarait, 1982.

Cintra, Luis Filipe Lindley, 'Sobre a formação e evolução da lenda de Ourique (até à Crónica de 1419)', *Revista da Faculdade de Letras de Lisboa*, 23 (1957), 168–215.

"A lenda de Afonso I, Rei de Portugal (origens e evolução)", *ICALP-Revista*, 16–17 (1989), 64–78.

Clough, Cecil H. (ed.), *Profession, Vocation and Culture in Later Medieval England*, Liverpool: Liverpool University Press, 1982.

Coelho, Maria Helena da Cruz, *O baixo mondego nos finais da idade média*, 2 vols., Coimbra: Faculdade de Letras, 1983.

Coelho, Maria Helena da Cruz and Armando Luís Carvalho Homem, 'Origines et évolution du registre de la Chancellerie royale portugaise (XIIIe–XVe siècles)', *Revista da Faculdade de Letras* (Oporto), 12 (1995), 47–74.

Coelho, Maria Helena Cruz and Armando Luís Carvalho Homem (eds.), *Portugal em definição de fronteiras (1096–1325): do Condado Portucalense à crise do século XIV, Nova História de Portugal*, vol. III, Lisbon: Presença, 1996.

A génese do estado moderno no Portugal tardo-medievo (séculos XIII–XV), Lisbon: Universidade Autónoma, 1999.

Colvin, H. M., 'Royal gardens in medieval England', in *Essays in English Architectural History*, New Haven and London: Yale University Press, 1999, pp. 1–12.

Colvin, H. M. (ed.), *The History of the King's Works*, vol. I, *The Middle Ages*, London: Her Majesty's Stationery Office, 1963.

Contamine, Philippe, *La Guerre au moyen âge*, Paris: PUF, 1980.

Corbin, Solange, *La Déposition liturgique du Christ au Vendredi Saint, sa place dans l'histoire des rites et du théâtre religieux (analyse de documents portugais)*, Paris: Les Belles Lettres, 1960.

Cordeiro, Luciano, 'Diogo de Azambuja' [1892], in *Questões histórico-coloniais*, vol. II, Lisbon: Agência Geral das Colónias, 1936, pp. 92–174.

Corominas, J. and J. A. Pascual, *Diccionario crítico etimológico Castellano e Hispánico*, 5 vols., Madrid: Gredos, 1980.

Correia, José Manuel Silva and Natália Correia Guedes, *O Paço Real de Salvaterra de Magos*, Lisbon: Horizonte, 1989.

Correia, Vergílio, *Três túmulos: uma arca tumular do Museu de Santarém. Sepultura de Fernão Gomes de Goes, em Oliveira do Conde. Moimento do Primeiro Marquês de Valença*, Lisbon: Portugália, [1921].

Monumentos e esculturas: séculos III–XVI, Lisbon: Férin, 1924.

Obras, 2 vols., Coimbra: Universidade de Coimbra, 1946.

Correia, Vergílio and A. Nogueira Gonçalves, *Inventário artistico de Portugal*, vol. II, *Cidade de Coimbra*, Lisbon: Academia Nacional de Belas-Artes, 1947.

Cortesão, Jaime, *História dos descobrimentos Portugueses*, 3 vols., Lisbon: Livros Horizonte/Círculo de Leitores, 1978.

Cortijo Ocaña, Antonio, 'La traducción Portuguesa de la *Confessio Amantis* de John Gower', *Euphrosyne*, 23 (1995), 457–66.

Coss, P. R., 'Bastard feudalism revised', *Past and Present*, 125 (1989), 27–64.

Costa, A. D. Sousa, 'O doutoramento em Bolonha do secretário de D. João I – Dr. Lançarote, Conde Palatino e embaixador ao Concílio de Pisa', *Itinerarium*, 3 (1957), 202–20.

'Mestre Afonso Dinis, médico e secretário de D. Afonso IV, professor da Universidade de Paris', *Itinerarium*, 3 (1957), 310–47, 510–607.

'D. Gomes, reformador da Abadia de Florença, e as tentativas de reforma dos mosteiros Portugueses no século XV', *Studia Monastica*, 5 (1963), 123–60.

'O célebre conselheiro e chanceler régio Doutor João das Regras, clérigo conjugado e prior da Colegiada de Santa Maria da Oliveira de Guimarães', *Itinerarium*, 18 (1972), 232–59.

'Bispos de Lamego e de Viseu no século XV', *Itinerarium*, 34 (1988), 232–73.

'D. João Afonso da Azambuja, cortesão, bispo, arcebispo, cardeal e fundador do Convento das Dominicanas do Salvador de Lisboa', *Arquivo Histórico Dominicano Português*, 4 (1989), 1–150.

Portugueses no Colégio de S. Clemente e Universidade de Bolonha durante o século XV, 2 vols., Bologna: Real Colegio de España, 1990.

Costa, Avelino Jesus da, 'La chancellerie royale portugaise jusqu'au milieu du XIIIe siècle', *Revista Portuguesa de História*, 15 (1975), 143–68.

Costa, Maria Yolanda, 'Diogo Lopes Pacheco: subsídios para o estudo da acção política de um magnate português do seculo XIV', Dissertação de Licenciatura, Universidade de Coimbra, 1967.

Costa, Mário Júlio de Almeida, *Raízes do censo consignativo: para a história do crédito medieval Português*, Coimbra: Atlântida, 1961.

Costa Gomes, Rita, 'As elites urbanas no final da idade média: três pequenas cidades do interior', in *Estudos e ensaios em homenagem a Vitorino Magalhães Godinho*, Lisbon: Sá da Costa, 1988, pp. 229–37.

'Virtuosa Benfeitoria', in Giulia Lanciani and Giuseppe Tavani (eds.), *Dicionário da literatura medieval Galega e Portuguesa*, Lisbon: Caminho, 1993, pp. 681–3.

'Cerimónias da realeza nos finais da idade média', *Penélope*, 14 (1994), 129–36.

'Invocar o rei na idade média: breve nota de antropologia jurídica', *Revista Portuguesa de História*, 31 (1996), 195–207.

'A curialização da nobreza', in Diogo Ramada Curto (ed.), *O tempo de Vasco da Gama*, Lisbon: CNCDP–Expo 98, 1998, pp. 179–87.

'A reflexão antropológica na história da realeza medieval', *Etnográfica*, 2 (1998), 133–40.

'Monarquia e território. Residências reais Portuguesas (séculos XIV–XVI)', in *Lugares de poder/Lieux de pouvoir/Places of Power*, Lisbon: Fundação Calouste Gulbenkian, 1998, pp. 85–105.

'Um acontecimento: as Cortes de 1481–82', in Diogo Ramada Curto (ed.), *O tempo de Vasco da Gama*, Lisbon: CNCDP–Expo 98, 1998, pp. 245–64.

'A realeza: símbolos e cerimonial', in M. H. Cruz Coelho and A. L. Carvalho Homem (eds.), *A Gênese do estado moderno no Portugal tardo-medievo (séculos XIII–XV)*, Lisbon: Universidade Autónoma, 1999, pp. 201–13.

Coulet, Noël, 'De l'intégration à l'exclusion: la place des Juifs dans les cérémonies d'entrée solennelle au moyen âge', *Annales ESC*, 34 (1979), 672–83.

Crouch, David, D. A. Carpenter and P. R. Coss, 'Debate: bastard feudalism revised', *Past and Present*, 131 (1991), 165–203.

Cruselles, Enrique, *El maestre racional: función política y desarollo administrativo del oficio público*, Valencia: Edicions Alfons el Magnànim, 1989.

Cruz, António, *Santa Cruz de Coimbra na cultura Portuguesa*, Oporto: Biblioteca Pública Municipal, 1964.

Cunha, António Geraldo da (ed.), *Índice do vocabulário do Português medieval*, Rio de Janeiro: Fundação Casa de Rui Barbosa, 1988.

Cunha, Mafalda Soares da, *Linhagem, parentesco e poder: a Casa de Bragança (1384–1483)*, Lisbon: Fundação da Casa de Bragança, 1990.

'A nobreza Portuguesa no início do século XV: renovação e continuidade', *Revista Portuguesa de História*, 31 (1996), 219–52.

Curto, Diogo Ramada, 'Ritos e cerimónias da monarquia', in Francisco Bethencourt and Diogo Ramada Curto (eds.), *A memória da nação*, Lisbon: Sá da Costa, 1991, pp. 201–65.

'A Capela Real: um espaço de conflitos (séculos XVI a XVIII)', in *A espiritualidade de corte em Portugal, séculos XVI–XVIII*, supplement to *Revista da Faculdade de Letras*, 5, Oporto, 1993, pp. 143–54.

Dakhlia, Jocelyne, 'Dans la mouvance du prince: la symbolique du pouvoir itinérant au Mahgreb', *Annales ESC*, 43 (1988), 735–60.

Le Divan des rois: le politique et le religieux dans l'Islam, Paris: Aubier, 1998.

Daveau, Suzanne, 'Géographie historique du site de Coruche, étape sur les itinéraires entre Évora et le Ribatejo', *Revista da Faculdade de Letras*, 5th series, 2 (1984), 115–35.

David, H., 'L'Hôtel ducal sous Philippe le Bon. Mœurs et coutumes. Les offices', *Annales de Bourgogne*, 37 (1965), 241–55.

David, Henrique and José Augusto Sotto Mayor Pizarro, 'Nobres Portugueses em Leão e Castela (século XIII)', *Revista de História* (Oporto), 7 (1987), 135–50.

David, Pierre, 'Français du midi dans les évêchés portugais (1279–1390)', *Bulletin des Etudes Portugaises*, 39 (1942), 16–70.

De Martino, Ernesto, *Morte e pianto rituale: dal lamento funebre antico al pianto di Maria*, Turin: Boringhieri, 1975.

De Witte, Charles Martial, *Les Bulles pontificales et l'expansion portugaise*, offprint of *Revue d'Histoire Ecclésiastique*, Louvain, 1958.

Del Re, Niccolò, *La Curia Romana: lineamenti storici-giuridici*, Rome: Edizioni di Storia e Letteratura, 1970.

Delpech, François, 'Un souverain, un ange et quelques folies: avatars d'un *exemplum* médiéval', in Augustin Redondo and André Rochon (eds.), *Visages de la folie (1500–1650)*, Paris: Pub. de la Sorbonne, 1981, pp. 55–65.

Demurger, Alain, *Vie et mort de l'Ordre du Temple*, Paris: Seuil, 1989.

Descalzo, Andrés, 'La música en la corte de Pedro IV "el Ceremonioso"', *Acta Historica et Archeologica Mediaevalia*, 11–12 (1990–91), 401–19.

Devy-Vareta, Nicole, 'Para uma geografia histórica da floresta portuguesa', *Revista da Faculdade de Letras – Geografia*, 1 (1985), 47–67; 2 (1986), 5–39.

Dias, Isabel, *A arte de ser bom cavaleiro*, Lisbon: Estampa, 1997.

Díaz Martín, Luis Vicente, *Los oficiales de Pedro I de Castilla*, Valladolid: Universidad de Valladolid, 1987.

Díaz y Díaz, Manuel, 'La lengua institucional en la Hispania de los siglos VI–XI', *Ideologie e pratiche del reimpiego nell'alto medioevo*, XLVI Settimana di Studio del Centro Italiano di Studi sull'Alto Medioevo, Spoleto, 1999, vol. I, pp. 435–60.

Dicionário enciclopédico da história de Portugal, 2 vols. published, Lisbon: Edições Alfa, 1985.

Dinis, A. Dias, 'Quem foi o bispo de Coimbra nos anos de 1386 a 1398?', *Colectânea de Estudos*, 3 (1952), 67–109.

'Ainda sobre a identidade de Frei João Verba', *Itinerarium*, 3 (1957), 486–90.
Estudos Henriquinos, Coimbra: Universidade de Coimbra, 1960.
À volta do casamento do Infante D. Duarte (1409–1428), offprint of *Revista Portuguesa de História*, Coimbra, 1974.
Dios, Salustiano de, *El Consejo Real de Castilla (1385–1522)*, Madrid: Centro de Estudios Constitucionales, 1982.
'La evolución de las cortes en Castilla durante el siglo XV', in A. Rucquoi (ed.), *Realidad e imágenes del poder: España a fines de la edad media*, Valladolid: Ambito, 1988, pp. 137–69.
Dominguez Casas, Rafael, *Arte y etiqueta de los Reyes Católicos: artistas, residencias, jardines y bosques*, Madrid: Alpuerto, 1993.
Douglas, Mary, *In the Active Voice*, London: Routledge and Kegan Paul, 1982.
Du Cange, C. D., *Glossarium Mediae et Infimae Latinitatis*, ed. L. Fabre, 10 vols., Paris: Librairie des Sciences et des Arts, 1938.
Duby, Georges, 'La vulgarisation des modèles culturels dans la société féodale', *Niveaux de culture et groupes sociaux. Actes du Colloque*, Paris: Mouton, 1967, pp. 33–41.
La société chevaleresque, Paris: Flammarion, 1988.
Duby, Georges (ed.), *Histoire de la vie privée*, vol. II, *De l'Europe féodale à la Renaissance*, Paris: Seuil, 1985.
Duggan, Anne J., *Queens and Queenship in Medieval Europe*, Woodbridge: Boydell, 1997.
Duindam, Jeroen, *Myths of Power: Norbert Elias and the Early Modern European Court*, Amsterdam: Amsterdam University Press, [1994].
Dumont, Louis, *Homo hierarchicus: le système des castes et ses implications*, Paris: Gallimard, 1995.
Dvornick, Francis, *Early Christian and Byzantine Political Philosophy*, 2 vols., Washington, DC, Dumbarton Oaks Center for Byzantine Studies.
Echaniz Sanz, María, *Las mujeres de la Orden Militar de Santiago en la edad media*, Salamanca: Junta de Castilla y León, 1992.
Eis, Gerhard, *Mittelalterlische Fachliteratur*, Stuttgart: Sammlung Metzler, 1967.
Forschungen zur Fachprosa, Ausgewhälte Beiträge, Berne and Munich: Francke, 1971.
Eisenstadt, Schmuel N. and L. Roniger, *Patrons, Clients and Friends: Interpersonal Relations and the Structure of Trust in Society*, Cambridge: Cambridge University Press, 1984.
Elias, Norbert, *What Is Sociology?*, London: Hutchinson, 1978.
The Civilizing Process, 2 vols., Oxford: Blackwell, 1978, 1982.
The Court Society, Oxford: Blackwell, 1983.
'Figuration', 'Soziale Prozesse', 'Zivilisation', in Bernhard Schäfers (ed.), *Grundbegriffe der Soziologie*, Opladen: Leske und Budrich, 1986, pp. 88–91, 234–41, 382–97.
'The retreat of sociologists into the present', *Theory, Culture and Society*, 4 (1987), 2–3, 223–49.
The Society of Individuals, Oxford: Blackwell, 1991.
Elliot, J. H., 'The court of the Spanish Habsbourgs: a peculiar institution?', in P. Mack and M. Jacobs (eds.), *Politics and Culture in Early Modern Europe: Essays in Honour of H. G. Koenigsberger*, Cambridge: Cambridge University Press, 1987, pp. 5–58.
Elze, Reinhard, 'Le Consacrazione Regie', in *Segni e riti nella Chiesa altomedievale occidentale*, Spoleto: Settimane di Studio del Centro Italiano di Studi sull'Alto Medioevo, 1987, pp. 43–55 and 57–61.

'Ein krönungsordo aus Portugal', *Memoria Sanctorum Venerantes: Miscellanea in onore di Monsignor Victor Saxer*, Rome: Pontificio Istituto di Archeologia Cristiana, 1992.

'*Sic transit gloria mundi*: la morte del papa nel medioevo', *Annali dell'Istituto Storico Italo-Germanico in Trento*, 3 (1977), 23–41.

Encyclopédie de l'Islam, new edn., 10 vols. (in publication), Leiden and Paris: Maisonneuve et Larose, 1954–98.

Entwistle, W. J. and P. E. Russell, 'A rainha D. Felipa e a sua corte', in *Congresso do Mundo Português*, vol. II, Lisbon: Comissão Executiva dos Centenários, 1940, pp. 317–46.

Erdmann, Carl, *A ideia de cruzada em Portugal*, Coimbra: Instituto Alemão da Universidade, 1940.

Esch, A., 'Dal medioevo al Rinascimento: uomini a Roma dal 1350 al 1450', *Archivio della Società Romana di Storia Patria*, 94 (1971), 1–10.

Espanca, Túlio, *Palácios Reais de Évora, cadernos de história e arte Eborense* 2, Évora: Edições Nazareth, 1946.

Estepa Díez, Carlos, 'Formación y consolidación', in *En torno al feudalismo Hispánico*, Ávila: Fundación Sánchez-Albornoz, 1989, pp. 158–256.

Ewert, Ulf Christian and Stephan Selzer (eds.), *Ordnunsformen des Hofes*, Mitteilungen der Residenzen-Kommission der Akademie der Wissenshaften zu Göttingen 2, Kiel, 1997.

Ewig, Eugen, 'La monocratie dans l'Europe occidentale (Ve–Xe siècles)', in *La Monocratie*, Recueils de la Société Jean Bodin 21, Brussels: Université Libre, 1969, vol. II, pp. 57–105.

Facinger, Marion F., 'A study of medieval queenship: Capetian France, 987–1237', *Studies in Medieval and Renaissance History*, 5 (1968), 1–47.

Fantoni, Marcello, 'L'economia delle splendore. La corte medicea fra Cinque e Seicento', in Maurice Aymard and Marzio Romani (eds.), *La Cour comme institution économique*, Paris: Maison des Sciences de l'Homme, 1998, pp. 115–24.

Farinha, António Dias, 'Contribuição para o estudo das palavras Portuguesas derivadas do Árabe Hispânico', *Portugaliae Historica*, 1 (1973), 244–65.

Ferreira, Manuel Pedro, 'Da música na história de Portugal', *Revista Portuguesa de Musicologia*, 4–5 (1994–95), 167–216.

Fichtenau, Heinrich, *Living in the Tenth Century*, Chicago: University of Chicago Press, 1991.

Figueiredo, José Anastácio de, *Synopsis chronologica de subsídios ainda os mais raros para a história e estudo crítico da legislação Portugueza*, vol. I, Lisbon: Academia Real das Ciências, 1790.

Fleckenstein, Josef, *Die Hofkapelle der Deutschen Könige*, Stuttgart: Hiersemann, 1959.

'*Rex Canonicus*. Über Entstehung und Bedeutung des mittelalterlichen Königskanonikates', in Peter Classen and Peter Scheibert (eds.), *Festschrift Percy Ernst Schramm*, vol. I, Wiesbaden: Steiner, 1974, pp. 57–71.

Fleckenstein, Josef (ed.), *Curialitas: Studien zu Grundfragen der höfischen-ritterlichen Kultur*, Göttingen: Vandenhoeck and Ruprecht, 1990.

Fogel, Michèle, *Les Cérémonies de l'information dans la France du XVIe au milieu du XVIIe siècles*, Paris: Fayard, 1989.

Folz, Robert, 'Le régime monocratique en Allemagne (XIe–XVe siècles)', in *La Monocratie*, Recueils de la Société Jean Bodin 21, Brussels: Université Libre, 1969, vol. II, pp. 241–327.

Les Saints Rois du moyen âge en occident, Brussels: Société des Bollandistes, 1984.

Fonseca, Luis Adão da, *O Condestável D. Pedro de Portugal*, Oporto: INIC, 1982.

'Algumas considerações a propósito da documentação existente em Barcelona respeitante à Ordem de Avis: sua contribuição para um melhor conhecimento dos grupos de pressão em Portugal em meados do século XV', *Revista da Faculdade de Letras* (Oporto), 1 (1984), 19–56.

Forey, Alan, 'Women and the Military Orders in the twelfth and thirteenth centuries', in *Military Orders and Crusades*, London: Variorum, 1994, [IV], pp. 63–92.

Fradenburg, Louise Olga (ed.), *Women and Sovereignty*, Edinburgh: Edinburgh University Press, 1992.

Frazer, James G., *The Golden Bough: A Study in Magic and Religion (Abridged Edition)*, London: Macmillan, 1933.

Freire, Anselmo Braamcamp, 'A Chancelaria de D. Afonso V', *Arquivo Histórico Português*, 2 (1904), 479–87.

A Honra de Resende, offprint of *Arquivo Histórico Português*, Lisbon, 1906.

Brasões da Sala de Sintra, 3 vols., Lisbon: Imprensa Nacional–Casa da Moeda, 1973.

Freitas, Judite Gonçalves de, *A burocracia do 'Eloquente' (1433–1438): os textos, as normas, as gentes*, Cascais: Patrimonia, 1996.

Galego, Júlia, João Carlos Garcia and Maria Fernanda Alegria, *Os itinerários de D. Dinis, D. Pedro e D. Fernando: interpretação gráfica*, Lisbon: Centro de Estudos Geográficos, 1988.

Ganshof, F. L., 'La *Tractoria*. Contribution à l'étude du droit de gîte', *Revue d'Histoire du Droit*, 8 (1927), 69–91.

García de Valdeavellano, Luis, *Curso de historia de las instituciones Españolas. De los orígenes al final de la edad media*, Madrid: Revista de Occidente, 1977.

Historia de España: De los orígenes a la baja edad media, 2 vols., Madrid: Alianza, 1980.

El feudalismo Hispánico y otros estudios de historia medieval, Barcelona: Ariel, 1981.

García Marín, J. M., *El oficio público en Castilla durante la baja edad media*, Seville: Universidad de Sevilla, 1974.

García Oro, José, *La nobleza Gallega en la baja edad media*, Santiago de Compostela: Bibliófilos Gallegos, 1981.

Garin, Eugenio, *La cultura filosofica del Rinascimento Italiano*, Florence: Sansoni, 1979.

Garrigou, Alain and Bernard Lacroix (eds.), *Norbert Elias: la politique et l'histoire*, Paris: La Découverte, 1997.

Geertz, Clifford, 'Centers, kings and charisma: reflections on the symbolic of power', in J. Ben-David and T. Nichols Clark (eds.), *Culture and Its Creators: Essays in Honour of Edward Shils*, Chicago: University of Chicago Press, 1977, pp. 150–71.

Negara: The Theatre State in Nineteenth Century Bali, Princeton: Princeton University Press, 1980.

Local Knowledge, New York: Fontana, 1983.

Genet, J. P. and B. Vincent (eds.), *Etat et église dans la genèse de l'état moderne*, Madrid: Casa de Velázquez, 1986.

Génicot, Léopold, *La Noblesse dans l'occident mediéval*, London: Variorum Reprints, 1982.

'La noblesse médiévale: encore!', *Revue d'Histoire Ecclésiastique*, 88 (1993), 173–201.

Gerbet, Marie-Claude, *La Noblesse dans le royaume de Castille: étude sur ses structures sociales en Estrémadoure de 1454 à 1516*, Paris: Sorbonne, 1979.

Gierke, Otto, *Political Theories of the Middle Ages*, Cambridge: Cambridge University Press, 1987.

Giesey, Ralph, *If Not, Not: The Oath of the Aragonese and the Legendary Laws of Sobrarbe*, Princeton: Princeton University Press, 1968.

Le Roi ne meurt jamais, Paris: Flammarion, 1987.

'Modèles de pouvoir dans les rites royaux en France', *Annales ESC*, 41 (1986), 579–99.

Girão, A. Amorim, Vergílio Correia and Torquato de Sousa Soares, *Coimbra e Arredores*, Coimbra: Universidade de Coimbra, 1939.

Girardi, Nelly Porro, *La investidura de armas en Castilla, del Rey Sabio a los Católicos*, Valladolid: Junta de Castilla y León, 1998.

Given-Wilson, Chris, *The Royal Household and the King's Affinity: Service, Politics and Finance in England, 1360–1413*, New Haven and London: Yale University Press, 1986.

Godinho, Vitorino Magalhães, *A expansão quatrocentista portuguesa: problemas das origens e das linhas de evolução*, Lisbon: Empresa Contemporânea de Edições, 1944.

'Finanças públicas e estrutura do estado', in *Ensaios II: sobre a história de Portugal*, Lisbon: Sá da Costa, 1968, pp. 25–63.

A construção de modelos para as economias pré-estatísticas, offprint of *Revista de História Económica e Social*, Lisbon: 1985.

Mito e mercadoria: Utopia e prática de navegar. Séculos XII–XVIII, Lisbon: Difel, 1990.

Gomes, José da Costa, *Collecção de Leis da Dívida Pública Portugueza*, vol. I, Lisbon: Imprensa Nacional, 1883.

Gomes, Saul António, *O Mosteiro de Santa Maria da Vitória no século XV*, Coimbra: Universidade da Coimbra, 1990.

'Percursos em torno do panteão quatrocentista de Avis', *Biblos*, 70 (1994), 197–242.

Introdução à história do castelo de Leiria, Leiria: Câmara Municipal, 1995.

Gómez Izquierdo, Alicia, *Cargos de la casa y corte de Juan II de Castilla*, Valladolid: Universidad de Valladolid and Cuadernos de la Cátedra de Paleografía y Diplomática, 1968.

Gonçalves, A. Nogueira, 'O tesouro de D. Catarina de Eça', *O Mundo da Arte*, 12 (1982), 3–10.

Gonçalves, Iria, *Pedidos e empréstimos públicos em Portugal durante a idade média*, Lisbon: Ministério das Finanças, 1964.

As finanças municipais do Porto na segunda metade do século XV, Oporto: Câmara Municipal, 1987.

Imagens do mundo medieval, Lisbon: Horizonte, 1988.

O património do Mosteiro de Alcobaça nos séculos XIV e XV, Lisbon: Universidade Nova de Lisboa, 1989.

Alguns aspectos da visita régia ao Entre Cávado e Minho, no século XIII, offprint of *Estudos Medievais*, Oporto, 1993.

Goodenough, W. H., *Basic Economy and the Society*, New Haven: Yale University Press, 1941.

Goody, Jack, 'Religion and ritual: the definitional problem', *British Journal of Sociology*, 12 (1961), 142–64.

'Against ritual: loosely structured thoughts on a loosely defined topic', in S. Moore and B. Myerhoff (eds.), *Secular Ritual*, Amsterdam: Van Gorcum, 1977, pp. 25–35.

Gordon, Daniel, *Citizens without Sovereignty: Equality and Sociability in French Thought, 1670–1789*, Princeton: Princeton University Press, 1994.

Gouldner, Alvin, 'The norm of reciprocity: a preliminary statement', *American Sociological Review*, 25 (1960), 161–78.

Grassotti, Hilda, *Las instituciones feudo-vasalláticas en León y Castilla*, 2 vols., Spoleto: Centro Italiano di Studi sull'Alto Medioevo, 1969.

'Apostillas a "El Prestimonio" de Valdeavellano', in *Estudios medievales Españoles*, Madrid: Fundación Universitaria Española, 1981, pp. 133–58.

Graus, František, 'Littérature et mentalités médiévales: le roi et le peuple', *Historica*, 16 (1969), 5–79.

Gray, Victor, *Glossaire archéologique du moyen âge et de la Renaissance*, 2 vols., Paris: Picard, 1928.

Green, Richard Firth, 'The *familia regis* and the *familia cupidinis*', in V. J. Scattergood and J. W. Sherborne (eds.), *English Court Culture in the Late Middle Ages*, London: Duckworth, 1983, pp. 82–108.

Grossi, Paolo, *L'ordine giuridico medievale*, Bari: Laterza, 1995.

Groten, Manfred, 'Königskanonikat und Krönung', *Deutsches Archiv für Erforschung des Mittelalters*, 48 (1992), 625–9.

Grottannelli, C., 'Divisioni delle carni, organizzazione del Cosmo, dinamica sociales', *Studi Storici*, 25 (1984), 824–33.

Gual Camarena, Miguel, 'El hospedaje hispanomedieval. Aportaciones para su estudio', *Anuario de Historia del Derecho Español*, 32 (1962), 527–41.

Guenée, Bernard, *L'Occident aux XIVe et XVe siècles: les états*, Paris: PUF, 1971.

'Le roi, ses parents et son royaume en France au XIVe siècle', *Bullettino dell'Istituto Storico Italiano per il Medio Evo e Archivio Muratoriano*, 94 (1988), 439–70.

Guenée, Bernard and Françoise Lehoux, *Les Entrées royales françaises, de 1328 à 1515*, Paris: CNRS, 1968.

Guevara y Valdés, Eduardo, 'Los Castro Gallegos del siglo XIV. Apuntes para un análisis de su proyección en la historia política de Castilla', *Hispania*, 45 (1985), 161, 477–511.

Guglielmi, Nilda, 'La curia regia en León y Castilla', *Cuadernos de Historia de España*, 33–4 (1955), 116–267; 38 (1958), 43–131.

'Posada y yantar. Contribución al estudio del léxico de las instituciones medievales', *Hispania*, 26 (1966), 5–40, 165–219.

Guillaume, Jean (ed.), *Architecture et vie sociale: l'organisation intérieure des grandes demeures à la fin du moyen âge et à la Renaissance*, Paris: Picard, 1994.

Guillemain, Bernard, *La Cour pontificale d'Avignon, 1309–1376: étude d'une société*, Paris: Ecole Française de Rome, 1962.

Hall, Edward T., *The Hidden Dimension*, New York: Doubleday, 1966.

Halphen, Louis, 'Le "*De Ordine Palatii*" d'Hincmar', *Revue Historique*, 183 (1938), 3, 1–9.

Hamilton, E., 'Origin and growth of the national debt in Western Europe', *American Economic Review*, 37 (1947), 118–40.

Hauf, Albert, 'El *Ars Praedicandi* de Fr. Afonso d'Alpão, O.F.M. Aportación al estudio de la teoría de la predicación en la Península Ibérica', *Archivum Franciscanum Historicum*, 72 (1979), 233–329.

Heers, Jacques, *Escravos e servidão doméstica na idade média*, Lisbon: Dom Quixote, 1983.

Heleno, Manuel, *Antiguidades de Monte Real*, Lisbon: Imprensa Nacional, 1922.

'Antiguidades de Monte Real (aditamentos)', *O Arqueólogo Português*, 26 (1924), 331–45.

Héliot, P., 'Sur les résidences princières bâties en France du Xe au XIIe siècle', *Le Moyen Age*, 61 (1955), 27–61, 291–317.

Herculano, Alexandre, *Opúsculos*, 10 vols., Lisbon: Ailland and Bertrand, 1873–1908.

Hersch, Philip, Angus MacKay and Geraldine MacKendrick, 'The semiology of dress in late medieval and early modern Spain', *Razo*, 7 (1987), 95–100.

Hespanha, António Manuel, *História das instituições: épocas medieval e moderna*, Coimbra: Almedina, 1982.

Heusch, Luc de, *Ecrits sur la royauté sacrée*, Brussels: Université Libre, 1987.

Hicks, Michael, *Bastard Feudalism*, New York: Longman, 1995.

Hirschbiegel, Jan, 'Der Hof as soziales System', *Mitteilungen der Residenzen-Kommission der Akademie der Wissenschaften zu Göttingen*, 3 (1993), 1, 11–25; 2, 15–19.

Hobsbawm, E. J. and T. Ranger (eds.), *The Invention of Tradition*, Cambridge: Cambridge University Press, 1983.

Hocart, Arthur, *Kings and Councillors: An Essay in the Comparative Anatomy of Human Society*, Chicago: Chicago University Press, 1969.

Kingship, London: Oxford University Press, 1970.

Homem, Armando Luís de Carvalho, *Subsídios para o estudo da administração central no reinado de D. Pedro I*, offprint of *Revista de História*, Oporto, 1978.

'O Doutor João das Regras no desembargo e no conselho régios (1384–1404). Breves notas', in *Estudos de História de Portugal: Homenagem a A. H. de Oliveira Marques*, vol. I, Lisbon: Estampa, 1982, pp. 241–53.

Conselho real ou conselheiros do rei? A propósito dos 'privados' de D. João 1, offprint of *Revista da Faculdade de Letras*, Oporto, 1987.

O desembargo régio (1320–1433), Lisbon: INIC, 1990.

Para uma abordagem da burocracia régia: Portugal, séculos XIII–XV, offprint of *Revista Portuguesa de História*, Coimbra, 1996.

Homem, Armando Luís de Carvalho, Luís Miguel Duarte and Eugénia Pereira da Mota, 'Percursos na burocracia régia', in Francisco Bethencourt and Diogo Ramada Curto (eds.), *A memória da nação*, Lisbon: Sá da Costa, 1991, pp. 403–23.

Hourlier, Jacques, 'Famiglia', in *Dizionario degli Istituti di Perfezione*, Rome: Edizioni Paoline, 1980, vol. II, 1390–95.

Hughes, Andrew, 'The monarch as the object of liturgical veneration', in Anne Duggan (ed.), *Kings and Kingship in Medieval Europe*, London: King's College, 1993, pp. 375–424.

Inwood, Brad, 'Politics and paradox in Seneca's *De Beneficiis*', in André Lacks and Malcolm Schofield (eds.), *Justice and Generosity: Studies in Hellenistic Social and Political Philosophy*, Cambridge: Cambridge University Press, 1995, pp. 241–65.

Jaeger, C. Stephen, *The Origins of Courtliness: Civilizing Trends and the Formation of Courtly Ideals, 939–1210*, Philadelphia: University of Pennsylvania Press, 1985.

The Envy of Angels, Philadelphia: University of Pennsylvania Press, 1994.

Jenkinson, Hilary, 'Medieval tallies, public and private', *Archaeologia*, 84 (1923–24), 289–351.

Johnstone, Hilda, 'The wardrobe and household of Henry son of Edward I', *Bulletin of John Rylands Library*, 7 (1922–23), 384–420.

'The queen's household', in J. F. Willard and W. Morris (eds.), *The English Government at Work, 1327–1336*, Cambridge, MA: The Medieval Academy of America, 1940, vol. I, pp. 250–99.

Jouanna, Arlette, 'Des réseaux d'amitié aux clientèles centralisées: les provinces et la cour (France, XVIe–XVIIe siècle)', in Charles Giry-Deloison and Roger Mettam (eds.), *Patronages et clientélismes, 1550–1750 (France, Angleterre, Espagne, Italie)*, Villeneuve d'Ascq and London: Centre d'Histoire de la Région du Nord et de l'Europe du Nord-Ouest/Institut Français du Royaume-Uni, 1995, pp. 21–124.

Kaminski, Howard, 'Estate, nobility and the exhibition of estate in the later middle ages', *Speculum*, 68 (1993), 684–709.

Kantorowicz, Ernst, *Laudes Regiae: A Study in Liturgical Acclamations and Mediaeval Ruler Worship*, Berkeley and Los Angeles: University of California Press, 1946.

The King's Two Bodies: A Study in Political Medieval Theology, Princeton: Princeton University Press, 1957.

Selected Studies, New York: Augustin, 1965.

Kaye, Joel, *Economy and Nature in the Fourteenth Century: Money, Market Exchange, and the Emergence of Scientific Thought*, Cambridge: Cambridge University Press, 1998.

Kazhdan, Alexander P. and Michael McCormick, 'The social world of the Byzantine court', in Henry Maguire (ed.), *Byzantine Court Culture from 829 to 1204*, Washington, DC: Dumbarton Oaks, 1997, pp. 167–97.

Keen, Maurice, *Chivalry*, New Haven and London: Yale University Press, 1984.

Nobles, Knights and Men-at-Arms in the Middle Ages, London and Rio Grande: Hambledon, 1996.

Kern, Fritz, *Kingship and Law in the Middle Ages*, Oxford: Blackwell, 1939.

Kerscher, G., 'Die Strukturierung des mallorquinischen Hofes um 1350 und der Habitus der Hofgesellschaft', in Holger Kruse and Werner Paravicini (eds.), *Höfe und Ordnungen 1200–1600.* 5 Symposium der Residenzen-Kommission der Akademie der Wissenschaften in Göttingen, Sigmaringen: Thorbecke, 1999, pp. 77–89.

Kipling, Gordon, *Enter the King: Theater, Liturgy, and Ritual in the Medieval Civic Triumph*, Oxford: Clarendon, 1998.

Klapish-Zuber, Christiane, 'La *mattinata* médiévale', in *La Maison et le nom: stratégies et rituels dans l'Italie de la Renaissance*, Paris: Ecole des Hautes Etudes en Sciences Sociales, 1990, pp. 229–46.

Kleinbauer, W. Eugene, 'Charlemagne's palace chapel at Aachen and its copies', *Gesta*, 4 (1965), 2–11.

Knecht, R. J., 'The court of Francis I', *European Studies Review*, 8 (1978), 1–22.

Knighton, Tess, 'Ritual and regulations: the organization of the Castilian royal chapel during the reign of the Catholic Monarchs', in *De musica Hispana et aliis: Miscelánea en honor al Prof. Dr José López-Calo, S.J.*, vol. I, Santiago de Compostela: Universidad de Santiago de Compostela, 1990, pp. 291–320.

Köhler, Erich, 'Senso e funzione del termine *joven*', in *Sociologia della fin'amor: saggi trobadorici*, Padu: Liviana, 1976, pp. 233–56.

Korrodi, Ernesto, 'A Alcáçova do Castelo de Leiria e a sua significação social e política', *Boletim da Academia Nacional de Belas-Artes*, Lisbon, 13 (1944), 12–28.

Koselleck, Reinhart, *Le Futur passé: contribution à la sémantique des temps historiques*, Paris: Ecole des Hautes Etudes en Sciences Sociales, 1990.

Krus, Luis, *A concepção nobiliárquica do espaço Ibérico (1280–1380): geografia dos Livros de Linhagens medievais Portugueses*, Lisbon: Fundação Calouste Gulbenkian, 1994.

Passado, memória e poder na sociedade medieval Portuguesa: estudos, Redondo: Patrimonia, 1994.

Krynen, Jacques, '"Naturel". Essai sur l'argument de la nature dans la pensée française de la fin du moyen âge', *Journal des Savants*, 2 (1982), 169–90.

Labbé, Alain, *L'Architecture des palais et des jardins dans les Chansons de Geste: essai sur le thème du roi en majesté*, Paris and Geneva: Champion-Slatkine, 1987.

Ladero Quesada, Miguel Angel, *Fiscalidad y poder real en Castilla (1252–1369)*, Madrid: Editorial Complutense, 1993.

Lafortune-Martel, Agathe, *Fête noble en Bourgogne au XVe siècle: le banquet du faisan (1454)*, Montreal and Paris: Bellarmin-Vrin, 1984.

Lanciani, Giulia and Giuseppe Tavani (eds.), *Dicionário da literatura medieval Galega e Portuguesa*, Lisbon: Caminho, 1993.

Larcher, Jorge, *Castelos de Portugal: Distrito de Leiria*, Lisbon: Imprensa Nacional, 1933.

Lasswell, Harold D., Daniel Lerner and Hans Speier (eds.), *Propaganda and Communication in World History*, vol. II, Honolulu: University of Hawaii, 1980.

Le Bras, Gabriel, 'Institutions ecclésiastiques de la Chrétienté medievale', in A. Fliche and V. Martin (eds.), *Histoire de l'église depuis les origines jusqu'à nos jours – XIV*, 2 vols., Paris: Bloud & Gay, 1959–64.

Le Goff, Jacques, 'Le roi dans l'occident médiéval: caractères originaux', in Anne J. Duggan (ed.), *Kings and Kingship in Medieval Europe*, London: King's College, 1993, pp. 1–40.

Leclercq, Jean, *L'Idée de la royauté du Christ au moyen âge*, Paris: Editions du Cerf, 1959.

Leite, A. P. Sousa, 'O Bispo de Lamego D. João da Costa e a sua compilação de livros de cetraria no manuscrito Sloane 821 do Museu Britânico', *Boletim da Academia Portuguesa de Ex-Libris*, 12 (1967), 18–30.

Lekai, Louis, *The Cistercians: Ideals and Reality*, Kent, OH: Kent State University Press, 1977.

Lemoine, Henri, 'Les écuries royales sous Charles VI et Charles VII', *Bulletin Philologique et Historique* (1928–29), 130–7.

Leroy, Béatrice, 'La cour des rois Charles II et Charles III de Navarre (vers 1350–1425), lieu de rencontre, milieu de gouvernement', in Adeline Rucquoi (ed.), *Realidad e imágenes del poder: España a fines de la edad media*, Valladolid: Ambito, 1988, pp. 233–48.

Lévi-Provençal, E., *Histoire de l'Espagne musulmane*, vol. II, *Le Califat Umayade de Cordoue (912–1031)*, Paris and Leiden: Brill, 1950.

Lewin, Kurt, *Field Theory in Social Science: Selected Theoretical Papers*, New York: Harper, 1951.

Linehan, Peter, *History and the Historians of Medieval Spain*, Oxford: Oxford University Press, 1993.

'The politics of piety: aspects of the Castilian monarchy from Alfonso X to Alfonso XI', *Revista Canadiense de Estudios Hispánicos*, 9 (1985), 385–404.

'The king's touch and the dean's ministrations: aspects of sacral monarchy', in Miri Rubin (ed.), *The Work of Jacques le Goff and the Challenges of Medieval History*, Woodbridge: Boydell and Brewer, 1997, pp. 189–206.

Lino, Raúl, *Os paços reais da vila de Sintra*, Lisbon: Valentim de Carvalho, 1948.

Lisboa Quinhentista: as imagens e a vida da cidade (exhibition Catalogue), Lisbon: Câmara Municipal, 1983.

Little, Lester K., *Religious Poverty and the Profit Economy in Medieval Europe*, Ithaca: Cornell University Press, 1994.

Lobo, A. S. Costa, *História da sociedade em Portugal no século XV*, reprinted, Lisbon: Editora História Crítica, 1979.

Lombard-Jourdan, A., *Mont-Joie et Saint-Denis! Le Centre de la Gaule aux origines de Paris et Saint-Denis*, Paris: CNRS, 1989.

Lopes, Flávio (ed.), *Património arquitectónico e arqueológico classificado: inventário*, 3 vols., Lisbon: Instituto Português do Património Arquitectónico e Arqueológico, 1993.

López, A., 'Confesores de la familia real de Castilla', *Archivo Ibero-Americano*, 31 (1929), 6–75.

López Estrada, Francisco, 'Corte y literatura en las *Siete Partidas*', in Monique de Lope (ed.), *Littérature et institutions dans le moyen âge espagnol*, Montpellier: Université Paul Valéry, 1991, pp. 9–46.

Lorenzo, Ramón, *Sobre cronologia do vocabulário Galego-Português*, Vigo: Galáxia, 1968.

Lot, Ferdinand and Robert Fawtier, *Histoire des institutions françaises au moyen âge*, vol. II, *Institutions royales*, Paris: PUF, 1958.

Lourie, Elena, 'Jewish participation in royal funerary rites: an early use of the *repraesentatio* in Aragon', *Journal of the Warburg and Courtauld Institutes*, 45 (1982), 192–4.

Lowe, Kate (ed.), *Cultural Links between Portugal and Italy in the Renaissance*, Oxford: Oxford University Press, 2000.

Luchaire, Achille, *Manuel des institutions françaises: période des Capétiens directs*, Paris: Hachette, 1892.

Luhmann, Niklas, *The Differentiation of Society*, New York: Columbia University Press, 1982.

Essays on Self-Reference, New York: Columbia University Press, 1990.

Lukes, Stephen, 'Political ritual and social integration', in *Essays in Social Theory*, London: Methuen, 1977, pp. 52–73.

Lupis, Antonio, 'Per una storia della caccia aragonese', *Quaderni Medievali*, 11 (1981), 86–101.

Lyon, Bryce Dale, *From Fief to Indenture: The Transition from Feudal to Non-Feudal Contract in Western Europe*, Cambridge, MA: Harvard University Press, 1957.

Lyon, Bryce Dale and Mary Lyon, *The Wardrobe Book of William Norwell, 1338–1340*, Brussels: Académie Royale de Belgique, 1983.

MacCormack, Sabine, *Art and Ceremony in Late Antiquity*, Berkeley and Los Angeles: University of California Press, 1981.

McCormick, Michael, 'Analyzing imperial ceremonies', *Jahrbuch der Österreischen Byzantinistik*, 35 (1985), 1–20.

McFarlane, K. B., *The Nobility of Later Medieval England*, Oxford: Oxford University Press, 1973.

England in the Fifteenth Century: Collected Essays, London: Hambledon Press, 1981.

Machado, J. Montalvão, *Dom Afonso primeiro Duque de Bragança: sua vida e obra*, Lisbon: Edição do Autor, 1964.

'O Paço Real de Frielas', *Olisipo*, 28 (1965), 187–94.

Alguns acontecimentos esquecidos do tempo do rei D. Fernando, offprint of *Anais da Academia Portuguesa da História*, Lisbon, 1982.

MacKay, Angus, 'Ritual and propaganda in fifteenth-century Castile', *Past and Present*, 107 (1985), 3–43.

'The lesser nobility in the kingdom of Castile', in *Society, Economy and Religion in Late Medieval Castile*, Aldershot: Variorum, 1987, [IV], pp. 159–80.

Macpherson, I. R., '*Amor* and Don Juan Manuel', *Hispanic Review*, 39 (1971), 167–82.

Maczak, Antoni, *Klientelsysteme im Europa der frühen Neuzeit*, Munich: Oldenbourg, 1988.

Madden, James Eugene, 'Business monks, banker monks, bankrupt monks: the English Cistercians in the thirteenth century', *The Catholic Historical Review*, 49 (1963–64), 341–64.

Major, J. Russell, 'Vertical ties through time', *French Historical Studies*, 17 (1992), 63–71.

Makarius, Laura, 'Du roi magique au roi divin', *Annales ESC*, 35 (1970), 668–98.

Mantini, Silvia, 'Notte in città, notte in campagna tra medioevo ed età moderna', in Mario Sbriccoli (ed.), *La notte: ordine, sicurezza e disciplinamento in età moderna*, Florence: Ponte alle Grazie, 1991, pp. 30–45.

Maravall, José Antonio, 'Relaciones de dependencia e integración social. Criados, graciosos y pícaros', *Ideologies & Literature*, 1 (1977), 3–32.

Estudios de historia del pensamiento Español: edad media, Madrid: Cultura Hispánica, 1983.

Marques, A. H. de Oliveira, *Ensaios de história medieval Portuguesa*, Lisbon: Vega, 1980.

A sociedade medieval Portuguesa, Lisbon: Sá da Costa, 1981.

Introdução à história da cidade medieval Portuguesa, offprint of *Bracara Augusta*, Braga, 1981.

Portugal na crise dos séculos XIV e XV, Nova História de Portugal IV, Lisbon: Presença, 1986.

As cidades Portuguesas nos finais da idade média, offprint of *Penélope*, Lisbon, 1992.

Hansa e Portugal na idade média, Lisbon: Presença, 1993.

'Depois da Reconquista. A cidade na baixa idade média', in Irisalva Moita (ed.), *O Livro de Lisboa*, Lisbon: Horizonte, 1994, pp. 89–113.

Marques, José, *A propósito dos recomendados de D. Luís da Guerra (1434)*, offprint of *Bracara Augusta*, Braga, 1977.

'A Colegiada de Guimarães no Priorado de D. Afonso Gomes de Lemos (1449–1487)', in *Actas do Congresso Histórico de Guimarães e da sua Colegiada*, vol. II, Guimarães, 1981, pp. 239–325.

A Arquidiocese de Braga no século XV, Lisbon: INCM, 1988.

O Testamento de D. Lourenço Vicente e as suas capelas na Sé de Braga e na Lourinhã, offprint of *Homenagem à Arquidiocese Primaz*, Lisbon: Academia Portuguesa da História, 1993.

Martimort, G., *Les Ordines, les ordinaires et les cérémoniaux*, Typologie des Sources du Moyen Âge Occidental 56, Turnhout: Brepols, 1991.

Martin, José Luis, 'El Rey ha muerto. Viva el Rey!', *Hispania*, 51 (1991), 5–39.

Martínez Sopena, Pascual, 'La nobleza de León y Castilla en los siglos XI y XII. Un estado de la cuestión', *Hispania*, 185 (1993), 801–22.

Martins, Mário, *Laudes e cantigas espirituais de Mestre André Dias*, Roriz: Edições Mosteiro de Singeverga, 1951.

O ciclo Franciscano na nossa espiritualidade medieval, offprint of *Biblos*, Coimbra, 1952.

Estudos de cultura medieval, 3 vols., Lisbon: Brotéria, 1969–83.

Dum poema Inglês de John Gower e sua tradução do Português para o castelhano, offprint of *Didaskalia*, Lisbon, 1979.

Guia Geral das Horas del-Rei D. Duarte, Lisbon: Brotéria, 1982.

Mateu Ibars, Josefina, 'La *confirmatio* del *signifer, armiger y alferez* según documentación Asturleonesa y Castellana', *En la España Medieval*, 1 (1980), 263–316.

Mathew, Gervase, *The Court of Richard II*, London: J. Murray, 1966.

Mattoso, José, *Le Monachisme ibérique et Cluny: les abbayes du diocèse de Porto de l'an mil à 1200*, Louvain: Publications Universitaires, 1968.

'Testamentos de D. Sancho I', in Alexandre Herculano, *História de Portugal desde o começo da monarquia até o fim do reinado de D. Afonso III*, vol. III (Nota Final III), Lisbon: Bertrand, 1980, pp. 570–4.

Ricos-homens, infanções e cavaleiros: A nobreza medieval Portuguesa dos séculos XI e XII, Lisbon: Guimarães Editores, 1982.

Identificação de um país, 2 vols., Lisbon: Estampa, 1985.

Fragmentos de uma composição medieval, Lisbon: Estampa, 1987.

'A coroação dos primeiros reis de Portugal', in F. Bethencourt and D. Ramada Curto, *A memória da Nação*, Lisbon: Sá da Costa, 1991, pp. 187–200.

Portugal medieval: novas interpretações, Lisbon: Imprensa Nacional Casa da Moeda, 1993.

'O poder e a morte', *Anuario de Estudios Medievales*, 25 (1995), 395–427.

'O mosteiro de Rendufe (1090–1570)', in *Religião e cultura na idade média Portuguesa*, Lisbon: Imprensa Nacional Casa da Moeda, 1997.

'Perspectivas actuais sobre a nobreza medieval Portuguesa', *Revista de História das Ideias*, 19 (1997), 7–37.

'A nobreza medieval Portuguesa (séculos X a XIV)', in *La nobleza peninsular en la edad media: VI Congreso de estudios medievales*, Avila: Fundación Sánchez-Albornoz, 1999, pp. 9–32.

Mattoso, José, Luis Krus and Amélia Andrade, *A terra de Santa Maria no século XIII: problemas e documentos*, s.l.: Comissao de Vigilância do Castelo de Santa Maria da Feira, 1993.

Melville, Gert, 'Hérauts et héros', in Heinz Duchhard, Richard A. Jackson and David Sturdy (eds.), *European Monarchy: Its Evolution and Practice*, Stuttgart: Steiner, 1992, pp. 17–25.

Menéndez Pidal de Navascués, Faustino, 'Heráldica funeraria en Castilla', *Hidalguía*, 13 (1965), 133–44.

Menjot, Denis, 'Un Chrétien qui meurt toujours. Les funérailles royales en Castille à la fin du moyen âge', in *La idea y el sentimiento de la muerte en la historia y en el arte de la edad media*, Santiago de Compostela: Universidad de Santiago de Compostela, 1988, pp. 127–38.

'Enseigner la sagesse. Remarques sur la littérature gnomique castillane du moyen âge', in Nilda Guglielmi and Adeline Rucquoi (eds.), *El discurso político en la edad media*, Madrid: CSIC/CNRS, 1995, pp. 217–31.

Meouak, Mohamed, 'Notes historiques sur l'administration centrale, les charges et le recrutement des fonctionnaires dans l'Espagne musulmane (2e/VIIIe–4e/Xe siècles)', *Hesperis-Tamuda*, 30 (1992), 9–20.

Merêa, Paulo, *Introdução ao problema do feudalismo em Portugal*, Coimbra: França Amado, 1912.

'Génese da lei mental (algumas notas)', *Boletim da Faculdade de Direito da Universidade de Coimbra*, 10 (1926–28), 1–15.

Para um glossário do nosso Latim medieval, offprint of *Biblos*, Coimbra, 1940.

Sobre a aclamação dos nossos reis, offprint of *Revista Portuguesa de História*, Coimbra, 1962.

Mertes, Kate, 'Aristocracy', in Rosemary Horrox (ed.), *Fifteenth-Century Attitudes: Perceptions of Society in Late Medieval England*, Cambridge: Cambridge University Press, 1994, pp. 42–60.

Michaud-Quentin, Pierre, *Universitas: expressions du mouvement communautaire dans le moyen âge latin*, Paris: Vrin, 1970.

Miglio, Massimo, 'Liturgia e cerimoniale di corte', in Giovanni Morello and Silvia Maddalo (eds.), *Liturgia in figura: Codici Liturgici Rinascimentali della Biblioteca Apostolica Vaticana*, Rome: Biblioteca Apostolica Vaticana/Edizioni De Luca, 1995, pp. 43–50.

Millar, Fergus, *The Emperor in the Roman World*, Ithaca: Cornell University Press, 1977.

Mitre Fernández, Emilio, 'La emigración de nobles Portugueses a Castilla a fines del siglo XIV', *Hispania*, 26 (1966), 513–25.

Mitteis, Heinrich, *The State in the Middle Ages: A Comparative Constitutional History of Feudal Europe*, Oxford and New York: North Holland and Elsevier, 1975.

Molénat, Jean-Pierre, 'La volonté de durer: majorats et chapellenies dans la pratique tolédane des XIIIe et XIVe siècles', in *En la España medieval*, vol. V, *Estudios en memoria de Claudio Sánchez-Albornoz*, Madrid: Universidad Complutense, 1986, vol. II, pp. 683–96.

Molho, Anthony, *Marriage Alliance in Late Medieval Florence*, Cambridge, MA: Harvard University Press, 1994.

Moniz, M. Carvalho, *O Convento e a Igreja de S. Francisco de Évora*, offprint of *Boletim da Junta da Província do Alto Alentejo*, Évora, 1959.

Monteiro, Fernando Sá, 'Os Sás e as suas origens', *Armas e troféus* (5th series), 1 (1981), 205–27.

Monteiro, João Gouveia, 'A cultura militar da nobreza na primeira metade de Quatrocentos', *Revista de História das Ideias*, 19 (1998), 195–227.

A guerra em Portugal nos finais da idade média, Lisbon: Editorial Notícias, 1998.

Os castelos Portugueses dos finais da idade média, Coimbra: Colibri, 1999.

Moore, Sally and Barbara Myerhoff (eds.), *Secular Ritual*, Amsterdam: Van Gorcum, 1977.

Moraes, M. A. Pereira, 'Capelas vinculadas na Colegiada de Nossa Senhora da Oliveira', in *Actas do Congresso Histórico de Guimarães e sua Colegiada*, vol. II, Guimarães, 1981, pp. 451–80.

Morato, Francisco Manuel Trigoso Aragão, 'Memória sobre os escrivães da puridade dos reis de Portugal, e do que a este officio pertence', *Memórias da Academia Real das Ciências*, 12 (1837), 91–107.

Moreno, Humberto Baquero, *Os itinerários do Infante D. Pedro (1438–1448)*, offprint of *Revista de Ciências do Homem da Universidade de Lourenço Marques*, Lourenço Marques, 1968.

'A conspiração contra D. João II', *Arquivos do Centro Cultural Português*, 2 (1970), 56–66.

Os itinerários de El-Rei D. Duarte (1433–1438), Lisbon: Academia Portuguesa da História, 1976.

A Batalha de Alfarrobeira, 2 vols., Coimbra: Imprensa da Universidade, 1980.

Novos dados sobre as exéquias solenes de D. Afonso V, offprint of *Bracara Augusta*, Braga, 1982.

Itinerários de El-Rei D. João I, Lisbon: Instituto de Cultura e Língua Portuguesa, 1988.

'La lutte de la noblesse portugaise contre la royauté à la fin du moyen âge', *Arquivos do Centro Cultural Português*, 26 (1989), 49–65.

Moreta Velayos, S., 'La sociedad imaginada de las Cantigas', *Studia Historica – Historia Medieval*, 7 (1990), 117–38.

Morgan, D. A. L., 'The house of policy: the political role of the late Plantagenet household, 1422–1485', in David Starkey (ed.), *The English Court from the Wars of the Roses to the Civil War*, London: Longman, 1987, pp. 25–70.

Moroni, Gaetano, *Dizionario di erudizione storico-ecclesiastica*, 103 vols., Venice: Tip. Emiliana, 1840–79.

Morreale, Margherita, *Castiglione y Boscán: el ideal cortesano en el Renacimiento Español*, Madrid: Real Academia Española, 1959.

Mousnier, Roland, *La Vénalité des offices sous Henri IV et Louis XIII*, Paris: PUF, 1971.

Moussy, Claude, *Gratia et sa famille*, Paris: PUF, 1966.

Moxó, Salvador de, 'La nobleza Castellana en el siglo XIV', *Anuario de Estudios Medievales*, 7 (1970–71), 493–511.

'La promoción política y social de los "letrados" en la corte de Alfonso XI', *Hispania*, 35 (1975), 5–29.

'El auge de la nobleza urbana de Castilla y su proyección en el ámbito administrativo y rural a comienzos de la baja edad media', *Boletín de la Real Academia de la Historia*, 178 (1981), 407–510.

Feudalismo, señorío y nobleza en la Castilla medieval, Madrid: Real Academia de la Historia, 2000.

Mozzarelli, Cesare (ed.), *'Familia' del principe e famiglia aristocratica*, 2 vols., Rome: Bulzoni, 1988.

Mozzarelli, Cesare and Giuseppe Olmi (eds.), *La corte nella cultura e nella storiografia: immagini e posizioni tra Otto e Novecento*, Rome: Bulzoni, 1983.

Muir, Edward, *Civic Ritual in Renaissance Venice*, Princeton: Princeton University Press, 1981.

Muratori, Ludovico Antonio, *Dissertazioni sopra le antichità Italiane*, 3 vols., Monaco: Agostino Olzati, 1765.

Musacchio, J. M., *The Art and Ritual of Childbirth in Renaissance Italy*, New Haven: Yale University Press, 1999.

Myers, A. R., *The Household of Edward IV: The Black Book and the Ordinance of 1478*, Manchester: Manchester University Press, 1959.

Nassiet, Marcel, 'Parenté et succession dynastiques aux XIVe et XVe siècles', *Annales HSS*, 50 (1995), 621–44.

Natividade, Vieira, *As granjas do Mosteiro de Alcobaça*, offprint of *Boletim da Junta da Província da Estremadura*, Lisbon, 1944.

Naz, R. (ed.), *Dictionnaire de droit canonique*, 7 vols., Paris: Letouzey et Ané, 1935–65.

Nelson, Janet L., *Politics and Ritual in Early Medieval Europe*, London: Hambledon Press, 1986.

'The Lord's anointed and the people's choice: Carolingian royal ritual', in David Cannadine and S. Price (eds.), *Rituals of Royalty: Power and Ceremony in Traditional Societies*, Cambridge: Cambridge University Press, 1987, pp. 137–80.

'Kingship and empire in the Carolingian world', in Rosamond McKitterick (ed.), *Carolingian Culture: Innovation and Emulation*, Cambridge: Cambridge University Press, 1994, pp. 52–87.

'Early medieval rites of queen-making and the shaping of medieval queenship', in Anne J. Duggan (ed.), *Queens and Queenship in Medieval Europe*, London: Boydell Press, 1997, pp. 301–15.

Nemésio, Vitorino, *Almirantado e portos de Quatrocentos*, Lisbon: Faculdade de Letras, 1961.

Neves, C. M. Baeta, *Subsídios para a história da falcoaria em Portugal*, offprint of *Boletim da Sociedade de Geografia de Lisboa*, Lisbon, 1984.

Niederehe, Hans J., *Alfonso el Sabio y la linguística de su tiempo*, Madrid: Sociedad General Española, 1987.

Nielsen, Inge, 'Royal banquets: the development of royal banquets and banqueting halls from Alexander to the Tetrarchs', in I. Nielsen and H. Nielsen (eds.), *Meals in a Social Context: Aspects of the Communal Meal in the Hellenistic and Roman World*, Aarhus: Aarhus University Press, 2000, pp. 102–33.

Niermeyer, J. F., *Mediae Latinitatis Lexicon Minus*, Leiden: Brill, 1997.

Nieto Soria, José Manuel, 'La monarquía bajomedieval castellana. ¿Una realeza sagrada?', in *Homenaje al Profesor Juan Torres Fontes*, vol. II, Murcia: Universidad de Murcia, 1987, pp. 1225–37.

'La capilla real Castellano-Leonesa en el siglo XV: constituciones, nombramientos y quitaciones', *Archivos Leoneses*, 43 (1989), 7–54.

Ceremonias de la realeza: propaganda y legitimación en la Castilla Trastámara, Madrid: Nerea, 1993.

Nieto Soria, José Manuel (ed.), *Orígenes de la monarquía Hispánica: propaganda y legitimación (ca 1400–1520)*, Madrid: Dykinson, 1999.

Nussdorfer, Laurie, 'The vacant see: ritual and protest in early modern Rome', *Sixteenth Century Journal*, 18 (1987), 173–89.

Oexle, Otto Gerhard, 'Les groupes sociaux du moyen âge et les débuts de la sociologie contemporaine', *Annales HSS*, 47 (1992), 751–65.

Oliveira, António Resende de, *Depois do espectáculo trovadoresco: a estrutura dos cancioneiros peninsulares e as recolhas dos séculos XIII e XIV*, Lisbon: Colibri, 1994.

Trobadores e xograis: contexto histórico, Vigo: Edicións Xerais de Galicia, 1995.

Oliveira, Luis Filipe, *A Casa dos Coutinhos: linhagem, espaço e poder (1360–1452)*, Cascais: Patrimonia, 1999.

Orcástegui Gros, Carmen, 'La coronación de los reyes de Aragón. Evolución político-ideológica y ritual', in *Homenage a Don Antonio Durán Gudiol*, Huesca: Instituto de Estudios Aragoneses, 1995, pp. 633–47.

Oro, Cesar, 'Las formas del verbo Galaico-Portugués *teer* según los textos, siglos XII y XIII', *Cuadernos de Estudios Gallegos*, 31 (1978–80), 293–328.

Osório, Jorge Alves, 'Cantigas de escarnho Galego-Portuguesas: sociología ou poética?', *Revista da Faculdade de Letras – Línguas e Literaturas*, 3 (1986), 153–99.

Otero, A., 'La patria potestad en el derecho histórico Español', *Anuario de Historia del Derecho Español*, 26 (1956), 208–41.

Palacios Martín, Bonifacio, *La coronación de los reyes de Aragón, 1240–1410: aportación al estudio de las estructuras políticas medievales*, Valencia: Anubar, 1975.

'Investiduras de armas de los reyes Españoles en los siglos XII y XIII', *Gladius* (número especial *Las Armas en la Historia*) (1988), 153–92.

Papagno, Giuseppe and Amedeo Quondam, *La corte e lo spazio: Ferrara estense*, 2 vols., Rome: Bulzoni, 1982.

Paravicini, Werner, 'Expansion et intégration. La noblesse des Pays-Bas à la cour de Philippe le Bon', *Bijdragen en Medelingen betreffende de Geschiedenis der Nederlanden*, 95 (1980), 298–314.

'Structure et fonctionnement de la cour bourguignonne au XVe siècle', in J. M. Cauchies (ed.), *Le Duc, son entourage, son train*, Turnhout: Brepols, 1998, pp. 1–8.

Paravicini-Bagliani, Agostino, *Cardinali di curia e 'familie' cardinalizie dal 1227 al 1254*, Padua: Antenore, 1971.

La Cour des Papes au XIIIe siècle, Paris: Hachette, 1995.

The Pope's Body, Chicago: University of Chicago Press, 2000.

Parkin, David, 'Ritual as spatial direction and bodily division', in David Coppet (ed.), *Understanding Rituals*, London and New York: Routledge, 1992, pp. 11–25.

Parsons, John Carmi, *The Court and Household of Eleanor of Castile in 1290*, Toronto: Pontifical Institute of Medieval Studies, 1977.

'Ritual and symbol in the English medieval queenship to 1500', in Louise Olga Fredenburg (ed.), *Women and Sovereignty*, Edinburgh: University of Edinburgh Press, 1992, pp. 60–77.

Parsons, John Carmi (ed.), *Medieval Queenship*, New York: St Martin's Press, 1993.

Pastor, Reyna (ed.), *Relaciones de poder, de producción y parentesco en la edad media y moderna*, Madrid: CSIC, 1990.

Pastoureau, Michel, *Les Armoiries: typologie des sources du moyen âge occidental*, fasc. 20, Turnhout: Brepols, 1976.

Pásztor, E., 'Funzione politico-culturale di una struttura della chiesa: il cardinalato', in *Aspetti culturali della società italiana nel periodo del papato Avignonese*, Todi: Centro di Studi sulla Spiritualità Medievale, University of Perugia, 1981, pp. 199–226.

Patlagean, Evelyne, 'De la chasse et du souverain', *Dumbarton Oaks Papers*, 46 (1992), 257–63.

Peck, Linda L., *Court Patronage and Corruption in Early Stuart England*, London and Boston: Unwin, 1990.

Peck, Russell A., *Kingship and Common Profit in Gower's Confessio Amantis*, London and Amsterdam: Southern Illinois University Press, 1978.

Pereira, Gabriel, *Pelos subúrbios e vizinhanças de Lisboa*, Lisbon: Clássica Editora, 1910.

Peres, Damião (ed.), *História de Portugal*, 7 vols., Barcelos and Oporto, Portucalense Editora, 1928–37.

Pérez de la Canal, Miguel Angel, 'La justicia de la corte en Castilla durante los siglos XIII al XV', *Historia, Instituciones, Documentos*, 2 (1975), 387–441.

Peristiany, John G. and Julian Pitt-Rivers (eds.), *Honor and Grace in Anthropology*, Cambridge: Cambridge University Press, 1992.

Pessanha, José, 'Uma reabilitação histórica. Inventários da Torre do Tombo no século XVI', *Arquivo Histórico Português*, 3 (1905), 287–303.

Petit-Dutaillis, Charles and Georges Lefebvre, *Studies and Notes Supplementary to Stubb's Constitutional History*, Manchester: Manchester University Press, 1930.

Picard, E., 'L'écurie de Philippe le Hardi, Duc de Bourgogne', *Mémoires de l'Académie des Sciences, Arts et Belles-Lettres de Dijon*, 10 (1905–6), 307–439.

Piel, Joseph M., *'Paço' e 'Milhafre': história de duas palavras e de alguns termos congéneres*, offprint of *Revista da Faculdade de Letras de Lisboa*, Lisbon, 1971.

Sobre a origem do antigo Galego-Portugês 'ovença' e 'ovençal', offprint of *Revista Portuguesa de História*, Coimbra, 1978.

'Considerações sobre o Hispano-Godo *Sala, Gal.-Port. *Sáa, Sá*, etc', in *Estudos de Linguística Histórica Galego-Portuguesa*, Lisbon: Imprensa Nacional Casa da Moeda, 1989, pp. 123–7.

Pimenta, Alfredo, *Idade media: problemas e soluções*, Lisbon: Edições Ultramar, 1946.

Pinto, Augusto Cardoso, *A Guarda del Rei Dom João II: notas e documentos para a história das Guardas Reais Portuguesas*, Lisbon: Centro Tipográfico Colonial, 1930.
Pipponier, Françoise, *Costume et vie sociale: la cour d'Anjou, XIVe–XVe siècles*, Paris: Ecole des Hautes Etudes en Sciences Sociales, 1970.
Piskorski, Wladimiro, *Las cortes de Castilla en el período del tránsito de la edad media a la edad moderna*, Barcelona: El Albir, 1977.
Pizarro, J. A. Sotto Mayor, 'Os patronos do Mosteiro de Grijó', Dissertação de Mestrado, Universidade do Porto, 1987.
D. Dinis e a nobreza nos finais do século XIII, offprint of *Revista da Faculdade de Letras*, Oporto, 1993.
Polanyi, Karl, *The Great Transformation*, New York: Rinehart, 1944.
Porsia, Franco, *I cavalli del re*, Fasano: Schena Editore, 1986.
Post, Gaines, *Studies in Medieval Legal Thought: Public Law and the State, 1100–1322*, Princeton: Princeton University Press,1964.
Pradalié, Gérard, *Lisboa, da Reconquista ao fim do século XIII*, Lisbon: Palas, 1975.
O Convento de S. Francisco em Santarém, Santarém: Câmara Municipal, 1992.
Price, Simon, *Rituals and Power: The Roman Imperial Cult in Asia Minor*, Cambridge: Cambridge University Press, 1984.
Privat, Jean-Marie, 'Rois mages, images des rois (matériaux pour une recherche)', in Jean Dufournet, Adelin Fiorato and Augustin Redondo (eds.), *Le Pouvoir monarchique et ses supports idéologiques aux XIVe–XVIIe siècles*, Paris: Sorbonne Nouvelle, 1990, pp. 213–31.
Procter, Evelyn S., 'The use and custody of the secret seal (*sello de la puridad*) in Castile from 1252 to 1369', *The English Historical Review*, 217 (1940), 194–221.
Curia and Cortes in León and Castile, 1072–1295, Cambridge: Cambridge University Press, 1980.
Prodi, Paolo, *Il sacramento del potere: il giuramento politico nella storia dell'ocidente*, Bologna: Il Mulino, 1992.
Proença, Raul (ed.), *Guia de Portugal*, vols. I and II [1924–27], Lisbon: Fundação Calouste Gulbenkian, 1983 edition.
Quintanilla Raso, María Concepción, 'La tenencia de fortalezas en Castilla durante la baja edad media', in *En la España medieval* vol. IV: *estudios en memoria del Profesor Claudio Sánchez-Albornoz*, vol. II, Madrid: Universidad Complutense, 1986, pp. 861–97.
'La renovación nobiliaria en la Castilla bajomedieval. Entre el debate y la propuesta', in *La nobleza peninsular en la edad media. VI Congreso de estudios medievales*, Ávila: Fundación Sánchez-Albornoz, 1999, pp. 257–95.
Raffestin, Claude, *Pour une Géographie du pouvoir*, Paris: Librairies Techniques, 1980.
Ramos, João, 'Genealogia dos reis de Portugal', *Biblos*, 10 (1934), 331–57, 608–34.
Rau, Virgínia, *A Casa dos Contos*, Coimbra: Faculdade de Letras, 1951.
Estudos de história medieval, Lisbon: Presença, 1985.
Ravegnani, Giorgio, *La Corte de Giustiniano*, Rome: Jouvence, 1989.
Rebello, João António, *Capella Real Portugueza: sua origem, progresso, esplendor, decadencia e estado actual*, Lisbon: Tip. Minerva, 1878.
Rebelo, Luís de Sousa, *A concepção do poder em Fernão Lopes*, Lisbon: Livros Horizonte, 1983.
'A alegoria final do *Livro da Virtuosa Benfeitoria*', *Biblos*, 69 (1993), 367–79.
Reuter, Timothy (ed.), *The Medieval Nobility*, Amsterdam and New York: North Holland, 1979.

Reydellet, Maurice, *La Royauté dans la littérature latine, de Sidoine Apollinaire à Isidore de Séville*, Rome: Ecole Française de Rome, 1981.

Reynolds, Susan, *Fiefs and Vassals: The Medieval Evidence Reinterpreted*, Oxford: Clarendon, 1996.

Kingdoms and Communities in Western Europe, 900–1300, Oxford: Clarendon, 1997.

'The historiography of the medieval state', in Michael Bentley (ed.), *Companion to Historiography*, London and New York: Routledge, 1997, pp. 117–38.

Ribeiro, João Pedro, *Dissertações cronológicas e criticas sobre a história e jurisprudencia eclesiástica e civil de Portugal*, 5 vols., Lisbon: Academia Real das Ciências, 1810–36.

Reflexões históricas, 2 vols., Coimbra: Imprensa da Universidade, 1835–36.

Ricard, Robert, *Les Portugais au Maroc de 1495 à 1521*, Rabat, 1937.

Riché, Pierre, 'Les représentations du palais dans les textes littéraires du haut moyen âge', *Francia*, 4 (1976), 161–71.

Riley, Carlos, 'A Inglaterra como espaço de projecção da memória e imaginário linhagísticos da família Almada', *Actas do Colóquio Comemorativo do VI Centenário do Tratado de Windsor*, Oporto: Faculdade de Letras, 1988, pp. 161–72.

Riquer, Martí de, *Cavalleria fra realtà e letteratura nel Quattrocento*, Bari: Adriatica, 1970.

Robin, Françoise, 'Les chapelles seigneuriales et royales françaises au temps de Louis XI', *La France de la fin du XVe siècle: renouveau et apogée*, Paris: CNRS, 1985, pp. 237–52.

Rodrigues, Maria Teresa Campos, *Aspectos da administração municipal de Lisboa no século XV*, offprint of *Revista Municipal*, Lisbon, 1968.

'O itinerário de D. Pedro I, 1357–1367', *Ocidente* (n.s.), 82 (1972), 147–76.

Itinerário de D. Fernando, 1367–1383, offprint of *Bracara Augusta*, Braga, 1978.

Rodrigues, Ana Maria, *Torres Vedras: a vila e o termo nos finais da idade média*, Lisbon: Fundação Calouste Gulbenkian, 1995.

Rodríguez-Salgado, Mia, 'Honour and profit in the court of Philip II of Spain', in Maurice Aymard and Marzio A. Romani (eds.), *La Cour comme institution économique*, Paris: Maison des Sciences de l'Homme, 1998, pp. 67–86.

Roncaglia, Aurelio, 'Le corti medievali. Premessa', in *Letteratura Italiana I: il letterato e le istituzioni*, Turin: Einaudi, 1982, pp. 33–6.

Rosa, Maria de Lurdes, *O Morgadio em Portugal, séculos XIV–XV: modelos e práticas de comportamento linhagístico*, Lisbon: Estampa, 1995.

Pero Afonso Mealha: os bens e a gestão de riqueza de um proprietário leigo no século XIV, Redondo: Patrimonia, 1995.

Rosário, António do, *Letrados Dominicanos em Portugal nos séculos XIII–XV*, offprint of *Repertorio de las Ciencias Eclesiásticas*, Salamanca, 1979.

Roth, Cecil, 'The qualification of Jewish physicians in the middle ages', *Speculum*, 28 (1953), 834–43.

Rubin, Miri, 'Small groups: identity and solidarity in the late middle ages', in Jennifer Kermode (ed.), *Enterprise and Individuals in Fifteenth-Century England*, Stroud: Alan Sutton, 1991, pp. 132–50.

Rucquoi, Adeline, 'Noblesse urbaine de Castille (XIIIe–XVe siècles)', in *Les Pays de la Méditerranée occidentale au moyen âge. 106e Congrès national des sociétés savantes*, Paris: Comité des Travaux Historiques et Scientifiques, 1983, pp. 35–47.

'De los reyes que no son taumaturgos: los fundamentos de la realeza de España', *Temas Medievales*, 5 (1995), 163–86.

Ruggieri, Jole Scudieri, *Cavalleria e cortesia nella vita e nella cultura di Spagna*, Modena: Mucchi, 1980.

Ruiz, Teófilo, 'Une royauté sans sacre: la monarchie castillane du bas moyen âge', *Annales ESC*, 39 (1984), 429–53.

'Unsacred monarchy: the Kings of Castile in the late middle ages', in S. Wilentz (ed.), *Rites of Power: Ritual and Politics since the Middle Ages*, Philadelphia: University of Pennsylvania, 1985, pp. 109–44.

'Fiestas, torneos y símbolos de la realeza en la Castilla del siglo XV. Las fiestas de Valladolid de 1428', in A. Rucquoi (ed.), *Realidad e imágenes del poder: España a fines de la edad media*, Valladolid: Ambito, 1988, pp. 249–65.

Rusconi, Roberto, 'De la prédication à la confession. Transmission et contrôle de modèles de comportement', *Faire croire: modalités de la diffusion et de la réception des messages religieux du XIIe au XVe siècle*, Rome: Ecole Française de Rome, 1981, pp. 62–87.

Russell, Peter E., 'João Fernandes Andeiro at the court of John of Lancaster', *Revista da Universidade de Coimbra*, 14 (1940), 20–30.

The English Intervention in Spain and Portugal in the Time of Edward III and Richard II, Oxford: Clarendon, 1955.

Prince Henry the Navigator: A Life, London and New Haven: Yale University Press, 2000.

Ryder, Alan, *The Kingdom of Naples under Alfonso the Magnanimous: The Making of a Modern State*, Oxford: Clarendon Press, 1976.

Sabaté, Flocel, *Lo Senyor Rei es mort! Actitud i cerimònies dels municipis Catalans baix-medievals davant la mort del monarca*, Lerida: Universitat de Lleida, 1994.

Sahlins, Marshall, 'On the sociology of primitive exchange', in *Stone Age Economics*, London and New York: Routledge, 1972.

Sampaio, Alberto, *Estudos económicos*, vol. I, *As vilas do norte de Portugal*, Lisbon: Vega, 1979.

Sánchez-Albornoz, Claudio, *La Curia Regia Portuguesa: siglos XII y XIII*, Madrid: Centro de Estudios Históricos, 1920.

Investigaciones y documentos sobre las instituciones Hispanas, Santiago: Edición Juridica de Chile, 1970.

'El *Palatium Regis* Asturleonés', *Cuadernos de Historia de España*, 59–60 (1976), 6–104.

Sánchez Casabón, Ana Isabel, 'Los cargos de mayordomo, senescal y dapifer en el reinado de Alfonso II de Aragón', in *Aragón en la edad media*, vol. VIII, *Homenage al Profesor Emérito Antonio Ubieto Arteta*, Saragossa: University of Saragossa, 1989, pp. 599–607.

Santos, Domingos Maurício Gomes dos, *D. Duarte e as responsabilidades de Tânger (1433–1438)*, Lisbon: Comissão Executiva do V Centenário da Morte do Infante D. Henrique, 1960.

Santos, Maria José Azevedo, 'O peixe e a fruta na alimentação da corte de D. Afonso V', *Brigantia*, 3 (1983), 307–43.

Santos Diez, José Luis, *La encomienda de monasterios en la Corona de Castilla, siglos X–XV*, Rome and Madrid: Instituto Jurídico Español, 1961.

São Payo, Marquês de, 'A heráldica nos usos e costumes funerários', *Armas e Troféus*, 6 (1965), 220–30.

Saraiva, António José, *História da cultura em Portugal*, vol. I, Lisbon: Jornal do Foro, 1955.

Sawyer, P. and Ian Wood (eds.), *Early Medieval Kingship*, Leeds: Leeds University Press, 1977.

Scaglione, Aldo, *Knights at Court: Courtliness, Chivalry and Courtesy from Ottonian Germany to the Italian Renaissance*, Berkeley: University of California Press, 1991.

Schena, Olivetta, *Le Leggi Palatine di Pietro IV di Aragona*, Cagliari: Istituto sui Rapporti Italo-Iberici, 1983.

Schena, Olivetta and Josep Trenchs, 'Le Leggi Palatine di Giacomo III di Majorca nella corte di Pietro IV di Aragona', in *XIII Congrès d'Història de la Corona d'Aragó*, vol. II, Palma de Mallorca: Institut d'Estudis Baleàrics, 1990, pp. 11–119.

Schmidt, Steffen W., Laura Guasti, Carl H. Landé and James C. Scott (eds.), *Friends, Followers and Factions*, Berkeley, Los Angeles and London: University of California Press, 1977.

Schramm, Percy, *Kaiser, Rom und Renovatio: Studien und Texte zur Geschichte des Romischen Erneuerungsgedankens vom Ende des Karolingischen Reiches bis zum Investiturzeit*, 2 vols., Leipzig: Teubuer, 1929.

Las insignias de la realeza en la edad media Española, Madrid: Instituto de Estudios Políticos, 1960.

Selle, Xavier de la, 'La confession et l'aumône: confesseurs et aumôniers des rois de France', *Journal des Savants*, 2 (1993), 255–86.

Sena, Jorge de, *Estudos de história e de cultura*, Lisbon: Revista Ocidente, 1967.

Sénellart, Michel, *Les Arts de gouverner: du régimen médiéval au concept de gouvernement*, Paris: Seuil, 1995.

Sequeira, Gustavo de Matos, *Inventário artístico de Portugal*, vol. V, *Distrito de Leiria*, Lisbon: Academia Nacional de Belas-Artes, 1955.

Serrão, Joaquim Veríssimo, *Portugueses no estudo de Toulouse*, Coimbra: Imprensa da Universidade, 1954.

Serrão, Joel (ed.), *Dicionário de história de Portugal*, 4 vols., Lisbon: Iniciativas Editoriais, 1971.

Sherborne, J. W., 'Aspects of English court culture in the later fourteenth century', in V. J. Scattergood and J. W. Sherborne (eds.), *English Court Culture in the Later Middle Ages*, London: Duckworth, 1983, pp. 1–27.

Sills, David (ed.), *International Encyclopedia of Social Sciences*, 9 vols., New York: Macmillan, 1968.

Silva, António de Morais e, *Grande dicionário da língua Portuguesa*, 10 vols., Lisbon: Confluência, 1949–59.

Silva, Augusto Vieira da, *O Castelo de S. Jorge em Lisboa*, Lisbon: Empresa Nacional de Publicidade, 1937.

Dispersos, 3 vols., Lisbon: Câmara Municipal, 1968–70.

A Cerca Fernandina de Lisboa, 2 vols., Lisbon: Câmara Municipal, 1987.

A Cerca Moura de Lisboa: estudo histórico-descritivo, Lisbon: Câmara Municipal, 1987.

Silva, Eugénio de Figueiredo e, *Os Estaus de Tomar*, offprint of *Anais da União dos Amigos dos Monumentos da Ordem de Cristo*, Tomar, 1961.

Silva, José Custódio Vieira da, *Paços medievais Portugueses*, Lisbon: IPPAR, 1995.

Silva, M. J. Branco, 'A procissão na cidade: reflexões em torno da Festa do Corpo de Deus na idade média Portuguesa', in *Actas das Jornadas Inter e Pluridisciplinares sobre a Cidade*, vol. I, Lisbon, 1993, pp. 195–217.

Silva, Manuela Santos, *A região de Óbidos na época medieval: estudos*, Caldas da Rainha: Património Histórico, 1994.

Silva, Nuno Espinosa Gomes da, *Bártolo na história do direito Português*, offprint of *Revista da Faculdade de Direito*, Lisbon, 1960.

João das Regras e outros juristas Portugueses da Universidade de Lisboa (1378–1412), offprint of *Revista da Faculdade de Direito*, Lisbon, 1960.

Humanismo e direito em Portugal no século XVI, Lisbon: Edição do Autor, 1964.

O Chanceler João das Regras: Prior da Igreja da Oliveira em Guimarães, offprint of *Revista da Faculdade de Direito*, Lisbon, 1974.

História do direito Português, vol. I, *Fontes de direito*, Lisbon: Fundação Calouste Gulbenkian, 1985.

Simmel, Georg, *On Individuality and Social Forms: Selected Writings*, Chicago: University of Chicago Press, 1971.

'La différentiation sociale', in *Sociologie et épistémologie*, Paris: PUF, 1981, pp. 207–22.

Simões, Veiga, 'O Infante D. Henrique. O seu tempo e a sua acção', in António Baião, Hernâni Cidade and Manuel Múrias (eds.), *História da expansão Portuguesa no mundo*, vol. I, Lisbon: Ática, 1937, pp. 311–56.

Smith, Pierre, 'Aspects de l'organisation des rites', in M. Izard and P. Smith (eds.), *La Fonction symbolique*, Paris: Gallimard, 1979, pp. 139–70.

Soares, Sérgio Cunha, 'Nobreza e arquétipo fidalgo. A propósito de um Livro de Matrículas de Filhamentos (1641–1724)', *Revista de História das Ideias*, 19 (1997), 403–55.

Sommé, Monique, 'L'alimentation quotidienne à la cour de Bourgogne au milieu du XVe siècle', in *Actes du 93e Congrès des sociétés savantes – Bulletin Philologique et Historique*, 1 (1971), 103–17.

'Le cérémonial de la naissance et de la mort de l'enfant princier à la cour de Bourgogne au XVe siècle', in *Fêtes et Cérémonies aux XIVe et XVe siècles: Rencontres de Lausanne, Septembre 1993*, Neuchâtel: Centre Européen d'Etudes Bourguignonnes, 1994, pp. 87–103.

Isabelle de Portugal, Duchesse de Bourgogne: une femme au pouvoir au XVe siècle, Villeneuve d'Ascq: Presses Universitaires du Septentrion, 1998.

Sousa, Armindo de, 'O mosteiro de Santo Tirso no século XV', *Estudos Medievais*, 1 (1981), 95–156.

'As cortes de Leiria-Santarém de 1433', *Estudos Medievais*, 2 (1982), 71–224.

A morte de D. João I (um tema de propaganda dinástica), Oporto: Centro de Estudos Humanísticos, 1984.

As cortes medievais Portuguesas (1385–1490), 2 vols., Lisbon: INIC, 1990.

Sousa, Bernardo Vasconcelos e, 'O sangue, a cruz e a coroa: a memória do Salado em Portugal', *Penélope*, 2 (1989), 27–48.

Os Pimentéis: percursos de uma linhagem medieval Portuguesa (séculos XIII–XIV), Lisbon: Imprensa Nacional Casa da Moeda, 2000.

Sousa, J. Cordeiro de, 'Andanças de Nun'Álvares (1373–1422)', *O Instituto*, 129 (1967), 108–55.

Sousa, João Silva de, *A casa senhorial do Infante D. Henrique*, Lisbon: Horizonte, 1991.

Spiegel, Gabrielle M., *The Past as Text: The Theory and Practice of Medieval Historiography*, Baltimore: The Johns Hopkins University Press, 1997.

Starkey, David (ed.), *The English Court from the Wars of the Roses to the Civil War*, London: Longman, 1987.

Storia dell'urbanistica: le residenze collettive, in *Urbanistica*, 42–3 (1965), thematic volume.

Strayer, Joseph (ed.), *Dictionary of the Middle Ages*, 12 vols., New York: Scribner's, 1984.

Suárez Fernández, Luis, 'Don Pedro Tenorio, arzobispo de Toledo (1375–1399)', in *Estudios dedicados a Menéndez Pidal*, vol. IV, Valladolid: University of Valladolid, 1953, 601–27.

Juan I, Rey de Castilla (1379–1390), Madrid: CSIC, 1955.

Tambiah, Stanley Jeyaraja, *Culture, Thought, and Social Action: An Anthropological Perspective*, Cambridge, MA: Harvard University Press, 1985.

Tamm, Birgitta, *Auditorium and Palatium: A Study on Assembly-Rooms in Royal Palaces during the 1st Century BC and the 1st Century AD*, Stockholm: Almqvist and Wiksell, 1963.

Tardits, Claude, 'L'invitation au comparatisme. Marc Bloch et les anthropologues', in Hartmut Atsma and André Burguière (eds.), *Marc Bloch aujourd'hui: histoire comparée et sciences sociales*, Paris: Ecole des Hautes Etudes en Sciences Sociales, 1990, pp. 135–46.

Tarouca, Carlos da Silva, *A Graça de Santarém: fundadores e fundações*, offprint of *Brotéria*, Lisbon, 1942.

Tavares, Maria José Ferro, 'A revolta dos mesteirais de 1383', in *Actas das III Jornadas Arqueológicas de 1977*, Lisbon: Associação dos Arqueólogos Portugueses, 1978, pp. 359–83.

Os Judeus em Portugal no século XV, 2 vols., Lisbon: Universidade Nova/INIC, 1982–84.

'A nobreza no reinado de D. Fernando e a sua actuação em 1383–1385', *Revista de História Económica e Social*, 12 (1983), 45–89.

'As minorias religiosas no reinado de D. Fernando e em 1383–85', in *Actas das Jornadas sobre Portugal medieval*, Leiria, 1986, 469–77.

Távora, Luis Gonzaga de Lencastre e, 'Mestre João Afonso, Chanceler do rei D. João I', *Arquivos de Cascais*, 1 (1980), 91–120.

Teyssier, Paul, 'Estrados e cadeiras: estudo de alguns objectos culturais em Gil Vicente e na escola Vicentina', in *Studies in Portuguese Literature and History in Honour of Luis de Sousa Rebelo*, London: Thamesis Books, 1992, pp. 63–71.

Theuws, Frans and Janet L. Nelson (eds.), *Rituals of Power: From Late Antiquity to the Early Middle Ages*, Leiden: Brill, 2000.

Thomassin, Louis, *Ancienne et Nouvelle Discipline de l'Église*, 6 vols., Bar-le-Duc: Guérin, 1864–66.

Thompson, I. A. A., 'The institutional background of the rise of the Minister-Favourite', in J. H. Elliot and L. W. B. Brockliss (eds.), *The World of the Favourite*, London and New Haven: Yale University Press, 1999, pp. 13–25.

Tilley, Christopher, *A Phenomenology of Landscape: Places, Paths and Monuments*, Oxford and Providence, RI: Berg, 1994.

Todeschini, G., '*Oeconomica* Franciscana. Proposte di una nuova lettura delle fonti dell'etica economica medievale', *Rivista di Storia e Letteratura Religiosa*, 13 (1977), 461–94.

Tomás y Valiente, Francisco, 'Origen bajomedieval de la patrimonalización y la enajenación de oficios públicos en Castilla', in *Actas del I Symposium de Historia de la Administración*, Madrid: Instituto de Estudios Administrativos, 1970, pp. 123–59.

Manual de historia del derecho Español, Madrid: Tecnos, 1986.

Torre, A. de la, *La Casa de Isabel la Católica*, Madrid: CSIC, 1954.

Torre, A. de la (ed.), *Cuentas de Gonzalo de Baena, tesorero de Isabel la Católica*, 2 vols., Madrid: CSIC, 1955–56.

Torres Balbás, Leopoldo, *Ciudades Hispanomusulmanas*, 2 vols., Madrid: Instituto Hispano-Árabe de Cultura, 1971.

Torres Balbás, Leopoldo, L. Cervera and F. Chueca, *Resumen histórico del urbanismo en España*, Madrid: Instituto de Estudios de Administración, 1954.

Torres Fontes, J., 'La conquista del Marquesado de Villena', *Hispania*, 13 (1953), 37–151.

'Los condestables de Castilla en la edad media', *Anuario de Historia del Derecho Español*, 41 (1971), 57–112.

Tout, T. F., *Chapters in the Administrative History of Mediaeval England*, 6 vols., Manchester: Manchester University Press, 1967.

Tovar, Conde de, *Estudos históricos*, vol. III, *O escrivão da puridade*, Lisbon: Academia Portuguesa da História, 1961.

Treitinger, Otto, *Die Oströmische Kaiser- und Reichsidee nach ihrer Gestaltung im höfischen Zeremoniell*, Darmstadt: Geutner, 1956.

Trexler, Richard C., *Public Life in Renaissance Florence*, New York: Academic Press, 1980.

Trexler, Richard C. (ed.), *Persons in Groups: Social Behavior and Identity Formation in Medieval and Renaissance Europe*, Binghamton: Center for Medieval and Early Renaissance Studies, 1985, pp. 39–45.

Türk, Egbert, *Nugae Curialium: le règne d'Henri II Plantagenet et l'éthique politique*, Geneva: Droz, 1977.

Turner, Victor, *Dramas, Fields and Metaphors: Symbolic Action in Human Society*, Ithaca: Cornell University Press, 1974.

From Ritual to Theatre: The Human Seriousness of Play, New York: Paj Pub., 1982.

Urríez y Azara, J. Jordán de, 'Las ordenaciones de la corte Aragonesa en los siglos XIII y XIV', *Boletín de la Real Academia de Buenas Letras de Barcelona*, 13 (1913), 220–9, 284–92.

Vale, Malcolm, *War and Chivalry: Warfare and Aristocratic Culture in England, France and Burgundy at the End of the Middle Ages*, London: Duckworth, 1981.

van den Bergh, Godfried von Benthem, *The Structure of Development: An Invitation to the Sociology of Norbert Elias*, The Hague: Institute of Social Studies, 1971.

van den Bosch, J., *Capa, basilica, monasterium et le culte de Saint Martin de Tours: étude lexicologique et sémasiologique*, Utrecht: Dekker & Van de Vegt, 1959.

Van Gennep, Arnold, *Les Rites de Passage*, Paris: Emile Nourry, 1909.

Van Winter, J., 'The knightly aristocracy of the Middle Ages as a "social class"', in T. Reuter (ed.), *The Medieval Nobility*, Amsterdam and New York: North Holland, 1979, pp. 313–29.

Varela, Javier, *La muerte del Rey: el ceremonial funerario de la monarquía Española (1500–1885)*, Madrid: Turner, 1990.

Vasconcelos, Joaquim de, *A Ourivesaria Portuguesa*, s.l.: s.d. [1882].

Veiga, A. Botelho da Costa, *Estudos de história militar Portuguesa*, vol. I, Lisbon: Tip. Henrique Torres, 1936.

Veloso, Maria Teresa Nobre, 'D. Afonso II: relações de Portugal com a Santa Sé durante o seu reinado', Doctoral thesis, University of Coimbra, 1988.

Ventura, Leontina, 'A nobreza de corte de Afonso III', Doctoral thesis, University of Coimbra, 1992.

'Testamentária nobiliárquica (séc. XIII). Morte e sobrevivência da linhagem', *Revista de História das Ideias*, 19 (1997), 137–56.

Verbecke, Gérard, *The Presence of Stoicism in Medieval Thought*, Washington, DC: Catholic University Press, 1983.

Vercauteren, F., 'L'Hôtel du Roi (à propos d'un livre récent)', *Le Moyen Age*, 74 (1968), 577–97.

Verdon, J., 'Recherches sur la chasse en occident', *Revue Belge de Philologie et d'Histoire*, 56 (1978), 805–29.

Verlinden, Charles, *L'Esclavage dans l'Europe médiévale*, vol. I, *Péninsule ibérique. France*, Bruges: De Tempel, 1955.

'Les découvertes portugaises et la collaboration italienne d'Alphonse IV à Alphonse V', in *Actas do Congresso Internacional de História dos Descobrimentos*, vol. III, Lisbon, 1961, pp. 593–610.

Vermers, Manuel Maria, 'Nun'Álvares Pereira. A sua cronologia e o seu itinerário', *Lusitania Sacra*, 5 (1960–61), 7–99.

Versnel, H. S., *Inconsistencies in Greek and Roman Religion*, vol. I, Leiden: Brill, 1990.

Veyne, Paul, 'Propagande, expression, roi, image, idole, oracle', *L'Homme*, 114, 30 (1990), 7–26.

Vieira, Yara Frateschi, 'O escândalo das amas e tecedeiras nos cancioneiros Galego-Portugueses', *Colóquio-Letras*, 76 (1983), 18–27.

Viollet, Paul, *Histoire des institutions politiques et administratives de la France*, 3 vols., Paris, 1890–1903.

Viterbo, Francisco Marques Sousa, *A livraria real, especialmente no reinado de D. Manuel*, offprint of *Memórias da Academia das Ciências de Lisboa*, Lisbon, 1901.

'A cultura intelectual de D. Afonso V', *Arquivo Histórico Português*, 2 (1904), 255–68.

Duarte Galvão e a sua família, offprint of *História e Memórias da Academia Real das Ciências*, Lisbon, 1905.

A armaria em Portugal, 2 vols., Lisbon: Academia Real das Ciências, 1907–9.

O rei dos Charamelas e os Charamelas-mores, offprint of *Arte Musical*, Lisbon, 1912.

Amas, amos e colaços de pessoas reaes e personagens illustres, offprint of *Revista de História*, Oporto, 1914.

Calígrafos e iluminadores Portugueses: ensaio histórico-bibliográfico, Coimbra: Imprensa da Universidade, 1916.

Subsídios para a história da música em Portugal, Coimbra: Imprensa da Universidade, 1932.

Dicionário histórico e documental dos arquitectos, engenheiros e construtores Portugueses, 3 vols., Lisbon: Imprensa Nacional–Casa da Moeda, 1988.

Viterbo, Joaquim Santa Rosa de, *Elucidário das palavras, termos e frases que em Portugal antigamente se usáram, e que hoje regularmente se ignórão*, ed. Mário Fiúza, 2 vols., Oporto: Civilização, 1962.

Voci, Anna Maria, 'La cappella di corte dei primi sovrani angioini di Napoli', in *L'Etat angevin: pouvoir, culture et société entre XIIIe et XIVe siècle*, Rome: Istituto Italiano per il Medio Evo, 1998, pp. 447–67.

Vogel, Cyrille, *Medieval Liturgy: An Introduction to the Sources*, Washington, DC: The Pastoral Press, 1986.

Walker, Simon, *The Lancastrian Affinity, 1361–1399*, Oxford: Oxford University Press, 1990.

Wallace-Hadrill, J. M., *Early Germanic Kingship in England and on the Continent*, Oxford: Clarendon Press, 1980.

The Long-Haired Kings, Toronto: University of Toronto Press, 1982.

Warnke, Martin, *The Court Artist: On the Ancestry of the Modern Artist*, Cambridge: Cambridge University Press, 1993.

Weber, Max, *Economy and Society*, ed. G. Roth and C. Wittich, 2 vols., Berkeley and Los Angeles: University of California Press, 1978.

Weinberger, Stephen, 'The ennoblement of the aristocracy in medieval Provence', *Medievalia et Humanistica*, 20 (1994), 1–14.

Werner, Karl Ferdinand, 'L'historien et la notion d'état', in *Einheit der Geschichte: Studien zur Historiographie*, Sigmaringen: Thorbecke, 1999, pp. 709–21.

White, Lynn, 'The flavor of Early Renaissance technology', in Bernard Levy (ed.), *Developments in the Early Renaissance*, Albany: State University of Nebraska Press, 1972, pp. 36–57.

Willard, James F. and William A. Morris (eds.), *The English Government at Work, 1327–1336, I, Central and Prerogative Administration*, 2 vols., Cambridge, MA: Medieval Academy of America, 1940.

Winterling, Aloys, *Zwischen 'Haus' und 'Staat': antike Höfe im Vergleich*, Munich: Oldenbourg, 1997.

Wolfram, Erwig, 'The shaping of the early medieval kingdom', *Viator*, 1 (1970), 1–20.

Woolgar, C. M., *The Great Household in Late Medieval England*, New Haven and London: Yale University Press, 1999.

Zabalo Zabalegui, Javier, *La administración del reino de Navarra en el siglo XIV*, Pamplona: Universidad de Navarra, 1973.

Index

1429483R0

Printed in Great Britain by
Amazon.co.uk, Ltd.,
Marston Gate.